ELEMENTARY SCHOOL LANGUAGE ARTS:
SELECTED READINGS

31

ELEMENTARY SCHOOL LANGUAGE ARTS: *SELECTED READINGS*

Paul C. Burns
The University of Tennessee

Leo M. Schell
Kansas State University

Rand McNally & Company
Chicago

Preface

This anthology attempts to be truly supplementary—and therefore as specific as possible in enlarging and extending upon ideas in the most widely used language arts professional textbooks. The editors have deliberately avoided and rejected general, overall, summary-type articles which duplicate content usually found in good language arts textbooks in favor of clear, specific, concrete, detailed essays with a unique focus that have 'classroom relevancy' to a prospective or practicing teacher.

Our method of selecting the final readings may be of interest to the reader.

(a) The relevant, published literature over the past decade was identified with particular attention given to writings since 1960.

(b) The materials were organized into appropriate categories on the basis of the content and approach of the article.

(c) The articles judged best on the basis of the criteria suggested above were selected from each category for inclusion in the anthology.

(d) The remaining articles were screened for the listing called Selected References.

The anthology is oriented around transfer-into-action materials and particularly emphasizes such topics as (a) applications from the study of language and its components (the 'new' English); (b) influences of cultural variations; (c) creative writing, especially in the primary school years; (d) newer trends, materials, and resources, and (e) a few controversial topics. Various types of essays were deliberately chosen. Besides the customary explanations of most textbooks, included are: reports of research, 'how-to-do-it' descriptions, historical surveys, exhortations, points of view, and challenging, in-depth explorations. The editors recognize that they were not able to touch upon all possible areas, due to the facts that language arts is such a vast field and some topics are more adequately treated in the periodical literature.

Short chapter introductions are provided which give a concise summary of the areas of concern in each section. Brief article introductions contain questions designed to help the reader think critically, to compare viewpoints in other articles or sources, and to encourage him to take a stand on controversial or unanswered topics. These questions may be of most value after the article has been read. The Selected References stress supporting or contrasting viewpoints as well as pinpointing other notable articles.

The practical problem of teachers in conducting undergraduate and graduate courses in the teaching of language arts figured prominently in the decision to compile this volume. Wide reading in such courses seems a must, yet university and college or local school libraries usually contain but one or two sets of any given periodical. Group consideration of a recent essay at a given time in a course is almost impossible in most situations. The sheer availability of current articles, representing important statements and trends, is a problem this anthology was designed to solve in some measure. Finally, although the various essays represent individual viewpoints, it should be no surprise that many of them appeared in *Elementary English*. This official publication of the National Council of Teachers of English has long represented a cross section of the thinking of the teaching profession in the United States. Other publishers and organizations to whom we are indebted for permitting their material to be reprinted in this book are: *Annual Conference and Course on Reading* at the University of Pittsburgh; *Atlantic Monthly; California Teacher Association Journal;* Center for Applied Linguistics; *Childhood Education* (ACEI); *College English* (NCTE); *Education* (Bobbs-Merrill Company, Inc.); *Elementary School Journal* (University of Chicago Press); *English Journal* (NCTE); *Grade Teacher* (Teachers Publishing Corporation); *Instructor* (F. A. Owen Publishing Company); *Journal of Educational Research* (Dembar Educational Research, Inc.); *Journal of Psychology* (Journal Press); *Language Learning; Library Quarterly* (University of Chicago Press); *NCTE Research Reports; Review of Educational Research* (AERA); *Teachers Service Division Bulletin* (Allyn and Bacon). Without their cooperation, this venture would have been impossible.

PAUL C. BURNS
LEO M. SCHELL

Knoxville, Tennessee
Manhattan, Kansas

Table of Contents

ELEMENTARY SCHOOL LANGUAGE ARTS:
SELECTED READINGS

Part One

Introduction

Any claims that a revolution is sweeping elementary school language arts seem premature. True, some stimulating innovations are taking place—attitudes toward teaching usage and grammar are changing, once neglected topics are being stressed (*e.g.*, listening and creative writing), certain individual differences are receiving special attention, new media and organizational plans are being tried, and research is replacing exhortation as a criterion for change— but these hardly constitute a large-scale reform movement permeating elementary school classrooms no matter how new or exciting they may be. By focusing on the past, present, and future, it is hoped this part of the anthology will present a balanced, realistic picture of the language arts curriculum that is informative and inspirational and which sets the stage for and the tone of the remainder of the book.

Knowledge of the past may not be *essential* to understand the present or to prophesy the future but it is helpful in gaining a perspective on and an overall view of a situation. Current goals, materials, and procedures did not spring full blown into existence but neither were they the product of a systematic, sequential development; if anything, they more resembled Topsy and "jes' growed." As dominant philosophies, societal demands, available information and tools, and educational values changed, additions, deletions, and modifications resulted. Some periods thus emphasized the child, others teacher preparation; some stressed repetitive drill while others focused on functional opportunities for expression. And some were more productive and influential than others. Mackintosh focuses on this multifaceted development of the language arts curriculum from 1910 to 1960 in the introductory essay of this anthology.

1

In a large nation such as ours with a highly decentralized educational system, large-scale reform is most difficult and even vital changes may occur with excruciating slowness. One solution for more rapidly effecting change has been to establish a number of large, independent centers staffed by educational specialists and financed by the federal government whose responsibility is to create and evaluate materials and methods and to disseminate their products and findings. Such solutions have worked advantageously where there are myriad topics awaiting investigation—as there are in present day language arts. Project English is such a program encompassing varied elements of the language arts from kindergarten through college at curriculum centers throughout the country. Slack reports on the goals, products, and possible ramifications of this immense undertaking.

One of the most productive ways to improve language arts instruction is through research. Project English is an example of large-scale experimentation. But Singleton, Diederich, and Hill feel that significant research contributions do not require a laboratory, advanced university training, the intellect of a genius, or access to thousands of subjects—although these may help. They point out that teachers informally participate in research daily, although usually unknowingly. All that is needed to transform everyday procedures into research capable of producing valid—although tentative—conclusions is to follow a series of simple steps, essentially a recipe, which they outline in the third article in this part.

Surveys of pupil preferences of the curricular areas have repeatedly and consistently shown lack of pupil fondness for the language arts. With the exception of spelling which rates highly, children rank the language arts at the lower end of the scale—often last of eight to ten curricular areas. One reason suggested for this lack of appeal is that present teaching methods bore the pupils. Too often, it is asserted, English classes seem caught in a perpetually repeating cycle of "tell-drill-test" from which there is no escape (short of graduation or truancy!). Professors of educational psychology proclaim the values of motivation; methods textbooks repeatedly declare the need for active pupil participation; teachers awesomely describe the power of piqued curiosity to stimulate even the dullest. Yet there is little evidence that these universally recognized techniques are systematically used in any degree in language arts instruction. Carlsen deplores this state of affairs, and taking his cue from recent developments in the teaching of mathematics and science, recommends that teachers maximize use of methods first suggested by Socrates and later formalized by John Dewey. And he provides some provocative illustrations of how this could be done.

Since the quality of education is felt to be highly related to and influenced by the nature of teacher preparation, there needs to be, in the absence of definitive research, a consensus of professionals on the general characteristics desired in English teachers. The fifth article in this part, the result of a two-year project by outstanding specialists in English, English education, and teacher certification, specifies some broad guidelines for the preparation of teachers of English.

The world of language arts instruction cannot be contained between the covers of any single book; educators desiring to increase their professional competence and to improve their language arts program need access to a variety of professional reference books from several disciplines. Evertts and Moore provide a handy list of sources minimally required to achieve these dual goals.

1 Language Arts Curriculum: Fifty year highlights of the elementary program

Helen K. Mackintosh

To best understand current programs and newer trends, one must know the past. Dr. Mackintosh succinctly pinpoints significant events in the language art curriculum from 1910 to 1960.

What were the most important happenings in each decade? Which recommendations have still not been fully implemented? What themes seem to recur in each decade? Why? For information about curriculum developments in the 1960's, read the article by Jones cited in Selected References for Part One.

Fifty years is a long time when one is actually living it, but a relatively short time when it is put in the perspective of history and of education in the United States of America. The decades from 1910–1960 reflect many changes and many developments characteristic of a society in a country that fought three wars, experienced a major depression, and moved from an agricultural and industrial age to the atomic era. At the same time it must be clear that these exciting fifty years depend in a number of respects upon the events, educationally speaking, of the 1890's and the first decade of the Twentieth Century.

In a bulletin issued in 1949, Harlan Shores[1] reviewed research on elementary school curriculum covering the period of 1890–1949. He pointed out that in the 1890's, "Teachers tended to be impartial umpires between pupils and textbook in the recitation process." As a reaction against such practices, John Dewey and his disciples, in a sense paralleling the emphasis of G. Stanley Hall on the value of studying children's interests, were the godfathers of the experience curriculum. Over the period 1910–1960, such a curriculum was developed in forward-looking elementary schools.

From *Elementary English* 40:5-14; January 1963. Reprinted with the permission of the National Council of Teachers of English and Helen K. Mackintosh, Retired from U.S. Office of Education, Washington, D.C.

If the definition is accepted that the curriculum is the sum total of experiences provided the child by the school, it is evident that regardless of what exists on paper, the nature and quality of the child's education depends primarily upon the breadth of vision and experience of his teacher. During the years 1910–1960 it is evident that there were many influences at work in the field of the language arts that touched the supervisor and, ultimately, the classroom teacher.

Research and experimental studies, the growth of professional organizations and of professional magazines; the publication of professional books, especially yearbooks of the National Society for the Study of Education; the increasing importance of libraries and of the production of more and more books for children; the pronouncements of groups such as the National Council of Teachers of English through its commissions and committees; and the emphasis on the production of curriculum guides by State departments of education, and by city and county school systems, made a contribution to the nature and scope of children's experiences in the language arts.

Period of 1910–1920

One of the early courses of study published in 1909 came from the city of Boston.[2] This course of study gave two-thirds of the time in English to reading and literature, except in grades one and two, where half of the time was given to oral and written English. The purpose set forth was to unify the work in English throughout the grades in the fields of spelling, handwriting, spoken and written English, reading, literature, dictionary work, technicalities (grammar), and dictation. Some of the suggestions offered are as sound today as they were in 1909. For example, "In conversational exercises involving questions, pupils should not be required to answer in complete sentences. Such use of language is unnatural, unusual in life, and peculiar to the schoolroom." And another statement reads, "There should be in every school some uniform method of correcting compositions to make the work most successful." The majority of the work in spelling was to be written rather than oral, and not only textbooks, but supplementary books, the school library, poems and prose were to be used in the program.

It is of interest to note that in this bulletin of 102 pages, 43 pages are devoted to various aspects of English. An inspection of time allotments, which provided 1,500 minutes per week in grades one through eight, reflects this same strong emphasis on English, even though all the subject areas (with some slight variations in label) that are part of the typical elementary school program were included in the child's school day in Boston in 1909. However, in large black type, attention is called to the fact that within the 1,500-minute time allotment, 240 minutes in the eighth grade should be devoted to independent study by each pupil, "neither assisted by nor interrupted by the teacher."

States as well as cities were producing general curriculum guides for teachers with emphasis on English. In 1910 Alabama[3] published such a course of study for teachers in that state. Some of the statements that seem to reflect the purpose and suggested use include ones such as the following: "These manuals should be carefully studied every day by all teachers who desire to become more efficient in their work. They constitute the basis of work in any teachers' institutes." Any interested teacher was invited to send for a copy of the manual and to include seven cents for postage. Some of the words and phrases that reflect the character of the material, largely written by a number of specialists, include, "the school as a socializing agency," and "thought-getting and thought-giving, the basis of the course of study." Listed were The Alabama Teachers' and Pupils' Reading Circle, School Improvement Associations, and Educational Journals as aids to the teacher.

Courses of study from Baltimore County, Maryland,[4] appeared first in 1909 and were revised in 1915. It is interesting to read statements such as the following: "The modern course of study makes it imperative for the teacher to have a broader view of the topic to be treated than that given in the text and supplementary books to which the pupils have access. . . will be subject to revision from time to time as experience shows its points of strength and weakness."

Reading, stories, and poems are given an important place in the work of first and second grades. Dramatization is mentioned. In grades one through four the course of study is outlined in respect to reading and literature, and language. In grades five through eight, "grammar" is added to language. Throughout the publication the suggestions are specific for each grade.

Some of the pertinent statements found throughout the course of study seem to express the philosophy of those who prepared it. For example:

Langage is learned largely by imitation; the child absorbs from all about him—his home, his classmates, his teachers, his books (Grade One).
Teachers should exercise discrimination and judgment in selection of subjects suited to children (Grade Two).
The reading should never become a mere rote or mechanical exercise (Grade Three).
Abundant knowledge, purposeful arrangement, spontaneity, a characteristic style, free use of related knowledge, expression of personal experience, judgment or preference sought as essentials (Grade Four).
Interest and delight must accompany all work done in literature (Quoted from Percival Chubb) (Grade Five).
It is well to postpone the systematic treatment of formal grammar until the seventh year in school (Grade Five).

In the sixth grade teachers were urged to use all subject areas as a basis for teaching language. The seventh grade outline mentions voluntary and pleasure reading as recommended, as does the eighth grade. At this point spelling is discussed from the standpoint of selecting words from the daily lessons in other fields, as appropriate in grades 5, 6, 7, and 8.

Certainly most of the statements or points of view quoted would be equally sound today in a discussion of the content of the language arts and the philosophy that is represented in methods of teaching.

The 1915 revision of the 1909 course of study[5] carried the names of Lida Lee Tall and Isobel Davidson, names that would be known to persons of a certain vintage even today. The authors pointed out that in making the revision great care had been taken to secure unity from grade to grade; that outside specialists had been consulted; and that some "new departures" were incorporated. Among these were the use of "silent and oral reading," the school library, how to study, scientific testing, and use of standardized spelling scales.

It was in this decade that yearbooks of the National Society for the Study of Education dealt with problems in spelling and handwriting—time allotments, word selection, and methods of teaching.

In her book, *American Reading Instructions,*[6] Nila B. Smith traces the development of the teaching of reading in the United States. On page 149 she mentions the Reading-Literature series by Margaret Free and Harriette Treadwell as appearing first in 1910; and the Elson Readers appearing from 1909 through 1914. The former series emphasized myths, some stories by American authors and with perhaps less than a fourth of the space devoted to stories of child life, and of nature. The latter series was designed to present a broader reading program with cultural emphases covering science, transportation and communication, history, biography, citizenship, industry, invention, adventure, humor, travel and world friendship.

Rather than attempt to trace the developments in reading as Dr. Smith viewed them, in terms of the decades, a brief summary is offered here. Books such as Huey's[7] led to interest in scientific investigation, which in turn influenced the development of standardized texts. . . . Seat work came into being. . . . There was recognition of the fact that reading must meet the practical needs of life. . . . Remedial reading was born. . . . Names such as those of Willis F. Uhl, Mary E. Pennell, and Alice M. Cusack appeared as the authors of books. . . . During the 1920's teachers' manuals came into general use, accompanied by supplementary material. . . . There was a trend toward the use of factual and informational material as appropriate for silent reading exercises. . . . In using these, teachers came to give an emphasis to speed of reading. . . . The Picture-Story Reading Lessons by Courtis and Smith emphasized reading as a tool in a reading program that was aimed at self-directed child activity. . . . At this point literary appreciation was somewhat overshadowed.

. . . For the first time ability grouping was recommended. . . . Integration, both the term and the practice, was about to be adopted. . . . There was evidence of teachers' concern with child development. . . . At this point the *Twenty-Fourth Yearbook of the National Society for the Study of Education, Part I,* was published in 1925. . . . The objectives set up in this volume have continued to influence the nature and quality of reading instruction even down to the present time. . . . Many professional books were published, courses of study increased in number, with greater emphasis given to literature again. . . . Optional procedures were suggested for the teacher's use. . . . Pre-primers appeared. . . . Dr. Florence Bamberger, in a significant experimental study, discovered that a book bound in a cover of highly saturated blue had greatest appeal for children and thereby established a new style for use of gay colors, with blue in the lead. . . . More attention was given to the physical features of the book, to the development of basic vocabulary lists. . . . There were more attempts at integration of reading with other subjects. . . . There were discussions of the place and use of phonics. . . .

In 1934 when Dr. Smith's book was published, reading was recognized as a tool. . . . However, the importance of children's interests was clearly recognized. . . . The on-going importance of reading in the total program of the school was clearly determined.

It is significant to note that the year 1918 marks the beginning of the annual celebration of Book Week, which annually has an important place in every local community, as well as nationally. To trace the developments and contributions of this movement would be a story in itself.

1920–1930

Although the importance of this ten-year period might well include description and analysis of courses of study and curriculum guides, there are a number of "firsts" that should receive attention in these particular years. Of comparable value to curriculum workers, and to classroom teachers, are publications and new developments or modifications in philosophy, materials, and methods. Referred to earlier was the *Twenty-Fourth Yearbook*.[8] The influence of the pronouncements in this volume tied together much of the thinking that had been expressed by individuals in books or articles. But in the Yearbook a committee gave prestige to the objectives and to the nature and content of reading experiences.

Published in 1921 were two experimental studies that revived an emphasis on the importance of children's reactions to books, stories, and poems, and their voluntary choices of such materials. Dunn[9] studied children's interests in grades one, two, and three, in selections which possessed such qualities as good story, action, humor, repetition, and others. Jordan[10] studied library withdrawals made by children over a period of several weeks' time, sitting unobtrusively in the children's section where he could observe, as well as listen to comments made. Authors of literary readers made use of the findings of such studies as these, in selecting material of known interest to children.

An important "first" was the establishment in 1921 of the Newberry Medal Award by Frederick G. Melcher, publisher and editor, for the most distinguished contribution to American literature for children. The first book to be so distinguished was *The Story of Mankind* by William Hendrick Van Loon. The American Library Association, through a committee established for that purpose, makes the selection annually. In 1951 the chairman of this committee commented, "Looking back over the nominations of other years, we see issuing trends, new currents of thought, and reflection of national interest of people who work with books."[11]

Sterling Andrus Leonard published a book[12] in 1922 which exerted strong influence over a period of years in the field of teaching literature especially, but in other aspects of reading as well. He helped readers to distinguish between and among purposes for reading. Too, he offered guidelines in methods of teaching that were developed in keeping with the belief that teachers must begin with children where they are, not where the teacher wishes them to be.

It was during the early 1920's that manuscript writing was imported from England to displace cursive writing, at least in grades one and two, and the early part of three, of the elementary school. Although at present, the majority of schools introduce cursive writing at some time during the third grade, the manuscript form is usually retained for use in those situations where it is appropriate, such as labeling, or the making of titles, or the preparation of written material for display purposes.

Although it cannot be labeled as a "first" in the strict sense of the word, the publication in 1923 of the story of an experiment by Ellsworth Collings[13] beginning in 1917, offered some specific help for teachers in knowing just how one can provide children with real experiences that are nevertheless genuine learning situations. This experiment carried on in a rural school reports in detail how children and teacher worked together. Oral and written expression were highly functional as described in this volume.

But the most important event between 1920 and 1930, from the point of view of the National Council of Teachers of English, was the establishment of *The Elementary English Review* by C. C. Certain, of Detroit, who throughout his lifetime continued the publication of this magazine for the guidance of elementary teachers. After Mr. Certain's death the magazine became the official organ of the National Council of Teachers of English in the elementary school field. Although the content includes research studies, the descriptive articles written by teachers themselves represent concrete help for both those who are experienced and those who are beginners. Today *Elementary English*, as the title now reads, keeps teachers up-to-date with respect to books for children, audio-visual aids, free and inexpensive materials, and any growing edges in language arts of value to the elementary school program.

The first issue of the magazine, Vol. I, No. 1, appeared in March 1924. The advisory board included names familiar to many Council members: Sterling A. Leonard, Orton Lowe, Florence Bamberger, R. L. Lyman, W. W. Hatfield, Patty Smith Hill, and Walter Barnes.

In describing the purpose and need for such a publication, the following statements were included: "A new magazine to fill a long-felt need in a field not previously served by professional journals. . . . The *Review* is devoted exclusively to teaching of English in elementary schools with emphasis upon social well-being of children." Listed are (1) study of literature; (2) silent and oral reading; (3) dramatics, composition, grammar, spelling; (4) standard tests; (5) scientific procedures for experimental teaching; and (6) more effective organization of Elementary Teachers of English.

It should be a matter of interest for present-day teachers to take a look at the titles of the articles that appeared in the first issue of *The Elementary English Review* and to compare them with the issue for November 1960.

Teaching Literature for a Fuller Experience
Stage Craft for the Elementary School Teacher
Silent Reading in the Elementary Grades
The Creation of Dr. Doolittle, by Hugh Lofting
A Spelling Procedure with Social Values
Intelligence and Problems of Instruction in English
Fun for Children
Practical Exercises for Classroom Use
Classroom Observations
Reviews and Abstracts
Shop Talk

1930–1940

A significant development in the early 1930's was the organization of the National Conference on Research in Elementary School English on February 23, 1932, in Washington, D. C. Later the words "Elementary English" were dropped from the name, but many of the continuing contributions of this organization have been focused on the elementary field. Today it is one of the organizations with which the NCTE actively cooperates.

Of interest to those concerned with the problems of helping children to develop legible handwriting were the experiments reported in 1932 on the use of the typewriter[14] in elementary schools. Although there has been no wholesale invasion of elementary school classrooms by the typewriter, further studies have been made and are being made. A recent study indicates that an extensive bibliography is available. For children with handwriting problems that are difficult to solve, the use of a typewriter may be a real motivation for written expression.

In 1935 Wilbur Hatfield edited for the Council a volume[15] which had been several years in the making with participation of many members of the organization. The use of the word "Experience" in the title signaled the fact that the thesis to be discussed was a more realistic approach to teaching and learning. Since this publication should be well known to Council members, no further discussion is needed at this time.

It was in 1937 that the Association for Childhood Education International issued its first *Bibliography of Books for Children*[16] with classification of titles in terms of children's interests, with brief annotations, and with a suggestion of the age range to which each book would appeal. Interestingly enough, the NCTE published its first book list in this same year, under the title *Reading for Fun*.

In the same year Frederick Melcher established the Randolph Caldecott Medal for the artist who had contributed the most distinguished picture book for American children during that year and annually thereafter. The first award was made in 1938 to Dorothy P. Lathrop for the book, *Animals of the Bible*.

In 1938 the Office of Education made an important contribution to the curriculum field in the publication of a survey of courses of study.[17] As the title indicates, the materials represent courses published during 1935 and 1936. The author classified 1,262 pieces of material as deserving the label "curriculum." Dr. Leary reported that 88 per cent of courses were organized by subjects, and 53 per cent of all courses, whether organized by subject or otherwise, included units of work. One section of the survey made a general statement concerning the character of the courses in English. There was no mention of literature in the elementary school.

The author pointed out that the Minneapolis, Minnesota, course of study for elementary and junior high schools included activities shown by investigation to be those of major importance in everyday life: (1) conversation (including telephoning); (2) discussion; (3) explanation, description, directions; (4) storytelling and dramatization; (5) short talks and reports (including announcements); (6) meetings; (7) note taking; and (8) letter writing. Other cities and counties are listed as following a similar practice.

Courses in handwriting received mention in terms of the suggestions for diagnostic and remedial work, some consideration of lefthandedness, functional teaching, and suggestions for correlating handwriting with other school activities. More of the groups that had prepared courses were reported as favoring cursive rather than manuscript writing at this time.

In *reading* there were a number of trends indicated: (1) provision for wide reading experience; (2) organization of reading in large areas of interest; (3) building a background of experience before introducing first-grade children to reading; (4) recognition of the importance of reading readiness in all years beyond the first, extending into high school. Approximately half of the courses made some provision for individual needs of pupils.

As for *spelling*, there was some provision for correcting cases of spelling disability; there was a trend toward functional spelling, with emphasis on the importance of seeing words in context.

It was in 1939 that the Council, through a committee chaired by Angela Broening, issued a report[18] designed to show to what extent *The Experience Curriculum* of 1935 had made an impact on the teaching of English in the United States. The Committee studied the questions of thousands of persons interested in the problems of teaching and learning English. In the summary it was stated that flexibility in experience-centered units was an outstanding characteristic of current practice as evidenced by wide differences in method. All that was good in traditional methods had been absorbed into the experience curriculum.

Significant for elementary school teachers at the end of the 1930's was the publication of the handbook[19] for use of middle grade children. This book was designed to give children answers to their questions on form and usage largely by means of illustrations. It was to be a reference book and not a text.

Since the study by Dr. Leary summarized, in a sense, certain characteristics of curriculum in this period, only brief attention can be given to individual courses. However, Pasadena[20] made use of the term "language arts" in the title of its course, stressed need for understanding what reading readiness means, distinguished between learning to read and reading to learn, and provided suggestive criteria for evaluation. One quotation from the bulletin indicates the spirit of the publication—"Purposeful, persistent and properly directed practice is important for effective skill learning. Insight into pertinent relationships and meanings involved in a total situation is essential to any effective functional learning." This point of view may well be used to summarize many of the developments in this period.

1940–1950

Perhaps the most significant contribution to the curriculum in the field of English occurred in 1945 when the Executive Committee established a Commission on the English Curriculum, with Dr. Dora V. Smith, of the University of Minnesota, as Director. Three volumes have been published, another has been completed, and another is in process. For purposes of this paper it is sufficient to mention the volume[21] for the elementary school. This volume was the cooperative product of a committee of elementary school persons who viewed elementary language arts as consisting of listening, speaking, reading, and writing interwoven into the total curriculum, with emphasis on the child development point of view.

In a Directory of the Council in the 1940's there appears mention of the Committee on Elementary School Reading List, established for the following purpose: "To prepare, with the aid of committee representatives from the American Library Association, classified and annotated book lists for elementary school pupils." Lists and supplements have been published and revised from time to time. *Adventuring with Books*, the current book list, is one in which the would-be purchaser may find titles, annotations, publishers, prices, and suggested age levels for each book.

It is sometimes difficult to place a new development as to time. This is true of the studies dealing with research in reading published by Traxler. The first of these, says the author, covered a period of ten years, beginning in the 1930's, but including part of 1940. The second covered the period 1940–44. The third[22] was concerned with research published from 1945 to 1952; and the most recent volume was available in May 1960. In each of these studies, the author provides an overview of the period which the study covers; discusses in summary form the outstanding developments; and provides a selected, carefully annotated bibliography. Each issue presents an accurate and comprehensive picture of the highlights in reading research for the period covered.

This was the period, too, when the *Forty-Eighth Yearbook, Part II*,[23] was devoted to reading in the elementary school. As the foreword indicates, the volume was designed to realize ". . . the primary objective of providing an authoritative interpretation of the significance of new knowledge and of emerging problems in the field of reading." Dr. William S. Gray served as chairman of the committee. A quick glance through the table of contents brings to the eye such headings as child development, literature and personal reading, evaluation of pupil growth, in-service growth of teachers, and interpreting reading to the public.

Although the published bulletin[24] did not appear until 1952, a survey of courses of study made by Merritt and Harap covered the period 1948–50. Previously, Dr. Harap had reported such studies in professional magazines. Of a total of 543 guides reviewed in this bulletin, 82 were in English, 38 of them for the elementary school, and 28 of these using a combination of reading, writing, listening, and speaking. The authors noted the increase in number of language arts courses; commented on a trend toward sequential development; noted that 5 of the 82 courses were for grades 1–12. Of the 543 guides, 51 per cent contained suggestions for adjusting teaching to individual differences, especially in reading.

In a comparable study covering the years 1951–53, these same authors noted 112 teaching guides in language arts, 52 of these for the elementary school.

During the ten-year span of the 1940's, there are perhaps fewer new developments because of the fact that during the wartime years, professional groups did not have an opportunity to meet, but shared ideas in their publications.

1950–1960

In this period there are many new developments brought about by the entry of the whole world into the space age. Teachers, children, and parents are confused by some of the proposals made to take steps backward rather than forward in the development of curriculum. But some of the contributions made in the early 1950's should be enumerated. The International Reading Association became an entity during these years, having been formed through co-operation of existing groups. Through the *Reading Teacher* and annual conferences, this organization has made an important contribution to the language arts.

In 1953 the National Education Association, through its member departments of classroom teachers and the research groups, began the production of a series[25] of thin pamphlets, each easily read at one sitting, and directed to the teacher. The first of these was devoted to reading. Others in the series that related to language arts were on spelling, handwriting, and teaching composition. Each bulletin includes careful documentation.

In 1953 the Association for Supervision and Curriculum Development issued a bulletin[26] dealing with research in the language arts, a publication again written to the classroom teacher. At present, even more than in the past, there is a continuing need for the translation and interpretation of research in the language arts in order to make an improvement in classroom practices.

It was in 1954 that *Language Arts for Today's Children*[27] was published in the late fall.

In 1957 Dr. Pooley's volume on grammar[28] made its appearance. In the chapter devoted to the elementary school, he points out that all the evidence is against the teaching of grammar at that level. He says, "If there were any demonstrable evidence that the teaching of grammar in the grades up to and including six resulted in superior writing and speaking on the part of the children, such instruction might be justified." Dr. Pooley gives a birds-eye glimpse of linguistics in his discussion of new views on English grammar. Linguistics represents one of the growing edges for elementary school language arts.

Mention should be made especially of the studies conducted by Paul Witty and his associates of children's looking, listening, and reading habits. Each year beginning in 1951 and continuing yearly[29] these educators have made studies in the Chicago area of children's use of TV, and for a number of these years have also made studies of radio and the comics. It is stated that TV represents children's strongest interest, although whether in spite of it or because of it, librarians report that children are reading more books. Schools have the responsibility to capitalize on the wholesome interests developed from this source of stimulation, and to guide children by means of the language arts program.

Another contribution that should not be overlooked is in the form of compilations of research studies[30] made by the National Conference on Research and the Research Committee of the National Council of Teachers of English. The first appeared in the 1957 issue of *Elementary English*, reporting 289 studies under way in 1956. In the 1959 compilation, 284 research studies are reported for 1958. No breakdown is given with respect to those studies that are in the elementary school field.

We are now in the era of the ballpoint pen and of the teaching machine. It is the period of controversy with respect to philosophy, content of learning, and methods of teaching. At every turn there is need to support one's opinion or judgment with research. And, as this discussion has indicated, research is perhaps the most important earmark of the period 1950 to 1960. In view of the fact that some may feel that child growth and development as an influence has not been stressed sufficiently, it is important to reaffirm that this emphasis has probably contributed more than any single factor to the basic philosophy of the total elementary school program, and thereby to language arts as well. But, this movement has been present throughout the Twentieth Century. Whether it is the battle of the alphabet versus readiness, or creativity versus academic achievement, or individualized reading versus the three-group method, or the array of proposals for reorganizing the school or the class, there is never a dull moment in teaching, and especially in the field of the language arts. As Mrs. Partington might have said, "New names and new nostrums everywhere!"

Footnotes

[1] Harlan Shores, *A Critical Review of the Research on Elementary School Curriculum, 1890-1949*. College of Education, Bureau of Research and Service. University of Illinois Bulletin, Vol. 47, No. 8, September, 1949, Urbana, 1949. 29 pp.

[2] Boston, Massachusetts. *A Provisional Course of Study for the Elementary Schools*. Boston: Printing Department, 1909. 102 pp.

[3] Alabama *State Manual of the Course of Study for the Public Elementary Schools of Alabama*. The Department of Education. Montgomery: Brown Printing Co., 1910. 255 pp.

[4] *Outline Course of Study for the Public Elementary Schools of Baltimore County, Maryland*. Grades I-VIII. Towson, Md.: Democrat and Journal Printers, September, 1909. 345 pp.

[5] *Course of Study—Public Schools, Baltimore County, Md.* Grades I-VIII. Baltimore: William and Wilkins Co., September, 1915. $1.50 ppd. 653 pp.

6 Nila Banton Smith, *American Reading Instruction*. New York: Silver Burdett and Company, 1934. 287 pp.

7 Edward Burk Huey, *The Psychology and Pedagogy of Reading*. New York: The Macmillan Company, 1908. 469 pp.

8 *The Twenty-Fourth Yearbook of the National Society for the Study of Education, Part I*. Bloomington, Illinois: Public School Publishing Company, 1925. 335 pp.

9 Fannie W. Dunn, *Interest Factors in Primary Reading Material*. New York: Teachers College, Columbia Univ. Contributions to Education, No. 113, 1921. 70 pp.

10 A. M. Jordan, *Children's Interests in Reading*. New York: Teachers College, Columbia Univ. Contributions to Education, No. 107, 1921. 143 pp.

11 Mary Peters, "The Newbery-Caldecott Awards—The Effect on Children's Literature." *Chicago Schools Journal*, January-February 1952, pp. 101-105.

12 Sterling A. Leonard, *Essential Principles of Teaching Reading and Literature*. Philadelphia: J. B. Lippincott Co., 1922. 437 pp.

13 Ellsworth Collings, *An Experiment with a Project Curriculum*. New York: The Macmillan Company, 1923. 346 pp.

14 B. D. Wood and F. N. Freeman, *Experimental Study of the Educational Influences of the Typewriter in the Elementary School Classroom*. New York: The Macmillan Company, 1932. 214 pp.

15 W. Wilbur Hatfield, *An Experience Curriculum in English*. New York: D. Appleton, 1935. 323 pp.

16 Association for Childhood Education International, *Bibliography of Books for Children*. Washington, D.C.: The Association, 1937. 76 pp.

17 Bernice Leary, *A Survey of Courses of Study and Other Curriculum Materials Published Since 1934*. Bulletin 1937, No. 31. U. S. Washington, D.C.: Department of the Interior, Office of Education. 185 pp.

18 Angela M. Broening, *Conducting Experiences in English*. A Report of a Committee of the National Council of Teachers of English. Based on Contributions of 274 Cooperating Teachers of English. New York: D. Appleton-Century, 1939. 394 pp.

19 Delia Kibbe, Lou L. LaBrant and Robert C. Pooley, *Handbook of English for Boys and Girls*. Chicago: Scott, Foresman and Company, 1939. 128 pp.

20 Pasadena, California. *Language Arts in the Elementary School Curriculum*. Pasadena, 1936. 187 pp.

21 The Commission on the English Curriculum of the NCTE. *Language Arts for Today's Children*. New York: Appleton-Century-Crofts, Inc., 1954. 431 pp.

22 Arthur E. Traxler and Agatha Townsend, *Eight More Years of Research in Reading*—Summary and Bibliography. Educational Records Bulletin, No. 64. New York 32. Educational Records Bureau, 21 Audubon Avenue, January 1955. 283 pp.

23 *The Forty-Eighth Yearbook of the National Society for the Study of Education, Part II, Reading in the Elementary School*. Chicago: The University of Chicago Press, 1949. 343 pp.

24 Eleanor Merritt and Henry Harap, *Trends in Production of Teaching Guides—A Survey of Courses of Study Published in 1948 Through 1950*. Nashville, Tennessee: George Peabody College for Teachers, 1952. 31 pp.

25 Arthur I. Gates, *What Research Says to the Teacher. Teaching Reading*. Washington, D.C.: The National Education Association, 1953. 29 pp.

26 Harold G. Shane, *Research Helps in Teaching the Language Arts*. Washington: The Association, 1953. 80 pp.

27 Ibid.

28 Robert C. Pooley, *Teaching English Grammar*. New York: Appleton-Century-Crofts, Inc., 1957. 207 pp. (p. 126)

29 Paul Witty and others, "A Tenth Yearly Study and Comments on a Decade of Televiewing." *Elementary English*, Vol. 38, No. 8, December 1959, pp. 581-586.

30 Ralph C. Staiger, "Language Arts Research, 1958." *Elementary English*, 36 November 1959, pp. 502-510.

2 A Report on Project English

Robert C. Slack

A current significant force in all phases and levels of education has been projects financed by the federal government. Project English is one of the largest of these and, although its influence is just beginning to be felt, it could determine to a great extent the direction of future language arts instruction. Even though relatively few Curriculum Study Centers are exclusively concerned with the elementary school, many of the ideas generated in Centers dealing with the secondary school will undoubtedly both filter down to and influence elementary programs. Educators should be aware of current trends and potential influences; hence the inclusion of this article.

Why do you believe the Centers chose to produce materials rather than to conduct experiments comparing different methods of instruction? How do you think these materials will influence language arts textbooks of commercial publishers? Since this is a federally financed project, does it seem possible that a national language arts curriculum might emerge? For a sample of the type of material being produced by one Center, see Evertts' article in Part Four of this anthology, "Literature and Composition in the Elementary Grades." Another look at the role of government in language arts instruction is provided by Haven's article listed in Selected References for Part One. Also see Wachner for a description of a school system's improvement program in a large city.

The question "What is Project English producing?" has been appearing frequently at all levels of the profession. In the spring of 1962, the first three Curriculum Study Centers sponsored by the Office of Education of the Department of Health, Education, and Welfare were established. By now nine more Centers have been added to the list, each with a different concern (though at first glance some of them may appear to overlap the territory of others). A broad picture of the activities and plans of these twelve Centers has been almost impossible to obtain until quite recently. There are understandable reasons for

From *Elementary English* 41:796-800; 807; November 1964. Reprinted with the permission of the National Council of Teachers of English and Robert C. Slack, Professor of English, Carnegie-Mellon University, Pittsburgh, Pennsylvania.

this. Some Centers have been too busy setting up shop and getting their programs under way to pause and give outside inquirers a comprehensive picture of their activities. Others wrote into their original contracts the condition that they would not release their materials until these had been tried in the classroom, revised, and then justified by a comprehensive testing program.

In early May, 1964, a general conference of the first eleven Centers was held at Carnegie Institute of Technology. For the first time it was possible to hear reports on the activities of every Project English Center. The pattern which emerged was both varied and comprehensive.

K Through Twelve

Two Centers have concerned themselves with the whole range of the public school curriculum—one located at the University of Nebraska and the other at the University of Wisconsin.

The Nebraska Center, one of the first established under Project English, originally proposed to make composition the center of its interest. It has, however, developed several pathways to composition and thus has employed a different focus of emphasis in the three large divisions of the overall curriculum. In the elementary school the focus is on children's literature of a high order, in the junior high school the emphasis moves toward language study, and in the senior high school special attention is given to rhetorical studies. All of these studies channel into the overall aim of developing the students' compositional skills. This Center also proposes to give attention to the freshman year of college. The operating personnel of the Nebraska Center constitute a large complex, involving Nebraska teachers, Nebraska University professors, and prominent consultants from the country in general. The activities of the Center are supported not only by Project English funds, but also by the Woods Charitable Fund and the Hill Family Foundation. The Center has been prolific in the production of curricular materials—over 5,000 pages of such materials, which are being used, partly or wholly, in over fifty Nebraska school systems.

The other Center with a broad area of concern is the Wisconsin English-Language-Arts Curriculum Project, sponsored jointly by the University of Wisconsin and the State Department of Public Instruction. This Center is directing a significant portion of its effort into establishing a mechanism for making curricular plans and materials (K through 12) available to every teacher in the state. In addition to designing plans which may result in the recommendation of a state-wide curriculum, the personnel of this project are busy visiting schools and faculties, conducting conferences on various areas of the English-arts program, and preparing educational bulletins for state-wide distribution.

The Elementary School

Two Centers are preparing materials for use in the elementary school. One of these is located at the University of Georgia. The Georgia Center is developing curriculum materials related to written composition in the elementary school. Its first task has been the identification of concepts from several disciplines—such as psychology, sociology, anthropology, and linguistics— which may be used in connection with composition for the elementary school children. This Center is also analyzing, and planning to incorporate into its program, certain creative aspects of language. This is a recently established Center, in the early stages of its operation.

A quite different concern with the needs of the elementary school is being undertaken by the Columbia University Center. Actually, though its work is intended to be useful for early elementary school children from a wide range of linguistic and cultural backgrounds, this Center is developing a program not strictly limited to the public school curriculum. The aim of the Columbia Center is to develop materials for teaching English as a second language. The very nature of this aim widens its horizons to the international scene. The materials developed here will be used not only in New York City, in New Mexico, in Mississippi—but also in Nigeria, Ethiopia, New Guinea, Peru, and other test centers throughout the world.

The TESL Project (as the Columbia project, Teaching English as a Second Language, is widely known) has chosen as its guiding principle to focus upon language as an act of communication. A great deal of its program is oral. Statements are made which call upon the student to perform an action. The following instance was cited at the Carnegie Conference: The instructor says: "My cigarette lighter is in my right jacket pocket; get it for me, please." The student shows his understanding of the statement by doing as he is requested.

This Center, of course, is engaged in developing many approaches to its aim. It intends to complete 100 lesson units during the summer of 1964, as well as playlets, reading materials, recordings, and ancillary materials for composition. These materials will be tried in the various worldwide test centers.

The Junior High School

The curriculum of the junior high school (grades 7 through 9) is the area of concern of two of the Centers—one at the University of Florida and one at Hunter College. Their aims, however, are quite dissimilar. The Florida Center is studying the comparative effectiveness of three different English curricula designed for the junior high school. The first curriculum is organized according to the logic of the subject; that is, it is divided into blocks of content—into units in linguistics, written composition, and literature. The second curriculum is literature-centered and organized into thematic units; in this curriculum, language study and writing are generally related to the literature. The third curriculum is a spiral approach, based on certain cognitive processes which seem related to the study of language and literature. For all three curricula, the seventh-grade courses are now planned in detail and were tried in classrooms beginning in the fall of 1964. Since a comparative evaluation of the three curricula is an essential goal, it is necessary that the Florida Center develop and conduct a comprehensive testing program; one test already developed is concerned with the ability to read poetry.

The Center at Hunter College has chosen to develop an English program for a special group of junior high school students—those whose achievement in English is hampered by environmental and educational disadvantages. Such children do not identify with the reading materials usually provided them. They require reading which, on a high interest level, deals with the kind of problem and environment with which they are familiar. The Hunter Center has begun to select and to create appropriate readings and is giving considerable attention to related audio-visual aids; it has ordered the seventh-grade materials into curriculum units, and will proceed to do the same for the other grade levels. The Center has found also that teachers benefit from guidance in the use of these materials, and it is producing a number of handbooks and video tapes for their use.

The Junior-Senior High School

The greatest number of the Centers have concerned themselves with the full span of the high school years (grades 7 through 12). Four universities house these centers: the University of Oregon, the University of Minnesota, Northwestern University, and Indiana University.

The Oregon Center is preparing a sequential curriculum in language, literature, composition, and speech that will be usable for 85 per cent of the high school students. The assumption here is that, with different expectations at different ability levels and with some adjustment of content,essentially the same program can serve the needs of all students except small groups at the extremes of the spectrum.

Two grades of the curriculum are being planned each year, and in summer institutes pilot teachers of the corresponding grade levels are being prepared to introduce the courses in seven cooperating school systems. The language program consists mainly of transformational grammar, plus supplementary study of social levels in language, the history of language, and similar materials. The literature program is built around the three concepts of Subject, Form, and Point of View. The rhetoric curriculum contains assignments in both writing and speaking, with provision for special training in speech in the eleventh grade. The Center plans to build a testing program to evaluate the curriculum.

The Minnesota Center is developing a curriculum for the junior-senior high school which uses language study as its focal point. Specifically, the Center is developing a series of language-centered units and study guides which will supply a core of continuity for the high school English program. Fourteen such units were used by cooperating schools during the 1963–64 school year; a total of 41 units is projected. Selected high-school teachers are paid to attend summer programs during which they take courses and write drafts of units. The Center is looking forward to the next stage of the project in which data will be analyzed. The final stage will concern the publication of materials and the dissemination of research results.

The Northwestern Center has done some special studies on composition in the high school—particularly in the junior high school. There has been special interest in informal writing (essays concerned with personal experience) and with the writing of narrative. A thesaurus of successful poetic images arranged topically has been begun. The Center has begun work also on exercises dealing with the process of writing and on a set of essays on the problems of composition.

The fourth Center working with the junior-senior high school curriculum is that at Indiana University. This Center is developing three English programs —one for the slow learner, one for the average student, and one for the academically talented. At the outset, of course, it has had to establish criteria for grouping students by ability. The Center has apportioned the curriculum building to three committees, each developing materials suitable for the appropriate ability level. Over fifty pilot schools will test the trial programs for a period of three years. It is planned that the final courses of study will be printed by the Indiana State Department of Public Instruction and distributed to all junior and senior high school teachers of English in the state. The Indiana Center is engaging also in two other activities, sponsored by private foundations. It is developing a journalism course of study under the auspices of The Newspaper Fund of *The Wall Street Journal*. Also, it is developing elective courses in speech and drama under a grant from the Cummins Engine Foundation. Future plans call for workshops and in-service training programs which will be widely available to teachers of English in Indiana.

The Senior High School

The curriculum most limited in scope is that being developed by the Center at the Carnegie Institute of Technology: a cumulative and sequential English curriculum for able college-bound students in senior high school (grades 10 through 12). The Carnegie Center has built around a core literature program which stresses World, American, and English literature in the three years; a second movement in the literature program proceeds from a study of characterization and certain universal themes (10th grade), through the relation of the literature to the culture that produced it (11th grade), to a concern with literary genres and forms (12th grade). The composition program is, for the most part, closely related to the literature. Language study—centered on structure the first year, on semantics the second, and on rhetoric and the history of English the third—is undertaken in three- to six-day units of work strategically spaced throughout the school years.

The entire program has been planned cooperatively by the staff at the Center (four professors of English at Carnegie Tech) and by teachers from seven Pittsburgh area high schools. It has been taught in pilot sections in the cooperating schools, and will be undergoing revision during the third Summer Planning Session. After this revision and another year of teaching the program, the Carnegie Center will be in a position to release its materials to interested schools.

The Carnegie Center is designing a testing program which has a double objective. Using some standardized tests and some newly devised tests, the Center is seeking to measure the effectiveness of the experimental curriculum as compared to that of the standard courses given in the cooperating schools. In developing new tests the Center has the further aim of coming closer than available tests do to measuring subtle skills of reading, writing, and apprehending the nature of the language—all of which constitute the subject English.

Evaluation

At the Carnegie Tech Conference, while the subject matter persons from the several Centers were reporting to one another on curriculum concerns, the psychometricians met separately to consider problems they face in evaluating the newly developed curricula. Their problems are particularly knotty, and some indication of them is instructive to persons whose main professional concern is the teaching of English.

A major problem for evaluators is that the subject matter planners are unable (or unwilling) to define the goals of the new curricula in behavioral terms. That is, they do not (or are not able to) tell the evaluators specifically how a student who has been "taught" a novel or a poem behaves in a way different from that of a student who has not been so "taught." Perhaps it is not possible to state this in behavioral terms; but whether it is or not, it is clear that the evaluators are put into a disadvantageous position if statements of goals are not made in terms that they can measure.

The evaluators also found that the establishment of control groups brought on many problems. In theory, the matching of a group of students who take the "traditional" English course with the group taking the newly developed course should give evidence about the comparable effectiveness of the two courses. But in actual practice, the "traditional" English course defies definition; it might be or become anything. Teachers of such courses are quickly influenced by ideas and practices of the new curriculum (which they are sure to hear of as soon as an experimental course is offered), and consequently they tend to alter their own courses in the new direction. Thus the reason for establishing a control group is seriously vitiated.

Undoubtedly, evaluators have severe handicaps in the context of Project English. They have the very real problem of establishing full rapport with the subject matter people who tend to distrust their method of procedure. But they have not given up hope that they can bring some revealing measurements to bear on the program. They see possibilities for meaningful "clinical" studies of a small group of students; they still suspect that they can pinpoint and measure certain key aspects of the new curricula; they feel that close observation of teacher-student relationships may produce profitable perceptions.

Conclusion

It is clear, certainly, that Project English is producing; that it is actively developing materials for all the years of the school program. Every grade level is receiving careful attention from at least four Curriculum Study centers; the junior high school years—sometimes referred to as the educational no man's land—are of concern to eight of the eleven Centers. The range of the developmental work is broad also, spanning all the main areas within the subject of English. Language study and composition are the areas of prime interest; these two appear prominently in the programs of eight Centers each. The development of programs in literature is of major importance in seven of the Centers.

Project English promises to be an effective force in the development and training of English teachers. Every Center has built into its functional operating procedure a reciprocally beneficial process whereby public school teachers are not only receiving specialized higher education but are also contributing to the developmental work. Through these cooperative endeavors, large segments of the teaching profession are growing in stature and competence, and their influence is bound to be felt in the thousands of schools that they represent. Moreover, built into the plans of many of the Centers is the establishment of some mechanism whereby such teachers, through conferences, demonstrations, in-service training, and the like, will meet with and influence a much broader proportion of the profession. In addition to direct personal influence, of course, the distribution of curriculum materials by the Centers is bound to have an enormous influence upon education in the United States, whether these materials are wholly or partly used, or whether they serve only to arouse thoughtful discussion amongst teachers who reject them.

Indeed, a new Center . . . is devoting its central effort to the preparation of secondary school English teachers. Located at the University of Illinois, this Center represents a state-wide effort of twenty colleges and universities to bring about improvements in their programs for preparing teachers. Both undergraduate and graduate programs will receive their attention, as well as programs for upgrading teachers presently employed.

If every Center were really to succeed in bringing its hopeful plans to a wise and just fruition, Project English could lead us into the Promised Land. Assuredly, we will have to settle for less than this. However, to judge from the content and the tone of the eleven reports, we may not have to settle for much less. The people of the United States are getting more for their money than they might reasonably have counted on.

3 The Classroom Teacher as a Researcher

Carlton M. Singleton, Paul B. Diederich, and Walter Hill

Anyone who believes that all the answers about language arts instruction are already known or who is unwilling to change his present teaching procedures need not read this article.

Why do you think the editors of this anthology included this article in the introductory part? Have you read any research reports within the past six months that you believe could make a significant difference in language arts instruction? What limitations are inherent in single classroom research? Refer to article 5 noting particularly guideline II C for a related idea. After reading this article, formulate a problem you can research in your classroom and outline a suitable methodological procedure encompassing the do's and don't's mentioned in this article. For a review of some significant language arts researches, see the article by Burns listed in Selected References for Part One.

Classroom-centered research is not new. Educational research has always been concerned with the teaching-learning process in the places where it occurs. Each classroom is a possible research laboratory. The important corollary is that each classroom teacher is a possible researcher.

Educational research has taken on a false aura of grey-bearded, library-centered mysticism. It is not mysticism. It is not mysterious, nor need it be library-centered, nor does the researcher need to be grey-bearded. Much of what is important in educational philosophy, psychology, and methodology has come from the ideas and hunches of classroom teachers. Tryouts of their ideas have formed the bases for larger studies which in turn have become the cornerstones of our teaching practices.

From *Elementary English* 38:330-335; May 1961. Reprinted with the permission of the National Council of Teachers of English and Carlton M. Singleton, President, Education, Inc., Charleston, West Virginia; Paul B. Diederich, Senior Research Associate, Educational Testing Service, Princeton, N.J.; and Walter Hill, Professor of Education, University of New York at Buffalo, New York.

The teaching of English is in desperate need of the kind of research that is best done in the individual classroom. The plain fact is that the average recipient of today's English teaching does not use English skillfully. It is the task of teachers of English to develop in all students the ability to read intelligently, to write clearly, and spell correctly, to listen well, and to speak effectively. That these attributes are not shared by all adults is obvious. Considerable debate ranges as to whether students are more skilled or less skilled than they were fifty years ago. This is unimportant. It is important that large numbers of our graduates at any level do not read intelligently, write clearly, listen well, or speak effectively. The number is large because we do not know how to develop these abilities as well as is desirable or necessary.

Finding out how to teach better is the task traditionally set for educational research. In our present ignorance it is more specifically the job of the classroom teacher. Only at the classroom teacher level do we possess the man-power and the facilities to do the vast amount of preliminary work necessary to effect any real improvement in the teaching of English.

The methods used to teach English now differ little, if at all, from the methods in vogue at the turn of the century. (The teaching of reading and spelling in the elementary school are exceptions.) We use the same methods, not because they have demonstrated their effectiveness, but because better ones have not yet emerged from the cauldron of preliminary tryout and rigorous investigation.

The formation and tryout of ideas form the very core of educational research. If the desperately needed improvement in methods of teaching is to come, the direction of improvement must be based upon research. To be effective and useful, such research must be based on good ideas that have withstood the test of preliminary tryout.

The challenge is great. The need is crucial, but despite this obvious need, classroom teachers are notoriously unwilling to research. The unwillingness may be traced to a variety of fears, most of which fit under one of two headings: the fear that the teacher is not fulfilling her responsibilities toward her students; and the fear of research itself.

The responsibility of a teacher to her students is to guide them to the most efficient learning of which they are capable. Such guidance must necessarily be different for different individuals, else all we have learned and subscribed to concerning individual differences is false. It is unfortunate that this basic and simple responsibility is often forgotten in the idea that certain material "must be covered" and/or that the colleges "require certain things." The idea that a course of study is the total diet for any group at any age directly opposes the truth of individual differences. It leads to the shocking pattern of the teacher who plunges into her course of study in September and emerges from the end, in June, triumphant and alone.

Guiding students to efficient learning requires that the teacher search out and apply variations in teaching methodology. It is because this guidance is necessarily different for each individual that the teacher will always be essential to the teaching process. If the course of study contained all that was necessary for each student in a group then the teaching machine could supplant, rather than supplement, the teacher.

The classroom teacher must, to fulfill her appointed task, search out and apply new techniques of teaching. Such endeavor is precisely the kind of educational research this [article] is proposing. To make the ideal of classroom research a reality, it is necessary to add only the activities of describing and evaluating the process. This can and should be as simple as writing a grocery list or taking attendance.

The fact that a full-scale educational investigation designed to test a major hypothesis is involved, time-consuming and difficult to conduct does not affect teacher-directed, classroom-centered research. These are two separate and distinct *levels* of research. At one level the classroom teacher tries out a new idea or technique, evaluates the results, and keeps records of the experiment. At another level a research specialist notes the findings, forms a hypothesis and proceeds to test that hypothesis as rigorously as he knows how. It is apparent that one level is as important as the other, since the second relies so obviously on the first.

Thus, the fears of teachers regarding research are groundless. Our responsibility to our students demands that we do research rather than avoid it. The kind of research we should do is simple, not rigorous, but it is, nonetheless, essential for guiding the total process.

The requisites for good classroom-centered, teacher-directed research are three in number: an idea; a statement of the idea; and a method of determining the effect of the procedure suggested by the idea.

The idea may come from anywhere. It need not be original. In fact, it has been said often that no new ideas exist in education but simply old ideas in new words. The idea may come directly from another teacher's experience, either at first hand or through a journal. It may be an adaption of another's idea. It may come from sensing an educational use of a technique used in business or another profession. The source of the idea is unimportant. It is important that the teacher find an idea that in her judgment is worth trying.

Stating the idea clearly is the next step. It should be phrased as a simple purpose usually in the form of a question. Some examples follow:

1. Would my pupils make fewer errors in punctuation and capitalization if they wrote three 100-word themes each week instead of one 300-word theme?
2. Would my pupils' handwriting improve faster through five minutes of practice each morning or one 30-minute period once a week?

3. Would my pupils make fewer spelling errors in their free writing if I counted such spelling errors in setting their spelling grade?
4. Would my pupils make better progress in written expression by working as parts of teams of two or three than by writing independently?
5. Would my class make faster progress in spelling by mastering 5 words each day than they make using the pattern of 25 words studied in one list all week?
6. Would my class do more independent reading if I read them portions of books than if I assigned them to read a book a month?

These questions are simple and one may well wonder why the answers are not already known. The answers are not known because sufficient research has not been done. The answer to any one may be either yes or no depending upon other circumstances. It might be yes for particular students in a particular place. It might be no for students with differing backgrounds.

The simplicity of these questions makes apparent two important characteristics that distinguish educational research from research in other areas. The teaching-learning process is so complicated that very little is known and established as fact concerning it. The educational researcher is forced to work with little bits of the final results in an effort to establish facts to guide further research. The second characteristic is that educational research, since it is concerned with living people who lead their own lives away from the experiment most of the time, can never control all the variables that may be affecting the experiment. In contrast to a typical educational experiment, a biological or chemical experiment starts with the materials carefully provided for in a lock and key environment that effectively rules out of the experiment any outside interference. The educational experimenter must realize that in his research the results he obtains may have been caused by something completely outside of his experiment. Consequently, a part of the design of full scale educational research must always be provision for duplicating the experiment under widely differing environmental conditions. Only as the technique works anywhere and with anyone can we be sure that the technique itself is important.

Each of the questions posed above are not only simple but posed in terms of the teacher's own class. So stated, the results apply only to the particular class but the value to the profession lies in the possibility that many teachers might reach the same results with many classes. This is called either duplication or replication of research. Classroom teachers can perform a great service to their profession by repeating experiments tried successfully elsewhere, fitting them to the classroom environment within which they are teaching.

The questions listed are samples of the kind of classroom-teacher designed research that is most worthwhile. They are limited in scope as they must be if the results are to be valuable in face of the classroom-group limitation. This does not mean that problems with a broader scope are valueless—it means simply that problems with a larger scope have to be repeated a great many more times before their results can be considered important. As a general rule the smaller the scope the more likely it is that a single classroom experiment offers indications of lasting value.

Another virtue of simplicity in the statement of a problem for classroom research is that the method of technique to be tried is apparent. Ideally, another teacher should be able to tell from the statement alone the basic technique to be attempted. A simple way to check the clarity of a research statement is to ask another teacher to read it and then tell you what she thinks you are going to do. If what she suggests is alien to your plan rewrite your statement.

The third requirement of a good research study is evaluation—finding out what happened. One needs to find out whether the technique worked—did the students learn what they were supposed to or did their behavior change in the way we had hoped? Then one needs to find out whether or not the new method worked better than some other means.

The simplest way to find out whether or not students have learned something is to test them. If tests are available that cover the exact material taught then they can be used. More often the classroom teacher has to build her own tests. . . . For the one time study the first attempt at a teacher-made test must be used and therefore it should be built as carefully as possible. Teachers have been building and relying upon their own tests for years.

Basically, the building of a test over a narrow range of subject matter requires the inclusion of as many facets of the learning as there are. The best classroom test is an exact inventory of all that has been taught. The validity of such a test is reasonably assured if the total content is represented. Generally this ideal is not achieved because teachers tend to regard testing time as non-teaching time and therefore their tests are too brief. Testing time is actually learning time, particularly so if the tests are corrected in class so that each student learns where he went wrong and what he should have done. The recommendation is, then, that the teacher-made test be as comprehensive as possible even if it means testing over two or three classroom periods.

Of the sample questions proposed only Number 5—the one concerned with spelling words in a spelling list—is susceptible to teacher-made test evaluation. Number 2—the handwriting question—could be resolved by using a standardized measure against which to grade handwriting samples. The evaluation would be improved by collecting and grading handwriting samples from a variety of situations including occasions when the students were unaware that their handwriting was to be graded.

The other questions posed call for observations of behavior. Each one suggests that the teacher count errors or books read or some other easily collected data. Such counts should be made both before and after the experiment. Error counts can usually be reduced to a so-many-errors per 100 written words base so that different samples can be compared directly. Such counts serve to answer the first question posed to any evaluation—has the technique accomplished the expected result?

The second facet of evaluation—has the experimental technique done the job better than another method—can be accomplished only partially in the classroom-centered, teacher-directed study. The importance of outside factors is larger when two or more methods are compared. The research specialist allows for this by carefully controlling all the factors he can and then attempts to control the rest by statistical procedures.

The best thing the classroom teacher can do is attempt to evaluate her results against "normal" expectancy. She can define normal expectancy as the progress her last year's group made or the progress this year's group has made during a previous period. Such progress is determined by results on achievement tests. If she has a group with a normal range and mean of mental ages the assumption is reasonable. Most of the questions posed earlier are concerned with learning that is measured in achievement tests. The mechanics of written language and spelling are usually measured directly in such a test. If this year's group makes 18 to 20 months gain against the normal expectancy of 12 months gain, then the indications are that this year's teaching was more successful than last year's. Beyond this rather mild statement no further conclusions are warranted in the single classroom experiment. If the teacher secures the same results in several succeeding years then somewhat stronger claims can be made although they still apply only to the type of group the teacher meets. If her success with a particular technique causes other teachers to try it and they in turn meet with success then even stronger claims are possible. Each success, whether it be in an ensuing year by the same teacher or in other classrooms by other teachers, makes the results more and more conclusive. This duplication or replication of an experiment can be the strongest possible kind of research because good results time after time and in place after place make possible the conclusion that it is the technique itself that is strong despite the many factors which may have influenced it.

Teacher-directed, classroom-centered research is important. As pressures upon us to teach more and more in less time continue to increase, such research becomes crucial. The classroom teacher must search for ways of using teaching time more efficiently. We are confronted with the fact the general level of competence in English is low. It is too much to expect that the remedy will come from the handful of people on college campuses who devote their full time to research in English. It must come from the classroom teachers who have accepted responsibility for teaching English.

The kind of research that is necessary is directly in line with the teaching philosophy general in our schools. It is the searching out of the particular technique, or combination of techniques, that will best fit the individuals in a class.

The formal requirements of scientific investigation are out of place in this kind of research. All that is necessary is an idea, a statement of the idea, and simple evaluation. If the results suggest that the idea is good then is the time to consider a more formal evaluation.

There are many ways in which this simple kind of research can be expanded as individual teachers become research-minded. Another teacher in the same school system may become interested in a direct comparison of method. Co-operative research across a whole school, or school system, is an excellent way to broaden the base of a study. A mutual project in which two or more teachers who teach in different schools may try an idea together but on differing populations, can be valuable. The cooperation of a University in broadening a project by enlisting other teachers and by providing statistical and technical aid can turn a simple study into an extremely important guidepost to the mysteries of the teaching-learning process.

But basically it is the simple study which is important even with its limitations because so many thousands can be done in the time it takes to get one broad research study completed. The challenge offered by the present status of the tea˜hing of English is one that can be successfully met only as each of us, who has accepted the responsibiltiy of teaching English, realizes that research is part of that responsibility.

4   How Do We Teach?

G. Robert Carlsen

Teaching methods can energize desire, sustain effort, and transform the seemingly trivial and mundane into significant adventures. Or they can sow the seeds of lethargy and inertia while making the monumental and gigantic seem dreary and tedious. They can make thinking and problem-solving a way of life or they can change natural inquisitiveness into dulled, unquestioning acceptance. A practitioner and scholar, Carlsen examines some recent methodological changes in the teaching of mathematics and science and challenges teachers to apply these to the teaching of English.

Do you agree with Carlsen that English teaching at present is 95 per cent telling and molding? Examine Carlsen's illustrations; what elements do they all have in common? Are there any particular reasons why the approach advocated by Carlsen should have been pioneered by mathematics and science teachers rather than English teachers? Are all aspects of the language arts program equally suited to the 'discovery' approach? Why or why not? If textbooks tend to be descriptive and declarative, how can they best be adapted to an inductive approach? How does Carlsen's theme relate to Postman's contention in his article cited in Selected References for Part Five? Sabol's article cited in Selected References for Part One is germane to this topic. Try to formulate a 'discovery' situation for one or more of these areas: literature, spelling, composition, grammar, handwriting, and usage.

We all know that a minor revolution has taken place in the teaching of science and mathematics in American schools. Those of us interested in English suddenly find ourselves faced with a desperate need to catch up. But our attempts to imitate the revolutions in science and math have been based on an inadequate understanding of the changes in those fields. While these two areas have changed their content to some extent, they have changed their methodology to a greater extent. The mathematicians and scientists saw clearly that the way

From *English Journal* 54:364-369; May 1965. Reprinted with permission of the National Council of Teachers of English and G. Robert Carlsen, Professor English Education, University of Iowa, Iowa City.

a student studies the subject is fundamental if he is to learn to think within the subject. In English most of our recent efforts have been in the area of content to be taught. It is time that methods of teaching English again became a major concern within our profession.

Methods can usually be described as a choice of one of three roles the teacher selects for himself and his students.

Role I. The Teacher Tells: The Student Memorizes and Stores

Mankind has accumulated vast stores of knowledge. The teacher has accumulated some of this information. Education is the transmission of knowledge from those who have to those who have not. The process is a one-way flow of pre-determined and pre-digested information, whether it is conveyed by the use of the lecture, the recitation, the latest in audio-visual media, or the textbook. The student is given information that someone has accumulated. Father Ong, in a meeting of the new NCTE Commission on Literature, made an interesting point. Not only is new information being created at a fantastic rate, but also old information is being rediscovered to an extent never before undertaken by any former civilization. Archeology, for example, is only 100 years old. We know far more about the past of man than did people during the nineteenth century. There is not only more of the "new" to be transmitted to boys and girls, but there is more of the "old" as well.

Role II. The Teacher Molds: The Student Conforms

This process is not unlike that of orthodontistry. The dentist begins with a preconceived idea of the perfect conformation of the teeth. He constructs a system of wires that can be slowly tightened to exert force on the teeth so that they can be moved closer and closer to the pattern. Once the pattern is attained, the teeth are held in position for a number of years until they will remain in place without the aid of braces.

The whole process of learning language is best described in this kind of construct. The child gains his skills in language by the process of infinitesimal changes that take place as the results of the language molds surrounding him, both in his school and outside school environment. Obviously, for any social order to exist, there has to be some molding: these are the puberty rites by which the young are inducted into the patterns of the tribe. But we might question a bit, particularly at the upper levels of more complicated and involved language skills, whether the vision of perfection on which the molds are built aren't really somewhat artificial. Are we a bit like a fanciful dentist who has a personal predilection for V-shaped sets of teeth and proceeds to move all his patients' teeth into such a configuration?

Role III. The Teacher Stimulates: The Student Teaches Himself

Plato defines the teacher as an "intellectual midwife." He does not create the baby; he does not determine its sex or the color of its hair or its body configuration; he does not even determine its time of arrival; but he does ease the pangs of birth for the mother. Kahlil Gibran says that no man can give another of his understanding; he can only lead another to the brink of his own understanding. Sooner or later, most people who think at all deeply about the problems of education come to believe that the process of inquiry and self-discovery are the central part of the educational endeavor.

Perhaps because we pay singularly little attention to educational history, each new generation of educators has to discover this old truth. In essence this is what the mathematicians and scientists are talking about in their new classroom methods. The School Mathematics Study Group says in the introduction[1] to one of their junior high school volumes: "Mathematics is fascinating to many persons because of its opportunities for creation and discovery as well as for its utility. . . . Even junior high school students may formulate mathematical questions and conjectures which they can test and perhaps settle."

Although I shall focus on this last point of view about education, obviously all three approaches are important in the education of the child. We all admit that we have learned from people who told us what they knew. We have a cliché in our language, however, that acknowledges the limitation of teaching by telling. As parents and teachers, we are all guilty sooner or later of saying, "Look, I told you and I told you, and I told you, but you didn't seem to learn." Obviously students are also aided by some practice in conforming to pre-determined molds. The very nature of language as a shared human activity requires conformity to a pattern. But the whole excitement and ultimate significance of an educational enterprise is lacking unless the third ingredient is there as well.

My feeling is strong that English at present is structured to use *telling* and *molding* about 95 per cent of the time. We have not really learned as yet how to set up situations in which students are stimulated and permitted to make discoveries on their own.

Let's see what is happening in methodology in the fields we profess to admire. A 1964 mathematics text[2] begins something like this:

> Let's suppose that a Cro-Magnon man found it necessary to leave valuable possessions, such as his collection of skins, when he went off hunting. He wanted to be sure when he returned that no one had slipped in and taken some of the skins, but he didn't have any way

of counting. So he devised the idea of putting a bone on each skin, then taking the bones and putting them in a bundle and burying them in the back of the cave. When he returned, he could dig up the bones, put one on each skin and see if they were all there. But after a time, he had so many skins that the "one bone to one skin" method wasn't very effective. Now what do you suppose he might do?

I assume that students start to give answers. Someone suggests the idea that the man might use a bone for every two skins. Another counters with the opinion that there might not be an even number of skins. And the third proposes that an extra skin could be represented by a twig. So now they have the proposition that a bone equals two skins and a twig represents one. Thus through induction, students discover for themselves the concept of a number system built on base units—a concept that I myself didn't understand until I helped my daughters work through their math books.

The School Mathematics Study Group presents this problem in *Mathematics for Junior High School*:[3]

> One sunny day a boy measured the length of the shadow cast by each member of his family. He also measured the length of the shadow cast by a big tree in their yard. He found that his father, who is 72 inches tall, cast a shadow 48 inches long. His mother, who is 63 inches tall, cast a shadow 42 inches long. His little brother, who is only 30 inches high, cast a shadow 20 inches long. He didn't know how tall the tree was, but its shadow was forty feet. Let us arrange this information in a table.

While the table leads to stated generalizations, the intention of the teaching is obvious: that from the table young people would make as many observations on their own as possible and, bit by bit, figure out something about ratios and how they operate mathematically.

A 1965 math book[4] takes this approach:

> When you buy a pair of gloves, do you count the fingers to see if there are the correct number? Can you think of an easier way to find out if the number of fingers is correct? A teacher walks into the classroom carrying a seating chart for the class. Can he tell immediately who is absent, just by looking at the empty chairs and at the chart? If so, how? Does he need to call the roll or to count?

These questions, of course, lead the student to develop the concept of one-to-one correspondence between the elements of two sets.

Many of us have been intrigued with Suchman's demonstrations of teaching inquiry using scientific materials. One of his favorites consists in showing a brief film clip of a knife blade which bends down when held in a flame. Water straightens it out. The blade is turned over and held in the flame once again. This time it bends upward. He then says to the class: "Let's try to figure out why this happens. You ask me any questions you want to and I'll give you the answer if I know it."

As the questions come, he suggests that some of the questions are fact questions and some are theory questions. He answers the theory questions by asking the student what other questions he might need to ask to substantiate or refute the theory. Students quickly differentiate between the two kinds of questions. Excitement runs high. It is important to note that in Suchman's approach he is not asking students to look things up, thereby discouraging them from asking questions. He is posing as a source of information to which they can turn directly for an immediate answer to an immediate question, but he does not offer information unless they ask for it.

These illustrations highlight, I think, how differently instruction is being oriented in the sciences from what it is in English. I can find almost none of this kind of teaching in our newest textbooks or in the day-by-day observations I make of classroom practice. Let's take some samples from recent English texts:[5]

> The climax of the story occurs when your suspense is greatest, when Rainsford's Uganda Knife trick has failed to kill Zaroff, when Zaroff and the dogs have Rainsford at bay on the edge of a cliff, when Rainsford must either jump into the sea or be killed. At the climax of the story, you learn that Rainsford "leaped far out into the sea." Although you stay in suspense until the end of the story, from the climactic point in the action, the outcome of the story is determined.

Notice how the above study materials tell the student everything. Nothing is left for his own creative thinking or initiative. Take another example from a 1963 English literature text. Students are told before reading *Macbeth:*

> William Shakespeare's *Macbeth* is a powerful drama of a man whose weakness first brought him power, then defeat. As a play for acting, it outdistances most because of its admirable construction and its many scenes that are theatrically powerful as well as inherently dramatic. . . . Alive with the passions of eleventh century Scotland, yet timeless in its impact, *Macbeth* is one of the most gripping of Shakespeare's tragedies.

These are statements of what someone *else* has found out. The student feels no necessity to find out anything for himself. From the same book:

> In "The Cloud," consider the unusual meter and the internal rhymes in alternate lines. What swing and gusto these give to the constantly shifting life of the cloud! The whole poem moves with the speed of racing clouds on a windy day.

The student is told. He does not discover anything.

Let's look now at a 1964 language text which prides itself on including newer grammatical approaches. It states categorically:

Most English words belong to one of four large groups—nouns, verbs, adjectives, and adverbs. These groups are often called form classes because many of the words in them have special forms: for example; *man* and *men, go* and *going, blue* and *bluest.* A relatively small number of English words do not belong to any form class. These words are called structure words and are divided into several structure groups. . . . A word can be identified as belonging to one form class or another on the basis of the following characteristics: . . . *etc.*

In spite of these categorical statements, the book says thirty pages later: "A noun is a word used as the name of a person, place, or thing."

From a widely used composition textbook students are told how to write a composition. Section titles are: *List Your Ideas, Group Related Ideas under Headings, Arrange Ideas in Order, Make an Outline.* Each of these injunctions is developed through a series of more refined procedures which, in effect, tell the student exactly what the author feels he must do.

The textbooks from which I am quoting are not bad as English books go. Some of them are the best we have available, but they are certainly different in their implied methodology from the math and science texts. Notice that in every one, students are told what someone else has found to be true. They set up no situations in which the student must think his way through to his own understanding. They rely heavily on statements of conclusion. "*Macbeth* is a powerful drama of a man whose weakness first brought him power, then defeat." Since this statement precedes the play, why bother to read it at all when you are told exactly what you will find?

Without straining to create, let's try imitating some of the techniques used in science and math in our own subject matter field. What might happen? "Supposing," we might say to a class, "that pre-historic man is at a point where he makes sounds . . . he even imitates sounds, but he hasn't yet invented language. One day he returns to his cave in great excitement and tries, through pulling and nipping, to get his family to come with him deeper into the cave because he has seen a hungry saber tooth tiger lurking nearby, watching every move. But the family is not about to be moved by this nipping and pulling since they do not understand the situation. What could he do to communicate the idea of imminent danger?"

Some student will be sure to suggest acting the danger out and still another may propose drawing a picture. But the class can be led to see that either procedure would take too long . . . the family would be destroyed before the idea could be conveyed. So then the student could be led to discover for himself, how sounds come to stand for things; how sounds are combined with one another to mean still other things; how language needs words for different functions.

Let's take another example. We might say: "Here are two sets of sentences. Notice that set A sentences all have commas within them. Set B sentences express similar ideas but do not have commas. Your job is to figure out what differences between the two sets may account for the differences in their punctuation. You can ask me questions to help you gather the facts you need to construct your theory or principal."

Or we might say: "Suppose on Saturday you were buying gas and the attendant said, 'That don't cost very much.' On Sunday the minister said, 'John doesn't come to church much anymore.' In the newspaper you read: 'The committee doesn't have its report completed.' On Tuesday your friend said to you: 'Hey, that crazy English teacher don't have any assignment for us.' That same day the vet remarked: 'The cat don't really seem to have a broken leg.' Let's arrange these in a chart showing the instances of use of *don't* and *doesn't*. Let's also include the speaker's level of education and probable ability to use language, the number of people present, the formality of the situation. Now what observations can you make from the chart?"

A possible situation in composition might go something like this: "Suppose you have written the sentence, 'Climbing the tower I thought ahead to the dive I was about to make.' Now write five different sentences, any one of which might logically be the next sentence. Now consider how the use of each different second sentence would change the direction of the third sentence which you might write."

And of course, literature should be a continuing process of discovery. My son says that a work of literature is like the closed door leading into a wonderful palace he has not visited before. Each book is the opening on something to be discovered for the first time. Mrs. Maxine Delmare of the Kirkwood Schools in St. Louis once said that literature was like a mathematical model, abstractly conceived. Each reader is in the process of testing the accuracy of the model against his own reality . . . sometimes rejecting the model and sometimes rejecting his own view of reality because of the model. Inquiry and discovery are the very essence of the reading of literature, yet here too, we as teachers have substituted didacticism and molding. Try a short lyric sometime and ask students to jot down in columns after reading it what they saw, what they heard, and what they felt. Now check. How many of the items are not directly mentioned in the words? Where do you suppose these ideas came from? How many things did you miss that are directly mentioned in the poem? Why do you suppose you missed them?

I am sure that we need to supply students with information. I am sure that we must also build molds and braces to bend them to given patterns. But I am also sure that we miss the heart of education if we do not stimulate them to make their own discoveries through the process of their own inquiries. I am sure that we know almost nothing of how this method might best be applied to the subject matter of English. We are woefully behind the refined techniques now standardly used in math and science. And I am sure that until we learn how to use this method, we can do little to improve the curriculum in English. We will simply turn out a student who remains bound by his imitation of certain patterns.

The mathematician says: "Mathematics is fascinating . . . because of its opportunities for creation and discovery. Even junior high school students may formulate mathematical questions and conjectures which they can test and perhaps settle."

When will English teachers be able to make this statement: "English is fascinating because of its opportunities for creation and discovery. Even students may formulate linguistic, literary and composing questions and conjectures which they can test . . . perhaps settle"?

Footnotes

[1] School Mathematics Study Group, *Mathematics for Junior High School*, Vol. I, Part I, Revised Ed. (New Haven, Conn.: Yale University, 1960), p. v.

[2] Marie Wilcox and John Yarnelle, *Basic Modern Mathematics* (Reading, Mass.: Addison-Wesley Publishing Co., Inc., 1964).

[3] School Mathematics Study Group, *Mathematics for Junior High School*, Vol. I, Part II (New Haven, Conn.: Yale University, 1959), p. 383.

[4] H. Vernon Price, *Mathematics, An Integrated Series*, Book I (New York: Harcourt, Brace and World, 1965).

[5] Quotations similar to these given from several English textbooks could have been collected from most series now in use in the schools. Since the intent is not to ridicule any particular series, the sources of these quotations are omitted. They are in the possession of the editor of the *English Journal* and can be supplied by the author on request.

5 English Teacher Preparation Study: Guidelines for the preparation of teachers of English

Probably no other curricular area includes as many components, each of which is exceptionally vital for the effective functioning of human beings in society, as the language arts curriculum. This singular quality demands a scope and depth of teacher preparation not required by other elementary school curricular areas. The following guidelines were the result of a project conducted jointly by the National Association of State Directors of Teacher Education and Certification, the National Council of Teachers of English, and the Modern Language Association of America, with the cooperation of Western Michigan University. They are not intended to be applied arbitrarily to the certification of English teachers at either the elementary or secondary level but rather to set a context within which teacher preparation programs can be evaluated with discretion and imagination.

What recommendations reflect a changing view of the task of the English teacher? Do you believe the guidelines are arranged in their order of importance? If not, which ones do you consider most important? Least important? Consider the breadth of the elementary language arts program; are there any areas you feel deserve more attention? Are any overemphasized? How would your teacher preparation rank if evaluated by these guidelines? Can all guidelines be met by enrollment in a series of college or university courses? An article by Squires cited in Selected References for Part One is germane to this topic.

Guidelines for English Teacher Preparation

I. The teacher of English at any level should have personal qualities which will contribute to his success as a classroom teacher and should have a broad background in the liberal arts and sciences.

A cooperative study by the National Association of State Directors of Teacher Education and Certification, the National Council of Teachers of English, and the Modern Language Association of America, centered at Western Michigan University. The Guidelines have been endorsed by the three sponsoring organizations. Reprinted with permission from *Elementary English*, October 1967 (*English Journal*, September 1967 and *College English*, October 1967).

II. A. The program in English for the elementary school teacher should provide a balanced study of language, literature, and composition above the level of freshman English. In addition, the program should require supervised teaching and English or language arts methods, including the teaching of reading, and it should provide for a fifth year of study.

B. The program in English for the secondary school teacher of English should constitute a major so arranged as to provide a balanced study of language, literature, and composition above the level of freshman English. In addition, the program should require supervised teaching and English methods, including the teaching of reading at the secondary level, and it should provide for a fifth year of study, largely in graduate courses in English and in English Education.

C. The teacher of English at any level should consider growth in his profession as a continuing process.

III. The teacher of English at any level should have an understanding and appreciation of a wide body of literature.

IV. The teacher of English at any level should have skill in listening, speaking, reading, and writing, and an understanding of the nature of language and of rhetoric.

V. The teacher of English at any level should have an understanding of the relationship of child and adolescent development to the teaching of English.

VI. The teacher of English at any level should have studied methods of teaching English and have had supervised teaching.

Guideline I

The teacher of English at any level should have personal qualities which will contribute to his success as a classroom teacher and should have a broad background in the liberal arts and sciences.

A. Like all other teachers, he should be able to work successfully with children or adolescents and with his peers. He should have a mature personality and possess such important qualities as creativity, a sense of humor, self-discipline, and a genuine appreciation of the variety of linguistic and cultural backgrounds of his students.

B. He should be an educated person who has a critical awareness of himself and of the world in which he lives. Careful counseling should help him plan a balanced program from among the many disciplines which can contribute to his intellectual growth and to his effectiveness as a teacher of English.

1. History, speech, fine and applied arts, and foreign language would be particularly appropriate in a program for the teacher of English at any level.

(a) Because American literature is an integral part of the curriculum in the secondary school, the teacher of English would benefit from a study of American social, cultural, and intellectual history, as well as political history. The inclusion of the works of many British authors in the curriculums of American elementary and secondary schools suggests the value of the study of British cultural history. The increasing appearance of African, Asian, and Latin American literature in the curriculum makes courses in the cultural history of non-English speaking peoples useful for all, and essential for some, teachers.

(b) Preparation in speech should help the prospective teacher listen more critically, speak and read aloud more effectively, and assist students in developing these proficiencies. Such preparation should also broaden the teacher's knowledge of the process of oral communication, help him relate these processes at both theoretical and functional levels to other uses of the English language, and provide him with the means of assessing the effectiveness of his own use of spoken language in varying teaching situations.

(c) Study and practice in the fine and applied arts, valuable in themselves, would enhance the teacher's ability to recognize, to nourish, and to evaluate students' creative work and artistic techniques.

(d) A knowledge of at least one foreign language should not only broaden the cultural background of the secondary school teacher, but also supplement his knowledge of the English language and of literature written in English. Instead of merely reading or hearing about the difficulties and deficiencies of translations and about the differences between the structure of English and that of other languages, he should learn about these matters directly through study of another language, classical or modern. Especially appropriate is the study of a foreign language having a literature that has significantly influenced English and American literature. But in the present world, important advantages accrue from a practical command of any living foreign language.

The increasing frequency and intensity of problems of bilingualism and multi-dialectalism in American schools make it virtually imperative that both the elementary school teacher and the secondary school teacher of English be familiar with a foreign language, with the methods by which English is taught to speakers of another language or dialect, and with the psychological processes involved in learning a second language or dialect.

2. Philosophy, history, sociology, psychology, anthropology, and geography, valuable in themselves, would help the prospective teacher become

familiar with a growing body of information that contributes to our understanding of man, his languages, and his literature.

3. The sciences and mathematics would give the prospective teacher some knowledge of these subjects, an understanding of their importance in the modern world, and an introduction to methods of scientific analysis.

Guideline II

A. The program in English for the elementary school teacher should provide a balanced study of language, literature, and composition above the level of freshman English. In addition, the program should require supervised teaching and English or language arts methods, including the teaching of reading, and it should provide for a fifth year of study.

   1. The elementary school teacher spends between 40 and 60 per cent of his time teaching English and related skills in almost any pattern of school organization.

      (a) His preparation program should, therefore, develop his own skills and increase his knowledge of the components of English.

      (b) His program must, in addition, include study of materials and methods for teaching English to elementary school children.

   2. The fifth-year program may be taken either prior to teaching, during summers, or through accredited extension or in-service courses taken during the school year, but it should ordinarily be completed within the first five years of teaching. The elementary school teacher should study English and English Education to supplement his basic preparation. His needs, deficiencies, or special interests, determined through careful counseling, may suggest undergraduate or graduate work in these or other areas.

B. The program in English for the secondary school teacher of English should constitute a major so arranged as to provide a balanced study of language, literature, and composition above the level of freshman English. In addition, the program should require supervised teaching and English methods, including the teaching of reading at the secondary level, and it should provide for a fifth year of study, largely in graduate courses in English and in English Education.

   1. The secondary school teacher of English is a specialist in English:

      (a) His preparation program should, therefore, develop his own skills and increase his knowledge of the components of English.

      (b) His program must, in addition, include study of materials and methods for teaching English at the secondary level.

   2. The fifth-year program may be taken either prior to teaching, during

summers, or through accredited extension or in-service courses taken during the school year, but it should ordinarily be completed within the first five years of teaching. The secondary school teacher of English should ordinarily study English and English Education at the graduate level. His needs, deficiencies, or special interests, determined through careful counseling, may, however, call for undergraduate or graduate studies in these or other areas.

C. The teacher of English at any level should consider growth in his profession as a continuing process.

  1. He should broaden his knowledge and understanding of the content and teaching of English through reading, observation, research, formal course work, in-service study, workshops and institutes, and travel.
  2. He should read publications which report investigations of the organization and content of the English curriculum, describe new and improved methods and materials for the teaching of English, report relevant research, and examine the philosophical bases for the teaching of English.
  3. He should seek further professional growth through such activities as membership in local, state, and national professional organizations, study in the United States and in foreign countries, and experience as an exchange teacher.

Guideline III

The teacher of English at any level should have an understanding and appreciation of a wide body of literature.

A. His undergraduate program should have prepared him to read for his own enjoyment, to gain insight into himself and the world around him, and to understand and appreciate how writers order experience.

  1. He should have developed a strong commitment to literature as an experience to be enjoyed both in and out of school classes.
  2. He should have developed the habit of reading beyond classroom necessity so that he can bring to his teaching a wide experience with literature and with the means of stimulating his students' creative responses and reactions to literary works.

B. He should have studied literature systematically.

  1. He should know a wide range of significant works of literature recognized as classic and, in addition, examples of other well-written discourse.
  2. He should have studied such major literary genres as drama, poetry, fiction, and the essay.
  3. He should be able to relate contemporary writing to the traditions from which it grows.

4. He should have studied important writers and writings of English and American literature both to extend his knowledge of literary history and convention and to develop his critical skill.

5. He should have studied some representative works from literatures other than English and American.

6. He should have studied in depth some major authors (such as Shakespeare) and at least one literary period.

C. He should have acquired critical and scholarly tools.

1. He should be able to use his knowledge of language and rhetoric to analyze literature more perceptively.

2. His study of different ways of analyzing a work of literature should include some formal training in the theories of literary criticism and practice in close textual criticism.

3. He should be able to analyze and discuss language as it is used in various media and literature as it is presented in such media as radio, television, motion pictures, and theater.

D. He should know literary works appropriate for the level at which he teaches.

1. The elementary school teacher should know a wide body of children's literature.

2. The secondary school teacher of English should know a wide body of literature for adolescents.

E. He should have studied and practiced the strategies of teaching literature to students who have a wide range and variety of individual and group differences.

1. He should be able to foster in his students a taste for literature.

2. He should be able to demonstrate processes of literary analysis to his students through critical techniques appropriate to the literary work and to the level at which he is teaching.

3. He should have a knowledge of the theories and methods of teaching children and adolescents to read literature with skill and perception.

4. He should be able to insure a fuller understanding of literature through his own oral reading and through classroom activities such as individual oral interpretation, choral reading, and appropriate dramatic activities of all kinds.

Guideline IV

The teacher of English at any level should have skill in listening, speaking, reading, and writing, and an understanding of the nature of language and of rhetoric.

A. He should have developed skill in speaking and writing.

1. He should have had supervised practice in speaking and writing in a variety of modes.

2. He should have acquired a functional understanding of the activities essential to the composing process, and of the qualities and properties of children's writing.

3. He should have had supervised practice in describing, analyzing, and evaluating, for purposes of teaching, various kinds of speaking and writing, both historical and contemporary.

4. He should have had special work appropriate to the level at which he will teach:

   (a) to develop his skill in reading aloud and in storytelling;

   (b) to develop his ability to help students control and expand their linguistic resources for conversation and other forms of oral discourse, such as storytelling, informal or structured discussions and reports, or fully developed speeches for public occasions;

   (c) to develop his ability to help students find adequate means of expression in both imaginative and factual writing;

   (d) to increase his awareness of the origins, the objectives, and the potentialities of composition teaching in the schools;

   (e) to prepare him to teach spelling, handwriting, and other conventions of written expression.

5. He should have had instruction in writing beyond the college freshman level, either through an advanced course in composition or through supervised individual instruction and practice.

B. Not only should he be prepared in the technical and expository aspects of composition, but he should also have explored the creative and liberating functions of speaking and writing and the relations between such creativity and other forms of expression, e.g., painting and pantomime.

C. He should have a well-balanced descriptive and historical knowledge of English language.

1. He should have some understanding of phonology, morphology, and syntax; the sources and development of the English vocabulary; semantics; and social, regional, and functional varieties of English usage.

2. He should be acquainted with methods of preparation and uses of dictionaries and grammars.

3. He should be well-grounded in one grammatical system and have a working acquaintance with at least one other system.

4. He should have studied basic principles of language learning in order to apply his knowledge at various grade levels to the problems of those learning to speak, listen, read, and write to a variety of audiences.

5. He should have an understanding of the respective domains of linguistics

and rhetoric, and of the range of choice available within the structure of the language.

D. He should be able to utilize his knowledge of language and of language learning to develop his own and his students' ability to read and to listen. His knowledge should include an understanding of the components of reading and listening processes and of the variety of ways in which people read and listen.

E. He should have acquired a functional understanding of the nature and substance of rhetoric.

   1. He should have some acquaintance with the principles of classical rhetoric, and should understand their relationship to modern rhetorics.
   2. He should have some acquaintance with the influence of rhetorical theory on the teaching of composition.
   3. He should have sufficient acquaintance with the principles of rhetoric and the nature of the writing process to be able to use the former, where relevant, in analyzing the latter or products thereof, whether written or oral.
   4. He should have sufficient acquaintance with the principles of rhetoric, as related to the writing process, to be able to use them, where relevant in his own writing and speaking, and also in his teaching.

Guideline V

The teacher of English at any level should have an understanding of the relationship of child and adolescent development to the teaching of English.

A. He should in a formal way have studied human behavior, with emphasis upon the age level at which he plans to teach, and should explore relevant research on child and adolescent development for its possible implications for the curriculum in English.

   1. He should have studied the language development of children and adolescents: their interest in language, their growth in using vocabulary and syntax, in understanding and using figurative speech, as well as their growth in the ability to distinguish among several varieties of usage.
   2. He should be aware of the growing knowledge about the relationships between language development and personal development.
   3. He should be aware of the growing knowledge about the specific relationships between control of spoken language (sentence patterns, vocabulary, dialect) and success in reading.
   4. He should recognize aspects of child development that will help the teacher select literature which children or adolescents are likely to understand and enjoy.

B. Because he must constantly evaluate the performance of his students and the effectiveness of his own teaching, both subjectively and by diagnosing and measuring student performance, he should understand the techniques, possibilities, and limitations of testing and of grouping students by interest, aptitude, achievement, and task.

C. He should be familiar with theories of reading and be able to apply appropriate methods to improve the reading abilities of students at various levels of achievement and with various rates of progress.

    1. The elementary school teacher should have an understanding of developmental reading from early childhood to adolescence and be able to utilize that understanding in his teaching.

    2. The secondary school teacher of English should have an understanding of developmental reading, particularly at the junior and senior high school levels, and be able to utilize that understanding in his teaching.

Guideline VI

The teacher of English at any level should have studied methods of teaching English and have had supervised teaching.

A. He should have considered and analyzed the purposes of English instruction in the schools.

B. The elementary school teacher should have had supervised teaching or an internship which includes the language arts guided by teachers and supervisors prepared in this area, should be able to relate the language arts to other elements in the curriculum, and should be aware of recent developments in the teaching of English.

C. The secondary school teacher of English should have had supervised teaching or an internship at the level at which he plans to teach. He should be guided by a supervisor who has successfully taught English at that level and is aware of recent developments in the teaching of English.

D. He should have learned to use in his teaching what he knows about children, adolescents, and the psychology of learning.

E. He should have learned to analyze units of instruction, to prepare individual lessons and teaching materials, and to understand and evaluate the development and design of courses of study.

F. He should know how to create or find, evaluate, and use significant instructional materials from various media: texts of all kinds, films, kinescopes, tapes, records, slides, and programmed materials.

G. He should know how to select, adapt, and develop activities and materials appropriate to different age groups distinguished by maturity, culture, ability, and achievement, and to individual students.

H. He should have learned how to recognize students who have the kinds of differences or disabilities in the language skills which should be referred to specialists for attention.

I. He should have analyzed and practiced a range of teaching techniques, with particular attention to the techniques of inductive teaching.

J. He should have learned how to correlate the contents and skills of listening, speaking, reading, and writing with one another and with other subjects in the curriculum.

K. He should have studied and practiced ways to foster creativity in· the speaking and writing of his students.

L. He should understand the kinds of problems which censorship and propaganda can bring to the school and have learned procedures for handling specific situations.

6　A Minimal Professional Reference Library on the Language Arts for Elementary School Teachers

Eldonna L. Evertts and Walter J. Moore

No single book can adequately cover the broad range of topics included in the elementary school language arts program; hence this list. But neither can even the most recent books incorporate the dynamism which pervades the language arts today; hence the inclusion of professional journals in the list and the implication that additions must be made as they become available in the future.

With which of these references are you familiar? Unfamiliar? Why are references on curriculum and language included as well as ones on methodology? Do the compilers imply that this list is designed for individuals, elementary schools, or college libraries? Are there any professional references omitted which you believe should have been included?

Suggested only as a basic list of minimum essentials to which schools may add titles as funds become available.

Professional journals

Subscription to *Elementary English*
Subscription to one or two periodicals which regularly feature articles on aspects of the language arts: *The Reading Teacher, Childhood Education, The Horn Book, Elementary School Journal.*
Subscription to the journal of the state English association.

The curriculum series of the
National Council of Teachers of English

The English Language Arts. New York: Appleton-Century-Crofts, 1952. (Perspective on the total English program)
Language Arts for Today's Children. New York: Appleton-Century-Crofts, 1954.

From *Elementary English* 44:536-539; May 1967. Reprinted with the permission of the National Council of Teachers of English.

General books on methods of teaching about curriculum in the language arts

Anderson, Paul S., *Language Skills in Elementary Education.* New York: The Macmillan Company, 1964.

Anderson, Verna Dieckman, *et al., Readings in the Language Arts.* New York: The Macmillan Company, 1964.

Burns, Paul C. and Alberta L. Lowe, *The Language Arts in Childhood Education.* Chicago: Rand McNally & Co., 1966.

Crosby, Muriel, *Curriculum Development for Elementary Schools in a Changing Society.* Boston: D. C. Heath and Company, 1964.

Fleming, Robert S. (ed.), *Curriculum for Today's Boys and Girls.* Columbus, Ohio: Charles E. Merrill Books, Inc., 1963.

Herrick, Virgil E. and Leland B. Jacobs (eds.), *Children and the Language Arts.* Englewood Cliffs, N.J.: Prentice-Hall Inc., 1955.

MacCampbell, James C., *Readings in the Language Arts in the Elementary School.* Boston: D. C. Heath and Company, 1964.

Russell, David H., *Children's Thinking.* Boston: Ginn and Company, 1956.

Strickland, Ruth G., *Language Arts in the Elementary School,* Second Edition. Boston: D. C. Heath and Company, 1957.

Taba, Hilda, *Curriculum Development Theory and Practice.* New York: Harcourt, Brace & World, Inc., 1962.

Tauger, Wilmer K., *Language Arts in Elementary Schools.* New York: McGraw-Hill Book Company, 1963.

Watts, A. F., *The Language and Mental Development of Children.* London: George G. Harrap and Company, Ltd., 1944, 1966.

Specialized books and references

One or two reference books in each area, such as in:

Reading

Harris, A. J., *Effective Teaching of Reading.* New York: David McKay Co., Inc., 1962.

Harris, A. J., *How to Increase Reading Ability,* Fourth Edition. New York: Longmans, Green and Company, 1961.

Jennings, Frank G., *This Is Reading.* New York: Bureau of Publications, Teachers College, Columbia University, 1965.

Reeves, Ruth, *The Teaching of Reading in Our Schools.* New York: The Macmillan Company, 1966.

Robinson, H. Alan (ed.), *Recent Developments in Reading.* Chicago: The University of Chicago Press, 1965.

Robinson, H. Alan (ed.), *Reading and the Language Arts.* Chicago: The University of Chicago Press, 1963.

Russell, David H., *Children Learn to Read,* Second Edition. Boston: Ginn and Company, 1961.

Smith, Nila Banton, *American Reading Instruction.* Newark, Del.: International Reading Association, 1965.

Smith, Nila Banton, *Reading Instruction for Today's Children.* Englewood Cliffs, N. J.: Prentice-Hall, Inc., 1963.

Spache, George, *Reading in the Elementary School.* Rockleigh, N.J.: Allyn & Bacon, Inc., 1964.

Tinker, Miles A. and Constance M. McCullough, *Teaching Elementary Reading,* Second Edition. New York: Appleton-Century-Crofts, 1952, 1962.

Veatch, Jeanette, *Reading in the Elementary School.* New York: The Ronald Press Company, 1966.

Writing and Speaking

Applegate, Mauree, *Easy in English.* New York: Harper and Row, Publishers, 1960.

Burrows, Alvina T., *They All Want to Write: Written English in the Elementary School,* Third Edition, pap. New York: Holt, Rinehart, and Winston, Inc., 1964.

Burrows, Alvina T., *et al., Children's Writing: Research in Composition and Related Skills.* Champaign, Ill.: National Council of Teachers of English, 1961.

Clegg, A. B., *The Excitement of Writing.* London: Chatto and Windus, 1964.

Corbin, Richard, *The Teaching of Writing in Our Schools.* New York: The Macmillan Company, 1966.

Cutforth, John A., *English in the Primary School.* Oxford: Basil Blackwell, 1964.

Huckleberry, Alan W. and Edward S. Strother, *Speech Education for the Elementary Teacher.* Boston: Allyn and Bacon, Inc., 1966.

Siks, Geraldine Brain, *Children's Literature for Dramatization.* New York: Harper and Row, Publishers, 1964.

Ogilvie, Mardel, *Speech in the Elementary School.* New York: McGraw-Hill Book Company, 1954.

Ward, Winifred, *Play Making with Children, from Kindergarten Through the Junior High School,* Revised Edition. New York: Appleton-Century-Crofts, 1957.

Language, Grammar, and Usage

Allen, Harold B. (ed.), *Readings in Applied English Linguistics,* Second Edition. New York: Appleton-Century-Crofts, 1964.

Anderson, Wallace L. and Norman Stageberg, *Introductory Reading on Language.* New York: Holt, Rinehart and Winston, Inc., 1966.

Dean, Leonard F. and Kenneth G. Wilson, *Essays on Language and Usage,* Second Edition. New York: Oxford University Press, 1963.

Emig, Janet A., *et al., Language and Learning.* New York: Harcourt, Brace & World, Inc., 1966.

Folsom, Franklin, *The Language Book.* New York: Grosset & Dunlap, Inc., 1963.

Goldstein, Miriam B., *The Teaching of Language in Our Schools.* New York: The Macmillan Company, 1966.

Language Programs for the Disadvantaged. Champaign, Ill.: National Council of Teachers of English, 1965.

Malmstrom, Jean, *Language in Society.* New York: Hayden Book Company, Inc., 1965.

Malmstrom, Jean and Annabel Ashley, *Dialects—U.S.A.* Champaign, Ill.: National Council of Teachers of English, 1963.

Marckwardt, Albert H., *Linguistics and the Teaching of English.* Bloomington: Indiana University Press, 1966.

Pooley, Robert C., *Teaching English Usage.* New York: Appleton-Century-Crofts, 1946.

Research on Handwriting and Spelling. Champaign, Ill.: National Council of Teachers of English, 1964-1966.

Rycenga, J. A. and J. Schwartz, *Perspectives on Language.* New York: The Ronald Press Company, 1963.

Shuy, Roger W. (ed.), *Social Dialects and Language Learning.* Champaign, Ill.: National Council of Teachers of English, 1964.

Literature

Arbuthnot, May Hill, *Children and Books,* Revised Edition. Chicago: Scott, Foresman & Company, 1964.

Arnstein, Flora J., *Poetry in the Elementary Classroom.* New York: Appleton-Century-Crofts, 1962.

Fenner, Phyllis, *The Proof of the Pudding: What Children Read.* New York: The John Day Company, Inc., 1957.

Frank, Josette, *Your Child's Reading Today,* Revised Edition. Garden City, N. Y.: Doubleday & Company, Inc., 1960.

Haviland, Virginia, *Children's Literature: A Guide to Reference Sources.* Washington: Library of Congress, 1966.

Huber, Miriam Blanton, *Story and Verse for Children,* Third Edition. New York: The Macmillan Company, 1965.

Huck, Charlotte and Doris Young Kuhn, *Children's Literature in the Elementary School.* New York: Holt, Rinehart, & Winston, Inc., 1963.

Jacobs, Leland B. (ed.), *Using Literature with Young Children.* New York: Teachers College Press, Columbia University, 1965.

Smith, Dora V., *Fifty Years of Children's Books.* Champaign, Ill.: National Council of Teachers of English, 1963.

Smith, Lillian H., *The Unreluctant Years: A Critical Approach to Children's Literature.* Chicago: American Library Association, 1953.

Aids for selecting books for children

Two or three recent annotated book lists, such as:

A Basic Book Collection for the Elementary Grades. American Library Association, 50 East Huron Street, Chicago, Illinois 60611.

Adventuring with Books. National Council of Teachers of English, 508 South Sixth Street, Champaign, Illinois 61820.

Best Books for Children, 1966 Edition. R. R. Bowker Company, 1180 Avenue of the Americas, New York, New York 10036.

Book Selection Media. National Council of Teachers of English, 508 South Sixth Street, Champaign, Illinois 61820.

Bulletin of the Center for Children's Books. University of Chicago Graduate Library School, University of Chicago Press, 5750 Ellis Avenue, Chicago, Illinois 60637.

Reading Ladders for Human Relations, Fourth Edition. American Council on Education, 1785 Massachusetts Avenue, Washington 36, D. C.

Part Two

Language Learning and Linguistics

Two interrelated topics are the focus of this section: (1) the how and what of children's language learning, and (2) the science of linguistics and some of its concerns that are particularly relevant to language arts instruction.

Many words stand for abstractions, for constructs for which there may be no concrete referent in reality. Such words easily come to mind: *enemy, intelligent, ugly, depressed, wealthy*. Such words imperceptibly influence how we see our world and what we think of it—ourselves included. And even though these abstract descriptions may bear little or no resemblance to reality, they nevertheless are a powerful determinant of our thinking—and our behavior. And the social group from which experiences arise and from whom language is learned shapes both the thought and language of its members. Cohen examines these interrelationships in the first essay in this part of the anthology.

Smith, extending some of the foundations laid by Cohen, gives a broad overview of the conditions, sequence, and operation of children's language learning with particular attention to the relationship between thought and structure of language. Because, by and large, children's language growth is sequential, teachers can anticipate language difficulties typically met by children at differing stages of development. This allows the teacher to select the content and procedures best suited for coping with these problems. But instruction is not sufficient. Because language is a social instrument, Smith points out that teachers must provide opportunities for expression and then guide that expression so as to achieve maximal language growth. And all of this must be so done that language engenders desirable, more mature thought patterns—and vice versa. Truly a gigantic task demanding intimate knowledge of children's language!

Certain elements in our culture seem to contribute to small but persistent differences between the sexes in language development: girls, as a group, consistently use more words and more mature sentence structure than do boys. And even though schools have made various adjustments in attempting to cope with varied differences such as intelligence, achievement, interests, and skills, they have done relatively little to provide for these language differences. And yet, if perception, thought, and behavior are shaped by the language that is used, it seems reasonable to assume that when special provisions are not made for any language deficiencies boys may have, development in these extremely vital areas is inhibited. McCarthy examines some possible causes of language differences, but educators must apply her conclusions to school situations.

Socially disadvantaged children have more conspicuous language and speech deficiencies than any other large identifiable population segment. Born into a quantitatively and qualitatively deficient family, they interact with equally deficient peers, receive little direction in expressing themselves coherently and lucidly, and fail to develop certain cognitive abilities common to and prized by the rest of our society. And these deficits appear to be cumulative with age. In a world of individual differences, disadvantaged children—with regard to language—may definitely be unique; their handicaps and the causes of them may defy conventional understanding. We may need a totally new orientation toward language learning, its effect on cognitive development, and adequate instructional procedures if we are to begin to help these children. Raph, in a comprehensive review of recent research, provides some much-needed background on the language development of socially disadvantaged children.

A plethora of influences are working to re-shape the language arts curriculum but none is currently more potent or widespread than linguistics. Because it deals with the language people use rather than a set of rules or a system to be adhered to, an introduction to it seems logically to follow a section devoted to understanding children's language.

Educators, like the rest of our society, tend to be faddish: if it is new, has publicity value, a scholarly lineage, or claims as a panacea, it is good. Whether content or method, little attention is typically given to a thorough, critical scrutiny of it; frequently labels are adopted without understanding what they represent or their implications. Because the entire conception of linguistics breaks so sharply with traditional models of viewing language, we must understand it if we are to best apply its findings, methodology, and point of view to language arts instruction. Owen's article summarizes the outstanding characteristics of linguistics and provides information about the fundamental ideas necessary to comprehend this unique discipline.

Even though there are a few dissenters and doubting Thomases, the linguistics bandwagon is accelerating rapidly. A hodge-podge of materials and activities—all purported to be derived from linguistics—threaten to flood the educational scene. Many of these materials and ideas are based on an over-simplified, naive belief that linguistics is a 'thing' which has given final simple answers to vexing, complex problems. Roberts cautions against such simplistic notions and notes some possible applications of linguistics to the teaching of English in his essay.

Another case of English teachers trying to repeal or ignore reality is illustrated by Kurath who points out that standards for both pronunciation and usage differ widely within the United States and that a man's meat may be his poison if he moves to another region. The United States has not been a total melting pot for the numerous national languages spoken by its immigrants and Kurath points out that any teacher or textbook who holds to a single, undeviating standard of usage or pronunciation may produce only teacher frustration and not pupil change.

7 Language and Experience: The setting

Dorothy H. Cohen

If, as Cohen maintains, experiences, perception, and language interact to form patterns unique to each social subgroup, children's language reflects infinitely more than merely the models they have unconsciously imitated. Additionally, each subgroup should have its own peculiar language 'system' which diverges in differing degrees from that of other subgroups.

How does cultural experience influence language usage? Can you think of any ways in which language influences your perception (and consequently your behavior)? What implications do these facts have in terms of methods and materials as we seek to expand and improve children's language learning? Does this article stress or de-emphasize the need to provide for individual differences? How is this article related to the succeeding ones by Smith and McCarthy? Articles by Bacher, DeBoer, Deutsch, McDavid, and May in Selected References for Part Two are all germane to the points made in this essay.

In translating the idioms of one language into another, some persons complain that something is lost, a certain comprehensibility, and that the full flavor of the original does not come through. Those attempting to clarify the meaning of certain words in a foreign tongue are often reduced to the helpless "There is no word for it in your language." And this common experience occurs despite the fact that each of the almost three thousand languages is a grammatically complete language, fully expressive of the communicative needs and purposes of the people who use it.

From *Childhood Education* 42:139-142; November 1965. Reprinted with the permission of Dorothy H. Cohen, Bank Street College of Education, New York, New York and the Association for Childhood Education International, 3615 Wisconsin Avenue, N.W., Washington, D. C. Copyright © 1965 by the Association.

Differences in Purpose

It is in the differences in need and purpose, rather than in vocabulary, syntax and grammar, that the significant differences among languages, and even within the same generic language, should be sought. Suzanne Langer[1] has suggested that language is a form of symbolization of experience and occurs inevitably because the need to transform experience into symbols is a biologically determined characteristic of man. Clearly enough, despite the universality of basic human needs, experience has varied considerably in certain details in the climatic and historically shaped subgroups that make up the genus Man. The many languages in the world reflect these differences in specific aspects of experience as well as in the cumulative totals. Syntax, grammar, vocabulary and the use of modifying words of all kinds are unique to the cultural group or subgroup for whom they represent a reflection of experience.

Thus the Eskimos have many words for *snow*, each one a separate tool to describe various conditions that must be carefully defined within a snow-bound culture, whereas people not so basically affected by conditions of snow might have the separate words *snow* and *slush* but use adjectives for further precision. North American children, who can tell with their fingers and palms what the special consistency of snow must be like for proper packing into snowballs, have no word to help them refer to this special consistency. In the Jewish culture and language there is a word that describes a kinship between the parents of a bride and the parents of the groom. But in the English language bride and groom each acquire a pair of in-laws whose new relationship to each other cannot be discussed with economy of words.

Yet the English language is richly descriptive in many ways, a result no doubt of turbulent history which brought encounters both unexpected and sought after with people of other cultures and langages which added a steady infusion of new and "foreign" words into the basic stock. Regarded as a result and/or a continuation of experience a language is neither right nor wrong; it either suits the purpose of its users or it changes to do so. Language is passed on to children by their parents just as it exists in the community.

> Content, form and uses of the language of each community mirror its physical setting, its historical events or contacts, its cultural level and mental climate, its cultural history and texture. . . . The language of a group or community is an index of its characteristics. . . . Conversely, the very form, extent and complexity of the social structures, and the functions these perform, vary with and are affected by the language system. . . . The defects, distortions and inadequacies of language, or the inadequate command of language,

retard cultural development and culture acquisition, and impair societal organization and operation. . . . Thus the language system and the socio-cultural texture and context of a society or even a group cannot be separated. Each reflects the other; each is both cause and effect of the other.[2]

Given this context, the language of the socio-economic classes in society, as well as of the groups of differing ethnic origin, can all be seen to stem from different batteries of total experience and therefore to have different perceptions in certain areas. Such an approach to the comparison of language usage has been suggested by several sociologists, anthropologists and linguists. An important sociologist, Basil Bernstein, noting differences in the language of working- and middle-class people,[3] associates style of language usage with child-rearing practices.[4] To give an illustration of the approach, he points to time-orientation as a base of perceptive possibilities. The middle-class groups, future oriented and planning ahead, see things differently from lower-income groups who are more heavily rooted in the immediately basic problems of living.

This syndrome in turn affects disciplinary practices and in turn language. Thus, according to Bernstein, the middle-class group tends more toward directing children to consistent goals of behavior approved in middle-class adulthood, using mainly words to do so; whereas low-income parents tend more to punish in response to immediately felt irritations and probably physically. In the one case the statement, "I'd rather you did not go on the hike this time because you are not really over your cold; there will be other opportunities," includes concepts of degree, relationship, future goal, rationality and organization. In the other, where the directive might be, "You can't go. Stop your crying," the immediacy of the expressive meaning, the omission of cause and effect or of degree and comparison present to the child a bounded and therefore limited perception of possibilities. At the same time the child learns a limited use of the tools of language to express no more than the descriptive, the commanding or the demanding. Out of such subtleties and relationships between parents and children, subtleties which are themselves a reflection of the life view of the parents, comes a communicative mode that serves the purposes of the way of life and sets a linguistic style for the child.

Style and Usage

Another study focused on language style and usage in two socio-economic groups drew its material from story interviews recorded after an entire community had been struck by a tornado.[5] The significance of this study is in the models that children of educated and uneducated parents have available as they learn to speak and the support this lends to Bernstein's hypothesis concerning differing perceptive bases in the middle and working classes.

The recounting of the common disastrous experience was analyzed for ways in which people expressed their thoughts and feelings about the same event. Four significant categories reflecting thought processes and to some extent interpersonal relations showed differences in quality and degree according to the level of education, in turn related to economic conditions. In all four categories,

- the standpoint from which a description is made
- the ability to see what the other person can comprehend
- information about classes of persons
- organizing frameworks and stylistic devices,

the people of higher education tended toward a more objective, better detailed, more cohesive and more clearly organized verbal presentation of the events experienced physically by all. This difference in the variability of human perception and the way in which language reflects it can be a fascinating topic of study in and of itself. It poses serious questions as to ways in which children perceive and handle the chosen language of the schools, that is, *book language,* a language which has grown out of the need to pass on to others the distillation of experience in increasingly abstract classifications. To quote Watts,[6]

> If therefore we wish to make any considerable progress in the attempt to find our way about the world of general and abstract ideas, we must become masters of the language which has been devised for the purpose of describing them.

But if, as Kluckhohn[7] confirms,

> Every language . . . is a special way of looking at the world and interpreting experience . . .

and Hoijer[8] adds,

> A language, then, more or less faithfully reflects the structuring of reality which is peculiar to the group that speaks it,

what shall we make of Sapir's[9] statement? He says:

> To pass from one language to another is psychologically parallel to passing from one geometrical system of reference to another. The environing world which is referred to is the same for either language; the world of points is the same in either frame of reference. But the formal approach to the same item of experience is so different that the resulting feeling of orientation can be neither the same in the two languages, nor in the two frames of reference. Entirely distinct, formal adjustments have to be made and these differences have their psychological correlates.

Thus the problems of methodology which confront us as we attempt to educate so variable a population as the American school community are real indeed. We must ask ourselves whether we are dealing with the enlargement of perception when we attack the specific grammatical errors of children whose English is substandard. Does the way to increasingly abstract classification of experience lie through a formal study of the mechanics of expression? There is no doubt that acceptable grammar and usage and a good vocabulary are important assets for precision and expression of perspective. But is the road to thought, inextricably bound up with mechanics, best followed by drill in the mechanics? Or, as in life outside school, is it possible that language to express experience will be most meaningfully and efficiently learned when the experience the language must convey is meaningfully and clearly understood?

In the course of their normal development in the use of symbols, children begin by understanding *meaning* in babyhood, go on to using *oral language* as toddlers, and eventually recognize and utilize *symbols* for words in their school years. In an ongoing study of children's vocabulary,[10] this vertical development appeared horizontally in children of the same age and socioeconomic class who were categorized by school placement as slow, average and bright learners. In the course of the experimental program, language growth seemed to move from increase in *comprehension* of book words through oral usage and to eventual skill in reading and writing, with a dramatic change in comprehension among the slowest. *Meaning*, so often described in educational literature as basic to growth in the language arts, is seen once again as the key to helping children cross the divide from egocentric, limited perception and use of language to the more objective use of classification, comparison, analysis and synthesis of experience. If we concentrate on comprehension, oral expression and finally symbolic learning, not by grade level alone or by age, but by stage of need in which we find each child, we will be starting with the child's perception of life and use of language which to him seems natural and "right" because he learned it from his parents. As we accept him as a phemonenon of experience, we will not challenge the "rightness" of his perception but will open additional possibilities for him to examine and assimilate as he will, beginning with his childhood comprehension and oral expression and leading to his use of the symbols that deal with both.

Footnotes

[1] Suzanne Langer, *Philosophy in a New Key* (Cambridge: Harvard University Press, 1948).

[2] J. O. Hertzler, "Toward a Sociology of Language," *Social Forces*, December 1953, V. 32, pp. 109-119. By permission of University of North Carolina Press, Chapel Hill.

3 Basil Bernstein, "A Public Language," *British Journal of Sociology*, December 1959, pp. 311-327.

4 ———, "Some Sociological Determinants of Perception," *British Journal of Sociology*, V. IX, 1958.

5 L. Schatzman and A. Strauss, "Social Class and Communication," *American Journal of Sociology*, January 1955.

6 A. F. Watts, *The Language and Mental Development of Children* (London: George G. Harrap and Co, Ltd., 1944).

7 Clyde Kluckhohn, "The Gift of Tongues," from *Mirror of Man* in *Introductory Readings on Language*, ed. Anderson and Stagers.

8 J. O. Hoijer, "Relation of Language to Culture," in *Anthropology Today*, ed. A. L. Kroeber (Chicago: University of Chicago Press, 1953).

9 Edward Sapir, "The Grammarian and His Language," as quoted in Hoijer.

10 Dorothy H. Cohen, "Effect of a Special Program in Literature on the Vocabulary and Reading Achievement of Second-Grade Children in Special Service Schools," U.S. Office of Education Cooperative Research, Project S-254 in progress.

8 Developmental Language Patterns of Children

Dora V. Smith

*Without a sure grasp of the significant phases of children's language develop-
ment, teaching objectives' may be irrelevant, expectations unrealistic, instruction erroneous, and improvement nil. An acknowledged authority on both
children and language arts outlines some of the major aspects of children's
language growth.*

*If the home is so influential in children's language development, how
might the school better harness its potent force? What implications for elementary school language arts instruction can be drawn from the statement that
language and thought are inextricably intertwined? In Loban's study (reported later in this part) and that of DeLawter and Eash's in Part Three, the use
of subordination to indicate language maturity plays a major role. Why? Have
you ever tried to measure in some way variances in children's language at different chronological ages or intellectual levels? If you wish to read further on
this topic, the articles cited in Selected References for Part Two by Church,
Deutsch and Cherry-Peisach, McCarthy, Menyuk, and Strickland may prove
enlightening.*

We in the schools face one of life's greatest challenges—to help boys and
girls to lay hold on life through the development of language power, remember-
ing that it is from the materials of experience that the child must evolve meaning
and concepts by attaching them to verbal symbols.

Beginning with the birth cry, the infant gains control over volume, pitch
and sound through babbling and cooing; he uses both vowels and consonants
as he emits noises for their own sake. The coming of teeth paves the way for
articulation as the child embarks upon a process of imitation of adult speech.
Toward the end of his first year, he forms his first word, and by the age of two,

From *Reading and the Related Arts*, A Report of the Twenty-first Annual Conference
and Course on Reading, University of Pittsburgh, 1965, pp. 19-28. Reprinted with permission
of Donald L. Cleland, editor, and Dora V. Smith, Professor Emeritus in English Education,
University of Minnesota, Minneapolis.

he has made what one psychologist calls the greatest discovery of his life—namely, that things have names. To these he soon adds actions and qualities. "Dog," he says, pointing to emphasize his point, "two dogs." Perhaps a bird flies overhead. It is big and black. "What is dat?" he demands. "A crow," his mother patiently replies—but back comes the inevitable question—"Why?" Obviously the child has begun an intensive use of language to explore his relations with people and things.

Ultimately he finds out that not all words name objects. A friend offers to bring him a present from California. What it is to be is a *secret*. He associates the word with the cricket which appeared on the hearth the night before. What the present later turns out to be is a box of mud-pie tins in the shape of animals. He picks out his storybook friends—Timothy Turtle and Old Mr. Bullfrog—and then demands emphatically, "But where's the secrick" (25)? It will take several presents from California to establish the generalization. During the second year, also, most children develop what one linguist has called "telegraphic" English—"Baby sleep." "Push car." "No, I doot!" meaning "No, I do it."

Recently, Brown and Bellugi at Harvard studied the sentence structure used by a gifted boy and girl from highly intellectual families (5). They recorded and transcribed everything said by each child and by his or her mother in two hour interviews over a period of thirty-eight weeks. At first, a simple repetitive dialogue ensued in which the mother's sentences were structurally about a year in advance of the child's.

> "I see truck," says the child.
> "Did you see the truck?" asks the mother.
> "There go one," says the child.
> "Yes, there goes one," replies the mother (5).

The child's sentence, even with the mother's example, is a reduction of hers. He seems unable to reproduce the whole statement. "Fraser will be unhappy," says the mother. "Fraser unhappy," repeats the child. The mother's speech is always an imitation with expansion of the child's words. Later the youngster's effort to reproduce a negative results in, "No, I see a truck," to which the mother replies, "No, you didn't see a truck" (5).

At one point, when the recorders were unable to tell whether Adam understood the semantic difference between putting a noun in subject or object position, they set him two tasks: "Show us the duck pushing the boat," and "Show us the boat pushing the duck" (5). He did both without any difficulty. Later the child appeared to understand and to construct sentences he had never heard before, modelling them apparently from a latent pattern evolved from previous experience. It is clear from this example that the child's early linguistic environment is crucial.

At this stage, also, experiments in the Bank Street Nursery School recorded the children's efforts to express cause, purpose, result, and condition in such sentences as "What for Lois crying?" or one of them takes off her coat, saying, "Janet's too warm a coat" (22).

A significant improvement in recent studies of the language of children lies in their emphasis upon positive elements of growth rather than upon so-called "errors" in English usage. The trend is due partly to the methods of study used in structural linguistics or transformational or generative grammar. Paula Menyuk at the Massachusetts Institute of Technology reports an analysis of the speech of nursery school and first grade children according to the techniques of Chomsky's transformational grammar (21). The study involved forty-eight children from a private nursery school and the same number from a first grade room. All of them came from upper class families and had IQ's of 120 or above. Selection made possible the discovery of the heights children can reach in imitation of adult speech.

Two hours of speech from a single day were recorded for all the children in addition to the language they used in response to projected pictures, individual responses in a personal interview between the experimenter and each child, and conversation within the group during role playing in a family setting. All responses were analyzed by Chomsky's techniques of transformational grammar into (1) simple, active, declarative sentences, and (2) the transformations derived from each. The recorder separated what she called "children's grammar" from adult constructions; for example:

> He'll might get in jail.
> I see a dog what's white.
> Him's stomach hurt.
> He growed.
> He liketed it (21).

The nursery school children used all the basic structures employed by adults. The most common difficulties were in substituting *ed* for irregular forms of the past tense. The mean number of sentences said by the nursery school children was 82.9, and by the first grade 95.7.

Evidences of growing maturity in the first grade were complete mastery of the passive voice and partial use of *if* and *so* clauses, use of the auxiliary, *have*, of a series like *She does the shopping and cooking and baking*, and of a participial complement such as *I like singing*. There was no difference in performance between boys and girls. Mean sentences length and total number of sentences increased with age. However, greater length was sometimes achieved by joining a series of remarks together by "and," for example, "I have a big, big teddy bear and I have a little doggie and he's named Blacky-Whitey and there's this big dog and he's named Peppermint" (21).

Dr. Menyuk summarizes her findings with this significant comment:

Most of the structures are used at an early age and used consistently. If we look at the nature of the structures which are used by all the children (for example, negation, contraction, auxiliary *be* and the like) it would seem that the theory of Piaget and others, which states that language is an expression of children's needs and is far from a purely imitative function even at a very early age, is a valid one. A need for social instrumentation and a method of categorizing the environment would motivate the usage of these structures (21).

Dr. Mildred Templin points out in her study of children three to eight that all grammatical constructions used by adults appear at least in rudimentary form in the speech of eight-year-olds, and their articulation is practically mature (27). Children from lower socio-economic levels were retarded one year. Boys matured in expression a year later than girls, a situation which has appeared less frequently in recent studies.

Ability to discriminate among sounds improves somewhat after eight while vocabulary increases to adulthood and probably throughout life in a scientifically oriented world. For most children, future growth in language, Dr. Templin notes, will be in the perfection of forms already used rather than in the introduction of new types of linguistic expression.

Comparison of her results of 1957 with those of Dr. Davis collected in 1932 is encouraging to teachers today (7). Six-year-olds today use sentences longer than those of nine-and-one-half-year-olds twenty-five years ago. Use of compound-complex and elaborated sentences increased substantially from year to year, children in 1957 using twice as many as children in 1932 (27). Deviations from standard English decreased over the years from 52 per cent at age three to 26 per cent at age six and to 23.9 per cent at age eight. There was, however, a startling increase in the use of slang and colloquialisms of fifty per cent among children from three to six and a similar increase from ages six to eight (27). Dr. Templin attributed the significant improvement over a period of twenty-five years to the increased linguistic stimulation from motion picture, radio, and television and to the greater permissiveness in the relationships of children and adults. Presumably the slang came from the same sources (27).

Dr. Walter Loban of the University of California has in progress a fascinating study of the language of the same children from their entrance into kindergarten through their graduation from high school. Results are available for the first six years (19).

The pupils were asked in an interview to tell what they saw in a carefully selected group of pictures and what they thought about them. The responses were recorded and the language analyzed by a scheme set up by a board of linguists.

One of the major problems in any such analysis is the presence in the speech of children and young people of certain "tangles" of language. They are hesitations, false starts, and meaningless repetitions which interrupt the sentence patterns. These "tangles" were removed and studied separately from the remaining sentences. During kindergarten and the first three grades, the total group and the high subgroup showed a steady decrease in the number of mazes (35 per cent) and the number of words per maze (50 per cent) (19). The low group, on the other hand, increased both the number of mazes and the average number of words per maze during the same four year period. Throughout the study, the low group, writes Dr. Loban, "says less, has more difficulty saying it, and has less vocabulary with which to say it" (19).

The high group was distinguished from the kindergarten up by the ability to express tentative thinking as revealed by such words as *perhaps, maybe,* and *I'm not exactly sure.* The gifted sensed alternatives; the weak made flat, dogmatic statements (19). Although the pictures invited generalizations and figurative language, little of either was used by any of the children (19).

"Language," Dr. Loban points out, "is more than uttering whatever perceptions or thoughts rise by chance to the surface of expression. The content requires organization" (19). Use of the dependent clause helps to subordinate ideas, but use of dependent clauses is not in itself a sufficient index of subordination. Grammatical complexity is revealed also by use of modifiers or verbals or the clause within a clause. This latter fact is one of the chief contributions of Dr. Loban's study. Meta Bear (1), Lou LaBrant (18), Ellen Frogner (9) and others long ago found progressive use of subordinate clauses to be one measure of growing maturity in children's writing. Dr. Loban points out, however, that compression of ideas into more succinct form may represent a higher level of thinking than use of the clause. For example, one child may write, "Mary was in such a hurry that she fell over the chair," while another uses the more compact form: "In her hurry, Mary fell over the chair." One may say, "When he had finished his breakfast, Tom set off for school," while another compresses the clause into a participial phrase: "Having finished his breakfast, Tom set off for school" (19). One significant measure of growing maturity in language is ability to find more and more succinct means of expressing relationships between ideas.

Similar studies were made of the children's ability to use and to vary the basic structural patterns of English, and the dexterity each showed in varying elements such as movables within the patterns. Use of nouns amplified by modifiers, compound nouns, clauses, and infinitives was characteristic of the high as contrasted with the low groups.

Dr. Ruth Strickland used the same analytical scheme for her study of the oral language of children from sixteen public schools in Bloomington, Indiana (26). Her purpose was to contrast the intricacy of children's patterns of speech with the simplicity of sentence structure in reading textbooks commonly used in Grades 1 through 6. The latter proved to be extremely simple in contrast to forms used by the children in their own speech. Whether they should be or not seems to be a question still in the realm of dispute.

At the University Schools of Florida State University in Tallahassee Dr. Kellogg Hunt compared the maturity in sentence building of nine boys and nine girls in each of three grades, IV, VIII, and XII (13). Their IQ's ranged between 90 and 110. After trying sentence length, clause length, and frequency of subordinate clauses, he found the best index of maturity was the so-called single clause T unit, that is, a unit which is in itself a sentence. These he isolated by ignoring punctuation (of which the fourth graders had too little) and co-ordinating conjunctions between main clauses (of which the fourth graders had too many), and then cutting up the material into short grammatical sentences with a capital at one end, and a period or question mark at the other, with no fragment left over (13). As in Dr. Loban's study Dr. Hunt found it necessary to eliminate "mazes," which he called "garbles."

Doubtless, if one did this to the compositions of fourth graders, his respect for their achievement in language would greatly increase. Perhaps, too, if he showed the results to the children, it would increase their own respect for them-selves. These "ands" Dr. Hunt thinks children use chiefly as a stopping place during which they can decide what they want to say next. Results showed that successively older boys and girls used more and more subordinate clauses and many more non-clause modifiers than the younger pupils did (13).

Dr. Hunt found fourth grade pupils employing noun clauses chiefly to indi-cate what people said and did, whereas older students tended to talk of what they thought or asked or believed—an interesting element in growth toward maturity (13). In all these sentences, the majority of noun clauses are direct objects. Use of noun clauses in any other position is a mark of maturity. Fourth graders used it fifteen times in such positions; twelfth graders, sixty-three times. This factor may also be related to reading difficulty.

Although practically all structures appear somewhere in the writing of fourth grade children, younger pupils tend to write as sentences what older chil-dren reduce to phrases and single words; for example, "The fireplace gave the most light in the room, but away from it they had to use the candle," as con-trasted with "Aside from the fireplace, the candle was the chief source of light." This is what Hunt calls "greater density of grammatical structures" by means of which the older student "can incorporate a larger body of thought into a single intricately related organization" (13). In the work of the older students non-clauses such as infinitive or participial phrases, appositives, and the like are found in larger proportions than clauses.

Study of the growth of pre-school and elementary school children in language brings dramatically to the fore factors which are pertinent to im-provement at any level of instruction. They include: (1) a social setting which stimulates constant practice in the use of language; (2) an environment rich in the things, the experiences, and the ideas, for which words stand; and (3) adult example and assistance in the clearly motivated maturing of language skills. If there were time, it would be valuable to examine in the light of these criteria the setting in which language is supposed to grow in our own classrooms.

A most telling study of this problem was carried on by Dr. Luria in Russia (20) with twins, who, finding their own phonetic grunts and gesticulations sufficient for their life together, hardly spoke at all with others up to the age of two, and at four barely differentiated sounds in reply to questions. Sounds, separate words, direct actions, and lively gesticulations were enough for their purposes. Present objects they could name, but absent ones confused them. When they entered the same kindergarten, they had no understanding of narrative speech and refused to listen to storytelling, which they could not follow.

Finally, they were placed in separate kindergartens where association with others was imperative. "The new objective situation," says the author, "gave rise to a need for verbal speech and became the most significant factor in its development" (20). Communication through speech also led to significant improvement in the organization of their mental processes. Imaginative play, Dr. Luria believed, was a fundamental element in lifting the children to greater heights both in thought and in language. The new situation in which speech was interlocked with action in company with other children developed first narrative and then planning speech. Findings from studies such as these may have some bearing upon the question of whether reading should be taught in the kindergarten.

The influence of the home on the children's language is fundamentally important. A child of four, one investigator found, is probably silent some nineteen minutes of his waking day (4). Such oral practice works wonders, with the aid of an intelligent mother. Milner, studying the relationship between reading readiness and patterns of parent-child relationships, found that children who engage in two-way conversation at mealtime with parents who encourage them to talk can be distinguished from others in a reading readiness program (23). Helen Dawe, experimenting with orphanage children, who have little contact with adults, gave one group of institutionalized children of nursery-school age approximately fifty hours of (1) looking at and discussing pictures, (2) listening to poems and stories, (3) going on short excursions, and (4) training in understanding words and concepts (8). These children made significantly greater gains than a control group in the same institution.

Enriching the child's environment, encouraging conversation about it and pushing through to adequate expression of the experience in words are major elements in the growth of language. Dr. Watts, in England, also found storytelling and reading aloud to children useful for the development of language in pre-school years (28). Forty nursery rhymes, he maintains, introduce four hundred new words.

Together with intelligence, socio-economic status seems to be the most influential factor in the child's development of language. This problem is one of particular moment at a time when the education of the underprivileged is in the forefront of attention. Contact with others and an enriched environment where association with the things words stand for is made possible may be the most important elements in the education of these children and young people.

Even in the kindergarten Mahmaud Khater found that upper class children talked more about themselves and their possessions while lower class youngsters talked of the outside world of people, of the immediate present, or what they would do in the future (17). Upper class youngsters listened to each other and commented freely and spontaneously; whereas lower class children remained silent until they were drawn out. Upper class children could discuss procedures, sticking to the subject, and contributing to the problem; whereas lower socio-economic groups tended to drop the problem and engage in narratives of personal experience. Such children often rely on gestures or on "you know what I mean" instead of coming to grips with the expression of an idea.

Bernstein in England has been much interested in this problem because differences due to socio-economic status are often progressively reinforced through the years (3). In the lower levels of society, he believes, the command "Shut up!" not only conditions the child's relations with his parents, but cuts off any intellectual approach to the problem; whereas in an upper class home in England, the mother's "I'd rather you'd make less noise, my dear" is less damaging to the ego of the individual and leaves room for decision on his part (3). Different kinds of mental functions result from such treatment.

Berg (2) and Havighurst (11) discuss this problem at length in the 1964 proceedings of the University of Chicago Reading Conference, indicating the effect of stultifying experience on language and reading at a time when one child in three in the public schools of our country's fourteen largest cities is culturally deprived.

All the evidence points to the need of psychological understanding on the part of those who presume to plan for improving the language of the underprivileged.

Martin Joos of the University of Wisconsin has penned a tirade against the grammar of correctness and the effect of it in causing school drop-outs. "Teachers must simply abandon the theory that usages differ in quality as between good and bad, correct and incorrect, and instead build their methods and reconstruct their emotional reactions on the plain facts that are already known in part to their pupils . . . that usages can be learned without condemning those which they replace, that the learner has an indefensible right to speak as he likes without school penalties, while the teacher has no rights in this respect, but only to demonstrate what usages are profitable in the adult world" (16).

The United States Office of Education recently called a conference on improving English skills of culturally different youth. The first seventy pages of its report set forth the need of understanding the nature, the values, and the attitudes of the culturally different, whose social backgrounds are frequently more of a detriment than their intelligence (15). Allison Davis of Chicago has a particularly telling article in the bulletin, emphasizing the differences in thinking to be expected of pupils from different walks of life and the danger of attempting to fit all young people into a particular academic mold (15).

In 1963 Frank G. Jennings wrote in the *Saturday Review of Literature* a fascinating account of Dillard University's pre-freshman program for those Negro students who wish to offset a dearth of language, little access to books and inadequate opportunity to think about and discuss current affairs with six weeks of intensive work before entering college in the fall (14). Requirements of the program are that the students read two hours a day from books in the library and talk over with a teacher what they have read, and that each evening they join with the group in listening to selected television broadcasts on contemporary affairs, discussing together later under the direction of a teacher what they have heard. In addition, each student may take another course of his own choosing. The program is interesting because it uses the techniques which research and common sense suggest are important for the development of language power and thinking.

Another problem in current language teaching stems from the fact that the linguist has been particularly concerned with the development of accepted forms of *structure* in the use of language, but tends to ignore the *power of words* in the expression of meaning. Does it make any difference whether a child says, "I wish you could see my nice little dog with legs four inches long," or whether he writes, "I wish you could see my beady-eyed black Scottie with the sad bewhiskered look"? The structure of these two sentences is identical, but what a world of difference there is between them as communication! Again, whereas a mature speaker says, "His ultimate destination was uncertain," an immature one remarks, "He did not know which place he would have to go to in the end" (28). The mature sentence is one of the simplest which could be found. The difference lies in the individual's command of words and of thinking.

As teachers we are deeply concerned with the development of vocabulary —not alone with how many words children know but with how well they understand those with which they are familiar, and what skills they need to increase the number, the breadth and the depth of concepts with which they have a sketchy acquaintance. Children become much interested in words from the days of Mother Goose and " 'Twas the Night before Christmas." They are captured by much more than the story of the annual visit of Santa because of the dramatic power of the words with which his housetop ride is described. From the mere names of things little children move into the realm of words which have a hypnotizing appeal to the senses. Modern poetry for boys and girls is full of such words, and children should enjoy it and the colorful picture books with stories rhythmically told, which open to them a fascinating world of language to offset the often dull vocabulary of their early readers. Both are necessary to the well-rounded development of their use of language.

In their readers, too, primary children learn to separate the roots and endings of words, to find two words in *afternoon* and *sometimes*, and ultimately to discover prefixes that alter meaning, so that large numbers of words can be made from a single root.

The intermediate grades are crucial ones for vocabulary building because words which once had a single meaning bob up in new and strange situations. An eight-year-old boy was told by his father that a building they were passing housed a Finnish bath. Incredulously, the child replied, "Is it because it's the last one he'll ever have?" Children make a game out of words with double meanings: "What is black and white and red (read) all over?" appears in every generation. And what child has not repeated the rhyme about the peach which, on falling to the ground, became a squash? Teachers should encourage such fun and participate in it.

But the real business of grades IV through XII is to lead children to a mastery in context of the significant vocabularies of the various fields of study with which they are concerned—science, geography, history, mathematics, composition and literature. One obvious tool is the dictionary, in the use of which they should be schooled in every year from the primary grades up. Children's encyclopedias are also helpful and the many books for elementary and junior high school pupils such as *The Tree of Language* by Helene and Charlton Laird (World, 1957), *The First Book of Words* by Samuel and Beryl Epstein (Watts, 1954), and *Words from the Myths, Words from Science,* and *Words on the Map* by Issac Asimov (Houghton, 1961; 1959; and 1962).

Important vocabulary development comes from clarification of concepts in relation to the daily mastery of each subject of study. Ernest Horn has inveighed against memorization of empty words and the complacent possession of flagrant misconceptions and vague ideas which come from lack of attention to specific meanings in the social studies (12). He found one child who interpreted the sentence, "The French Revolution corresponded in a rough way with the American Revolution" (12), to mean that they wrote insulting letters to one another.

The late David Russell gave us one of the most useful studies we have of the development of vocabulary from the fourth grade through the twelfth. He called it an analysis of the *dimensions* of children's vocabulary, that is, a study of the breadth of meaning a word may have in a wide-range sampling of meanings from science, social studies, mathematics, and sports and recreation; analysis of *depth* of meaning, that is, going beyond superficial recognition of a synonym to some measure of how much a child understands about the word; *precision* of meaning, such as ability to make fine discriminations in use of the word in different situations; and finally the ability to use it in one's own, meaning vocabulary in speaking, writing, and reading. This he calls the "availability" of the word (24).

In testing for proficiency in vocabulary in Grades IV through XII he found that both boys and girls improved their scores in different subject matter areas rather consistently from grade to grade though they often slowed down somewhat in the senior high school. To test vocabulary adequately in high school requires special tests in each subject-matter. Boys in general were somewhat above girls, especially in the areas of science, sports, hobbies, and recreation. Girls' vocabularies became specialized earlier than boys'. Depth of vocabulary proved difficult to test. In breadth of knowledge of words pupils showed more growth in grades IV through VI than they did in the junior and senior high school.

Development of concepts—that is, abstract meanings—is one of the major goals of education. No one has defined this task more concretely than Dr. John Carroll (6). "For development of a concept," he says, "the individual must have a series of experiences that are in one or more respects similar. From this constellation of similarities the concept evolves. After that a mixture of positive and negative instances insures the adequate learning of the concept. For example, take the meaning of *tourist* as contrasted with that of *immigrant*. One child describes a tourist as a 'well-dressed person who drives a station wagon with an out-of-state license.' " He has seen American tourists but no foreign immigrants. To another a tourist may be well dressed and an immigrant poorly dressed. Both could be, of course, from a foreign country, and both could be American or Mexican, but the child has seen only foreign immigrants and American tourists. Ultimately, in order to develop a correct concept the reader must sense the fact that the distinction is not one of nationality or dress but of purpose, the immigrant's seeking to change his residence and the tourist in search of pleasure with no thought of altering his address. The example shows clearly what a complex task it is to help children develop accurate and specific concepts.

Finally, what is the significance of the fact that no study except Dr. Loban's mentions figurative language (19) and he found that no child used it? Figurative language is all about us. We cannot read modern advertising without it. Little children use it constantly like the child who watched the burning ashes fly up from the fireplace and come down again from the chimney. "They go up red birds," she said, "and they come down black birds." A gifted child of six once startled the writer by not understanding the expression: "Let's not cross that bridge till we come to it." "What bridge?" he asked with a puzzled look (25). Miss Gill of California has written two illuminating articles on the difficulties of teaching current American fiction to high school seniors who do not know how to respond to figurative language (10). I am not arguing for classifying and naming figures of speech, but merely for teaching how to "figure out," as the child says, "what they say." Has the reading of literature as literature with an imaginative quality to its language been neglected in our elementary and junior high schools? If so, it seems to me there is no time like the present for repairing the damage.

Study of the linguistic development of children from infancy through high school is one of the most rewarding experiences any adult can pursue. Besides that, it will guide him more expertly to help the child progress in ways that will enrich experience for him as long as he lives.

References

1. Bear, Meta. "Children's Growth in the Use of Written Language," *Elementary English Review*, XVI (December, 1939), pp. 312-219.
2. Berg, Paul Conrad. "The Culturally Disadvantaged Student and Reading Instruction," *Meeting Individual Differences in Reading* (Proceedings of the Annual Conference on Reading, Vol. XXVI, Supplementary Educational Monograph, No. 94). Chicago: University of Chicago, December, 1964.
3. Bernstein, Basil. "Social Class and Linguistic Development: A Theory of Social Learning," *Education, Economy, and Society*, Halsey, A. H., *et al.* (eds.). The Free Press of Glencoe, Inc., 1961, pp. 218-315; pp. 293-294.
4. Brandenburg. "The Language of a Three-Year-Old Child," *Pedagogical Seminary*, XXII (March, 1915), pp. 89-120.
5. Brown, Roger, and Bellugi, Ursula. "Three Processes in the Child's Acquisition of Syntax," *The Harvard Educational Review*, XXIV (Spring, 1964), pp. 133-151; p. 135; p. 143; p. 134.
6. Carroll, John B. "Words, Meanings and Concepts," *Harvard Educational Review*, XXXIV, No. 2 (Spring, 1964), pp. 178-202; p. 194.
7. Davis, Edith A. *The Development of Linguistic Skill in Twins, Singletons, Singletons with Siblings, and Only Children from Age Five to Ten Years* (University of Minnesota, Institute of Child Welfare Monograph, No. 14). Minneapolis, Minnesota: University of Minnesota Press, 1937.
8. Dawe, Helen C. "A Study of the Effect of an Educational Program upon Language Development and Related Mental Functions in Young Children," *Journal of Experimental Education*, XI (December, 1942), pp. 200-209.
9. Frogner, Ellen. "Problems of Sentence Structure in Pupils' Themes," *English Journal*, XXII (November, 1933), pp. 742-749.
10. Gill, Naomi. "Depth Reading," *English Journal*, XLII (September, 1953), pp. 311-315; "Depth Reading II: The Figures," *English Journal*, XLIII (September, 1954), pp. 297-303, 323.
11. Havighurst, Robert. "Characteristics and Needs of Students That Affect Learning," *Meeting Individual Differences in Reading* (Proceedings of the Annual Conference on Reading, Vol. XXVI, Supplementary Educational Monograph, No. 94). Chicago: University of Chicago, December, 1964.
12. Horn, Ernest. *Methods of Instruction in the Social Studies*. New York: Charles Scribner's Sons, 1937, p. 172.

13. Hunt,Kellogg W. *Differences in Grammatical Structures Written at Three Grade Levels.* Tallahassee, Florida: Florida State University (Cooperative Research Project 1,998), 1964, pp. 11-12; p. 110; pp. 57-59; p. 139.
14. Jennings, Frank. "For Such a Tide Is Moving . . ." *The Saturday Review* (May 16, 1964).
15. Jewett, Arno, *et al. Improving Skills of Culturally Different Youth in Large Cities.* Washington, D. C.: U. S. Department of Health, Education, and Welfare, Office of Education Bulletin 1964, No. 5, pp. 10-21.
16. Joos, Martin. "Language and the School Child," *Language and Learning, The Harvard Educational Review,* XXXIV, No. 2 (Spring, 1964), p. 209.
17. Khator, Mahmaud. "The Influence of Social Class on the Language of Kindergarten Children": Unpublished Ph.D. dissertation, University of Chicago, 1951.
18. LaBrant, Lou L. *A Study of Certain Language Developments in Grades IV to XII, Inclusive, Genetic Psychology Monographs,* XIV (November, 1933), pp. 387-491.
19. Loban, Walter D. "The Language of Elementary School Children," *A Study of the Use and Control of Language Effectiveness in Communication and the Relations Among Speaking, Reading, Writing, and Listening.* Champaign, Illinois: National Council of Teachers of English (Research Report, No. I, 1963), pp. 8-32-33; p. 43; pp. 53-54; p. 58; p. 55.
20. Luria, A. R., and Yudavich, F. *Speech and the Development of Mental Processes in the Child.* London: Staples Press, 1959, p. 122.
21. Menyuk, Paula. "Syntactic Structures in the Language of Children," *Child Development* (Society for Research in Child Development, XXXIV), 1963, pp. 407-422; pp. 411-412; p. 418.
22. Merry, Frieda K. and Ralph V. *The First Two Decades of Life.* New York: Harper, 1950, p. 17.
23. Milner, Esther. "A Study of the Relationship Between Reading Readiness in Grade One School Children and Pattern of Parent-Child Interaction," *Child Development,* XXII (June, 1951), pp. 95-112.
24. Russell, David. *The Dimensions of Children's Meaning Vocabularies in Grades IV Through XII.* Berkeley, California: University of California Publications in Education, Vol. XI, No. 5, pp. 315-414.
25. Smith, Dora V. "Growth in Language Power As Related to Child Development," *Dora V. Smith: Selected Essays.* New York: The Macmillan Company, 1964, pp. 15-83.
26. Strickland, Ruth. *The Language of Elementary School Children: Its Relationship to the Language of Reading Textbooks and the Quality of Reading of Selected Children.* Bloomington, Indiana: Bulletin of the School of Education, Indiana University, Vol. XXXVIII, No. 4, July, 1962.
27. Templin, Mildred C. *Certain Language Skills in Children; Their Development and Interrelationships.* Minneapolis, Minnesota: The University of Minnesota Press, 1957, pp. 83-93; pp. 99-100; p. 151.
28. Watts, A. F. *The Language and Mental Development of Children.* London: George C. Harrap and Company, Ltd., 1964, p. 40; p. 31.

9 Some Possible Explanations of Sex Difference in Language Development and Disorders

Dorothea McCarthy

For over fifty years educators have been aware of significant differences be-tween the sexes in language development and academic achievement. An emi-nent child psychologist elucidates her position—based on research and experience—that these differences are cultural artifacts rather than biologically determined traits.

Why is it important to determine whether these differences are environ-mentally or hereditarily determined? Should these differences cause us to make any adjustments in the materials, procedures, organization systems, or levels of expectation? In general, have they? From your experience, do you believe these differences increase or decrease during the elementary school years? In light of Cohen's thesis in an earlier article in this part, might these differences be more noticeable in some subgroups in our society than in others? What are some educational changes which you would advocate on the basis of this article?

There has appeared in the literature considerable evidence indicating that American white boys are slightly later than girls in practically all aspects of language development which show developmental trends with age (3, pp. 551-555). These differences seldom are statistically significant, but the careful observer cannot ignore the amazing consistency with which these small differ-ences appear in one investigation after another, each being conducted by a different experimenter, employing different techniques, different subjects, and sampling different geographical populations.[1]

Sex differences in favor of girls are present as soon as children begin to talk; that is, at about the age of onset of true language as distinct from pre-linguistic utterances. Irwin and Chen (5) present curves showing the number

From *Journal of Psychology* 35:155-160; January 1953. Reprinted with permission of *The Journal Press* and Dorothea McCarthy, Professor, Fordham University, New York, New York.

of speech sounds from birth to 2½ years, which are practically identical for the two sexes for the first year of life, but these curves begin to diverge in favor of the girls in the second year of life when true speech emerges.

Although the developmental differences between the sexes are small in magnitude, they seem to be of considerable importance for the later acquisition of the more complex and secondary language forms for the effect seems to be cumulative. All statistics on the incidence of language disorders, particularly on the incidence of stuttering and of reading disabilities, reveal that language disturbances occur much more frequently among boys than among girls in most American reports (2, 6, 13). Series of case studies of language disorders show that rather than being evenly divided between the sexes, from 65 to 100 per cent of such disorders occur among boys.

The roots of the sex differentiation in language development must be sought in early infancy, for the differences appear at an extremely early age and the vital importance of imitative babbling in the establishment of language patterns is well recognized. Stengel (9) has stressed especially the importance of the so-called "echo-reaction" stage in which the baby babbles back to the mother approximations of the sounds made by her. This is pleasant and satisfying to the infant and is considered to facilitate identification with the adult who provides the language model. Wyatt (12) also emphasizes the importance of the emotional quality of the early mother-child relations and the fact that the learning of the mother's speech is achieved through a process of unconscious identification. The mother is thus the child's first language teacher and as such is the first mediator of this vital cultural heritage.

The usual environmental situation in our culture is somewhat different for the boy infant than for the girl infant. Children of both sexes are usually cared for by, and have the constant companionship and speech model of, the mother. This experience in early language development is likely to be more satisfying for the girl than for the boy infant as she identifies more readily with the mother. The boy baby, on the other hand, needs to identify with, and to imitate the father's speech, of which he is likely to hear a minimum in our culture. When he does hear the father's speech and tries to imitate it, the experience must be much less satisfying for him than for the girl who can produce a fairly satisfactory echo-reaction of the mother's voice. The tremendous difference in voice quality of the adult male whose voice has changed with the attainment of maturity, and the small high-pitched voice of the boy infant certainly must make the echo-reaction stage much less satisfying for the male infant. It may even be quite confusing and perhaps even fear-producing, since loud sounds often produce fear in the young child. It may be argued that girls also experience the father's voice, about as much as do boys, but they probably feel less need to imitate and to identify with him than do boys for they are already making good progress in echoing the speech of the mother, and are finding considerable security and satisfaction in so doing. It is conceivable therefore, if this interpretation is correct, that contacts with the father would be less disturbing and less confusing to girl than to boy infants.

The writer has elsewhere (7, 8) pointed out that language disorders in older children seem to be due to emotional insecurity based on attitudes of parental rejection. A second hypothesis which could account at least in part for the observed sex difference in language is that it may be due to differential parental attitudes towards the two sexes. Adoption agencies in the American culture usually have many more requests for girls than for boys for placement. If the same sex preference is present among true parents (that seems evident in instances in which prospective parents have their choice) it is reasonable to assume that girl babies are more often welcomed, and hence are given greater warmth, affection, and security from the very beginning, than are boys in our present day society.

One of the reasons which may account for this preference is that boys are usually more active physically, and hence more difficult to control. Goodenough (4) has shown that boys have more frequent and longer anger outbursts than girls, that they are the objects of more disciplinary measures, and are usually handled more harshly than are girls. This would seem to indicate that they are more often frustrated by parental treatment, and must therefore experience a greater degree of emotional insecurity, which could lay the groundwork for later language disabilities as well as other behavior disorders.

If, as was pointed out above, the boy child finds less satisfaction in echoing the mother's speech, he will presumably repeat the activity less often than the girl who, as pointed out above, finds such activity more pleasant. Thus, there may be a differential in amount of linguistic practice, and in the degree of satisfaction derived therefrom by the two sexes in our culture which may tend to make a cumulative difference in experience in favor of girls.

In our culture, the boy is encouraged in active games, and even at the nursery age, when he is acquiring language skill, he is sent outdoors to play more often than the girl. This separates him from further adult linguistic stimulation. Boys are also more likely to engage in play with blocks and wheel toys and objects low in conversational value. Girls on the other hand are encouraged in indoor play with dolls, household toys, and table-play which have been shown to be of high conversation value (10). Girls too are more likely to be permitted around the kitchen and other centers of household activity, and thus to have more constant adult attention. Girls are then more likely to be found within question-asking range of the mother and thus are more likely than their brothers to enjoy maternal contact and linguistic stimulation.

As the child finds satisfaction in echoing back the mother's utterances, the mother in turn finds it satisfying to engage in vocal play with the child. The girl child, however, being better able to identify with the mother, will probably be more responsive than the boy, so that the mother again may unconsciously give more linguistic practice to the girl than she does to the boy. Thus, it is conceivable, if these hypotheses are correct, that the groundwork is laid for greater conversation and companionship between mother and daughter than between mother and son. Such factors certainly seem worth considering in attempting to interpret the dynamics of the sex differences which are found. It becomes more understandable, in the light of such factors, why boys often interpret maternal behavior as rejecting and hence more of them feel insecure in their family relationship than is the case among girls.

There are of course some instances of language disorders among girls. One may ask, in the light of the above interpretations, how the relatively rare occurrence of language disabilities among girls can be accounted for. In the writer's clinical experience girls with language disorders have always had severely disturbed relationships with the mother so that the identification with the mother through language probably never occurred or was seriously distorted. Usually the relationships with the father were either non-existent or contacts were so infrequent or of such poor quality that they in no way compensated for the deprivation of maternal care, affection, and opportunity for identification.

Many language disorders are first noticed at the time of school entrance. Retardation and poor articulation which have been tolerated within the family circle become obvious. Unfavorable comparisons with other children contribute still further to the insecurity of already insecure children. At this time, adjustment must be made, not only to a new group of one's peers, often in a highly competitive situation, but also to another adult, usually another female, who becomes identified in the child's mind with the mother. When the mother-child relations in the preschool period have been of a wholesome quality, and a secure child enters the school situation, little difficulty arises. However, as has been outlined above, the average boy is more likely to enter school feeling somewhat insecure and rejected and to have had a less healthy relationship with his mother than the average girl. His predispositions therefore toward the female teacher are more likely to be fraught with a greater degree of anxiety, which may interfere with effective learning; and hence he is somewhat more likely to have difficulty with reading and other verbal skills in the academic situation than the average girl. Being about six months less mature linguistically than the average girl with whom he now has to compete in oral language, he is slower in beginning reading. His performance with the primer is likely therefore to be frustrating to the teacher whose aim is often centered on teaching reading skills early, and her behavior toward the boy is therefore likely to be one of further rejection, contributing still more to his insecurity. The basic anxiety so accumulated interferes with effective learning and the stage is set for the problem or typical boy behavior which Wickman (11) found so frustrating to teachers. If the child happens to encounter a teacher who is not well adjusted, who lacks insight into his behavior and into her own attitude, she will behave in what Anderson (1) describes as a "dominative" rather than an "integrative" way, and the vicious circle of frustration and aggression in the school situation becomes well established, and another non-learner in verbal skills, a potential problem child, is added to the rolls. It should also be remembered that the physical limitations of the classroom are undoubtedly more frustrating to the naturally more active boy than they are to the girl who is accustomed to and accepts sedentary play.

It is always possible to postulate differences in native endowment to account for the sex differences observed. Yet, it does not seem as though this explanation should be resorted to until account has been taken of the various environmental factors which certainly are operative in present day American culture. These interpretations are offered as tentative explanations which may operate as indicated in the long run when averages for large numbers of cases are considered. They are advanced in an effort to harmonize evidence from genetic studies on the one hand, and from various clinical investigations on the other hand. They must not be construed as operating in every individual case, for the individual differences within each sex group are indeed great, and hence almost everyone can point to individual cases of boys who are accelerated and girls who are retarded for their ages in language. It seems to the writer, however, that such dynamisms as have been outlined in this paper probably operate in the directions indicated with sufficient frequency to account for the small differences found in the averages for the two sexes at early ages in the genetic studies, and for the resultant cumulative effects observed in the clinical data at later ages.

Footnote

[1] An investigation by Anastasi and D'Angelo (*J. Genet. Psychol.*, 1952) reports a sex difference in favor of boys among five-year-old Negroes.

References

1. Anderson, H. H. The measurement of domination and of socially integrative behavior in teacher's contacts with children. *Child Devel.*, 1939, 10, 73-89.
2. Bennett, C. C. An inquiry into the genesis of poor reading. *Teachers College Contribution to Education, No. 442*, 1938.
3. Carmichael, L. *(Ed.) Manual of Child Psychology.* New York: Wiley, 1946.
4. Goodenough, F. L. Anger in young children. *Institute Child Welfare Monog., Ser.* 9. Minneapolis: Univ. Minnesota Press, 1931. Pp. xiii & 278.

5. Irwin, O. C., & Chen, H. Development of speech during infancy: Curve of phonemic types. *J. Exper. Psychol.*, 1946, 36, 431-436.
6. Loutitt, C. M. *Clinical Psychology*. New York: Harper, 1947. Pp. xviii & 661.
7. McCarthy, D. The psychologist looks at the teaching of English. *Indepen. Sch. Bull.*, 1946-47, No. 5.
8. ———. Personality and learning. *Amer. Coun. Educ. Stud.*, 1949, 35, 93-96.
9. Stengel, E. A. clinical and psychological study of echo-reactions. *J. Men. Sci.*, 1947, 93, 598-612.
10. Van Alstyne, D. *Play Behavior and Choice of Play Materials of Preschool Children*. Chicago: Univ. Chicago Press, 1932.
11. Wickman, E. K. *Children's Behavior and Teachers' Attitudes*. New York: Commonwealth Fund, 1928.
12. Wyatt, G. L. Stammering and language learning in early childhood. *J. Abn. & Soc. Psychol.*, 1949, 44, 75-84.
13. Yedinack, J. G. A study of the linguistic functioning of children with articulation and reading disabilities. *J. Genet. Psychol.*, 1949, 74, 23-59.

10   Language Development in Socially Disadvantaged Children

Jane B. Raph

Much has been written and spoken about the verbal deficiencies of socially disadvantaged children. Most has been accurate but incomplete while some has bordered on myth. What has been missing is a compendium of reliable information discovered through research. In the best summary of research available, Raph provides some informative data and challenging interpretations which should allow teachers to more squarely base instructional programs on facts rather than guesses.

Do language deficits cause lowered intelligence or only lowered intelligence quotients? How do the language models of impoverished children influence both their thinking and their behavior? Does it necessarily follow that because disadvantaged children learn better through visual and motor than auditory avenues we should stress the former two and de-emphasize the latter? How is this article related to those by Cohen and Smith earlier in this part? To Ruddell's and Loban's in Part Three? What unanswered questions could you investigate in your classroom using action research? Articles cited in Selected References for Part Two which deal with this same general topic include those by Cazden, Church, DeBoer, Deutsch, May, and Metz. For some practical suggestions for helping the disadvantaged build language, read Wilson.

Conspicuous deficits in language and speech are a handicap which socially disadvantaged children often have. Because adverse environmental circumstances have not equipped many of these children to conceptualize clearly or to verbalize adequately, their ability to profit from compensatory opportunities provided them, especially those of the school, seems to be limited. Two main questions then become relevant for an understanding of their difficulties: (a) How is the language acquisition of these children different from that of

From *Review of Educational Research* 35:389-400; December 1965. Reprinted with permission of American Educational Research Association and Jane B. Raph, Professor, Graduate School of Education, Rutgers University, New Brunswick, New Jersey.

middle class children? (b) How do language and speech characteristics vary according to social class? Since studies pertaining to middle class children have been summarized elsewhere (McCarthy, 1954), this review will be limited to a presentation of investigations concerned specifically with language development and characteristics in children of low socioeconomic status.

Background Studies

In the 25-year period between 1930 and 1955, research on children has focused to a limited degree on the effects lower social class, institutionalization of infants, and minority membership have on language development. The classic studies of McCarthy (1930), Day (1932), and Davis (1937), which utilized paternal occupation as a criterion of selection in efforts to secure representative samplings, concur in indicating that group differences favor children from the upper socioeconomic levels on practically all aspects of language studied. Irwin (1948a, b) also showed the superiority of the speech sounds of infants whose fathers were in a business or profession over those of infants whose fathers were skilled, semiskilled, or unskilled. That the absence of verbally oriented interactions between a significant adult and a very young child can have lasting and detrimental effects on his language has been documented by research done on infants cared for in hospitals or orphanages (Brodbeck and Irwin, 1946; Dawe, 1942; Fleming, 1942; Goldfarb, 1943, 1945; Williams and McFarland, 1937).

Membership in minority groups and its adverse influence on language facility was first pointed out by Klineberg (1935) in regard to interpretation of mental tests administered to Negro children. Brown (1944) and Anastasi and D'Angelo (1952) compared young Negro and white children on the relationship of language development to IQ measures. In a longitudinal study of a low socioeconomic Negro group in New Haven, Pasamanick (1946), Pasamanick and Knobloch (1955), and Knobloch and Pasamanick (1953) pointed out that at the end of two years the infants' language behavior, though not retarded, was significantly lower than were other fields of behavior. Anastasi and Cordova (1953) and Anastasi and de Jesús (1953) dealt with the effects of bilingualism on intelligence in two groups of Puerto Rican children. The older group of sixth graders showed a lower level of intellectual functioning than normal, an effect ascribed in part to a very low socioeconomic level and to severe language handicaps during initial school experiences. The younger group, however, did not differ in IQ measures or in language from a white and Negro group studied previously (Anastasi and D'Angelo, 1952).

The outcomes of the work done in the two and a half decades summarized above were to foreshadow much contemporary work. The finding that children from the middle class with adequate mothering revealed marked and persistent superiority in language facility over those who for reasons of low socioeconomic level or institutionalization had received less than adequate mothering was to contribute to a revival of interest in the whole area of educability of preschool-age children (Fowler, 1962; Hunt, 1961). In addition, the frequently reported finding that socioeconomic status and racial or ethnic membership appeared to be important correlates of performance on measures of ability—measures known to be highly dependent on verbal factors—served to stimulate research designed to identify the particular environmental factors which enhance or inhibit language development.

Antecedents of Language Deficiency

The following factors will be considered in the review of current studies on the process of language acquisition under socially disadvantaged circumstances: infant vocalization, development of comprehension, development of cognition, and family interactive patterns.

Infant vocalization

Knowledge regarding some determinants of vocal output in infants and the relationship of vocalization to the development of language has been extended by several experimental studies. Rheingold, Gewirtz, and Ross (1959) demonstrated the responsiveness of vocalizations to conditioning in the three-month-old infant. Irwin (1960a) showed that in homes of lower occupational status the phonetic production of infants between 13 and 30 months could be increased beginning around 18 months by systematic reading to and talking with the infant for a short period each day, an increase greater than would occur without the sound enrichment. Rheingold and Bayley (1959), in a follow-up at 18 months of 16 institutionalized infants who had received attentive care by one person from the sixth to the eighth month of life, found that more of their experimental subjects vocalized during the social test procedure than of the control subjects, who had been cared for under the usual institutional routine. Other differences in social responsiveness and developmental status were not found, suggesting that verbal behavior of infants appears to be more sensitive to interactive influences in the environment than are other classes of behavior, a conclusion confirmed by Pringle and Tanner (1958) and Pringle (1959). To the extent that the lack of attentive mothering in an institution resembles the minimal care a child receives in a lower class home—where marginal income, crowding, and noise often make it difficult for the caretaker to give the infant much beyond bare sustenance—the likelihood of language and speech impairment in the lower class child is evident.

Development of comprehension

Comprehension and verbal responsiveness through language represent two different functions and as such need to be considered separately with regard to facility in lower class children. Pasamanick and Knobloch (1955) divided language behavior items on the *Gesell Developmental Schedules* into three spheres: language comprehension, verbal responsiveness, and reported language behavior. They found that their two-year-old Negro subjects excelled to a statistically significant degree in the sphere of comprehension in comparison with verbal responsiveness. Reported verbal behavior did not differ significantly from the other two spheres of language behavior. Such findings have to be interpreted in the light of developmental expectations, however, where comprehension tends to precede verbalization in the normal course of events. Carson and Rabin (1960), in a comparison of school age Negro and white children equated for comprehension and from different geographical locations, showed marked difference favoring Northern white children with respect to communication on the Vocabulary subtest of the *Wechsler Intelligence Scale for Children* and on a qualitative scale applied to the oral definitions in the *Ammons Full-Range Vocabulary Test*. Here results appear to be a bona fide function of socioeconomic factors.

John and Goldstein (1964) noted the disproportionate reliance the lower class child has on what he hears for his learning in contrast to the middle class child, who has the benefit of numerous conversational dialogues with adults to assist him in his verbal responses. While it might appear likely that the lower class child begins to grasp meanings in advance of any opportunity he has for verbalizing them, even here a lack of differentiation among mental abilities based on lower verbal meaning and lower fluency scores was found to be characteristic of low status children compared with high status children studied by Mitchell (1956). Pavenstedt (1965) described children from low class families as frequently not attending to instructions and needing to rely on concrete demonstrations to translate instructions into action, a conclusion which could, however, reflect short attention span rather than comprehension difficulties. The language models to which impoverished children are exposed are often not only meager, restricted, and incorrect grammatically but also punitive, according to Gray and Klaus (1963) and Bernstein (1961), limiting divergence and elaboration in children's thinking, and thereby inhibiting the development of their ability to comprehend.

Development of cognitive behavior

The Verbal Survey project being conducted by Deutsch and associates at the Institute of Developmental Studies of the New York Medical College is generating a number of investigations regarding the relationship of language development and cognition. John's (1963) and John and Goldstein's (1964) extensive work on certain patterns of linguistic and cognitive behavior in children from various social classes showed some of the specific limitations in the disadvantaged group's acquisition of the ability to label, discriminate, categorize, and generalize. Brown and Deutsch (1965), drawing from the same sample, demonstrated that within a socioeconomic status group particular levels of cognitive performance reflected certain specific environmental characteristics such as race and relative deprivation. Deutsch and Brown (1964) noted additional elements of preschool educational experience and family stability as sources of variance in IQ scores; IQ scores were higher among those children who had attended a day care center or a nursery school and among those whose fathers had been present in the home.

From the above series of studies employing a first and fifth grade core sample of 292 children and an extended population of about 2,500 children of various racial and social class groupings, Deutsch (1965) concluded that the cumulative deficit effect advanced by Klineberg (1963) does indeed exist. On the basis of a large number of measured variables studied, with language functioning at the core, Deutsch (1965) inferred that children from low socioeconomic backgrounds and minority status became less able to handle intellectual and linguistic tasks as they moved through school.

Effects of family interactions

Studies on the effect of the family on language development have centered around three main variables: the frequency, quality, and continuity of interactions. McCarthy (1961) emphasized the relationship between verbal skills and parental availability, particularly the amount and kind of contact the child experiences with his mother. The small amount of contact between parent and child with many siblings seemed to explain in part Nisbet's (1961) finding that a large family is a handicap to verbal development. Walters, Connor, and Zunich (1964) supported the same hypothesis of significantly fewer interactions between lower class mothers and children than between mothers and children in other social groups, on the basis of an experimental study of the observed facilitating-inhibiting behaviors used by lower class mothers in the guidance of their preschool children. Although the authors' categories did not differentiate between verbal and nonverbal interactions, the lack of communication between mother and child was clear.

Two studies penetrate beyond the fact of relative frequency of verbal exchange to the quality of the contact maintained. Milner (1951) offered promising retrospective information on the specific value of early language experience. She compared the social backgrounds of two groups of first grade Negro children who scored contrastingly high and low on language development tests. The high language scorers were found to have participated more widely in adult family conversation and to have received more overt demonstrations of affection. Bernstein (1961), a British sociologist, compared the language of working class and middle class groups of adolescents. From his work he deduced a series of highly provocative postulates pertinent to origins of language deficiencies in culturally impoverished groups. He noted the tendency of the lower class parents to exercise arbitrary authority and categorical demands in disciplining their children, without giving any explanation or allowing the child to deviate or question. In this way, children were thought to be deprived of the opportunity to explore alternatives verbally and to lack experience in conceptualizing and reasoning.

One study of lower class children was concerned with the duration of the adult-child relationship. Pringle and Bossio (1958) in their study of 8-, 11-, and 14-year-old orphans examined the effects of regular contacts with adults living outside the orphanage. Backwardness in language development was least marked among those children who, since their removal from home, had maintained a continuing relationship with a member of their family or family substitute.

Characteristics of Language Deficiency

The general picture of language inadequacy in lower class children is currently being subject to scrutiny not only in an effort to determine why language and speech vary according to social class but also to ascertain what the distinctive qualities of the various groups may be. Studies which relate to these efforts will be reported below according to sensory modalities, quantitative language usage, qualitative language usage, and articulatory characteristics.

Sensory modalities

It has been hypothesized that sensory modalities contribute differentially to learning. The work of Sievers (1955) on the *Illinois Test of Psycholinguistic Abilities (ITPA)* based on the formulations of Osgood (1954) has made it possible to test how children of varying intellectual endowments utilize their abilities differently. Weaver (n.d.) studied the psycholinguistic abilities of three groups of culturally deprived children. Their performance on the *ITPA* showed a similarity of language patterning with relative strength in the visual-motor channels and relative weakness in auditory-vocal channels. Moreover, children in the study who had been exposed to an early training project (Gray and Klaus, 1963) did significantly better than did those in the control group. C. P. Deutsch (1964) investigated auditory discrimination as a factor in verbal behavior and in reading achievement of a lower class group. She postulated that children raised in a very noisy environment with little directed and sustained speech stimulation might well be deficient in their discrimination and recognition of speech sounds, and that they would also be relatively inattentive to auditory stimuli and would have difficulty with any other skill which is primarily or largely dependent on good auditory discrimination. Her well designed study employing poor readers and good readers at grades one, three, and five indicated the poor readers had poorer auditory discrimination and greater difficulty shifting from one modality to another than did the good readers. Her results again confirm the apparent importance of auditory discrimination and general auditory responsiveness for verbal performance and reading ability. Inferences to be drawn from these studies point to the advantages of employing visual and motor avenues in dealing with socially deprived children.

Quantitative characteristics of language usage

Thomas (1962) studied sentence development and vocabulary usage in the spoken language of white and Negro kindergarten children from low socioeconomic circumstances in a Midwestern urban setting. Verbal utterances were obtained in a structured oral interview conducted by the investigator. The traditional measures of length of verbal responses, complexity of sentence structure, proportion of parts of speech, and types and frequency of grammatical errors yielded a large number of comparisons. Notable among these was the finding that his subjects used significantly fewer words per remark than did Templin's (1957) subjects drawn from a middle class socioeconomic group. Of importance to the process of beginning reading was Thomas' finding that his subjects failed to use 20 to 50 per cent of the words contained in five of the standard word lists recommended for primary grades.

Deutsch and others (1964) evaluated selected aspects of expressive and receptive speech in 167 pupils from 12 New York City public schools chosen to represent various combinations of two school grades, three socioeconomic levels, sex, and Negro and white race. Continuous speech samples were obtained by use of two reinforcement techniques and were recorded on tapes. Twenty measures were applied to the transcribed language protocols including such variables as total verbal output, mean sentence length, number of different word uses, and so forth. On the basis of numerous correlations applied to these variables and the use of a factor analysis, they found that differences in language performance which correlate with social class or race also correlate with significant differences in IQ performance. This relationship is even more clear in the fifth grade than in the first grade. Such a finding suggests the importance of improving language skills if IQ scores are to be raised, a task which would need to be undertaken during the crucial preschool years.

Qualitative characteristics of language usage

Qualitative characteristics of language have not been considered to any extent in relation to the culturally impoverished but are useful for tapping certain features of the way they talk, particularly to their peers. Bernstein's (1961) theoretical formulations refer to a number of dimensions of linguistic behavior in British working class children which he sees as responsible for the large proportion of educational failures in that group. Their inability to plan verbally, to develop and maintain a sequence of thought, and to deal cognitively and conversationally with specificity and relativity were proposed as barriers to academic achievement. Riessman (1962) observed that such children have considerable facility with informal language expressed best in unstructured spontaneous situations and give unusual and original responses in word-association tests. Such distinctive properties of communication as presented by these two authorities, however, are not yet substantiated through systematic research.

Articulatory characteristics of language usage

There are few current studies on the pronunciation and articulation aspects of the speech of the lower class child. Davis (1937) showed that the percentage of children with good articulation was higher among upper occupational groups than among lower. Beckey (1942) found that significantly more children with retarded speech belonged to lower socioeconomic groups. Templin (1953) demonstrated a significant difference between children of upper and lower socioeconomic groups on both screening and diagnostic tests of articulation, the difference being in favor of the upper group. She stated that according to her extensive data children of the lower socioeconomic group take about a year longer to reach essentially mature articulation than do those of the upper group. Pavenstedt (1965) said children from very low class families form their words so poorly as to make it almost impossible to understand them at three and four years of age.

The sparseness of information in this area is due probably to several factors. (a) The presence of subcultural variation in pronunciation, while known generally to act as a crucial deterrent to learning and to later vocational adjustment, has only very recently received any major or focused consideration as it occurs in underprivileged groups. (b) Problems of unclear or unintelligible pronunciation have not usually been brought to the attention of the speech therapist or psychologist prior to the lower class child's entrance to school; a body of knowledge emanating from study of such problems, therefore, does not yet exist. Once these culturally disadvantaged children are in school their problems have been so great and severe as to render largely ineffective the usual services the school might have available for dealing with their needs, especially in the congested urban schools and the substandard schools in the economically poorer sections of the country. (c) The speech problems posed by groups of children from different low socioeconomic circumstances vary with geographic location, race, and ethnic origin. It has not been clear where responsibility for remediation should be assigned. The regular classroom teacher, through no fault of his own, has been largely ineffective. The time of the speech therapist has, of necessity and by training, been devoted to remediation of organic and functional speech pathologies not primarily cultural in origin.

Conclusions and Needed Research

Research to date indicates that the process of language acquisition for socially disadvantaged children, in contrast to that of middle class children, is more subject (a) to a lack of vocal stimulation during infancy, (b) to a paucity of experiences in conversation with more verbally mature adults in the first three or four years of life, (c) to severe limitations in the opportunities to develop mature cognitive behavior, and (d) to the types of emotional encounters which result in the restricting of the children's conceptual and verbal skills. Distinctive qualities of their language and speech include (a) a deficit in the auditory-vocal modality greater than in the visual-motor areas; (b) a meagerness of quantity and quality of verbal expression, which serves to depress intellectual functioning as they grow older; and (c) a slower rate and lower level of articulatory maturation.

In view of the recognized communication difficulties of lower class children, there is a pressing demand for both developmental and cross-cultural studies on the multiple factors related to their language and speech. Methodology needs to be developed which will make possible age and subgroup comparisons through carefully controlled standard-stimulus situations. These situations should be sufficiently simple and practical to be easily used in a variety of settings and with many types of disadvantaged children. Techniques such as those described by Irwin (1960b) for obtaining and transcribing accurately taped recordings of language samples need to be further refined to tap spontaneous language behavior among children rather than to elicit only the more stereotyped responses obtained through adult questions. Procedures need to be developed which will enable researchers to investigate the various modes of verbal functioning and adaptation employed by the child, including attention to his language in the context of his activities with peers. The gesture accompaniments of his talking should be studied. This suggests the possibility of combining narrative and descriptive methods of describing total behavior with use of mechanical recording devices. Lastly, investigation is needed into the influence of adult models on child language and the extent to which the patterns and expressions of the parents are imitated and modified by the child.

Bibliography

Anastasi, Anne, and Cordova, Fernando A. "Some Effects of Bilingualism upon the Intelligence Test Performance of Puerto Rican Children in New York City." *Journal of Educational Psychology* 44: 1-19; January 1953.

Anastasi, Anne, and D'Angelo, Rita Y. "A Comparison of Negro and White Preschool Children in Language Development and Goodenough Draw-a-Man IQ." *Journal of Genetic Psychology* 81: 147-65; December 1952.

Anastasi, Anne, and de Jesús, Cruz. "Language Development and Nonverbal IQ of Puerto Rican Preschool Children in New York City." *Journal of Abnormal and Social Psychology* 48: 357-66; July 1953.

Beckey, Ruth Elizabeth. "A Study of Certain Factors Related to Retardation of Speech." *Journal of Speech Disorders* 7: 223-49; September 1942.

Bernstein, Basil. "Social Class and Linguistic Development: A Theory of Social Learning." *Education, Economy and Society.* (Edited by A. H. Halsey, Jean Floud, and C. Arnold Anderson.) New York: Free Press of Glencoe, 1961. Chapter 24, pp. 288-314.

Brodbeck, Arthur J., and Irwin, Orvis C. "The Speech Behavior of Infants Without Families." *Child Development* 17: 145-56; September 1946.

Brown, Bert R., and Deutsch, Martin. "Some Effects of Social Class and Race on Children's Language and Intellectual Abilities: A New Look at an Old Problem." Paper read at the Biennial Meeting of the Society for Research in Child Development, March 1965. New York: Institute for Developmental Studies, Department of Psychiatry, New York Medical College, 1965. 9 pp. (Mimeo.)

Brown, Fred. "An Experimental and Critical Study of the Intelligence of Negro and White Kindergarten Children." *Journal of Genetic Psychology* 65: 161-75; September 1944.

Carson, Arnold S., and Rabin, A. I. "Verbal Comprehension and Communication in Negro and White Children." *Journal of Educational Psychology* 51: 47-51; April 1960.

Davis, Edith A. *The Development of Linguistic Skill in Twins, Singletons with Siblings and Only Children from Age Five to Ten Years.* Institute of Child Welfare Monograph Series No. 14. Minneapolis: University of Minnesota Press, 1937. 165 pp.

Dawe, Helen C. "A Study of the Effect of an Educational Program upon Language Development and Related Mental Functions in Young Children." *Journal of Experimental Education* 11: 200-209; December 1942.

Day, Ella J. "The Development of Language in Twins: I. A Comparison of Twins and Single Children." *Child Development* 3: 179-99; September 1932.

Deutsch, Cynthia P. "Auditory Discrimination and Learning: Social Factors." *Merrill-Palmer Quarterly* 10: 277-96; July 1964.

Deutsch, Martin. "The Role of Social Class in Language Development and Cognition." *American Journal of Orthopsychiatry* 35: 78-88; January 1965.

Deutsch, Martin, and Brown, Bert. "Social Influences in Negro-White Intelligence Differences." *Journal of Social Issues* 20: 24-35; April 1964.

Deutsch, Martin, and others. *Communication of Information in the Elementary School Classroom.* Cooperative Research Project No. 908. New York: Institute for Developmental Studies, Department of Psychiatry, New York Medical College, 1964. 133 pp. (Mimeo.)

Fleming, Virginia Van Dyne. "A Study of Stanford-Binet Vocabulary Attainment and Growth in Children in the City of Childhood, Mooseheart, Illinois, as Compared with Children Living in Their Own Homes." *Journal of Genetic Psychology* 60: 359-73; June 1942.

Fowler, William. "Cognitive Learning in Infancy and Early Childhood." *Psychological Bulletin* 59: 116-52; March 1962.

Goldfarb, William. "Infant Rearing and Problem Behavior." *American Journal of Orthopsychiatry* 13: 249-65; April 1943.

Goldfarb, William. "Effects of Psychological Deprivation in Infancy and Subsequent Stimulation." *American Journal of Psychiatry* 102: 18-33; July 1945.

Gray, Susan W., and Klaus, Rupert. *Early Training Project: Interim Report.* Murfreesboro, Tenn.: The City Schools and George Peabody College for Teachers, November 1963. 25 pp. (Mimeo.)

Hunt, J. McV. *Intelligence and Experience.* New York: Ronald Press Co., 1961. 416 pp.

Irwin, Orvis C. "Infant Speech: The Effect of Family Occupational Status and of Age on Use of Sound Types." *Journal of Speech and Hearing Disorders* 13: 224-26; September 1948. (a)

Irwin, Orvis C. "Infant Speech: The Effect of Family Occupational Status and of Age on Sound Frequency." *Journal of Speech and Hearing Disorders* 13: 320-23; December 1948. (b)

Irwin, Orvis C. "Infant Speech: The Effect of Systematic Reading of Stories." *Journal of Speech and Hearing Research* 3: 187-90; June 1960. (a)

Irwin, Orvis C. "Language and Communication." *Handbook of Research Methods in Child Development.* (Edited by Paul H. Mussen.) New York: John Wiley & Sons, 1960. Chapter 12, pp. 487-516. (b)

John, Vera P. "The Intellectual Development of Slum Children: Some Preliminary Findings." *American Journal of Orthopsychiatry* 33: 813-22; October 1963.

John, Vera P., and Goldstein, Leo S. "The Social Context of Language Acquisition." *Merrill-Palmer Quarterly* 10: 265-76; July 1964.

Klineberg, Otto A. *Negro Intelligence and Selective Migration.* New York: Columbia University Press, 1935. 66 pp.

Klineberg, Otto. "Negro-White Differences in Intelligence Test Performance: A New Look àt an Old Problem." *American Psychologist* 18: 198-203; April 1963.

Knobloch, Hilda, and Pasamanick, Benjamin. "Further Observations on the Behavioral Development of Negro Children." *Journal of Genetic Psychology* 83: 137-57; September 1953.

McCarthy, Dorothea A. *The Language Development of the Preschool Child.* Institute of Child Welfare, Monograph Series No. 4. Minneapolis: University of Minnesota Press, 1930. 174 pp.

McCarthy, Dorothea A. "Language Development in Children." *Manual of Child Psychology*. (Edited by Leonard Carmichael.) Second edition. New York: John Wiley & Sons, 1954. Chapter 9, pp. 492-630.

McCarthy, Dorothea A. "Affective Aspects of Language Learning." Presidential address, Division of Developmental Psychology, American Psychological Association, September 1961. *Newsletter*, APA Division of Developmental Psychology, Fall 1961, pp. 1-11.

Milner, Esther. "A Study of the Relationship Between Reading Readiness in Grade One School Children and Patterns of Parent-Child Interaction." *Child Development* 22: 95-112; June 1951.

Mitchell, James V., Jr. "A Comparison of the Factorial Structure of Cognitive Functions for a High and Low Status Group." *Journal of Educational Psychology* 47: 397-414; November 1956.

Nisbet, John D. "Family Environment and Intelligence." *Education, Economy and Society*. (Edited by A. H. Halsey, Jean Floud, and C. Arnold Anderson.) New York: Free Press of Glencoe, 1961. Chapter 23, pp. 273-87.

Osgood, Charles E., issue editor. "Psycholinguistics: A Survey of Theory and Research Problems." *Journal of Abnormal and Social Psychology*, Vol. 49, Supplement 1954, No. 4. October 1954. 203 pp.

Pasamanick, Benjamin. "A Comparative Study of the Behavioral Development of Negro Infants." *Journal of Genetic Psychology* 69: 3-44; September 1946.

Pasamanick, Benjamin, and Knobloch, Hilda. "Early Language Behavior in Negro Children and the Testing of Intelligence." *Journal of Abnormal and Social Psychology* 50: 401-402; May 1955.

Pavenstedt, Eleanor. "A Comparison of the Child-Rearing Environment of Upper-Lower and Very Low Lower Class Families." *American Journal of Orthopsychiatry* 35: 89-98; January 1965.

Pringle, M. L. Kellmer. "Comparative Study of the Effects of Early Deprivation on Speech Development." *Perceptual and Motor Skills* 9: 345; December 1959.

Pringle, M. L. Kellmer, and Bossio, Victoria. "A Study of Deprived Children: Part II. Language Development and Reading Attainment." *Vita Humana* 1: 142-70; 1958.

Pringle, M. L. Kellmer, and Tanner, Margaret. "The Effects of Early Deprivation on Speech Development: A Comparative Study of Four Year Olds in a Nursery School and in Residential Nurseries." *Language and Speech* 1: 269-87; October–December 1958.

Rheingold, Harriet L., and Bayley, Nancy. "The Later Effects of an Experimental Modification of Mothering." *Child Development* 30: 363-72; September 1959.

Rheingold, Harriet L.; Gewirtz, Jacob L.; and Ross, Helen W. "Social Conditioning of Vocalizations in the Infant." *Journal of Comparative and Physiological Psychology* 52: 68-73; February 1959.

Riessman, Frank. *The Culturally Deprived Child.* New York: Harper & Row, 1962. 140 pp.

Sievers, Dorothy Jean. *Development and Standardization of a Test of Psycholinguistic Growth in Preschool Children.* Doctor's thesis. Chicago: University of Illinois, 1955. 148 pp. (Abstract: *Dissertation Abstracts* 16: 286-87; No. 1, 1956.)

Templin, Mildred C. "Norms on Screening Test of Articulation for Ages Three

Through Eight." *Journal of Speech and Hearing Disorders* 18: 323-31; December 1953.

Templin, Mildred C. *Certain Language Skills in Children.* Institute of Child Welfare Monograph Series No. 26. Minneapolis: University of Minnesota Press, 1957. 183 pp.

Thomas, Dominic Richard. *Oral Language, Sentence Structure and Vocabulary of Kindergarten Children Living in Low Socio-Economic Urban Areas.* Doctor's thesis. Detroit, Mich.: Wayne State University, 1962. 393 pp. (Abstract: *Dissertation Abstracts* 23: 1014. No. 3, 1962.)

Walters, James; Connor, Ruth; and Zunich, Michael. "Interaction of Mothers and Children from Lower-Class Families." *Child Development* 35: 433-40; June 1964.

Weaver, S. Joseph. *Interim Report: Psycholinguistic Abilities of Culturally Deprived Children.* Nashville, Tenn.: George Peabody College for Teachers, n.d. 3 pp. (Mimeo.)

Williams, Harold M., and McFarland, Mary L. "A Revision of the Smith Vocabulary Test for Preschool Children, Part III." *Development of Language and Vocabulary in Young Children.* (Edited by Harold M. Williams, Mary L. McFarland, and Marguerite F. Little.) University of Iowa Studies in Child Welfare No. 13. Iowa City: University of Iowa, June 1937, pp. 35-46.

11 Linguistics: An overview

George D. Owen

Linguistics, the study of language, has begun—and undoubtedly will continue —to exert powerful influences over both the content and the methods of the language arts program. It is incumbent upon educators to understand something about this discipline, its point of view and its basic tools and concepts, if they are to use and realize its potential in vitalizing language arts instruction.

Does Owen contradict himself when, on one hand, he says language is systematic but then states, on the other hand, that it is arbitrary and illogical? Why is it important to distinguish between linguistically correct and socially acceptable language? What implication does the fact that language is habitual have for teaching usage and grammar to elementary school pupils? What besides the basic sounds of a language—phonemes and morphemes—do linguists study? Why? Articles cited in Selected References for Part Two which give additional information about linguistics are by Chomsky, Laird, and Wetmore. For a lucid polemic on linguistics, read the article by Tillery.

I

Today no one can claim to be a linguist without qualifying his terms carefully. John Carroll, whose book, *The Study of Language,* is an exposition of the various facets of language study, discusses descriptive linguistics, psycholinguistics, historical linguistics, comparative linguistics, and a host of other subdivisions of linguistics. Certainly all of these disciplines make interesting and valuable contributions to our understanding of language and its use, but the American teacher of English might find little that would help her in her classroom tomorrow morning from reading tonight a technical discussion of the differences between the morphemes of Tagalog and those of English. She might find the interspersed Greek and English dialogue of a movie like *Never on Sunday* more instructive, and the hours devoted to the instruction would cer-

From *Elementary English* 39:421-425; May 1962. Reprinted with permission of the National Council of Teachers of English and George D. Owen, Director of Continuing Education, Detroit Public Schools, Michigan.

tainly be more entertaining. Before anyone can talk about linguistics, there-fore, and especially, talk *briefly* about linguistics, he has to limit his field.

II

First, then, let us consider the *attitudes* toward language which character-ize linguistics. No discussion of linguistic theory will make much sense until we first understand the philosophy toward language out of which this theory grows. I am not going to try to arrange these attitudes in any order of im-portance, but certainly one of the most fundamental beliefs of linguists is that *language is speech;* that the spoken form of any language is more nearly *the language* than the written form. Speech, they point out, is older than writing. Speech satisfies the total communication needs of millions of human beings scattered all over the face of the globe who will never read or write a single word in their entire lives. Where once we used to say that writing is permanent and therefore enables us to communicate at a distance and at different periods of time, the development of telephones, radio, and tape recorders has extended these capabilities to speech. Speech is primary; writing develops from speech but can never be more than an approximation of speech. It never reproduces all of the factors of speech; gestures, stresses, speech tones, and intonation can-not be accurately recorded. Writing is slow and laborious and its difficulty of production hampers its value as a vehicle of communication. The permanency of writing limits its changes of form. Speech, on the other hand, changes con-stantly. Because of these differing characteristics, the degree to which writing approximates speech becomes smaller and smaller with every generation. For all of these reasons, linguists believe that language is speech and most of their efforts, therefore, are devoted to the study of speech. They do not ignore writ-ing as they are sometimes accused of doing, but their interest in writing is in the ways in which, successfully or unsuccessfully, it reproduces speech.

A second fundamental attitude of linguistics toward language is that lan-guage is *systematic.* Specific principles govern its operation and these principles are all intertwined and interrelated. If this were not so, no one could ever learn by pure memorization the almost infinite number of combinations that are possible in every language. Actually, many of us know that language is sys-tematic even though we rarely think about it. We know, for example, that to form the past tense of a verb in English, the *ed* suffix is usually added: *plan* becomes *planned, iron* becomes *ironed, flunk* becomes *flunked.* When a child learning to speak says *runned* ("We runned all the way home"), his parents smile and indulgently "correct" the little darling. But the child has caught one facet of the system of operation of the English language, and "correction" is not what he needs. He must now begin to learn the modifications of the inflectional system for the past tense in English. When he has really mastered the system, he will recognize that the change of *run* to *ran* is one of the fifty-two possible modifications of the inflectional system for the past tense in English. Most of these modifications he will learn to make accurately and fluently early in his life. A few of the modifications for the past tense, such as the distinctions between *sat* and *set*, *lay* and *laid*, he may not learn to make until he enters high school.

The system is a powerful force, however, in our use of our language. All of you listening to me today know that the verb *slay*, for example, has a past tense, *slew*. If I tested you on the sentence "David slew the giant, Goliath," you would all get the verb form right. But a few years back when a popular comedian coined a new meaning for *slay* and made the expression "You slay me" a household phrase, it was not long before thousands of persons, English teachers included, were saying "He slayed me with that answer" and "That slayed me." Youngsters who have heard the verb *slay* only in this context will find it doubly difficult to learn that the "correct" past tense is *slew*. And teachers who understand the systematic nature of the productive process in language change will find it easier to teach the verb form *slew* indulgently, rather than regarding their students' use of *slayed* as another indication of the complete stupidity of the younger generation.

Linguists think that language is speech and language is systematic. These concepts are clearly definable and therefore arguable even to those who insist they are not linguists. A third attitude of linguistics is harder to illustrate. It may be best to think of this attitude as a cluster of three related concepts. This cluster of three concepts may be stated briefly: language is *symbolic*, language symbols are *arbitrary*, and the symbolism of any language is *complete*. What does this mean?

Many words in English refer directly to objects that can be seen or touched. A *cat*, for example, is an object we all recognize. The recognition is so instantaneous for most of us that the word and the object blend together in our minds. When we see the animal, we think the word simultaneously; when we use the word, its referrant is recalled immediately. This stimulus-response pattern is so unconscious that we tend to forget that the word is not the object but is only a sound symbol or a written symbol for the object. This point may be a little clearer if we consider the morpheme *ed* for the past tense of the verb. Clearly this is a symbol. There is nothing about the sound of *ed* or its appearance in writing that intrinsically means anything related to the past. The words of a language, the inflectional changes, the prefixes and suffixes, all of these are symbols that speakers of English agree on and can manipulate in patterns of such great complexity that fluent language use is in reality a miracle.

Now, if language is symbolic, where did these symbols come from? In the very dim past, words may have evolved from pictures of objects or from attempts to reproduce the sounds that primitive man heard around him: the dog says "bow-wow" and the cat says "meow," for example. Historically, I believe this is uncertain, but it is perfectly obvious that no such relationship exists today between the words of a language and the objects which they symbolize. The word for *cat* might just as well be *geb* as *cat*. The symbols, in other words, are arbitrary. If they are arbitrary, then a person learning a language must learn it from some other person, either directly or from books or tapes or some other humanly developed vehicle. He cannot learn it by himself through observation or listening to the sounds of nature around him. If this is true, then language is the language that people use, the English that they speak in 1962. . . . It is not the language of Shakespeare, of George Washington, of Franklin Roosevelt. Students learn the language of their parents, their friends, their community. If the language they learn is not the language their teachers speak, then they may have to learn a second language in school. But the language they bring with them is in every *linguistic* respect as good a language as the language of their teachers. Socially, it may not be as acceptable, but linguistically it is equally useful.

And, like all language, it is *complete*. It is capable of expressing every idea or feeling that its users wish to express. This does not mean that it is capable of expressing every idea that a poet, engineer, or a physician wishes to express, but then the ancient Greeks did not have a word for *TV* or *Sputniks* either. And we as teachers might as well admit that we ourselves cannot express every idea a nuclear scientist might wish to express. But the ancient Greeks could have invented a word for *TV* if they had needed it, we could learn to talk like a physicist, and our students can learn to express the new experiences they undergo in school. At each stage of their experience, however, their language is complete: capable of expressing any experience they encounter in symbols which are arbitrarily selected.

As part of their approach to language, linguists also accept two concepts which are shared with other intellectual disciplines. The first of these is that language use is *habitual*, not logical. All of us learn to use our language by slow steps, but we cannot be fluent in that language until we can manipulate it without conscious effort. By the time we are adults, this effortless, habitual use of our language is so deeply embedded in our subconscious mind that we never think about how we are using it. That is, we never think about it until we get in an English class and are told to "correct" our English by applying the rules that are listed in our textbooks. This implies that language use is logical: "Think, man, think!" "Here's the rule; now apply it next time you speak or write." Generations of teachers notwithstanding, students don't think when they speak. Neither do you nor I. Our attention is fixed on what we are saying, not the way we are saying it. And this is as it should be. If we need to change a student's use of language, the way to do it is the way we would change any habit: the habit of smoking, the habit of driving with a standard shift after we have been used to an automatic transmission, the habit of shifting our fork from our left hand to our right hand when we have cut up our meat and are now ready to eat it. Break down the old habits and build new ones, step by step, say the psychologists, and linguists agree with them.

Finally, linguists insist that any description of the way in which a language operates, that is, a grammar of the language, must be developed through the techniques of science. These, of course, are the techniques of inductive reasoning: careful observation and collection of data until a pattern begins to emerge, the formulation of a hypothesis to explain this pattern, the testing of the hypothesis against new data. The alternative is to start from premises and arrive at conclusions by deductive reasoning. This latter process has been the one by which most English grammars have been written. Linguists reject it.

III

The application of these five attitudes toward language, that language is *speech;* language is *systematic;* language is *symbolic, arbitrary* and *complete;* language use is *habitual,* not logical; and language descriptions must be *scientific,* has led linguists to some very precise analyses of English. While these analyses help us as teachers to understand how the language operates, they do not tell us how to teach English. They tell us a great deal about what is significant in our language, and therefore, what must be taught and what can be left out, but they do not tell us the best way to teach English phonology or syntax. In spite of ambiguities in popular use, we do not teach "linguistics" instead of grammar, "linguistics" instead of literature, "linguistics" instead of speech. Linguistics has given us much more precise descriptions of the way our language operates. Naturally these descriptions will change what we teach and how we teach it, but these changes are in the realm of pedagogy, not linguistics.

No brief paper on the theory of linguistics can possibly present completely the descriptions of English that linguistic scientists have been developing. But perhaps a brief outline of the major subdivisions of the work in structural linguistics will be helpful.

Linguistic analysis starts with the basic sounds of the language. Which sounds in the language are significant, it asks, and what is the system within which they operate. Obviously, all the sounds that we make as we speak do not contribute to conveying meaning. We could do without the "ahs" and "ohs" many of our friends insert in their speech, for example, or without the clicking of dentures. These sounds are not significant; they have no part in transmitting meaning. The sounds that do transmit meaning in English are the consonant and vowel sounds, the stresses and pitches, and the junctures, the ways in which we interrupt and break off the stream of speech. These significant sounds are the phonemes of the language.

The significant sounds are organized in a system of sound usage. Many linguists have worked out descriptions of this system. Today the most widely accepted phonology of English is the one published by George Trager and Henry Lee Smith in 1951. This phonology is logical, complete, and adequate to deal with the complexities of English speech. While many technical arguments have swirled around the Trager-Smith conclusions, their phonology will not be superseded until someone succeeds in putting together a better organization of all of the complexities of the sound system of English. American students who speak English as a native language know the language's sound system intuitively, and, therefore, do not have to be taught how to produce or understand its sounds, but there may be some advantage to them in understanding intellectually what they do when they speak. And, certainly, all English teachers should have this information as part of their technical background.

The phonemes of a language, its significant sounds, do not of themselves transmit meaning. The /k/, /t/, and /æ/ sounds, pronounced individually and in this order, are meaningless. Put together in the pattern /kæt/, however, they do transmit meaning: *cat*, a furry animal that drinks milk, or *cat*, as in *that cool cat*, a thumb-and-finger snapping version of a human being, who, we are told, is unusually sensitive to the complexities of modern jazz. Combinations of phonemes which do transmit meaning are called morphemes, and the system of organization within which these morphemes operate is the morphology of a language. Many morphemes are words, but not all words are morphemes: *joy*, for example, is a morpheme which is a word but *enjoy* is two morphemes although still only one word. A morpheme does not have to be a combination of phonemes. The /s/ on the end of *cats*, for example, is a morpheme. It transmits the meaning that there are more than one of this animal. This same phoneme can be heard at the end of the noun *cat* in *My cat's bed, my two cats' feeding bowl*, and at the end of the verb *drink* in *my cat drinks milk*. The phoneme is the same, but in each of these examples the meaning transmitted is different. The single phoneme /s/ in these examples is four different morphemes.

The morphology of English is not complete when we have catalogued all the words, their possible prefixes and suffixes, and the various inflectional changes. Any native speaker of the language knows that it's not just what we say, but also how we say it, that counts. We know what the Western Badman means when he sneers, "Smile when you say that, pardner," and all of us can distinguish between "Really!" and "Really?" or "The rat," and "The rat ! ! !" If the words are the same but the meaning is different, obviously something other than words is transmitting meaning. Careful analysis will show that it is the intonation patterns, the combination of stresses, pitches, and junctures, which are morphemic in these examples. A complete morphology of English would have to include a cataloguing of these patterns in addition to the words and word changings, and a description of the intonation system of English.

Finally, morphemes are put together in larger patterns which transmit ideas. These patterns linguists often call utterances. The study of the way utterances are created, the structures of which morphemes are the building blocks, is called syntax. Linguists working on a description of English syntax attempt to chart the various word order patterns in English, the functioning of the various parts of speech in English utterances, the uses English makes of function words, the connecting signals between parts of speech in English utterances, and the devices for compounding and modifying the patterns of English. In syntax, as in phonology and morphology, linguists are concerned not only with accurate observation of the phenomena of English speech, but with the discovery of the interrelations of the system within which the language operates.

12   The Relation of Linguistics to the Teaching of English

Paul Roberts

Linguistics per se *has nothing to do with the teaching of English; it is a science concerned with studying language. A task for educators operating in conjunction with linguists is to apply linguistic findings to utilitarian classroom situations. Knowledgeable in both linguistics and English education, Roberts shares a few of his insights and opinions about what linguistics can—and cannot— contribute to language arts instruction.*

Why are traditional definitions weak, incomplete, and misleading? What is necessary if one is to be able to categorize words as nouns or verbs or to recognize complete sentences? What phases of language arts instruction does Roberts believe linguistics can contribute most to? Why do you believe Roberts never spells out in detail what he believes to be the relation of linguistics to teaching English? Do Roberts, Owen (previous article), and Kurath (following article) all make consistent statements concerning linguistics? Articles by Hamp and Strickland cited in Selected References for Part Two further explicate this topic. The one by Tibbetts is a caustic attack upon Roberts' article while the one by Rosenbaum is an effective companion piece to this Roberts article.

It is probably fair to say that linguistics is the hottest topic on the English teacher's agenda at the present time. It is the one topic almost certain to be on the program wherever English teachers come together, and articles on the subject claim an increasing share of the space in our professional journals. Linguistics is hot also in the sense that it gives off heat. Views tend to be extreme and to be extremely held. From one side we gather that linguistics is about to clear away all the problems of teaching English, to show us delightfully simple ways of bestowing literacy on the illiterate; from the other it is disclosed that linguists are satanically in alliance with progressive educationists bent on the destruction of humanism and the corruption of the youth. Whichever side you

From *College English* 22:1-9; October 1960. Reprinted with permission of the National Council of Teachers of English.

are on, it is perfectly clear to you that holders of opposing views are willful idiots and probably venal to boot.

The worst possible position to occupy in this struggle is that of the wise moderate, skillfully mediating between the extremists. Such a person is certain to get clubbed mercilessly from all directions and is likely to end screaming louder than anybody. I have no intention of falling into this snare. Forsaking, if necessary, any claims to either wisdom or moderation, I must ally myself with the linguists and say that I think they have much the better of the argument— that, indeed, I can see no real argument against them. But I take this position at some cost. I have no natural bent for controversy and take no pleasure in being the object of attack either in school board meetings or in the pages of [professional journals.] I could wish for a cooling off, based on a greater measure of understanding than has so far been obtained.

Whether any great measure of understanding is actually obtainable seems sometimes doubtful. It may be that ultimately the differences are temperamental rather than rational, that those whose major professional commitment is esthetic can find no common ground with those whose commitment is scientific. Perhaps what is required for a lying down together of traditionalists and linguists is nothing less than the long-sought rapprochement of the humanities and the sciences, and this may be altogether beyond our powers. Still I cannot give up hope of persuading my colleagues in the humanities that linguists, though working in a different direction, may yet be friends to their ground and liegemen to the Dane.

It seems to me that the major points at issue may be indicated in a series of three questions:

1. What essentially are the differences between linguistic grammar (or whatever you call it) and traditional grammar (or whatever you call *that*)?

2. What is the linguistic view on correctness?

3. What exactly is the application of linguistics, supposing its views to prevail, to the teaching of English?

It is easy to exaggerate the weakness of traditional grammar and the superiority of linguistic grammar, as it is easy to exaggerate the differences between them. They are similar in the important sense that they come out with by and large similar answers. A traditionalist can tell an English verb or an indefinite relative clause when he sees one just as well as a linguist can. They may have different names for these categories, but surely we can agree that differences in terminology are trivial differences.

What is not trivial, however, is the framework in which the concepts are described and discussed. It has been traditional practice to describe such concepts as *noun, verb, subject, sentence* with what are called notional definitions —i.e., definitions based on the supposed meaning of the classes. These definitions have certain weaknesses. For one thing, they are invulnerable statements: one can never conclude an argument about their truth or falsity, and arguers must end by simply stamping their feet. It may be true that sentences are groups of words expressing complete thoughts, as it may be true that angels are incorporeal beings, but such statements can be pursued only to tautology: what is a complete thought?—that which a sentence expresses; what is an incorporeal being?—an angel.

What can, I think, be demonstrated is that such definitions are altogether unusable and that in fact nobody ever uses them. No one can learn the definition "a sentence is a group of words expressing a complete thought" and then use that as a criterion to sort out sentences from non-sentences in some particular language. Anyone who tried to apply it seriously would find himself instantly in serious perplexity. For instance, in what sense is the first sentence of this paragraph a complete thought? It could certainly not stand alone, since the word *such* necessarily implies a preceding statement. If we were to take this definition seriously, we would have to conclude that the sentences of a paragraph have no relation to one another and that there is no connection between paragraphs.

Similarly, no one can actually apply such a definition as "a verb is a word that expresses action." If he did, he would have to list as verbs such English words as *arrival, operation, action*. There must be some sense in which the word *action* expresses action. We do not count these words as verbs, not because they do not express action, but because they do not occur in what we recognize (somehow or other) as verb structures: we do not say "He will arrival," "They were afraid to operation," "I actioned."

Such traditional definitions as are not notional are relational, and these lead to another difficulty, that of mixing hierarchies in the analysis. *Adjective* and *adverb*, for example, are defined relationally, in terms of what is modified: an adjective is a word that modifies a noun. This leads us to conclude that "dirty sink" and "kitchen sink" are identical structures, each consisting of a noun modified by an adjective. But our intuition tells us that they are in some way different, that *dirty* is somehow a different kind of word from *kitchen*. If we were given a third structure, say "empty sink," we would, I suppose, not hesitate to say that it is more like "dirty sink" than like "kitchen sink." The traditional definition of adjective—anything that modifies a noun—simply buries and conceals a large and important part of English expression, throwing together such quite different structures as "our sink," "dirty sink," "kitchen sink," "leaking sink," "scrubbing sink," "repaired sink," "sink upstairs." All are different, and the difference is that in each case the modifying word belongs to a different class or subclass. I am aware that traditional grammarians can perceive and express such differences, using such terms as "limiting adjective," "descriptive adjective," "participle," "gerund," but they can do so only clumsily and with clear contradiction of earlier statements.

The basic fallacy here is a mixing of levels of description. English structures can be analyzed on the word-class level into such categories as *noun, verb, adjective*. They can also be analyzed on a relational level into such categories as *modifier of a noun, modifier of a verb, subject, object*. Both classifications are logical and both are necessary to a description of English syntax. But to mix them is like sorting the students of a college into the categories *men, women,* and *commuters*. To ask, in the traditional framework, whether *kitchen* in "kitchen sink" is a noun or an adjective is like asking whether John Jones is a man or a commuter.

To point out the weakness of traditional definitions is to invite the question —with what do you propose to replace them? The answer to this is—nothing. We must, I think, give up hope of finding definitions for such concepts as *noun, adjective, subject, sentence* which are both short and operable, which can actually be used to sort out the members of the categories. It is not hard to frame rational definitions for these concepts. A modern dictionary, for example, will give for *sentence* some such definition as this: "A structure in a language which is not shown by some grammatical feature to be a part of a larger structure." But this of course is not applicable as a criterion until we outline the grammatical features which do or do not make a structure part of another structure. To make the definition operable, we should have to describe such features as subject and predicate, modification, subordination, conjunction, transformation. In other words, we cannot really define the concept "sentence in English" short of describing English grammar.

Linguists have not, I fear, always been clear on this point. We have sometimes talked as if we had, or were on the point of getting, short and usable tests for determining whether items belong to one category or another. Thus we say "a noun is a word that can fill the blank in 'The _____ was interesting.'" Or "a noun is a word that forms a plural." But as definitions such statements fail in both directions. It is true that any item, any noise, that occurs in the blank in "The _____ was interesting" will be construed as a noun. But there may be nouns that do not occur there (some things may not be interesting) and there are many other positions in which nouns occur.

Definitions based on morphology—inflectional endings and the like— seem to me to lead to error. If *noun* is defined as "any word that forms a plural," then *chaos* cannot count as a noun. This would appear to go contrary to our intuition as speakers of English. Adjectives have sometimes been defined as words that add the endings /-er/ and /-est/, as *small, smaller, smallest*. This also fails in both directions. It has been pointed out that if we were to apply it literally we would have to take *tear* as an adjective: *tear, terror, terraced*. Even worse, it requires us to put *beautiful, courageous, hopeful,* in a different class from *pretty, old, sad,* which, again, is contrary to our intuition.

What is true, it seems to me, is that in a real language it is only rarely that word classes or other structures are signaled by some simple and unique signal. If we were making up a language, creating an artificial language, we might wish to order things differently. We might, for example, make a rule that all nouns end in –a and that no other words end in this sound. Then we could always tell by the occurrence or nonoccurrence of –a whether a word was a noun or not.

But no real language has such a simple structure. In English, we must always know whether a word is a noun or not; otherwise we shall not be able to understand the sentence. But the signals which sort out nouns from the other classes with which they might be confused—verbs and adjectives, particularly— are multiple. The signal might be an inflectional ending, like the plural or the possessive; it might be a derivational ending, like -ness or -ation; it might be position; it might be the fact that our only previous experience with the word is in noun uses, so that we take it as a noun even when it occurs in a position in which other classes occur. Thus *Jones* in "It was Jones" is clearly a noun. But *Green* in "It was Green" could be taken, in speech, as an adjective. For any particular unambiguous sentence we could specify exactly how we know that a word is a noun and not an adjective or a verb, but there is no short and simple way of saying how we know in all sentences.

Similar remarks can be made about the concept *sentence*. One can imagine an artificial language in which sentences are marked in a simple way. Suppose that we had the custom, in English, of beginning every sentence with the expression *eek* and concluding it with the expression *awk*: "Eek, I ran into Sam Jones today, awk. Eek, he's been visiting his mother in Plainsville, awk. Eek, that's not far from Toledo, awk." Then we could easily define *sentence*: a structure that begins with *eek* and ends with *awk*. Students would memorize this definition at the age of six and never thereafter write comma faults or fragments.

Unfortunately, no real language has a simple and unique signal marking the sentence unit, either in the intonation or in the segmental structure. There is such a thing as "sentence in English," but it is marked as such in multiple fashion. "I have some" is a sentence; "if I have some" is not; "I have some—" (with the pitch staying level) is not; "I have some money" is; "Have some" is; "Is some" is not. There is simply no way of comprehending the concept "sentence in English" short of learning English grammar, either unconsciously, as a child learns it, or through explicit instruction. Certainly nobody learns or teaches the concept "sentence in English" through steady repetition of the incantation "a sentence is a group of words expressing a complete thought."

Traditional teachers do teach the concept "sentence in English," as they teach such other concepts as *noun, verb, adjective, subject*. Some of their students, at least, come to recognize these structures and to be able to identify them in a more or less uniform way. A linguist should recognize this success. But he must point out that it is achieved not because of the definitional apparatus but in spite of it. The traditional teacher has the students learn the definitions, but must then take care that they never apply them. The learning comes not from definition and discussion of the concepts but from illustration, correction of mistakes, and the like. The whole burden of generalization is placed on the student, who must work through the examples to an understanding of what the teacher means when he says "a sentence is a group of words expressing a complete thought," "a verb is a word that expresses action, being, or state of being."

People nowadays frequently make remarks like "Linguistics may be all right but we had better not give up traditional grammar until we are provided with something to take its place." This is reasonable enough, unless by "something" is meant something similar, a comparable battery of short definitions. But neither linguistics nor anything else can ever provide such an apparatus. The classes English noun and English sentence are exactly as complicated as they are, and linguistics has no way of making them simpler. What linguistics does suggest is that the complexities be directly faced, not obscured in a fallacious philosophy. What a grammarian is—or ought to be—interested in is not meaning directly but the structure through which meaning is expressed, the mechanism by which meanings are distinguished. Every teacher of grammar must deal with structure and is therefore in some sense a structural linguist. But it is clear that the study could proceed much more efficiently, and infinitely more interestingly, if we could get through the philosophical fog and focus on the actual signals of the language.

The debate about correctness has been with us much longer than the debate about structure, but it seems no nearer conclusion. The difficulty seems to be at least partly a matter of misunderstanding, for which linguists are no doubt at least partly to blame. For one thing, linguists use the terms "correct" and "incorrect," but their usage departs considerably from the common one. By "incorrect English" a linguist is likely to mean such a mistake as might be made by a foreigner or a child learning the language. Thus both "I it bought" and "I buyed it" are incorrect sentences. But a linguist, as a linguist, would not say that "I done it" or "I brung it" are incorrect sentences. They are correct in relation to the dialects in which they occur, and the question of whether the dialects are admired in the nation as a whole is a sociological, not a linguistic, question.

Linguistics simply has to work in this way or it cannot operate as a science. To ask it to condemn "I done it" is like asking botany to condemn weeds. This is not to say that schools should not correct students who say "I done it." Those who go into college or into business saying "I done it" are clearly headed for difficulties which ought to be pointed out to them. There is a correlation, though not a perfect one, between the achievement of material success and the avoidance of expressions like "I done it," and therefore there is a strong sense in which "I done it" is incorrect. But the reason is purely sociological. The best people—so defined by wealth or education or some other criterion—don't say it, and that is all there is to it.

What more might be supposed to be to it, I simply can't figure out. We are not concerned here with "good" and "bad" sentences. If we are talking about good and bad, we can bring in such criteria as clarity, grace, euphony, economy, discrimination. But if we are talking about correctness, there is simply no criterion but somebody's usage. If a student asks me whether an expression is correct or not, I have no resource but to reflect on whether I use it or whether I hear it in the conversation of my friends, a small but select group of professors of English. If my answer does not satisfy, and it often does not, I am quite at a loss. There is no other principle I can invoke. Certainly not an historical one—I cannot suppose it proper that everyone speak Elizabethan English. Not an analogical one—if I insist on *bring/brought* on the analogy of *think/thought*, I should also, I suppose, have to campaign for *cling/clought* and *sting/stought*. So I answer according to the only principle I know—the usage of the best people, i.e., my friends and me. If the student persists—"I don't care what you and your friends say, what I want to know is which is *correct*"—I can only suppose him to be asking what God says.

If we knew what kind of English God speaks, we would have no problem, but we don't, and so we are reduced to figuring out who the best people are and reporting their English and persuading our students to emulate it. This is difficult, and perhaps linguistics will again be accused of destruction without replacement. But how is it a loss to be without what one never had? There has never been any criterion of correctness but somebody's usage. Linguistics does not create this complication; it merely points it out. Surely the first step in solving a problem is to discover the nature of the problem.

The problem is no doubt more complicated in the United States than it is —or at least than it has been—in England and on the continent of Europe. In countries with an aristocracy, it is relatively simple to define correct language: it is the language of the aristocracy, which is partly synonymous with the educated class. But in the United States, which has no visible aristocracy and where the tides of anti-intellectualism sometimes run strong, the situation is quite different. To decide what correct English is, we must in some sense decide who the best people are. I think this is what makes the subject explosive. Professors of English probably sometimes feel that linguists are somehow traitors to their class, pandering to the masses. I should like to point out that such a position is no necessary consequence of linguistics. It is possible to be both a linguist and (in some sense) a purist. I myself am in no doubt about who the best people are. They are the intellectuals, like Jacques Barzun and my friends and me.

It should be noticed that the problem of correctness becomes much simpler when we are careful to discriminate between speech and writing. Usage governs both, but in quite different ways. We must be forever in disagreement among ourselves and with our fellow citizens on what is correct in speech. It depends on who and what and where we are and on who and what and where we want to be. But in writing, and particularly in certain aspects of writing, we can achieve very considerable agreement. Nowhere are items more clearly right or wrong than in spelling. With a very few exceptions, all English words are correctly spelled in only one way. Like correctness in pronunciation, correctness in English spelling has no logical basis, but unlike pronunciation, spelling is uniform, and the agreed on system is knowable. The same is true, though to a lesser extent, of punctuation, word forms, sentence structures that occur in writing.

Yet in writing as in speech it is usage that controls, the difference being that in writing it is the usage of a relatively small and easily discernible group—the publishing industry largely—that matters. The question "Is this correct written English" can be more specifically phrased: "Would a copy editor pass this?" "Does this accord with the style books of the publishing houses?" One cannot change speech or retard its development by taking thought about it. It is doubtful that all the not inconsiderable efforts of mass education have had very much effect on the speech of the population as a whole. But the writing system is very largely controllable. It changes, but it changes very slowly, compared to speech. If we wanted to change it radically—e. g., if we wanted to reform our spelling— we could do that.

The last of the three questions posed was, what exactly is the application of linguistics, supposing its views to prevail, to the teaching of English? First of all, it must be said that this is a question that no linguist, as a linguist, can answer, just as no mathematician, as a mathematician, can say what the applications of mathematics should be. The application is a question for the teacher of English, and I speak from here on as a teacher of English and not as a linguist.

I think that the effect of linguistics on the teaching of English may be profound but that it will not be the sort of effect commonly expected. There seems to be a widespread hope that the teaching of grammar according to linguistic principles will lead directly to a great improvement in writing, a falling off in comma faults, fragments, dangling modifiers, and such errors. I think that linguistics might make some contribution in this direction, but I doubt that it will be substantial. Certainly I know of no way in which punctuation can be taught or in which "sentence sense" can be communicated to those who haven't got it, except through some kind of teaching of the grammar; and it is reasonable to suppose that a good grammar will serve better here than a confusing one. . . .

13   Area Linguistics and the Teacher of English

Hans Kurath

The lack of uniformity in usage and pronunciation within the United States becomes more acute as both pupils and teachers become more mobile. An expert in regional linguistics, Kurath cautions teachers not to set standards in usage and pronunciation without regard for differing regional backgrounds of the children.

  What pronunciations or usages are peculiar to your part of the United States? Do textbooks make provisions for differences such as these? Does the pronunciation key of your classroom dictionary conform to your pronunciation of words? If not, why? How do you think mass media such as movies and television will influence these regional variations? How does this article relate to the ones by Kenyon and McDavid cited in Selected References for Part Two? To that by Pooley in Part Five?

It should be obvious that the teacher of English in grade school, high school, or college should know the usage of the area in which he does his teaching before he undertakes to 'mend' the speechways of his pupils. If there is a class cleavage in usage within the area, he should be aware of it, so that for the good of his students he can set 'better' or 'cultivated' usage over against socially less desirable practices. If several regional dialects are current within the area (as for instance in Detroit, with its large groups of recent immigrants, black or white, from south of the Ohio), he should be familiar with them in order to deal sensibly with his wards.

How does the teacher of English get the information he needs to do a good job? Can he rely upon the ordinary textbooks, the desk dictionaries, Kenyon and Knott's *Pronouncing Dictionary*, Craigie and Hulbert's *Dictionary of American English*?

From *Language Learning* 2:9-14; March 1961. Reprinted with permission of Hans Kurath, Professor of English, Emeritus, Ann Arbor, Michigan, and *Language Learning*, Special Issue No. 2, March 1961, pp. 9-14. © 1961 by the Research Club of Language Learning. One footnote has been omitted.

Yes, to some extent. However, the *DAE* deals with American vocabulary without identifying regional usage or the social standing of the expressions, though a check of the quotations often permits an inference; Kenyon-Knott is adequate for Northern pronunciation, including Eastern New England's, but fails to deal satisfactorily with usage in Metropolitan New York and the South; the desk dictionaries, though registering some variant cultivated pronunciations, give no indication of their habitat; the ordinary textbook is tailored for the national market and is apt to gloss over regional differences, even if the author knows better.

Two recent textbooks on American English (Hill and Francis) practically obliterate regional differences current in cultivated use by imposing Trager's 'over-all' nine-vowel system. Only 'incidental' differences are admitted, and rather effectively concealed by the transcription at that.

Clearly, the teacher of English must be given better information than he now has at his disposal. What can area linguistics, the study of regional and social dialects, do to help him? I shall try to show, by dealing with differences in pronunciation current in the Eastern States, how a useful body of information can be made available, and how this sort of information can be instrumental in developing a scholarly, and therefore salutary, point of view.

Some sections of the Eastern States (all of the South and the South Midland) have a /j/ after the initial alveolar consonant (as in *tube, due, new*) on all social levels, others not (as Pennsylvania and eastern New England). Should a teacher in Boston or Philadelphia make his students adopt the /j/? In other sections usage is divided, as in Middle New York: Should the teacher insist upon one or the other of these pronunciations in such a community?

In eastern New England, Middle New York, Virginia, and South Carolina, postvocalic /r/, as in *ear, care, four, poor*, is not pronounced as such by a considerable majority. Should the minority be urged to 'drop the /r/,' i.e., substitute unsyllabic /ə/, in this position when no social stigma attaches to pronouncing the /r/? What should be done when /r/ is an index of rusticity, as in most of eastern North Carolina and parts of South Carolina and Georgia?

In the greater part of the South and the South Midland the diphthongal vowel in *down, owl, crowd* begins like the vowel of *man* on all social levels, whereas in New England and elsewhere this pronunciation is confined to folk speech. How should a teacher behave under such diverse circumstances? What should he do in Michigan, where [æu] is uncommon, except among recent immigrants from south of the Ohio?

Eastern New England and western Pennsylvania have the same vowel in *law, caught, salt* and in *lot, cot, rod*, whereas all other sections of the Eastern States have contrasting vowels in these two sets. If a Michigan student lacks the contrast, as many do, should he be taught to distinguish *caught* from *cot, taught* from *tot?*

On the Atlantic seaboard, the vowel in *care, chair, stairs* ranges regionally all the way from the /æ/ of *cat* to the /ɛ/ of *get* and the /e/ of *gate* without social implications. Should one insist upon one of these pronunciations in view of the fact that, except for parts of South Carolina and Georgia, no regional dialect has more than one vowel phoneme between high and low before historical /r/, pronounced regionally as /r/ or unsyllabic /ə/?

Hoarse and *horse, mourning* and *morning* are homophonous in an area extending from the Potomac northward to Middle New York and westward throughout Pennsylvania, but not elsewhere in the Eastern States. For the sake of a few homonyms, or for some other reason, should one undertake to teach contrasting vowels in *four* and *forty* in the schools of Michigan, if usage is divided among the student body?

If a student pronounces *Mary* like *merry* and *fairy* like *ferry*, or rimes *story* with *sorry*, should he be urged to differentiate them, as Southerners, New Yorkers, and most New Englanders do? Or is Pennsylvania usage good enough?

When a Michigan student says *he et (=ate) it, he dove (=dived) right in,* and *he hadn't ought to (=ought not to) talk so much,* like his Yankee forebears, should the teacher 'correct' him or merely point out to him that others say *ate, dived,* and *ought not to*? If his own usage is in line with that of well educated New Englanders, why should he change his ways? On the other hand, if he says *he eat it all up, he clumb a tree, he driv in the nail,* he should be told to avoid these past tense forms if he wants to appear to advantage, since they are strictly folk forms, though they are of venerable vintage, being derived by normal phonemic change from standard forms of earlier English.

These examples and queries have probably suggested to you the drift of my thinking in this matter. Unless a variant is clearly marked as 'low class' or 'rustic' within the area in which one teaches, it should be tolerated. To fight it is not only a waste of time, but an insult to students coming from well educated families or from other sections of the country. It breeds confusion, if not resentment, in the student body. On the other hand, a teacher who can say: 'Your family must come from New England,' or 'Did you grow up in New York City?' or 'That's the way they say it in Virginia,' will command the respect of his class. In any event, he will stimulate the interest of his better students in our language, if he can tell them that well educated New Englanders, New Yorkers, Pennsylvanians, and Virginians don't talk exactly alike (although they understand each other quite easily), and point out some of the salient differences.

To put the teacher of English into a position to make pertinent comments on usage, we need better textbooks; and before we can produce better textbooks we must have more adequate information on regional and social differences in usage than we now possess. We are making progress in that direction, but we still have a long way to go.

We must realize that the linguistic situation in this country is rather different from that in England and France, and even from that in Germany. The former have *one* unquestionably dominant social dialect, and German-speaking Europe has at least the *Bühnenaussprache* (stage pronunciation) as a guide, though Bavarians, Austrians, and Swiss don't hew exactly to the line. On the other hand, we have rather well marked regional types of cultivated speech, and there is no reason for assuming that in matters of pronunciation Virginians will bow to New Yorkers, or Detroiters to Bostonians, within the foreseeable future. It is equally unlikely that the Ohio Valley will conform in usage to the Great Lakes Basin. Though postvocalic /r/ is fairly regularly used in both of these major areas, there are many differences in the incidence of the vowels and in their phonic character . . . the common fiction of a 'General American' type notwithstanding.

Part Three

Listening and Speaking

This section is devoted to the oral language arts which include listening (auding), choral speaking, and speech therapy as well as topics commonly termed oral communication (reporting, discussing, announcing, etc.). Not covered in this section are topics incorporating both oral and written aspects of language: vocabulary, semantics, usage, and grammar. These are dealt with in Part Five.

Compared with written aspects of the language arts, oral language skills appear elusive and difficult for direct instruction. Many teachers believe they can be developed satisfactorily merely by providing pupils with experiences and situations which encourage communication and expression. But without some direction and instruction, children are unlikely to develop the full powers of their language. Certain difficulties may prevent them from attaining mature levels of expression. In the first article in this part, DeLawter and Eash report the results of a study analyzing prevalent communication errors made by elementary school children.

But oral language is valuable not only for itself; it apparently is highly generalizable and transferable to non-oral situations such as listening, reading, and writing. In general, all of the language arts are highly interrelated, but we have not yet fathomed the maze so that we understand what each contributes to the others and what is unique to each one. Ruddell examines the contributions of oral language to the development of other language skills.

A problem in analyzing children's language is that in sampling a random group of different-aged children, the researcher is never sure that the same variables are operating at the different levels. Factors which influenced the older children may now be absent or no longer potent while new factors may be influencing the language learning of the younger subjects. The most valid way to circumvent this problem is to conduct a longitudinal study, following the same subjects for a period of years. But there are numerous drawbacks to this approach and few such studies have been done. Loban not only tackled such a study but he also stratified his subjects by social class, thereby making intra-cultural comparisons possible. Some findings were contrary to expectations, others substantiated known facts, and still others revealed unsuspected insights. These, and other results, should help teachers to provide some semblance of meaningful, individualized instruction in oral language.

Oral language usage should not be thought of as being restricted to struc-tured, reportorial situations; valid opportunities exist for incorporating it into a myriad of everyday activities. The more natural these situations, the better suited they are to oral expression because the focus is on the activity rather than artificially being on oral language. This fact coupled with knowledge of how children clarify reality and the power of their imagination leads to the conclu-sion that creative dramatics is an ideal vehicle for oral expression—as well as a meritorious activity in its own right. But not all topics are worthy of being dramatized; nor do children participate with the same enthusiasm in all stories. McIntyre's article elucidates children's preferences and shows how creative dramatics can become an integral part of curricular areas other than the lan-guage arts.

Human beings try and do manipulate other human beings in order to achieve certain goals. Even infants adopt manipulative techniques during their first months of life. But much organized manipulation is insidious and unrecog-nized as propaganda. Analyses of manipulative literature have isolated ways in which language is used to beguile, delude, and control thought and behavior and many people—educators and non-educators alike—are convinced that pupils' awareness of these techniques need to be increased. Lundsteen reports an experiment which tried to do this through listening lessons.

It has been recognized for years that learning and retention are facilitated by practice and use in functional, meaningful situations; drill on items in iso-lated, arbitrary situations is usually wasted. No aspect of the language arts pro-gram is better suited to functional, meaningful usage than oral language skills. In other words, oral language should breach the confining walls of the language arts 'period' and be incorporated into all curricular areas and school activities, but a program relying on only incidental instruction will probably be weak and ineffective. In her article on oral reporting, Millsap, rather than halting with mere admonitions, describes some practical and specific techniques which can help assure a coherent, high level program in one of the most frequently needed —and poorly developed—facet of the oral language program.

Communication is hindered not only by incoherence but by speech handi-caps which may make listening difficult and unpleasant. And speech handi-capped children, presumably because they recognize their deviancy from the norm, are more susceptible to emotional disturbance than are the non-handi-capped. Thus, a variety of reasons demands that help is provided for these children. But classroom teachers need information about different causes of speech disorders, which require referral for special treatment, which can be dealt with in the classroom, and what type of remediation and special help are needed by these children. Anderson's article provides some challenging answers to these issues.

14   Focus on Oral Communication

Jayne Anne DeLawter and Maurice J. Eash

DeLawter and Eash claim that even though highly structured curricula are provided for reading and writing, in oral language teachers have leaned heavily upon the 'improvement by accident' approach; not systematically giving instruction in the basic components of this skill which are necessary for children to learn to express themselves with clarity and precision. In fact, the writers contend that the fundamental errors which children make which need to be the focus of instruction have not been really identified. They make a tentative list of seven pervasive errors as revealed by their research and give some suggestions for effecting improvement.

Do you believe these categories are stable at all grade levels? Are some more prevalent among certain social subgroups than among others? Are any categories so developmentally determined that maturation rather than instruction may produce improvement? (See the article by Smith in Part Two.) Do you agree that direct instruction is necessary to eradicate these errors or would incidental methods be equally effective? Is this a problem which a single teacher in one classroom can successfully treat or would a system-wide program be essential?

In the literature and in practice the improvement of oral language has received little attention in the full scope of the language arts program. Reading, seen by many as the key to academic success, is emphasized heavily in each grade of school. Spelling also has a period set aside specifically for its study, and handwriting usually is given particular attention through a period of formal instruction. Creative writing, though not a major part of the curriculum, nevertheless, is often found in extensive units throughout the elementary years. Comparatively then, it can be seen that development of oral communication skills has been seriously neglected in relationship to the time spent in these other

From *Elementary English* 43:880-883; December 1966. Reprinted with permission of Jayne Anne DeLawter, Teachers College, Columbia University, New York, and Maurice J. Eash, Associate Professor, Hunter College of the City University of New York, New York, New York.

areas. The tragedy of this neglect is further compounded when one considers the time spent by individuals in the areas of language arts, reading, spelling, writing, and oral communication, with the latter accounting for more of the communication process than the sum total time in other areas.

With this apparent lack of emphasis in formal oral language instruction, it is inescapable that many children's ability to handle oral communication is poorly developed. Although outwardly few children have little problem communicating with other people, an analysis of language reveals repetitions, disorganized explanations, and lack of focus in ideas; all of which are a handicap to communicator and listener alike.

The approach to oral language instruction suggested in this article is an outcome of a broader study in the area of linguistic analysis of patterns of speech.[1] In this study a sample of children's language was gathered and analyzed for the structure of the language and expressions of authoritarianism. Working with these data the authors discovered common errors in oral language which would serve as a basis for oral language instruction in the classroom. The techniques used in the study can be employed in the classroom as a teacher seeks to analyze her students' speech for specific errors or problems in oral language.

In obtaining a language sample, the authors planned a situation where children were encouraged to speak freely. A method which promotes fluency in speech is the use of unfinished stories as a stimulus for oral response. Stories such as the "Anderson Incomplete Stories"[2] present a conflict situation between adults and children which the respondent must resolve in some way. An example of one of these stories is titled "The Missing Money" story. In it, a teacher finds that fifty cents has disappeared from her desk. She doesn't know what happened to it. In the interview the child is asked, "What happened to the money?" "What does the teacher do?" "How does the teacher feel?"

This type of story is desirable for several reasons. First of all, it gives the child a definite focus for his reply. It also encourages an uninterrupted flow of speech which is more easily analyzed than scattered statements in response to general questioning. Aside from the linguistic content of the responses to these stories, much can also be learned about the child's cultural background and value system from a content analysis of the responses. The authors have found these stories to be of high interest to all children and to encourage lucid expression.

In order to preserve the speech samples of the children, tape-recorded interviews are essential. Previous research finds that note-taking obtains only a selective 10 per cent to 20 per cent of free flowing responses. In contrast, a taped interview captures the full response, retains the emotional tone and spontaneity of the child, and provides a listening sample which can be reviewed when desired. Certain precautions were observed in the interviews in order to obtain reliable samples. Interviews were done individually in a school setting familiar to the students. Initial curiosity about the tape recorder was satisfied by a brief discussion, a previous experience with the machine. In this case since the interviewer was someone other than the classroom teacher, rapport with the students was built by conversation, observation, and participation in classroom procedure prior to the interview.

After the data had been collected in the interviews, the responses were typed on protocols, using a format that captured as accurately as possible the student's responses. A sample from a protocol is reprodu..ed below.

Interviewer: What does the teacher do?
Respondent: She . . . she would just . . . she would ask 'em . . . they was doin' their arithmetic, she could just ask 'em to stop for a minute and she could say that . . . the money was gone off her desk. And if somebody had it, they could give it back to her. And nobody say nothing . . . maybe who got it would have a smile on their face or she can tell.
I. How does the teacher feel?
R. Sad . . . and mad. Because no one tell her who got it.
I. What will she do then?
R. Go around the room—look in the desks and then if nobody had it, she can say—look in their shoes. And if she still don't find it, I don't know.
I. Can you think of an ending for this story?
R. Ending of it? She feel real—very sad. She wished—she wished that she would know who'd—who were—who it was.

Linguistic studies involving elaborate analysis can be done of the prepared protocol.[3]

However, this linguistic approach does not indicate how a child can organize and handle ideas; it primarily outlines the dominant patterns in his speech.

To improve the child's language in terms of handling ideas, the teacher needs to look for basic errors in oral communication. Some of the errors which are critical to more mature speaking are:

1. Failure to focus

The ability to focus on the major point may relate to the type of stimulus given. However, the failure to focus seems to be related to immaturity of speech habits or inadequate experience in extended conversations. Failure to focus carries over into adult conversations which, when recorded, reflect tangency and indirection.[4] The ability to focus can be tested by using specific or general questions. For example, a direct question, such as "Why did the children run?" elicits a different type of response than a general directive, such as "Name three reasons why the children ran."

2. Poor organization of ideas

This error relates quite closely to the failure to focus. Many children begin speaking before they think through any organization of a response or before they examine the intent of the question or questioner. This leads to unnecessary repetition and rambling in the response. This is seen in the following interview sample:

I. Tell me more about the teacher.
R. O.K. And then the teacher . . . and then he takin' up lunch money and this boy was poor and anyway he had to get his book rent paid. He had an uncle and he was a movie star and. . . .

3. Failure to clarify questions

Again this error comes from instantaneous response with no thought about what the questioner had asked. Misunderstandings often arise from hasty replies which have little relationship to the question at hand. The protocols reflect lack of questioning before responding, or any interaction which would draw the questioner out—literally no active effort to determine the intent of the questioner. Frequently the response does not seem to fit the inquiry, and the responder seems insensitive to the questioner.

I. How would that person feel?
R. She couldda said that they shouldn'ta been playing in the yard.

4. Lack of supporting ideas

This mistake is another characteristic of immature speakers. Common to this mistake is using a general blanket statement as sufficient to prove a point or to express their position. Opinion and fact are confused in presentation. Mastery of this phase of oral communication is crucial to critical thinking and can be taught quite early in the elementary grades. Getting students to question the support for a position is essential to critical thinking on any social problem. An error of this type can be seen in the following protocol illustrating the mistaken belief that relationship means friendship, where the story implied rather poor relationships between father and son.

I. How do you know John and his father are good friends?
R. Cause that's his son.
R. Cause it's his father.

5. Inadequate descriptions

The ability to visualize and describe a scene, person, or attribute takes a high degree of awareness and mental acuity. A contributor to clear and precise detail-giving is considerable past experience in reading and analysis of reading for description. However, oral language ability will not necessarily develop from reading, if attention is not directed to the function of description. Many immature speakers tend to personalize the description if they lack words to express the ideas they hold.

In a discussion of a story involving bicycles, the substitution of personalizing the response for adequate description is seen:

I. What is a skinny wheel?
R. It's a big bike—handbrakes on it. Some of 'em have hand brakes, some have foot brakes. I like hand brakes; you don't have to put your feet back.

6. Lack of subordination

The use of subordination to divide run-on units into more precise sentences is one mark of a mature speaker. Subordination is a problem with many children as they run many sentences and ideas together. This is seen in the following example:

> And then they went through it again and their mother was mad. And then they go out and play football and they wouldn't go around the house no more cause the window might get broke again and they had to stay in. And then they don't want no more whippings cause it hurts.

As the response shows, this child failed to differentiate between the level of ideas. In an attempt to maintain fluency the child has used a series of conjunctions to combine unrelated ideas.

7. Stereotyped vocabulary

The vocabulary of a child seems to be quite heavily related to his environment. An abundance of first-hand experiences is a major factor in the use of a variety of words. Children rarely used words which have no personal relevance to their own lives. Therefore, if actual experiences are not adequate, and if books or other vicarious experiences are not provided, a child's vocabulary remains that of his immediate environment, and words do not carry precise connotation. The lack of definitiveness of descriptions and stereotyping in description of human behavior is evident in the following description of a teacher's actions.

> She look in her desk and look in her pocketbook again and look in the kids' desk and pockets and look in her pocket and coat pockets until she finds it.

No claim is made that these categories are mutually exclusive, and the teacher should not become bogged down in attempting to maintain a tidy classification scheme. A gross lumping of errors, however, does give a starting point for working with children on oral communication.

Approaches to Language Improvement

After the basic errors in the children's expression have been identified and studied, the teacher is then faced with the most crucial question in the improvement of the oral language of her students—how will she use the information found in the language analysis to best approach the problem of her students? Some suggestions for beginning work are given here.

1. Small group instruction is essential for oral language development. It is advantageous to both the teacher and the student. The teacher can focus specific problems in one group and concentrate on individual communication errors. Also, more important in a small group, each child can get experience in speaking and listening. He can practice new patterns with the teacher's guidance until the patterns become almost automatic. Furthermore, the student's level of sensitivity to language can be developed without the undue embarrassment often found in speaking and being corrected in the larger class.

2. The use of devices to help the children see and/or hear their own speech patterns can be exciting and profitable. Tape recorders offer one method in this approach. The teacher and students can listen to their own conversations and analyze oral language errors. Also, with some training, students can analyze their conversations and class discussions along the lines of the analysis in this paper.

3. Another method incorporating the children's own language is the extensive use of experience charts, even in the intermediate grades, providing teachers use the children's language. This approach involves the children as they compose stories, poems, or conversational dialogues. The content of such compositions is of immediate relevance to their lives and maintains a high degree of interest. It also allows the children to analyze their own speech patterns as a part of their language arts work.

If improvement of oral communication is to be effective, the teacher must have a program that provides for an analysis of basic errors. After discovery of the basic errors, a systematic program of instruction must be provided which sensitizes children and provides opportunity to learn better systems of expression. Improvement in oral communication is not fortuitous, although present instructional patterns have leaned heavily upon the improvement by accident approach. The framework described in this article which evolved from a research study provides a systematic approach and places the teaching of oral language upon a more secure base. There is further reason to believe that improvement in performance in oral language will carry over into the other language arts areas of reading, writing and listening.

Footnotes

[1] Jayne Anne DeLawter, *A Study of Language Patterns and Expressions of Authoritarianism in Workingclass Children,* unpublished honors thesis. Ball State Teachers University, May, 1964.

[2] Harold H. Anderson and Gladys L. Anderson, "Anderson Incomplete Stories," mimeograph, Michigan State University, 1959.

[3] Ruth G. Strickland, "The Language of Elementary School Children: Its Relationship to the Language of Reading Textbooks and the Quality of Reading of Selected Children," *Bulletin of the School of Education,* Indiana University, 38 (July, 1962).

[4] Anselm Strauss and Leonard Schatzman, "Cross-Class Interviewing: An Analysis of Interaction and Communitive Styles," *Human Organization Research,* edited by R. N. Adams and J. J. Preiss. Homewood, Illinois: Dorsey Press, 1960, pp. 205-213.

15   Oral Language and the Development of Other Language Skills

Robert B. Ruddell

Ruddell not only surveys research to delineate the varied interrelationships among the language arts, he also emphasizes that the levels achieved in all language arts are highly dependent upon the quality of oral language which has been attained and he draws from his findings some challenging implications for language arts instruction.

What specific aspects of language seem crucial to achieve high level language functioning? Does this review agree or conflict with DeLawter and Eash's thesis in a preceding article? How might the discipline of linguistics contribute to increasing our understanding of these relationships and to helping formulate appropriate instructional procedures? Brown's article in Selected References for Part Three pinpoints some problems in the improvement of oral language presented by pupil textbooks while the articles by Loban, Manolakes, Munkres, and Ogilvie further elucidate the role of oral language in the language arts curriculum. And the article by Petty and Starkey looks at oral language from another perspective: how it contributes to personal and social development.

Understanding the contribution of oral language to the development of other basic communication skills is vital to the classroom teacher. Such an understanding should enable the teacher to utilize better the transfer potential present in the interrelatedness of all communication skills.

A major purpose of the language arts program in the elementary school is the development of each child's ability to utilize his skill in oral and written expression for effective communication. This communication can be considered to be of two major types: first, interpersonal communication (verbal interaction

From *Elementary English* 43:489-498; May 1966. Reprinted with permission of the National Council of Teachers of English and Robert B. Ruddell, Associate Professor, University of California, Berkeley.

with others); and second, intrapersonal communication (verbal interaction with self). Research studies focusing on the interrelationships of language skills in achieving the communicative objective have been described; this report is an extension of past writing with emphasis upon oral language skills as related to the development of other language skills.[1]

Vocabulary and Syntactical Language Development

The five to seven years of pre-school experience has afforded most children opportunity for vigorous oral language interaction with environment and self. During these years the average child's vocabulary increases dramatically from a minute number of words used by the one year old to many hundreds of basic and derivative words recognized by the average first grader.[2] The grammatical development of children's language likewise increases at a rapid rate from one word utterances at the end of the first year to lexical class substitution by the second year.[3] The mastery of most basic grammatical fundamentals has occurred by the fourth year.[4] By the time the child enters the first grade, he has achieved a high degree of sophistication in his oral language development.[5]

It must be recognized of course that these findings represent the language development of "average" children.[6, 7] The very nature of inferential research requires that the researcher test major hypotheses by relying on significant differences derived from large sample averages, which may result in conclusions of a general nature. Thus the practitioner must be alert to the developmental ranges in language growth as related to factors in each child's language environment. For example, Bernstein's research with British youth points to middle and lower working class language differences.[8] The speech patterns of the middle-class children reflected greater individual variation and greater meaning clarity through the utilization of the available possibilities of sentence organization. This presented a marked contrast with patterns of lower working class children who were found to have a comparatively rigid and limited use of the organizational possibilities of sentence construction. Templin's findings also suggest that socioeconomic level is related to the grammatical complexity of responses and vocabulary development of children.[9]

The frequency of the child's opportunity to participate verbally with adults in the family and the language model available would appear to have a direct bearing on the rate of language development.[10] In families with a single child, the child's language facility was found to develop more rapidly than that of children with siblings; the latter children were found to develop language facility faster than twins only.

Thus oral language development of the individual child must be carefully assessed for present achievement and for future potential in light of related environmental factors. The following discussion will focus on research dealing with the relationship between the development of oral language skills (speech, listening) and written language skills (reading, writing), the interrelatedness of language skill development, and the implications from this research for the teaching of language skills.

Oral Language Development and Reading Achievement

The relationship between oral language development and reading achievement is evidenced either directly or tangentially from a number of significant investigations.

Strickland's study of children's oral language development and reading achievement at the sixth-grade level revealed a significant relationship between the use of movables and elements of subordination in oral language and oral reading interpretation.[11] Children who ranked high on measures of comprehension in silent reading and listening were found to make greater use of movables and elements of subordination in their oral language than did children who ranked low on measures of these variables. This finding suggests that a child's ability to utilize subordination and movables in oral expression is closely related to his ability to comprehend written language.

The longitudinal study of children's language development by Loban revealed that children who were advanced in general language ability, as determined by vocabulary scores at the kindergarten level and language ratings by teachers, were also advanced in reading ability.[12] The inverse was found for those low in general language ability. Language achievement differences between the high and low groups were found to increase from year to year with the low group using many more partial expressions or incomplete sentence patterns. Loban concluded that competence in spoken language appears to be a necessary base for competence in reading.

Further evidence of this relationship was supplied by Milner's investigation of the use of language in the home and reading achievement at the first-grade level.[13] She found that the high achieving readers came from an enriched verbal environment which, as contrasted with that of the low achieving readers, included having more books available and being read to more often by high-esteemed adults. The high-scoring children also engaged in conversations with their parents more often than the low-scoring children.

Gibbons used a "disarranged phase test" to study the relationship between third-grade children's ability to understand the structure of sentences and their reading achievement. She found a correlation of .89 between the ability to see the relationship between parts of a sentence and the ability to understand the sentence, when intelligence was partialled out. A correlation of .72 was found between the ability to see the relationship between parts of sentences and total reading achievement.[14]

The significant finding highlighted in both Strickland's and Loban's studies, emphasizing the relationship between children's demonstrated use of movables and subordination in oral language and their reading and listening achievement, has an interesting parallel in Thorndike's early descriptive study of mistakes in paragraph reading.[15] Thorndike concluded from his study of sixth-grade children that in "correct reading" each element of meaning must be given appropriate weight in comparison to other elements and that ideas presented must be examined and validated to make sure that they satisfy the mental set or purpose of reading. He further concluded that understanding a paragraph is dependent upon the reader's selection of the right elements and synthesizing them in the right relationships. These conclusions point to the importance of seeing relationships among contextual elements—the movables and various forms of subordination—to reading comprehension. Again it would seem to follow logically that the child who demonstrates control over movables and subordination in his oral language will better comprehend written or spoken language emphasizing these features than will the child who has little facility in using movables or in subordinating.

A reading program encompassing oral patterns of language structure, identified by the Strickland study, was developed at the first-grade level by Ruddell.[16] In the early stages of the program, meaning change in oral and written language as conveyed by intonation patterns (pitch, stress, juncture) and punctuation was stressed. In a later phase of the program, emphasis was placed on the relationships which exist among words in sentences by developing meaning change through manipulation of specific elements in the sentence. The sentences used were developed in the context of a paragraph or story. Findings at midyear in this first-grade study showed significant differences in reading comprehension skills favoring the basal reading programs using the special supplement emphasizing language structure as related to meaning when contrasted with identical basal reading programs not using the special supplement. This study reported correlations of .68 and .44 between children's syntactical language development measured early in grade one and the respective factors of vocabulary achievement and comprehension achievement measured at midyear.

At the fourth-grade level the same researcher examined the effect on reading comprehension of patterns of language structure which occur with high and low frequency in children's oral language.[17] When the readability level of reading passages was controlled, comprehension scores on material written with high frequency patterns of language structure were found to be significantly superior to comprehension scores on passages written with low frequency patterns of language structure.

The research reviewed here strongly suggests that facility in oral expression, particularly vocabulary knowledge and an understanding of sentence structure, is basic to the development of reading comprehension skill.

Listening Development and Reading Achievement

Kelty investigated the effect of training in listening for certain purposes upon the ability of fourth-grade pupils to read for the same purposes.[18] She found that practice in listening to note the details of a selection produced a significant gain in reading for the same purpose. However, training in listening to decide upon the main idea and to draw a conclusion produced a positive but not significant change in reading for these purposes.

The research by Hampleman indicated that the listening comprehension of fourth- and sixth-grade children was superior to their reading comprehension of easy material when compared to the comprehension of more difficult verbal context.[19] Listening comprehension was found to be significantly superior to reading comprehension for both fourth- and sixth-grade pupils, but an increase in mental age resulted in a decrease in the difference between listening and reading comprehension.

Young[20] found that children retained more from an oral presentation by the teacher than from silent reading by themselves. The oral presentation plus simultaneous silent reading by the pupils was equally as effective as the oral presentation of the teacher alone. Children who did poorly in comprehension through listening were also found to perform poorly in comprehension through reading. Young concluded that throughout the intermediate grades children improve their ability to comprehend through reading at the same rate that they improve their ability to comprehend through listening.

A number of correlational studies have examined the relationship between listening and reading comprehension. At the fifth-grade level Lundsteen reported a correlation of .52 between critical listening and reading achievement.[21] Plessas reported correlation coefficients between a listening test and various aspects of reading achievement ranging from .27 to .80.[22] Trivette found a correlation between listening and reading comprehension of .61 and Hollow found a correlation of .55, at the fifth-grade level.[23, 24] From a study at the sixth-grade level, Pratt reported a correlation of .64, while Devine, at the high school level, found a correlation of .65.[25, 26] High relationships between listening and reading comprehension were also reported in early studies by Larsen and Feder and by Young.[27, 28]

The correlations from the majority of these studies suggest that factors in listening comprehension account for approximately twenty-five to sixty per cent of the variance in the reading comprehension scores, depending on the types of listening and reading skills measured. It must be emphasized, however, that correlational studies are limited as to the clarity of relationships between variables. This is to say that a cause-and-effect relationship is not established through correlational analysis. The common, but imperfectly defined, variable of intelligence, for instance, may account for a significant portion of the relationship observed between listening comprehension and reading comprehension.

The research of Caffrey and the study by Spearritt suggest that ability in listening, or "auding," may be constituted of verbal comprehension factors differing from those involved in reading.[29, 30] Russell has emphasized the need for a theory of listening which would enable researchers to generate fruitful hypotheses for examination and allow practitioners to apply findings in developing this phase of the language arts curriculum.[31]

In summary, the relationship between listening and reading is shown to be of significant magnitude, with common factors accounting for a degree of the positive correlations; however, the evidence indicates that each receptive skill may contain verbal factors individually unique.

Oral Language Development and Writing

The research evidence concerning the relationship between oral language and writing is comparatively limited. Loban reported from evidence obtained in his longitudinal study that children who were rated superior and above average in oral language usage were also rated above average in writing, and those below average in oral language were also below average in written language.[32]

Although specific data were not reported, Winter's findings of "low stable relationships" between oral language vocabularies and writing abilities of first- and second-grade children, substantiate Loban's research.[33]

Hughes also concluded from his investigation of 332 fifth-grade children that high achievement in any one of the language abilities examined (e.g., language usage) tended to be associated with above average achievement in the other areas studied (e.g., sentence sense, paragraph organization).[34] The inverse was true with low achievement in any one of the abilities. Correlations between language usage and the two factors of sentence sense and paragraph organization were found to be .46 and .39 respectively. The correlations reflected a positive relationship between each of the selected language variables independent of intelligence.

A detailed study by Harrell compared selected language variables in the speech and writing of 320 children of ages nine, eleven, thirteen, and fifteen. A short movie was used as the stimulus for securing the speech and writing samples.[35] The investigator found that the length of the compositions and clauses used in oral and written expression increased with age, with a larger percentage of subordinate clauses being used by the older children in both written and spoken composition. The children were found to use a larger percentage of subordinate clauses in writing than in speaking. More adverb and adjective clauses were used in written compositions while a larger number of noun clauses were used in speaking. A larger percentage of adverbial clauses, excepting those of time and cause, were used in the children's speech. The developmental increase of each language variable in relation to age was found to be greater for written compositions than for oral.

Working with tenth-grade students Bushnell compared each student's oral and written compositions on the same topic.[36] He found that higher scores on measures of thought content and sentence structure were obtained on the written themes than on the oral compositions. Correlations between the scores on oral and written thought content and oral and written sentence structure were found to be .42 and .35 respectively. Bushnell concluded that the most important difference between the two forms of expression was the more precise and logical organization of written language in contrast to the less precise and loosely organized oral language.

By examining research which contrasts the language development of children possessing defective hearing with that of children having normal hearing, the relationship between oral language development and writing achievement is brought into sharper focus. Heider and Heider used a motion picture as a stimulus for securing written compositions from 301 deaf and 817 hearing children ranging in age from eleven to seventeen years and eight to fourteen years respectively.[37] Although the deaf children were three years older their compositions were found to resemble the less mature hearing children. The deaf children were found to use fewer numbers of words and clauses than the hearing children. The hearing children used more compound and complex sentences with a larger number of verbs in coordinate and subordinate clauses, indicating a more advanced development in written language.

The written language of normal and defective hearing children was also examined by Templin.[38] Children having defective hearing were found to use more words in their explanations of natural phenomena than hearing children. This was interpreted as reflecting less adequate control over vocabulary, rather than representing a more complex type of expression. The children with defective hearing apparently needed more words to express a concept because of their inability to use precise vocabulary. Templin concluded that the written language of the defective hearing child is more immature than that of the hearing child of the same age, grade, and intelligence.

These investigations point to similarities in the growth patterns of oral and written language development. Achievement in oral language appears to be directly associated with written language achievement although some variance in the organizational quality of oral and written expression of older children is evidenced.

Summary: Interrelationships of Language Skills

Research evidence available strongly suggests a high degree of interrelatedness among the various communication skills. The functional understanding of vocabulary and the ability to comprehend relationships between elements of vocabulary in structural patterns appear to encompass common communication components in the language arts.

✗   The research reviewed indicates that oral language development serves as the underlying base for the development of reading and writing achievement. The child's ability to comprehend written material through reading and to express himself through written communication appears directly related to his maturity in the speaking and listening phases of language development.

The findings reported suggest that the receptive skills of listening and reading are closely related and utilize similar verbal factors but may encompass factors unique to each skill.

The relationship between the receptive skill of listening and the expressive skill of writing was explored in the research on normal and hearing handicapped children. Hearing children were found to use more complex types of language structure and more concise composition, reflecting a higher degree of maturity in written expression than that of deaf or partially hearing children.

The expressive skills of speaking and writing appear to parallel closely each other in developmental growth. With older children, however, some variance is noted in the types of subordination and the degree of organization utilized in oral and written compositions.

Interrelationships among the language arts skills are very much apparent in the research examined. These interrelationships deserve careful consideration by the classroom teacher if full utilization is to be made of the learning transfer potential in language skills.

Implications for Teaching the Language Skills

The research evidence presented in this discussion suggests a number of implications for teaching language skills. These include the following:

1. The teacher of basic language skills must be aware of the wide range in language development which can be anticipated in the elementary classroom. His understanding of individual children will be more complete, enabling the planning of a more adequate language program, if the possible factors which may have precipitated the range of individual language differences can be accounted for. These factors may include the language models presented in the

home, the degree of language interaction between the parents and the child, the value placed by the home on the importance of language development, the dialect differences between home and school, and individual pupil characteristics such as hearing acuity loss and intellectual development.

2. Children's language is greatly influenced by the models presented in their environmental settings. Although the early home environment plays a major role in a child's language development, it would seem that the teacher's model and that of other children could also exert a positive influence on children's language development in the classroom setting. Such devices as the tape recorder should be considered for individual or group listening activities in presenting appropriate and contrasting language models to the chldren. Oral language enrichment activities such as role playing, storytelling, and group discussions of direct experiences, deserve strong emphasis, particularly with children from culturally disadvantaged backgrounds. In this manner a language base can be established for the development of reading and writing skills.

3. Consideration should be given to language difficulties impairing children's reading and listening comprehension and clarity of oral and written expression. Vocabulary enrichment and the development of functional utilization of movables and subordinating elements in improving sentence meaning may require special emphasis. Consideration should be given to the following types of structural meaning changes: word substitution (*e.g.*, Bill hit the *ball*. Bill hit the *girl*.); expansion of patterns (*e.g.*, Tim had a wagon. Tim had a wagon *yesterday*. Tim *my brother* had a wagon yesterday.); inversion of sentence elements (*e.g.*, Sam hit the ball. *The ball* hit Sam.); transformations of basic structural patterns (*e.g.*, Ann is in the house. *Is* Ann in the house?). By a careful appraisal of language skill development, the language arts program can be based on the children's specific needs.

4. Oral language development can provide a basis for written language skill development in the integrated language skills curriculum. Oral language activities such as reading literature to children, dramatic play and dialogue, combined with extensive use of experience charts, can serve to help children understand how intonation and punctuation may be used to convey meaning in oral and written expression. Such activities also provide an excellent way to show children how descriptive language can be used in developing story characters and story settings, and how certain parts of sentences can be expanded to provide the listener or reader more precise information in an interesting way.

5. An increased awareness of the interrelatedness of listening comprehension and reading comprehension skills should be fostered in the classroom. Listening and reading activities should encompass a variety of purposes, ranging from direct recall to critical evaluation of material. In practice the development of these skills may evolve through the careful development of purposes for listening and reading. For example, news articles and advertisements found in the

daily newspaper or on television may be used in fostering critical comprehension skills. Listening comprehension skills can be taught and would seem to enhance reading comprehension skills. This consideration in the instructional program is essential if children are to obtain maximum benefit from the language environment which surrounds them.

6. Careful consideration should be given to children's concept development in relation to their own experiences. The child must have a firm grasp of the concept he is attempting to express in oral or written form if his communication attempt is to be successful. The teacher should attempt to develop and expand concepts through concrete experiences in the classroom and field trips, and by showing children how words convey different meanings in a variety of oral and written sentence contexts.

7. Language educators must consider the implementation of two types of research in the further exploration of the nature of interrelationships among the language arts and in testing the hypotheses embodied in the procedures and materials of language programs. The first type of research is the action research study carried out in individual classroom settings. In practice, this means using procedures and materials with children and noting in a descriptive manner the success and difficulty experienced in improving language skills within the limitations of the classroom. The second type of research is the carefully controlled research study carried out in an experimental setting. This type of evaluation must be effected with groups of children taught by distinct and contrastingly different programs with provision for control of important variables such as intelligence and socioeconomic background.

Although past research on children's language development has explored only a small segment of the vast cognitive realm, the high degree of interrelatedness between oral and written language skill development is evident. Through cooperative efforts psychologists, linguists, and language educators have recently forged new tools providing for more precise descriptive analysis of children's language. The value of such analysis techniques has been demonstrated in the studies of Strickland and Loban and should facilitate the exploration of the future language researcher. These techniques, new hypotheses, and development of new curriculum materials all require added understanding of factors leading to the improvement of children's language achievement. These must be carefully studied in classroom settings if knowledge is to be furthered and methodology of language arts instruction is to be improved.

Footnotes

[1] A. Sterl Artley, "Research Concerning Interrelationships among the Language Arts," *Elementary English*, 27 (December, 1950) 527-37.
Mildred A. Dawson, "Interrelationships Between Speech and Other Language Arts Areas," *Elementary English*, 31 (April, 1954) 223-233.

John J. DeBoer, "Composition, Handwriting, and Spelling," *Review of Educational Research*, 31 (April, 1961) 161-172.

Gertrude Hildreth, "Interrelationships among the Language Arts," *Elementary School Journal*, 48 (June, 1948) 538-549.

[2] Mary K. Smith, "Measurement of the Size of General English Vocabulary Through the Elementary Grades and High School," *Genetic Psychological Monographs*, 24 (1941) 311-345.

[3] Ruth Weir, *Language in the Crib*. The Hague: Mouton and Company, 1962.

[4] Susan M. Ervin and Wick R. Miller, *Language Development*. The Sixty-Second Yearbook of the National Society for the Study of Education, Part I. Chicago: University of Chicago Press, 1963, pp. 108-143.

[5] Ruth G. Strickland, "The Language of Elementary School Children: Its Relationship to the Language of Reading Textbooks and the Quality of Reading of Selected Children," *Bulletin of the School of Education*, Indiana University, Bloomington, 38 (July, 1962).

[6] *Ibid.*

[7] Smith, *loc. cit.*

[8] Basil Bernstein, "Language and Social Class," *British Journal of Sociology*, 11 (1960) 271-276.

[9] Mildred C. Templin, *Certain Language Skills in Children: Their Development and Interrelationships*. Minneapolis: University of Minnesota Press, 1957.

[10] Edith A. Davis, *The Development of Linguistic Skill in Twins, Singletons with Siblings, and Only Children from Ages Five to Ten Years*. Minneapolis: University of Minnesota Press, 1937.

[11] Strickland, *loc. cit.*

[12] Walter D. Loban, *The Language of Elementary School Children*. Champaign, Illinois: National Council of Teachers of English, 1963.

[13] Esther Milner, "A Study of the Relationship Between Reading Readiness in Grade One School Children and Patterns of Parent-Child Interaction," *Child Development*, 22 (June, 1951) 95-112.

[14] Helen D. Gibbons, "Reading and Sentence Elements," *Elementary English Review*, 18 (February, 1941) 42-46.

[15] E. L. Thorndike, "Reading and Reasoning, A Study of Mistakes in Paragraph Reading," *Journal of Educational Psychology*, 8 (June, 1917) 323-332.

[16] Robert B. Ruddell, "The Effect of Four Programs of Reading Instruction with Varying Emphasis on the Regularity of Grapheme-Phoneme Correspondences and the Relationship of Language Structure to Meaning on Achievement in First Grade Reading: A First Progress Report," *Psycholinguistic Nature of the Reading Process*, edited by Kenneth Goodman. Detroit: Wayne State University Press.

[17] Robert B. Ruddell, "The Effect of the Similarity of Oral and Written Patterns of Language Structure on Reading Comprehension," *Elementary English*, 42 (April, 1965) 403-410.

[18] Annette P. Kelty, "An Experimental Study to Determine the Effect of Listening for Certain Purposes upon Achievement in Reading for These Purposes," *Abstracts of Field Studies for the Degree of Doctor of Education*. Greeley: Colorado State College of Education, 15 (1954) 82-95.

[19] Richard S. Hampleman, "Comparison of Listening and Reading Comprehension Ability of Fourth and Sixth Grade Pupils," unpublished doctoral dissertation, Indiana University, 1955.

[20] William E. Young, "The Relation of Reading Comprehension and Retention to Hearing Comprehension and Retention," *Journal of Experimental Education*, 5 (September, 1936) 30-39.

[21] Sara Lundsteen, "Teaching Abilities in Critical Listening in the Fifth and Sixth Grades," unpublished doctoral dissertation, University of California, 1963.

[22] G. P. Plessas, "Reading Abilities and Intelligence Factors of Children Having High and Low Auding Ability," unpublished doctoral dissertation, University of California, 1957.

[23] Sue E. Trivette, "The Effect of Training in Listening for Specific Purposes," *Journal of Educational Research*, 54 (March, 1961) 276-277.

[24] Sister M. K. Hollow, "Listening Comprehension at the Intermediate Grade Level," *Elementary School Journal*, 56 (December, 1955) 158-161.

[25] Edward Pratt, "Experimental Evaluation of a Program for the Improvement of Listening," *Elementary School Journal*, 56 (March, 1956) 315-320.

[26] Thomas G. Devine, "The Development and Evaluation of a Series of Recordings for Teaching Certain Critical Listening Abilities," unpublished doctoral dissertation, Boston University, 1961.

[27] Robert P. Larsen and Daniel D. Feder, "Common and Differential Factors in Reading and Hearing Comprehension," *Journal of Educational Psychology*, 31 (April, 1940) 241-252.

[28] William E. Young, *loc. cit.*

[29] J. G. Caffrey, "Auding Ability as a Function of Certain Psychometric Variables," unpublished doctoral dissertation, University of California, 1953.

[30] Donald Spearritt, *Listening Comprehension—A Factoral Analysis.* Australian Council for Educational Research, Research Series No. 76. Melbourne: G. W. Green and Sons, Ltd., 1962.

[31] David H. Russell, "A Conspectus of Recent Research on Listening Abilities," *Elementary English*, 41 (March, 1964) 262-267.

[32] Walter Loban, *loc. cit.*

[33] Clotilda Winter, "Interrelationships among Language Variables in Children of the First and Second Grades," *Elementary English*, 34 (February, 1957) 108-113.

[34] Virgil Hughes, "Study of the Relationships among Selected Language Abilities," *Journal of Educational Research*, 47 (October, 1953) 97-106.

[35] Lester E. Harrell, Jr., "An Inter-Comparison of the Quality and Rate of the Development of Oral and Written Language in Children," *Monographs of the Society for Research in Child Development*, 22, No. 3, 1957.

[36] Paul Bushnell, *An Analytical Contrast of Oral with Written English.* Contributions to Education, No. 451. New York: Teachers College, Columbia University, 1930.

[37] F. K. Heider and Grace M. Heider, "A Comparison of Sentence Structure of Deaf and Hearing Children," *Psychological Monographs*, 52 (1940) 42-103.

[38] Mildred C. Templin, *The Development of Reasoning in Children with Normal and Defective Hearing.* Minneapolis: University of Minnesota Press, 1950.

Bibliography

Artley, A. Sterl, "Research Concerning Interrelationships among the Language Arts," *Elementary English*, 27 (December, 1950) 527-537.

Bernstein, Basil, "Language and Social Class," *British Journal of Sociology*, 11 (1960) 271-276.

Bushnell, Paul, *An Analytical Contrast of Oral with Written English.* Contributions to Education, No. 451. New York: Teachers College, Columbia University, 1930.

Caffrey, J. G., "Auding Ability as a Function of Certain Psychometric Values," unpublished doctoral dissertation, University of California, Berkeley, 1953.

Davis, Edith A., *The Development of Linguistic Skill in Twins, Singletons with Siblings, and Only Children from Ages Five to Ten Years.* Minneapolis: University of Minnesota Press, 1937.

Dawson, Mildred A., "Interrelationships Between Speech and Other Language Arts Areas," *Elementary English*, 31 (April, 1954) 223-233.

DeBoer, John J., "Composition, Handwriting, and Spelling," *Review of Educational Research*, 31 (April, 1961) 161-172.

Devine, Thomas G., "The Development and Evaluation of a Series of Recordings for Teaching Certain Critical Listening Abilities," unpublished doctoral dissertation, Boston University, 1961.

Ervin, Susan M. and Wick R. Miller, *Language Development*, The Sixty-Second Yearbook of the National Society for the Study of Education, Part I. Chicago: University of Chicago Press, pp. 108-143.

Gibbons, Helen D., "Reading and Sentence Elements," *Elementary English Review*, 18 (February, 1941) 42-46.

Hampleman, Richard S., "Comparison of Listening and Reading Comprehension Ability of Fourth and Sixth Grade Pupils," unpublished doctoral dissertation, Indiana University, 1955.

Harrell, Lester E., Jr., "An Inter-Comparison of the Quality and Rate of the Development of Oral and Written Language in Children," *Monographs of the Society for Research in Child Development*, 22, No. 3, 1957.

Heider, F. K. and Grace M. Heider, "A Comparison of Sentence Structure of Deaf and Hearing Children," *Psychological Monographs*, 52 (1940) 42-103.

Hildreth, Gertrude, "Interrelationships among the Language Arts," *Elementary School Journal*, 48 (June, 1948) 538-549.

Hollow, Sister M. K., "Listening Comprehension at the Intermediate Grade Level," *Elementary School Journal*, 56 (December, 1955) 158-161.

Hughes, Virgil, "Study of the Relationships among Selected Language Abilities," *Journal of Educational Research*, 47 (October, 1953), 97-106.

Kelty, Annette P., "An Experimental Study to Determine the Effects of Listening for Certain Purposes upon Achievement in Reading for These Purposes," Colorado State College of Education, Greeley: *Abstracts of Field Studies for the Degree of Doctor of Education*, 15 (1954) 82-95.

Larsen, Robert P. and Daniel D. Feder, "Common and Differential Factors in Reading and Hearing Comprehension," *Journal of Educational Psychology*, 31 (April, 1940) 241-252.

Loban, Walter D., *The Language of Elementary School Children*. Champaign, Illinois: National Council of Teachers of English, 1963.

Lundsteen, Sara, "Teaching Ability in Critical Listening in the Fifth and Sixth Grades," unpublished doctoral dissertation, University of California, Berkeley, 1963.

Milner, Esther, "A Study of the Relationship Between Reading Readiness in Grade One School Children and Patterns of Parent-Child Interaction," *Child Development*, 22 (June, 1951) 95-112.

Plessas, G. P., "Reading Abilities and Intelligence Factors of Children Having High and Low Auding Ability," unpublished doctoral dissertation, University of California, Berkeley, 1957.

Pratt, Edward, "Experimental Evaluation of a Program for the Improvement of Listening," *Elementary School Journal*, 56 (March, 1956) 315-320.

Ruddell, Robert B., "The Effect of Four Programs of Reading Instruction with Varying Emphasis on the Regularity of Grapheme-Phoneme Correspondences and the Relationship of Language Structure to Meaning on Achievement in First Grade Reading: A First Progress Report," *Psycholinguistic Nature of the Reading Process*, edited by Kenneth Goodman. Detroit: Wayne State University Press.

Ruddell, Robert B., "The Effect of the Similarity of Oral and Written Patterns of

Language Structure on Reading Comprehension," *Elementary English*, 42 (April, 1965) 403-410.

Russell, David H., "A Conspectus of Recent Research on Listening Abilities," *Elementary English*, 41 (March, 1964) 262-267.

Smith, Mary K., "Measurement of the Size of General English Vocabulary Through the Elementary Grades and High School," *Genetic Psychological Monographs*, 24 (1941) 311-345.

Spearritt, Donald, *Listening Comprehension—A Factoral Analysis*. Australian Council for Educational Research, Research Series No. 76. Melbourne: G. W. Green and Sons, Ltd., 1962.

Strickland, Ruth G., "The Language of Elementary School Children: Its Relationship to the Language of Reading Textbooks and the Quality of Reading of Selected Children." Bloomington: Indiana University, *Bulletin of the School of Education*. 38, No. 4 (July, 1962).

Templin, Mildred C., *Certain Language Skills in Children: Their Development and Interrelationships*. Minneapolis: University of Minnesota Press, 1957.

Templin, Mildred C., *The Development of Reasoning in Children with Normal and Defective Hearing*. Minneapolis: University of Minnesota Press, 1950.

Trivette, Sue E., "The Effect of Training in Listening for Specific Purposes," *Journal of Educational Research*, 54 (March, 1961) 276-277.

Thorndike, E. L., "Reading and Reasoning: A Study of Mistakes in Paragraph Reading," *Journal of Educational Psychology*, 8 (June, 1917) 323-332.

Weir, Ruth, *Language in the Crib*. The Hague: Mouton and Company, 1962.

Winter, Clotilda, "Interrelationships among Language Variables in Children of the First and Second Grades," *Elementary English*, 34 (February, 1957) 108-113.

Young, William E., "The Relation of Reading Comprehension and Retention to Hearing Comprehension and Retention," *Journal of Experimental Education*, 5 (September, 1936) 30-39.

16   Problems in Oral English

Walter D. Loban

Amazingly few details are known about the longitudinal growth patterns of children's language development and our ignorance is multiplied tenfold for children commonly labeled 'culturally disadvantaged.' Until more is known about common problems in oral English, instruction will tend to be arbitrary guesswork unlikely to focus on the real needs of pupils. This article is a summary of a study—well on its way to becoming a classic in its own time—which not only recorded and analyzed children's language over a ten year period but which also compared groups from different social backgrounds. This is the type of research which should make a significant contribution to the improvement of language arts instruction.

What are some errors common to all groups? To what might you attribute the primary difficulty found by Loban, that of lack of clarity and precision? What implications for junior high school teachers can be drawn from Figure 18? Even though frequent, how serious is disagreement between subject and verb in third person singular? Do textbooks typically tackle the major difficulties these children face? How do Loban's conclusions relate to the article by DeLawter and Eash in Part Two? You may wish to reread this article in conjunction with Brook's article in Part Seven. The complete report of Loban's research will be found in Problems in Oral English *published by the National Council of Teachers of English. Another equally interesting study of his is reported in* The Language of Elementary School Children, *also published by NCTE.*

A study was made of the nonstandard speech of four different groups of subjects during the years of their schooling from kindergarten through grade nine. All four groups were drawn from a larger sample of 338 children chosen to represent a range of socioeconomic background, intellectual ability, ethnic variety, and equal in number of boys and girls. The Random group was drawn

From *Problems in Oral English*, NCTE Research Report No. 5, 1966. Reprinted with permission of the National Council of Teachers of English and Walter D. Loban, Professor of English Education, University of California, Berkeley. Footnotes have been renumbered.

from this larger group as were the Caucasian group high in language proficiency, the Caucasian group low in language proficiency, and a Negro group, likewise low in language proficiency.

The examples of nonstandard oral usage—except for pronunciation, which was not considered—were classified, counted, and compared. . . . What conclusions, useful to teachers and others who determine the content of education, may be drawn from this examination of the subjects' oral language?

Subjects Speaking Standard English

For those children not handicapped by social dialect, most difficulties fall into five categories, occurring in the following order of frequency:

inconsistency in the use of tense
careless omission of words (excluding omission of auxiliaries)
lack of syntactic clarity
    ambiguous placement of words, phrases, and clauses
    awkward and incoherent arrangements of expression
confusing use of pronouns
trouble with agreement of subject and verb when using *there is, there are, there was,* and *there were*

It is immediately apparent that all these problems transcend usage. They are matters of sensitivity to clarity and precision of communication rather than problems of habit or usage. This is not at all what the researcher had expected. He had assumed that problems of usage—such as nonstandard verb forms and agreement of verb with subject *(It don't, I would've took him, I seen it)*—would constitute the major difficulty for most pupils who did not speak a social class dialect. Exactly the opposite proves to be the case. On every figure representing a category that tallies matters of habitual usage, the frequencies adhere to the horizontal line representing zero. Instead the major problems occur in categories related to clarity of expression. Even the confusion over *there is* and *there are,* properly understood for what it is, may be viewed as a problem in thoughtful arrangement and anticipation of sentence elements rather than a problem of proper habits. Bryant finds an overwhelming proportion for *there is* when the first member of the compound subject is singular (as in "There is the boy and his sisters.").[1]

How to label this distinction between usage and clarity of communication proves to be a problem. To most people, the term *usage* denotes the habitual ways an individual uses oral language, ways that are spontaneous rather than carefully chosen and considered. Usage fits very well such categories as subject-verb agreement, case of pronouns, and the use of verb forms in the past and past perfect tenses, but it applies much less appropriately to consistency of verb tense or skilled arrangement of the syntactical elements of sentences. For these latter problems in this research, the term *rhetoric* was used initially. However, rhetoric includes a connotation of overall artistry—the art of organizing logically and effectively the total structure of expression. Those who read early drafts of this manuscript considered rhetoric too large a concept to describe the problems of the standard-speaking subjects.

To avoid these issues, we will use the term *coherence* to designate the major difficulties of pupils who come from homes where standard English prevails. Such pupils in this study, except for those few whose scores fall distant from the mean, do not need drill or help with usage. What they do need is instruction concerned with increasing their coherence and effectiveness.

An empirical way to distinguish between the two kinds of oral language difficulties has been suggested by Robert F. Hogan, Associate Executive Secretary, National Council of Teachers of English. The simpler and less troublesome problems of usage fall within a single communication unit, e.g., "The calf don't want his milk." The more complex and persistent problems span two or more such units, e.g., shift of verb tense and faulty reference to an antecedent.

Subjects Speaking a Social Class Dialect

For children whose language is influenced by a social class dialect, a more complicated pattern of difficulties emerges. In this study, only one group, the Negro, has been studied, but the results lead one to believe that a similar complicated set of problems would be revealed for many Oriental, Hawaiian (Pidgin), Spanish-speaking, Cajun, and Appalachian subjects. For the Negro subjects in this study, what were the most troublesome difficulties in oral language? Their difficulties fall into ten categories in the following order of frequency:

lack of agreement of subject and verb, third person singular (other than forms of the verb *to be*)

omission of auxiliary verbs (especially those formed from the verb *to be*)

inconsistency in the use of tense

nonstandard use of verb forms

lack of agreement of subject and verb while using forms of the verb *to be*

careless omission of words (excluding omission of auxiliaries)

nonstandard use of pronouns

nonstandard use of noun forms

double negatives

omission of the verb *to be*

Of this list five out of the first six represent difficulties with verbs. Highly dramatic were the gains these Negro children made in conquering the problems of verb-subject agreement in the third person singular, the use of auxiliary verbs, and omission of needed words. Their persistent problem, one which does *not* show such a dramatic conquest, is the use of the verb *to be*. Actually this problem affects other categories and, in ways not at first apparent, causes the Negro child's main difficulties in achieving standard use of auxiliary verbs as well as some of his difficulties with consistency in verb tense.

For these Negro subjects both usage and coherence are involved in their oral language problems, but habitual use of standard forms is clearly a problem whereas it is not one for the Caucasian groups. For the Negro eight of the ten categories are problems of usage. Only consistency of tense and careless omission represent problems of a larger order. These children do indeed come from speech communities in which social class dialect rather than standard English is used. In ten years of schooling they make enormous improvement in subject-verb agreement and in using auxiliaries, yet almost no improvement in using the verb *to be* appropriately or in standardizing the verb forms. Except that their problem is more acute, they have the same difficulties as other subjects in confusing uses of pronouns and inconsistency of verb tense, particularly as they increase the length of their expression units in grades six, seven, eight, and nine.

In the categories that show difficulties but without such crucial frequencies —nonstandard use of noun forms and double negatives—the Negro subjects make almost no improvement. The double negative does almost disappear in grade seven, but as new complicated communication problems and larger units of expression require attention in grades eight and nine, the problem of the double negative springs back into place again.

Although this study has not been concerned with clear articulation of speech, one matter should be noted as a subject for future study. Anyone listening to the oral language of the Negro subjects would agree that many word endings and beginnings are missing in Negro dialect. These subjects are also uncertain when to use an *s* to end a verb and when not to use it, as in the following:

> My mother *look* at television a lot.
> We *likes* to ride our bikes in the park.

They tend to omit the required *s* on the third person singular verb and to add a superfluous *s* to verbs which agree with subjects not requiring an *s* to end the verb. They also confuse *a* and *an*, *sometime* and *sometimes*, and the phonemes *d, t,* and *th*. They have not acquired all the phonemes of standard English and do not, apparently, hear any difference between phonemes they use in nonstandard fashion and the corresponding phonemes in standard speech. These phonemic differences have been carefully described by Pedersen.[2] In this study, they have merely been noted, but no rigorous study has been made of them.

All Subjects

In some categories, *neither Negro nor Caucasian subjects* reveal any serious problems. Such categories are the following:

agreement between subject and predicate other than in the third person singular
connection through prepositions and conjunctions
modification with adjectives and adverbs
use of *that* instead of *who* as a relative pronoun referring to persons
nonstandard use of possessives

However, in the oral language of all these subjects, syntactic connection through conjunctions is practically limited to *and* and *but*. As the subjects begin to use more complex and lengthy units of expression in high school, the problem may change. This may also apply to the use of *that* and *who* if the increase in subordination, notable in grades seven through nine, continues. Because *that* can be accepted as standard, the problem does not seem to be one for instruction and drill but rather one to be noted as an example of disputed usage.

Although the prestige dialect groups have low frequencies on most of these categories, one must not forget that the figures are charted on mean scores. This indicates that even in the High Caucasian group there will be some individuals one or more standard deviations above the mean who will need individual instruction even when the group as a whole does not. The practice, so common among weaker teachers, of drilling all pupils on the same skill is not supported by this research.

Total Deviations

So far, in examining the subjects' problems of using standard spoken English, we have avoided combining the categories. Can anything be gained by looking at the totality of deviations from the prestige dialect? A summation of all the separate categories, most of which have been shown on individual graphs, is shown in Figure 18. As can be seen, the Negro group shows steady improvement through grade five but then abruptly increases its difficulties, not achieving the fifth grade level again until grade nine. The Low Caucasian group shows a similar abrupt increase after grade five and *remains* at a high level through grade nine. The High Caucasian group shows a slight but steady improvement until grade six and then moves upward slightly in grade seven. For

FIGURE 18

Total Number of Deviations per 1,000 Words of Spoken Volume
High Caucasian, Low Caucasian, Negro, and Random Groups
Grades Kindergarten through Nine

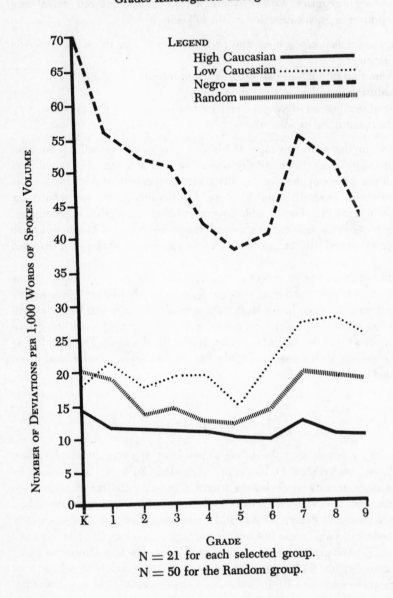

GRADE
N = 21 for each selected group.
N = 50 for the Random group.

the Random group as well as for both low groups, the dip in the curves followed by an abrupt upward trend in the total number of deviations seems to indicate that as complexity of sentence structure and total volume of spoken language both increase, there is a *more than proportional* probability of difficulty with certain problems—problems of clarity and precision, not problems of habitual usage. In other words, it is not logical to assume that the Random group and both low groups suddenly grow more inept in the use of language after grade five. The research clearly shows that as they speak with more complexity and in longer units of expression, their difficulties with coherence increase.

Total Deviations Apart from Social Class Dialect Problems

Certain departures from the prestige dialect, departures that are obviously a tremendous problem for the Negro group, represent a minor problem for *both* Caucasion groups. Specifically, these are the categories concerned with (1) agreement of the subject and verb in the third person singular, (2) omission of the verb *to be*, (3) omission of auxiliary verbs, (4) nonstandard use of verb forms, (5) double negatives. Figure 19 shows the result in total deviations when these five categories are subtracted on a year-by-year basis for all four groups.

Comparing Figure 18 to Figure 19 makes it obvious that the Low Caucasian group performs better than the Negro group in either case (with dialect categories retained or with dialect categories subtracted). However, on the total deviations the magnitude of difference between the two graphs is very great. When deviations which are primarily cultural are subtracted, all four groups move much closer together. In other words, the Negro group seems to be expending much of its energy *in overcoming problems the Caucasians subjects never encounter.*

A Concluding Statement

Because many English verbs form their principal parts irregularly, those occurring most frequently in English speech will always require high instructional priority for individual pupils who have not mastered them. The irregular verbs frequently used in nonstandard form are *lie, see, break, come, go, run, take, do, give, write, ring, sit, drink,* and *begin.* Other irregular verbs, less frequent in use but crucial when they do occur, are such verbs as *sneak, drown, sing, know, throw.* Individual pupils, but not whole classes of pupils, will need help if they are to use the standard forms of such verbs. Another troublesome

FIGURE 19

Total Number of Deviations per 1,000 Words of Spoken Volume
with Deviations of Ethnic Origin (1A, 1D, 1E, 1F, 8) Subtracted
High Caucasian, Low Caucasian, Negro, and Random Groups
Grades Kindergarten through Nine

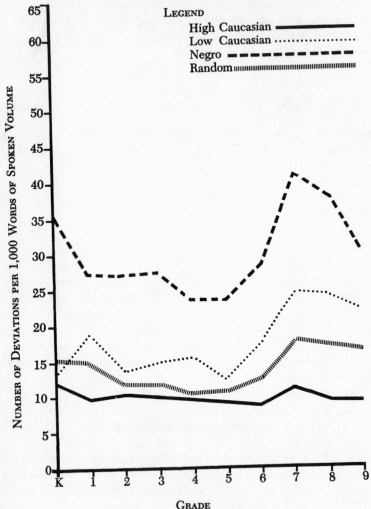

N = 21 for each selected group.
N = 50 for the Random group.

irregularity of the English language is the change occurring in the third person singular agreement of the verb with its subject (I do, you do, he *does*, we do, you do, they do.)

For those Negro pupils who speak a social class dialect, the overwhelming problem is standard use of the verb *to be:* omission as a linking verb; omission as an auxiliary with other verbs; agreement with subject; unusual uses. Other persistent problems of usage for this group are case of pronouns and the double negative.

Almost all the pupils whose parents speak informal standard English have little need of drill on usage. What they do need is help on coherence, and such help cannot be achieved through a drillbook approach. Improvement would seem most possible in situations where pupils are concerned with expressing thoughts and feelings so others will understand them. Such instruction, when successful, alternates skillfully between two polarities: one is the motivated class or group discussion, panel, or brief informal speech (usually impromptu or extempore, whether "sharing" in grade one or a "report" in grade nine); the other is the focused attention upon the strategies of coherence, using living examples, material just uttered, models, and examples. The tape recorder is invaluable for such instruction. For the pupil to become aware of how the same coherences occur in writing, listening, and reading would seem equally helpful. Here is the point at which all the language arts reinforce instruction in any one aspect of language. Dialect speakers need help with coherence, in addition to their need for changing nonstandard usage.

Whenever usage drill occurs, whether for dialect speakers or for the non-typical standard speaker, other research has shown that oral drill is more effective than workbook drills.

In societies organized for stability through caste and class, language is one means of maintaining the *status quo*. Even in a fluid society such as ours, where individual worth and aspiration are intended to count for more than fortunate or unfortunate birth, language still operates to preserve social class distinctions and remains a major barrier to crossing social lines. In a democracy schools should assist all other institutions in making equality of opportunity a reality. However, to do this teachers must begin to see how language and social caste are linked and why many people are inclined to condemn rather than accept the language of the least favored economic groups in any culture. On attitudes concerning language, teachers can learn much from sociology.

> We fear lower class speech and are inclined to give it no quarter. The more precarious our social status in the higher classes—that is, the closer we are to the line that divides the middle from the lower classses or the more recent our ascent from the lower strata—the more insistent we are on the purity of our linguistic credentials.[3]

Realizing that human worth cannot be measured by the language or dialect a man uses, teachers will be more likely to help children acquire standard

English without making them ashamed of their own language. Such change—not "improvement"—would seem to be much more possible in situations where drill and directed effort were oral and where they were not separated from language used to express ideas, attitudes, and values of genuine concern to the learners. Not only improved habits but also awareness of how listeners are helped or hindered by one's language proves to be the need of most learners. To improve language ability a pupil must apply whatever is studied to situations in which he has something to say, a deep desire to say it, and someone to whom he genuinely wants to say it.

Footnotes

[1] Bryant, Margaret M., *Current American Usage* (New York: Funk and Wagnalls, 1962), pp. 13-14.

[2] Pedersen, Lee A., "Non-Standard Negro Speech in Chicago," *Non-Standard Speech and the Teaching of English*, Language Information Series, 2 (Washington, D.C.: Center for Applied Linguistics, 1964), pp. 1-15.

[3] Cohn, Werner, "On the Language of Lower Class Children," *School Review*, 67 (Winter, 1959), pp. 435-440.

17 Creative Dramatics

Barbara McIntyre

Innumerable books purchased by parents have gathered dust because they lacked genuine child appeal—even though parents were attracted and elated by them. Apparently much the same is true of selections for creative dramatics; there is a discrepancy between teacher and pupil opinions. But the task is to identify the characteristics of a story which children prefer but which still meet the established criteria for quality creative dramatics. McIntyre presents the results of a unique research study which probed these issues and yielded concrete information usable by the classroom teacher.

What contributions can creative dramatics make to the oral language program? What controls did the author use to minimize bias and external influences? What factors may help explain the rank order of pupil preferences? How do the findings of this study relate to the teaching of the content fields (social studies, etc.)? What topics or stories are you familiar with which meet both the criteria set by McIntyre and the preferences expressed by the children? Do your experiences with creative dramatics affirm or refute McIntyre's findings? How does this article relate to Singleton's in Part One on the classroom teacher as a researcher? Graubard's article cited in Selected References for Part Three deals appealingly with pantomime, a facet of creative dramatics, while ones by Kane and Siks deal with values and techniques of creative dramatics.

Creative dramatics is informal playmaking which grows spontaneously from a simple plot (story) into a living experience through dramatization.[1] Utilized imaginatively, creative dramatics may become one of the teacher's most valuable techniques in stimulating interest in the social studies and enhancing interest in reading good literature.

Choosing material which will accomplish such lofty aims has always proved to be a problem. Children and adults frequently do not agree on the selection of stories. Adults are accustomed to this situation and often decide that they know best what is good for children and proceed to give it to them

From *Education* 49:495-498; April 1959. Reprinted from the 1959 issue of *Education* by permission of the publishers, The Bobbs-Merrill Company, Inc., Indianapolis, Indiana, and Barbara McIntyre, Professor, Northwestern University, Evanston, Illinois.

whether the children like. it or not. Such was the case of the writer when a beginning teacher of creative dramatics in the Evanston Public Schools.

As a special teacher in grades four, five and six, it was her duty to visit regularly three public schools and work with the classroom teachers in correlating the creative dramatics program with the regular work of the class. Sometimes the classroom teacher was interested in having the children play a story dealing with their current social studies program. At another time a teacher might suggest a story from the children's reader or other literature. There were occasions when the stories selected appeared to appeal to the children and others when the children were disinterested. Frequently when the material did not apppear to meet with the approval of the class some child would protest, "Why do we have to play that boring story? Let's have an exciting one." The suggested exciting one was frequently considered by the new teacher as unacceptable from the adult point of view.

It was this difference of opinion between the child and adult point of view that led to an investigation of the problem. The general purpose of this investigation was to try to discover what qualities according to the child's point of view makes a successful creative dramatics story. Specifically, it attempted to present reasonable answers to the following questions.

1. What types of story—true, fantasy and folk tale, nonsense or moralistic —do children prefer for creative dramatics?

2. Do stories selected for creative dramatics by adult evaluation agree with the child evaluation of such stories?

3. What main qualities present in a story make for successful playing in creative dramatics?

Stories from Adult Criteria

After careful consideration of opinions of recognized authorities in the field of children's literature and creative drama, it was decided that from the adult point of view a good story for creative dramatics should contain: 1) the elements of good drama; 2) much action; 3) brief and natural dialogue; 4) emotional appeal; 5) poetic justice.

Child Classification

In order to try to determine what types of stories children preferred, it was necessary to classify stories from the child's point of view. After several discussions with the members of the ten classes for which the writer was responsible, a classification was finally agreed upon by the children. According to these children, all children's stories could be placed in one of the following categories: true, fantasy and folk tale, nonsense and moral story. The true stories included stories "about real people who could have lived." The folk and fantasy group included stories "about people who couldn't really have lived on this earth." Nonsense stories were the ones "told because they are supposed to make you laugh." Moral stories the children agreed could be in the other categories but they wanted a fourth category to make the distinction in the story "that is supposed to teach us something."

Selection of Stories

The selection of the stories for the study was limited by two factors: 1) only short stories were practical; 2) only those stories which might interest the age group 9 to 11 years were applicable. After an investigation of approximately 500 stories, thirty-two were finally selected, eight in each of the categories of true, fantasy, nonsense, and moralistic. These thirty-two stories were divided into eight groups of four stories each. Each series of four stories contained a story chosen by chance from each of the above categories. One of the four did not meet the adult criteria of what constituted a good story. The inclusion of one story in each series which did not meet the five-point adult criteria was to create a control story within each series.

Testing of Stories

One of the greatest difficulties in the investigation was the obtaining of a true picture of the child reaction to the story itself. It was believed, however, that the first positive, undirected comments offered by a child with the spontaneous approval of several of his fellows would be valuable and would throw as clear a light as was generally possible upon the child's evaluation of the story. Since a reader or story teller may influence the child's evaluation by her interpretation, and since each group of children may differently influence the storyteller, a story may vary greatly from one telling to the next. In an attempt to eliminate this variable and to be sure that every class heard exactly the same story, recordings were made of all of the stories. These were recorded by the writer in a recording studio completely devoid of audience situation.

The members of the ten classes for which the writer was the creative dramatics teacher participated in the investigation. The records were played to the classes, one series a month for four months. No introduction or comment preceded the playing of the recordings. Immediately, at the conclusion of the playing, ballots containing the titles of the stories just heard were distributed.

Before there was opportunity for class or individual discussion, the children graded the stories in order of their preference: 1) being the story which the child wanted to play; 2) being his second choice; 3) being his third, and 4) being his last choice. The ballots were counted and the results scored. The story receiving the lowest numerical rating therefore indicated its popularity and was declared the story to be dramatized creatively.

Immediately after the collection of ballots an open discussion of the different stories was held. The first positive and spontaneous reactions which gained the general approval of the majority of the class were noted and tabulated. After the conclusion of the playing of the story a free discussion was held. The first positive, most generally accepted evaluations of the story were noted and recorded.

Results of the Testing

The numerical ratings given by the children upon hearing the stories read was of real importance in evaluating the child's point of view. The following scores indicate the number of times the type of story was chosen for playing: True stories—13; Moral stories—10; Fantasy and Folk Tale—10; Nonsense —7. These ratings combined with the comments which accompanied them presented a picture of the child's point of view and provided some answers to the questions which initiated the study.

Question 1. What types of stories—true, fantasy and folk tale, nonsense or moralistic—do children prefer for creative dramatics? According to the numerical ratings, the true stories were the most popular with this age group. The score alone, however, did not present the true picture. Almost every story chosen to be played was selected because of its elements of reality. Even some stories listed as fantasy were chosen because "there are some interesting real characters in the story." At no time was a story chosen to be played because of its elements of fantasy. The words "real," "true," and "alive" kept reappearing through the evaluations.

Another important and interesting factor was the interest in the known content of the stories. All groups chose to play the story of *William Tell*. Every class explained the choice not because it was a true story but because "We studied Switzerland in Social Studies and like Swiss stories." Two other true stories, *Antonio Canova* and *Murillo*, were chosen to be played by only one class and rejected by all the others. This was explained when the children in the one class said that they had chosen these stories because they were interested in a unit which involved great artists. The story *Pocahontas and Captain Smith* was chosen not because of the real individuals in the story but rather because the children had recently seen the Children's Theatre production of the *Indian Captive. Christopher Columbus*, on the other hand, was rejected by every class.

In each case the children claimed that "we are sick and tired of hearing about him." On the other hand, some of the folk tales were chosen on the basis of interest content. All but one class chose to play the Chinese fantasy *The Wise Girl*. This was not because it was a fantasy but rather they were interested in China.

Throughout the whole study it appeared that current interest in subject material rather than type of story was the dominant factor. Therefore, although we may conclude that at least for these children they prefer true stories, we must add that current influence in social studies, outside activities, and reading had great influence in selection.

Question 2. Do stories selected for creative dramatics by adult evaluation agree with the child evaluation of such stories? A possible answer to this may be found in noting the child's reaction to the "control" story in each series. This story did not meet the adult standard. It apparently did not meet the child's standard either. Only one of these stories was chosen for playing. After the dramatization of this story had been completed, the children claimed that they wished that they had chosen another story. "It didn't make as good playing as I thought it would." Therefore, it would appear for this group of children at least, that children tend to agree and accept the adult criteria of what makes a good story for creative dramatics.

Question 3. What main qualities present in a story make for successful playing in creative dramatics? This question seeks its answer in the evaluation of the first spontaneous comments made by the children at the conclusion of the playing of the story. The children's interest in and preference for "real and interesting characters" appeared twelve times in their comments following the final playing. Their desire for stories involving large numbers of characters so that all the children could play was expressed in ten different comments. Their interest in what they termed as "fun" appeared many times coupled with their interest in elimination of "dull" and "boring" stories. The children's wish for dramatic construction in a story was noted seven different times. It was expressed by such statements as "We want a story that builds to a climax," and "I like this kind of a story because it grows each time we play it." Therefore it would appear that according to this particular group of children the main qualities necessary for successful playing in creative dramatics are: 1) real and interesting characters; 2) large numbers of characters; 3) fun; 4) excitement and 5) opportunity of building to a climax.

Implications of This Study

Although this investigation did not completely solve the problem that elicited its birth, it did point toward a solution. It emphasized two factors that, when taken into consideration, tended to minimize the number of times children and teacher disagreed on material for creative dramatics. These two factors were the child's interest at this age in reality. True characters who really lived or characters "we see each day" proved more interesting to the children than the fanciful ones. The second factor which stood out was the desire of the child for stories dealing with his current and immediate interests. This points to the advisability of utilizing material from reading and social studies and further points to the possibility of greater correlation of creative dramatics with the rest of the basic curriculum. It suggests that from the child's point of view, at least, the integration of living, dramatic material within the curriculum might lead to an increased interest in social studies and dynamic classroom living.

Footnote

[1] Ward, Winifred, *Playmaking with Children*, Appleton-Century-Croft, New York, 1957.

18   Teaching and Testing Critical Listening in the Fifth and Sixth Grades

Sara W. Lundsteen

Some crucial language skills have been woefully ignored or relegated to incidental instruction only; listening is one of these. But listening is not a single global, unitary skill. It is composed of varied subskills, just as are speaking and reading, which require specific attention if they are to be best learned, retained, and used. Lundsteen describes how a series of direct lessons were effective in teaching some critical listening skills to intermediate grade pupils.

How did this study differ from earlier ones? What were the skills included in the instruction and testing? Do most available textbooks and courses of study include critical listening? Why? For a followup of this study, see the article by Lundsteen cited in Selected References for Part Three. Jacob's article in Part Five is also germane to this topic. The articles by Anderson, Brown, Canfield, Duker, Hoffman, Horrworth, and Lewis all treat different aspects of listening instruction. The article by Petrie takes a point of view quite different from Lundsteen's while the essay "Research Critiques" takes issue with Lundsteen's experiment and her results.

"Children are living, talking records of what we [advertisers] tell them every day." When we are confronted with this quotation from Packard's book, *The Hidden Persuaders*, it makes us feel that something is wrong. When television can be called the giant cookie cutter that shapes children's minds all in the same mold, something is wrong.

That is why we should be concerned with two questions: Can children be taught to listen critically, and can the results of this teaching be measured objectively? This report first examines assumptions on which answers to those questions are based. Then it describes an experimental study on testing and teaching critical listening abilities.

From *Elementary English* 41:743-747; 752; November 1964. Reprinted with permission of the National Council of Teachers of English and Sara W. Lundsteen, Associate Professor, University of Texas, Austin. Copyright, Sara W. Lundsteen, 1964.

Underlying Assumptions

Although investigators have only begun to explore listening, recently called the master key to all the language arts, there is agreement on these assumptions: (1) There is an identifiable factor of listening comprehension. Moreover, it can be tested objectively. It is distinguishable from other language factors, such as reading and verbal mental ability. (2) The process of critical listening has been observed in children, even pre-school children, although it may be restricted by lack of knowledge and experience. (3) Hoping for natural growth in listening abilities is not enough for our day and age. Just as systematic instruction is necessary in reading, so systematic instruction is necessary also in listening.

Background of Related Studies—Testing

Those assumptions are supported by evidence from research, such as the following. In 1953 Caffrey was not satisfied with proclamations from leading authorities that a distinguishable listening factor existed. Instead, he did a factor analysis of scores from a group of listening and related tests. He used correlations obtained from scores on his experimental test of general listening ability, the *California Auding Test,* the reading portion from the *Iowa Tests of Educational Development,* and the *Otis Quick Scoring* test of mental ability. His test of listening measured vocabulary, direction following, and lecture comprehension. Using data from a sub-sample of 287 students, he did find a separate listening factor. Moreover, he concluded that whether the test was taped or presented orally, listening ability could be objectively, reliably, and validly measured. Further, if he added mental and chronological age to *reading* ability, the composite score would predict *listening* ability with only 30 per cent efficiency.

To this evidence indicating the value of testing listening, was added further assurance of a distinguishable listening factor from an impressive study by Spearritt. In 1961 he used 10 classes of sixth-grade pupils in Australia and correlations from their scores on 34 measures of listening, reading, thinking, memory, and attention. What were a few conclusions? (1) Again, a separate listening comprehension factor was found in the listening tests. (2) He found no close relationship between attention and listening. (3) Children who did well on reading and reasoning tests and who could remember long sequences of symbols tended to do well on tests of listening comprehension.

Among Spearritt's measuring instruments was the *STEP Listening* test. Since this is the only nationally standardized test designed specifically to test listening comprehension of upper elementary school children, it warrants careful attention. This test measures a wide variety of skills: from plain-sense or literal comprehension to interpretation, application, and evaluation. There are four forms designed for fourth grade through college.

Hailed in 1958, the *STEP Listening* test has recently been under criticism as to its validity. Some items appear to be guessed readily by pupils who have not heard the selection on which the item is based. Other experimenters complain that the test is too long and possibly too easy.

Besides this standardized test of listening, there are at least four other experimental tests for the upper elementary grades that have reported statistical data (Young 1936, Pratt 1953, Wilson 1955, Biggins 1961). Finally, in 1958 and in 1961 two attempts to measure specifically *critical* listening were made by West and by Devine; but both were above elementary school level. The test reliabilities on the experimental tests just mentioned range from .64 to .91. From experimental listening tests at all grade levels, the correlations between listening, and reading and mental ability scores range from .22 to .81. Again, the correlations suggest a separate listening factor. Moreover, low subtest correlations tend to demonstrate differing listening abilities, including critical listening abilities.

Thus, there appears to be research to support the first assumption, the possibility of testing listening. But, what evidence exists to support the second assumption: What evidence exists that elementary school children can perform the demanding process of critical listening—a highly conscious process involving analysis, a questioning attitude, and keeping a standard in mind while judging? There is evidence in the area of critical reading. But there is other discussion that it is more difficult to *listen* critically than it is to read critically. Fortunately, the present study demonstrated that fifth- and sixth-grade pupils could perform the critical listening process.

Background of Related Studies—Teaching

Next, if critical listening exists, is within the grasp of children and can be measured, what evidence supports the third assumption, that it improves with instruction? At the upper elementary level, some representative studies in the teaching of listening abilities have been done by Pratt (1953), Hogan (1953) and Edgar (1961). In all these studies significant gains were made by the group having training, while the group having no training made little or no gain. The present investigation belongs in this category.

The Present Study

In a "world of many opinions and propagandas," augmented by television, authorities have urged experimentation in teaching critical listening to children.

Evidence from child growth and development studies implies that the upper elementary grades may be a crucial point for such instruction. Based on the studies of listening just mentioned, the following experimentation, sponsored by David H. Russell at the University of California, was conducted in 1963.

First, what was done? The initial hurdle was to choose from a variety of definitions of critical listening. In this study, critical listening was defined as the process of examining spoken materials in light of related, objective evidence, comparing the ideas with some standard or consensus, and then concluding or acting upon the judgment made. By this definition, it was a highly conscious, judging process. It involved not only a questioning attitude and analysis but also judgment. Earlier studies frequently stopped at "analysis" in the testing and teaching without proceeding to the "judgment" process. For example, the pupil might be led to analyze and detect the propaganda device, say, "name calling," in a "litterbug" campaign, or when a pupil is labeled "chicken" or a teacher, "communist." But no effort might be made to guide the next step: the use of a standard and the attempt to judge the propaganda as "useful," "harmless," or "injurious."

The sample for the experiment included almost 300 fifth- and sixth-grade pupils in a large Texas city. The twelve volunteer classes were randomly assigned to experimental and control groups. Measures of reading, general and critical listening, critical thinking through reading and mental ability showed no significant differences between the groups before instruction. The total sample scored well above average in mental ability and academic skills. Children recently arrived from many parts of the country were in the sample.

Derived from a survey of related literature and two years of empirical observation of pilot classes, 18 lessons were developed to teach critical listening. Lessons were given to the experimental group twice a week during a 40-minute period. The control group followed the usual English curriculum.

The first three weeks of lessons taught detection of a speaker's purpose. Pupils were led to analyze and to discover standards for judging a speaker's main purpose as humorous, factual, or persuasive. The lessons were organized to a large extent in program form, broken into small steps made up of a developing series of examples, prompts, and questions. If the pupils could not answer the questions, additional examples and "back-tracking" routes were frequently provided for the teacher.

Growing out of the speaker's persuasive purpose, the next three weeks dealt with propaganda. Pupils made individual and class investigations to test the hypothesis that "advertisers use many tricks of propaganda to sell their products, but present few facts."

The last three weeks dealt with the analysis and judgment of strong and weak arguments. Fallacies, such as using false cause, misusing expert opinion, and appealing to ignorance were discovered by the pupils. Finally, in order to point up the complexity rather than the dichotomy of most topics, a debate was held. This activity involved taped discussion and switching of sides.

The test of critical listening, developed by the experimenter, was administered on tape by the teachers as a pre- and post-test. Using electrographic pencils, pupils marked their answers on mark sense cards, a fully automatic device. No reading was involved. The test, 79 items, measured detection of the speaker's purpose, analysis and judgment of propaganda and arguments. Within the test, standards by which to judge were given to the pupil. For example, the first part of the standard for judging propaganda instructed the pupil to judge the propaganda selection as "bad" if the evidence in the selection showed: (1) that it was a lie, or (2) that it was harmful to physical or mental health. A sample test item follows. First the selection is given, then the question and multiple choices.

> Here is an actual criticism from a noted newspaper, dealing with a new movie, quote: "The movie, *Torrid Jungle,* is a magnificent *flop.*" Here is a speaker now, giving an advertisement. "Be sure to see the great movie, *Torrid Jungle.* A noted newspaper says, 'it's magnificent.' "
>
> Question 47: What method is the speaker using to persuade you?
> 1. Makes you want to do as other plain, average folks, as most of us do?
> 2. Has a famous person talk or give a testimonial in favor of the movie?
> 3. Repeats words and phrases over and over and over.
> 4. On purpose, the advertiser gave you only a part of the facts, a part of the quotation?
>
> Question 48: Using just the evidence given in the selection and using the standard given you, how would you judge this propaganda?
>   1. bad   2. harmless   3. good
>
> Question 49: Because:
> 1. Giving you only a part of the quotation, in this case, adds up to a lie.
> 2. Anything is fair in advertising as long as it sells your product.
> 3. It was a very clever way to get back at the critic, who may have been just an old fussbudget.

Moreover, each week data were collected from pupils and teachers on check sheets. They evaluated transfer of the lessons to other in-school and out-of-school activities and the programmed lessons themselves.

The Findings

1. The lessons were effective in improving listening abilities. The analysis of variance test showed a significant difference between the experimental and control groups at the .01 level.

2. Test data showed that critical listening scores for the sixth grade surpassed significantly the fifth grade.

3. The girls appeared to be slightly better critical listeners than the boys. A significant difference was found at the .05 level.

4. In evaluation of the test of critical listening, the test-retest method produced a reliability coefficient of .72. As evidence of test validity, opinions of judges, item analysis, and factor analysis appeared to indicate a satisfactory instrument. By factor analysis, based upon the intercorrelations of 16 test variables, four components were identified within the critical listening test. According to logical content, these factors were labeled: (1) General Analysis and Inference, (2) Value Judgment in Regard to Propaganda, (3) Factual Judgment in Regard to Arguments, and (4) Reasons for Fallacies in Arguments. The factors gave further assurance of a critical listening process and abilities.

Correlations Between Scores on the Lundsteen
Test of Critical Listening and Other
Experimental Variables
(N = 263)

The Pratt test of general listening	.64
The Hendrickson test of critical thinking	.52
The Stanford Achievement Test, Form N, total reading	.47
The California Test of Mental Maturity, Form E,	
Total: Verbal and Non-Verbal	.39
Verbal	.43
Non-Verbal	.26

In addition, the correlations of the scores on critical listening with other measures can be seen on this table. Ranging from .26 to .64, they are close to those found by another investigator, Devine. The relationships are positive and substantial, but are not so close as to refute the existence of critical listening abilities.

5. In evaluation of the lessons for teaching critical listening, the results of the content analysis of weekly pupil and teacher reports showed substantial evidence of transfer and the generally satisfactory nature of the lessons. For example, out of 50 reports, teachers indicated transfer from the lessons to other in-school and out-of-school activities on 90 per cent of the reports. The following comments from pupils reveal transfer.

Says one: "After the lessons, many TV commercials sound so stupid now. For example, you know that bread-tearing test on TV. . . ."

Another pupil commented: "Now I can decide better whether things are a fact or not. I listened critically to a man at the fair and. . . ."

Yet another commented: "I can see that many of my arguments with my brother and sister are weak. Instead of sticking to the point and getting facts, I just call them names, like, 'you cootie.' "

A teacher reported: "They've got it. By themselves, they decided they needed to set up a standard judging their storytellers for the younger grades."

Implications

This study has two main implications: (1) It is time to begin a more scientific, systematic, and developmental approach to the teaching of critical listening. A word of caution: this does not have to be an isolated attack. Rather, it should be an integrated one commingling all the language arts. (2) Long-range planning is needed, spiraling through the elementary school with varied teaching strategies and devices. In this study, devices such as the following helped: role playing to illustrate attitudes and fallacies, partner practice in judging examples, abstraction ladders, and a rumor clinic.

Conclusion

It has been demonstrated that given appropriate experiences and materials, the elementary school pupil has considerable ability to improve his critical listening. If this is a generation plagued with the dilemma of unconscious conformity created by mass media, if this is a generation confounded by the problems of "when to listen, what to listen to, and how to listen"—what exactly can we as language teachers do? The theme of this convention, a re-thinking of the English curriculum, offers us a summons, a challenge, and an opportunity to give children critical listening power.

Bibliography

Biggins, Mildred E., "A Comparison of Listening Comprehension and Reading Comprehension in Second and Third Grades," *The Teachers College Journal*, 33:54-55, December, 1961.

Caffrey, J. G., "Auding Ability as a Function of Certain Psychometric Variables," unpublished doctoral dissertation, University of California, Berkeley, 1953.

Devine, T. G., "The Development and Evaluation of a Series of Recordings for Teaching Certain Critical Listening Abilities," unpublished doctoral dissertation, Boston University, 1961.

Edgar, K. F., "The Validation of Four Methods of Improving Listening Ability," unpublished doctoral dissertation, University of Pittsburgh, 1961.

Hogan, Ursula, "An Experiment in Improving the Listening Skills of Fifth and Sixth Grade Pupils," M. A. Seminar Study, University of California, 1953.

Packard, V., *The Hidden Persuaders*, David McKay, New York, 1957.

Pratt, L. E., "The Experimental Evaluation of a Program for the Improvement of Listening in the Elementary School," unpublished doctoral dissertation, State University of Iowa, 1953.

Spearritt, D., "A Factorial Analysis of Listening Comprehension," unpublished doctoral dissertation, Harvard, 1961.

West, Dorothy A., "Report of Progress Toward the Experimental Development of an Elementary Evaluative Listening Test," master's thesis, South Dakota State College, Brookings, 1958.

Wilson, A. R., "Construction and Evaluation of a Test of Listening Abilities for the Third Through Sixth Grades," master's thesis, University of California, Berkeley, 1955.

Young, W. E., "The Relation of Reading Comprehension and Retention to Hearing Comprehension and Retention," *Journal of Experimental Education*, 5:30-39, 1936.

19   Oral Reporting

Lucille Millsap

*Oral expre sion—listening and speaking—is a skill whose value and potential
can be realized only if it is an integral part of the on-going, purposeful activities
of every curricular area and if its use permeates the school day. This essay gives
a series of concrete suggestions for improving oral reporting and increasing
pupils' interest in a curricular area by making speaking-listening activities more
meaningful, functional experiences.*

*How can language arts instruction be correlated with subject-matter fields
to the benefit of each? This article is aimed at grade three and above; what can
primary grade teachers do to lay a firm foundation for such activities? How
does this article relate to Mackintosh's introductory article in Part One? Would
Millsap's suggestions be more likely to prevent or to contribute to the errors
catalogued by DeLawter and Eash in an earlier article in this part of the anthology? Articles by Bloom, Munkres, and Ogilvie listed in Selected References
for Part Three all expand related aspects of this topic while those by Bany, Cox
and Hughes, and Crocker all describe unique ways to use and improve oral
language as a by-product of other activities. For a view of the treatment of
speech and listening in elementary school language textbooks, see K. Brown.*

When fully exploited in the classroom, oral reporting offers an abundance
of multiple, desirable learnings. Surely a proper place for the beginning of
improvement would be a thoughtful examination of the objectives for oral
reporting. These objectives in general terms would appear to be: (1) to provide
an opportunity for an individual pupil to share important and pertinent information with his classmates; (2) to give pupils a sense of responsibility for and a
satisfaction in obtaining and sharing such information with their classmates;
(3) to provide pupils with opportunities for cooperative problem solving, using
relevant information and utilizing purposes that are real and important to the
individual and to the class; (4) to teach the skills of research and a careful

From *Elementary English* 35:197-200; February 1965. Reprinted with permission of
the National Council of Teachers f English and Lucille Millsap, Professor of Education,
Oregon College of Education, Monmouth.

evaluation of relevant data in the preparation of a report; (5) to provide children with purposeful activities designed to improve oral language skills; (6) to provide the listeners with opportunities in learning to listen critically and appreciatively and, after the report has been concluded, of participating thoughtfully in a worthwhile discussion concerning the material presented.

When careful planning and effort have gone into a determined pursuit of these goals, many gratifying results are almost certain to occur. Observation and experience suggest that by directing attention and effort to certain fundamental procedures, much can be done to enliven and vitalize oral reporting especially in social studies and science.

Research has shown that children often do not like social studies, yet investigation reveals that they have a keen interest in the general content of the social studies.[1, 2, 3, 4] This apparent inconsistency implies that the difficulty lies with the way the social studies are taught.[5] It seems reasonable that one significant way of improvement could be made in oral reports. Some suggestions for improving such reports are offered here.

1. The pupil who is to report and those who are to listen should know how or where the individual's special report topic fits into the broad scheme of the unit or problem being studied. This means that before committees are organized, the class should acquire some general understanding of the entire area to be studied. A few filmstrips, a film or two, some assigned readings, class discussions, perhaps a resource person—these may suffice to give children an overview of the unit. A pupil can neither intelligently select report subjects, prepare and give an effective report, nor can others listen intelligently unless the class possesses a reasonably comprehensive understanding of the broad outlines of the chosen unit or problem.

2. The individual child should have a clear idea of how his topic is a part of the subject his committee has chosen. The teacher should not assume that such knowledge is automatic when a pupil selects to become a member of a particular committee.

3. Children should be given much directed, detailed practice and supervision in the preparation of a report. Some of this preparation should be done prior to the organization of committees and should be carried out as an activity involving the whole group. It hardly seems necessary to add that the preparation of a worthwhile report is a skill, and one or two class periods given to the problem will not go far in helping children acquire proficiency in it. Therefore, periodically throughout the year the teacher should devote time and effort toward helping children improve in their ability to construct a good report. They should be shown in detail, by participating in the activity, exactly what constitutes a fine report. They should be especially urged and shown how to apply such knowledge in preparation of individual reports to the class.

4. Children of elementary school age should be encouraged to use, if mate-

rials are available, at least two sources of information for their reports—and *the encyclopedia should not be one of these sources*. As teachers well know, when children are preparing a report they almost invariably turn to the encyclopedia whence they copy word for word gobs of material they often cannot read or fully understand. Therefore, they should use the encyclopedia only as a last resort when other materials do not offer needed information on the topic, and special help should be given in assuring their understanding of their material.

5. Moreover, children should present in a report only information they themselves understand. It seems a foregone conclusion that if the child reporting does not understand what he is talking about, neither will his classmates understand. Holding children to such a standard means that reports will probably be somewhat shorter than usual, but this is no loss if the teacher reminds himself of what his goals really are for children's reports.

6. Children should practice their reports before they appear in front of the group. No child should be permitted to stand before his class and read or attempt to read in an inaudible or incoherent manner the contents of his report. To allow a pupil to perform in any such way is to cheat him and his classmates and to blight the possibilities in the learning situation.

The teacher may exclaim that he does not have time to hear each individual practice his report. He may not have time to hear him as he obtains all the practice he needs, but the teacher can have read his report and offered suggestions if any are needed on its contents. In addition, he can and should see to it that the members of a committee practice and evaluate their reports among themselves. If teachers are tempted to protest that in the crowded daily schedule there just is not time for the practice of oral reports, it can only be maintained that if the justifiable goals of oral reporting are to be attained, then time must be taken for thorough preparation. One report prepared and presented well is worth a dozen of the other kind.

7. Pupils and their teachers should cooperatively establish criteria for a good report. Almost intuitively children seem to know the chief elements of effective reporting, and they are often amazingly verbal about them. The children's suggestions will cover most of the salient features, but it is always the teacher's responsibility to offer others he recognizes as important.

These criteria should be thoroughly discussed before any reports are given and, once determined upon, such criteria should be summarized. They should be few rather than numerous and should be succinctly stated. Moreover, they should be made into a chart. (Individual copies of such standards might be dittoed and given pupils.) The chart should be visible to all, and the criteria set forth on it should be referred to frequently when preparation for reporting gets underway. Too many times, it would seem, class standards are proposed but are often shunted aside and more or less forgotten. Children should not be permitted to forget that these standards are guides, and efforts should be made to follow them. Most children thoroughly enjoy trying to live up to certain attainable goals once they know what is expected of them.

The criteria set up should include not only those for content but for the presentation as well. If the criteria chosen are appropriate and if the children have had a hand in establishing the standards, the class as a whole will feel itself committed to such standards. Under those circumstances individuals tend to feel keenly the sense of commitment to the group and as a result strive to reach the class-formulated goals.

8. In the process of preparing a report, every pupil should be expected to supplement his report with some audio-visual aid in the form of graphs, or charts, maps, pictures, models, realia, filmstrips, films, murals, and so on to accompany and enhance the information he seeks to impart. Such supplementary aids may sometimes consist of no more than two or three pictures in a book previously located and easily found. One teacher recommends that children begin early in the preparation of a report collecting in a large envelope materials which heighten their reports.[6]

In addition, committees as a group should be encouraged to present their reports in a variety of ways such as dramatizations, panels, interview techniques, and other even more imaginative ways.

9. When a pupil presents a report, all children should be expected to sit quietly with a semblance of attention. Although no teacher can compel a child to listen, the child can at least sit reasonably quietly so that he does not interfere with those who are listening. The class members, for example, should not be permitted to turn the pages of a magazine, read a storybook, play with clay, or occupy themselves with similar activities while another member is reporting. In general, desks should be cleared although there seems no reason to object to simple doodling during a report. Moreover, some teachers may wish pupils to record some brief notes.

10. Children should tell the main points of their reports rather than read them. If one of the significant objectives of oral reports is that of sharing information which contributes to the solution of the class problem, it must be recognized that such information presented in a clear and interesting manner will be more readily applicable, longer remembered, and more impressive if it is told rather than read. At any rate, children should be encouraged to read only parts, if any. No teacher, however, should deny a child the opportunity to have his written report with him as he stands before the group. He should feel free to turn to it and should not feel ill at ease if he forgets. The specific, direct, and supervised help mentioned earlier in the preparation of a report should include instruction in making and using a brief outline.

11. Pupils should write on the chalkboard or present on a chart the unusual but highly pertinent vocabulary and concepts especially peculiar to their

reports. These need not be defined on the board or chart, but they should be explained in the course of the report.

12. The pupil who is to report should expect to conduct a discussion following the report he has given. When his report is concluded, he should call for questions and comments. He and he alone should be in charge of this discussion. The kind of questions and comments which will be offered depend upon the pattern of questions and comments the teacher initiates at this point. Children are quick to sense the nature and kind of responses the teacher makes and to follow his lead in developing worthwhile comments and questions.

13. The pupil's report should be evaluated by the teacher and the children.[7] Here again the teacher sets the trend for the kind of evaluation he wishes. Children should be praised for what is genuinely praiseworthy, and they should be told in a kindly and objective manner ways in which their reports might be improved.

14. Teachers should make use of summarizing activities at the end of the report and discussion. These may be brief and cooperative endeavors of the class or they may be a short summary given by the child who is reporting.

15. When a report has been given, the teacher should be alert to opportunities for further utilization of the information presented. This not only serves to reinforce the learnings gained but it also serves to emphasize the importance attached to oral reporting. (All too often when a report has been given, the "giving" is the end of the matter.) Also, from time to time a child should feel an obligation to seek further information on some of the questions raised following his report. In any case, when the report has been presented, it should be carefully copied and placed in an individual, committee, or class booklet. This booklet may be attractively decorated, and it should be available as a reference or for browsing.

The opportunities for learning which lie inherent in well-organized, well-presented, and adequately understood oral reports are many. Time and effort expended in helping children make the most of these learning activities can surely convert oral reporting into one of the most valuable classroom procedures.

Footnotes

[1] Robert L. Curry, "Subject Preferences of Fifth-Grade Children." *Peabody Journal of Education*, 41:23-27, July, 1963.

[2] Charles A. Harper, "Why Do Children Dislike History?" *Social Education*, 1:492-494, October, 1937.

[3] Wayne L. Herman, Jr., "How Intermediate Children Rank the Subjects." *The Journal of Educational Research*. 56:435-436, April, 1963.

[4] Arthur T. Jersild and Ruth J. Tasch, *Children's Interests and What They Suggest for Education*. New York: Bureau of Publications, Teachers College, Columbia University, 1949, pp. 27-36.

⁵ Richard E. Gross, "Social Studies." *Encyclopedia of Educational Research*, Chester W. Harris, ed. Third Edition. New York: The Macmillan Company, 1960, p. 1305.

⁶ Edith F. Miller, "Stimulate Reading with Individual Research Projects." *Grade Teacher*, 79:28-29, 84-85, December, 1961.

⁷ John Jarolimek, *Social Studies in Elementary Education*. New York: The Macmillan Company, 1967, pp. 221-222.

20 The Speech Handicapped Child in the Classroom

Virgil A. Anderson

*Even though children with certain types of speech defects are frequently seg-
regated for special instruction, they still spend the major part of their school
day in regular classrooms. This demands classroom teachers who are empathetic
with these children, who know how to assist the special teachers, and who are
prepared to shoulder a large part of the instructional burden. This essay, by a
recognized authority in speech education, deals with these topics and reflects
his point-of-view as expressed in greater detail in* Improving the Child's Speech,
New York: Oxford University Press, 1953.

*To what extent do you believe classroom teachers should try to diagnose
the causes of speech disorders? Why is the development of social and emotional
maturity so important with a speech handicapped child? What are some undesirable ways of dealing with speech handicapped children, not mentioned by
Anderson, that unwary teachers may fall prey to? For additional ideas on dealing with children with speech problems in the regular classroom, see the articles
by Emerick, Hollingsworth, and Leutenegger cited in Selected References for
Part Three.*

There is little question that the ultimate salvation of the child with a serious
speech handicap rests with the specialist in speech correction. It is not conceivable that the average classroom teacher will ever be able to acquire a sufficient
background in this relatively complicated and technical field to enable her to
deal satisfactorily with the more severe types of speech and hearing disorders
found among the public school population. The specialist we must have, but
the specialist alone is not enough.

In the first place, the problem as a whole is too extensive. The results of
actual surveys lend credence to the estimate that at least 10 per cent of the

From *Education* 77:103-107; October 1965. Reprinted from the October, 1965, issue of
Education. Copyright, 1965, by the Bobbs-Merrill Company, Inc., Indianapolis, Indiana.
Virgil A. Anderson is Professor Emeritus, Stanford University, Palo Alto, California.

elementary- and secondary-school population suffer from speech deficiencies sufficiently serious to be classed as speech defects. This would mean approximately 2,500,000 speech-defective school-age children in the United States— over 40,000 in a city the size of Los Angeles, for example. It is highly unlikely that within the foreseeable future a sufficient supply of specialists in speech correction will be available to take care of this large number of children who need help. The responsibility for the ultimate welfare of the major portion of these speech handicapped children must rest with the classroom teacher.

Even if there were enough speech therapists to give specialized help to all of the large number of children needing it, this in itself is not enough. It is difficult and, to a degree, futile to attempt to teach a skill or an ability in a situation apart from that in which the skill is eventually to be used. It is not enough that the speech correction teacher gets the child to the place where he can speak adequately in the carefully controlled and restricted environment provided by the short meeting once or twice each week which her crowded schedule makes possible. This is no guarantee that the child will use his newly acquired good speech when he goes back to the classroom or goes home after school. The person best qualified and most strategically situated to assist the child in this "carry-over" of his good speech habits into real-life situations is the classroom teacher, since she is with the child throughout a large portion of his day and can thus control and supervise many of his activities in which speech is used.

The responsibilities of the classroom teacher must extend beyond merely assisting the special teacher, however. She must be prepared to do a great deal of constructive speech teaching herself in connection with the normal curricular and extra-curricular activities in which speech plays a part, or can be made to play a part. It must be remembered that speech, as a basic function of the individual, cannot be separated from his other activities. Speech training must be an integral part of normal and everyday uses of speech, in situations in which speech skills function as means to an end, not merely as "exercises" to be done in a special "lesson." Speech training, including much of speech correction, must be integrated, to use an over-worked term, into other activities of the curriculum, particularly those portions of it known as the language arts. Thus, the classroom teacher acquires a responsibility for the speech welfare of her pupils —a responsibility that cannot be shrugged off nor successfully delegated, even to the special speech teacher. And in those areas in which there is no special teacher, or at least not enough to go around, the classroom teacher represents virtually the only hope for the child handicapped in speech.

To what extent can the teacher deal successfully with the average run of speech problems found in the schools? With a minimum basic knowledge of speech defects and speech correction, the answer is, more than one would think. Fortunately, most speech defects found among the school population are not particularly complicated or deep-seated, and a large proportion of them respond readily to intelligent handling, especially if dealt with in time. Only about 15 per cent of the defects have any structural basis, and only approximately 25 per cent could be called involved, complicated, or difficult to correct. The implications are obvious—in the majority of cases of speech defects found among school children there is nothing "wrong" with the speech mechanism and a large percentage of them are correctible if (a) they are recognized in time, and (b) the proper methods are used.

One point should be made clear, however—there is still a sizeable number of speech defects which are really complicated and require highly specialized knowledge and skills on the part of a well trained therapist. Training given to the classroom teacher, therefore, should make clear to her her limitations as a speech therapist and should teach her where to turn for help when she discovers a case she is not equipped to handle herself.

One of the first responsibilities of the teacher is, of course, to recognize a speech defect when she hears one, so that she can either deal with it herself or refer the child to someone who can. The teacher will be aided in this process if she is aware of the categories into which speech deficiencies fall and is familiar with the chief identifying characteristics of each. On the basis of symptoms, or the way speech sounds, speech defects can be classified as: (1) phonatory, or voice defects, such as hoarseness, nasality, breathiness, or too-high pitch; (2) articulatory, or defects in the production of speech sounds, such as occurs in lisping, the omission of sounds or the substitution of one for another, or in regional or foreign dialect; (3) linguistic, or language disorders, in which the individual cannot express himself because he has lost, or has never had, the necessary command of words; and (4) defects of rhythm, of which stuttering is the prime example.

Except for certain types of nasality, voice defects are likely to be relatively complicated and involved, and there is always the possibility that certain voice quality disorders such as hoarseness may have a serious physical basis. For this reason the teacher would be well advised to refer children with such problems to a physician or a speech therapist or both. It is with problems involving articulation that the classroom teacher can accomplish the most, although she can often be of great help to the child exhibiting symptoms of stuttering as well as to the child whose language development is retarded.

One of the first steps in the treatment of speech disorders is to determine the cause, or causes, of the condition with a view toward eliminating or alleviating them. The possibility that a speech deficiency may have a physiological or structural basis should never be overlooked by the teacher. Articulatory disorders, for example, can be caused by malocclusions and dental irregularities, or by hearing loss, or certain forms of paralysis. Voice defects may result from infection or structural irregularities in the larynx, from cleft palate, or paralyzed velum. Many of these conditions are remediable, and the teacher should be alert to the advisability of having the child examined by such specialists as the orthodontist, the otologist or audiologist, and the pediatrician, if there is the least indication that the speech problem is physically based. It is always discouraging, often futile, and sometimes dangerous to attempt to deal with speech and voice defects if there is a physical cause still operating.

Other possible causes of a wide variety of speech and voice disorders are mental retardation and emotional maladjustment. If these conditions are suspected, the teacher should seek help from the psychologist or psychiatrist before attempting to deal with the situation herself. As was mentioned earlier, however, many speech deviations result from nothing more serious than poor speech models in the home, poor methods of training on the part of the parents, or from other causes that often remain obscure. In these cases the teacher can often accomplish much to improve the speech, and thus head off what might become a much more serious problem later if allowed to persist. Even when other serious conditions exist to cause or complicate the speech problem, the teacher can often render invaluable service to the child and his parents by instilling healthy attitudes toward the handicap in the child and his parents, relieving anxieties and tensions, and enhancing the child's environment at school by improving the attitudes of his playmates toward him and thus modifying their behavior. All that is needed is some recognition of the problem and the application of common sense and certain basic principles of mental hygiene and good counseling.

Along the line of the above, it is well known that symptoms of personality and emotional maladjustment are found much more frequently among speech defectives than among normal speakers. Whether the maladjustment has caused the speech defect, or whether the opposite, or some other, relationship is true, cannot always be readily determined. More important—the teacher should recognize the presence of the maladjustment and the importance of dealing with it if the child is to be helped with his speech problem. There is often much the teacher can do for such a child within the limitations of her background of training and the routines of the school environment.

Perhaps one of the most constructive steps she can take is to assist the child in developing social and emotional maturity. The parental attitude and pattern of behavior that emerges most clearly from environmental studies of children with certain types of speech problems, especially delayed speech and stuttering, is that of over-protection and over-supervision, which, of course, amounts to a form of parental domination. The effect upon the child is to keep him dependent and immature, perhaps with marked feelings of inferiority and insecurity. Such attitudes and behavior patterns very easily manifest themselves in certain speech and language deviations. The role of the teacher here is to counteract, as best she can, whatever detrimental influences there may have been at home. Many suggestions will occur to her of ways in which she can assist the child in developing self-confidence, social competence, and emotional maturity. Through encouraging the child to participate in school activities, assisting him in developing his strong points through hobbies, special interests and abilities, and assuring the child that the teacher has a genuine, sympathetic interest in him and holds out high hopes for him, she can do much to help the child mature and assume his normal place and responsibilities. This may be more important, especially in the lower grades, than more formalized speech training, although often both approaches must be followed simultaneously.

Much of what was said in the previous paragraph applies with considerable aptness to the child who stutters. Such an individual characteristically suffers from feelings of embarrassment, apprehension, personal inferiority, and social inadequacy. Anything that can be done, therefore, to "build him up," both in his own and his classmates' estimation will be all to the good. More specific suggestions for assisting the stutterer in the classroom are presented in the following paragraphs:

1. Relieve the child's apprehensions by pointing out to him that his speech isn't as bad as it seems to him. Remind him that other people often hesitate in their speech and "hem and haw" and think nothing of it. He should not be ashamed of his speech nor try to hide his trouble or cover up when he does have some difficulty; such attempts at avoiding stuttering may well make his speech worse. He must accept his problem, do the best he can, emphasize his strong points, and develop a healthy attitude toward himself and others. This approach should be followed, of course, only if the child is old enough to be aware of his problem and to understand the applicability of these points. With the younger child the approach must be much more indirect, and nothing should be done that will center the child's attention directly on his problem.

2. Everything feasible should be done to insure the most desirable attitudes and responses toward the stutterer on the part of his classmates. Perhaps a heart-to-heart talk with some of them will show them that they are only making matters worse when they laugh at the stutterer or make fun of him, treat him with pity or curiosity, or in any other way single him out as being different from any of the rest.

3. The teacher should set the stuttering child a good example by being poised and unhurried herself. Make it clear to him by example, as well as precept, that there is no need to hurry, that there is plenty of time to say what he has to say, and that no one is going to interrupt or grow impatient.

4. One of the most pressing problems facing the teacher of a stuttering child is whether to excuse him from oral recitations or put him through the regular routine with the rest of the pupils. There are disadvantages either way, but, in general, some concessions and special arrangements are usually necessary if the best interests of the child are to be served. The teacher should remember that any speech experience the stutterer can handle with reasonable

success will benefit him and add to his feelings of self-confidence, but any situation in which he fails and stutters badly will only increase his dread of speaking and his anticipation of failure in the future. Therefore the child should be encouraged to participate in those situations that offer the most promise of success. In this the child may be a better judge than the teacher, and therefore he should be encouraged to volunteer at such times as he feels he can manage adequately. In the end, the common sense and good judgment of the teacher must prevail, rather than a blind adherence to an arbitrary practice. The final guide is to do the thing that is most likely to benefit the child most in the end.

Finally, the teacher should keep in mind that of all the language arts, oral communication is the most vital for the child, especially in the lower grades, since it is through aural comprehension and oral expression that he functions in the learning situation. A child with a speech defect suffers from a basic handicap that may well function to retard him in all of his school work. To take reading as one example—there is considerable evidence to indicate that a child with a speech problem will present more reading deficiencies and will make slower progress than a child whose speech is normal. Stutterers have been found to be retarded from one to three grades in their general school development although they are the equal of normal speakers in intelligence.

The teacher has a serious responsibility, therefore, to do everything she can to help the child overcome his speech handicap before it can exert its adverse influence on his school progress, his social maturation, and his personality development. Without highly formalized training in speech correction, she will see many opportunities for assisting such a child in developing better attitudes and a more effective personality generally and for helping him improve his oral communication through attention to basic principles of good speech as the opportunities are presented in connection with the integral, as well as peripheral, activities of the school curriculum.

Bibliography

Anderson, Virgil A., *Improving the Child's Speech*, Oxford University Press, New York, 1953.

Beasley, Jane, *Slow to Talk*, Bureau of Publications, Teachers College, Columbia University, New York, 1956.

Irwin, John and Duffy, John, *Speech and Hearing Hurdles*, School and College Service, Columbus, Ohio, 1951.

Irwin, Ruth Beckey, *Speech and Hearing Therapy*, Prentice-Hall, Inc., New York, 1953.

Johnson, Wendell, ed., *Speech Handicapped School Children*, Harper and Brothers, New York, Rev. Ed., 1956.

———, *Speech Problems of Children*, Grune and Stratton, New York, 1950.

Minneapolis Public Schools, Minneapolis, Minnesota, *Speech Correction in Practice*, 1948.

Nebraska State Department of Education, Lincoln, Nebraska, *Speech Development and Correction*, 1955.

Scott, Louise B. and Thompson, J. J., *Talking Time*, Webster Publishing Company, St. Louis, 1951.

Van Riper, Charles and Butler, Katharine G., *Speech in the Elementary Classroom*, Harper and Brothers, New York, 1955.

Part Four

Literature and Creative Writing

Believing that children's literature and creative writing are inherently inter-related, each contributing to and building upon the other, the editors of this anthology have combined into one part articles dealing with these topics.

Just as children are introduced to great figures in history, they should also be acquainted with those stories which form a veritable literary heritage. Children never exposed to this treasure chest may not only be fixated at a low level of literary appreciation but they will have meager vocabularies, be puzzled by phrases such as 'sour grapes,' have restricted perceptions of the awe-inspiring breadth of variety in the world, develop superficial understandings of themselves and their emotions, and miss much of the fun and adventure available in life. In keeping with the supplementary nature of this book, the editors rejected the inclusion of articles which attempt to encapsulate a course in children's literature in some few pages. The question then arose: is a literature program a literature program? Maybe not if it is best suited for the culturally disadvantaged, 'children without.' What material will meet the objectives of the literature program yet appeal to the interest of these children, be readable in spite of their reading deficiencies, overcome some negative, undesirable images they have of themselves and their world, and create some attainable dreams where none now exist? Edman tackles some of these questions in a provocative article.

Arbuthnot's essay treats a significant but frequently neglected component of the literature program—storytelling—in an article which qualifies as both practical and truly supplementary, two important ingredients for inclusion in a book of readings.

McFadden's article on how to run a book fair qualifies as truly supplementary, one criterion for inclusion in this anthology. Textbooks cannot allot the space necessary to describe explicitly activities of this type, no matter how vital the details are to the success of the project or the project to the language arts program. There is a dearth of articles available on special topics; comprehensive, detailed descriptions such as this can produce instructional improvement just as surely as can vast research.

Creativity has received so much recent publicity that it threatens to become a vapid, educational cliché. But it is not important for itself. Its humanizing qualities seem urgently needed in a society that threatens to become increasingly depersonalized and its potential value as a problem-solving technique seems equally valuable to the individual and to society. But it is born and fostered only in an atmosphere currently not prevalent but which can be created if certain steps are taken. Wilt discusses and justifies the need for these steps. Applegate describes some unexpected but significant by-products of children's writing which can occur only under truly creative conditions.

Beginning first grade pupils cannot write, a problem that may seem insurmountable to many first grade teachers and which deters them from attempting creative writing activity. Yet if a curriculum is to be an articulated sequence, creative writing must be started here—and the earlier the better. Dictating stories and experiences to a teacher who records them on paper or charts is the beginning of a series of steps that culminates in independent writing for both functional and expressive purposes. Kelley tells 'how to do it.'

Astute observers of the language arts early realized the intimate relationships existing among all of them. Some of these have been taken advantage of in the classroom but others have languished, their potential unrecognized. Literature and composition are two of the latter. If language is viewed on the basis of an in-put, out-put model, it becomes obvious that children's expression is directly proportional to the amount and quality of linguistic reception. The better the patterns of oral and written language assimilated, the better the speaking and composing. And how better to provide children with incisive, coherent, imagination-stretching models than through immortal selections from children's literature? The articles by Evertts and Endres are similar; both apply this general idea to creative writing although Evertts focuses chiefly on stories while Endres deals only with poetry.

Providing the atmosphere and experiences conducive to creativity are hardly sufficient to produce quality composition; direct instruction is a must. Children must be acutely and accurately aware of their world and describe it precisely; they must use words which make characters and events real and vivid, and they must learn how to spin a cohesive, gripping story. Larom describes how these issues were approached in one sixth grade class. Evans argues that such an approach will result in better and more imaginative composition than any amount of encouragement can give or creative atmosphere can produce.

Poetry has some unique values unattainable through other forms of literature as Endres so ably points out. But it also presents some unusual and difficult compositional challenges not met in teaching other literary forms. By resorting to a unique type of poetry, Scofield was able to produce some outstanding results even with ordinarily reluctant boys.

21   Literature for Children Without

Marion Edman

Because of certain unique characteristics of culturally disadvantaged children, Edman contends they have special literary needs and that some procedures are better than others for introducing these children to and sustaining their interest in literature.

If Edman drew up a list of core books for disadvantaged children, how would it differ from Smith's list given in the article cited in Selected References for Part Four? What books do you know of which seem particularly appropriate for meeting the literary needs of 'children without'? How does this article relate to the one by Cohen in Part Two? The articles by Korey and Neville cited in Selected References for Part Four are also pertinent to this topic. Those by Beghe, Huck, McClelland, Neville, and Thornley also make a major contribution to understanding of the literature program and the role of the teacher.

The title for this paper calls to mind a statement attributed to John Ciardi, "Fools give short answers to long questions." Certainly either "literature for children" or "children without" requires long answers. It becomes increasingly clear as one tries to find published research and to tap the practical experiences of many people (primarily teachers and librarians) who for long years have tried to bring together the children in culturally deprived areas with the books in their libraries and school rooms. The research is pitifully lacking and the reports of experience almost completely contradictory.

This is a not uncommon frustration in our age when we seem to know the answers, but the questions we do not always know. The discussion of this topic, therefore, might most profitably point the way to questions that must be raised before they can be answered. Only rigorous research, highlighted by carefully evaluated practices in dealing with this special group of children and the ways that will lead them to books and reading, can give us the answers we earnestly seek.

This does not discount the honest efforts many conscientious librarians and

From *Library Quarterly* 37:32-45; January 1967. Reprinted from "Literature for Children Without" by Marion Edman, by permission of The University of Chicago Press © 1967 by University of Chicago Press and Marion Edman, Wayne State University, Detroit, Michigan. One footnote has been omitted.

teachers have long been engaged in. Perhaps they were the first to discover what the sociologists and the politicians have recently become excited about: the culturally deprived children in our society. It is they who have really understood the importance of bringing these children into the mainstream of American life, which the politicians and sociologists now believe necessary if this country is to be transformed into the Great Society.

There are numerous, generally well-known, sociological descriptions or definitions of the culturally deprived. It should be pointed out that cultural deprivation is not monolithic. This phenomenon has many faces and many degrees. While there are no exact figures on what proportion of children and youth might fall into the category of general deprivation, it is estimated to be between one-fifth and one-third of all our children. The proportion is expected to increase. Many, but not all, live in the inner core of our large cities. Despite the disadvantages these children may suffer in varying degree, it should be remembered that a considerable number do achieve success in school, graduate from high school (some even go to college), and find a happy place for themselves in adult life. They may find great pleasure in vicarious experiences far beyond their own circumscribed early beginnings, including their pleasure in the use of libraries and books. Because a child grows up in an area where there is no grass, does not mean, *ipso facto*, that he has become incapable of imagining a world that has luscious green fields. Sam Levenson, who grew up in Harlem, has made this point clear in his autobiography *Everything but Money*. Claude Brown, in the story of his childhood in the same city, *Manchild in the Promised Land*, and Betty Smith in *A Tree Grows in Brooklyn* have demonstrated that a degrading sociological and economic environment does not entirely mold the mental and spiritual life of the child. Cultural deprivation may even bring children certain advantages. These children may have seen more of the essential matters of life before they are ten than many more privileged children will see even as adults. Claude Brown speaks of his own experience:

> When I was very young—about five years old, maybe younger—
> I would always be sitting out on the stoop. I remember Mama telling
> me and Carole to sit on the stoop and not to move away from in front
> of the door. Even when it was time to go up and Carole would be pull-
> ing on me to come upstairs and eat, I never wanted to go, because there
> was so much out there in that street.
> You might see somebody get cut or killed. I could go out in the
> street for an afternoon, and I would see so much that, when I came in
> the house, I'd be talking and talking for what seemed like hours. Dad
> would say, "Boy, why don't you stop that lyin'? You know you didn't
> see all that. You know you didn't see nobody do that." But I knew
> I had.[2]

While Claude Brown does not say in his autobiography that he found books an extension or an explanation of the exciting life he was leading, doubtless there are today, in the slums and in the deprived areas in the rural sections of our country, numberless children who are able and eager to accept much of what we have in the way of books and reading to give them. Certainly many of them will look for greater sophistication in books than do usual children of their age. But it is well known that these children are only a part of the total group, perhaps a small minority, and that it is probably most often this minority who come to the minds of teachers and librarians when they discuss the culturally deprived, for these are the successes in the efforts of these workers. Who among us does not like to think about and talk about his successes?

The culturally deprived for whom books and reading might well be completely out of reach are those who are extremely deficient in their ability to use standard English (the ordinary language of books); those whose reading skills are so extremely limited that they have come to regard print as almost an exquisite instrument of torture; those whose lives have been so warped that they cannot think of themselves as anything but failures, in relation to what they believe society really wants of them; those whose relationships with other persons have been so unsatisfactory that they find it difficult, if not impossible, to identify with real human beings, to say nothing of fictional characters. These are the children with whom this paper is concerned. A brief discussion of their handicaps as they seem to relate to the children's ability to understand and to find empathy with literature follows.

Handicaps of Speech

In the area of speech handicaps there is good research. Let me review some of the more significant studies. Two studies by Strickland and Loban have attracted a great deal of attention. The first is a horizontal study, and the second is a longitudinal study of the actual speech patterns of children, using the techniques of modern recording equipment, modern linguistics, and computers. While these studies are not solely concerned with the culturally deprived, they do include children from this segment of society, and thus comparison is possible between them and more favored children.

Strickland found that practically all children in her sample used a wide range of language patterns but that there were differences in their ability to manipulate the variables. Furthermore, ability to use the variables was significantly related to intelligence, mental age, and the occupational status and education of the parents.[3]

Loban's study followed the speech development of some 250 individual cases through thirteen years: kindergarten through twelfth grade. To date two reports of his findings have been published, one for elementary-age children, one for the junior high level.[4] In both reports, Loban established that at all ages studied there was wide variation in children's ability to communicate orally.

This was reflected in the amount of speech used, range of vocabulary, complexity of sentence pattern, fluency, correctness of form, and the occurrence of "language tangles" or mazes. Particularly germane to discussion here are his findings relative to underprivileged children. Negro children, especially those newly emigrated from the South, had a number of peculiar difficulties, but particularly with the verb "to be." Loban concludes, "At the kindergarten level on the omission of auxiliary verbs, the low Negro group had five times as much difficulty as the low Caucasian group and sixteen times as much difficulty as the high Caucasian group."[5]

Loban cites numerous other language patterns where the difficulties of Negro children in using standard English are startling and concludes: "Negro children obviously need to listen and to communicate in situations where they can hear more standard usage—not because standard usage is 'correct' but because standard usage helps to provide access to opportunities and entrance to a wider range of social groups."[6] In other words, Negro children, more than any other group, have special need of becoming familiar with the way English is usually spoken and written.

Loban's study is also useful in establishing a positive relationship between proficiency in oral language and all other areas of the language arts: reading, writing, listening. He makes a plea for considering skill in speaking and listening the cornerstone of skill in writing and particularly in reading; in fact, he insists that the school must give children more help in developing facility in oral speech. He makes a special point concerning the culturally deficient child: "The persistently parallel variation of language proficiency and socio-economic status should not be overlooked. It appears entirely possible that language proficiency may be culturally as well as individually determined. If children reared in families at the least favored socio-economic positions receive a restricted language experience, if their early linguistic environment stresses only limited features of language potential, such children may indeed be at a disadvantage in the years at school and in the ones beyond school."[7]

A study of language involving only culturally deprived children of kindergarten age was made by Dominic Thomas at Wayne State University. Thomas' conclusions were (1) Culturally different children use a smaller number and variety of words to express themselves. They speak in shorter sentences. (2) They use a much larger proportion of incomplete sentences. (3) They use a smaller proportion of mature sentences and elaborate constructions. They tend not to elaborate their ideas. (4) They commit more errors such as verb and subject not in agreement, colloquialisms and slang, omission of auxiliaries, wrong word order, and misuse of prepositions.[8]

Numerous other studies similar in scope to those cited might be cited here, but perhaps these suffice to establish the fact that considerable research indicates that culturally deprived children suffer severe handicaps in their use of

language. Does not this research concerning the importance of the child's learning oral communication suggest that libraries, as well as classrooms, become
places for talking, as well as reading? Does it not mean that storytellling, reading aloud, dramatization, and discussing books in groups become activities of
paramount importance? That all sorts of audio-visual stimulation for talking
precede attempts to motivate reading? Perhaps in children's libraries, at least,
all "Quiet, Please" signs must come down.

The research cited does not mean that culturally deprived children cannot
communicate effectively in their own society. This they do in a kind of dialect that carries all the meaning they wish or need to convey to their listeners.
Linguists insist that for purposes of communication, any system of language
which enables the user to convey meaning is a perfectly permissible form of
speech. The only trouble with deviation from standard language is that it is not
acceptable in all circles and that it often presents barriers to the acceptance of
the deviant speaker. Such is the reception given the speech many children
bring to school. Worse still, the language that these children are asked to
read is not their language and as such cannot establish communication with
them. On many counts, it is almost a foreign tongue: there may be differences
of vocabulary, of usage, of pronunciation, of stress and rhythm. To the children, however, the books are wrong and they themselves are right, because
those individuals who are most important to them use this language.

How to deal with such discrepancies between the language of everyday
communication and the language of books is debatable. There are those who
insist that, particularly for the young child, we must begin by writing for him
in his own tongue. This practice is illustrated in some delightful reading materials prepared for Headstart children in Mississippi. Such sentences as these
are accepted as perfectly normal English: "We been swimming down at the
pond"; "Me and Jane killed that ole snake"; "This fish got a mouth like a big
smile."[9]

How and when to make the transition from this sort of language to the
standard language of literary materials is a subject in need of a great deal of
research. The research now available suggests that much work must be done
with children's oral speech before change becomes easy. Ruth Golden's efforts
in a Detroit high school bears witness to this fact.[10]

It seems important to point out one obstacle in initiating a program of producing and giving the children with deviant language the kind of reading
matter that really communicates with them. This is the intransigent position
taken by those teachers, librarians, and leaders of minority groups who see the
improvement of language as the *sine qua non* of upward mobility and release
from slum status. One linguist of note speaks rather bitingly to teachers on
this point:

There is one subcultural factor which does affect the language development of these children, and it is one which I wish to touch on now. This factor is the set of attitudes toward language held by the teachers whom Allison Davis would call "aspiring middle class"—as many teachers are. These attitudes are partly learned in the school and college training of English teachers with its monolithic fixation on "correct English" as the main proper outcome of education in English and the language arts. It is a fixation so deep that it is not felt as a subject for question: it overrides whatever work in child development, educational psychology, or methods the teacher may have had, even if these have been more enlightened about language than usual. It is a fixation often nourished in the teacher's own sense that only by parting with his origins, learning correct English, and moving out of the neighborhood has he been able to cut himself off from the foreign, rural, or working-class ways of his parents. And it frequently expresses itself as a demonstration of real love and concern for the children, that they, too, should come up and out and away from a manner of life that is poverty-stricken, universally condemned, and dead-ended. Negro teachers especially, insisting that they cannot even understand the children whom they understand only too well, bear down brutally on the divergent phonology, "grammar," and usage of Negro children, communicating their own tension to the construction of the child's ultimate trauma about language. In most instances, all the mores of the school sustain them in this unfortunate practice where they should resist it. The alternative to this overemphasis on conformity to "middle class" speech, too, is unfortunate—the idea that the children are so low on the intelligence scale that their case is hopeless, and that the most the school can do is prepare them for the same manual occupations their parents engage in, keeping them off the streets and out of trouble as long as possible.[11]

In summary, then the language disability of the culturally deprived child affects his use of books, perhaps most *particularly* those of literary value. As Artley points out:

Many children are in a position of learning to attach meaning to a printed symbol when the symbol lies outside their spoken vocabulary; to understand a printed ten-word sentence when normally they speak only a disjointed three-word sentence; to interpret a complex sentence when they have difficulty in using simple ones; to follow the organization of a new story they are trying to read when they are unable to tell in logical order the events in the familiar "Little Red Riding Hood"; to read complete sentences with expression when they are unable to give emphatic expression to their own ideas; to interpret punctuation marks when they attach no significance to gesture, pantomimes and free play.[12]

Do not these studies of the modern linguists, with their insistence that we respect the language of all children, no matter how "bad," and that we learn to regard their speech as legitimate communication, place upon teachers and librarians the responsibility to demand of authors and publishers the kind of language in books which these children really use? Do the studies not further sugggest that we might carefully consider our attitudes toward "proper" language? And, finally, do they not lay upon us the burden of discovering the techniques whereby the gradual transition from "slum" language to "acceptable" norms of speech is accomplished? Does this not all add up to the proposition that we help these children to become, in effect, bilingual?

Handicaps of Poor Reading Skills

It should be noted that for those children who have not mastered the basic reading skills, books of any sort are to be avoided because all they can do is to give the child a sense of shame and defeat. While the contention of modern reading experts that "Johnny really can read" is true, it is equally true that an appalling number of children are so handicapped in reading ability that they must be classed, at best, as semiliterate. In a recent newspaper release of reading levels for a high school in a depressed area of Detroit, the Board of Education indicated that in a graduating class of 260 seniors only 50 were reading at grade level on the standardized reading test given at the school.[13] One might well ask what kinds of books the students in such situations might read with guidance and help from teachers, what sorts of books librarians could beguile them into taking for voluntary and recreational reading. Even though the tests given might not be a fair measure of each child's real ability, and certainly not of his potential as a reader, harm has been done in establishing a label for him as an inadequate reader, of which he himself is more or less painfully aware.

While there is a paucity of research that is truly diagnostic in determining the real causes why the culturally disadvantaged child usually has such tremendous problems in learning to read, one fact seems quite clear and that is, as was pointed out earlier, that he has not begun reading with materials that make sense to him, either in language or in subject matter. He has never looked upon reading in terms of my favorite definition for that complex process—a child's definition: "Reading is talk wrote down."

A reading program in any language, at any stage in a student's career, is likely to be effective to the degree that it parallels the language habits that the student has acquired in speaking. In terms of the language usage of all children in relation to reading, many questions concerning needed research have been raised. One writer in the field lists these: (1) What is the process of learning to read, in linguistic and sociological terms? (2) What is dialectology? (3) What is the general dialectical situation in American English? (4) How does this situation affect the problem of the teacher? (5) How much do we know about regional kinds of dialect differences in American English? How much more can we hope to know? (6) How do these differences as we know them affect the problem of reading in the American dialectical situation?[14]

Has the time now come when the children's librarian, traditionally co-operative with teachers in schools, be provided with an additional staff member: namely, a person trained, not as a librarian, but as an expert who can analyze children's specific reading problems and who can analyze the difficulties that certain types of reading matter give him? In response to a questionnaire the writer sent librarians working with culturally deprived children, over and over the librarians said, "These children need individual help and guidance." However, librarians are not trained as reading specialists. An expert, such as the one proposed, might be able to co-ordinate, more effectively than is now possible, the efforts made by school and library to give children mastery of those basic skills, without which reading of any sort is impossible.

Psychological and Sociological Handicaps

But language is not the only area where the child needs to feel empathy with what he finds in books. Perhaps the psychological and sociological factors involved are far more important than the linguistic ones. The observation has already been made that because of his background the culturally deprived child may be far more sophisticated about some things than are normal children of his age. Are the pictures he sees, the characters he meets, the situations presented ones that he can understand and find meaning and delight in? With such questions in mind, several school systems have taken great pains to prepare special materials for the culturally deprived, sometimes with happy, sometimes with disastrous, results.

One program involving the careful preparation of special reading materials for culturally deprived children in Detroit has been described by Gertrude Whipple.[15] Careful consideration was given general content, characters, illustrations, stories, vocabulary, and the teacher's manual. These books thus prepared have now been used with apparent success through the second grade and hopefully will prevent many children from becoming crippled readers even at the earliest levels.[16] To what age levels such contrived material can be used successfully is not yet known.

Much of the work done along these lines, however, has been based on faith rather than on exhaustive research. Does the culturally deprived child gain more from reading that which gives him better understanding of his own world with its real, raw problems of life, exciting and challenging as they are, or should he learn to live vicariously in an entirely strange world of order and respectability, often (to his taste) humdrum and placid? Here the basic question of what our society wants of the culturally deprived becomes paramount: is it greater conformity by making more people middle class in values and habits or is it to play up the strengths of lower-class life, while minimizing its pain and vulgarity? Claude Brown, whose *Manchild in the Promised Land* was mentioned earlier, is one who is still earnestly seeking an answer to this basic question:

> Everybody I knew in Harlem seemed to have some kind of dream. I didn't have any dreams, not really. I didn't have any dreams for hitting the number. I didn't have any dreams for getting a big car or a fine wardrobe. I bought expensive clothes because it was a fad. It was the thing to do, just to show that you had money. I wanted to be a part of what was going on, and this was what was going on.
>
> I didn't have any dreams of becoming anything. All I knew for certain was that I had my fears. I suppose just about everybody else knew the same thing. They had their dreams, though, and I guess that's what they had over me. As time went by, I was sorry for the people whose dreams were never realized.[17]

The Handicap of a Poor Self-Image

An important factor in their development of values and goals in life is the kind of self-image children form.

In their excellent discussion of ego development among segregated Negro children, Ausubel and Ausubel report the consequences of factors that prevent the growth of normal human relationships and a feeling of inner-self worth for this type of youngster. The segregated Negro child often refuses to identify himself with his own group, because he believes his group is accorded little worth in general society.[18] He benefits little or nothing of derived status from his parents, and so early he associates himself with a peer group, where his activities are often unsuppressed. Here he experiences a freedom that middle-class children rarely have and develops a sure sense of independence; however, he ordinarily feels no great drive for academic success, although he often expresses unrealistically high vocational interests, which may not really be his true or functional level of striving. In general, he misses those "supportive traits [that] include habits of initiative and responsibility, the 'deferred gratification' pattern of hard work, renunciation of immediate pleasures, long-range planning, high frustration tolerance, impulse control, thrift, punctuality and willingness to undergo prolonged vocational preparation."[19]

Sexual differences in these matters are more pronounced for Negro children than for white because the Negro family pattern is more predominantly matriarchal. Bowman reports four negative aspects of the child's self-image in school: a sense of failure, alienation from people, a feeling of always being treated unfairly, and finally, hopelessness concerning the future.[20] Bowman lists five characteristics of a good school program that can help heal the bruised egos that the culturally deprived often bring to the learning tasks set for them, but none of his remedies indicates any part that the right books can play in this healing process.

There are those who feel that school and formal attempts at education of any sort, as presently constituted, do more to increase than to alleviate the feelings of insecurity and inferiority that the culturally deprived child brings with him as he enters into contact with this segment of his world. A recent book describing this process is titled *Education for Alienation*.[21] Many psychologists and sociologists insist that the kindergarten child from the slums is a far healthier individual in his personal and interpersonal relationships than he will be at any later stage of his school life. If this unhappy situation is now true and is to be reversed, what shall be the role of books? Is it by identifying with others in like trouble or is it by identifying with individuals who were successes that these children gain a more favorable perspective of themselves and their rightful place in the society? Should this identification be with their own race or minority group? Should it be with those whose achievements are within the realm of possibility for themselves or with those who were the particularly fortunate unfortunates? Answers to these questions seem now in the realm of the unknown. Here is probably the area where librarians can help most, but perhaps they will need the assistance of trained psychologists.

The Universality of Children's Interests

All studies of the general interests of culturally deprived children show that they do not vary markedly from those of so-called normal children. They enjoy television and look at the same programs. They laugh at humorous situations; they understand tragic and disappointing ones. They can be led, with appropriate methods, to enjoy rhyme and rhythm, stories of adventure, stories of animals, stories of real life. In other words, their interests are as broad as life and as wide as the subjects dealt with in books. The key to success here is now, as it has ever been, the interested and resourceful librarian who makes a real study of getting the right book to the right child. A real problem is how to multiply the number of such librarians available to children.

The Place of Literature

Just exactly what literature should be provided for the culturally deprived child is still a debatable matter among teachers and librarians. For this reason, the following definition of literature for children will be used: that body of children's books which, in the combined judgments of teachers and librarians, has been included in the lists compiled by respected and reputable professional organizations such as the ALA, NCTE, ACEI, and others. These lists include books of a wide variety of formats, dealing with a wide variety of topics and certainly far from equal is that elusive quality, "good literary style." These are the books found on the shelves of the average public library, the books in the school library or the classroom, the books that are being purchased for the special projects now being set up for the culturally deprived. These are the materials now available for use with children.

It is to our advantage, in dealing with culturally deprived children, that we have a broad spectrum of materials from which to choose rather than a narrow range of materials that somehow have been labeled "real" literature. Our clientele presents too broad a spectrum of special problems to be encompassed narrowly. It may well be that research will indicate that we need an even broader range of materials than we now have and that many books must be written with the culturally deprived particularly in mind: special subject matter, special language, special format, special illustrations. These will not be inferior materials, because they will be written by talented authors who are particularly sensitive to the needs of this large segment of our society and who will consciously make use of the extensive research of linguistics, reading experts, sociologists, and psychologists now available. But for here and now we must try to make optimal use of what materials we have: this is the best we can do.

The remainder of this paper describes some ways in which teachers and librarians are introducing literature to culturally deprived children and which practices seem to be bringing results. It is assumed that the work of teachers and librarians, whether public or school librarians, is basically the same, for both groups are seriously concerned with helping children to find meaning and pleasure in books. No attempt will be made to mention specific titles. Many excellent lists are in existence, some of which have been developed for special projects dealing with the culturally deprived.[22]

The Unique Contribution of Literature

One should, however, point out the importance of one role that literature, in its narrower definition, should play in the reading experience of children. Perhaps its unique function is to present a pattern for the development of those personal and interpersonal values commonly accepted as ideal in our culture.[23] The understanding that such values exist and that they have generally proved satisfying to human beings may be the greatest need of children without. If this be true, there is some evidence that current writers of children's books sidestep the presentation of such values. Chambers found in his study of the output of two major publishing houses for one year that the books he analyzed were typically amoral in the themes with which they dealt.[24] It is likewise true that authorities in the field are often in disagreement concerning the validity of the values that an author attempts to present. Such is the case of *The Empty School House*.[25] Perhaps it is not surprising then that general disagreement exists as to what these children need, what materials will meet their needs, and what the youngsters can and will read. We must have further and continuing dialogue on these matters.

Reading Interests and Habits of Children

It is striking to note that little has been done to identify the specific reading preferences of various groups of children.[26] We have many suggestions from authorities in the field but little or no evidence to support it. Norvell, reporting on the reading preferences of 24,000 students in the fourth, fifth, and sixth grades in New York, found a marked difference in what children preferred and what experts recommended.[27]

If such disparity between what children like and what experts *think* they *should like* is true for "average" children, what credence can be placed in opinions regarding the reading interests and habits of the culturally different? In attempting to answer this question, I submitted a brief questionnaire to librarians who work with culturally deprived children. These were the questions:

1. Is there any evidence that certain formats in books appeal particularly to these children: large print, many pictures, limited size, pages broken with wide margins, short paragraphs, etc?

2. What sorts of language barriers seem to inhibit their reading: vocabulary, many proper names, sentence structure, idioms, dialect of various kinds?

3. Do children of minority groups like to read about traditional figures representing their own group? About "real live heroes" of their group who have succeeded? Do they like pictures of their own race?

4. What kinds of humor appeal to these children? What kinds, if any, appeal particularly to Negro children?

5. Do they seem to prefer idealistic materials such as fairy tales and fantasy or, rather, realistic stories of real children in real-life settings?

6. Do they show any preference for stories laid in the urban living they know best rather than in settings quite unfamiliar to them?

7. Does television viewing seem to influence reading? Do the adult television programs that many of these children watch, with their emphasis on adult adventure and violence, seem to have much influence?

8. Do these children follow the usual sexual differences of boys and girls in

their reading interests, despite the fact that many of them are precocious in their knowledge of sex?

9. Do they show any interest in special literary art forms such as poetry or drama?

10. Can you honestly say slum children are a distinct reading group, or do they represent all the individual differences to be found in any "normal" group of children?

The most striking result obtained from this questionnaire was that there is no general agreement on answers to the questions asked among librarians who work almost solely with the culturally deprived in many different cities of the country; however, a few facts did become apparent as the interviews progressed and the questionnaires were analyzed. One was that all children with limited experience in reading, or those having reading difficulties, tend to choose picture books with large illustrations and a minimum amount of text. If this is typically characteristic of the disadvantaged child, then an emphasis on the picture book is not only important for the early reader but also for children at upper elementary and junior high levels. We must, therefore, reconsider our practice of placing all the picture books in one place for the younger child. Poor readers recognize that such titles are the baby books; thus, the non-reading older child will be found at the magazine rack looking at picture books for adults, rather than choosing what might be more suited to his interest and taste.

Another matter of some agreement is the interest of minority groups in reading specifically about themselves. Most of the experts, however, insisted that all groups in our society should be represented in books. In essence, these books should realistically portray our society today if the book is concerned with the present. All children like a good, adventurous hero regardless of origin. Illustrations should be true to the situation and mood.

Some librarians identified humor and nonsense books as being specifically of interest to these children, especially Negro children. Others objected and said no such preference could be discerned. All children like a funny story or non-sense book.

Statistics on attendance and circulation figures for children's rooms are not available in Detroit, and the questionnaire to other cities did not include this question, but Countee Cullen library in New York was able to report a sharp rise in library use when the staff was expanded.[28] This is significant because the cry is usually for more books and materials. The implication here is what is needed is a more effective job with what is available. One example cited by Countee Cullen librarians is the stress placed on local community organizations to encourage reading as a habit among disadvantaged youngsters. School visits, reading clubs, guest speakers, and community groups have stimulated a new interest in reading at Countee Cullen; this all demands an expanded staff and a reappraisal of the role of librarian. As was indicated earlier, perhaps in slum areas, librarians *are* more important than books, since it is only through guidance to the right books that many of these children will dare to attempt any reading at all, to say nothing of developing the habit of turning to books for profit and pleasure. Furthermore, all agencies interested in the slum child need to cooperate in encouraging him to read.

Reaffirmation of this viewpoint came while interviewing ninth, tenth, and eleventh grade boys in the "Upward Bound" program at Cranbrook School near Detroit.[29] These boys, who are certainly characteristic of children without, continually reiterated that they frequented only those libraries where the librarian was a sympathetic guide for their interests. Whether it was homework or reading for pleasure, they identified with the library where encouragement and interest were apparent on the part of a librarian. Some indicated that no place like this was available and therefore they did not use the library.

Good picture books, easy text, high interest, universal heroes, realistic situations: these are the materials that librarians say they need. Expanded, interested staff who make extended community contacts and who are creative and particularly sympathetic with the peculiar problems of children without are needed to get these materials into circulation. In addition to librarians, perhaps other highly trained workers are needed if the library staff is to deal effectively with children without.

Teaching Methods and Materials

Just as the traditional librarian must be remade to fit the new situations, so must the traditional teacher of literature, both in the materials used and in the methods followed, if he wishes to reach this type of child. The old "classics" will hardly do. While being interviewed, the boys at Cranbrook frequently mentioned the titles currently being read in their English classes: *Catcher in the Rye* and *Bridge over the River Kwai*. They were not only reading and discussing these books but were excited by them. Again and again the boys mentioned that *Catcher in the Rye* is about them and their world, that *Bridge over the River Kwai* is an exciting book.

It is important to note that these boys had all been tested and found to be reading far below grade level. Most of them were eleventh graders, but some were as low as fourth grade in reading skills. One was so low that he registered no grade level at all on the test used. It is likewise important to know that in this experiment classes are small and that teachers are well trained and enthusiastic about helping these boys succeed. Much time is spent in oral activities.

While many high schools in many cities have developed special reading materials and suitable methods for presenting these materials, one of special

merit has been worked out for the high schools in New York City. In an outline showing how methodology must be suited to characteristics of slow learners,
many of the problems of the culturally deprived are covered (although all slow
children do not fall into the category of the deprived). Such hints as these are
given to teachers: select varied materials that are not too long and that are in
line with youngsters' reading skills, interests, and experiences; work on skills
needed for understanding; stress experience values in literature rather than
literary forms or values; use audio-visual aids, reading by the teacher, class
dramatizations, and television to make verbalization concrete; stress successes
no matter how small; be generous with praise; make assignments short and
concrete.[30]

A teacher in the New York City schools has described his success in finding books that made sense to culturally deprived children in terms of their own
special concerns. The advice the children seem to be giving their teachers about
books was summed up in four points:

1. The subject had to be worth it to us. We like books about
animals, aviation, careers, hobbies, sports, the sea, westerns. We love
lots of adventure, plenty of excitement, slews of interesting facts about
science and things.
2. You couldn't treat us like babies. We may not be so "hot" as
readers, but that doesn't mean, if you give us an easy book about
ducks on a farm, we'll cackle over it gleefully. We had that stuff in the
third grade—remember?
3. You had to give us lots of good pictures, good drawings, and
big print. As one of the fellows said, "I can't read when the print on
page is so small. After a while I lose my eyesight."
4. You had to know how to write. Maybe the guy who likes to
read a lot will stand for some boring parts, but not us! If you want us
to read don't beat around the bush; come right to the point. Give us a
story that pushes us to go on to the next page and the next page, and
you're in![31]

The fact that teachers, as well as librarians, are particularly concerned about
these children and are developing special methods for helping them should
mean that even closer working relations between school and library will be
planned. For these children, more than other children, the right hand should
know what the left hand is doing to try to help them.

In conclusion, then, what do we make of the fact that we have in our
society a considerable number of children whom we designate as children
without? What do we wish to give them that books can supply? In a recent editorial discussing the computer age and what it might mean for man, Norman
Cousins speaks of the role of the poet, the man of literature, in our total society:
"The poet reminds men of their uniqueness. It is not necessary to possess the
ultimate definition of this uniqueness. Even to speculate on it is a gain."[32]

One main question now becomes crystal clear. How shall the books we give him help encourage the child who is without many of the trappings and certainly without some of the values and life patterns we hold dear in our society but who still possesses many ideals that have value for human life? How shall these books help him and us to cherish his uniqueness and special worth in our society?

Claude Brown reminds us that even in the murkiest slums people have their aspirations. He says, "Everybody I knew in Harlem seemed to have some kind of dream."[33] We teachers and librarians can only ask a question in reply: "What books can we find for creating finer dreams and for making these dreams come true for children that fate has given little but dreams to live by?"

Footnotes

[2] Claude Brown, *Manchild in the Promised Land* (New York: Macmillan Co., 1965), p. 415.

[3] Ruth G. Strickland, "Language of Elementary School Children: Its Relationship to the Language of Reading Textbooks and the Quality of Reading of Selected Children," *Bulletin of the School of Education, Indiana University*, Vol. 38, No. 4 (July, 1962), 131 pp.

[4] Walter D. Loban, *The Language of Elementary School Children* (Research Report, No. 1 [Champaign, Ill.: National Council of Teachers of English, 1963]), 92 pp., and Loban, *Language Ability: Grades Seven, Eight, and Nine* (Co-operative Research Project, No. 131 [Washington: U.S. Office of Education, 1963]), 248 pp.

[5] *Ibid.*, p. 236.

[6] *Ibid.*, pp. 237-38.

[7] *Ibid.*, p. 241.

[8] Dominic Thomas, "Oral Language Sentence Structure and Vocabulary of Kindergarten Children Living in Low Socio-Economic Urban Areas" (unpublished Ph.D. dissertation, Wayne State University, 1961).

[9] "Pond, Mississippi Action for Community Education" (Edwards, Miss.: Mace Press, n.d. [mimeographed]).

[10] Ruth I. Golden, "Ways to Improve Oral Communication of Culturally Different Youth," in Arno Jewett, Joseph Mersand, and Doris V. Gunderson (eds.), *Improving English Skills of Culturally Different Youth in Large Cities* (U.S. Office of Education Bulletin, No. 5 [Washington: U.S. Office of Education, 1964]), pp. 100-109.

[11] Donald Lloyd, "Subcultural Patterns Which Affect Language and Reading Ability," in Arno Jewett, Joseph Mersand, and Doris V. Gunderson (eds.), *Improving English Skills of Culturally Different Youth in Large Cities* (U.S. Office of Education Bulletin, No. 5 [Washington: U.S. Office of Education, 1964]), pp. 117-18.

[12] A. Sterl Artley, "Oral Language Growth and Reading Abiilty," *Elementary School Journal*, 53 (February, 1953), 321.

[13] *The Detroit News*, May 1, 1966, p. 1.

[14] Raven I. McDavid, "Dialectology and the Teaching of Reading," *Reading Teacher*, 18 (December, 1964), 206-13.

[15] *City Schools Reading Program* (4 vols.; Chicago: Follett Publishing Co., 1963).

[16] Gertrude Whipple, "The Culturally and Socially Deprived Reader," in H. Alan Robinson (ed.), *The Underachiever* (Supplementary Educational Monographs, No. 92 [Chicago: University of Chicago Press, 1962]), pp. 129-36.

[17] Brown, *op. cit.*, p. 414.

[18] David Ausubel and Pearl Ausubel, "Ego Development among Segregated Negro

Children," in A. Harry Passow (ed.), *Education in Depressed Areas* (New York: Bureau of Publications, Teachers College, Columbia University, 1963), pp. 109-41.

[19] *Ibid.*, p. 118.

[20] Paul H. Bowman, "Improving the Pupil Self-Concept," in Robert D. Strom (ed.), *The Inner City Classroom: Teacher Behaviors* (Columbus, Ohio: Charles E. Merrill Books, 1966), pp. 75-91.

[21] Nathaniel Hickerson, *Education for Alienation* (Englewood Cliffs, N.J.: Prentice-Hall, Inc., 1966).

[22] *Gateway English: Development of Reading and English Language Materials for Grades 7-9 in Depressed Urban Areas* (New York: Hunter College of the City University of New York Curriculum Study Center, October, 1965).

[23] May Hill Arbuthnot, "Developing Life Values through Reading," *Elementary English,* 43 (January, 1966), 10-16.

[24] Dewey Chambers, "An Exploratory Study into the Social Values in Children's Literature" (unpublished Ph.D. dissertation, Wayne State University, 1965).

[25] Compare Shelton L. Root, Jr.'s review (*Elementary English,* 43 [April, 1966], 433-35) of *The Empty School House,* by Natalie S. Carlson (New York: Harper & Row, 1965), with comments on the same book by Arna Bontemps, "Uncle Remus, Farewell," *Bookweek, Fall Children's Issue* (October 31, 1965), p. 3.

[26] Jean M. Lepere, "Review of Research in Children's Literature," *A Review of Educational Research,* 31 (1961), 179-87.

[27] George W. Norvell, *What Boys and Girls Like to Read* (Morristown, N.J.: Silver-Burdett Co., 1958), 306 pp.

[28] "Saturday's Children," *Library Journal,* 91 (March, 1966), 1581-90.

[29] Personal interviews with boys at Cranbrook, July 15, 1966.

[30] Joseph Mersand, "Teaching the Slow Learner in English," *High Points,* 49 (May, 1966), 38-53.

[31] Charles Spiegler, "Reading Materials for Retarded Readers," in Helen M. Robinson (ed.), *Materials for Reading* (Supplementary Educational Monographs, No. 86 [Chicago: University of Chicago Press, 1957]), p. 29.

[32] Norman Cousins, "The Computer and the Poet," *Saturday Review* (July, 23, 1966), p. 42.

[33] Brown, *op. cit.,* p. 414.

Author's note: I wish to acknowledge the very considerable help I received from Mr. William Curtis, doctoral student at Wayne State University, who interviewed teachers, librarians, and students in the Detroit area and who helped analyze questionnaires and answers from other cities. Thanks are also due the many librarians, teachers, and students who cooperated with us.

22   The Art of Storytelling

May Hill Arbuthnot

A curriculum in children's literature, no matter how rich and varied, remains incomplete if it includes only books and magazines and overlooks the oral aspects or storytelling, poetry reading, and choral speaking. Since storytelling is a behavior alien to many teachers, practical guidelines are needed if they are to feel secure and be successful. Arbuthnot, an acknowledged authority on children's literature—and an outstanding storyteller herself—succinctly provides these aids in this article.

Is storytelling restricted to the primary grades? What type of story might be most appropriate for you to select for your first storytelling experience? What environmental and audience factors help assure a well-told story? Why are folk tales especially suitable for storytelling?

One Northern tribe has a saying that in ancient times, to keep men from being weary-hearted, a kind god created the storyteller.[1]

An Ancient Art

Storytelling is one of the oldest and most intimate of the arts. Perhaps it began when the grannies of the tribe told stories to quiet crying children or scare them into proper behavior or answer their interminable questions. "How did the big chief kill the bear?" "What are the wolves saying when they howl like that?" "How did the stars get up in the sky?" "What happened to the little boy who disobeyed his granny?" Stories made up to answer such questions were compounded of facts, fancy, fear and wonder, and some of them were so spellbinding they were remembered and passed on by word of mouth. Storytellers for the grownups arose, and those with special skills became professionals who traveled from castle to castle or country to country—the bards, scops, troubadors, minstrels. They introduced adult themes of romance, infidelity,

From *Some Oral Aspects of the Language Arts Program,* A Report of the Thirteenth Annual Conference and Course on Reading, University of Pittsburgh, 1957, pp. 41-50. Reprinted with permission of Donald L. Cleland (ed.). Footnotes have been renumbered.

murder, revenge and the like, and gradually the hero tales developed into those hero cycles we call epics. But whether it was an old woman by a peat fire or a traveling minstrel in the great hall of a king or an Indian with his tribe gathered round him by a camp fire, the storyteller watched his audience, played on the emotions of the people and held them enthralled.

Padraic Colum suggests that when lights came into the cottage, storytelling went out.[2] Before lights, in an Irish cabin, when a storyteller came visiting, he was honored with the best the family could provide. All the neighbors were sent for to share this great privilege, so highly was the well-told story esteemed. Grace Penney in her collection of *Tales of the Cheyennes*[3] tells us that among these Indians, "Storytellers were honored old men, wise in their lore of the people, and stories were owned by certain tellers and might not be told by any other person. The owner might give the story to another, just as he might give a robe or any other gift." Then she describes a Cheyenne story time "with the old storyteller in the place of honor and after everyone was seated, no one was allowed to get up or leave or walk around or speak. It was believed that any distraction would bring great misfortune to the camp." This is a good picture of a story hour today. Any modern teller knows all too well how an interruption can upset the mood and bring grief to the story.

Why Tell Stories Today?

Teachers say, "Storytelling is all right for remote peasants or peoples of past generations or isolated tribes of Indians. But in the modern world, with television, moving pictures, radio and myriads of beautiful books, why should hard-pressed teachers tell stories? Storytelling requires careful preparation but books can be read aloud on the spur of the moment. Why tell when you can read?"

The first answer to that question sounds frivolous but is quite serious. Tell stories for enjoyment and fortunately, once your skill is sure, storytelling is as much fun for the teller as it is for the audience. There is no contribution you can make to children that will furnish you and them with more satisfaction than lively, imaginative storytelling. Try it and see. In the classroom, on journeys, round a camp fire, in hospitals, at a picnic, the grownup who can tell a good story for children or adults possesses a gift of great price. There is an informality about it that is not true of reading aloud. Facial expression and the occasional gesture are more natural and change more readily because there is nothing between the teller and his audience. The mood is homey, intimate and relaxed. It's fun!

The second reason for learning to tell stories is that this ancient art can do much for the teller. It sharpens the sense of the dramatic, of suspense, climax, humor or pathos, and the varied beauties of style with which different stories are told. It develops a sense of timing and an uncanny sensitivity to audience response. These are invaluable assets to a teacher. In fact it is safe to say that the better your storytelling becomes the better teacher you will be.

There are many other reasons for cultivating the art of storytelling. Folk tales, for instance, demand telling and suffer when they are read. They came into being as an oral art and the tight precision of the printed text takes something away from them. Oddly enough the modern child used to television is as naively impressed with a well-told tale as children were two generations ago. One nine-year-old said recently, "I'll never forget 'Budulinek.' I think it was the best story I ever heard." And the group agreed with her. Now, the Czech story of "Budulinek"[4] is not the greatest story in the world, but the intimacy of storytelling makes an emotional impact on the hearers that will outlast any Western TV can concoct.

Last of all, the stories you know, you have always with you. The children's picnic is interrupted by a heavy rain. Outdoor play is impossible and the shelter is too small for indoor games. No one has a book along, but you have a goodly stock of stories in your head. You gather the children round you in a close, cozy group. The rain hums an accompaniment to your words, and the age-old magic of "Once upon a time," takes over. The day is saved.

Elements of Good Storytelling

There are certain outward and inward qualities necessary to good storytelling. Tellers differ as widely as the tales they tell, but in general they need to have good voices, clear diction and a pleasant, unaffected appearance. The inner qualities are harder to define but two are essential—complete sincerity and joy in telling the story. This means forgetting self because you are absorbed and lost in the story. And it means respect both for the story and the audience. The storyteller who does not take his story seriously is doomed to failure. And the storyteller who talks down to his audience, is arch or patronizing, deserves to fail and will. Integrity is basic to any art, especially storytelling with its unusual intimacy.

Voice

Voice is of great importance. In *Children and Books*[5] I have described three famous storytellers as different from each other as they could well be. And there are many more varieties. But whether the voice is light and sweet or the laconic drawl of a mountain man or a mature voice with resonance and depth, the storyteller must make of it a flexible instrument to convey character and mood. The gradation of voices in "The Three Bears" is a nursery skill which mothers achieve almost instinctively. Even at the youngest level there are subtler examples. For example, in "The Lad Who Went to the North Wind," the story-teller's voice suggests the forthright courage and determination of the lad when he faces the mighty North Wind and declares, "I have come again because I want my rights for that meal you took away from me. As for the ram, it can't coin so much as a copper penny." Or in the story of "Budulinek," the unctuous voice of old Lishka the fox warns the children that she is a villain when she says, "You know me, Budulinek. I am Lishka the Fox, and if you'll open the door I'll give you a ride on my tail." Obviously, the voice is saying without words, she's up to no good. So, too, in the conversation between Budulinek and his granny before she goes to work and warns him that he must not open the door, he replies virtuously, "Oh, no, granny, I wouldn't do that." At which a little boy used to groan and mutter, "Uhuh, but he's going to!" So the storyteller's voice contin-ually reveals secrets that are not told in words.

No special voice is required for storytelling, just so it falls pleasantly on the ears and is neither monotonous nor overly loud. You can do much to improve the quality of your voice by listening to yourself when you practice your stories in privacy. Most women need to pitch their voices lower to avoid the shrill, high range so common to the feminine voice, especially when it is tired. If possible, make a tape recording of your storytelling, then work for better voice quality and articulation. Record again to see if you have improved. Listen also to the modern records of poets and actors reading poetry—Edith Sitwell, Archibald MacLeish, Robert Frost, Agnes Moorehead. Not that you will imitate any of these fine readers, but listening to them will train your ear and cultivate better standards of voice quality and enunciation.

Diction

This brings us to diction which is as important as voice. The storyteller's speech must be clear and vigorous so that every word carries and is effortlessly understood by the audience. But this never means loudness. A story that is told loudly is a contradiction in terms, for storytelling must always sound intimate and natural. But clear articulation will give carrying power to a small voice, which is another reason for trying to improve your diction.

As you work for crisp, agile speech be sure you avoid anything that smacks of artificiality. Don't strive for the accent of some other person, or area, or coun-try, but strive instead to achieve the most cultivated speech of your own par-ticular corner of the world—New England, Middle West, South, Canada or England. Forms of sloven, sloppy speech are common to all areas and all coun-tries. Fortunately, the careful purity of speech among gentle, educated people is also common to all areas, and it is for such speech we should strive.

Appearance

Finally, what about the appearance of the storyteller? There have been storytellers who costumed for the part—as Mother Goose, or in character with a Robin Hood tale or a Norwegian or French peasant or court story. Costuming smacks too much of the stage or a stunt. Storytelling is the art of the fireside, simple and homey. Your best everyday self, comfortable and unperturbed, is all it takes to put your audience and yourself at ease. For this reason avoid fussy clothes, especially hats, if you are a woman. They are strange concoctions at best and may prove distracting. Sit or stand naturally, if your posture is good. If not, study yourself in a mirror and improve. But don't slouch or lean heavily on desk or table and keep your hands free of all such impediments as handkerchiefs, or pencils, or dangling chains.

However, these are minor details. What really matters about your appearance is what comes from within. Your infectious enjoyment of the tale will show in the twinkle of your eye, the half-smile on your lips or the half-laugh in your voice. So, too, your facial expression will suggest fear or despair because you are living the story. You *are* the unhappy Goose Girl or the wicked and malicious Queen, but you only *suggest* these roles; you never act them. If the story says, "The lassie made a low bow," you do not bow, but your voice does it in the mood of humility or mockery as the story demands. This is of the utmost importance. To dramatize the story you are telling is completely false to this ancient and beloved art. If the story says, "The poor Goose Girl turned away and wept," don't do it. You make a spectacle of yourself and ruin the story. But if your voice has become a flexible instrument for characterization and mood, the drama will come through with little or no visible action.

How to Learn a Story

To memorize or not

Apparently no two people learn a story in quite the same way. To memorize or not to memorize is the first question. Some frown upon the practice; others believe it is the only way. It goes without saying that memorized or not, a story must be so thoroughly learned that no possible distraction can upset the teller's recall of his material. The chief argument against memorizing is that it kills the spontaneity and freshness of a story. But with genuine artists this is not so; with the less gifted it is apt to be true. Another point against memorizing is that recall may not be as durable as it is when the teller keeps the story somewhat fluid. You may have to test both methods and see which is safer and more effective for you. In general the majority of storytellers feel that a story which depends for its effect upon the exact words of the author should be read aloud and not told. If told, it becomes a recitation and storytelling is something different.

Making a story your own

If you don't memorize, you must still keep close to the original both in style and vocabulary. These differ in folk tales in different nations and in modern realistic stories. You must catch the peculiar cadence of an Irish story and keep it throughout the narration.

> The king was walkin' one mornin' by the edge of the lake, lamentin'
> his cruel fate, and thinkin' of drownin' himself, that could get no
> diversion in life, when all of a sudden . . . whom should he meet but
> a mighty decent young man coming up to him.[6]

In the Norwegian tales there is no substituting modern words for tapers, mare, goody, lassie and the like, although the first time you use such words you may paraphrase them: "So the goody, the old woman, said she," or "They said they would throw him down a well of scythes, you know, a well all lined with sharp knives." And ever after, you use the original word goody, scythe, mare, or whatever it is that makes a tale from the Arabian Nights quite different in flavor and style from an old tale of the German peasants.

Another must for non-memorizers is that the beginnings, conclusions and dialogue of every story must be polished to considerable exactness. This is because all that follows or has gone before must dovetail with these parts. Yet your version may not be in precisely the words of the text. That is true of the parts already quoted from "Budulinek," they are close to the text but not exact. In the dialogue of "The Pancake" the text follows a certain pattern which may be varied by the teller without harm to the spirit of the tale. It does not matter if, in answer to the "How-do-you-do" or the "Good day" of the various creatures, the Pancake says, "The same to you," or "As well as I may." The important thing is that each creature accosts him politely, even pleadingly and he gets cockier and cockier until he meets the pig, then all his insolence collapses and he says affrightedly, "How-do-you-do, Piggy Wiggy," and begins to roll on like mad. Dialogue that is kept fluid becomes uniquely your own, but it must not violate the content or style of the original.

All this is true of beginnings and conclusions. Take the opening paragraphs of the English tale, "Tom-Tit-Tot," the language is unique. It establishes the mood and reveals the dumbwittedness of the characters with which the story is going to deal and the absurd problem on which it turns. The teller has to keep pretty close to the original.

Once upon a time there was a woman and she baked five pies. And when they came out of the oven, they were that overbaked the crusts were too hard to eat. So she says to her daughter:

"Darter," says she, "Put you them there pies on the shelf and leave 'em there a little, and they'll come again,"—she meant, you know, the crusts would get soft.

But the girl, she says to herself: "Well if they'll come again, I'll eat 'em now. "And she set to work and ate 'em all, first and last.[7]

This feckless, daft beginning just can't be tampered with. It sets the mood for the whole mock-tragedy that is to follow.

Conclusions, too, must be polished and precise, both for a strong finale and also because children want everything accounted for—virtue rewarded and the villains neatly finished off. There is, for instance, the unfailing humor of "The Brementown Musicians" scratching, biting, knocking the robber down and calling out in good rooster language, "Cuc cuc cuc kadoo." Then the robber's report to his fellow brigands, "There was a witch who scratched me with her long nails, a man who cut me in the leg with a knife, a giant who knocked me down and beat me with a club, and finally, a terrible creature that called out, 'Cut cut cut the man in two!' " to the hilarious satisfaction of the children. Or there is the romantic conclusion of East o' the Sun, "And so the Prince took the lassie by the hand, and the two of them flitted far, far away from the castle that lies East o' the Sun and West o' the Moon." No trifling with such endings as these, but every teller must make them uniquely his forevermore. Ruth Sawyer says her Irish nurse always ended her stories with the traditional challenge, "Take it, and may the next one who tells it better it."[8]

Visualizing as you tell a story

Some people find it helps in learning a story if you deliberately visualize people, places and episodes as you go along. For instance, Hansel and Gretel, coming out of the dark woods upon the little gingerbread house all shining with sugar and candy, you see stuffing themselves happily not seeing as you do, the terrible old woman coming out of the door. You see her sharp beaked nose, cruel glittering eyes and terrible bony jaws, and you bring her more vividly to life because you see her so. This may help you or it may not. Try it and see.

Practice

One last word of advice, practice your stories aloud. Don't waste time reading it through silently more than once. Then, begin to tell with the book in front of you, to consult when you halt and stumble. Retell and polish parts and retell again until you are telling larger and larger blocks of the story. When you finally reach the point where you can stumble through it, then you are ready to begin your real work. Tell it and tell it again, when you are dressing or driving to school or taking a bath and always before you go to sleep at night. Listen to yourself and your re-creation of this delightful tale you like so much you wish to share it. Polish your weak points, heighten the humor or the pathos or the drama. Build up the suspense and begin to enjoy thoroughly your new creation. For that is what it is when you have made it uniquely yours, it is your own artistic creation.

What Stories to Tell

Sources

So far, the examples mentioned in this discussion have been folk tales, but there are many modern, realistic stories that lend themselves happily to the storyteller's art. Meindert DeJong's *Smoke Above the Lane*[9] tells beautifully, with some discreet cutting, and so does Marguerite Henry's *Benjamin West and His Cat Grimalkin.*[10] Stories as varied in style and content as *Burma Boy,*[11] *School Train*[12] and *Pinto's Journey*[13] will add richly to the storyteller's repertoire. At Christmas try Julia Sauer's fine story *The Light at Tern Rock*[14] or the fanciful *Torten's Christmas Secret*[15] and the almost fanciful "The Goldfish"[16] which is popular from the kindergarten to upper grades. You will find many other recent stories which with some cutting or adaptation are delightful to tell.

Undoubtedly, the largest and richest source of stories for telling is to be found in folk tale collections, especially nowadays when new ones are appearing with amazing frequency. One of the most notable is that series published by Oxford University Press of English, Scotch, Welsh, Irish, Norwegian, French and other national groups of Folk Tales and Legends.[17] These are not the familiar tales but chiefly fresh and unfamiliar material. For special countries notable recent collections are the Korean *Which Was Witch,*[18] the Jamaican *Anansi, the Spider Man,*[19] the Persian *Once the Mullah*[20] and the Canadian *Sashes Red and Blue.*[21] These contain a wide variety of amusing, beautiful and strange new tales. Of course, we won't forget our own tall tales built around such legendary figures as Paul Bunyan and Pecos Bill, wonderful for campfire telling.

The age appeal of folk tales is wider than we used to think. In such an anthology as *Time for Fairy Tales*[22] the stories range from such nursery favorites as "The Three Little Pigs" to stories that delight the sophisticated upper graders. Try with them that Danish version of "The Taming of the Shrew" called "The Most Obedient Wife" and the next day, turn the tables on the boys by telling "Clever Manka" in which the woman triumphs.

Even after you know many sources, the important element in your choice of a story for telling is you yourself. Learn your limitations and what you do best. Ruth Sawyer admits she cannot tell Hans Christian Andersen stories effectively. I cannot tell our tall tales happily, although I like them, as I am sure Mrs. Sawyer likes Andersen. Each storyteller comes to know in his heart what stories are not his and what stories are. Certainly, never waste your time and talent on mediocre tales. Be proud of your story because it can bring laughter or stir wonder or lift the heart with the marvel of man's goodness or courage or endurance. Be glad to tell your story because storytelling is a creative art like playing great music. It can kindle the imagination and warm the spirit of those who listen and him who tells.

Footnotes

[1] Deutsch, Babette and Yarmolinsky, Avraham. *Tales of Faraway Folk*. Harper, 1952.
[2] Grimm, Jacob and Wilhelm. *Grimm's Fairy Tales*, tr. by Margaret Hunt, rev. by James Stern. Pantheon, 1944.
[3] Penney, Grace. *Tales of the Cheyennes*. Houghton-Mifflin, 1953.
[4] Arbuthnot, May Hill. *Time For Fairy Tales*, p. 132. Scott, Foresman, 1952.
[5] Arbuthnot, May Hill. *Children and Books*. Revised edition, Scott, Foresman, 1957.
[6] Arbuthnot, May Hill. "King O'Toole and His Goose," *Time For Fairy Tales*. Scott, Foresman, 1952.
[7] Arbuthnot, May Hill. "Tom-Tit-Tot," *Time For Fairy Tales*. Scott, Foresman, 1952.
[8] Sawyer, Ruth. *The Way of the Storyteller*. Viking, 1942.
[9] DeJong, Meindert. *Smoke Above the Lane*. Harper, 1951.
[10] Henry, Marguerite. *Benjamin West and His Cat Grimalkin*. Bobbs-Merrill, 1947.
[11] Lindquist, Willis. *Burma Boy*. Whittlesey, 1953.
[12] Acker, Helen. *School Train*. Abelard, 1953.
[13] Bronson, Wilfred. *Pento's Journey*. Messner, 1948.
[14] Sauer, Julia. *The Light At Tern Rock*. Viking, 1951.
[15] Doblier, Maurice. *Torten's Christmas Secret*. Little, 1952.
[16] Street, Julian. "The Goldfish," *Time for True Tales*, by May Hill Arbuthnot. Scott, Foresman, 1952.
[17] Reeves, James. *English Fables and Fairy Stories*. Oxford, 1954; Wilson, Barbara. *Scottish Folk-Tales and Legends*. Oxford, 1954, and Walck, 1954.
[18] Jewett, Eleanore M. *Which Was Witch*. Viking, 1953.
[19] Sherlock, Philip. *Anansi, the Spider Man*. Crowell, 1954.
[20] Kelsey, Alice Greer. *Once the Mullah*. Longmans, 1954.
[21] Carlson, Natalie Savage. *Sashes Red and Blue*. Harper, 1956.
[22] Arbuthnot, May Hill. *Time For Fairy Tales, Old and New*. Scott, Foresman, 1952.

23 How to Run a Book Fair

Dorothy McFadden

One way to generate interest in and enthusiasm for books is to sponsor a book fair. McFadden not only details how to plan and conduct one but she encourages broad community cooperation and support by involving parents, public librarians, local mass media, and civic organizations.

Which suggestions seem most feasible in your current situation? Which could be omitted without seriously undermining the objectives of the fair? Would the articles by Arbuthnot and Edman in this part be of help in running a book fair? What kind of follow-up and evaluation do you think would be best after such an activity? For an annotated listing of other resources for stimulating interest in children's books, see the article by Sister Mary Nora and French cited in Selected References for Part Four.

Purpose of a book fair

Perhaps your main purpose is to raise money for the school library or some other worthy school or community project. This is fine, of course; but as parents and responsible citizens, it should be equally—if not more—important to you to stimulate reading among both children and adults. After all, you are going to put a lot of planning, time, and energy into your book fair. Why not aim at the greatest possible contribution to old and young alike—and count your results afterwards not merely in dollars and cents?

A well-planned book fair, whether held by one school or an entire city, can lead to greater use of school and public libraries; better selection of library books; wiser and more frequent book buying; more families reading together; interesting teen-agers, especially, in new leisure-time hobbies; opening the eyes of many children to the fun of reading something besides comic books.

Your book fair can do all these things—and make money besides—with only a little additional planning. This wider view of your project need not mean greater expense. Many excellent fairs have been put on by single parent-teacher

From *Elementary English* 35:168-175; March 1958. Reprinted with permission of Dorothy McFadden, Mendham, New Jersey.

associations when the only cost was the price of order blanks. It does, however, take time, imagination, and careful advance thinking to put on a successful book fair. So do discuss your purposes first, then shape your plans, always keeping these in mind.

Sponsorship

Even if your book fair is only a one-school project, be sure that the group of sponsors includes your town librarian, your school librarian, your school's reading co-ordinator, your youth groups—both for the sake of well-rounded publicity and for assistance in your initial planning. The more co-operative sponsoring organizations you can get to work with you, the bigger your attendance will be, and the closer you will come to fulfilling your purposes. We are taking it for granted that you have obtained the interest and approval of your school principal and superintendent, and their permission to have school classes visit the fair.

Do not expect to get good co-operation from your sponsors, however, if you present them with fully formed plans. Ask a representative of each group to sit in on your first meeting, so that all the sponsoring groups feel they really share in the project. Sponsors will help you by suggesting special features of local interest; rounding up literary celebrities; helping at a preview tea or other social publicity function; working out decorations which you could not otherwise afford—as well as giving the fair publicity at all community gatherings.

Where to obtain books

The sponsoring group should decide first on the number of books it wants to display, and whether books for adults as well as for children should be included. A one-school book fair usually has about 250 books; the big-city fairs show from 1,000 to 3,000. The greater the number of books, the bigger the publicity impact; but don't display more books than your space will allow for comfortable viewing. Every book should be laid out singly on tables or racks; piles of books will attract only those who already are bookworms—they will not tempt new readers.

Books may be secured from several sources. The following is a digest of information on sources from Children's Book Council reports which have appeared annually in *Publishers' Weekly*, also in *Junior Libraries* and *Top of the News:*

Books may be secured from your local booksellers; from dealers throughout the country who regularly specialize in supplying exhibits; from various special exhibitors and/or the State Library Commissions of Boards of Education in many states; and, for a limited number of very large fairs, from the

Children's Book Council. It is urgently recommended that books be secured from these sources, rather than from the individual publishers direct.

First, for fairs to be held in one school or a group of schools, your local bookseller will often give fine co-operation. He may arrange to order the books, give a commission on sales made or orders taken at the fair, and take back books unsold. Or he may simply arrange a school exhibit at which no sales are made, but publicity distributed announcing that all titles in the exhibit may be purchased in the store. These stores want to please you—their customers—and are accustomed to dealing with wholesalers who, in their turn, must keep the stores as customers.

Second, there are a number of dealers and jobbers who specialize in supplying exhibits of children's books over a wide area. A list of these—A List of Dealers Supplying Exhibits of Children's Books—is available on request from the Children's Book Council. If you are unable to secure books from your local bookseller, this list should prove helpful. The services of these dealers vary as described, but most will arrange an exhibit at which books may be sold or orders taken.

Your committee should investigate and compare arrangements offered by local stores, other dealers, and jobbers, finding out whether you must guarantee a minimum amount of books sold (this is dangerous if it is your first book fair experience!) ; whether books will be delivered and returned by your committee or the agency, and who pays for transportation; how long it will take for orders to be filled (important if before Christmas) ; and especially whether you must take a prepared exhibit or can make your own selection of books. In a small book fair, it is much better for your local book store and librarian to help you select books suited to your community, particularly if you want to make money on orders. They will help you avoid many pitfalls, such as— ordering too few of the types most in demand locally; omitting books by local authors and illustrators whom you wish to invite; ordering many trashy books not worth endorsing; simply duplicating what is available at drug stores and department stores; ordering books priced too high to sell in your school area; omitting favorite classics or the finest new books; ordering too few or too many in one age category, etc. Your committee should make every effort to arrange for an outstanding, inspiring, newsworthy selection of books.

Third, for those interested in exhibits at which no sales are made or orders taken, there are commercial exhibits, publisher-sponsored—that is, maintained by fees paid by subscribing publishers—as well as such regional educational exhibits as the Kansas State Teacher's Association Children's Traveling Book Exhibit. These are included among the "Miscellaneous Special Exhibits" attached to the "Dealer List" available from the Children's Book Council. Further, there are the State Traveling Exhibits of Children's Books maintained by the Publishers Liaison Committee (composed of school and public librarians and children's books editors), collections of current books provided by the publishers and available to educational institutions and civic and educational groups from the state library commissions or boards of education in a number of states. A list of these is also available from the Council.

Finally, books for a few large fairs—exhibiting from 1,000 to 3,000 books —are provided each year by the Children's Book Council, acting as a co-sponsor. (Sponsorship by the Council means that its member publishers, the children's book editors of over 60 publishing houses, select and provide the books on a proportionate basis.) These fairs are held either in major cities where they attract a large metropolitan and suburban audience, or in smaller cities where they also affect a large population, often state-wide, in localities where books are not widely circulated. Of necessity, the fairs which the Council can co-sponsor are limited in number, and they must be scheduled months in advance. Other co-sponsors of these fairs often include a large newspaper and a museum or other institution where the fair is held.

When you have decided what kind of a fair you want to put on and will find it practical to produce, decide on your source of books and get an agreement in writing, including dates and financial details, so that there can be no misunderstanding.

Possible costs

A one-school book fair, as was said before, need have no expense other than buying some order blanks for the "book salesmen" to use. However, even here, some of the following items which might cost the committee money should be considered, and the biggest fair would definitely need to reckon on many of them.

Decorations—many of these may be made by school children, but expenses may be incurred for paper, paint, balloons, flags, posters and other items.

Entertainment—records or juke box; film projectors and films; picture quizzes, puzzles; fees and/or transportation for drama and dance groups; fees and/or transportation for authors and illustrators. Many will give free programs for publicity but should be provided with travel expenses and appropriate hospitality.

Equipment—display tables and racks (well worth having made by vocational classes for big annual fairs) ; loud-speaker system for large halls; order blanks; pencils for order-taking or list-making by visitors.

Exhibition Room—rental of hall or, if donated, possible cost of heating and cleaning.

Insurance—on special exhibits or books; also liability for unusual crowds.

Publicity—postage for letters to sponsors, authors, book suppliers, social invitations; mimeographing and printing.

Refreshments—for social events, unless donated.

Special Fees—for museum custodians, janitors' fees or tips.

Transportation—of books, school classes, special exhibit material, entertainment group.

Date

This might be during or close to Children's Book Week, held usually during the third week in November (inquire of Children's Book Council). Equally successful fairs have been held in any month during the school season. If the added impetus to Christmas buying seems desirable, have the fair early in November or even in October if you are taking orders, for it takes time to order books, sort them and get them to the buyers.

Time length

This may be anywhere from three or four days to a week or more. The fair should be open during school hours if classes can be scheduled for visits; and after-school hours and at least one evening or weekend for parents and families.

Title

With your purposes clearly in mind, try to select a catchy title. If you are showing only children's books, we suggest "Boys' and Girls' Book Fair" as preferable to "Children's Book Fair" as the word *children* will keep teen-agers away. Other possible titles: "Book Festival"; "Book Bazaar"; "Pageant of Books"; "Books Around the World", or use a Book Week slogan like *The New York Times* "Reading is Fun" exhibits. The more exciting and glamorous the title, the more visitors will want to come.

Committees needed

General Committee: To run the book fair and appoint chairmen.

Book Display: To select, order, and transport books.

Book and Other Sales: To take orders on books at the fair, and keep accounts.

Decorations: To plan, secure, and arrange decorations.

Hostesses: To staff Information Booth, greet program participants, greet visiting classes.

Printing: To prepare fliers, lists, tags, tickets, etc.

Programs: To arrange entertainment.

Promotion: To set up contests, social functions.

Publicity: To release stories to press, present TV and radio program material.

School Relations: To schedule class visits, arrange for participation projects.

Special Exhibits: To obtain, insure, display, and return.

Participation projects

Besides showing posters, handicrafts, art work, etc. done by school children, as suggested above, or developing from school projects, there are several ways in which children and adults attending the fair can participate actively. Some of these are:

Book quiz games

These can be played in many ways by visitors, perhaps with a prize for the class—children and their parents—having the most correct answers. (Answers dropped in box.)

Picture quizzes and other book puzzles may be obtained from the Children's Book Council. Or you can make your own picture quiz, with the help of a librarian, by removing titles from jackets of well-known books, numbering them and mounting them on the wall. Book slogans or titles might be spelled out in international flag code on walls and ceiling, with the flag alphabet posted in several places.

A story-teller could describe book plots for those around her to guess.

Miniature scenes from books can be set up on tables for guessing.

Children in story-book costumes

These can parade to the fair—perhaps accompanied by a bookmobile, library float, etc. Or they can serve as junior hosts and hostesses at the fair. Or they can compete in a Pet Show, with pets also in costume, representing books (Mary and her Lamb, Red Riding Hood and the Wolf, etc.). Or a Story-Book Ball can open the fair, with a grand march, book prizes for the best cost mes, square dancing and ice cream—the ice cream served away from the books!

Guest authors' and artists' autograph

This should be forbidden except when visitors bring or buy books to be autographed. Signing little slips of paper that are usually thrown aside is a nightmare to authors.

Model libraries

Book and department stores may be willing to set up a model home library for a child. In one city several stores arranged such exhibits, each library being of a different type. Blanks were given out to fair visitors, who registered which library they would like to own and gave their reasons in 25 words or less. The actual libraries were the prizes.

Reading rate exhibit

Let visitors time their reading speed and find out how to increase it. Your teachers of reading will give you information and perhaps demonstrate at such a table.

Voting machines

This can be borrowed from election officials and used, not only to teach voting technique, but also to register choices on questions about reading. All questions must be designed for a "yes" or "no" answer or a check list. For example: "Do you read a book after you have seen it on TV or in a movie?" (Yes or No.) "Which of the following types of books do you like best?" (check list.) Age and sex should also be asked of voters, to make the totaling of answers more valuable. Results make interesting publicity stories. The local League of Women Voters would probably be willing to staff the booth.

Decorations, music

Even the smallest book fair can be made into a gay, festive occasion if the room is decorated and jolly marches and dances are played on a phonograph or juke box at various intervals. Decorations may consist only of balloons, flags, or well-placed book jackets. A large poster or montage of photographs of authors appearing at the fair will attract attention. Special murals or large cut-outs may be made in the schools, to be shown at the entrance or behind each table. The major colors from the annual Book Week poster and streamers, available from the Children's Book Council, may form the basis of the decorators' color scheme. Remember that if you use crepe paper, it must be the fireproof kind.

By choosing a different theme for each year, decorations at annual book fairs can be varied and exciting: "Treasure Island of Books," "Around the World in Books," "Cruise of the S.S. *Book Fair*," "Animal Fair"—all have good possibilities.

Information desk

It is important to have a table near the entrance, staffed with hostesses who can answer questions about coat rooms, washrooms, telephones; how books are ordered; where special exhibits are located; when programs are to begin and end. Answers to quiz games may be distributed here on request, or answers placed in a box; booklists, souvenirs, pencils given out; books in the exhibit looked up on the list or in a card file by authors or category, etc. This is the place for lost articles or lost children. If desired, printed booklists or other miscellaneous items can be sold here.

Hostesses and "book salesmen"

Every hostess, committee worker, or "book salesman" should wear a tag for identification.

Hostesses will take turns at the book tables and the Information Table; greet visiting celebrities and program participants; and help the general committee at any social preview function.

"Book salesmen" should have a special meeting before the fair, to discuss procedure in ordering books and become familiar with the order blanks, which should be made out in triplicate—one copy for the book fair committee, one for the book supplier, and one for the purchaser. You should decide whether you want to take cash for orders, or deliver them C.O.D. It is possible that your co-operating book store or department store would allow its charge customers to charge books. If orders are to be paid in cash, have plenty of change at every table; or let one person at a special desk take in all money and give out receipts. Book orders must be written out at the book table, however, either by the "salesman" or the purchaser, to make sure that title and author are listed correctly. The easiest way to deliver the books to individuals is to have them shipped to one place where the Book Sales Committee can sort and mark them for recipients, then ask purchasers to call for them. One caution: if books are bought by parents to give their children for Christmas, do not leave them with purchasers' name attached where children might see them!

Entertainment programs

Any entertainment feature which can be arranged at the fair will greatly increase the attendance. Many parents—who would not come just to look over some books—will bring children if they know there is to be a puppet show or a famous illustrator drawing pictures. Once there they will browse and make lists of books to buy.

One warning: *Please* plan only entertainment features that are related to children's books. Just having an array of magicians or trained dog acts is beside the point—which point throughout the fair should be to *stimulate reading*. Puppet shows or plays must be based on favorite books; animals can be shown if they are the pets of authors who wrote about them in their books; radio or TV personalities can be scheduled if they will act as masters of ceremonies for programs related to books, and so on.

Be sure to let your speakers know the age of their audience in advance.

Someone should announce and introduce each program over a loud speaker. A costumed herald with fanfare bugle adds color and drama. At large community fairs, tickets must carefully regulate the size of audiences in auditoriums.

Chest microphones are particularly helpful to illustrators who, when giving chalk talks (see below), must turn their backs to the audience at times. Any authors or illustrators who have never done programs of this sort but are willing to try, might like a free reprint of my article from *Publishers' Weekly*, July 25, 1953, "How Authors and Illustrators Talk to Children." Just address me at *The New York Times*, 229 West 43rd St., New York 18, N.Y.

Canvass the talents in your community—you will be surprised how much entertainment you can find, suitable to your book fair, that need not cost you a cent. Professional groups will often give performances free or for transportation only, if they get good publicity. Here are some suggestions to choose from:

In small space, perhaps in the same room with the books, preferably on a raised platform, short programs while visitors stand:

Bookmaking

Authors, publishers, or editors, showing how a book is made.

Story-telling

Professional story-tellers, authors or radio personalities telling stories.

Chalk talks

Illustrators drawing while visitors watch. (Drawings must be done swiftly.) Sometimes illustrators prefer to show materials illustrating how their original drawing progresses from sketch to finished printed product. If you or your librarian do not know where to locate illustrators and authors of children's books in your area, write to the Children's Book Council for a Speakers Request Form. When you fill this out and send it in, the Council's editor-members will contact you directly—if they have authors or illustrators available in the required area. Programs by authors and illustrators are often given in school assemblies just before children come to the fair, as well as at the fair itself.

Puppets

Puppet shows and puppet-making demonstration.

For seated audiences, in small or large halls with stage:

Book quizzes

Charades of titles; dramatized excerpts from children's books; parade of costumed characters; showing of objects associated with certain stories or characters—these are some of the ways of giving hints for books to be guessed. Two teams of children can do them for each other or children can do them for the audience to guess. The book answers must not be too old for the audience or too hard to guess.

Dance programs

Of book characters or stories.

Dramatizations

By professional or amateur groups of children or adults. Each day the play may be a framework for presenting different authors in person. Plays may relate to the fair's theme, be based on books by guest authors, or just based on popular books.

Films

On the history of printing or book-making; excerpts from famous books made into movies, etc. A list of films related to books and reading in general is incuded in the *Manual of Book Week Aids* issued annually by the Children's Book Council.

Speakers and panel discussions

For adult or child audiences. Speakers may be famous authors, editors, publishers, book reviewers, community leaders. Teen-agers may interview their favorite authors or discuss books. Possible topics for adult audience could be: "Designing Children's Books," "Writing and Publishing Children's Books," "Children's Taste in Books," "Can TV Stimulate Reading?" "Outstanding Books of the Year for Children," "The Art of Story-Telling," etc.

Fliers

An attractive announcement flier is a "must," whether it is mimeographed and sent home with every child from school, or printed and distributed throughout the community by mail or at meetings. It should be in color, have some sort of illustration, and be exciting, attention-getting. Just announcing a book fair with time and place will never get the attendance it should—use salesmanship! Stress your famous guests, entertainment features, the number of recent books, special exhibits. A bookmobile may help you distribute fliers.

Posters

These are often done in the schools, the best being shown in stores and on bulletin boards.

The official Book Week poster can be bought from the Children's Book Council at low cost. Throughout the year, streamers designed by leading children's book illustrators and carrying the annual Book Week slogan, but no dates, are also available from the Council. . . . And Scholastic Teacher Magazine includes a poster in its annual packet of Book Bazaar promotional materials.

Printed lists

Mimeographed or printed lists of the books shown at the fair will be needed by your "book salesmen" if they are taking orders. They are also very popular with visitors. Books should be listed alphabetically, grouped by categories. Sometimes these lists are sold at 10c each; or their cost is covered by a book store advertisement. A co-sponsoring newspaper may print the list in a special supplement. Or where there are only a few book stores in a community they may combine to sustain the costs of such a list, leaving space for visitors to jot down the books they will want to purchase.

Souvenir tags, memos on books to buy and borrow, bookmarks

Some fairs give away little tags that children tie on their clothes, showing that they have been to the book fair.

Most book fairs distribute something on which visitors can make lists of books they want to read. This may be in the form of a long, folded bookmark, with or without a pencil on a string. Or it may be a memo blank, headed "Books I Want to Read."

Newbery and Caldecott Medal bookmarks and Book Week bookmarks reproducing the Book Week poster are available from the Children's Book Council.

Contests

Contests for children's posters or essays about reading, with book prizes for the best in different age groups, can publicize the fair as well as serve educational purposes.

Social functions

A preview tea the day before the fair, inviting all sponsors and celebrities, will help spread the word and add a good newspaper story. Book-and-author luncheons also add interest. Inviting authors and others who give their time to your book fair without charge is a gracious way of thanking them.

Press stories

Stories about the fair should be sent well in advance to newspapers, magazines, and organizational bulletins, as well as daily to newspapers during the fair. Each press story should emphasize a different feature: contests, number of books, special exhibits, entertainment programs, author and illustrator guests (using biographical notes from book jackets and others sent out by publishers).

Interviews of authors and illustrators may be written by teen-age students. In some towns where the fair has been a community project, the mayor has proclaimed a special Book Fair Week. Quotations from city officials or local celebrities will assure newspaper attention. Remember that your first stories are the ones that will increase your attendance. Newspapers that are co-sponsors of children's book fairs usually print a special children's book section the week of the fair.

Photographs

Advise your newspaper when you are to have particularly good material for photographs, and interest your amateur camera fans and clubs also in taking candid shots, perhaps offering a book prize.

Television and radio

Women's hour program, book reviewers on the air, children's programs, and others will be delighted to publicize your fair if you have practical suggestions to offer: child contest winners showing posters, puppets, etc.; famous visiting authors, or illustrators who will draw on TV; general information about your fair and its special features, given by your committee chairman; a preview of some of the books to be seen at the fair, and so on.

Results of a book fair

You may think that the only results you can tabulate are the number of books ordered at a fair, and the attendance. By talking to all your librarians and book shops, however, you will find out how much reading and book buying have been stimulated. Lists that children or adults made at a book fair, indicating books they want to read or buy, will turn up for many months in libraries and stores. The fair may have instigated a number of school projects that had great educational value. Your local clubs will have found out about the talented writers and artists available in the area, and can draw on them again for good programs. If your committee has put real time, effort, and imagination into the project, it has certainly been a worthwhile civic contribution—which we hope will be continued year after year!

24   Shall We Let Them Create?

Miriam E. Wilt

We are in the middle of a crusade for creativity that has reached epidemic proportions. But the goals it originally aimed for may be endangered by rampant sloganizing and faddish bandwagonitis. In a lucid, tempered analysis, Wilt delineates the rationale behind the movement and describes six teacher characteristics crucial to a truly creative atmosphere.

Are schools more or less demanding of conformity than is adult society? Why? Can an atmosphere conducive to creativity also engender permissiveness? Are the characteristics necessary for creativity in agreement with or opposed to those required for efficient learning of information or skills? Why are the language arts peculiarly well suited to creative endeavors? Which of Wilt's teacher characteristics do you think would be easiest for you to achieve? Most difficult?

> I'm going out to clean the pasture spring
> I'll only stop to rake the leaves away
> And wait to watch the water clear, I may
> I shan't be gone long, you come, too.
> > Robert Frost[1]

Creative expression in the elementary school is that pasture spring. Raking away the leaves and waiting for the water to clear is the purpose of this article. Perhaps the spring is muddied because we have let our thinking be befouled by pressures from so many sources to return to the 3 R's. Perhaps we have too hurriedly jumped on the science, mathematics, and remedial reading bandwagons and so have lost sight of the humanities and specifically of personal expression. Perhaps we have lost sight of certain fundamental truths in the name of academic achievement and the social pressure for conformity. The rationale for critical independent thinking and endeavor has never been in question; the balance between conformity and creativity has. The muddiness is in our thinking, the fog a mist over our eyes. So, please, you come, too, and

From *Elementary English* 40:357-361; April 1963. Reprinted with permission of the National Council of Teachers of English and Miriam E. Wilt, Professor of Curriculum and Instruction, Temple University, Philadelphia, Pennsylvania.

perhaps we can find our way back to a more healthy point of view about creativity.

Not because it isn't known, but rather to bolster what has always been known, let us review the rationale for creative thinking and creative output in elementary classrooms. Many sources might be tapped, but the following generalizations are taken from Carl Rogers'[2] chapter "Toward a Theory of Creativity" from the symposium *Creativity and Its Cultivation* edited by Harold Anderson. Rogers says, "In education we tend to turn out conformists, stereo-types, individuals whose education is completed rather than individuals who are freely creative and original thinkers." Further, he describes leisure time as overwhelmingly devoted to regimented group action; the sciences producing technicians rather than those who creatively formulate hypotheses and theories; industry reserving individual critical creative thinking for the few, the man-ager, designer, or research departments; and in family living, food, clothing, books read, and ideas held following a rigid pattern of conformity in which those who dare to be different are frowned upon.

Harold Anderson[3] says, "That is to say, creativity was in each of us a small child. In children, creativity is universal. Among adults it is almost non-existent." Sylvia Ashton-Warner[4] states in the *Spinster*, "I see the mind of the child as a volcano with two vents, destructiveness and creativeness. And I see that to the extent that we can widen the creative channel we atrophy the de-structive one." Creative thinking is important in childhood because it teaches the small person that he is important; what he is; what he sees; what he does; and what he says.

At the time when the child is as fluid, flexible, and malleable as he will ever be, schools, society, and family patterns seem to be placing him on a mono-rail as inhibiting and constricting as the two rails of a train track. Robert Osborn[5] in a scathing cartoon on conformity warns that if it is too late to do anything about ourselves, then at least let's not put today's children, tomorrow's citizens, on the same unimaginative treadmill most adults are on.

Should the reader feel that conformity is an important ingredient for living in today's world, the writer must agree. However, when teachers and parents feel that conformity is of prime importance the ideas of children wither and die away before they are born.

Deeply concerned themselves and warned by the statements of serious thinkers in all disciplines, a growing body of elementary classroom teachers are mustering their forces to defend what they believe is a fundamental part of every learner's educational program. To answer their critics and strengthen their own beliefs they know that keeping abreast of the research and literature is as important as keeping the channels of independent thought and enterprise open for the children they teach.

In order to understand this process of which we speak, let us examine our own concepts as well as those of some of the writers and researchers. Let us look at definitions and descriptions of creative people and the creative act, and try to establish a common point of view. There are those who say, "Creativity is a way of life," and others who say, "It is life itself." A distinguished and formidable group of scholars have investigated traits displayed by creative people. There is uncommon agreement among them as to these traits. The traits of fluency, adaptability, originality, the ability to synthesize and analyze, fluidity, sensitivity, flexibility, and uniqueness are stated in many different ways; but they do appear again and again. Perhaps Olivia in Rumer Godden's[6] *Episode of Sparrows* has summarized them best when she says, "Everyone, everything, each thing is different. So, it isn't safe to know, you, you have to grope."

The creative process is not so easily described. Rogers[7] has said, "My definition then of the creative process is that it is the emergence in action of a novel relational product, growing out of the uniqueness of the individual on the one hand, and the materials, events, people, or circumstances of his life on the other."

He goes on to say that by its very nature its defies description but speaks of a quality in all creative products that he chooses to call an essence or selectivity of emphasis. Concomitant with this is the need to be alone, to say something and an inevitable feeling of ecstasy in the "I've got it, this is what I wanted to say."

In the attempt to distil a short understandable statement of creativity and the process, perhaps we have generalized far too much; but since anybody who reads this article with intent to understand will go to the original sources from which many ideas have been culled, we will go on to discuss the place of the teacher in fostering creativity and the atmosphere that permits individual critical thinking and creative expression. Loren Eiseley[8] in *The Mind as Nature* says:

> The teacher must ever walk warily between the necessity of inducing those conformities which in every generation reaffirm our rebellious humanity, yet he must at the same time allow for the free play of the creative spirit. . . . He too, amid contingencies and weariness, without mental antennae, and with tests that foil him, is a savior of souls . . . and the shapes themselves, driven by their own inner violence, wrench free of his control . . . must . . . surge like released genii from the classroom or, tragically, shrink to something less than bottle size.

We dare not discuss the creative potential of teachers. Too few of us would venture forth were we to feel that in order to maintain a climate necessary for creative endeavor, we ourselves have to be creative. Regardless of how much or how little creative ability a teacher may have there are situations, materials, time, and attitudes that he can provide. Perhaps the provision of these elements is a benchmark of a creative individual.

After long reflection, listening, reading, and observing teachers in action, we see the following characteristics as common in most classrooms in which children are free to think and express themselves. First, whether we look at Miss Vorontosov in fiction or Mr. Jones in Public School 44, we find that the more a teacher knows about the individual child, the more likelihood there is that the teacher values creative intent and creative output. When interests, desires, tolerances, and talents are suspected or known, the teacher is apt to provide the time and the psychological climate. The teacher who constantly attempts to learn the "why" and the "how" of behavior patterns in general and of each child in particular is more likely to value creative products than those who do not. The one who looks always for the elements that synthesize to make each child tick in his own unique way; the particular stimuli to which he responds, his threshold of fatigue, his pace, and the kind of atmosphere in which he operates best is most likely to encourage personal expression.

The second characteristic of this teacher is that he obviously values uniqueness. He encourages honesty and integrity, which is not always fully matured in the child. He neither preaches nor moralizes about these qualities, but rather he emphasizes them as part of the self-awareness that is always present in creativity. He prizes the growth he observes in this direction and by his support conditions the child to look within himself for a code to live by. He, the teacher, responds to original thought with appreciation and sincerity. The right word at the right time will sometimes carry the child over the last barrier to that wonderful "touché" moment when the child realizes it is mine, mine alone and I like it.

Nothing is more characteristic of the creative process than self-discipline. The third attribute of this teacher then is an honest concern for building habits of self-respect, direction, and control. Extrinsic control means death to creative thinking. In saying this we do not refer to those necessary conformities mentioned earlier. Here we speak of a built-in self-control and discipline that knows when to conform to societal pressures but reserves the right to be his own judge and jury in creative endeavors. The teacher recognizes that no more fertile soil exists for growth in these directions than in creative activities, for the most highly developed discipline in the world is required for genuine creative endeavor, intrinsically conceived and internally applied. Far more rigid rules are applied by the creator than any external force can ever apply.

Fourth, this teacher has humility. He recognizes clearly that he can't possibly know everything. His security is not dependent upon keeping a page ahead of the students. He knows that children can teach him much, that there is a great deal to be learned together, that he can never hope to equal some in perception and awareness. He will often stand in awe at the wonder in them. As Sara Teasdale[9] says it:

> Children's faces looking up
> Holding wonder like a cup

or Loren Eiseley,[10] saying, "I have had the experience of being labeled by that vague word 'mystic' because I have not been able to shut out *wonder* occasionally...."

Ah, would that we all could appreciate "another world of pure reverie of at least equal importance to the human soul."[11] As those boys and girls blast off for thresholds he, their teacher, will never know, he will applaud their flights. He will teach them to let no man be their measuring stick. Leonora Speyer[12] speaks for them all when she says:

> Measure me, sky!
> Tell me I reach by a song
> Nearer the stars;
> I have been little so long.
>
> Sky be my depth,
> Winds be my width and my height,
> World my heart's span;
> Loveliness wings for my flight.

Yes, the teacher who values creativity has great humility but no subservience.

What all this has to do with the teaching of English we now begin to see. As a sixth characteristic of the teacher seeking creativity on the part of his pupils, this teacher is a catalytic agent who brings children, experience and expression together. Expression requires symbols, and language is one system of symbols that is used for intake, thinking, and output. No one who understands creativity tries to teach creativity, for creativity cannot be taught; but more children than we care to admit must have proven to them that what they are, say, and do is important. The creatively oriented teacher opens doors to every media of expression, be it words, movement, color, form, shape, rhythm, melody, or chemical elements and sees that each child has opportunities to experiment with the media. Out of this experiencing, some time for some children, at least, will emerge a novel relational product. In *The Prophet,*[13] Kahlil Gibran says of teaching:

> [He] Gives not of his wisdom but rather of his faith and lovingness.
> [Tells not] but rather leads to the threshold of your own mind.
> [Gives not his vision] for the vision of one man lends not its wings
>   to another man.

The foregoing traits and habits it seems to the writer add up to just one thing and that is what Rogers labels psychological safety. The child is freed from external evaluation; he is accepted as of unconditional worth, and he finds empathy. A teacher so oriented makes no judgments of the end product of a creative process. While he often may, really must, react with honest feeling as to his likes and dislikes, there is absolutely no place for good-bad, beautiful-ugly, right-wrong, A-B evaluative comments. "This is what I wanted to say, it is mine, I like it," lies in the heart of the communicant. External evaluation of unique original endeavor is always a threat, always creates a need for defensiveness, always means that some private part of an experience must be denied the light of day. We speak of children's efforts, children in the elementary school who are not yet ready to enter competitive fields in personal expression, children who are learning to savor experience and dredge it up out of the well of the subconscious and after a fine frenzy of awareness, selection, and arrangement can be proud of what they have done. Says Mauree Applegate[14] "class evaluation shrivels the soul of the creator and miniscule corrections shorten the life of the teacher."

Throughout the writing one is constantly reminded of the aloneness, the loneliness of creating. When we consider how many times teachers and parents have forced children into groups, rather than accepting the need and right of people to isolate themselves from their fellows, one is ashamed. Some children must be shown that there is no stigma attached to a desire to be alone, that the ability to shut out an all too cacophonic world and retreat into oneself is sometimes healthy and desirable. Call this solitude what you will; place it geographically where you choose; it is the erection of walls. A. A. Milne[15] gives it to the child in "HalfwayDown":

> Halfway up the stairs isn't up,
> And isn't down.
> It isn't in the nursery,
> It isn't in the town.
> And all sorts of funny thoughts
> Run round my head:
> It isn't really anywhere!
> It's somewhere else instead!

Children who can be taught not to have a horror of being alone may find rich rewards in developing their own talents.

Sensory awareness, emotions, and imagination are the "stuff" out of which the child creates. As he savors these—chocolate and cinnamon, purple grapes wet with dew, an icy fairyland, a shroud of fog, a baby's lips, the crash of thunder, the joy of friendship, the sorrow of loss, the happiness of the warm puppy —and rolls them around in his mind and on his tongue, as he listens to poets and storytellers, as he tries out his own ideas, he is discovering himself.

Noncreative people seem to have a deep instinctive dread of the person who dares to be or think differently. Research shows children penalized at home and at school for this difference. If you, the teacher, positively wish to encourage creativity, you must help all children respect the right of the individual to his individuality. Whether the child himself will venture out.is not the problem, but that he as well as society generally must come to understand "that if a man seems too out of step with his fellows, it may be because as Thoreau said 'He hears a different drummmer. Let him step to the music which he hears, however measured or far away.' "[16]

NOW—

> I'm going out to fetch the little calf
> That's standing by his mother, it's so young
> It totters when she licks it with her tongue
> I shan't be gone long, you come, too.[17]

Perhaps the water in the pasture spring has cleared and the little calf (creativity) can stand alone.

As we hold the mirrors up to ourselves, we know that after we have sensed the wonder of opening doors and perhaps have "reached out and occasionally touched with a passing radiance, some other star in the night," we must borrow a black girl's estimate of what we have found.

Says Eiseley:

> In Bimini, on the old Spanish Main, a black girl once said to me, "Those as hunts treasure must go alone, at night, and when they find it they have to leave a little of their blood behind them." I have never heard a finer clearer estimate of the price of wisdom . . . for the girl had given me unknowingly the latitude and longitude of a treasure— a treasure more valuable than all the aptitude tests of this age.[18]

Footnotes

[1] Robert Frost, "The Pasture," *Favorite Poems: Old and New*, ed. by Helen Ferris. Garden City, New York: Doubleday and Co., 1957, pp. 230-31.

[2] Carl Rogers, "Toward a Theory of Creativity," *Creativity and Its Cultivation*, ed. by Harold H. Anderson. New York: Harper and Brothers, 1959, p. 69.

[3] Anderson, *op. cit.*, p. xii.

[4] Sylvia Ashton-Warner, *Spinster*. New York: Simon and Schuster, 1959, p. 221.

[5] Robert Osborn, "Conformity," *Better Homes and Gardens* (October, 1957), pp. 59-61.

[6] Rumer Godden, *An Episode of Sparrows*. New York: The Viking Press, 1955, p. 199.

[7] Rogers, *op. cit.*, p. 71.

[8] Loren Eisley, *The Mind As Nature*. New York: Harper and Row, 1962, p. 24.

[9] Sara Teasdale, "Barter," *Favorite Poems: Old and New*, ed. by Helen Ferris. Garden City, New York: Doubleday and Co., 1957, p. 21.

[10] Eiseley, *op. cit.*, p. 44.

[11] *Ibid.*, p. 45.

[12] Leonora Speyer, "Measure Me, World," *Favorite Poems: Old and New*, ed. by Helen Ferris. Garden City, New York: Doubleday and Co., 1957, p. 22.

[13] Kahlil Gibran, *The Prophet*. New York: Alfred A. Knopf, 1923, pp. 64-65.

[14] Mauree Applegate, *Everybody's Business—Our Children*. Evanston, Illinois: Row, Peterson and Co., 1952, pp. 220-21.

[15] A. A. Milne, "Halfway Down," *Favorite Poems: Old and New*, ed. by Helen Ferris. Garden City, New York: Doubleday and Co., 1957, p. 10.

[16] Henry Thoreau quoted in Carnegie Corporation of New York Quarterly, "Creativity," 11 (July, 1961).

[17] Frost, *loc. cit.*

[18] Eisley, *op. cit.*, pp. 59-60.

25   Hoppity, Skippity, Serendipity

Mauree Applegate

A long-time ardent proponent of children's imaginative writing points out that what this writing does for the child and what it tells us about his inner self may be as important as the literary quality of the product.

Has a child ever revealed any of his inner feelings to you through his writings? How valid and reliable are children's writings as expressions of their feelings? How should a teacher treat a child who pens a violent, hostile outburst? What can a teacher learn about pupils' feelings about school through their writings? In general, do Wilt and Applegate seem to agree or disagree on the essential requirements for creative expression? Miller's article, cited in Selected References for Part Four, deals with this same topic but from a slightly different point of view.

Horace Walpole started it—that word "serendipity." He wrote a short story about the princes of Serendip who, on their quest toward one type of goal, found so many unexpected pleasures along the way—little bonuses that turned out to be of greater importance than the goals they were seeking.

"Serendipity" is a lilting, dancing word, not shod in clumsy shoes as is "concomitant," the usual educator's word for the attendant rewards of any learning project. Concomitants of children's creative writing are indeed serendipities, since they are of far more importance than the end product—the writing itself.

The modern viewpoint toward imaginative writing in the classroom is: What does this writing do for this child? What growth does it register concerning him? What does it tell us about the kind of self he is, that we may learn to live with him and he with himself in growing comfort and peace?

Certainly the product a child creates is important—but only as it relates to the development of the child and can communicate to us concerning the state of his inner being, serving at the same time as a satisfaction to him.

From *Childhood Education* 37:259-262; February 1960. Reprinted by permission of The Association for Childhood Education International, 3615 Wisconsin Avenue, N.W., Washington, D. C. (Copyright © 1960 by the Association) and Maureee Applegate, retired from Wisconsin State College, LaCrosse, Wisconsin.

A child's creative writing builds a bridge from his inner self to a teacher's heart and mind—a fragile swinging bridge, easily destroyed by heavy steps.

My weekly radio program over The Wisconsin School of the Air, for grades four to eight, gives me an opportunity to become familiar with the writings of hundreds of children (50,000 children listen). The teachers are often kind enough to write a bit of a note on the side of the paper about the child who did the writing. One week last spring, from a program entitled, "If Dreams Were for Sale, What Would You Buy?" I received this poem from fourth-grade Patrick. The teacher's note explained that the lad was misshapen and short and very, very overweight and clumsy. She said he had a well-balanced personality, withal, and she never dreamed, until he wrote this verse, that he resented his bodily handicaps.

If Dreams Were for Sale

If I got a wish along the line,
I'd wish I wasn't a frankenstien
I'd wish I was short, but not too short,
I'd wish I was good at any sport.
If I had another wish,
I'd like to be a real cute dish.

The teacher reported that she was trying to build up the boy's status at school through his creative writing and extra assignments at which he could excel.

No cry from one human heart to another has ever affected me as this communication from sixth-grade Betty. The child's whole biography of heartbreak is written large here for all to read. It came from a broadcast, "Courage Has a Million Faces."

It Takes Courage

It was my birthday. I had invited everybody. It is first now that I realize what happened.

All of a sudden I was in the world I had always wanted. I was what you might say popular. Everybody who was invited to my party was my friend. I remember it so clearly, even though it has been three years now. The night of the party was excellent to every extreem.

After my party I started to loose all my friends, until I was back to the old routine! That wasn't all.

All my life I had been rather clumsy. I gradually grew worse until my muscles couldn't pull me up the stairs. Then the worst of it came. I was broken the news that I had muscular distrophy.

Every day I have to do exercises to help strengthen my muscles. The exercises seem so easy that even a baby could do them.

What can a teacher do to build status for this child? If nothing more she can show her a dozen times a day that she cares about her. As she passes her desk she can let gentle fingers brush her sleeve; she can often give her a secret understanding smile; she can make her feel important in many little ways. I know one teacher who placed a tiny occasional inexpensive gift in an unpopular child's desk, marked in "cut-out and pasted " newspaper words, "from a secret friend." The child thrived under the therapy. Betty doesn't need pity; she needs friends.

The personal writing of a sensitive child sends an SOS to the teacher, not for probing, not for exploring, but for friendly understanding and thoughtful therapy. And yet, a teacher must not feel that he has the whole story from one single clue on a child's paper. Each contact with the child adds still another clue to the mosaic of his personality.

Not only is the need for status communicated to a teacher through creative writing, but the beginning of mental illness usually shows itself in a child's paper—witness fourth-grade Jean's.

My Toys

I did not like my doll so I wanted to brack her head off. I would of nocked out her eyes, nose, and mounth but I could not. I liked my little doll better so I made a doll house for my little doll. Dolls are bad. Dolls are sad. Dolls are good.   The End

If professional help is not available to Jean, she can often be induced to draw, write out her fierce feelings, play them out in creative play or dramatics or with hand puppets. It seems evident that Jean is transferring her feelings about people to dolls. Maybe her home is more frustrating than she can bear, so she must be given many chances for success at school. I'm sure this teacher must have visited the home after this paper. I don't believe she could possibly *not* have done so.

Children who can learn to explode on paper often are able to keep from screaming at home or at school. On the "Let's Write" program we try to provide the children with one pop-off program each year. The therapy provided thus, say the teachers, has a healing effect. For when our inner hates and fears are subjected to the sun and air of another's reading they lose their musty odor of morbidity.

Fifth-grade Paul, a "Let's Writer," too, was far more able to treat his sister with respect after this unbrotherly but perfectly normal outburst:

My Sister

My Sister doesn't care if she gets to school ten hours late. She never hurries. She goes as slow as she can. She knows about as much as a mouse. She's what I call a mad sister. Always mad! I would like to give her one so hard she would fly to the moon and never come back.

Never be worried, teacher, about such unbrotherly attacks flattened out on paper. Just be honest with yourself and remember how often you have felt the same about a relative, a fellow teacher, or even about your life mate. Writing out one's feelings is good therapy for adults as well as for children—providing, of course, one destroys the evidence.

Fourth-grade Edward dared not tell his dad his true feelings, but one can easily feel vicariously his release after writing this paragraph!

Me and My Bank

My dad always keeps taking my money. One day I saw him taking some of it. About a week later, I found a mouse trap in the house. Then he put his hand in my bank and got his finger caught in it. Boy and did I get it from him. I could not seat down for 1 or 2 hours that day.

What needs does this story by sixth-grade Terry wig-wag to his teacher?

In Africa

One day I decided to go to Africa and hunt lions. I got there on Monday, November 15, 1948. I went hunting the next day. I was 20 feet from some bushes when a lion charged me, but I wasn't scared. I aimed my gun and shot it in the eyes. An hour later I had six lions, two tigers and one bullet left. What was I going to do? All of sudden two lions charged me, I shot one and then I was out of bullets. I dropped my gun and started to wrestle with it. As the rounds went on I got tired but I was going to stick it out. Gong! The tenth round is ready to start. I picked up a stick and put it in his mouth so he couldn't bite me but he bit my stick in two. I was scared. I started chewing my fingers until they were sharp. Then I dug my hand into him and killed him. I was the champ.

I went home and never went lion hunting again.

Only the meek and the fearful are so desperately brave as to write in this way. Could it not be that an exclusive diet of comic books and horror programs (or television in Jerry's case) needs supplementing with some almost-good books? Be careful, however, teacher, not to change reading diets too fast or too completely lest personality upsets develop.

Creative writing alerts sensitive teachers to other needs of children than friends, understanding and therapy. The need of a child's mind for standing on tiptoe, for being stretched to its utmost, is often communicated through his imaginative writing.

What does eighth-grade Jon's "Just How Does a Wheel Feel" suggest to a teacher about the need to personalize her teaching of geography and history so that a child feels that he has actually been there? How else can we ready hearts and minds for the gradually coming One World?

Just How Does a Wheel Feel?

I've often wondered just how it would feel to be a wheel zooming down the street supporting a car, a bus or a bike. The wear and tear those poor things take, all the glass and things that lay in the streets these days! I'll bet it really hurts when they get a blowout. I never hear a word but I know I wouldn't like a nail jabbed into me.

They see many things though and travel many places. And they see things from a different view, but I suppose things look pretty mixed up when they're spinning around so fast.

Another thing I wonder about is when I walk by the junkyard and see all those hundreds of tires piled up all over the place. I suppose to them its a big celebration, a get-together of all the old tires. They probably tell about all the places they've been and all the things they've seen. And I suppose just like humans some of them make their stories just a little exaggerated.

But I don't suppose I'll ever find out these things unless I become a wheel myself.

What need must sixth-grade Neil's teacher provide for the children in her room who long for enriched vocabulary and the taste of ripe words on the tongue?

My Garden

My garden is so gorgeous
With its sun-bloomed roses
Its rain-drenched daffodils,
The hail-hammered violets
Have almost lost their purpleness.
My flowers are like gems to me
My sister things they are the epitomy (e).

And the Jennifers in her room who so need music and the other arts for their soul's hunger. . . . What of the Jennifers, Teacher?

I think I'm playing the music, and in some music I think I'm dancing to it. I feel it in my heart. The swaying of the music. It feels so touching, that I like to play music all the time. I wish every one loved music as I do. I love to dance to music. When I'm alone I make my own music. I love the way the notes go from one to the other. I love to play my records over and over. I sing and dance to the music.

And the Carols in a fifth-grade room who need to touch, see, smell and feel in order to appreciate. What of the Carols, Teacher?

These I Love To Touch

I love the feeling of mother's furs
Of hands that's full of money,
I love the feeling that you get
When sticking clean fingers in honey.

I love the feeling of a nice, warm bath
Clean bedclothes on my bed,
I love the feeling that you get
With "shampooey" hair on my head.

I love to touch new dresses
Especially "netty" ones.
I love to touch the letter for me
Whenever the postman comes.

I love the feeling of soft, clean hair
I love the feeling of flowers
I also love the feeling of books
And to browse around for hours.

I love the feeling of a nice, cool lake
Most always on a "tropical" day,
I love the feeling that I get
When I go to the beach to play.

I love the feeling of lots of shells
And wiggling toes in the sand,
I love the feeling of shopping around
And taking my sister to a band.

All of these I love to touch
And many, many more
There are so many things people love to touch
Ever so many galore!

And the Roberts who are already thinking of their future roads. . . . Do you take plenty of time with them for fine literature, Teacher, or are you spending all your time on what businessmen call the essentials? There is a little of the Robert in every child. What of the Roberts?

Roadways

I don't know where my road leads to
It's an undiscovered trail
And can only be blazed by myself
But as I grow older
I hope to blaze it wide and clean of brush.

Ah, truly, to travel is better than to arrive, as Robert Louis Stevenson pointed out so long ago. At least this is true in the field of children's creative writing. What the children say between the lines is so much more important than the lines themselves.

If we teachers just had more time to listen to those "quiet ditties of no tune." . . . But a teacher's days go by . . . Hoppity, Skippity . . . Serendipity. . . . But then, so do everybody's.

26 Creative Writing in the First Grade

Julia D. Kelley

Some persons argue that creative writing is really only feasible after pupils have gained some competence in handwriting, spelling, and technical skills. But Kelley contends that a successful start can—and must—be made early in grade one even before pupils have mastered these skills. And she provides abundant examples to support her contention.

What kind of experiences are particularly conducive to generating a desire to write? How can a teacher take into consideration individual differences in interest and ability? Are there any guiding principles with which you disagree? How does this article relate to the preceding one by Applegate? To the one in Part Six by Burrows? Think about Ruddell's article in Part Three; what might he believe necessary for good creative writing besides experiences and encouragement? A more structured approach to beginning writing is advocated by Evertts in the article on primary composition cited in Selected References for Part Four while articles by Hill, May and Tabachnick, and Ross will also be helpful to primary grade teachers. Hildreth's article describes how early writing can aid in learning to read.

Creative writing *can* be done in the first grade. It is at this grade level that the children combine their initial attempts to compose and write independently.

Young children use oral language almost exclusively to communicate with others. As they mature, their experiences broaden and they need to be guided into expressing themselves in written form. Children progress at different rates of speed in written communication. The success of creative writing depends upon conditions within the child himself and upon the classroom atmosphere created by the teacher.

From *Elementary English* 41:35-39; January 1964. Reprinted with permission of the National Council of Teachers of English and Julia D. Kelley, teacher of first grade, Prospect Hill School, Pelham, New York.

Challenge Children

One of our aims is to challenge children to write. Therefore, each child must have freedom and encouragement to express himself. He needs stimulation to give an imaginative interpretation of his life. Diverse experiences, in and out of school, become the focal point for classroom discussion and thinking. As a child exchanges his ideas with others his imagination is stirred. Audiovisual approaches help to extend the child's background and knowledge. Through the reading of good literature the teacher helps him to develop attitudes and appreciation for what others have expressed and written. This exposure enriches his vocabulary and helps build standards for writing.

Children are encouraged to tell their own ideas and to dictate their impressions. When the teacher writes what the children dictate to her, they recognize what writing stands for; and as the children watch the teacher and others write, they may also develop a desire to write. With wise teacher guidance, children can be lead to tell or write about their experiences. A child's progress in language shows whether he should dictate his story to the teacher or be encouraged to write his own story. To force independent writing on the child who is not ready for it can instill a permanent dislike for writing. The teacher's role is to foster, not force.

Provide Experiences

Throughout the first grade, the teacher provides an experiential program which extends the previous learnings of children in a natural and functional situation. She teaches reading, penmanship, sentence structure, and some spelling, thus enabling the children to write their own ideas. The teacher and children develop charts cooperatively in relation to the class activities. These charts are written records of classroom and community experiences. Through these the children are made aware of the left to right progression in writing, general format, and the spacing between words. From these simple beginnings, children are made aware of the components that are important to writing. Effective instruction, enlightened guidance, and language of the teacher are contributing factors in fostering independent writing.

The timing for beginning writing is important. Some children are ready to write at an early age, while others, who have limited experiences, may not have much desire to write and have little knowledge of what writing is.

Give Encouragement

Children need encouragement to find something they really want to write about. Recent experiences provide a good beginning. One boy, who had spent the summer in Greece, shared his experiences orally with the class. By the middle of October he wanted to write. He wrote, "I sm in the Matrnen See." (I swam in the Mediterranean Sea.) He illustrated it with a boy swimming in blue water. This writing was enjoyed by the class and praised by the teacher. It was put on the bulletin board. No reference was made to the phonetic spelling, and no corrections were made.

The following day a girl wrote her story, "I sm a myl." She read her story to the group and told about being in a swimming race during the summer. These two writings started an interest in self-expression through writing. There were only a few children who were ready to attempt it at this time. One child copied from a color chart, "Carol sees colors. Red, Green, blue." Her attempt was praised, and she was encouraged to try to write some experience she had.

Evaluate the Writing

For evaluating the independent writing, each child has an individual folder in which his writings are kept and reviewed periodically. The following are examples of one child's writings through the months. It is particularly interesting to note the spelling, use of sentence structure, capitalization, punctuation, and an attempt to write in paragraph form. They show that in order to express himself freely, the child must have something which relates to himself to write about. Jerry wrote:

Nov. On Sunday I thnt to N.y.
  I saw the npierer S.t. bldin.
  I sm in the Meditrraean Sea.
  I was in Grrce This Summer.
Dec. I wint to the conchre clab (country club) and I saw santa clos.
  I gat a tag boat fram santa clos.
Jan. Yesterday I got a new ies bxi. (ice box)
  It was one pes. (piece)
  The man put it in the cold prch. My Mother told the man to put it theyr.
Feb. The snow is coming down. The ground is all wet. I like the snow. I like to run in the snow becoas I like to see the snow in frrant of me.
Mar.   My Brorther
  My borther is coming back June 18, 1962 for a vacation.

The vacation ends in Soptmber. I will have fun.

He will come back on a jet. Greec is about 6500 miels away.

Apr.   Once there was a very rich king. One of his slays said whane will I retier. So the king said in one year. After one year the slav was as rich as a king. Bat the king was very poor. (He had a drawing of a king on a throne with a slave in front of him.)

The children's interest and desire to write are stimulated by the writings of other children. Many children write their own stories using phonetic spelling. At the beginning most of the stories are one or two sentences. Most of them begin with a capital letter and end with a period.

Phonetic Spelling

In beginning writing the children are encouraged to use phonetic spelling. They are told to "Write it the way it sounds to you." The research skills begin at this time. The children are encouraged to find words neccessary for their writings in the many sources available in the room. They are to use picture dictionaries, charts, words around the room, individual word lists, and books. Each child also uses the *New York City Spelling Words List,* a booklet, as a reference. This booklet is in a dictionary form. The children, having been trained to use a vertical alphabet since September, are ready to use this speller to find some of the necessary words for their writings.

The children are taught, from the beginning, to write independently. Since words that are difficult to spell can present a mental block in writing, the children are trained to depend on themelves. So that the flow of writing will not be stopped, the teacher does not spell any words for the children. If it were necessary for them to wait until the teacher could provide the word, there would be prolonged periods of waiting in a class of twenty-nine children. Therefore, they are encouraged to look for the word or to spell it phonetically.

In the phonetic spelling of young children, there is a tendency to transpose letters in some words, such as: "I liek to paly. I aet dinr. I loev my baby. It is vrey niec." The children seem to know the letters in the words but are not aware of the correct placement of them. However, with many children, the transposition of letters corrects itself in a few months as the children gain power and experience in this written form of self-expression.

Praise Early Attempts

All of the children's writings are praised, especially the early attempts; no comments are made about the phonetic spelling, handwriting, sentence structure, or punctuation. The first-grade teacher needs to have an accepting and respective attitude toward the child's writing. With the child's permission, some writings are read to the group by the teacher in order to give proper inflections and emphasis. Then they are posted on the bulletin board. The children enjoy reading these stories in leisure time. Each child's story is meaningful to him. Although it may be a conglomeration of letters that are meaningless to others, he can read it to the group. One day some children, who had been reading the stories on the bulletin board, came to me with great excitement. One exclaimed, "Someone here writes in a foreign language. Charles can read anything, but he can't read this." This story was one that was unintelligible to anyone but the child who had written it.

At this level, children feel free to write when they know they will not be judged for incorrect spelling, penmanship, or content. The children who are afraid to take a chance are encouraged to try. It is important that each child's work be appreciated and praise be given for the slightest effort he makes. Otherwise, he may not continue to write. One child with poor muscular control in handwriting needed a great deal of encouragement before he would attempt to write. At the end of January he wrote: "I like my baby boy. he is qut." Through praise and encouragement he continued writing. Early in April he wrote this story:

Sool the princ. (Steal the Prince)

I day the princ whnt into the didb (deep) deark forest whr theyr loveed (lived) a princas. she loved in a casl. But the witking ound (old) which who was very witking (wicked) was theyr and she started (stole) the princ. Call the policeman. then they love happle every aftr.

The children liked this story so much they wanted it read a second time, and they requested that it be put on top of the other stories which were on the bulletin board. Although there were some remarks about the handwriting, the story was the important thing and so it was placed on top. It was amazing how Jeff's handwriting improved as a result of the children's criticism and approval of his story.

One day, the class wrote stories about a sad time. One child, who said he had never been sad, wrote a happy story. Leslie wrote "When nobode wantd to play with me." One child wrote about death.

A sad time

I had a gandmother she was very old. And one day she had to go the hospitle. And in the hoslpitl she deid. I was srie. everone cride. We saw hra wen she drid.

It was illustrated with a car, some people, a church and a clock. There is no lack of real situations in which children can be stimulated to do creative writing.

The teacher must try to handle the criticisms of the writings on an impersonal basis. Yet writings must be criticized in order to help the child to do better writing. In the first grade, a common fault is the tendency to repeat the word "and" and the words "I like." These repetitions can be eliminated by teaching and guidance.

One of the problems in beginning writing is training children to stick to one point. Through the reading of many stories children in time become aware of staying with one idea and an improvement can be seen in their writings.

All Writing at School

All the writings of the children are done in the classroom; nothing is accepted from home. In this way, the teacher is assured that all work done is exclusively the children's, with no outside help.

A teacher must provide varied opportunities for the children to write. The writing of letters is one excellent form of functional writing. Early in the year the children write a simple letter of invitation to their parents to visit school. Every opportunity for letter writing is used in order to foster a desire for the children to compose their own letters. The emphasis is placed on what is to be said. Thank you notes and letters of invitation are sent to other classes. These are group composed and copied from the board for correctness of form and content. After Glenn's orbital flight, the class wrote and mailed a letter to him, telling how proud they were of his flight. This experience proved the biggest incentive for letter writing that the children had ever had.

After a teacher from a neighboring school visited us, we had an opportunity to write to her and ask if her class would like to exchange letters with us. At the beginning these letters were group composed. Soon each child was writing his own letter to a pen pal in the other school. They answered questions asked, gave some interesting bit of their own news, and asked a question of the other child. These letters were written each week; and if the teacher forgot, the children were sure to remind her that they must write a letter.

By the middle of April, the children were writing without any help in the format of the letter. They all knew where the date, salutation, body of the letter, closing, and signature went. Most of them used correct punctuation for the letter. It had been stressed that when we send a letter to someone we must have correct spelling, punctuation, sentence structure, grammar, and our best handwriting. After each child composed his letter, the teacher made any corrections necessary and the child recopied it. This procedure did not seem to stifle creativity in any way. Very few mistakes were made at this time. A real purpose and proper incentive helped to make the children do their best work. Before the class wrote, the parts of the letter and the different types of punctuation were discussed. Some samples, as they were written before any corrections, are as follows:

April 2, 1962.

Dear Sally,
    I went to a ice skating rink. There were many children there. There were some people there too. I saw some little girls ice skating. They did not fall down. One of them could skate backwards. She can skate around. Have you ever went to a skating rink?
    Some of the children could not skate. They were lining. (learning)

Your freind,
Mary

May 10, 1962

Dear Peter,
    I went to a museum of nacharl history and I saw dinosoars. I just saw the sclatns of the dinasoors. They looked tarable. Did you go to the museum?

Your friend,
Jack

May 21, 1962

Dear Susan,
    My family is fine. I have for pople in my family. How many pople do you have in your family? These are the ones that I have in my family. I have my Mother and father and my brother and me. Who is in your family?

Your friend,
Joan

June 5, 1962

Dear Lanny,
    We have a little puppy. He is nice to us and our mother and father. We like him and he likes us. Do you have a puppy? our puppy is nice. If you have a puppy or if you have a dog tell me.

Your friend,
Jimmy

June 13, 1962

Dear Bobby,
    At our grandmas we like to ride on the horses. Are grandma has a born and on one side of the barn they have hay. James is alorgick to hay. Bob and I have fun, do you?

Your friend,
Ken

In Summary

If teachers strive to give the children every opportunity to write and express themselves in their own way it is a means of finding out the feelings, likes, and dislikes of children. Analysis of the writing enables the teacher to find where help is needed for individual children or for group instruction in the different areas: listening, speech, handwriting, spelling, sentence structure, or usage.

Primarily by rousing the children's desire to write, the teacher stimulates and guides them in the development of their abilities. The child who wants to communicate makes the necessary effort to learn the mechanics of writing. Thus, with the teacher's guidance, he becomes self-propelled.

27 Literature and Composition in the Elementary Grades

Eldonna L. Evertts

One aspect of the work on Project English by the Nebraska University Center was a large-scale investigation into whether elementary school pupils could improve their composition if they used as models patterns found in quality children's literature. This essay reports some of the central conclusions and suggestions of that group.

How does Evertts's underlying thesis relate to the article by Ruddell in Part Three? Can this approach effectively provide for individual differences in language ability, socio-economic level, and interests? Is there any danger in dissecting literature to find its fundamental components? Do Evertts's suggestions agree with Wilt's conditions necessary for creativity? How does this article relate to the one by Edman in Part Three? Evertts's article cited in Selected References for Part Four applies this approach specifically to the early school years while those by Tiedt and Carlson extend it to intermediate school years.

The interrelationship of the language arts has long been stressed by authorities in English and education; yet, too often the elementary teacher still tries to separate the language arts and to teach the skills of each area independently. However, if the nature of English and the role of language learning, as well as competence in the use of language, were really understood, administrators and teachers planning curricula would recognize this interrelationship and also plan concrete activities for it. Only recently, for example, educators have begun to sense the importance of beginning and continuing with oral language throughout the school program. The "story time" now introduces basic literary concepts to the elementary pupil, so that these, too, will help in the pupil's composition.

From *New Directions in Elementary English* (edited by Alexander Frazier), 1967, pp. 207-221. Reprinted with permission of the National Council of Teachers of English and Eldonna L. Evertts, Assistant Executive Secretary, NCTE, and Associate Professor, University of Illinois, Urbana.

All levels of instruction are indeed reflecting an increased emphasis on the importance of oral English. In the past, elementary teachers have probably given some consideration to oral language, but they have not really thought seriously of what this means in curriculum organization. If teachers were to accept the contention made by Ruth Strickland that no one will read well or write well who has not learned to talk well, then they would make sure that all phases of English instruction included both an oral and aural approach.[1] Walter Loban suggests that reforms in language arts curricula may be expected to reflect the powerful link between oral language and reading and writing skills.[2]

To prepare children for the enjoyment of literature and written communication, one must begin with oral language and continue to parallel the oral and the written. Oral language and written communication must be considered together as a sequential English program from kindergarten through high school and even into college.

Recent research shows that boys and girls can form basic sentence patterns in oral conversation when they enter the first grade.[3] As pupils mature in the use of language, they learn how to vary the construction or components within the fixed slots or elements comprising the basic patterns. That is, students illustrate their ability to handle language by expansion within the subject, verb phrase, and object or by subordination and coordination, rather than mere extension of sentence length and the use of a typical sentence pattern. Since children first gain control over language by oral experimentation before entering the classroom, is it not logical that they need to continue learning through oral experimentation with language? Even in the study of foreign languages, the approach has become an oral-aural approach rather than a solo task focused upon visual recognition.

Oral Language as the Base of Writing

Before a child can be expected to write expanded sentences, he should have the opportunity to "try" the sentences orally. At the primary level much more can be done than has been done with beginning chart stories written in the language of the child who dictates the story; there should be no restraint in either sentence structure or vocabulary. Recently a student teacher took her class to view an excavation and to watch the steam shovel at work. The children were delighted and were impatient to discuss what they had seen. But when they started to write the story, the supervising teacher restricted the vocabulary to that of the reading series. So instead of "We saw a steam shovel," one line of the chart read, "We saw something."

In contrast, consider this first grade story. The pupils had listened to "The Story of the First Butterflies" and "The Story of the First Woodpecker," which represent the simplest kind of myths. This particular class loved the "pourquoi" stories explaining the world about them. One child, with some help from classmates, told the original story that follows, illustrating his concept of a myth. (The teacher, as secretary, wrote the story exactly as it was told to her. This technique is used by all good teachers at all levels of instruction: to accept the child's contribution during the priceless moments of creativity and leave the editing and correction until the pupils ask for ways to express ideas clearly and accurately in written form.)

The Story of the First Jack-o-Lantern

Someone found some seeds. They didn't know what kind of seed it was. They said, "We'll plant it and find out."

They planted it. It grew and grew. They gave it some water. It grew into a vine. One day later a yellow flower grew on it.

A little, thin round thing came where the flower was. There wasn't anything left of the flower. The green ball turned into a yellow ball. A man gave it the name of pumpkin. He decided to make eyes, nose, and mouth on it. He found seeds inside. He planted them. They grew. They had baby seeds again. After they had so many seeds, they gave them to all the world. They had Halloween with them.[4]

As teachers work with the young child who is using substandard dialect, they are finding that the child must become familiar with the standard dialect before he can logically be expected to speak, dictate, or read in the accepted dialect. At times, the teacher may use the child's dialect to enable him to realize that his speech can be recorded and then read by others. There comes a time during the child's experience with dictation or with his own writing when the teacher can show that there are more ways than one to say something, and that one must then select the appropriate form for a specific occasion or for a specific audience. An abstract knowledge about dialect is useless; the ability to use more than a single variety of language indicates linguistic command. Of course, learning does not result because the teacher once illustrated an alternate choice which could be identified as standard language usage. Teaching and learning a new dialect involve many experiences—a variety of ways to make the "new" sound natural to the child. Teachers must be sensitive not only to the child's desire to learn more about controlling his language patterns but also the rate at which this learning can be economically or efficiently accomplished. Teachers must use a light touch; they must beware of making too much ado about form or usage when the child is deeply occupied with recording content, ideas, or emotions and feelings.

Together teachers and pupils can explore the manipulation and handling of language. This exploration can be oral as pupils rephrase sentences or substitute words and phrases for the ideas they are expressing. They could begin with a sentence such as this: "The girl went down the street." The teacher will ask the children what word or words could be substituted for "went" which would help them visualize how the girl went down the street. The pupils might suggest: "The girl skipped and hopped down the street." This sentence could be expanded to: "The new girl who lives next to us skipped down the street" or "The new girl with the tired puppy slowly sauntered along the cool, shady street."

While she was reading *Little Tim and the Brave Sea Captain* by Edward Ardizzone, one teacher tried to help pupils become aware of the many ways a single idea could be expressed and to experiment with varying sentence patterns. She began with the sentence in the book, "In the middle of the night was a terrible crash." The sentences which the class composed from this idea were these:

In the night there was a crash. It seemed to be about midnight.
A boat crashed on some rocks in the middle of the night.
A terrible crash happened in the middle of the night.
A terrible crash was heard about midnight.
About midnight a terrible crash was heard.[5]

Ruth Strickland has investigated most carefully the relationship between listening and oral reading, silent reading, and spoken sentence patterns. The ability to listen correlates highly with the degree of competence in these variables. Pupils who listen effectively are also able to read well orally, score high on tests of reading comprehension and vocabulary, and have mastered the use of the common patterns of sentence structure. Her findings would indicate that teachers could help pupils gain power in all the related language subjects by supplying suitable material for listening, and the field of literaure has much to offer that is worthy of "listening time." Through listening a child notices how others use language. Then he is ready to speak and write—to experiment with language on his own.

Recent research has reported many other important findings with accompanying implications for teaching and curriculum planning; now it is time for teachers and administrators to use these ideas creatively as they begin experimenting with new techniques relating and incorporating more oral language into the language arts curriculum. They must rid themselves, in light of current knowledge, of binding outdated concepts. They must be encouraged to try new ways of teaching in their own classrooms. They must be permitted individual experimentation and not be forced to transplant artificially the ideas or methods of others. Teaching is, after all, a personal act with the principal determining factors being the teacher and the pupil. However, the teacher must be informed as to what are academically respectable ideas and what are educationally sound practices; then he may apply these to the instructional task.

Sylvia Ashton-Warner, in her refreshing book, *Teacher*, gives us this insight:

We don't waste enough in school. We hoard our old ideas or charts to be used again and again like stale bread. Ideas are never the same again, even those of the masters; even if the only change is in our own mood of reapproach. Yet there's never a shortage of ideas if the stimulus is there. Waste the old paper and waste the old pictures and waste the old ideas. It's tidier and simpler.[6]

Sometimes teachers preserve too much when they should be trying to use better approaches and better organization. These teachers resemble a certain recluse living in New York City. After her death the police went into her overcrowded apartment. They found things neat and orderly, although she seemed to have saved everything. In one closet they found the acme of orderliness and preservation—a box labeled "String too short to use."

Structure in Literature and Composition

Before coming to school, many fortunate young children have listened to mothers or grandmothers read or tell stories. Through listening, these children have learned to differentiate a story, a poem, a Mother Goose rhyme. They have captured the delight of the old folktales and the Hollywood versions of these same stories. Since children can also learn how written language functions and in particular how words and phrases are put together to form sentences, paragraphs, and finally a complete story; there is much value in reading quantities of stories, poems, and books aloud in the classroom. While teachers have often read stories and books for general enjoyment or relaxation, they have not realized that quality oral reading and interpretation of literature can be a vital part of the English program.

What better way to help pupils learn about their language than to hear it read aloud in the classroom? What better way to learn about the structure of stories and plot motifs than through listening to the stories that illustrate these principles? Plot is basic to a story; it rises from conflict which is favorably or unfavorably resolved. When a pupil is asked to write a story, he must become increasingly able to handle plot development if his story is to be more than a mere recital of events. Pupils cannot apply a broad generalization to plot structure until they have had sufficient exposure to what constitutes plot or a basic structural plot motif. While the differences between stories must not be ignored or forgotten, pupils need some understanding of what James R. Squire calls "form consciousness," which is basic to the reading and understanding of literature and to the composing process.[7]

Edward Rosenheim has stressed the idea that *a story is made*.[8] The author not only tells a story but he also creates a work which follows certain conventions and fulfills certain expectations. Then if a pupil is asked to create, he must understand how literary plots are put together so that he can make his own story. He needs to understand the literary structures which he can use to convey his ideas; he needs to know what is meant by a "story" before he can compose a "story." Later he can distinguish a chronological series of events which he may have experienced from a "story" based upon these events.

Literary criticism can approach plot structures from various points of view, not necessarily compatible. However, the following is one system of classification of basic structural plot motifs of folk tales which has been successfully used with elementary pupils in an experimental curriculum study conducted at the University of Nebraska.[9] According to this classification, there are four basic plot motifs for folk tales and two for fables. Actually stories are rarely based upon a single motif. The motifs which follow merely serve as a central description upon which the individual story can be superimposed.

Plot motifs for folk tales

1. The journey from home to isolation. This motif seldom exists alone; in many folk tales the central character leaves his home and enters the world of danger, excitement, frustration, or adventure. Upon entering this cold, impartial world, the central character leaves the warmth, comfort, and security of his home environment. Sleeping Beauty only travels upstairs, but she leaves her secure home and enters partial and then complete isolation.

2. The journey from home to confrontation with a monster. In this motif the central character leaves a secure home and meets a monster—an animal, person or element of nature—which either destroys the central character or is overcome by the hero. This motif can be illustrated by "Little Red Riding Hood," "The Story of the Three Little Pigs," or "The Story of the Three Bears."

3. The rescue from a harsh home and the miraculous creation of a secure home. While the previous motifs began with a secure home, this motif involves a harsh, cruel, or unloving home. The central character leaves the harsh home, goes into the outside world and somehow miraculously finds a new home, superior in countless ways to the original home. "Cinderella" and "Mother Holle" are both illustrations of this motif.

4. The conflict between the wise beast and the foolish beast. In this motif there are two or more central characters which possess contrasting qualities with the action centering on these differences. The stepsisters in "Cinderella" and "Mother Holle" illustrate this motif. One folk tale may have elements of more than a single plot motif; it is the combination and variations which make each story unique. The wise beast-foolish beast motif, it may be noted, is commonly used in fables, as indicated in the next section.

Plot motifs for fables

1. Single character and single incident. This structural pattern of a fable expresses a moral lesson through a single impersonal character involved in a single incident. "The Fox and the Grapes" illustrates this pattern.

2. Wise beast-foolish beast. This structural pattern may involve a single incident or parallel incidents in which the foolish beast (or character) seems to have the advantage, but the qualities of the wise beast result in his receiving reward or victory, with the qualities of the foolish beast causing his downfall. This plot pattern is recognizable in "The Lion and the Mouse," "The Hare and the Tortoise," and "The Ant and the Grasshopper."

I will illustrate how an understanding of these plot patterns was used by a second grader when writing his own composition. The story begins in a secure home; the central character, Janet, takes a journey into the outside world where she meets a "friendly" monster; and at the end of the story we find that Janet has returned to her own safe and secure home. One can see elements of a number of stories which have been recently read to this group. Like the little boy in *The Bears on Hemlock Mountain*, by Alice Dalgliesh, Janet goes on an errand for her mother; the three rabbits have human characteristics like those in the *Just So Stories* by Rudyard Kipling; and the ending is similar to the one found in *And To Think That I Saw It on Mulberry Street* by Dr. Seuss, which brings one quickly back from the imaginative world to reality.

The Three Rabbits

Once upon a time there lived a little girl named Janet. Her mother said, "Janet, will you go to the little store to get some things we need?" "Yes," said Janet, "what do we need?" Mother said, "Janet, we need some sugar and a loaf of bread and a pound of sugar and some milk." "Oh," said Janet, "I'll go get the things." Then Janet started to go to the store. On Janet's way to the store she saw a little house. There was a little rabbit playing in the yard doing tricks and a mother rabbit watering the garden and a daddy rabbit filling the car. Janet made friends with the rabbits and talked to them. Soon it was getting dark out. The rabbits said that Janet could stay for the night. In the morning Janet went to the store and got the things and after she got the things she started home again. When she got home her mother was happy to see her but her mother wanted to know where she stayed overnight. Then Janet told her mother the whole story.[10]

In directing attention to plot structure, the teacher helps the child inductively; she plans carefully the stories she will read and the questions she will ask.

Repetitive Elements of Style

The next concept the teacher may wish to explore concerns the incremental patterns of repetition which occur in folk tales. Stories which are episodic—the plot structure involves a series of independent events which together comprise a single work—frequently make use of verbal repetition: phrases and parallel incidents are repeated. The repetition in episodic stories entertains and gets attention; it also contributes to the meaning of the story. Young children delight in these repetitive elements of style and are able to recite or tell many stories after hearing them only once or twice. Pupils can be led to recognize the repetitive elements in "Mother Holle," a story which contrasts two trips to the bottom of a well, and the contrasting description of the stepsisters in "Cinderella."

After pupils have discovered the devices of plot and repetition and realize that stories are "made" by the author, they often use these devices in their own writings or find additional examples in their books. Teachers should not expect a pupil to use a device in his own stories immediately after class discussion. Rather, teachers should respond favorably to those who have attempted to use a literary device which could be appropriately incorporated in the story and to continue to read other stories illustrating the concepts that are being developed. It is tragic to see pupils struggle with a writing device they do not understand or which is inappropriate for the topic or idea they are trying to express.

Stories can be used as models to help pupils build their own compositions *after* the pupils have had a rich experience with literature. Many literary selections should be enjoyed before the generalizations are exposed. An understanding of plot structure gives a new dimension to enjoyment of children's literature. One first grade teacher helped her pupils to observe the use of repetition as a structural device by telling and retelling "The Little Red Hen," "The Three Billy Goats Gruff," and "The Gingerbread Boy." These stories were told orally, and some children enjoyed taperecording and listening to their own retellling of these stories over and over. At the same time the group studied "The House That Jack Built." Then, hoping to get a composition modeled after it, the teacher began by introducing a picture of a birthday cake with a lighted candle and expected the children to mention the ingredients of the cake, such as, "This is the cow that gave the milk that went in the cake that Susie baked." However, the members of the class had their own ideas which, by the way, the teacher readily accepted. The composition, as the children told it, indicates that they understood the use of repetition. They made a long, thin picture with a birthday cake at the top. Underneath it was a candle, then a boy, a lady, a young man, and an old man.

Here is the composition:

> This is the cake that Susy baked.
>
> This is the candle on top of the cake
> That Susy baked.
>
> This is the boy who blew out the candle
> On top of the cake that Susy baked.

This is the mother who spanked the boy
Who blew out the candle
On top of the cake that Susy baked.

This is the father who kissed the mother
Who spanked the boy
Who blew out the candle
On top of the cake that Susy baked.

This is the grandpa who visited the father
Who kissed the mother
Who spanked the boy
Who blew out the candle
On top of the cake that Susy baked.[11]

The Fable: Example of Learning to Use a Form

The teachers who have worked closely with primary children frequently find that fables are difficult for young pupils to understand. Fables as a type of literature have a distinct form and contain highly intellectual qualities. Even though the fables use animals for characters and are very brief, they present an abstraction, moral, or sermon which young children are reluctant to accept. Abstract ideas are presented strikingly and with force by employing flat characters which represent a single quality.

Fables can probably best be presented to elementary pupils as short stories, one at a time, throughout the year. Before reading a new fable, the teacher should identify the selection as a fable, one type of literary form, and mention the titles of other fables which have been read. If the teacher reads books containing a single fable, such as *Once a Mouse* by Marcia Brown or *Chanticleer and the Fox* by Barbara Cooney or the books by Katherine Evans, these can be placed on the library table where pupils can handle the books, thus permitting those who are ready and have the maturity for the abstract concepts to react individually to the book. From a gradual introduction of the fable throughout the early grades and listening to tales like "Chanticleer and the Fox" from Chaucer and "The Bremen Town Musicians," the pupils can be prepared to enjoy the elements of a satiric fable in which human vices and follies are ridiculed or scorned, as in *Winnie-the-Pooh* by A. A. Milne, at a later grade level. As upper elementary pupils listen to *The Bidpai Fables* and the *Jataka Tales* from India and Japan, they can relate these fables to those they have heard in early grades, such as the fables of Aesop. These understandings of the qualities of classical antiquity and an understanding of the classical fable form can then be applied to *The Wind in the Willows* by Kenneth Grahame, a tale representing the good and bad in modern society. Pupils will be unable to understand many of the classics and selections of quality literature at the high school level if they are not given a broad background in understanding the fable form through a firsthand experience with many fables.

May Hill Arbuthnot equates writing an original fable to a mathematical procedure.[12] She suggests selecting some animal character and a moral, such as, "Pride goeth before a fall." If a rabbit is chosen, he cannot be a well-rounded individual with only one weakness; rather, he must be all weakness—and in this case the weakness is *pride*. So the mathematical equation becomes: Proud Rabbit + X (single episode) = Pride goeth before a fall. The writer must solve for X by finding an episode to explain the moral.

Teachers who wish to experiment with fables in their classrooms will find these seven steps for presentation and writing of fables helpful:

1. Read many fables scattered throughout several months.
2. Review the easier fables and those liked by the children. Write the lesson or moral on the chalk board.
3. List other lessons on the chalk board which could appear in a fable.
4. Select one lesson from either group of morals and write a fable together in class.
5. Let pupils select a lesson or moral from those on the board or suggest a new moral and tell how a story or fable could present the idea.
6. Let pupils work in groups or committees and write fables with one of the group acting as secretary or scribe. Go over the fables together in class.
7. Let pupils write their own fables after selecting a moral.

These steps should not be compressed into a tight time pattern but should be extended over a period of time since learning to write fables requires both experience with that type of literaure and the development of the intellectual discipline to stay within the form.

The fable which follows illustrates the first type of fable plot pattern. The characters are flat and impersonal, and no one regrets the fate of the lazy chicken. Like most simple fables, this composition by a fourth grade pupil is brief, involving a single incident, and the ending is expected and justifiable. The originality found in other types of writing is not often found in a fable because the form is restricting and the content is prescribed by the moral.

> Once there was a chicken who, even though chickens get up early, this chicken did not. She liked to sleep late in the morning. But her friends who got up early, got the best food. And one day the farmer who owned this chicken was discouraged with this chicken. "She never gets up early, or lays good eggs, or eats good food," said the farmer very discouraged. So the next Sunday that little chicken was on the farmer's plate.
>
> Moral: Laziness does not pay off.[13]

The second fable was also written by a fourth grade boy after a number of fables had been studied in class. Note that the young writer has developed a clear, concise plot and has concluded with a moral.

The Woodsman and the Hawk

There was once a woodsman who lived alone in a little hut.

One day he was out in front of his hut when all of a sudden he heard two things at once, a hawk screaming and gunfire. He looked around. All of a sudden he happened to hear some flapping of wings. He looked down. There beside him was a panting hawk. The hawk said breathlessly, "Please kind sir, could you help me; a couple of dogs and a hunter are chasing me. Do you have a place to hide me?" "Why of course I do. Go into the hut and eat as much meat from my dog's bowl as you want. But come out when I tell you." In a few minutes the hunter and his two dogs came by the hut. The hunter asked, "Have you seen a hawk in the sky or on the ground around here?" "No, I haven't," he said, but as the woodsman said these words he winked his eye and pointed towards the hut. Anyhow the hunter did not see these signs, and so went on. When the hunter was out of sight the woodsman told the hawk to come out. The hawk went on its way without saying a word. The woodsman asked, "Why do you go without thanking me for what I have done?" The hawk turned around and said, "I saw what you did as you said those words." Adding to that he said, "The tongue can be as sly as the hand."[14]

Pupils can achieve a sense of plot in their own writing, often done without conscious effort on their part, after studying many selections from children's literature. The fourth grade writer of "Benny the Rabbit" has attempted to condense a whole series of episodes into a single story, which is much like *Charlotte's Web* by E. B. White. At one point the time sequence is inaccurate, but this does not detract and probably would have been corrected if the pupil's attention had been called to it. There is a note of sadness when we learn that Mr. Shoe sold Benny and that Benny hurt his paw, endured hunger, and later was killed. Even the chickens sense that Benny's delight in the sunshine and green grass foreshadows a dark ending. Like *Charlotte's Web*, however, at the end of the story the writer views the entire situation from the abstract adult world.

Benny the Rabbit

Mr. Shoe had seven rabbits and wanted to sell one. So he found a girl who wanted him. The rabbits were playing leap-the-rabbit, which was the game they played all the time.

The next day Susy Ever came and got him. She took him home and showed her parents the rabbit. She named it Benny.

That afternoon her brother Russell built Benny his home. It was a cozy little place with a place to store carrots.

Tuesday Benny went out and said, "It's a beautiful morning."

The chicken replied, "Yes it is Benny."

Benny burst out saying, "O the grass is so green!"

"Yes it is," said the chicken.

Thursday Benny got his paw stuck in the door, but Susy fixed it up.

The next day Benny was boiling mad. Nobody came to feed him. One, two, three hours and still no food.

Saturday was Benny's birthday and he would be two years old. He got a carrot cake that was so good. He had a good time.

Friday Benny got away and when they found him a hunter had him and said that he was very poor and had one boy who needed gloves. Susy was very happy that they could use Benny to keep warm.[15]

Teaching Point of View

A story may be told from more than a single point of view, depending on the narrator and the audience. Pupils should be helped to recognize who is telling the story and the audience to whom the story is directed, both in literature and in their own written communication. Studying a story such as *The Bears on Hemlock Mountain* provides a way for helping pupils write about a single episode from more than one point of view. The story is about Jonathan, who crosses the mountain to get a large kettle for a christening. He tries to be brave and remembers that others have said, "There are no bears on Hemlock Mountain." But as dusk falls he discovers that there *are* bears on Hemlock Mountain and saves himself by upsetting the huge kettle and crawling under it; his father and uncles later find him.

Here are a few composition assignments using varying points of view which could be based on this story:

1. A newspaper account of Jonathan's experience. The news story should give the most important facts first, in this case the rescue, rather than appearing as a climax at the end of a story. The article would be written factually rather than imaginatively.

2. A letter written by Jonathan to Aunt Emma. To avoid frightening Aunt Emma, Jonathan would tell about his adventure with the bears but minimize the danger and seriousness of the situation.

3. A letter written by Jonathan to his Uncle James. Since Uncle James first mentioned the idea of bears on the mountain and is only six years older than Jonathan, he might want to impress him with his bravery and quick thinking and even exaggerate the facts in his letter.

4. A new chapter following the story. The story of the bear hunt by father and the uncles could be told in the third person and addressed to the same audience as the book.

5. Expository writing. An explanation of how food was prepared or a christening planned in pioneer times and how present-day plans differ

would require the pupil to explain, compare, and contrast ideas. Pupils might feel the need to do research, since this type of writing requires a knowledge of facts.

6. Imaginative writing. Pupils could write an imaginative and creative account of another adventure that Jonathan might have. It could be modeled after the core story and use a basic plot motif: leaving the secure home, going on an errand, meeting a monster, building suspense through real or imaginary danger, and finally returning home.

7. Descriptive writing. Pupils might wish to describe how Jonathan viewed the mountain in the bright sunshine during the morning or how Jonathan felt when the bears were walking around the kettle while he was crowded inside.

Evaluation of Composition

While the term *evaluation* has not been used to this point in the discussion of literaure and composition, this is exactly what has been done with the examples of children's writing which have been included in this article. Attention has been called to the content—to the ideas which the pupils were developing—and to the structural forms commonly found in literature. Indeed, instilling a sensitivity to these elements is the teaching objective. Therefore, pupils are given a rich background of experience with literature and are led to see, hear, feel, and recognize elements and events in their environment which they might never otherwise notice.

There are many practical writing situations when teachers should call attention to spelling, punctuation, or usage. As pupils continue to write and to share their stories with their teachers and their peers, eventually they will discover the value of punctuation and capitalization as stoppers and starters. That point is the opportune moment for teaching the skills of handwriting, spelling, or punctuation.

Evaluation concerns much more than judging mechanical skill. Evaluation includes an identification of the ideas, thoughts, feelings, and adventures which the writer has presented. To share an involvement with the reader and to see appreciation for his story are compensation for the effort required of the writer. In other words, the evaluation can be the writer's reward.

Sometimes the effort of writing is great. Even a third grade pupil often feels overwhelmed by writing requirements. Yet at that very moment he can compose a description of his feelings for his teacher as noted in the following essay:

Something to Do

Where is something to do? When I want something to do I can't, and when I don't want something to do there is something to do. I don't know why it is this way. Can anyone tell me? I am so weary.[16]

Footnotes

[1] Ruth G. Strickland, *The Language Arts in the Elementary School* (Second edition; Boston: D. C. Heath and Company, 1957), p. 152.

[2] Walter Loban, "Oral Language Proficiency Affects Reading and Writing," *The Instructor*, 75 (March 1966), 97ff.

[3] See, for example, Ruth G. Strickland, "The Language of Elementary School Children," *Bulletin of the School of Education*, 38, 4 (July 1962). This journal is published in Bloomington by Indiana University.

[4] Teacher: Mrs. Eleanor Fuhrman, Grade 1, Norfolk, Nebraska.

[5] Teacher: Mrs. Virginia Hamilton, Grade 1, Lincoln, Nebraska.

[6] Sylvia Ashton-Warner, *Teacher* (New York: Simon and Schuster, 1963), pp. 79-80.

[7] James R. Squire, "Form Consciousness, an Important Variable in Teaching Language, Literature, and Composition," in Russell G. Stauffer (ed.), *Language and the Higher Thought Processes* (Champaign, Illinois: National Council of Teachers of English, 1965).

[8] See Rosenheim, p. 50 of this volume.

[9] Nebraska Curriculum Development Center, Paul Olson, Director, "Elementary Units," *A Curriculum for English* (Lincoln, Neb.: University of Nebraska Press, 1966).

[10] Teacher: Miss Joline Beck, Grade 2, Lincoln, Nebraska.

[11] Teacher: Mrs. Alice Schnabel, Grade 1, Lincoln, Nebraska.

[12] May Hill Arbuthnot, *Children and Books* (Third edition; Chicago: Scott, Foresman, and Company, 1965), p. 304.

[13] Teacher: Mrs. Margaret Tatroe, Grade 4, Lincoln, Nebraska.

[14] Barbara Grothe, *Elementary Composition Evaluation Project* (Postdoctoral Study in Progress, The University of Nebraska).

[15] Teacher: Norma J. Cleary, Grade 4, Omaha, Nebraska.

[16] Eldonna L. Evertts, *A Longitudinal Study of the Syntax and Content of Children's Compositions* (Grades 2-6) (Postdoctoral Study in Progress, The University of Nebraska).

28 Sixth Graders Write
Good Short Stories

Henry V. Larom

There are academic disciplines other than linguistics from which elementary school teachers can borrow and adapt both content and method. In this article a college professor and an elementary school teacher cooperate to adapt some techniques commonly used in college composition classes to successfully improve the imaginative writing of intermediate grade pupils. While some facets of the experiment may seem too advanced for fourth graders, such a unit would be appropriate as an enrichment project for linguistically advanced pupils.

Do you think it is better to give a series of discrete lessons on different techniques and then write a story or to write a story and then study ways of improving it? Why do you believe nothing is mentioned about motivating pupils to want to write or about suggesting suitable topics? Think about the previous article by Evertts; how might she have modified this approach if she taught the unit? The articles by Bateman, Boesen, and Carlson cited in Selected References for Part Four are particularly suited for intermediate grade teachers.

A little story of mine for children was a selection of the Children's Weekly Reader Book Club, and as a result several elementary school teachers asked me to appear before their classes. This was a salutary and exciting experience for a college "comp" teacher used to dealing with reluctant freshmen, and when a grade school pupil asked me to tell him how to write a story, it became something of a challenge. Consequently, with the cooperation of Miss Gladys Trambly of the Lewis and Clark school in Missoula, we conducted an experiment. I adapted some techniques I use in a creative writing class at Montana State University and spent an hour a week for seven weeks working with Miss Trambly's class.

By the end of the sixth week I was astonished. I was getting material that

From *Elementary English* 37:20-23; January 1960. Reprinted with permission of the National Council of Teachers of English and Henry V. Larom, Chairman, Department of English, Rockland Community College, Suffern, New York.

was more creative and better written than much of the work I was receiving from my college freshmen. Experimenting further, the following quarter I worked with four advanced sections of fourth graders, and although the results were not, of course, as mature, they were still remarkable. At least, by the end of the program the six teachers I had collaborated with agreed that the course stimulated ideas, motivated children to write, made the majority of pupils more critical of writing, and increased their desire to read.

Now the problem becomes how to get some of these ideas on paper for possible use by other teachers. I find it is one thing to appear before a class as an "author" and to stimulate the children and quite another to communicate these ideas in cold type to other teachers. However, the following is an outline of our experiment which I hope can be useful.

Description

First, we had to slow the pupil down. The average sixth grader's idea of a "story," we found, was to make a fast-moving synopsis of a recent television show. Therefore, we started by having the children write a page or two of "description" using all the senses. We demanded that they look around them (Is grass always green? Are trees seen on a distant mountainside almost purple?); that they hear things, *feel* things. Having to stop, look, listen, and touch in their writing not only made them slow down, it killed a lot of clichés and brought new, concrete lively words into their writing.

Live verbs

Next we went into the subject of "live verbs." One illustration will suffice. On the board we wrote the sentence: "The horse is coming out of the barn." We identified the subject and verb, but we decided it was a dead sentence. So we took it out of the "progressive" form. This was better but still pretty dull. Then, with plenty of class help, we brought the verb to life: The horse (pranced, bucked, stumbled, rocketed) out of the barn. Later we added adjectives until the horse took on considerable character in one simple sentence. From then on the "dead verb" was anathema.

The happening

The next step, which is the hardest of all for writers, was to learn to "render," as Henry James called it. This means to have something happen, on stage, so that the reader actually participates. As Joseph Conrad expressed it: "My task which I am trying to achieve is, by the power of the written word, to make you hear, to make you feel—it is, before all, to make you *see*. That—and no more, and it is everything." It is, in a sense, the playing of a scene and is the opposite of "reporting." We compared newspaper accounts of something with an actual rendering of a scene, which we called "a happening." Space forbids illustrative material, but it is easy to find.

So now, using the senses and plenty of live verbs, we had the pupils write "a happening," with quite happy results—and much lively criticism from the floor. Incidentally, these youngsters learned to render or write a happening much faster than college students do.

Plot

Next we tackled an easy one—plot. Children love to plot wild stories, but now they were kept from telescoping the action. A plot in outline was one or more happenings connected by transitions which were to be "reported." Again we used illustrative material, with as much collateral reading as possible.

Suspense

If there is one thing that a story for (or by) children must have, it is *suspense*. This is easily illustrated by reading or telling a suspenseful story, then stopping just before the climax. The class will heckle you and keep after you until you finish it. We made them write happenings that would keep us in suspense, but in order to do this they were forced to make the most of every little incident within the happening. We called this "milking the scene." (When you milk a cow you get *all* the milk—or the cow will object.)

Characters

But stories are about *people* (even if a good many of them are also about dogs and horses) so that the next step was to discuss—at length—*characters*. For this we used part of a short piece by John Steinbeck called "How to Tell Good Guys from Bad Guys" (*The Reporter*, March 10, 1955). It deals with his son, Catbird, who watches television and points out to his father that you can always tell the plot of a western at the very start. The man in the white hat is the hero; the man in the black hat is the villain. The man in the grey hat is either good at the start and then turns bad, or he is bad at the start and turns good by the end of the program. This gave us a wonderful opportunity to open up criticism on the "corn" in television. Excellent and powerful destruction of the western, the police story, and the horror movie resulted. Of course, the children went on looking at them—but perhaps with a little more skepticism, a little more maturity, and certainly with a more critical eye. We found it a good chance to face up to the stupidities of TV and movies, and we made the most of it.

So now the poor story had "flat characters." We had to have people—or horses and dogs—who were real, with weaknesses as well as strengths.

This brought up the problem: How do you make a character come to life? This is achieved, we decided, by any combination of the following methods:

1. Describe the character—how he looks, etc.
2. Show him in action—what he does.
3. Tell what he says—this can lead into attempts at dialogue.
4. Show what other people think about him.
5. Tell what he thinks about—what goes on in his head.

Rather than have the pupil do a "character sketch," we had the character in a "happening," and the various methods of bringing him to life fell naturally into place. He looks a certain way, he does things, he says things—he is a human being in action.

Motivation

Next we tackled something I thought would be hard, if not impossible, to get across—*motivation. Why* does a character do and say what he does? Again, we read illustrative material and let the pupil explain why the character behaved the way he did. Then we demanded that all characters must have reasons for their actions.

Each week we went back over all these ideas and phrases, and many of the children took notes. In one case, a child was transferred from our school to another one nearby. The teacher in the second school found the notes and, with the help of the pupil, made them work in his own class. Therefore, review and note-taking seem to be effective.

Viewpoint

Before the children were ready to connect the happenings with transitional reporting into a story, they had to learn one more important step—one that causes trouble in many a university class—they had to decide on the *viewpoint*.

This means, of course, from whose point of view the story is told. If the student switches viewpoint in a short story from person to person, the focus blurs and the story loses interest. Although there are times, of course, when a writer must switch, it is unwise to do so unless absolutely necessary. Therefore, we broke viewpoint down into:

1. The first person singular—the author is "I" and the chief character in the story.
2. "I, the observer"—the author is there, but is not the main character. These two viewpoints limit the story to what "I" saw, did, heard, or thought about.

3. The writer is a god—he stands back away from his characters controlling them at will without in any way entering into the action. The tale, the fairy story, the once-upon-a-time stories are often written in this way.

4. Through the eyes, or at least from the viewpoint, of one of the main characters. This is usually the most successful method—the reader finds out what the character did, why he did it, what he thought, how he felt, what he said. Other characters revolve around him, but he is the main one, the person we are mainly interested in. The focus is consistently on "he" or "she" reacting against other people.

By this time most of our pupils were raring to go on a full story. We turned them loose—and the rest of the experiment consisted of reading and criticizing the results according to our now well developed criteria.

Theme

One final element entered many of the stories naturally—the *theme*, the insight, the meaning of the story. Love of animals, loneliness, achievement, success, even moral precepts appeared in many stories. We discussed theme, but it was our feeling that this comes last, otherwise the narratives may become little allegories full of clichés and lifeless characters. Left to themselves, the children discovered their own insights, and the results were far more real, human, original, and rewarding than if they had been forced to build their stories around a given subject.

The better writers did considerable rewriting which, of course, is for all writers a most important part of the struggle. And meanwhile Miss Trambly kept after the mechanics and grammar and spelling so that story-writing aided the pupil with the fundamentals as well as stimulating his ability to express himself.

If this outline is at all useful to other teachers, we hope they will use it and let us have any comments or suggestions. The program is still being developed and we will gladly swap further information with any teacher who is interested.

29   A Glove Thrown Down

Robert Evans

*Cogently, Evans argues that there is a vast difference between writing and learn-
ing to write and that elementary school teachers, by uncritically riding the creativity bandwagon, are doing irreparable damage to children's ability to compose and express themselves with accuracy and precision.*

*What unstated assumptions about the values and functions of elementary
school writing does the author make? What are some specific skills he would
want pupils to learn? Would his suggestions ultimately enhance or inhibit creative writing? Would there be any place in his writing program for self-
expression? On what points and to what extent do you believe he and Wilt
would disagree? Are his views similar or different from those of Evertts and
Larom? How does this article relate to those by Loban in Part Two and De-
Lawter and Eash in Part Three? How might Singleton, Diederich, and Hill—
authors of an article appearing in Part One—reply to Evans's assertions?*

That a college professor should venture some remarks on the teaching of
composition in the early grades will not be set down, I hope, either as trespass or
presumption. We share, after all, a common concern, and your present fourth-
grader may well turn up in my Freshman English class. If he is not greatly
different from those already there, his writing will show certain crucial inadequacies, and it is about these, and their origin, that I wish to speak out.

I shall not consider here errors in spelling, punctuation, and the elementary
decencies of grammar. These are indeed matters of grave concern, but they are
less disturbing than inadequacies of a more radical nature: imprecision in word
and idea, incoherence of structure and argument, the almost compulsive injec-
tion of wholly irrelevant personal attitudes into every piece of writing the
student does, and a conception of style that admits of but two alternatives to
dead-level flatness: inflated diction and "cuteness." None of these developed
overnight. They are the final sum in the slow but inexorable compounding of a

From *Elementary English* 44:523-527; May 1967. Reprinted with permission of the
National Council of Teachers of English and Robert Evans, Assistant Professor of English,
Ball State University, Muncie, Indiana. Author's emendations as of 1968 have been included.

legacy of error which derives from the student's earliest formal instruction in writing. His notions of what prose is and how he is to use it crystallize then, though neither he nor his teachers may realize that so crucial an event is occurring. In subsequent grades he continues to make the same basic kinds of error, though with a somewhat more fluent hand, and all of the teacher's red pencilings are in vain, because the initial erroneous conception of the *function* of language remains unidentified and unchallenged. Useless to crop at the endlessly proliferating leaves and stems of such rank growth. It is at the root we must strike.

And what is that root? A mistaken emphasis on "self-expression" and "imaginative" writing, to the virtual exclusion of guided exercises, however elementary, in such forms as objective description, comparison, contrast, definition, and explanation. This one-sided emphasis is far from accidental. It is much easier to say, "Write a story," or, "Tell how you feel about autumn," than to explain carefully how a good paper in comparison should be written. And, be it noted, even when the student is asked to write a story, rarely is he told how to do so. It is blandly taken for granted that having read stories, he can write one, though it has never yet been thought that, having eaten a cherry pie, a child is therefore able to make one. Not shown how to construct a simple plot, or create a character, or write interesting dialogue, not led, in short, to an early awareness that all writing needs direction and control, the child is at best helped to a general subject ("Write a story about Christmas.") and then left to his own devices. But of course he has no devices; it is precisely these that he needs to be *taught*! And the words will come down on paper just as they came into his head: unchosen, unordered, uncriticized.

But it is unfair to suggest that the teacher's convenience is the only, or even the most important, reason for this misplaced emphasis on such "free" forms of composition, in which the pupil is encouraged to go his almost wholly unguided and unstructured way. Far more important is the assumption, too widely and too uncritically held, I fear, that because the young child usually has a fairly lively imagination, "creative" forms are best suited to elementary writing instruction. I suspect that, in the first place, we are confusing imagination with fantasy.

Much of the child's world is indeed fantasy, and no small part of our obligation as teachers is gradually but firmly to disengage the child from such a world and help him relate to, and learn to deal with, a world of obdurate fact, where wishes win no prizes, and where fantasy, if unchecked, may be profoundly dangerous. Further, this notion of the child's imaginative powers will prove, to cooler judgments, both exaggerated and sentimental. I can think of no significant works of imagination produced by children. No one expects a *Lear* or a *Moby Dick*, of course, but one might expect something that would qualify as a permanent addition to our large and excellent body of children's literature. But the great children's classics—*Alice in Wonderland, Winnie the Pooh, A Child's Garden of Verses, The Wind in the Willows*—were all written by adults in the fullness of their powers, and no child seems ever to have written anything of wide appeal even to his contemporaries, much less to succeeding generations of young readers.

Let us confess it: the child's fantasies, often charming, often pedagogically helpful in providing insights into his interior life, are not works of imagination in the Coleridgean sense of that word. They are neither sustained nor shaped sufficiently to rank even as minor works of creative imagination. I do not at all suggest that they are therefore wholly worthless, nor would I advocate eliminating all "creative" writing in the early grades. But I do urge that we not sentimentally overvalue these fantasies, and above all that we not assume that their undirected writing will lead the pupil to a just understanding of what writing is and how it should be done. Instructional emphasis should be placed on other forms that require the pupil to come early to grips with prose as an indispensable tool, not a toy. For only if he learns early to respect prose as a flexible instrument of great practical value, rather than a vehicle for ego indulgence, will he be at all serious about mastering it.

This over-emphasis on "free" forms is encouraged by another assumption which I should like to challenge: the assumption that it is highly desirable to promote maximum self-expression in young students. While believing firmly that we should by no means stultify the learner, whatever his age, I also believe that we do a mortal disservice to the child when we allow self-expression to deprive him of both disciplined learning and the joy that comes in having mastered that discipline. An anecdote may be *a propos*. Picasso, visiting a progressive school, was shown a class of youngsters busily engaged in "abstract" art. No attention was being paid to line, to perspective, to the formal elements of composition; the pupils were drawing what they "felt" like. Picasso asked their age, and the instructor, confident of approval, said, "Only twelve!" But the master, shaking his head, replied, "What a pity! At twelve I was drawing like Michelangelo." It is a point worth long and sober reflection. At twelve, one of the giants of modern art was not "expressing." He was *learning*. Before his freedom came the submission of self (and who knows how long and perhaps chafing a process that was?) to the exacting discipline of craft, which alone made him able to recognize his freedom when it came and use it as it should be used. Freedom, which is to say mastery, in any field, including writing, depends paradoxically upon the imposition of limitations. But "self-expression," as it is usually and naively construed, knows no limitations and is impatient of all attempts to impose them, for criticism of the expression is invarably interpreted as criticism of the self, and hence is rejected.

Surely we are putting the cart squarely in the path of the horse. Our primary job is not the expression of the student's self, but its *expansion*. The grade school pupil's self is at once too meagre and too inchoate for meaningful expression. It is, in truth, not yet known to him, or accessible to him. He knows only the intense but transient emotions that burn, now darkly, now radiantly on the yet too narrow horizon of his intellectual life. We should liberate him from this cage of subjectivity, not conspire to keep him in it. The considered expression of self is the end of education, not its starting point. It is the last and most demanding stage of writing, one to which few may attain, for it presupposes mature judgment distilled from experience both broad and deep, and it proceeds from relentless and unsentimental self-examination. Without these qualities— and what grade school pupil has them?—self-expression is mere froth and self-indulgence.

What kinds of writing, then, should the elementary language arts curriculum stress? First, it could utilize much more fully than it now does papers requiring the precise statement of precise observations. The child already has a knack for shrewd observation, as many an adult has discovered to his embarrassment. Taking the world less for granted than we do, children often detect striking differences where we see only generalized resemblances, and in objects that seem to us distinct, they may find hidden points of identity.

This quality of vision deserves encouragement, and not the least means of encouragement would be to help the student capture his observations in the net of language, so that they might be returned to at leisure, sharpened and organized. For such exercises, the object observed is far less important than the quality of observation. One common weed, truly seen, puts to shame a whole garden of roses vaguely felt about.

It follows that the teacher should be as exacting in her standards for these papers as the student's level will permit. Errors in observation should be pounced upon, and the student made to look again, and yet again. In the labored revisions of his papers (and the practice of revision should by no means be deferred to later grades!), the student will come gradually to realize that language bears a meaningful relationship to the world in which he lives, and that, depending on its use, it may either falsify or faithfully report that world. Such a view of language, such a respect for language, developed early and become habitual, would make later writing instruction far easier by drastically reducing that blithe slovenliness that is the despair of all English teachers.

It may often happen that these papers will fall short, not because the student has not seen, but because he lacks words or language structures to express clearly what he does see. It is precisely here that the paper in observation is pedagogically more useful than exercises in self-expression. First, it can be dealt with more rigorously, and with less danger of antagonizing the student, because the writer's private feelings are not at issue. Teacher and student stand together, looking out to an object external to them both, and they can discuss it without danger of a chasm of subjectivity opening beween them. Even more importantly, the kind of vocabulary needed for papers of observation is far easier to teach than that required by papers of self-expression, for the latter report highly subjective states to which the teacher has no direct access and which she therefore cannot verify. Whatever the problems involved in teaching a vocabulary adequate to the external world, they are as nothing compared to the mare's nest we create when we try to distinguish the fine shades of gray in such terms as *sad, wistful, pensive, discontented, morose,* etc.

Another sort of paper well within the grade school pupil's range of ability is that dealing with processes: how to make something, how to play a particular game, how to train a pet, or solve a problem in long division. Such papers give opportunity for combining careful observation with precise temporal sequences, and they also demonstrate vividly the importance of clarity of statement. Suppose, for example, that a student has explained how to fold a piece of paper so as to make a toy airplane. The adequacy—or inadequacy—of his instructions can be dramatized by having another student follow them to the letter. No step should be allowed that is not unambiguously described, so that "Fold back two of the corners" would be challenged (by the teacher or any of the pupils) with "*Any* two corners? Fold them back how far? And at what angle?" Or the pupil carrying out the instructions might be told to misunderstand them if he possibly could, so that the writer would be challenged to devise a set of instructions that would be proof against even the most determined misinterpretation. Criticism and revision of the paper would thus proceed simultaneously, and the product of such a demonstration would be a model, tested under fire, of one kind of writing which, in increasingly sophisticated forms, will be of immense and lasting value to the student. Emerging triumphant from such an ordeal, he will have learned a lesson that few of my freshmen composition students seem yet to have mastered: he will have learned how to write a sentence that says exactly what he wants it to say, and he will have learned how to write it so that it cannot possibly be misunderstood.

Such writing, clean in line, eloquent in its simplicity, will bear the stamp of integrity in its every part, and its writer will advance from strength to strength. But for the student who has never mastered this fundamental lesson in writing, every new technical resource proferred for his linguistic salvation will but serve as an instrument for his further damnation. Try to enlarge his vocabulary and he will pack his line so thick with misused words that one could not even begin to guess what poor groat's worth of wit might lie crushed beneath that vast slag pile of language. Try to teach him how to vary his sentence structure and he will splinter syntax mercilessly, jumbling together constructions that could be rivalled—if at all—only by a madman's translations from Chaldean or Bantu.

I would argue further that, though they might seem on first consideration to be restrictive or cramping, these elementary exercises in description and process are more genuinely liberating than the so-called "free" forms. However well intended, emphasis on "self-expression" forces the child constantly back into himself, and this is the wrong direction for him to take. This endless internal rummaging about is neither wholesome nor helpful at this stage of his development. Objective papers, requiring him to look steadily and to speak truthfully about what he sees, are papers worthy of the man we want the child to grow into, and they will help him grow. Step by step, they will lead him into the ever-widening world that is his birthright and enable him to discover how rich and various that world is, and how much there is to say about it. Properly used (and what, in teaching, does not ultimately depend for its success on the skill and tact of the teacher?), they will not stifle his imagination; they will kindle and fuel it. And if anyone supposes that true creativity is incompatible with precise observation and the controlled use of language, he would do well to rethink his ideas very carefully and turn once more the pages of Fabre and Gilbert White, of Gustav Eckman's "Two Lives," or of the last three essays in Loren Eiseley's *The Immense Journey*.

For far too long, to his irreparable harm, the grade school pupil has been deprived of the chance to roll up his sleeves and get down to the business of learning how to use his language in a serious and controlled manner. Misled by an understandable desire to arouse interest and provide motivation, his teachers have unduly encouraged a random and unstructured kind of writing assumed, on no clear grounds, to be "creative," and they have minimized or wholly neglected guided exercises in precisely those forms of writing more closely related to the rest of the child's present and future needs, both in school and out.

For the reasons advanced earlier, I am convinced that the elementary student's writing would improve rapidly—even dramatically—if his training in composition were to stress language as a means of dealing with the external world: of objectively reporting events, explaining processes, describing objects. From the teacher's point of view, such writing is both easier to teach and easier to criticize effectively. In criticizing subjective papers, she will all too often encounter the easy reply, "But that's what I feel!"—a reply which slams the door hermetically shut on all further discussion by implying, indignantly or plaintively, that the teacher is being wholly unreasonable in expecting the pupil to feel any other way. With objective exercises, however, this reply must yield to, "That's what I saw!" and this is easily dealt with. One has only to point and say, "But look here! And here! And here!"

If our schools are to graduate competent and responsible writers (which means competent and responsible thinkers), then the job must be begun, consciously and actively, in the elementary grades. It cannot be deferred to later years, for the child's ways of thinking about and using language will be by then too firmly fixed and will resist all but the most trivial changes. The first and just possibly the most important lesson the child must learn is that language is an instrument of many uses, and that all of these uses demand of him attention and control. And one of the best ways of teaching such a lesson is to require the pupil to write clearly about what is clearly and permanently there for all to see, rather than vaguely about his private, everchanging, and usually irrelevant feelings.

I have cast my glove into the arena. Pick it up who will.

30   Children and Poetry

Raymond J. Endres

Because poetry is such a miniscule part of many teachers' reading diets, it is usually not understood as a literary genre nor does it receive proportional and appropriate attention in the language arts program. The writer not only shows how poetry speaks a special language, expresses emotions and insights present but rarely communicated in everyday life, and has its own unique appeals and delights, but he elucidates how poetry can make important contributions to the language development of elementary school children.

What is the difference between poetry and verse? Can you think of any poems undeserving of the title? How might Endres judge your knowledge of and attitude toward poetry? In what ways is Endres's argument similar to Evertts's, Larom's, and Evans's? How does this article relate to Arbuthnot's earlier one in this part? Do you share Endres's opinion about most choral reading selections?

We live in an age of communications glut. In such an age we find it difficult, even as adults, to separate the wheat from the chaff; to discriminate, that is to say, between the relevant and the trivial, the cogently human, and the appetitively animal. Children, with limited experience to help them differentiate, find themselves bogged down in the mud of Captain Sacto or Bos'n Bill, to name two local TV children's programs. Day in and day out children submit themselves, or are submitted by unwitting parents, to oral communication that has been largely reduced to trivia.

This constant bombardment of persons to language that is basically connotative and appetitive rather than denotative and cognitive is, to use a term popularized by the existentialists, *depersonalizing*. In time the process of conditioning does its work: the hearer is hooked, an addict. Addiction to trivialized language stimuli, Hayakawa points out, is best termed *semantic thumbsucking*: going through the motions of nutrition without getting any.

From *Elementary English* 40:838-842; December 1963. Reprinted with permission of the National Council of the Teachers of English and Raymond J. Endres, Associate Professor, Bowling Green State University, Ohio.

Teachers with a proclivity to garrulousness must be aware that their rambling discourse, so innocent on the surface, may contribute to this general semantic environment. We should try to hear ourselves as others hear us, to coin a truism. We should constantly look for ways of making more relevant those parts of the school program dealing with oral language stimuli. I am led thus, circuitously, to my topic: poetry and children in an age of turgid prose. Poetry, if it is really poetry, may be humorous, or it may be fetching, or it may be tragic; it is never trivial. Poetry can be an effective means of beefing-up the oral language experiences of children.

My general thesis is this: children and youth who do not have rich and varied experiences with poetry lose contact with a most edifying and important segment of their heritage. This is true at each of the several levels of human experience, whether the poetry deals with the immediate community and time, with the world community, or with the world of the ancients. I am disposed to view the loss in its universal sense, the loss of contact with the heritage of the race, as this heritage runs its course throughout history.

The importance of poetic language in the education of children should not be misinterpreted to mean that every teacher should somehow punch the button that releases an indeterminant number of poetic stimuli. I do not believe every elementary or upper-grade teacher is a teacher of poetry. It is my fond hope, however, that my children in their elementary and upper-grade experiences will have one or two teachers—sensitive to the nuances, the history, the beauty of language—who will teach poetry to them.

I should like to tie down the relation of poetry to oral language. This is not difficult when we remember the genesis of poetry; it is among the most primitive art forms, originally found in a common pot with dancing and music in primitive societies. It is, at any rate, much older than prose; its appearance antedates by many millenia written language. The heritage of the tribe, its traditions and mores, were passed on from father to son, through these primitive forms. Of the three—poetry, music, and dancing—the first, usually as narrative, became a special and highly important form because of the medium of language upon which it depended. To be sure, each of the forms communicated, but only poetry—utilizing language—described, denoted, told, directed. And it was oral, that is spoken, rather than written.

Poetry is heightened speech. It is heightened by the rudiments of poetic form: imagery (real, abstract, imaginative) and rhythm. Through imagery we come to view life—that is, the lives of men—not in the particular sense, but in the universal. Images are generic, just as most language is generic. In the words of Brother Antoninus, "In the depths of his imagery the poet cannot lie because his imagery is formed below all the manipulation of the ego and comes out of him with that impetus which is the universality of the man himself in the quest for his own." The development of language, of words or concepts that are abstractions and that allow us to imagine, indicate a commonality of experience. The poet senses this generic quality of experience. The common experience is, however, more for the poet; he expresses his anguish at our failure to intensify the particular experiences of our lives. He despairs at our dragging down shared human and personal experience to the level of the pedestrian:

> A primrose by a river's brim
> A yellow primrose was to him,
> And it was nothing more.

Rhythm remains an important ingredient of poetry. But, whereas the original importance was more closely related to the emotional aspects of poetry, in a latter day it has taken on added significance. If the intention of the author is to connote feeling, his rhythm and meter will be steady, intense, or fast. Think of Lindsay or Poe. If, on the other hand, the intent is to get us to think, the poet will vary the meter and the rhythm. The resultant pattern will be an ebb and flow, a smooth-running channel, and a turbulent rapids. The reader or listener has time to reflect in these pauses, in those silences that come between the words. R. P. Blackmur makes these comments on the language of silence:

> We translate most in our own language, and so little of it gets into our words. If there were no gaps between our words—in which silence speaks, and in which we recollect ourselves (by tranquility Wordsworth must have meant a gap)—we should never find our thoughts or recognize the thoughts of others: the rhythm would not transpire. In verse—the oldest discipline of words we have, older than grammar, and reaching the naked syntax—in verse the silences animate with rhythm the variations of the meter, enlivening the metronome. Rhythm is how we feel and how we translate what moves us, but we move it through silence into words and when it is there the words remain alive.[1]

Poetry in its very primitiveness deals with those facets of man's experience that are basic, those elemental experiences that are at man's existential core: despair (oh, much about despair) and exultation, happiness and sadness, beauty and ugliness, sublimity and madness, tranquility and anger, life and death. Consider these two passages. As he looks around him, he views the earth, and Hamlet says:

> How weary, stale, flat, and unprofitable,
> Seem to me all the uses of this world!
> Fie on't! O fie! 'tis an unweeded garden,
> That grows to seed; things rank and gross in nature
> Possess it merely.

That swinger of birches, Robert Frost, comments:

> Earth's the right place for love.
> I don't know where it's likely to go better.

Poetry runs the full gamut of human emotions, feelings, thoughts. It is in its great range, alas, that poetry runs into difficulty, for it is the unfortunate truth that many teachers take a much narrower view of this form of art. The responses that some teachers make to poetry are, more frequently than not, stereotypical. Some female elementary teachers, on the one hand, believe the proper ingredients of poetry to be sweetness, light, beauty, virtuousness; this is the bountiful hand of God group, positive thinkers, who choose not to see the seamy side of life. These good ladies choose some second-rate versifier as the laureate of the land.

Some men teachers, already suspect because they *are* male and they *are* elementary teachers, try to assuage feelings of doubt about their manhood by rejecting as sissified and dandified any positive feelings toward poetry. Poetry, they feel, is for women. Indeed, most of their poetic experiences have been with women. Despite the several levels of meaning of that statement, I think I've made my point, to wit: poetry cannot be dealt with in terms of stereotypes. Poetic language can at once be beautiful *and* deal with man's most utter feelings of rejection: by man, by the world, by God. Poetry deals with these feelings, furthermore, with a succinctness and a poignancy absent in most prose.

Current practice in teaching poetry to children in elementary classrooms leaves much to be desired. Observation leads me to conclude that these factors obtain in many classrooms: first, most teachers have a severely limited knowledge of poetry; second, such knowledge as they have comes to them by way of language arts or children's literature classes; third, teachers who possess inadequate knowledge of poetry pass off their stereotypical notions about poetry to children; fourth, many teachers' oral interpretation of poetry reflects their feelings of inadequacy in this area; fifth, many teachers employ methods of teaching poetry which seem designed to drive children away from this form of expression; and sixth, teachers frequently approach poetry with trepidation rather than with quiet anticipation. My suggestions for improving current practice stem from these observations.

It is imperative that teachers try to improve their general knowledge of poetry. This may be done in several ways. Some take courses in poetry. There are obvious advantages in extending our knowledge in this way; we are forced to read, to place ourselves on schedule. There are also obvious disadvantages. For example, we are placed more or less at the mercy of an instructor as to the kinds of poetry we shall read and to his interpretation of this poetry. A second method, which is a real test of whether or not we've been liberally educated, is to place ourselves on a reading schedule that includes poetic expression of various types.

Sometimes a commentary of a well-known interpreter will help us in our efforts. If our interpreter is a good one, he will engender in us a curiosity and a thirst to read poetry which, paradoxically, will be whetted and quenched as we move from timid beginnings to full-fledged ingestion. Edith Hamilton is such a person; at least this is how her books about the Greeks affect me. I am driven to reread Aeschylus, Sophocles, Euripides. I may agree or disagree with her interpretation; but, frequently for the first time, I find myself reading Greek drama critically; and, frequently for the first time, I see the relation of the classics to my own life and to the life of the race. For the first time, moreover, I understand what classic means.

A word of caution. Increased insight and appreciation of poetry will not come if done primarily for utilitarian ends; that is, knowledge of the poets is important to us, not to enable us to teach children poetry more effectively, but to gain insight about the ambiguities of our lives in relation to our world and to other human beings. To learn poetry for utilitarian ends means that we have not learned it at all; *we* should be the end of our search. I think teachers too frequently look only for ways, gimmicks, or methods of improving instruction; we spend so much time in fruitless effort that we fail to learn that improved instruction is always related to how effectively we've kept alive our motive to learn, from which stems that curiosity and thirst of which I spoke earlier. Too frequently we live a double standard: it is important for the children to learn, but we no longer feel it is important for us. Do as I say, not as I do: this is our motto; and thus we perpetrate a fraud.

General knowledge of poetry is only somewhat less important than specific knowledge of a single poet. Choose a poet. Become thoroughly at home with his poetry. The poet should be one who captures your imagination and peaks your curiosity. He need not be a contemporary poet; poetry has the unique attribute of timelessness (or timeliness, if you prefer). You may choose, on the other hand, Auden or Frost. I would like you to become quite familiar with the poetry of a single author for several reasons. All poets write generally about the same symbols, or at least they use these symbols in their poetry. Thus, to become knowledgeable of a single poet is to become more familiar with all poets. There is, that is to say, a community of poets and within this community, a real and tangible communication. We are tempted when we read something of a particular poet, our poet, to say: "I seem to recall that Milton had something to say about that." Or, "Dante put it another way." Universality of theme is accompanied by uniqueness of expression. Two passages may deal with identical topics; the first may have been dealt with humorously by one poet and the second with deep seriousness by another.

Build a background knowledge of poetry which seems particularly adaptable to children. Learn those poets who have either written expressly for a children's audience or whose poetry can be used with children: De La Mare, Christina Rosetti, Stevenson, Frost, Daly, Ciardi, to name but a few. Sometimes it is a good idea to depend initially on an anthology, such as Arbuthnot's; but an anthology can be too restrictive. Remember: the better background you bring to choosing selections, the more independence you can exercise free from the restraints of the experts. Don't depend on others to tell you what good poetry for children is. Use the poetry that seems to satisfy the natural longing for rhythmic expression that the children in your classroom have. Don't be afraid to experiment with the poetry of different authors.

Keep balance in the selections you use with children. Remember that poetry expresses the broadest possible range of human experiences ranging from despair to ecstasy. Guard against developing among children stereotyped responses to poetry; it is important, therefore, not to demand that every child enjoy all forms of poetry. Such a demand is ludicrous. On the other hand, try to insure that the child's breadth of interest is expanded.

Poetic expression is rich. The diet of language can be enriched and fortified through poetry, but use it judiciously. Better to be a bit niggardly than to have to supply an emetic later.

Develop a repertory of poems for use with children which you have committed to memory. These are poems which, proven in the crucible of classroom experience, you know children will respond to. Several reasons seem apparent for such a repertory. There is, first of all, often a unique time to insert a particular poem. At such times we can't go fumbling about a file or anthology in a frantic search. As an example, the following might be used when a little boy (or girl) has been unusually stubborn:

> I shoot the hippopotamus
> With bullets made of platinum,
> Because if I use leaden ones
> His hide is sure to flatten 'em![2]

Another point. The poem which you can recite from memory allows you to watch your audience to check the reaction of the children. How do they respond, verbally and nonverbally? Finally, the memorized poem allows you to play on the feedback you get from the children; it allows you to pause, to use expression more freely, to concentrate on oral interpretation.

Work on your oral interpretation. Are you enunciating properly? Are your pauses effective? Are you giving proper emphasis to those words which need emphasis? Are you using your eyes, your expression, your stance to help put across the message of the poem?

Give children a chance to work at poetry. If they appreciate hearing you recite a poem, give them several chances to hear it. Any poem is worthy of repetition; if you can't repeat it, eliminate it from your repertory. Chances are, once children have heard a poem they like several times, they start making responses when they hear it. Watch for lip movement, expression, a light in the eyes, a movement of the head. These are your clues. When you see them, give the youngsters a chance to say the poem with you. This is probably one of the most effective ways to develop choral reading selections.

Use choral reading judiciously. In my opinion many of the selections in collections of verse for choral reading are not poetry; often they are verse, and poor verse at that. I am bothered, furthermore, by the way in which these selections, even the good ones, are cut up for parcelling out to individual members or groups in the class. "Line-a-child" or "antiphonal" selections are frequently second-rate. The Greeks in their drama, highly classical in style, could mix group and individual passages. I would guess, however, that elementary teachers would refrain from using Prometheus or Antigone with young children. Choral reading is best, in my judgment, when the chorus predominates. I've been most impressed with choruses where solos have been kept to a minimum, where the poem hasn't been chopped to pieces. In Thayer's *Casey at the Bat* the umpire says, "Strike three!" That's a solo line!

In developing your repertory, try to anticipate the varied feelings that children have during the year. Obviously these feelings will not be all of a kind; some will be happy, others sad, some dreamy, others definite. Find poems to fit these moods, these feelings, whether they be seasonal or cyclical. Chances are you'll be able to use the same poems from year to year. Likely, moreover, you'll gain in appreciation of them as you continue to use them.

In a recent issue of *Saturday Review*, Ivor Brown wrote of one of his teachers:

> Another eye-opener was Gilbert Murray, a Hellenist with a light in his eye and gold in his voice. Again schooling had been gloomily deterrent and the Greek drama became a series of "difficult passages" for translation and comment on the syntax. Fortunately, while still at school I came across Murray's *History of Ancient Literature*, which he wrote as a quite young man. . . . With this and subsequent attendance at his lectures in Oxford I was shown the miracle of the Greeks' sudden grasp of knowledge and their swift achievement of a new thing called liberty. "Freedom, the very name of it is beautiful," one said.[3]

It is just that we teachers must not make of poetry a dead and lifeless thing, but, like Murray, breathe life into it. Most of us have to satisfy our creative urgings in this way. For most of us, that is sufficient.

Footnotes

1 R. P. Blackmur, "The Language of Silence," in Ruth Nanda Anshen, Editor, *Language: An Enquiry into Its Meaning and Function*. New York: Harper, 1957, p. 152.

2 Hilaire Belloc, "The Hippopotamus," in William Cole, Editor, *Humorous Poetry for Children*. Cleveland: World Publishing, 1955, p. 32.

3 Ivor Brown, "Critics and Creators," *Saturday Review*. 46:39 August 10, 1963.

31 Haiku, a New Poetry Experience for Children

Elizabeth Scofield

Introducing children to poetry as literature presents few problems, but how to get children to produce anything other than doggerel or rhyme eludes many teachers. In this essay a former elementary school teacher shares her experiences and insights into how to help pupils compose—and understand—true poetry.

Why may Haiku be so eminently more suitable than other poetic forms for fostering poetic expression by elementary school pupils? What ideas seem most appropriate to expression by Haiku? Least appropriate? Might certain characteristics of Haiku make it a poor choice to use with certain kinds of children? What techniques have you successfully used to encourage children to write poetry? The article by H. Miller cited in Selected References for Part Four gives some specific suggestions on helping children express themselves poetically.

On a grey spring morning, framed against mist swept hills, the first acacia gleamed yellow from the night rain. Only a few words were needed to trace the delicate outline of that moment. A Haiku was waiting to be written, and that poem, still with me when I arrived at school, became the starting point of a new creative writing experience in my classroom.

For some time, I had been acquainted with Haiku, finding it the most satisfying medium for suggesting feelings which are inexpressible; for capturing essence in an exquisitely tiny frame. I had not thought of giving this experience to children, as it seemed so highly personal. Haiku is difficult to talk about. One reads or listens, and if he is open, he will experience it. However, my desire to create something beautiful that day made me decide to try. Little did I dream it would bring forth beauty in such abundance!

Haiku is one of the oldest types of Japanese poetry. In its present form, there are three lines consisting of seventeen syllables—five in the first and third

From *Elementary English* 38:24-26; January 1961. Reprinted with permission of the National Council of Teachers of English and Elizabeth Scofield, free-lance writer, Palo Alto, California.

lines, and seven in the second line. The subject is always clearly stated and the location, time of day and season are either mentioned or suggested. Usually a comparison is made between the temporal and the eternal. In Japanese, the poem does not rhyme, but some English translators have rhymed the first and third lines. Also, in English, the 5-7-5 syllabication may or may not be followed. This Haiku by Basho is often used as an example:

> On a withered branch
> a crow has settled—
> autumn nightfall.

Haiku is meant to be repeated many times in order to experience its full implications. Because of its brevity, it allows the reader to add subtleties of his own feelings to the already potent symbols.

In class, the first Haiku produced many startled reactions among the children, but interest ran high! We discussed the importance of poetry to the Japanese people. Everyone in Japan writes poems, and one of the most exciting national events is the Emperor's Poetry Contest, held each January. Nature plays an important part in Haiku, and using the book, *Little Pictures of Japan*, edited by Olive Beaupré Miller, we read aloud, finding that insects, animals, flowers and stars are all poems in themselves. This book with its lovely illustrations was particularly interesting to the children. Unfortunately it is now out of print, but can be found in many libraries. We also read from Harold Henderson's, *An Introduction to Haiku*, which has excellent translations in rhyme.

After listening to the poems and discussing them, these rules were listed: 1.) Write the poem in three lines; 2.) Tell what the subject is; 3.) Tell where the subject is; 4.) Tell when the action is taking place. The most important rule came out in our discussion, although it was not verbalized as such. The poem must be something expressed from one's heart. We did not attempt the 5-7-5 syllabication, but did stress that the poem be rhythmical. We talked about ways of suggesting seasons in our part of the country. Sometimes it makes a better poem to suggest rather than to state directly. In California for example, rain would indicate winter and early spring. Brown or gold hills would indicate summer and fall. Time of day can also be suggested in ways such as starlit sky, eastern sun, church bells, etc.

Upon finishing the presentation, I had a few moments of doubt as to whether the mood of this delicate medium would be picked up by the children. Then one of the girls handed me her first Haiku which she began as I was still talking, and from that moment, I was to experience a wonder seldom felt in teaching. Here is her poem:

> From the mountain
> the moon
> slowly goes to the stars.

Everyone was busy writing. There was no question as to what to write about. I went around the room, helping the children divide their poems into three lines and editing. Some immediately sensed the simplicity of the form. Others needed more help in eliminating excess words. There was almost a total response from the class, and many wrote five or six Haiku in the one lesson.

Because of the success we had in fourth grade, Haiku was presented to four other classes, grades three to five, with similar results. It seems possible that it could be used at any grade level, if adapted by the teacher to her particular class.

Although at times it is difficult to motivate boys in creative writing, they responded well to Haiku. The following are examples:

> The deer!
> Look how gaily he bounds—
> then goes.

> Petals on the ground—
> beautiful, so beautiful!
> birds singing in the starlight.

One boy confided to me with great seriousness, "You know, I really get romantic feelings when I write like this!"

In evaluating the use of Haiku as a poetry medium for children, I found there were reasons why it was successful. As something new, it is fresh to both the teacher and the students. Because it does not have to rhyme, it is easier to concentrate on images and rhythm. Some children will rhyme naturally, but those who have difficulty are not handicapped. The subject matter used is very close to children—specific things in nature. Seldom does the author state a feeling directly about these things, and in the presentation this objectivity was stressed, which perhaps saved embarrassment. The purpose was to paint a word picture without explaining one's own feelings. It is doubtful if the third grade boy who wrote of the sadness we witness each spring as rain destroys the blossoming trees would have said the same thing directly:

> Rain—
> the sight of flowers
> dies away.

Haiku must be brief. How often do we hear children ask in quiet desperation, "Is this long enough?" after pouring their energies into a writing project. And what a release to cast away words, to carve out unnecessary letters, leaving a picture of beauty etched in fine, clear lines! A Haiku usually comes all at once, or at least the total picture appears in the mind as a whole. It is possible to write it first as a sentence, afterward editing and placing the words rhythmically in three lines. Also, Haiku demands words that children know well. There is no need for long adjectives or complicated phraseology to make the poem beautiful. Words such as "oh" and "look" find their true meaning as expressions of wonder, and no other words could take their place in Haiku. Some of the less verbal children tended to write better poems as their images were more direct and clear:

> The blue blue sky
>   and the black black tree
>   with its long long arms.

> The clouds are pale;
>   in the bushes there's a rabbit;
>   it hopped!

Along with the poetry, we did some Japanese brush painting, keeping in mind the same approach of simplicity. Haiku can be used as a new writing experience alone, or included within a study of Japanese culture.

At the end of this article, there is a list of books which would be helpful to the teacher interested in further study of Japanese literature. One of the best is Harold Henderson's, *An Introduction to Haiku*, which is printed in pocket book form. Aside from its value for children, Haiku can be an exciting adventure for anyone who loves beauty and is seeking new ways of expression.

I often reread the Haiku we wrote in class, for they are not merely children's poems or clever imitations of an adult medium. They are beautiful fragments from other minds and hearts which have enriched my life with their loveliness.

Suggested Reading

Harold G. Henderson, *An Introduction to Haiku*, Doubleday Anchor Books, Doubleday & Company, New York, 1958.

Olive Beaupré Miller, editor; *Little Pictures of Japan*, The Book House for Children, Chicago, 1925.

Takamichi Ninomiya and D. J. Enright, editors; *The Poetry of Living Japan*; *An Anthology*, Grove Press, Inc., New York, 1957.

Donald Keene, editor; *Modern Japanese Literature*; *An Anthology*, Grove Press. Inc., New York, 1956.

Part Five

Words and Their Use

This part is devoted to certain oral and written aspects of the language arts: vocabulary; semantics; usage and grammar.

Vocabulary may be defined as the stock of words used by a person, class, or profession. Almost every individual uses several different vocabularies, all having much in common, yet each distinctly different. The most basic of these are often designated as hearing, speaking, reading, and writing vocabulary. Words are the symbols of ideas. To express and communicate ideas, one needs facility in the use of words. Teachers must give attention to developing vocabularies of each child through carefully planned instruction and they should be aware of modern media's influence on children's vocabulary development. This is the focus of the Mason article.

Recent attention has been focused upon the verbal disadvantages of the deprived child. He is said to have had limited opportunities for conceptualizing and for utilizing the labels (words) which are conventionally used in the society for its things and actions; often overuses simple, monosyllabic words; rarely uses descriptive or qualifying terms; and, in general, uses a smaller number and variety of words to express himself. On the positive side, the language of the culturally different may be rich and inventive, particularly in unstructured, spontaneous, out-of-school situations. Such ideas are critically analyzed by Dale.

Increasing vocabularies is an important task, but responsible and humane use of words is perhaps even more important. Students of semantics have become more vocal in recent days about the school's responsibility for freeing children from manipulators of language whose use of emotive language and connotative terms are everywhere. Some of the new English programs have incorporated aspects of semantics for elementary school study: understanding of symbol and referent; denotative and connotative meanings; slang and technical language; propaganda techniques. While Jacob's article is not an outline for such a formal program of study, nonetheless it presents the multiple opportunities available for helping the child become word-sensitive.

Usage and grammar are usually differentiated in meaning. Usage refers to the established oral language habits of an individual; grammar is a careful description and analysis of the structure of a language—its sound structure; word structure; phrase and sentence structure. A linguistically sound attitude toward usage is a part of a modern English program. This does not mean that usage standards not be established, for as Pooley states, "We are committed by duty and by conscience to bring every student as close as possible to the attainment of a decent standard of English usage by every means at our command." Pooley's article should help in clarifying current usage standards for today's language. Follett's essay indicates dissatisfaction with tolerance of "sloppy American usage."

There is a need for professional books and articles which present general and specific procedures for teaching the 'new' English that are in keeping with the spirit of the new English. Many articles are available which give an explanation of distinctive features of the new English but few tell how these distinctive features might be taught in the classroom. In the main, they leave the impression that the telling, showing type of instruction is appropriate. Use of tell and show for introduction of new content gives little encouragement to a pupil's thinking, to his originality. In contrast to telling, newer approaches should put a premium on pupil thinking and pupil seeing a need for the use of the content. Such approaches are in keeping with the spirit and content of the best elementary school language arts program.

Borgh's article exemplifies some traits mentioned above and while it is placed in this part with grammar, her essay is equally well suited to the part devoted to literature and creative writing for indeed the major purpose of syntax instruction is its value and application to the written aspects of language. It is believed that relating writing to the study of language is one new source to draw upon for composition study. Making sentences tighter or more succinct, providing variety in sentence structure, and achieving richness of detail by adding or combining relevant structural elements—these are ways of helping pupils learn more about how words are put together.

The implications for classroom application of the Owen article may be a bit more obscure. His lucid explanation of the grammars should stimulate readers to try to keep up with changing emphases and ideas in order to explore all avenues that appear relevant to the child's growth in power to use language.

32   Television's Contribution to Vocabulary Development in Children

George E. Mason

Various ways of increasing vocabularies have been proposed—first hand experiences, books, visual aids, study of content fields, oral and written expression, 'word campaigns,' exercises and direct teaching. As yet there is not sufficient evidence to suggest which methods of vocabulary instruction are most effective at different age levels and with pupils of differing degrees of ability.

Mason points out how the newer medium of television may promote vocabulary development. Just how does his essay relate to Part Two, Language Learning? What specific suggestions are offered for the teacher—and what other suggestions can you offer? How can television make a "contribution to vocabulary development of children"? What other possibilities has television—such as presentation of literature?

Television and school achievement

Children have often been compared to little blotters because of the way they soak up and display the environment to which they are exposed. Often they surprise their elders with perceptive or enlightened comments that suggest a wisdom beyond their years, comments stemming from their exposure to adult vocabulary, concepts, and language patterns. The advent of radio increased the amount of this exposure. The vicarious experiences provided by radio, however, could not approach in intensity those now available through television. Yet recent research suggests that television viewing may be detrimental in some ways to student achievement, especially in the field of reading.

Witty[1] has reported the results of several surveys of the television viewing

From *Teachers Service Division Bulletin* No. 124, 1966. Reprinted from Mason, George E., "Television's Contribution to Vocabulary Development in Children," *Reading Bulletin No. 124*; Published by Allyn and Bacon, Boston, 1966. George E. Mason is Associate Professor, The University of Georgia, Athens.

habits of children. He concurred with Scott's[2] conclusion that excessive viewing is associated with lower achievement in reading. Moreover, Sutton[3] reported the research finding that having a television set in one's house was negatively correlated with success in reading.

It is important to bear in mind, however, that correlational studies do not indicate cause and effect relationships. It is entirely possible that poor reading skills are conducive to more viewing than would have been done had the reading skills developed more favorably. There is even a possibility that a larger amount of television viewing might stimulate higher grades. In 1959, one research group reported that in their sample the children who viewed the most television in elementary school were those who had the higher grades.[4]

The thoughtful reader of such research must conclude that television, like most of man's inventions, can be both good and bad. The effect of television viewing may be that of a stimulant to the pursuit of further learning, or it may be a means of shutting out the real world and escaping to a world of adventure and fantasy. The use of television viewing as a tool for learning is thus a proper field of exploration for the educator.

Television as a mode of enriching concepts

In the act of reading, the would-be reader uses his sensory impressions of the black letters on the white pages to estimate the meaning intended by the author at the time of his writing. One of the difficulties in this mode of communication is the difference between the experience background of the author and that of the reader. The author may choose a word (such as "tough") which in his social stratum has a negative connotation but which has a positive meaning to members of another group. As a result, the members of this other group may encounter difficulty in comprehension.

Television viewing is common to most of our country's people. Network programs carry the same vicarious experiences to a large part of the population, and so provide a more common cultural background or body of experiences than would be otherwise possible. This provision of common experience should enable writers to produce materials much more comprehensible to their readers, because the experiences of the readers are more nearly alike. The reader's concepts are enlarged by the vicarious experience of television viewing.

Television as experience with standard English

One of the factors which tend to depress reading comprehension scores among children of minority groups is the difference between their oral language vocabulary and structure and the vocabulary and structure used by the writers of textbooks and literature. The children of such groups may have heard only a foreign language or a sub-standard variety of English from their parents, siblings, and peers.

These children cannot be expected to make maximum use of context clues to unfamiliar vocabulary. Their oral reading may be halting and lacking in intonational qualities essential for the conveying of meaning. They may easily become verbalizers who habitually recite the lines from a printed page without attempting to determine the meaning, because the words and structure being deciphered are uncommon to their experience with oral language.

However, television actors and announcers generally speak standard English. Their writers originate and perpetuate a nationwide idiomatic speech and provide common referents for analogies and puns. Some televised games involve panelists and viewing audiences in competitive situations in which language mastery is rewarded and even glorified. Watching some television programs should enrich the language of most children. As a matter of fact, one study showed that vocabularies are thirty per cent higher for first graders in towns receiving television programs than in similar communities without television reception.

On the other hand, many school teachers complain that television has taught children not to listen. Some point to the skill many people develop in "talking around" the television sound and ignoring the auditory stimuli coming from the television set. They blame this phenomenon for children's failure to listen well in the classroom. Their contention may be valid, but it does not exhaust the possibilities. An equally valid explanation might be that the television set exposes children to carefully planned and produced programs which, in terms of "showmanship," are vastly superior to the classroom program enacted by the teacher and sponsored by the Board of Education. Failure to attend in the classroom could then be interpreted as a rejection of inferior "staging," "acting," and/or "production."

The fact remains that television does invade most homes with a variety of sights and sounds. For many children it provides the only real chance to learn standard English other than that offered by the school, and the only chance for learning it before they start grade one.

Television as simultaneous visual-auditory presentation of vocabulary

It has long been believed by linguists that experience leading to concept formation is completed by the assignment of language labels to the generalizations elicited by experience. Many parents have noted that their children have learned to read common brand names and program titles which are simultaneously spoken and flashed on the screen every time a program is on the air. For example, it is common for preschoolers to be able to "read" such words and phrases as GREEN GIANT, KELLOGG'S, MICKEY MOUSE, and POST-TENS. After one brief survey[5] of such learning, it was reported that kindergartners and first graders could identify a very large proportion of the words thus presented during television commercials.

At the onset of the study, the teachers involved believed that duller or less attentive children (in the classroom) might learn words from television viewing as well as children who were more attentive and learned better in school. However, the results suggested that the same children who learned to read easily and well were those who learned words easily from viewing television.

Research studies by John and Matilda Riley[6] and by Eleanor Maccoby[7] make clear that social class and peer relationships are modifiers not only of the television viewing choices of children, but also of the reasons for these choices. Himmelweit,[8] in a most comprehensive study, found that the higher a child's intelligence, the less he viewed, and that his choices seemed to be modified much by parental example. She believed that television stimulates *interest* rather than activity. Her outstanding finding, however, was how little could be confidently stated about the effect of television on children.

All three of the research studies cited in the preceding paragraph seem to indicate that an extremely large amount of time spent in viewing is common to children who are not satisfactorily adjusted to their environments. This may, of course, indicate that the environment itself is inadequate for the normal development of the individual. If either of these tenets is true, the choices of favorite program should be of two types: (1) adventure and mystery, which provide vicarious activity and excitement, and (2) family serials providing a sense of warmth through vicarious "belonging" to a family.

This research may be considered at least a partial explanation as to why television viewing is not as great a modifier of vocabulary learning as many might believe. Apparently the same factors which would tend to inhibit language mastery (social maladjustment, lower social class, lower intelligence, deprived environment) are those which tend to promote extensive television viewing. The viewing is thus seen to be a symptom, rather than an illness.

Increasing learning from television

According to Schramm[9] most children develop a "set" (a readiness to respond) to television as a tool for fantasy, escape, and recreation. When his viewing time is reduced, a child first gives up programs designed to provide him with information or instruction leading to effort. Typically, he rejects educational television programming.

The teacher is thus working against the status quo in attempting to make television a direct educational tool. Yet the effort must be made in several areas. One of these is selective viewing. Teachers can read the weekly announcements of forthcoming television presentations and notify parents that certain programs would benefit their children. Teachers can also provide "previews" which would cause children to want to watch educationally stimulating programs. Discussions by the students can also be structured around popular programs.

By promoting such activities, the teacher is providing a "set" for the use of television for intellectual stimulation. One of the problems of cultural deprivation is that the deprived can "look but not see." Someone must help by pointing out what can be seen if one knows where and how to look. Someone must provide the background which can enable the young viewer to understand what he looks at. Parents of culturally deprived children cannot and do not do this. Teachers of culturally deprived children must try.

Television can be a tool for better understanding of the student we would teach. We can estimate his sleeping hours, his psychosocial adjustment, and the social characteristics of his family by learning his viewing habits. His understanding of some programs will indicate his understanding of the majority cultural group. Since teachers can never learn enough about their students, they should capitalize on the opportunity presented by the presence of television sets in the homes by learning about the viewing habits of their classes.

Summary

Television can be used by children to increase their knowledge of the world around them. It can also be used as an escape from that same world. Many children increase both their speaking and reading vocabularies by watching television programs and commercials. Others watch longer and watch more programs, but appear to learn less. The teacher's role is to assess what learning accompanies further viewing. Thus the teacher can insure that television *does* make a contribution to the vocabulary development of children.

Footnotes

[1] Witty, Paul A., "Children, TV and Reading," *The Reading Teacher*, 11 (October, 1957), 11-16.

[2] Scott, Lloyd F., "Television and School Achievement," *Phi Delta Kappan*, 38 (October, 1956), 25-28.

[3] Sutton, Rachel S., "A Study of Certain Factors Associates with Reading Readiness in the Kindergarten," *Journal of Educational Research*, 48 (March, 1955), 531-538.

[4] Stanford Institute for Communication Research, Preliminary Report No. 2, "Television," The San Francisco Study of Children and Mass Communication, Palo Alto, California (Mimeo Report, 1959).

[5] Mason, George E., "Children Learn Words from Commercial Television," *Elementary School Journal*, 65 (March, 1965), 318-320.

284   MASON

6 Riley, M. W. and Riley, J. W., Jr., "A Sociological Approach to Communication Research," *Public Opinion Quarterly*, 15 (1951), 445-460.

7 Maccoby, E. E.,"Why Do Children Watch Television?" *Public Opinion Quarterly*, 18 (1954), 239-244.

8 Himmelweit, Hilde T. et al., *Television and the Child*, London; Oxford University Press, 1958.

9 Schramm, Wilbur, "Television in the Life of the Child—Implications for the School," pp. 50-70 in *New Teaching Aids for the American Classroom* (a symposium). Washington; U.S. Government Printing Office, 1962, 173 pp.

33 Vocabulary Development of the Underprivileged Child

Edgar Dale

The cogent discussion in this essay on vocabulary development of the under-privileged child is based on the belief that "sharp changes can be made in the background of experiences of these students, in their school and out-of-school learning. . . ." Written by a foremost authority on children's vocabulary, this essay gives the writer's recommendations for bringing about these changes.

How do the characteristics of the underprivileged child relate to vocabulary development? Why does the writer believe that dullness or brightness will not be "the major conditioning factor" in vocabulary growth? What is meant by "inventive word power" of the deprived? What further research is needed in understanding the language of the deprived child? Compare this article with Cohen's in Part Two of this anthology and note articles by the following authors cited in Selected References: Part Two, DeBoer, May, and Ponder; Part Seven, Clubb.

Our concern as teachers is to see that our students live a fulfilled life, that they develop their potential. The job of the teacher is to liberate them from the bonds of ignorance, ineptitude, prejudice, irrationality; to develop the skills, attitudes, and information necessary for the citizen in a democracy. Unless this philosophy actively infuses programs for vocabulary development (or any kind of development of the underprivileged child), we shall be wasting our efforts. Further, nothing less than a revolutionary effort will do much toward the solving of this problem. The following suggestions, then, should be seen in the light of such a possibility.

When I speak of the underprivileged child I mean the children usually of the inner city, those farthest away from the suburbs, the children of migrants. Often we are talking about Negroes, Puerto Ricans, Mexicans, white children

From *Elementary English* 42:778-786; November 1965. Reprinted with permission of the National Council of Teachers of English and Edgar Dale, Professor of Education, Ohio State University, Columbus.

from the South. I know that when I use the term "underprivileged child" and sometimes "lower-class child" there is a genuine hazard of stereotyping. It suggests that *all* children who live in slums or in the inner city are very much alike. Actually they are quite different.

Let me point out first that nearly all writers dealing with the underprivileged child believe that environmental rather than genetic factors account for the general differences that are found, and find no evidence in the science of heredity to cause them to think otherwise. We start, therefore, with the hypothesis that sharp changes can be made in the background of experience of these students, in their school and out-of school learning, and consequently in their IQ's or other tests of mental and educational development. The basis for such a sweeping conclusion has been presented by Benjamin Bloom of the University of Chicago in his volume *Stability and Change in Human Characteristics*. He says:

> The absolute scale of vocabulary development and the longitudinal studies of educational achievement indicate that approximately 50 per cent of general achievement at grade 12 (age 18) has been reached by the end of grade 3 (age 9). This suggests the great importance of the first few years of school as well as the preschool period in the developing of learning patterns and general achievement. These are the years in which general learning patterns develop most rapidly, and failure to develop appropriate achievement and learning in these years is likely to lead to continued failure or near failure throughout the remainder of the individual's school career. (p. 27)

Let's look first at some of the characteristics of the underprivileged child. These are findings of Martin Deutsch of New York Medical College, Gertrude Whipple of the Detroit Public Schools, Roger Brown and Ursula Bellugi of Harvard, John B. Carrol of Harvard, and Basil Bernstein of the University of London. I do not mean that this is a consensus of all of their writing, but rather that these are the chief sources of the following statements:

1) Models of excellence in use of vocabulary or sentence structure are not easily available to these deprived children.

2) They come from broken rather than intact homes. Often there is a nonexistent or weak father image.

3) Underprivileged children stay closer to home, in their own neighborhood. Their physical ranging is limited.

4) They have a negative self-image.

5) Their auditory span, their capacity for sustained attention is less than middle-class or upper-class children.

6) They use a smaller number of less varied words to express themselves.

7) Their sentences are shorter and more categorical. There are more incomplete sentences.

8) These children meet limited variability in the kinds of problems they

face, have no opportunity to be challenged by the complexities faced by middle-class children.

9) Home tasks tend to be motoric, not motivated by distant goals. There is emphasis on the immediate.

10) There is probably less listening to TV or radio, but here the data are limited.

11) There is a lack of manipulable objects in the home.

Given this background, let us see how it relates to the development of vocabulary. It is in the environing culture that we must look for those factors which inhibit the language development of underprivileged children—with resultant meager vocabulary and inadequate syntax. The underprivileged are usually ghettoized, concentrated in the inner city or its fringes, do not freely associate with suburban children. There is little communication, defined as "the sharing of ideas and feelings in a mood of mutuality."

The average Negro adult has approximately an eighth-grade education: the white adult has almost a twelfth-grade education. One is an eighth grader, the other a twelfth grader. To be a parent with a twelfth-grade education means that you can usually read with relative ease and understanding such magazines as *Time, Life, Newsweek*, and others. Data regarding the readers of these magazines show that those below the eighth grade represent only a small proportion. Indeed, we know that about 70 per cent of the readers of "slick paper" magazines are high school graduates. The same point could be made about the reading of serious political, economic, or governmental articles in the daily press. The average Negro parent cannot bring these complicated ideas to his children.

Second, words name things and actions with which we come into physical contact, within our perceptual range. As I noted earlier, the actual physical range of the underprivileged child is restricted. He doesn't move as far away from home base as does the middle-class child. An example is the learning of animal concepts. The middle-class child tested on the names of animals may do very well. One boy, when questioned as to why he knew the names of so many animals, said: "My parents always stop at animal farms so that we can see them."

But who takes the lower-class child to see the animals in the zoo? If he lives in a broken home, there may be no father to do this. Or even if he is in an intact home, there may be no method of easy transportation, such as the middle-class child has. How would the child of the inner city or slum get farm experiences? It would have to be a part of a planned school program. The effectiveness of such a program was well illustrated by the experience of a Cleveland teacher who sharply increased the reading and vocabulary level of a group of second graders by this approach. These experiences were needed because the downtown school in which she worked was dominated by warehouses, produce and grocery markets, and other business establishments.

Forty pupils in her group were at a low level of the second grade and could not master simple reading books suited to their age. The activities they engaged in included planning and making a visit to a farm, meeting the farmer and his family, exploring the barn, operating a water pump, riding on a tractor, looking at the combine, seeing "real" cows and a baby calf, playing in the straw.

Returning to the school, they recorded in pictures and on tape what they liked best. Willie said, "I liked the cows." Ronald said, "I saw a apple tree. It was full of blossoms, so pretty, and after while the tree will have apples and I would like to go back and eat them apples." Stanley described a rake as "a thing that you make a garden with. Got a long handle, look like a comb, and you put the points on the ground, pull the dirt along when the farmer makes a garden." Fanny Mae found out that a duck is a "quack-quack who swim in the water." She also learned about a silo: "I know what that is now. It's a big high thing out beside the barn, and it's a big old round thing the farmer cuts up corn stalks and puts them in and save them all winter for the animals to eat." All but three of the forty children were brought up to the standard reading level by the end of the year.

The deprived child, then, has actually been physically restricted in the number of things he has seen, heard, touched, and tasted. He lacks perceptual experience. There is also a lack of sequencing, the giving of order to these experiences. The child does not have a satisfactory filing system for storage or retrieval of experiences. This, after all, is what is meant by vocabulary and syntax—putting new and old ideas into new and varying patterns.

But perceptual experience is not enough. Furthermore, perceptual experience is not guaranteed by the presence of things to be perceived, or we would all be able to name the trees, the flowers, the birds around us. Martin Deutsch has pointed out in *Education in Depressed Areas* that the child not only lacks perceptual experience but sustained attention as well, the perseverance necessary to master these experiences.

Why do lower-class children often do poorly on the Metropolitan Reading Readiness Test? One Negro educator with whom I discussed this question showed me the test and reasoned this way: "Here is a picture of a wagon with three wheels. What is wrong with it? The child sees nothing wrong with it. He often plays with a wagon with no wheels at all. Here is a table with three legs. This is not uncommon in his home. Why should he see anything wrong with it?"

The answer may be more complicated than this. Adults in primitive cultures who are shown a photograph of themselves may not know who it is. They learn this by having someone note the congruence of the various items in the photograph with the individual himself. Certainly the deprived child would not choose an *actual* wagon with three wheels if one with four wheels was available. But he may not be able to perceive the line drawing of a wagon as representing the same wagon which he chose or failed to choose. This must be learned, and the difficulty the typical pupil has in reading graphs and charts indicates the problem faced. Can you easily understand the symbols used on a blueprint or in a wiring diagram?

We may be able to see differences in the real things but not in their representation. That persons of limited ability can make complicated discriminations is illustrated by an experience I had walking through the woods in Ohio with a boy whose IQ was about 60. He had left school in the fourth or fifth grade. He named all the trees as we went along—chestnut, ironwood, beech, pin oak, wild cherry, black walnut, etc. Then I said, "I don't know how to tell the difference between the wild cherry tree and the black walnut. How do you tell the difference?"

His answer was simple. "You look at them." To him this was just as stupid a question as it would be to ask a fourteen-year-old boy, "How do you tell the difference between a Chevrolet and a Pontiac?" He would reply, "You look at them."

I am making the point that if we stay at the concrete level, dullness or brightness will not be the *major* conditioning factor of growth in vocabulary. If we set up an environment for children in which they can taste and touch and smell, manipulate, see, feel, work on materials, they will be able to name and to label. The brighter may learn faster than the duller, but all will be able to learn.

This would suggest, of course, that a program of nursery school education should enable children to work with wood of various kinds, to paint, to cut out things with scissors, to eat varied foods or prepare foods within the school, make visits, go on study trips—and to discuss all these activities. This is important because children learn by active contact with things that make a difference to them.

The teacher's role, then, is one of aiding the child to self discovery. He observes the child's rate of development and moves the child on to the next task when he is ready. He listens to the child as the child discovers writing and reading. He works with the child to help him see the relationship between sound and symbol.

The early vocabulary of children shows an emphasis on nouns. The relational terms, the qualifying terms, the complex sentences come later. So we may set up the basic premise that a major factor in the early development of language will be rich, concrete experience in which the child is involved and in which there is an explicit plan to name and to discuss.

Now we come to another critical factor in concrete experience. We may think, for example, that the word *pet* is a concrete, clear-cut name that all children would easily learn. Not so. Many children in a deprived area in Washington, D. C., did not know the word *pet*, according to a study made by the teachers. Further, even when some teaching was done with this term, it showed limited growth over a period of time.

Why? We must realize that many words which *seem* quite concrete to the middle-class teacher or to the middle-class child are indeed abstractions to the deprived child. The child living in an overcrowded apartment does not usually have pets. A dog requires a license, purchased foods, medical attention, *etc.* The word *pet* is an abstraction. It is an abstraction which applies not merely to a dog or a cat but it might apply also to a lizard, a frog, to any animal requiring constant care and given a certain amount of affection.

I asked my four-year-old granddaughter what a pet was. She looked at me with an air of disbelief and curiosity which said, "Is grandfather playing a trick on me?" Of course she knew what a pet was, and she knew it because she had had pets and they had been so named. The idea of pet was internalized, in her bones.

As we work with deprived children we must realize that some terms which we assume are concrete, are abstract and unknown to them. At this point we may ask whether the premise of providing rich school experience is enough. Does this furnish us with adequate guidelines for the curriculum? I don't think it does. We must have an alert teacher who is aware of the out-of-school experiences of the child and how these experiences can be enriched.

There must be close cooperation with the home—difficult as this may sometimes be. There must be enhanced opportunities to make and hear increasingly complicated sentences. This means listening to recordings, making recordings, doing role-playing, putting on plays, viewing specially designed films, filmstrips, and television programs. It means more questions and answers about things that matter, more riddles, more jokes.

Usually when the issue of the vocabulary of the deprived child is discussed I am told that the Negro child knows certain words that the white child does not; that he has a unique, concrete, expressive language. Are there key areas where the deprived child is likely to have vocabulary not possessed by the middle-class child? Does the deprived child have a skill in creating metaphors not possessed by the middle-class child? John Brewer, of the Miller Elementary School in Pittsburgh, has listed a number of synonyms which pupils use for common words:

    cigarette—bush, joint, weed, tips, butt, charge
    teacher—mink job, moose, sad sack, Smokey the Bear
    a retarded person—way out, goof, knuckle head, lame, hole-in-head
    gasoline—soup, thunder, lightning
    suit—cloth, the vine
    teeth—ivory, snags
    mustache—brush
    skin—soft stuff, velvet
    club—muscle, wood
    happy—he's gone, reefer head, he's groovy
    crying—kleenex job
    overcoat—winter heat

toothbrush—pearl pusher
run—took off, and away we go, split, fade out
pencil—stick
matches—fire
strong—iron head, cement job
outwitted—scooped, tank job, paying his dues
work—sweat job
make-up—bucket of paint
thief—glue, sticky, chicken-picker
hat—lid, sky
water—wet stuff, rock on rye
pop—oil, sweet water, bubble
movie—flip time, flicker
house—shack, pad, hole in the wall, crib
snow—white stuff, rice
magistrate—fine peeler, the heat, the man
bald—shine, sunny side up, Mr. Clean
mouse—tiny tim
coins—jingle, hopping Johns, dust
sleep—cat eye, shut eye, knock myself out, red eye
ice cream—snow

Some other examples which I have picked up include the following:

ace—a good friend, companion
everything's everything—everything is wonderful or good
grays—white people
happy shop—liquor store
pull his coat—to bring to someone's attention
the man—the police or a policeman, also a nab
bread ain't done—not very smart
mac—immaculate
walking on the wall—nervous
juiced up—drunk
finger popping—snapping fingers to music
pounding brick—looking for a job

In Jamaica, "big eye" means greed; "strong eye," domineering. In Columbus, I have heard "sure knows his way to High Street" and "keeps his shoe laces tied" used to mean, "He's plenty smart."

It is possible, too, that the child living in the inner city has a perceptive understanding of emotion not possessed by middle-class children. Perhaps he can size up situations better. Certainly he has been subjected to much more vital experience about the realities of life and death than has his middle-class counterpart. This is worth exploring further. Has the underprivileged child learned to read *people*, that is, to interpret skillfully the rejection and acceptance in the faces and behavior of those with whom he comes in contact?

Basil Bernstein, an English sociologist, has pointed out that at school the underprivileged children must learn a second language—the middle-class language of the school and textbook. Here logical modification is expressed in complex grammatical constructions. Symbolism of a high order of generality and a large discriminating range of adjectives and adverbs are now expected of him. This is a language that middle-class children have heard from their first months, and they have fewer problems with it than do the lower-class children.

At school the teacher says, "John, would you mind closing the window?" Whether he minds or not is of little consequence. Think of how often we say: "John, is your desk clean?" meaning, "Clean up your desk"; "Are we all paying attention?" meaning, "Get with it!" Bernstein says that the lower-class child must learn a middle-class way of talking about things. He is thus penalized much as is an immigrant child coming to this country from an alien culture.

Bernstein states that the lower-class parent may say to his child, "Don't sit there." "If the child says, "Why?" the parent says, "Because I said so." He is merely being told that he must obey. The middle-class parent, however, may give a reason, namely, "Because you will get too cold," or something else. In short, the middle-class parent tries to state a cause-and-effect relationship, whereas the lower-class parent may merely say: "Because I told you to do it." No new information is gained; there is merely an extension of a command. Thus the middle-class child learns to link cause and effect.

Third, it is likely that the lower-class child will not use the variety of tenses that the middle- or upper-class child will use. He may say, "Baby come" instead of "The baby is coming." He may say, "I go" instead of "I will go." He will also often omit articles, as in the speech of very young children, saying "I dig hole" instead of "I dig the hole." And the deprived child may carry this immature speech into the school. Roger Brown and Ursula Bellugi point out in the *Harvard Educational Review*, Spring 1964, that sometimes children will know the articles in a sentence but will not repeat them after the adult because of meager attention span. As they learn to keep more things in mind, the articles are then put in.

Brown and Bellugi also point out that adults tend to stress orally the words carrying the content and include articles and auxiliary verbs and verb endings which the child may omit. The difference then between child language and adult language is not necessarily a difference only in word order. The adult, correcting something the child said, tends to supply needed articles, auxiliary verbs, *etc.*, thus providing a model of how it should be done. How does the deprived child get this experience? Often he doesn't.

Where might we go from here in studying the language of the deprived child? First of all, we need adequate analyses of this language not only in terms of words and their level of generality but also in terms of syntax. I mean the kind of study that Ruth G. Strickland reported in "The Language of Elementary School Children: Its Relationship to the Language of Reading Textbooks and the Quality of Reading of Selected Children" (see bibliography; also Walter Loban, *The Language of Elementary School Children*).

Perhaps one of the reasons that differences grow greater in the upper grades is that the concrete vocabulary of the deprived child becomes increasingly inadequate in meeting language problems faced in school, especially those related to reading. Somewhere around the fourth or fifth grade the words learned by speaking and listening decrease in proportion to words learned by reading. Some of this reading vocabulary consists of synonyms of well-known spoken words, and the underprivileged child can learn them.

But a number of the critical new words are conjunctions. As long as they are the simple conjunctions such as *and*, there may be no problem. Difficulties arise, however, when conjunctions indicating pairing or casual relationship are developed. A time lag occurs before the meaning can be grasped, *e.g.*, "He was not only a scholar but also a gentleman." The idea must be held in mind to the end of the sentence. There are conjunctions of alternates such as *neither . . . nor*, and there are the conjunctions of inference. Some conjunctions are confusingly abstract little words such as *for, or* and *so*. Some are not usually heard in conversation, such as *consequently, hence, therefore, as a result*. The conjunction often introduces a high level of abstraction, something for which the limited reading and perhaps the limited attention span of the deprived child is a serious handicap.

Another area needing careful study is that of inflectional suffixes used to indicate tense. Berko, for example, in "The Child's Learning of English Morphology," *Word*, (August–December, 1958), has made such a study of children's oral language. However, we cannot assume that a child able to make oral inflectional changes in suffixes can make these changes in writing. Gerhard Eichholz has carried on some studies in this field, working with noun plurals, past tense of verbs, comparatives and superlatives, possessive singular and plural. More critical, expanded studies are needed in this area.

It is easy to say that too little is known about the vocabulary development of the deprived, that we need a great deal of research, *etc*. Since only a few persons are going to do this research, it seems to absolve us of responsibility for doing something about this problem. The term "deprived," however, is a relative one. There are deprived persons in our high school and college classes, in wealthy suburban schools, even in our graduate schools. The dynamic potential of these students has not been reached and may not be reached unless we as individual teachers are able to help them see what they can do to remedy past weaknesses and build new strengths.

It is possible that we are overvaluing the verbal, the formal, the highly symbolic language, as contrasted both with informal, expressive, tangible, descriptive language and with non-verbal language. "The oral tradition is still strong," notes Richard Hoggart in *The Uses of Literacy* as he discusses the British "working class." Certainly formal language is good for much, but it is not good for everything. I think of the little Japanese boy described in the book *Crow Boy* by Taro Yashima. Chibi's playmates reject him and he spends his time thinking, listening, watching. The author writes:

> Just the ceiling was interesting enough for him to watch for hours. The wooden top of his desk was another thing interesting to watch. A patch of cloth on a boy's shoulder was something to study. Of course, the window showed him many things all year round. Even when it was raining the window had surprising things to show him. On the playground, if he closed his eyes and listened, Chibi could hear many different sounds, near and far. And Chibi could hold and watch insects and grubs that most of us wouldn't touch or even look at.

When a new teacher came, however, Chibi became important.

> Mr. Asobe, the teacher, often took his class to the hilltop behind the school. He was pleased to learn that Chibi knew all the places where the wild grapes and wild potatoes grew. He was amazed to find out how much Chibi knew about all the flowers in our class garden.

But Chibi's great triumph came when he imitated the crows:

> First he imitated the voices of newly hatched crows, then he made the mother crow's voice, then he imitated the father crow's voice. He showed how crows cry early in the morning. He showed how crows cry when the village people have some unhappy accident. He showed how crows call when they are happy and gay. Everybody's mind was taken to the far mountainside from which Chibi . . . came to the school.

The story is a parable. It is the story of those who take excessive pride in their indirect knowledge of the world, its symbols and signs, but ignore the rich experience all around them. Don't forget, too, the growth and development that can come from music, drama, the tenderness and compassion of sensitive human relationships.

I suggested at the outset that we need a revolutionary change in order to meet the problems of underprivileged children, youth and adults. We could get it if we were all convinced that (1) there should be universal access to excellence; (2) we should place a high priority on funds for compensatory education of underprivileged children and their parents. If this means delaying putting a man on the moon, let us delay.

The place where you are born in the United States should not dictate educational opportunity. We can move immediately to the equalizing of all educational instructional materials. We have made a good beginning in doing this through providing NDEA funds, through language laboratories, films, and the like. We should proceed speedily to make equality a reality.

Finally, I counsel a tough-minded attitude toward the problem and a tender-minded attitude toward the child. Further, the job of the teacher is not to pick the winners, and this is what we are often doing both in the first grade and in the graduate school. We honor "being on top" and consider it almost immoral to be at the foot of the class. To live a fulfilled life we must share our fulfillment with others. The best symbol for democracy is not a circle, but a ladder.

Finally, and this is the most difficult of all, we must be willing to develop radically new educational patterns to solve these probems. It won't do to put frosting on a stale cake. We must not do better the things we should not be doing at all. Our society itself must be transformed. A friend of mine, the late Bent Taylor (who had a distinguished career in national social work), told me that his high school principal in Louisville, Kentucky, once said to him about an important job that needed to be done: "Bent, if you and I don't do this, who will?"

Bibliography

Berko, Jean, "The Child's Learning of English Morphology," *Word*, 14 (August–December, 1958), 150-177.

Bernstein, Basil, "The Public Language," *British Journal of Sociology*, 10 (1959), 311-323.

———, "Social Class, Linguistic Codes and Grammatical Elements," *Language and Speech*, 5 (1962), 221-240.

———, "Sociological Determinants of Perception," *British Journal of Sociology*, 9 (1950), 159-174.

Brown, Roger and Ursula Bellugi, "Three Processes in the Child's Acquisition of Syntax," *Harvard Educational Review*, 34 (Spring, 1964), 133-151.

Carroll, John, "Words, Meanings and Concepts," *Harvard Educational Review*, 34 (Spring, 1964), 178-201.

Cohn, Werner, "On the Language of Lower Class Children," *School Review*, 67 (Winter, 1959), 435-440.

Davis, Allison, *Social Class Influences upon Learning*. Cambridge, Mass.: Harvard University Press, 1948.

Davis, Allison and Kenneth Eells, *Intelligence and Cultural Differences*. Chicago: University of Chicago Press, 1951.

Deutsch, Martin, "Minority Groups and Class Status as Related to Social and Personality Factors in Scholastic Achievement," Society of Applied Anthropology, Monograph No. 2. Ithaca, New York: Cornell University, 1960.

Hunt, J. McV., "The Psychological Basis for Using Preschool Enrichment as an Antidote for Cultural Deprivation," *Merrill-Palmer Quarterly* (Spring, 1964).

Jewett, Arno, Joseph Mersand and Doris Gunderson, *Improving English Skills of Culturally Different Youth in Large Cities*. Washington, D.C.: U.S. Department of Health, Education and Welfare, 1964.

Loban, Walter, *The Language of Elementary School Children*. NCTE Research Report No. 1. Champaign, Illinois, 1963.

Newton, Eunice, "Culturally Disadvantaged Child in Our Verbal Schools," *Journal of Negro Education*, 31 (Spring, 1962), 184-187.

Passow, A. Harry (ed.), *Education in Depressed Areas*. New York: Bureau of Publications, Teachers College, Columbia University, 1963.

Riessman, Frank, *The Culturally Deprived Child*. New York: Harper and Brothers, 1962.

Schreiber, Daniel (ed.), *The School Dropout*. Washington, D.C. Project: School Dropouts, National Education Association, 1964.

——— and Bernard A. Kaplan, *Guidance and the School Dropout*. Washington, D.C. Project: School Dropouts, National Education Association and American Personnel and Guidance Association, 1964.

Strickland, Ruth, "The Language of Elementary School Children," *Bulletin of School of Education*, Bloomington, Indiana, 1962.

Whipple, Gertrude, "Culturally and Socially Deprived Reader," in *Underachiever in Reading*. Proceedings of the Annual Conference on Reading, v. 24, Supplementary Educational Monographs, No. 92. Chicago: University of Chicago Press, 1962. (Chapter 10, pp. 129-136.)

Wilkerson, Doxey A., "Bibliography on the Education of Socially Disadvantaged Children and Youth," *The Journal of Negro Education*, 33 (Summer, 1964), 358-366.

34 Teaching Children More About Words and Their Ways

Leland B. Jacobs

It is not enough that children enlarge their vocabularies in both quantity and quality of word meanings; they must see the awesome power of words in influencing thought and behavior. In this article, Jacobs, a noted writer, pleads for teacher effort in helping each pupil become a more sophisticated and discriminate user of language.

What specific suggestions can you offer to help a child see words as "a language invention of man"? That "change is an aspect of human language as regular and relentless as the birth and death of man"? Of what importance is the categorizing of words as labels, as fences, as vehicles? Would linguists generally agree or disagree with Jacobs's suggestions? What trade books about language might be of help to the pupil? To the teacher? The article by Everhart cited in the Selected References for Part Five provides additional information on this topic.

As a child learns to listen, speak, write, and read, he has so many things to do, to hold in mind, to be aware of. He has to be able to recognize and identify words, pronounce words, combine syllables, categorize words, put words together into phrases, sentences, and paragraphs. Each of these accomplishments is, in and of itself, a great feat, a notable achievement. Why, then, ask for more? Indeed, dare teachers ask for more?

Teachers must do more. If, through the language arts, a child is to bring meaning to and take meaning from word signs, signals, and symbols, he must know many things about words and their ways which will help him to be a sophisticated and discriminative user of language as well as an efficient, skillful one.

From *Elementary English* 41:30-34; 94; January 1964. Reprinted with permission of the National Council of Teachers of English and Leland B. Jacobs, Professor of Education, Teachers College, Columbia University, New York.

What to Teach

What, precisely, are some important aspects of the more that we shall teach to children? In the first place, we shall want children—at their appropriate point of development—to see words as a language invention of man. They need to be quite clear that language makes man human, that without language it would be very difficult to get along personally or to share many of his experiences with another person. It would be difficult for one to communicate his ideas and feelings to his family and his friends. Without language it would be practically impossible for people to live together in an orderly, cooperative community life, based on commonly accepted governmental rules and regulations. In his personal living, how would he communicate his needs, his hopes and ideals, his plans, his concerns, his likes and curiosities, and his intentions without words? Yes, words are today—and have been for a long time in the history of the world—an invention of tremendous importance to man in his daily personal living and in his life as a citizen of the nation and the world.

Civilization has been a long time growing. Children, to be wise about words, will need to be taught that from a simple primitive civilization, a world of few necessary words, our present living has so changed and has now become so very complex that we live in a world of many necessary words. The present state of civilization, moreover, is sandwiched in between the past and the future. Our life today, if we stop to think about it, differs markedly from the life of our grandfathers, and the life of our great-grandchildren will, again, differ in many ways from ours. There seems to be nothing quite so sure in this world as change. New discoveries, inventions, experiments, and ideas all make a difference in how we live and how we act and how we denote and connote that living and those actions. Every new scheme or plan put into practice changes the ways of our living and our language. To live richly in this day and age, then, the child must recognize and be prepared for a world of change and so adapt to significant changes that he "keeps up with the times" in deed and in word.

As life changes language must change also. When new experiences call for new words, men invent the words that are needed. *Oleomargarine, penicillin, facism, atomic power, sputnik* are examples of words of fairly recent stock. If others are to know what we are talking about, words must somehow help people "get hold of" the ideas that we are trying to express.

Words and Things

Words are often closely related to things that can be seen and touched. A Puritan ancestor, for instance, would have great difficulty in making sense from talk about plastics, carburetors, television, Hollywood, or high school. Such things were unknown to him in his day; the words would not tie to anything in his experience. Likewise there were things within his experience that no longer are closely associated with our living. His words for such experiences no longer convey much meaning to us: *piggin, wort, gaffer, tithing-man*, or *dame school*. Children have not had the experiences that help these new words to "make sense." Similarly, our great-grandchildren will coin new words for new discoveries and ideas so remote from us that we cannot, at the present time, even guess what they will be. We do know that new discoveries and practices will beget new words, and that those new words will have meaning for their times as our words have meaning for us. And we can also be sure that words and their meanings will change. All this is important for children to comprehend.

Probably most children have never given much thought to this unique and wonderful invention of man—words—even though they have been using them freely every day. What are *words?* If they are so important in our personal living, surely teachers will want to help children understand something of the nature of words and their uses.

For one thing, a word is a label. It is not the experience itself, but it is an identification tag for an experience. It is a verbal sign, signal, or symbol. The word *cat* is not a cat at all. It is just our label for an animal that we happen to designate by that spoken or written sign. In other words, the label *cat* is useful only to the extent that it "calls up" an experience for both the speaker and listener or writer and reader so that they can both be sure that they are thinking about the same animal. What a dilemma a person would be in if *cat* meant mouse to a writer but meant elephant to a reader!

When one sees or hears *cat*, it brings to mind a picture of an animal with which the reader or listener has had enough experience that, in general, he gets some idea of what is being talked about. He knows that here is the label for an animal that has certain well-defined characteristics. But even then he will probably interpret the meaning of this three-letter word in terms of his personal experience rather than that of another speaker or writer. If one should happen to be a keeper of a zoo he might mean "lion." If he is a cat fancier, he might have in mind "thoroughbred." If he doesn't like gossip, he might be applying this label to a nosy neighbor. Or he might mean just the ordinary house pet with which most people are quite familiar.

There is another kind of word which, as a label, ought to be looked at carefully. *Board* is such a word. By itself, this word does not mean very much because it can refer to any one of several possible experiences. Just think what different things *board* might mean to a carpenter, a trainman, an actor, a bank executive, and a rooming house keeper. When one sees the word *board* all by itself, does it mean a piece of wood, food, a planning group, or mounting steps? And what about such other common words as *run, fast, play*, and *pass?* Each of these also has so many different meanings. It is only when the reader knows who is using the word, in what situation, and in what mood that he can see just how this label is being used and what another person seems to be trying to say. The receiver has to see or hear such words in context to know what they mean.

Words and Ideas

There is yet another kind of word label that is the trickiest of all to deal with. Such words as *generosity, patriotism, truth, wrongdoing,* or *happiness* do not refer to any one concrete thing in the way that words like *cup, sweater, hand, radio,* or *grandmother* do. When people use words like *good* and *bad, democracy* and *facism, strong* and *weak,* it is difficult indeed to be sure of what they mean. To put the finger on the exact experience from which such words come is impossible. Words like *cooperation* never mean any one thing to all people. What such a label means will certainly depend upon who uses the word, what this person values, his purpose for using the word, and his definition of the word. Sometimes such words are used just to stir up people's emotions and thus hinder thinking. Sometimes these words are used to express opinions rather than to state facts. Sometimes even the users of such abstract words are not themselves very clear about what they mean.

Whenever a writer or speaker uses such abstract terms, it is necessary to pause and check up. We may well teach children to say to themselves, "Stop. Look. Listen. Here is a tricky word crossing. Just what does this person mean? Does that word seem to mean to him what it seems to mean to me? Do I really understand what he is saying?

Yes, words are a kind of label. Words are man's invention for dealing with a world of real things by means of verbal signs, signals, and symbols. Words are labels for reality; they are not the reality itself at all. And new word labels are added to the language as new ideas, experiments, and experiences demand distinction.

Word Walls

Children need to know that words are not only labels, however. They are also walls or fences in the sense that they have the job of helping us to see what something may or may not be. A hotel is a dwelling, a stopping place for travelers, a place to get food. At the same time it is not an apartment house, a tourist camp, an inn, a flat, a restaurant, a castle, or a rooming house. An ostrich has in common certain characteristics of all other birds, but it differs markedly, at the same time, from a blue jay, a heron, an eagle, or a parrot. There are boundary lines between the meanings of words. When we use words we really are indicating what something *is* and *is not, seems to be* and *seems not to be.* Running is, in certain respects, like all other ways of moving about on legs, since one goes on "shank's mares," but it is obviously not the same as skipping, hopping, sauntering, or sprinting.

An individual uses this "word wall" every day when he reads, writes, speaks, or listens, whether or not he is conscious of doing it. Words that name kinds of automobiles, breakfast cereals, wearing apparel, writing equipment, school activities, and family relationships all illustrate the point that every word has its fences. Such fences are for the purpose of helping us in our communication with others toward clearer and more exact dealings with ideas and feelings. Without such walls or fences, words would so spread out in all directions that it would be like trying to mark off a square yard of ocean with a stick. No one would quite know what the limitations of any word might be. To avoid confusion in communication, words must live within their boundaries so that in our daily use of language others can map out the territory that we intend to cover in our speaking, writing, reading, and listening.

Word fences, however, do not wall out just one alternative. *White* does not wall out just *black;* it walls out *yellow, pink, green, etc.* as well. A movie is not necessarily either *good* or *bad.* A person is not just either *rich* or *poor, honest* or *dishonest, alert* or *stupid, attractive* or *unattractive.* Children sometimes get the notion that one word walls out just one other word, when in actuality such a word fence always offers many possible alternatives, as has just been pointed out. There is danger in thinking that a thing can be only *either* this *or* that— the danger that a person is not seeing all around the word fences to the neighboring fields on many sides. When we use words to think straight we recognize and use word fences to make our ideas as discriminative as possible. And we avoid "either-or" thinking because then we have not taken the time and energy to look all the way around the fence, something which a thinker always tries to do. A good thinker avoids "either-or" because he realizes that, in this complex world, situations, quite likely, won't be that simple.

Words as Vehicles

In looking still further at the words we use, children can be led to see that they are more than labels and fences. Words are also a most important part of our transportation system for ideas. Words are the vehicles that carry our verbal or written messages. Words are the verbal means of taking our listeners or readers along with us to our destination in communication. If the other person cannot or does not "ride along" with the words we are using, he will not cover the same territory and hence will not understand what we are trying to express in words to him.

When a child recognizes words as vehicles, he learns to ask himself, critically, "Where are these words taking me?" For words can sometimes carry us in directions in which we really do not wish to go. They can sweep us off our feet and head us in a wrong direction so swiftly that we hardly know just what has happened. This is possible because part of the carrying power of words is their emotional effect. Some words have more emotional charge—carry us faster in the direction that the speaker or writer would have us go—than other words do. Of course, for every person the words of strong emotional charge will be different from those of every other individual. But there are certain areas where, for the most part, one can be sure to get some high-powered emotional reactions. Family relationships, friendship, love, patriotism, religions, beliefs, ideals, and morality are some such areas in which words possess high emotional tone. Examples of words that may easily carry us away are: "Old Glory," "Brotherhood of Man," "Mother," "My Buddy," "Purity," "Good Citizen."

As carriers of meaning, words can also be used for more than the presentations of facts that can be observed and proved in the world as it exists. Words can be used to state personal opinion about the reality of the world. In such cases, if the words used are not clearly marked "Personal Opinion," there is always the danger that they will be mistaken for fact. Think of the reactions likely to be associated with such statements as "That government official is crooked," or "He is a bad boy." Children need to be taught to ask for the evidence. They need to learn to label many statements "Personal Opinion Only" until convincing evidence is given.

Children can learn that *is* and *are* are tricky as carriers of meaning. Consider the following sentences: *There are fifty states in the United States. Washington is the capital of the United States.* In these cases *is* and *are* are vehicles for statement of fact for which proof can be offered. But what about the following statements? *Orientals are all alike in appearance. He is untrustworthy.* Without evidence, these statements can be treated as no more than one person's opinion, though they are stated as facts. There is considerable difference between saying "John *is* lazy" and "John seems lazy to me." Is the lake blue or does it just appear blue to you at this particular moment? Is any particular nationality group really inferior, in terms of available evidence, or is it just personal opinion that this group is less capable or less talented? Children need to see that, as vehicles, words may have tremendous carrying power. As they develop as more mature thinkers they will be aware of this language problem and interpret more shrewdly the differences between facts, opinions, judgments, wishes, and the like.

Inadequacies of Words

One more observation needs to be made about words as vehicles. When a person takes a trip on a main highway through a state, he does see many interesting and important phases of life in that state, but he does not see all that there is to be seen. When one takes a walk through a woods with his friends, each person will probably notice certain colorful or exciting things. But there will be certain other things in the woods that only one or a few of the group will see. In other words, no individual ever sees and understands all that there is to be seen and understood about any one object, idea, or experience.

Likewise, no words ever convey *all* that there is to be said about anything. Words give the general map of the territory, but they do not give all the details. Words always leave some things unsaid. Whenever words are used to communicate ideas, one must recognize that more *could* have been said than was said. When we talk and write, we always must depend upon our listeners and readers to cover some territory that we have hurried or skipped over or have not mapped out carefully at all. When anyone implies that he has told us all that there is to be known about any topic, subject, object, or idea, we will need to realize that he may be misleading himself, or that he may be trying to mislead us, or that it is his opinion that there is no more to be said on the subject, or that there may be personal reasons why he would have us think, "This is all there is to know." As a child observes advertisements, listens to and looks at television, or reads information or fiction, it is useful for him to remember that when words are used as vehicles, "the last word" has never been said.

Word Ways: A Summary

Words certainly do have their ways. They grow out of human experiences and are used as an invention of man to communicate experiences. They may be regarded as labels. They are used as walls or fences. They are intended to be vehicles for the conveyance of ideas—sometimes facts, sometimes opinions, sometimes sales talks, sometimes directions, sometimes feelings. Words do make a difference in how we live and how we behave.

It is, therefore, very important that children understand what words are, how people react to them, what they may do to our thinking, our feelings, and our actions. Over and over again, in the language arts, the teacher will be able to point up the ways in which words may make a difference in what one understands or feels. The teacher will want to help children learn ways by which they can become "word wise." The teacher can thus unravel the mysteries of words and their ways so that, like Sherlock Holmes, children can detect chief word clues, so that they can get on the right track for understanding what words are up to and how they are influencing people's thoughts and feelings, their behavior, and their personalities.

35   Dare Schools Set a Standard in English Usage?

Robert C. Pooley

Pertinent and specific answers are given to the question posed in the title of this essay. The writer examines the nature of a language standard; changes with time; the range of deviation; and then defines a standard of usage for the classroom teacher.

How does the list of 25 items differ from the list of 8 items? How might the lists differ for extreme achievers—the linguistically advanced and retarded? Why is there an absence of grade placement for the various items on each list? How do Pooley's usage proposals compare with recent English textbook coverage? (See Malmstrom in Selected References, Part Five.) Would a survey or inventory of pupils' usage against Pooley's listing be an appropriate first step in planning the usage program for a group of pupils? What would be appropriate next steps? Articles by Bostain, Joos, Norman, and Pooley (Selected References for Part Five) are germane to this topic.

The topic is "Dare the School Set a Standard in English Usage?" I shall answer this question Yankee-fashion with another question: Do we dare *not* to set a standard? To this there seems to me to be but one answer: We should not and cannot fail to set a standard. To do so is to abandon the very core of our obligation to the youth we are employed to teach. We are committed by duty and by conscience to bring every student as close as possible to the attainment of a decent standard of English usage by every means at our command. But what is this decent standard and by what terms do we describe it?

One of the commonest misunderstandings of the point of view of the linguistic scholar with regard to English grammar and English usage is that when he observes and reports changes which take place in the English language, he thereby weakens the position of the English teacher and lowers standards. It is

From *The English Journal* 49:176-181; March 1960. Reprinted with permission of the National Council of Teachers of English and Robert C. Pooley, University of Wisconsin, Madison.

extremely important to us all to correct this misapprehension and to recognize why the objective study of our language properly interpreted results in a strengthening of standards rather than in laxity. To do so we shall need to examine more closely what is meant by a standard. It may well be that a misconception of the nature of a language standard is at the root of the misunderstanding.

Range of Latitude in Standards

In all matters concerned with human behavior to which standards may be applied, it will be found that such standards, far from being fixed and unchangeable, are actually only approximations within a fairly wide range of latitude and tolerance. A standard, in human conduct, is a sort of gentleman's agreement as to the norm reasonably expected, but behavior superior to this norm and behavior inferior to it are tolerated to a fairly wide degree. When the behavior exceeds the limit of tolerance to the point of becoming noticeable, amusing, embarrassing, or annoying, the standard is violated. But when deviate behavior remains within the range of normally accepted tolerance, the standard may be said to be maintained.

To cite some instances: a gentleman when seated is expected to rise when a lady enters the room. This is the standard. What are the degrees of tolerance? Behavior may and often does range from a ceremonial rising with a bow and offering of a chair to a half-hearted semi-squat movement as a sort of grudging recognition of the standard. The latter behavior is on the edge of tolerance; if it becomes habitual and noticeable the offender may be considered a boor. On the other hand, excessive politeness and ceremonial attached to this simple standard becomes amusing or annoying, and thus violates the standard of behavior. But within the range between these extremes, the standard is considered to be met. Yet within this tolerable range there are troublesome variations. Does a male guest rise when an eight-year-old daughter of the house is introduced? Does a husband rise every time his wife enters the room? At what point in a daughter's age does a father rise for her entrance? Is he a boor if he does not rise when she is fourteen, sixteen, or eighteen? I do not need to elaborate further to illustrate that a standard of behavior such as this has considerable latitude.

Another example may be observed in the so-called "bread and butter" note—the note of thanks sent to one's hostess when one has been a dinner guest or a house guest. Punctilious meeting of this standard requires a note to be written within three days. A formal note sent the day after the engagement may have a tone of rigidity and coldness, as though one were getting a disagreeable task out of the way; failure to respond within a month is a laxity beyond tolerance within the standard. With considerable variation between these extremes is the friendly note of thanks and acknowledgment of courtesies, differing in degree of formality in proportion to the degree of acquaintanceship of the correspondents. It is almost impossible to write exact rules to cover the variety of situations within which this standard must function. Nevertheless, it is a standard whose performance one neglects only at his social peril. Parental instruction, experience, and general good taste determine the readiness to meet this standard; but the standard must be met if one is to remain within the ranks of the socially acceptable.

I have spoken of the two examples above as if they were unchangeable with time. But we are still aware that behavior patterns change with time and that the norms of expected behavior, in other words the standards, shift from one period to another. When I was a young man a formal dinner required a black dinner coat with formal trousers, a black vest, a black tie, and a starched white shirt with jewelled studs and cuff links. I recently attended the Captain's dinner (which was announced as formal) on board a cruise ship of the Norwegian-American line. The passengers were from the ranks of those Americans who may be called the privileged class. Less than a third of the gentlemen were arrayed in the dinner costume of my youth. The black vest has almost disappeared. In its place a cummerbund is worn. Nor need this be black. A number of guests wore dark maroon, deep blue, or plaid cummerbunds, with ties to match. The starched shirt has almost disappeared; soft shirts with studs and links are rare; soft shirts with ordinary buttons are common. Moreover, there were dinner jackets not black, but deep blue, dark maroon, and a few in resplendent plaid. Does this variety and differentiation mean that gentlemen no longer dress for dinner; that anything goes? Not at all; the standard is perfectly clear, but a range of deviation within the standard is now acceptable which a few years back was not.

In contrast, I would remind you that before the turn of the century every hotel, restaurant, and public parlor in which gentlemen gathered was adorned with cuspidors, and most private homes possessed them, even if discreetly concealed. A pattern of behavior once tolerated or taken for granted is today outside the pale; a hostess would be shocked to be asked to produce a cuspidor.

In the realm of social behavior most of us accept the two principles governing standards which I have illustrated; namely, range of tolerance within the standard at any one period of time, and change in the description of the standard from one period to the next. Any wise parent knows that to insist upon the details of a standard as observed a generation before is to breed rebellion at home and ridicule abroad; the essence is to teach the standard as it is observed today by persons of taste, refinement, and social experience. And as part of the teaching the latitude which exists in the performance of any standard should be included. Our aim for our children and ourselves is neither heel-clicking regimentation, nor loutish laxity. Between these undesirable extremes lies a range, not a point, of tolerated behavior within the standard.

Now we return to language, a form of human behavior, to observe that standards of language, unlike those of other behavior, are considered by many to be rigid and fixed with no range of tolerance, and no change of pattern from one period to another. But because language is a form of human behavior, such fixity of standard is an untrue fiction. It cannot be, it never has been, it never will be. At no time in the history of English can the most intolerant investigator find a time or a place where all the polite, educated elite employed exactly the same usages. On the contrary, the investigator finds volume after volume of writings criticizing the "errors" of the great authors and men of distinction of the previous generation. Apparently, to the neutral historical scholar, the only ones who ever spoke purely correct English were the authors of the books condemning their predecessors and contemporaries for gross errors, and of course, no two of them agreed with each other!

Let us face the facts in all seriousness. What we call "good English" is a gentleman's agreement covering a range of acceptable behavior, exactly parallel with the observance of standards in other types of human behavior. This range can be described, it can furnish a pattern of behavior, it can set a standard of the sort that an intelligent scholar of English can accept and use.

Standards for Classes

It remains to define and describe the standard of English usage we may properly set for our classes, and are indeed obliged by our duty to maintain so far as we are able. I would like to define this standard first in general, universal terms to lay the foundation for particulars. To this end I quote a definition I wrote nearly thirty years ago . . . : "Good English is that form of speech which is appropriate to the purpose of the speaker, true to the language as it is, and comfortable to speaker and listener. It is the product of custom, neither cramped by rule nor freed from all restraint; it is never fixed, but changes with the organic life of the language."[1] You will note that this definition allows for a range of latitude within tolerable limits, and provides for the changes which are inevitable in a spoken language. But a definition so broad leaves the classroom teacher with a great many specific decisions to make, and it is to clarify these decisions that the following specific matters are presented.

In proceeding from the most elementary details to the more complex, I do not intend to imply a grade level distribution, for some usage items are easily overcome and others tend to persist into adult life. The order of presentation is roughly that in which the usage matters become significant in the student's command of his language.

The standard we can rightfully set for ourselves, our colleagues in other departments, and our students, for public and private use, contains at present these particulars:

1. The elimination of all baby-talk and "cute" expressions.
2. The correct uses in speech and writing of *I, me, he, him, she, her, they, them.* (Exception, *it's me.*)
3. The correct uses of *is, are, was, were* with respect to number and tense.
4. Correct past tenses of common irregular verbs such as *saw, gave, took, brought, bought, stuck.*
5. Correct use of past participles of the same verbs and similar verbs after auxiliaries.
6. Elimination of the double negative: we don't have no apples, etc.
7. Elimination of analogical forms: *ain't, hisn, hern, ourn, theirselves,* etc.
8. Correct use of possessive pronouns: *my, mine, his, hers, theirs, ours.*
9. Mastery of the distinction between *its,* possessive pronoun, and *it's, it is.*
10. Placement of *have* or its phonetic reduction to *v* between *I* and a past participle.
11. Elimination of *them* as a demonstrative pronoun.
12. Elimination of *this here* and *that there.*
13. Mastery of use of *a* and *an* as articles.
14. Correct use of personal pronouns in compound constructions: as subject (Mary and I), as object (Mary and me), as object of preposition (to Mary and me).
15. The use of *we* before an appositional noun when subject; *us* when object.
16. Correct number agreement with the phrases *there is, there are, there was, there were.*
17. Elimination of *he don't, she don't, it don't.*
18. Elimination of *learn* for *teach, leave* for *let.*
19. Elimination of pleonastic subjects: *my brother he; my mother she; that fellow he.*
20. Proper agreement in number with antecedent pronouns *one* and *anyone, everyone, each, no one.* With *everybody* and *none* some tolerance of number seems acceptable now.
21. The use of *who* and *whom* as reference to persons. (But note, *Who did he give it to?* is tolerated in all but very formal situations. In the latter, *To whom did he give it* is preferable.)
22. Accurate use of *said* in reporting the words of a speaker in the past.
23. Correction of *lay down* to *lie down.*
24. The distinction between *good* as adjective as *well* as adverb, e.g., He spoke *well.*
25. Elimination of *can't hardly, all the farther* (for *as far as*) and *Where is he (she, it) at?*

This list of twenty-five kinds of corrections to make constitutes a very specific standard of current English usage for today and the next few years. Some elements in it may require modification within ten years; some possibly earlier. Conspicuous by their absence are these items which were on the usage lists by which many of us were taught and which survive today in the less enlightened textbooks.

1. Any distinction between *shall* and *will.*
2. Any reference to the split infinitive.
3. Elimination of *like* as a conjunction.
4. Objection to the phrase "different than."
5. Objection to "He is one of those boys who *is.*"
6. Objection to "The reason . . . is because. . . ."
7. Objection to *myself* as a polite substitute for *me* as in "I understand you will meet Mrs. Jones and myself at the station."
8. Insistence upon the possessive case standing before a gerund.

These items and many others like them will still remain cautionary matters left to the teacher's discretion. In evaluating the writing of a superior student I would certainly call these distinctions to his attention and point out to him the value of observing them. But this is a very different matter from setting a basic usage standard to be maintained. I think it is fair to say that the items I have listed in the basic table lie outside the tolerable limits of acceptable, current, informal usage; those I have omitted from the base table are tolerated at least, and in some instances are in very general use.

I would like to conclude with a very useful distinction in usage made by one of the distinguished members of our profession, Louis Zahner of Groton School. In the *Atlantic Monthly* for November 1959, he points out the difference between "inventive language," that is, language created to produce a desirable effect, as for example, *to pussyfoot,* or, a *lounge lizard;* and "preventive language," words which defeat meaning by abandoning it: "Isn't it a terrific day:" "He was terrific:" etc. The teacher who loves English will do well to recognize and on occasion praise an unorthodox expression which is creatively effective; but he will condemn with all his force the substitution of meaningless cant for meaningful words.

Let Geoffrey Chaucer have the last word on standards in English:

> Ye knowe ek, that in forme of speche is chaunge
> Withinne a thousand yeer, and wordes tho
> That hadden pris, now wonder nice and straunge
> Us thinketh hem; and yit they spake hem so,
> And spedde as wel in love as men now do.

Footnote

[1] Robert C. Pooley, *Grammar and Usage in Textbooks on English, Bureau of Educational Research Bulletin,* No. 14, University of Wisconsin. August 1933, p. 155.

36 Bargain Basement English

Wilson Follett

In this essay, an author who believed that English should be accurate takes issue with Bergen and Cornelia Evans for what he regards their tolerance of careless American usage. Though not essential to understanding this article, the reader might be interested in reading Bergen Evans's article cited in Selected References which appeared in print the month following the Follett article. The underlying assumption of Follett's article—that language should be used in an orderly way with strict attention to grammatical and semantic propriety—is set out in a clear fashion. It suggests modern trends in structural and descriptive linguistics have had a detrimental influence on usage, and is unashamedly prescriptive.

What similarities and differences are there between this article and the one reprinted from Pooley? And the one by Joos cited in Selected References for Part Five? What are teacher attitudes toward current usage? (See Womack cited in Selected References, Part Five.) If feasible, compare Bergen and Cornelia Evans's A Dictionary of Contemporary American Usage *(New York: Random House, 1957) and Wilson Follett's* Modern American Usage *(New York: Hill and Wang, 1966).*

Linguistic scholarship, once an encouragement to the most exacting definitions and standards of workmanship, has for some time been dedicating itself to the abolition of standards; and the new rhetoric evolved under its auspices is an organized assumption that language good enough for anybody is good enough for everybody. We have come into a time when the ideals preached and, sometimes, practiced by exalted authority can only take shape in uses of English that are at best tolerable and at worst revolting. Such official pressure as is now put on the young learner is no longer in the direction of forcing him to ask himself whether his way of saying something could have been made better at a bearable cost—as, in a language so rich and various as ours, it generally could

From *The Atlantic Monthly* 205:73-76; February 1960 under the title, "Grammar Is Obsolete." Reprinted with permission of Mrs. Wilson Follett. Copyright © 1960, by The Atlantic Monthly Company, Boston, Massachusetts 02116.

have. Everything now taught him concentrates on the lowly question, Will it do in a pinch?

For the handiest possible conspectus of what the new ideal is, one can do no better than to glance at a comprehensive manual of rhetorical practice. *A Dictionary of Contemporary American Usage*, by Bergen Evans and Cornelia Evans, comes from authors of prestige and influence, one of them a university professor of English and conductor of a radio and television program devoted to questions of spoken and written usage, the other a writing consultant in the Department of Health, Education, and Welfare and a prize-winning novelist. The reason for turning to this 570-page, 600,000-word volume is not that its publisher proclaims it to be "up-to-date, complete, authoritative"—an assertion of three attributes inherently unattainable by any such work compiled by mortals —but rather that it is described with strict accuracy to be "based on modern linguistic scholarship." It is essentially a popularization of findings about modern English arrived at and promulgated by contemporary philologists, semanticists, virtuosos of historical and descriptive (as opposed to prescriptive) grammar and morphophonetics, and learnedly implacable assailants of the discarded idea that to speak or write well means hard work, the taking of sometimes painful thought, the constant rejection of labor- and thought-saving alternatives, and the practice of canons that are mastered only by arduous self-cultivation and discipline.

The Evanses manage to convey, along with many shrewd discriminations and salutary warnings often very engagingly phrased, an overall impression that acceptable usages are arrived at by a process about as automatic as breathing; that to torment oneself with questions of better and not so good is to be a seeker after gratuitous trouble and, what is worse, a purist; and that the way to attain effective expression is to keep our ears open, bank on our natural and inescapable linguistic inheritance, and cultivate an English that will make us indistinguishable from the ostensibly educated surrounding majority. Let us see where anyone will come out if he accepts and applies the combination of what these authors recommend, what they defend or condone, and what they do themselves. He will come out speaking and writing an American English faithfully represented by the scattering that follows:

"Ask whoever you see." "He had as much or more trouble than I did." "He works faster than me"; "he is taller than me." "More unique." "Different than." "The reason is because. . . ." "I can't imagine it being him." "Let's you and I"; "let's you and me." "Bob as well as Frank were there." "Neither D. nor A. are at home"; "neither he nor I are timid"; "either of them are enough to drive a man to distraction"; "neither of them had their tickets"; "I do not think either of them are at home"; "each carried their own pack"; "each of the men were willing to contribute." "Every member brings their own lunch"; "either the boy or the girl left their book." "I cannot help but think." "Nobody was killed, were they?" "Less than three." "If one loses his temper." "We did not find a one." "The sheriff with all his men were at the door." "Not one of them were listening." "Some grammarians claim that this is not permissible." "He allowed that we were right." "Refer back to." "Back of" (behind). "Between each house"; "between every pause." "He blamed it on me." "I haven't but a minute to spare." "I don't doubt but that you are surprised." "Who did you see?" "Who are you looking for?" "Children whom we know are hungry." "Everyplace"; "anyplace"; "someplace"; "someway"; "noplace"; "I have looked everyplace." "It is not I who is angry." "These kind of men are dangerous." "You don't know Nellie like I do." "It is you who will be blamed for it, not them." "That's her at the door now." "A minimum of sufficiency." "We most always go shopping on Saturday." "Very amused." "Overly cautious." "Datas"; "phenomenas"; "much data"; "very little data"; "the data is now in." "I asked him what was he doing." "The rationale for his attack on the President." "As regards." "Somebody left their umbrella." "I will get one someway." "There will only be him left." "Subsequent to his release from the Air Force he got a job with a commercial air line." "A continuous use [of a word in a specified way] is vulgar." "He went no further than Philadelphia." "Neither of these reasons justify the use of the present tense." "He failed, due to carelessness."

This little anthology could be several times multiplied from the same source; thus much will do to imply a general pattern. Some of the specimens are patently better, or less bad, than others. Say of the whole, if you wish: "Some of it might be worse." There is no point in using a microscope on the gradations or on the merits of the arguments used to defend this locution or that. It is enough if we perceive—as we cannot very well escape doing—that collectively they define a stratum of diction that invites defense and seems to require it, one that it is now fashionable to defend with all the resources of specialized learning. No one could possibly contemplate any such handful and then declare its components above challenge and in no need of condoning; no one could associate them with an unremitting effort to discover and to utilize the best that our common language is capable of. A collection of the same size could hardly vary much from this one if it deliberately set out to specialize in the marginal, the dubious, the suspect. What it seems to represent is the pattern of habits deliberately adopted by the educated when they set out to show that they are no better than anyone else, if as good. It goes to show the lengths to which we can carry conformism and the terror of being noticeable in a society that is (as Bierce said of the republic long before H. L. Mencken was heard of) daft with democracy and sick with sin.

If anyone wanted to execute a piece of writing that would be from beginning to end the densest possible concentration of what the elder rhetoricians classified as solecisms, he could hardly do better than to attune his prose to the dicta laid down in *A Dictionary of Contemporary American Usage*. The book is an astute, artful, and tireless harvesting of whatever in American speech is barely tolerable to those who do not make a virtue of pushing either tolerance or intolerance to pathological extremes. And it is a translation into practical advice of what the most erudite philologists and lexicographers have for some time been telling us about the sources of health and vitality in our language. The great nuclear principle seems to be that we should speak and write not as well as we can learn how, but ignobly enough to escape notice.

Now, a resort to this kind of first aid may result in some tactical advantage to the purveyor of insurance or real estate, the chairman of a fund-raising campaign, the soapbox orator, the candidate for minor office. Even that advantage can be doubted: there seems to be a fairly powerful undertow of envious popular respect for the man who uses language with easy distinction, provided that he does it in quiet assurance with no air of showing off or of spitting on his hearers to see if they can swim, as the rude old Yankee folk saying has it. An instance is the standing that ex-Governor Adlai Stevenson seems to have had with all classes of his fellow countrymen, whether they applauded his political opinions or not. But whatever the practical momentary advantages of slovenly diction, what is its long-range bearing on education, on the language itself, on its literature? Will, say, two or three consecutive generations of calculated effort to speak and write without excellence enhance the prospect of our producing an Irving, a Hawthorne, a Melville, a Henry James, a Howells, a Sarah Orne Jewett, a Willa Cather? Or will it tend to blight that prospect? Did the virtue of English prose, from Sir Thomas Browne and the King James translators to Bernard Shaw, come out of the acceptance of language on the permissive or lowest-common-denominator basis—out of a preoccupation with what was tolerable, what could barely be endured in default of better?

Is it not one of the shames of modern scholarship that it has so little to say for what is really good, what is best, and so much to say for what is merely allowable or defensible? Scholarship is trying, of course, to discount the factor of taste as nonscientific; but is it scientific to discount it? Taste is the faculty of criticism, the faculty of intelligent choice; and to it belongs the last word about any given use of language. After all, the argument from usage carries only a permissive force, not a mandatory one. Even if it were possible to prove an overwhelming preponderance for "He failed, due to carelessness" and "You don't know Nellie like I do," the proof could mean only that one may use these expressions without being condemned. There would be nothing to say that anyone has to use them, and all of us would still have the freedom of "His failure was due to carelessness" or "Carelessness caused him to fail" and "You don't know Nellie as I do" or "the way I do," which will never raise any problems or any eyebrows.

Nobody is under compulsion to like a construction just because it exists or to use it if he does not like it. This is a principle that applies equally to present and to past usages. We have the whole range of linguistic resources at our disposal; and there is no virtue in flirting with ways of expression that we think dubious or inferior when there are alternative ways—as there always are—to which no exception can be taken. The formation of any style, even a bad one, is an affair of constant acceptances and rejections; and everyone has to lean on his own taste for acceptance of the better and rejection of the worse.

The discussion of usage was probably never shrouded in more fog than it is now. Those who want to fling wide the gates to all manner of laxity maintain firmly that change is the great inescapable law, that the only criterion is what people are doing with language *now*, and they can find no words severe enough for resistance to change, especially when resistance takes the form of quoting classic sources; but if they can unearth in Chaucer or Wycliffe or Donne or Hazlitt some parallel to whatever change is being resisted, they cite it as if it settled the matter forever. Whether the use cited was typical or exceptional in that author is a question not raised; it is enough that the passage exists. The Evanses give us a list of twenty authors, Shakespeare to Maugham—a list as easily extended back to Chaucer—who use *like* as a conjunction, but there is no attempt to show that any one of them regularly or even frequently used it so. A dictionary that illustrates a secondary meaning with a quotation may, for all we can tell, be using the only known occurrence of the word in that sense.

The radical, the innovator, the grammatical iconoclast and libertine is ready to beat down all opposition as tradition-bound and ridiculously conservative, but he is equally ready to demonstrate that whatever is objected to has been English for four or five hundred years. Both forms of argument are supposed to be unanswerably crushing. If some locution now current defies a past consensus, so much the worse for the past; but at the same time any locution ever written by a good writer is *ipso facto* attack-proof, and if a precedent can be adduced for anything, however shabby, the case is closed.

Actually not everything ever written by a good writer, or even by quite a number of good writers, is good, any more than everything ever written by a bad writer is bad. Every good writer has committed himself at one time or another to practices without which he would have been a better writer. It is our privilege to pick and choose, alike from the superior and the inferior, alike from the past and the present. For the winnowing of the past we have the guidance of perspective in addition to taste; for the present, taste alone has to suffice. For taste there is no substitute, nor is there any excuse for not using as much of it as we have. The unexpressed excuse that underlies most refusals to use it is the delusive feeling that every demolition of a barrier, old or new, is a freeing of the language from needless restraints and a further emancipation of its users.

What is overlooked is that language and its users grow by restraints, too. Especially in a time when looseness of many kinds is a dominant fashion, it may be salutary to cultivate a tightness and exactitude not customarily demanded. Linguistic resources are expanded not only by the seizing of new liberties as fast as they become available but also by the rejection of liberties that may be only license. A writer is not alone what he writes; he is likewise everything that he will not write because he finds it not good enough, and his power may be as much a function of his renunciations as of his self-indulgences. The libertarians will pity him as self-deprived and call his austerity a crotchet, but he and we are the gainers by his discriminations, and the language may be the loser by the indiscrimination of the loose constructionist.

In no domain is there a clearer illustration of the power of negative choice than in the domain of diction. Good writing has always been marked, and is marked today, by selection of words for their central and not their peripheral meanings. A word, particularly an abstract word, has a core of meaning from which it gradually spreads over associated meanings, perhaps in several directions, until it overlaps words that have likewise spread out from entirely different, possibly remote centers.

The liberalistic view now regnant ranks all such extensions as improvements of language, all as equally good. But the fine writer or speaker is habitually aiming at bull's-eyes, not at general target areas, and he does not care for the idea of shelling the woods with language. His dictionary gives *apparent* as one synonym of *evident,* and vice versa, but he still finds an important kind of integrity in applying *apparent* to the thing that seems to be so whether it is or not and in saving *evident* for that which both seems to be and is so. *Infer* once meant exactly what *imply* means now—it is generally, perhaps always, so used in the seventeenth-century plays of John Ford—but the two words have developed a clear differentiation whereby *imply* goes with the transmitting end and *infer* with the receiving end of the same process of deduction; smoke *implies* fire, but when you smell smoke you *infer* fire. It is a clear loss, not a gain, when we ignore the differentiation in such sentences as these from the best-selling murder story of the decade: "The defense is trying to infer that the prosecution is trying to conceal something." "And surely you do not mean to infer that it would be an unjust verdict if X. were acquitted on the ground of temporary insanity?" *Infer* is being so chronically abused by many who should know better that lexicography no longer quite sees what to do with it, but a decent writer sees, and he is well aware that the widespread confusion makes the English vocabulary not richer, but poorer. True, "language grows," as Greenough and Kittredge said in 1901, "by the felicitous misapplication of words"; but there is no profit to be had out of misapplication per se, without the felicity—a reservation that brings us straight back to the necessity of taste.

The obvious and growing indifference of many publishing houses to hundreds or thousands of such distinctions as those illustrated cannot be called one of the most gladdening signs of the times. No practicing editor of any great competence ever sees a book manuscript for which he could not do appreciable favors if he had a free hand and time, and ninety-nine of any hundred published books could have profited by good offices that they never received. But these phenomena, depressing as they are, seem not quite so shocking as the latter-day hospitality of the very learned to every popular usage that volunteers to make the language more fuzzy, inarticulated, and fumbling.

What steadily preoccupies everyone fit to be called a writer is the possibility of improving everything in his work that is improvable. In no other way can he contribute his much or his little to the effectiveness of language as an instrument of precision combined with power. The linguistic scholarship that impedes and discourages where it might help him is operating beneath its privilege, not to say beneath its obligation. Let those who choose define usage as what a swarm of folk say or write by reason of laziness, shiftlessness, or ignorance; the tenable definition is still what the judicious do as a result of all that they can muster of conscious discrimination. It is time we had a philosophy of usage grounded in the steadfast conviction that the best, whether or not we have it in us to attain it, is not too good to be aspired to.

37   The Case for Syntax

Enola M. Borgh

*Understanding the relationships among words in complicated sentences may
well be one of the most important functions of language learning. Borgh examines the need for this type of learning and suggests some practical exercises
to help children improve their use and understanding of syntax.*

*What is meant by "system, tune, and words" as three elements of a lan-
guage? How do the Strickland and Loban studies support the thesis of the
article? Do you agree that study of "basic patterns" should precede individual
word analysis? What language strengths are developed through study of means
of expanding basic patterns? Strickland's article cited in Selected References
for Part Five presents a supporting point of view while those by Geist, Hatfield,
Hayes, Jacobs, and Mooney provide additional information on this general
topic.*

Twice a year the teacher of freshman composition at *the* University—which
may be Texas or California or Illinois or Wisconsin—faces a crop of young
hopefuls, products of our many-faceted public and private school systems. Their
formal training in the English language varies greatly, not merely from community to community but even from school to school and teacher to teacher.
There is very little the freshman instructor can take for granted, except that this
rather bewildered group of adolescents knows with the certainty of divine in-
spiration that there is a difference between *can* and *may* and that no decent
sentence is ever begun with a conjunction or concluded with a preposition. These
particular shibboleths of language have long been retired by the linguists. Yet
they persist in the elementary and secondary textbooks, although the validity
of this continuing assault is contradicted by scientific study.[1]

Much more laudable, of course, is the time devoted to word study. Students
at all age levels find a certain fascination in the picturesque origins of many
words, in the historical events which controlled the introduction of our Latin

From *Elementary English* 42:28-34; January 1965. Reprinted with permission of the
National Council of Teachers of English and Enola M. Borgh, University of Wisconsin at
Milwaukee, Milwaukee, Wisconsin.

and Norman-French heritage, in the many foreign words which have found their way into English through exploration and colonization. Word lists, crossword puzzles, and dictionary exercises are but a few of the techniques used to help students build a wide vocabulary. Yet only infrequently are they encouraged to draw upon this hoard of meaning and use a "big" word in a syntactic structure; the wide gap between the recognition vocabulary and the working vocabulary remains.

The Neglect of Syntax

The neglect of syntax is characteristic not only of our teaching but even of our literary criticism. In his recent book, *Language, a Science of Human Behavior,* Warfel says,

> There has been bred in us an excessive adoration of words and ignorance of or distaste for the systematic organization of words into syntax. If one follows Otto Jespersen in "Shakespeare and the Language of Poetry," Chapter X in his *Growth and Structure of the English Language,* the major element in the greatest of all English poets' works is words. The few references to the master's grammar and syntax are unperceptive . . . Jespersen, of course, was caught up in the late nineteenth century preoccupation with morphology ("the internal structure and forms of words"), so that he never quite saw the language system which makes possible the tension in words and meanings. Usage study is predicated upon the wholly false notion that words have the power to operate *sui generis,* as if the panes in a window exist apart from the frame. The three elements in a language—in descending order of importance—are the system or code, the tune, and the words. . . . The "big" words are only as important as the system makes them.[2]

Today teachers of reading and literature tend to repeat Jespersen's error, concentrating their attention and that of their students on lexical matters and assuming that the syntax will take care of itself.

At a very early age children should see that words themselves can have only limited meaning without the language system. A simple word like *run,* for example, can mean: "They run down the street"; "it was a short run to school"; "I have a run in my stocking." Grammar studies then should encompass much more than fragmented drills on words and their forms; they should at least attempt to show how the system operates.

Language Studies

Studies in education and linguistics have shown that young children are capable of absorbing such instruction and have verified what parents of young children already know: that even the preschooler has caught on to the basic patterns of his language. Many of his amusing mistakes are thoroughly logical in the light of the system, as "Please higher my swing"; "I runned all the way home"; "It's not in my downer drawer." Before he appears at school for formal training, a child is able to generate his own sentences and to make simple transformations.[3] It seems a pity that this innate power is not immediately encouraged to develop.

Elementary school teachers are particularly fortunate to have available two studies on the language of school children: Walter D. Loban's *The Language of Elementary School Children*, published in 1963 by the National Council of Teachers of English, and Ruth G. Strickland's *The Language of Elementary School Children: Its Relationship to the Language of Reading Textbooks and the Quality of Reading of Selected Children*, published in 1962 by Indiana University. Both researchers have actually measured children's growth in manipulating syntactic structures, and their findings are significant to all teachers of the language.

One of Professor Loban's significant findings involves syntax. He discovered that although both his high group and his low group used the same general structural patterns, his high group was able to achieve greater flexibility within the pattern. For example, students in the high group used more structures of subordination, more nominals, more movable units.[4] The language skills of these gifted children might logically serve as some kind of a goal, for studies seem also to indicate that poor language skills are less related to intelligence than to environment.[5] The earlier the study of syntax is begun the less likely a child will become frozen in the syntactical patterns of his home environment.

The Strickland study points out that children at all age levels can expand and elaborate their sentences through movable units and elements of subordination.[6] Significantly, the study reveals that there appears to be no scheme for the development of control over sentence structure which parallels the generally accepted scheme for control over vocabulary.[7]

Suggested Procedures

What can the elementary school teacher do, then, in the absence of controlled teaching materials in the area of syntax? The answer to this rhetorical question is, "Possibly a great deal." The oral language that children use is structurally more advanced than that which they find in their books,[8] so little help can be expected there. But early work in oral and written composition will provide opportunity for the teacher to examine the child's syntax. There are several points of departure.

Tune and syntax

A logical beginning for the elementary school teacher could be the tune of language. Here a skillful teacher could make an easy approach from the work in reading, which seems to be divorced from the work in language. That this dichotomy does exist, even at the fourth-grade level, is unfortunate; for much of the work in the reading books, which seem to be more linguistically oriented than many of the language books, could be utilized to present an early introduction to syntax. For example, students in reading are asked to examine the rhythmic patterns of an English sentence by choosing between the following:

1. Once there was a king   who behaved in a strange way.
2. Once there   was a king   who behaved in   a strange way.

Intuitively, native speakers of English, even at the age of nine, will prefer sentence one. No one needs to know the elaborate interworking of the suprasegmental phonemes to understand that sentence one conforms to the basic patterns of the language. Once this point is established, children can quite easily see that the rhythmic patterns and the syntactical patterns are closely related. That is, sentence two would have to be rejected on two counts: the unnatural interruption in the main statement and the separation of a preposition from its object. Such an early introduction to syntax might prevent many problems in composition which persist through high school, such as the misplaced modifier and some of the perennial questions in the punctuation of nonrestrictive modifiers. Actually, sound and syntax can be used to reinforce one another, for surely a recognition of syntactic structures could also be useful in improving oral and silent reading.

Basic patterns

When the student has reached the fifth or sixth grade he should be able to recognize that these intonational units which he has been calling sentences tend to pattern themselves into recurring structures which can be called "basic patterns," those simple, active statements of the language which are familiar to any native speaker. Grammatical analysis should logically begin here, rather than with parts of speech which represent a more complex phase of analysis and present more detailed problems. Further, the ability to spot-check each word in a sentence and give it a name does not help to improve either reading or writing skills. (Some of this formal analysis is even misleading. A seventh-grade language book, for example, in one place asks the student to identify the word *story* as a noun, as in "Tell me a story," and in another place as an adjective, as in "I have a storybook." Most grammarians today would prefer the term "noun adjunct" for the second use, though perhaps any distinction is relatively un-important.)

Simply by examining the sentences in their reading books, students can see that there are five patterns that seem to recur with great frequency. It is useful to work with these basic patterns, though there is no certainty about the actual numbers of patterns possible for the English sentence. These declarative patterns can be designated as follows:

I.	N	V	
	Skaters	perform	
II.	N^1	V	N^2
	Cats	eat	fish
III.	N^1	V or *be*	N^1
	The boys	became	friends
	Father	is	a lawyer
IV.	N	V or *be*	Adj
	The doll	looks	pretty
	The doll	is	pretty
V.	N	*be*	Adv
	Mother	is	away

There is nothing sacred about the presentation of the formulas, but they demonstrate some simple observations about the sentences. First, the subjects remain the same, but the predicates differ in their relationships to the subjects. For example, in Pattern II, the noun in the predicate is numbered N^2 to indicate that it represents a distinct entity, while in Pattern III it is numbered N^1 to show that this pattern is, in effect, a grammatical equation and that the subject and the noun in the predicate have identical reference.

Sentence expansion

After children are thoroughly familiar with these patterns and can write them easily, teachers can demonstrate how these patterns are readily expanded into the more complicated sentences which the children actually read and compose orally. Without getting technical about prepositional phrases, infinitives, or participles, a teacher can show that there are open points in the basic patterns where subordinate units can be inserted. For example, the first sentence, "Skaters perform," can be expanded by inserting modifiers before the subject, after the subject, before the verb, and after the verb.

Every day graceful skaters, who belong to the girls' athletic club, skillfully perform on the school rink.

Students can now see that there are different kinds of modifiers, that there are several open points in a sentence, and that some of these modifiers can be

shifted to several points; that is, they are movables. Thus the student is introduced to the idea of options. The sentence could read: "Graceful skaters, who
belong to the girls' athletic club, every day perform skillfully on the school
rink." This type of classroom demonstration is merely an inductive device to
prove to children a fact which both the Strickland and Loban studies emphasize:
at all age levels children can expand and elaborate their sentences through movable syntactic units and elements of subordination. The teacher's role is to bring
to the conscious level something which children can do intuitively.

Transformations—substitutions

Expanding the basic patterns is the easiest way of showing children how
sentences structure. Another way is transformations. That is, these patterns can
be manipulated or changed at will according to obligations or options. At this
higher level of analysis, the more complex structures of language can be produced by rewriting. In other words, ideas can be expressed in different ways: as
passive constructions, as questions, as negative or emphatic constructions. There
is no need to develop the rather complicated rules of transformation which control these changes, for the native speaker already knows that he can make them.
The important thing for the teacher is to make the child realize that he can perform these miracles at will, that he has, in effect, a genie's control over his
language.

For example, Pattern II sentences occur most frequently in English, since
they represent the actor—action—goal type of situation and are the only sentences which can be transformed into the passive. The sentence, "Cats eat fish,"
can be transformed as follows:

> Fish is eaten by cats. (passive)
> Do cats eat fish? (question-active)
> Is fish eaten by cats? (question-passive)
> Cats do eat fish. (emphatic)
> Cats do not eat fish. (negative)
> Don't cats eat fish? (negative question)
> Cats are fish eaters. (Pattern III)

Substitutions and style

This matter of substitution, or of learning to say things in different ways,
is one of the most important aspects in developing style, which after all implies
something individual or "chosen.'" Most writers in a given context will prefer
one version to all others, but no one can choose unless he knows what his choices
are. In English these are many and varied and in a degree involve morphemic
as well as syntactic structures. One can say "the stealth of a cat" or "cat-like
stealth"; "the laughter of girls" or "girlish laughter"; "the structure of a
molecule "or "molecular structure."

The sentence, "To play tennis well requires frequent practice," can be restated as follows:

Those who play tennis well practice frequently.

Tennis is practiced frequently by those who play it well.

Frequency of practice is required by those who play tennis well.

The teacher of composition may wince a little at the last two versions, but unfortunately students do write such sentences and they are syntactically sound. It is often a genuine insight for a youngster to learn that he can say the same idea somewhat more gracefully than in his first awkward attempt.

Three approaches to syntax have been suggested for the teachers of younger children: the relationship of syntax to sentence rhythms, sentence expansions, and substitutions. Older children, perhaps at the seventh- and eighth-grade levels, can be introduced to coordination and subordination as two additional methods of developing their sentences.

Transformations—coordination

Young children employ coordination with *and* to such a degree that it may even sound superfluous to suggest that this can be a rather sophisticated way of manipulating sentences. It is, in fact, a characteristic of Hemingway's style and is used effectively to create tensions in meaning. Notice the coordination in the opening paragraph from *A Farewell to Arms:*

> Troops went by the house and down the road and the dust they raised powdered the leaves of the trees. The trunks of the trees too were dusty and the leaves fell early that year and we saw the troops marching along the road and the dust rising and the leaves, stirred by the breeze, falling, and the soldiers marching and afterward the road bare and white except for the leaves.

It is important to teach coordination as a method of syntax because it is basic to the rhetorical concepts of parallelism and balance. Actually, however, it is such a simple method that children have little difficulty in seeing how it works. First, it is important to demonstrate that any syntactic structure can be compounded, from the entire sentence to the single word functioning in a slot as subject, object, modifier, *etc.* Sometimes coordination is merely a question of addition, of linking two sentences:

The trees are bare.   The trees are bare, and
The grass is brown.   the grass is brown.

At other times the process involves subtracting repeated words and linking like syntactic structures. (Arrows mean "rewrite as.")

Father was strict. ⎯⎯⎯⎯⎯⎯⎯⎯⎯⎯⎯⎯   Father was strict, and ~~father~~
Father was fair. ⎯⎯⎯⎯⎯⎯⎯⎯⎯⎯⎯⎯⎯⎯⟩   ~~was~~ fair, and ~~father was~~ kind.
Father was kind. ⎯⎯⎯⎯⎯⎯⎯⎯⎯⎯⎯⎯

Father was strict, fair, and kind, *or* Father was strict, but fair and kind.

The house was neat. ────────▶ The house was neat, and the
The yard was neat. ──────────▶ yard was neat, and the barn
The barn was neat. ──────────▶ was neat.
The house, yard, and barn were neat.

When similarly patterned sentences are linked together, chainlike, obvious repetitions are revealed. If these can be canceled, as the illustrations show, economy of expression results. Note that in the second group an obligatory change in the number of the verb takes place to restore concord between the now plural subject and the verb.

This process of addition and subtraction can, of course, take place anywhere in the sentence and can involve any structures. If students can see exactly what transformations are involved they may perhaps be spared the problem of faulty parallelism later. For example, the child who wrote, "We marked our puppy's grave with a wooden cross and covering the grave with flowers," could easily have avoided this sentence if he had seen it like this:

We marked our puppy's ────▶ We marked our puppy's grave
grave with a wooden cross.   with a wooden cross and we
We decorated our puppy's   covered our puppy's (the)
grave with flowers. ──────▶   grave with flowers.

Here we can substitute the noun determiner *the* for the possessive phrase. To avoid possible ambiguity, *grave* is repeated.

Transformations—subordination

Coordination, then, can help writers to avoid repetition and redundancy and to achieve parallelism or balance in structure. Subordination, a more complicated type of transformation, shows the relative importance of ideas and maps out their relationship. Rhetorically, it helps by permitting variation in sentence openers and in the rhythmic patterns. The Loban study points out that the adverbial and noun clauses were used more frequently by the children studied than the adjective clause and that the use of subordinating connectors increased with age, ability, and socio-enocomic status.

Sentences transform into modifiers of nouns something like this:

The book was a copy of
Alice in Wonderland.
which ─────────────────────▶ The book which was in Fa-
The book was in Father's   ther's coat pocket was a copy
coat pocket. ──────────────▶   of *Alice in Wonderland.*
                                        or
                               The book in Father's coat
                               pocket was a copy of *Alice in
                               Wonderland.*

The first sentence is considered the consumer sentence, which has an open point between *book* and *was*. If the second sentence is to be inserted at this point, certain changes in syntax must be made to reduce the sentence to a subordinate position. This is done by the substitution of *which* for the noun and its determiner, *the book*. Because the word order makes the relationship of ideas perfectly clear, the words, *which* and *was*, which carry little or no lexical meaning, can be eliminated in the second transformation and the input sentence finally has become a prepositional phrase.

Often sentences transform to modifiers of verbs simply by the addition of a subordinator which in a sense lowers the status of the word group from a sentence to a subordinate clause. It can be demonstrated like this:

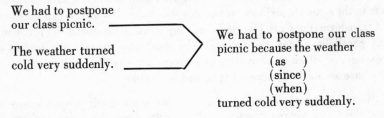

We had to postpone our class picnic. / The weather turned cold very suddenly. → We had to postpone our class picnic because the weather (as) (since) (when) turned cold very suddenly.

The two separate sentences give no indication of the thought relationship between them. As soon as the subordinator *because* is introduced, the cause-to-effect relationship is immediately emphasized. Other subordinators indicate other relationships:

> *although, though* (concession);
> *until, after, before, as, when, while* (time);
> *if, unless* (condition); *so* (result).

Application to Composition

It is possible in the elementary school to introduce these methods of improving the composition of the sentence, for verbal youngsters somehow manage to employ these syntactic structures without much tutorial help. Here is a composition of a second grader:

> Georgia is a pet mouse. We feed her cornflower seeds and dried out corn. We change her water in the morning and night. We put her cage in my dad's workshop. At night we let her run on the workbench. She loves to take my dad's nails. When she gets a nail in her mouth, she runs to the back of her cage. Then she drops it. After my dad puts her back in her cage he has to pick up all the nails. When you pick her up you feel a lot of pricks because she has such little claws.

Notice here that the young writer possibly tired of the subject opener, especially of the repetition of *we*. Then he began with a prepositional phrase, *at night*. Three of the sentences begin with adverbial clauses which sound idiomatic and unforced but which certainly vary the rhythmic pattern. The last sentence contains two adverbial clauses. A child who can intuitively or imitatively write such sentences at the age of seven or eight should certainly be exposed to the study of syntactic structures at the elementary level. The increasing control of structure may then enable him to use the vocabulary he has gained in his reading experience. And children who are less gifted verbally deserve some help in developing their power over language.

Footnotes

[1] See Margaret Bryant, *Current American Usage*. New York: Funk & Wagnalls Company, Inc., 1962, p. 48 and pp. 162-64.

[2] Henry Warfel, *Language, a Science of Human Behavior*. Cleveland: H. Allen, 1962, p. 141.

[3] See Jerome Bruner, *The Process of Education*. Cambridge: Harvard University Press, 1962, p. 8.

[4] Loban, p. 84.

[5] *Ibid.*, p. 64.

[6] Strickland, p. 106.

[7] *Ibid.*, p. 104.

[8] *Ibid.*, p. 106.

38   *Grammatici Certant*

Owen Thomas

*In this article, Thomas clarifies the assumptions and nature of four grammars
—traditional, historical, structural, and generative. Even though this part of
the anthology focuses upon application of grammars rather than grammars
themselves, this succinct and well-organized article may provide some background to clarify the concept of grammar and to inculcate a thoughtfully flexible
attitude toward language usage.*

*As one judge, what is your verdict on grammar? Does Thomas imply that
only four kinds of grammars are possible? To a linguist, what is the difference
between grammar and usage? For an application of structural grammar in
teaching elementary school pupils (sixth graders), see the Geist article cited in
Selected References for Part Five. The articles by Binney, Dykema, Gleason,
Jacobs, Johnson, and Lees may be of value to readers interested in pursuing this
topic further while other readers may want to compare and contrast this article
with the Wolfe essay cited in Selected References.*

> Grammarians dispute, and the case is still before the courts.
> Horace, *Ars Poetica*

Thanks to Harold B. Allen, we now have a method of identifying the major disputants in the current controversy over English grammar. Briefly, they
include the following:[1]

1. Grammar A: the "traditional" grammar which has its foundations in
   the eighteenth century. The major figures are Joseph Priestley (1761),
   Robert Lowth (1762), George Campbell (1776), and Lindley Murray
   (1795).
2. Grammar B: the "historical" grammars of the late nineteenth and early
   twentieth centuries, particularly the comprehensive grammar of the
   Danish scholar, Otto Jespersen (1914).

From *The English Journal* 52:322-326; May 1963. Reprinted with permission of the
National Council of Teachers of English and Owen Thomas, Professor of English, Indiana
University, Bloomington.

3. Grammar C: the "descriptive" grammars which are generally based upon the theories of Leonard Bloomfield (1914, 1933).

4. Grammar D: the "generative" (or, less accurately, "transformational") grammar of Noam Chomsky (1957) and Robert Lees (1960).

Defining the philosophies behind these grammars is somewhat difficult, certainly too difficult for a brief article. Yet some portions of these philosophies are integral to the current dispute and, consequently, such portions command our attention. Grammars A, B, and C are sufficiently well developed and well known so that we can make reasonably acceptable statements about them. These statements should suggest the kinds of statements that can be made about Grammar D, and ultimately, the relation between Grammar D and the earlier grammars.

Traditional Grammar

The grammarians of the eighteenth century tried to formulate definitive rules of syntax and usage. Such men as Lowth and Campbell were classical scholars and their grammars were based upon classical models. They were prescriptive, and their rules assumed the existence of an ideal language; that is, they either ignored historical change in language, or they viewed such change as inimical to good usage. In a very important sense, then, Grammar A incorporates intuition. Traditional grammarians based their rules partly on the rules of Latin, but partly also on their intuitive knowledge of "correctness" in language. Consequently, many of their rules may be understood as an attempt to articulate or to explain their intuition.

Current "traditional" textbooks incorporate the same kinds of rules. For example, one such textbook, intended for use in the secondary school, states: "The present tense is used to express action (or state of being) occurring now, at the present time."[2] And in discussing the difference between the active and passive voices, the same text states:

> A verb is in the *active* voice when it expresses an action performed *by* its subject. A verb is in the *passive* voice when it expresses an action performed *upon* its subject or when the subject is the result of the action. (p. 144)

Two facts may be noted in these explanations. First, traditional grammar does not hesitate to appeal to meaning (or semantics) in its rules of usage. (We may also note that the traditional definitions of "noun" and "verb" are also semantic.) Second, the traditionalists intuitively perceive an organic relationship between certain kinds of constructions, in this case between the active and passive voices, and this perception is reflected in their explanations.

The traditionalist's attempt to explain is pedagogically appealing. As teachers, we should be concerned with "how," but we should be much more concerned with "why." We like to feel that language has a rational basis and that we can appeal to this basis in teaching grammar.

Historical Grammar

Grammar B also sought to explain some of the intricacies—and apparent irregularities—of English. In this case, however, the explanations were based on history rather than intuition. In the nineteenth century, as every college sophomore knows, several philologists (including the Brothers Grimm) noticed that certain words in apparently quite different languages were amazingly similar. They developed the hypothesis of language families and successfully illustrated how certain word forms have gradually changed over the course of centuries.

Grammar B thus destroyed the myth of the ideal language, a basic supposition of Grammar A. In effect, Grammar B posed the rhetorical question: how can Latin (or Greek) be the ideal language when both of them (as well as Sanskrit, Italic, Celtic, Germanic, and others) developed—through gradual changes—from a single "parent" language (now called "Indo-European"). Because of the findings of Grammar B, we have been forced to re-evaluate the source of our standards of usage.

In addition, Grammar B has provided the answers to many questions that cannot be answered by Grammar A because of its prescriptive nature. Grammar B explains why certain verbs are regular while others are irregular, why we don't always pronounce words according to the way they are spelled, and even why we say "It's me" when (according to the eighteenth century logic of Grammar A) the first person pronoun should be in the nominative case.

For the linguist, and ultimately for the grammarian, Grammar B also answers other important questions. For example, we can ask: is there anything regular in the notion of plurality? In other words: can we speak of the *idea* of plurality? Does plurality recur regularly throughout English? The answer to all three questions is "yes." With the exception of a very limited number of words (such as "chaos") all nouns have a means of incorporating plurality; consequently, the notion of plurality is an identifying feature of nouns because it recurs regularly throughout the language. Plurality (again, with very few exceptions, most of which can be explained historically) is indicated in one of two ways: (1) by the addition of -s (or its spelling variant -es) to the end of a word, or (2) by mutation, i.e., the change of a vowel. Even the mutation is regular: the vowel in the plural form is always "fronted"; i.e., the vowel which, in the singular, is formed in the center or back of the mouth (as is the case with "man," "foot," and "tooth") is replaced by a vowel which is formed in the front of the mouth ("men," "feet," "teeth").

Structural Grammar

Such discoveries prepared the way for Grammar C. Early in this century, Leonard Bloomfield (among others) noted that it was both possible and valuable to separate the form or structure of language from the meaning of language. Thus, he divided language study into "syntax" and "semantics." Syntactically, we can speak of the notion of plurality in nouns or the notion of past time in verbs without referring to the semantic content of a particular noun or verb. Bloomfield, and his many followers (including such linguists as Charles C. Fries, H. A. Gleason Jr., Archibald Hill, John P. Hughes, James Sledd, and Harold Whitehall) then began to describe the language as it actually exists. They were not interested in making judgments about correct or incorrect usage; they sought, rather, to record and describe all usage (ignoring whether it might be "correct" or "incorrect" according to the standards of Grammar A).

They were accused, quite unfairly, of advocating anarchy in usage. This was the beginning of the current controversy over grammar.

The descriptivists found that Grammar A was inadequate to *their* purposes since Grammar A attempted to explain and prescribe while Grammar C attempted only to describe. Consequently, the descriptivists were required to develop new ways of discussing language. In particular, they developed the notion of "syntactic levels." The first level of Grammar C deals with the basic sounds (or "phonemes") of language. Most linguists agree that there are approximately forty phonemes in English. The second—and higher—level deals with regular combinations of phonemes called "morphemes." For example, the phonemes /b/, /e/, and /t/[3] may be combined to form the morpheme /bet/. Most descriptivists define a morpheme of a language as the smallest element which has meaning. (Other linguists, notably Chomsky and Lees, dispute this definition, but *this* dispute, at least, need not concern us here.)

The descriptivists also speak of two kinds of morphemes: "bound" and "free." A free morpheme is one which (like /bet/) can stand by itself in a sentence. A bound morpheme is one which (like the *-ly* ending on many adverbs or the *-s* ending on many nouns) cannot stand by itself but must, rather, be joined to a free morpheme.

The third level of Grammar C deals with combinations of morphemes and is called the "phrase structure" level. Where the phonemic level permits us to discuss sounds, and the morphemic level permits us to discuss words, the phrase structure level provides a means of discussing groups of words such as noun phrases, verb phrases, and prepositional phrases.

The descriptivists have used the concepts inherent in the various levels to redefine some of the terms originally advanced in Grammar A. They have applied the three scientific criteria of "simplicity, consistency, and completeness," and in doing so they have made their definitions completely syntactic. That is, their definitions make no appeal to meaning.

Thus, James Sledd defines a noun, not as "the name of a person, place, thing, or idea," but rather as:

> a word inflected like *man* or *boy*—any word that fits into the inflectional series which is built, like *man, man's, men, men's* or *boy, boy's, boys, boys'*, on either or both of the contrasts between singular and plural numbers and between common and genetive cases, and on no other contrasts.

The traditional definition is based on semantics; we must know the meaning of a word before we can classify it as a noun. Sledd's definition is based on syntax; if we can change a word to indicate plurality or to indicate possession, then the word is a noun, even if we don't know its meaning.

Grammar C, then, makes use of the notion of plurality which we discussed in connection with Grammar B. We can speak, quite consistently, of the "plural morpheme" as that element which, when added to a noun, changes the noun (in some fashion) so that it indicates "more than one."

As long as we limit ourselves to sounds, words, or phrases, Grammar C enables us to make significant observations about our language. But Grammar C, like Grammars A and B, should not be expected to accomplish more than it is designed to accomplish. Grammar C cannot explain relationships between, for example, the active and passive voice; it can simply describe such differences as may exist in construction.[4] Grammar C also becomes cumbersome in attempting to deal with sentences because, at least so far, it incorporates no well defined level for treating combinations of phrases.

To summarize briefly, Grammar A is intuitive, Grammar B is historical, and Grammar C is descriptive.

Generative Grammar

What, then, is Grammar D? According to Noam Chomsky, Grammar D is a device for producing (or "generating") English sentences.

In *Syntactic Structures* (The Hague, 1957), Chomsky refers to the "natural tripartite arrangement" of grammars (p. 45). He calls these three parts: (1) "phrase structure," (2) "transformational structure," and (3) "morphophonemics." The "phrase structure" part of Grammar D deals with the most elemental forms of language; it incorporates some of the descriptions of morphemes (according to Grammar C) and it presents rigorous rules for combining morphemes into simple phrases. For example, according to Part I of Grammar D, a "noun phrase" consists of a "determiner" (i.e., a word like "the," "my," "a," etc.), plus a "noun," plus a "morpheme" which indicates whether the noun is singular or plural. (Thus, on the phrase structure level, the noun phrase incorporates *no* adjectives.) Chomsky presents a similar description of a verb phrase.

Part II of Grammar D presents rigorous rules for combining phrases. We know (Grammar A would say we know "intuitively") that when we combine a subject and a predicate, the verb must agree with its subject in "number and person." The rule which guarantees such agreement is included in Part II of Grammar D. Part II also contains rules for adding adjectives to noun phrases, for transforming a sentence from the active to the passive voice, and other similar rules. Part II, then, presents (in the abbreviated notation system also used in symbolic logic) explanations of grammatical relationships, and the goal of Part II is similar to the most important goal of Grammar A. For example, as we have already noted, traditional grammar seeks to explain the relationship between active and passive voices; Chomsky's "passive transformation" has the same goal, but it differs from the traditional explanation chiefly by being more rigorous (and for this reason the explanation is syntactic; i.e., it avoids all reference to meaning).

Finally, Part III of Grammar D incorporates additional developments of Grammar C (notably, those concerned with phonemics) as well as the historical discoveries of Grammar B. Thus, the rule which says *"man* plus the *plural morpheme* equals *men"* would be included in Part III, as would the rules which indicate the phonetic pronunciation of "man" and "men" (similar to the pronunciations found in dictionaries but presented, probably, according to the conventions of the International Phonetic Alphabet).

Grammar D thus combines precise definitions with rigorous rules that are based on an understanding of the history of English as well as on current—and "socially acceptable"—usage. Briefly, the grammar operates as follows: the rules of Part I produce the elemental phrases that are part of the core (or "kernel") of our language. Part II contains two types of rules: obligatory transformations and optional transformations. Agreement between subject and verb is obligatory; the inclusion of such words as adjectives or negatives is optional. If we apply the obligatory transformations of Part II to the phrases produced in Part I, and if we then apply the approriate word-form rules of Part III, the result will be a grammatical English sentence; and since we apply only obligatory transformations, the sentence will be a "kernel" sentence. A kernel sentence is simple, active, declarative, with no complex noun or verb phrases (i.e., no adjectives, adverbs, conjunctions, prepositions, etc.). According to Grammar D, all sentences in English are either kernel sentences or are developed ("generated") from kernel sentences by optional—but invariable—transformations.

Thus, the sentence: "The boy is eating the cake" is a kernel sentence, and the following sentences are all transforms of the kernel:

1. The tall boy is eating the cake.
2. Is the boy eating the cake?
3. The boy isn't eating the cake.
4. What is the boy eating?
5. The cake is being eaten by the boy.

Grammar A seeks to explain the relationships between these sentences through a commendable but vague "intuitive feeling" for what is correct in language. Grammar C provides the rigorous definitions needed to describe the various elements of the sentences. And Grammar B tells us, for example, why we say "eaten" (instead of "eated"). But none of these grammars does all three. Grammar D does. Grammar D, I believe, is a synthesis of the best features of Grammars A through C.

Two observations remain to be made. First, Grammar D is not complete; much work remains to be done. Equally important, the findings of Grammar D must be applied to the teaching of grammar in the elementary and secondary schools, and the best methods of teachings must be developed—with the cooperation of experienced teachers—through experiment. Second, Grammar D is, at best, only part of the study of language. As teachers of composition and literature, we must be concerned with meaning as well as with grammar, with semantics as well as with syntax. But Grammar D can provide an excellent basis —perhaps the best available basis—for the study of meaning.

Perhaps, two thousand years after Horace, the courts are finally ready to hand down a verdict on grammar. And perhaps the pronouncement will include another phrase from *Ars Poetica*, where Horace stresses the importance of *usus*, "usage."

Usus quem penes arbitrium est et jus et norma loquenni.
(Usage, in whose hands lies the judgment, the law, and the rule of speech.)

Footnotes

[1] The dates following the names are the years in which the authors published their major works.

[2] John E. Warriner and Francis Griffith, *English Grammar and Composition, Complete Course* (New York, 1957), p. 137.

[3] The slant lines are used to indicate that the enclosed symbols represent phonemes.

[4] For example, Grammar C cannot explain the difference between "The girl was seated by the window" and "The wagon was pulled by the boy" because, on the level of phrase structure, the two sentences are syntactically identical.

Part Six

Spelling and Handwriting

This part of the anthology is devoted to the topics of spelling and handwriting. A succinct summary of the areas of concern presented herein may be presented in question form:

a. What are some practical interrelationships of the language arts, such as spelling and composition, where each can be used to give support to the other?

b. What are some basic issues in learning to spell? What specific spelling method is superior for the primary years?

c. What are the advantages of linguistically oriented spelling programs? What are the disadvantages?

d. What adjustments are crucial to consider in teaching left-handed writers? Does manuscript have advantages over cursive?

The first question—interrelationships—has been a major concern for teachers for many years. This anthology attempts to give some emphasis to practical aspects of this problem such as in several articles in Part Four where composition draws upon literature and the article by Bloom in Part Three relating oral aspects of language to social studies and other curricular areas. The article by Ruddell in Part Three is yet another example, as well as a number of articles found in Selected References for the various parts of this volume. The first article in this part, written by Alvina Burrows, is another attempt to emphasize the interrelationships of the language arts.

In spelling, various questions involving methodology remain controversial issues. Two articles (T. Horn and Reid) raise further questions and provide some tentative answers. Certainly the issue of linguistically oriented or a social utility approach to spelling is not a particularly new one. In 1953, Hanna and

Moore wrote an article (P. R. Hanna and J. T. Moore, "Spelling—From Spoken Word to Written Symbol," *Elementary School Journal*, Vol. 53 (February 1953), pp. 329-337) emphasizing the appropriateness of linguistic cues in teaching spelling. The Hodges and Rudorf article contained in this anthology is based on a study, on the order of Hanna's ideas, that sought to reveal any patterns of regularity in spelling. Ernest Horn's "Phonetics and Spelling" remains perhaps the finest rebuttal to the earlier position taken by Hanna and Moore.

Few persons have provided more information about the left-handed writer than has Enstrom. It has been found that about every classroom will have at least one and possibly two or three children who are left-handed. Our systems of handwriting have been developed for the majority who are right-handed. Improper left-handed writing habits can impede a child's speed in handwriting as well as its quality. This need not happen to pupils if teachers make provisions for them as suggested in the research report by Enstrom. In general, Hildreth's theme is that manuscript style may have advantages over cursive and the need for change (or addition of cursive) may not exist.

39 Spelling and Composition

Alvina T. Burrows

Even though different components of the language arts may be allotted their individual periods during the school day, one of our main goals is that pupils transfer their learnings to situations in which they actually use their learned skills. Burrows makes a strong case for the relationship of spelling and composition, suggesting that "self respect and pride resulting from spelling accuracy often moves many elementary school children to a greater flowering of inventive power."

Do you agree with the underlying premises of the article? What procedures can help pupils proofread for spelling errors? (See Frash's article cited in Selected References for Part Six.) How is the use of reference skills related to spelling? Does Burrows believe there is a place for isolated drill on spelling? How can acquisition of spelling power be correlated with composition instruction to their mutual advantage? How does this article relate to that by Fitzgerald cited in Selected References? Readers may want to compare Burrow's article with Lamana's on the relationship of spelling to other language arts.

Three premises underlie this treatment of spelling in relation to writing in the elementary school: (1) We learn to spell in order to write, and secondarily so that we can locate materials in indexes and reference files. (2) Children's limitations in spelling vocabulary should not limit what they write and conversely, children's here-and-now writing interests should not limit their study and control of a body of words of high frequency in common usage. (3) The elementary school program should build increasing accuracy and independence in spelling skills and contribute to a lively interest in words as symbols of communication.

From *Education* 79:211-218; December 1958. Reprinted from the December 1958 issue of *Education* by permission of the publishers, The Bobbs-Merrill Company, Inc., Indianapolis, Indiana, and Alvina T. Burrows, Professor of Education, New York University, New York, New York.

The Program in the Primary Grades

Most children come to school wanting to read and write. Their dramatic play at four and five years of age often includes writing lengthy letters with pencil or crayon. Occasionally a typewriter is used by some pre-schoolers resulting in a page of scrambled letters or the neat repetition of one or two characters. Sometimes these writings are "read" aloud by the young writers, each time with somewhat different phrasing, to be sure, but with sufficient earnestness of intent to offset shifts of content. The process is clearly a demonstration of an urge to communicate. However, when children in school struggle through their first attempts at composing with conventional spelling, their fatigue can become overwhelming. The strain of making a pencil reproduce letters similar to those on a copy close at hand or on the chalkboard is far different from that of writing a letter of colorful, jagged scribbles. On the other hand, to reduce spelling and handwriting at this stage to repetitive practice, thus omitting the fundamental experience of composition, is to risk losing the satisfaction of writing to say something that the beginner *wants* to say. An equally serious risk is that of losing self-confidence. Children should be insured against both risks.

Dictation, a transition to written composition

Many teachers find children's dictation a productive step toward eventual independent writing (1). The composing activity remains the child's; indeed, often the final writing on paper is his, but spelling errors are largely precluded through the teacher's furnishing correct forms on chalkboad or paper. Even here a long exercise should be avoided and the child's copy must be actually used, not done merely for practice. The following progression in dictation and copying activities suggests varying amounts of effort and kinds of difficulty.

1. Children dictate a group letter which the teacher writes on the board and reads aloud. It is then duplicated, the children sign their own names, and "decorate" their sheets in some individual way. Such letters may ask for some needed materials to be brought from home, such as scrap paper, paste jars, string, or other items. The beginner may further identify himself with the group composition by checking the thing he will try to bring.

2. After some facility has been gained in writing one's name on belongings or on practice sheets, a dictated letter or memo may be copied from the board. This, of course, should be very brief. Perhaps it says "Bring an apple" or "I need 2¢" or "No school Friday." Even these brief notes to take home offer difficulty to most beginning writers. Commendation should be given for large free letter formation and for getting all the letters in the right order. Many

children run words together which should be largely ignored in the first weeks. Seeing words as units develops with experience and guidance in spacing.

3. Dictation and copying of longer messages, memoranda, signs, captions, greeting cards, or explanations should be introduced very gradually. Children should be keenly aware of their need for the writing. They should see their exhibit of leaves, or dolls, or torn-paper shadows put up in the hall with their labels. Letters should be sent by mail or carried "by hand" and should be part of a situation the youngster senses as real. Two sessions may be needed by some children to do a letter of five or six sentences even at the end of first grade. At times the teacher needs to take over completion of the child's copy. Increasing power in correct letter formation and in spacing words should receive appreciative comment. Clear handwriting is an important aid to spelling for primary age children.

4. Choose one or two words to "proofread" as a class exercise. Have each child check letter by letter as the word is spelled aloud. Select words that you are sure will occur again in children's writings.

5. Make a class directory showing each child's drawing of his house or apartment, a picture of himself or his family and his address. Children do their own drawing and get help with spelling family names and streets. These may be written on slips for individuals. Some common ones may be placed on charts for group reference. Additional practice in correct spelling and writing may be gained by making a second directory for the school office, listing only names and addresses.

6. Dictated stories and verses should not be copied; they should be put into good form by the teacher. Here length should not be curtailed except as the teacher's time prevents. Stories or verse are read to the class and filed. This sort of composition keeps alive interest in rounding out narrative expression, as well as affording opportunity for more detailed and complex organization of ideas.

7. Combination of dictating-copying and independent writing will be begun by able first graders and used by many second graders. Dictating the beginning of a report and then taking over its completion independently may be a first step. Or the reverse procedure of starting with one's own writing of a sentence or two, may grow into dictating the remainder when fatigue becomes a serious hurdle to thinking on paper. The teacher should offer help in spelling needed words in these first steps toward independent written composition.

Drawing, dictating, and writing to express ideas

Children's drawings have excited much interest not only as art forms but also as evidence of immature ways of perceiving the world. Their clarity of expression is often admirable. This form of composition should be used to precede or to support writing so that limited control of verbal symbols may be enriched and clarified. Much pictorial narration of ideas also offers practice in eye-hand coordination in which apparently tremendous amounts of practice are needed.

1. A story often grows out of a picture as the ideas become more vivid on paper. Dictating an interesting bit of fantasy or narrative related to the picture should be encouraged.

2. Reports on a trip or an experiment in science can be pictured and labels added by copying or by dictation. At first the teacher will write the needed labels directly on the child's paper. Later the youngster may copy or write independently on his picture and check spelling with chart or blackboard.

3. A narrative cartoon telling about a real experience or a much-enjoyed story offers opportunity to organize the sequence in episodes, to highlight the important and the interesting detail, and to formulate brief conversation to fill the balloons.

Spelling lists in primary grades and their use in writing

When children show readiness for spelling, that is, when reading skill has gotten a good start, when confidence has been established and satisfaction from writing has been enjoyed, then the study of spelling lists can be really useful to children. After children have savored a feeling of power through language, the mastery of words becomes a means of furthering one's power, not an insurmountable obstacle. How fast to move into isolated spelling cannot be prescribed by day and date. The guides indicated above can be applied through observation of children's interests, their questions, and their growing independence. Merely by writing in meaningful situations children learn some words. The growing acuity of word perception encouraged in a good reading program and through correcting words in written messages is heightened by the repeated "proofreading" of selected words in functional writing.

One of the best signals that children are ready for study of isolated words is their boastful declarations that "I can spell all the words in the world" or "I can spell all the words in this room—or in my reader" or whatever all-inclusive sweep the young enthusiast indicates. Let the children write all words they think they can spell. In addition, dictate some of common usage they have overlooked. Keep the activity relaxed, avoiding tensions of competition or of too long a writing period. One first grade thus challenged in early spring ranged from 12 to 184 words spelled correctly. Obviously many were ready to study spelling lists. After such an exercise, appraise results and assure the children they are ready to study words. Plan a program of systematic work on lists selected from children's and adult's usage. Since this phase of the spelling program is treated in detail elsewhere . . . it will not be pursued further here.

In the beginning study it is useful to examine each list with the children. Have them tell words they have written before and ones they remember having to get help with, if any. From time to time, after a systematic approach to weekly or semi-weekly lists has been established, re-affirm the usefulness of study lists. The necessity of reviewing words one "knows" but misses in the haste of writing ideas should be pointed out.

It is rewarding to see that some shy children who have not flowered in dictated composition often become more articulate as they gain power in independent spelling. However, most children remain much more articulate composing through dictation than through independent writing throughout the entire six grades of the elementary school (2). Some adults retain this feeling of freedom and fluency in composing through dictation, as the popularity of recording machines attests.

Reference skills in primary grades

One acute limitation of children's reference skills in first grade is, very simply, that they can't find a word in a list unless they can spell it and if they can spell it they don't need to find it in a list! Whereas the adult can find a word knowing only its beginning and an approximation of its precise spelling, this does not hold for the beginner. Just how much of a stock of words a child needs to know by sight and by spelling before this more generalized faculty emerges is not yet established by research. Indeed, using a dictionary for spelling remains one of its most baffling services even to upper grade children.

In view of the phenomenon noted above, beginners should not be confused by a too early requirement of dictionary usage, even with a short dictionary. Exploring a picture dictionary and finding meanings of words are surely to be recommended. Making a class dictionary of "circus words" or "animal homes" can be an enjoyable activity and can demonstrate how reference books are organized. Moreover, these activities add to interest in words and their systematic arrangement. A class directory, mentioned before, is another useful aid.

When a considerable sight vocabulary has been mastered, finding words in limited lists can be undertaken. Typically, this seems a reasonable expectation in second grade for many children. In some classes an index file is made of cards approximately 6x8 inches. Words often called for are neatly lettered by the teacher. Large markers for the letters of the alphabet protrude above the cards to facilitate finding the words. Teachers emphasize finding first the beginning letter, then the word.

Advantages of this arrangement include the children's participation, flexibility in arranging boxes where needed in the room, and the possibility of partners helping each other find words. If not continued for too long a time this reference system has merit. Continued beyond the time when the cards become soiled and dog-eared, and beyond the time when a large list makes for cumbersome handling of many boxes, it is wasteful.

Another caution needs to be voiced. When children write they can rarely wait to find a word before the idea escapes them. Children have been seen to change their entire plan or to plead "nothing to say" rather than to be bothered looking up words. There are broad individual differences in this respect, but the risk of losing enthusiasm when detoured to searching out words is a serious risk, indeed. With children, timing is always important; in writing timing is strategic. Moreover, the great range of words asked for by a first or second grade in any realistic or fanciful writing far out-distances the number they can handle efficiently in a reference list. Moderation in the use of short indexes, just enough to begin to get the feeling of system, is in order for most primary children and, indeed, for the later grades as well. When young children write, most of the time the teacher must be their dictionary.

The Program in the Middle and Upper Grades

Greater dexterity of middle-grades children coupled with an increasing spelling vocabulary naturally results in longer writing. Certain problems peculiar to these grades need continuing attention throughout the elementary and junior high grades. Both the work-a-day practical writing, largely objective in essence, and the more subjective personal expression need to be considered.

Objective, practical writing

Most composition of middle-grades children, whether a business-like request for a change of playground rules or an exhibit illustrating and explaining solar energy, needs to be written in first draft and corrected. Both mechanics and meaning need to be clarified in this re-working and checking.

Several ways can be arranged to provide the teaching needed before a "good" second draft can be made.

1. The teacher and pupil both read the work draft, one of them reading aloud. At first the teacher must do a great deal of the reading. He must offer encouragement in voice and manner. He must also fill in omissions, asking for clarity where needed, and correct spelling. If a child can correct some words, he should. If he can't, the teacher does. As power grows, the child may consult a short list of words. Only a few very competent sixth graders can afford the time to search for correct spelling in a dictionary. In general this adult use of the dictionary must be reserved for secondary school training.

2. Several pupils act as "editor" to check spelling and point out omissions. This obviously is not as productive as (1) above but may be necessary in excessively large classes. A combination of pupil-editor help and

teacher conference can assure adult assistance at some time to every individual. A class chart of much-needed words can serve this plan economically.

3. The teacher corrects and returns the first drafts. Those children needing few obvious corrections of spelling and punctuation can proceed independently. Those needing much help or clarification of ideas may confer with the teacher. Rotation of teacher time to different pupils over a semester's work should be arranged. No matter what scheme is used to manage the checking and correcting in the classroom, the spelling correction is a central part of it. A few words commonly misspelled may be made the subject of a class or group lesson. Some words may be placed on individual lists if this practice is systematically carried through. The important goal is for children to develop a feeling that spelling is important in all work shared with others and in all permanent records. Moreover, children need to learn that spelling needs to be rechecked by another person before public exposure or filing.

4. Writing a correct second draft should help the learner forward to a pleasing product and toward increasing independence. Proofreading the finished copy is a necessity and should usually be done the day after the labor of writing it. A friendly comparison between the "rough" copy or work draft and the finished letter or report should highlight the careful attention the writer has given his work and afford him real satisfaction.

Proofing the final draft needs energizing satisfaction, for this needed last step may seriously tax the staying power of the middle-grades child. For immature children, the teacher may need to do the proofreading, pointing out words to be corrected. The more mature children can proofread line-by-line for spelling errors. Each child works from his own corrected first draft.

A class exercise pointing up certain much-missed words may be part of this activity. The children dictate a list of words which offered difficulty. This class list may be written on a chart and may vary from four or five to twenty words, depending on the situation and the power of the children. These words may be used for further reference for all, and for study by children able to go beyond ordinary requirements.

Personal, subjective writing and spelling power

Writing one's fanciful or imaginative ideas and feeling in story or verse stands in clear contrast to the essential character of the objective writing experience. In this more ephemeral visioning of thought and emotion the difficulties of spelling should be obviated as completely as possible. Teachers should supply needed words freely, writing words on slips of paper or spelling a very short word orally. In most cases writing on a slip or on the chalkboard is more helpful.

Since stories have served their purposes when they have been read to an audience, copying is unnecessary. Only enough correction of the first and only draft is needed to make smooth oral reading possible. Stories are filed in individual .folders so that the author may refer to them again. When a class anthology is made or a story sent to an absent friend it should, of course, be carefully copied and the spelling checked on the final draft.

Reference skills in upper grades in relation to writing

Children can use longer reference lists of words in middle grades and should have some experience in this skill as an assistance to their own writing and correcting. Gradual growth in use of the dictionary for verifying meanings, for syllabication at the ends of lines, and for other purposes will bring a few sixth-grade children to the point of using a dictionary to check spelling. Dictionary reference should be practiced systematically and dictionary use thoroughly respected. All signs of independence should be encouraged. However, most children in elementary school fall short of true independence in finding words they can't spell. Even standard school dictionaries with their forty or more thousands of words offer children excessive time loss in locating words whose spelling they do not know. Directed class exercises in finding words can give children a start in this important adult activity, but only a few pupils in elementary school can find words fast enough to facilitate the creative act of composition. A minimal listing in a spelling text or a class list of frequently used words can be handled successfully by many semi-independent writers. Patience is needed in building the transition from the teacher-dictionary to the book-dictionary!

Spelling lists and children's writing

Experience in correcting children's here-and-now errors in spelling parallels the findings of Horn in the efficacy of the corrected test as a method of teaching spelling (5). The added motivation of the communication's being important appears to step up the learning. Children who have shown gross carelessness in spelling lessons which had no apparent significance to them have written club rules, signs, and tickets of admission with painstaking effort to be accurate (3).

In addition to the correction of words in writing, spelling lists are, however, a necessity. Massive use of words in writing does not guarantee their correct spelling as is attested by continued error in *their, because, girl, library*, and even such high frequency items as *the* or *and!* To establish the serviceability of lists derived from common usage, class exercises should at times direct children's attention to their own use of words on study lists. Which of these words have you used in recent writing? Which would you be likely to use in reporting or letter writing? With which have you had to have help in writing? Questions of this sort have appeared to increase pupil awareness of the highly functional quality of some study lists in texts or workbooks.

Middle graders can occasionally plan to use some of the words of a given list. Either as committees or as individuals they can compose a paragraph that is interesting and that "makes sense." The utilitarian purpose is clear: to make up a reasonable test of words in written discourse. The class as a whole or the teacher selects the paragraph to be used; the paragraph is dictated and individuals score their own accuracy. Partners re-check for additional certainty. Activities of this sort are often enjoyed by a class. They add the challenge of a puzzle and the variety heightens interest. While such writing embodies more artifice than art its occasional use can contribute to a critical questioning of word meanings and usage, and hence, to clearer expression.

Does it help children to keep individual lists of words misspelled in their writing? Techniques for studying and testing these personal lists are possible but cumbersome. Children often study incorrect forms because their lists have not been adequately checked. Merely recording a word correctly helps to learn it but recording it on a permanent list after correcting it on the paper on which it was first written is most uncertain. The custom of requiring individual study lists needs careful appraisal in view of pupil resistance and of the consumption of both pupil and teacher time.

Though some very creative writers have been poor spellers, teachers need not assume that learning reasonable discipline in spelling must render their pupils less inventive. Acquisition of satisfactory spelling skills need not and should not deter the beginning writer; on the contrary, the self-respect and pride resulting from spelling accuracy often moves many elementary-school children to a greater flowering of inventive power.

References

1. Betzner, J. *Content and Form of Original Compositions Dictated by Children Five to Eight Years.* Teachers College, Columbia University, New York, 1930.
2. Burrows, A. T., Ferebee, D. J., Jackson, D. C., and Saunders, D. O. *They All Want To Write.* Prentice-Hall, 1952.
3. Burrows, A. T. *Teaching Children in the Middle Grades.* D. C. Heath, 1952.
4. Howell, M. M. "Differentiating Variables in Compositions of Seven-Year-Olds," *Elementary School Journal* 57, No. 3 (Dec., 1956), pp. 145-149.
5. The University of Texas, Group Study: *The Test-Study Method Versus the Study-Test Method of Teaching Spelling in Grade Two;* Study I—Gladys Hibler; Study II—Margaret Montgomery; Study III—Bernice Ledbetter. February-April, 1956.

40 Some Issues in Learning to Spell

Thomas D. Horn

In this essay, Horn argues for the need upon the part of children to develop both a "consciousness of spelling" and a "conscience for spelling." Then he points out seven recommendations made by spelling authorities which have not been widely incorporated into instructional programs.

What are some desirable spelling practices and procedures frequently overlooked or ignored by teachers? How can the schism between theory and practice in the teaching of spelling be narrowed? Is there more of a need for further spelling research or for application of known effective procedures? What do Hanna and others (cited in Selected References, Part Six) suggest as questions for further research in spelling? The article by Bremer elaborates the general theme of this article, giving a comprehensive overview of spelling procedures designed to enhance spelling achievement.

Recent evidence indicates that spelling achievement in the United States is lower now than it was thirty or forty years ago (10). There are a number of reasons for this. For one thing, there is certainly decreased emphasis on spelling in comparison with other curricular areas. The breadth of education very rightly has been greatly expanded in more recent years.

Unfortunately, along with the decreased emphasis on spelling has come a lowering of the prestige value of spelling insofar as pupils are concerned. Although no one is likely to suggest we go back to the "spelling school" days, children must develop both a consciousness of spelling and a conscience for spelling (23). The lack of these two things results in poor spelling accuracy.

Considerable misunderstanding of the nature of incidental learning has apparently been a major cause of the growing opposition to systematic teach-

From *Education* 79:229-233; December 1958. Reprinted from the December 1958 issue of *Education* by permission of the publishers, The Bobbs-Merrill Company, Inc., Indianapolis, Indiana, and Thomas D. Horn, Professor and Chairman, The University of Texas, Austin.

ing. This is coupled with a lack of systematic appraisal, largely because of a mistaken opposition to spelling lists and tests (21). The end results of unsystematic teaching and appraisal are fatal to spelling achievement (4, 6).

While the number and kinds of words taught have decreased, the benefits of integrated spelling instruction have not generally been used effectively. As a matter of fact, there now exists widespread acceptance and use of teaching methods which have been shown to be *inferior*. It is over some of these issues that subsequent discussion takes place.

1. To learn to spell effectively, you study first, then test over what has been studied (5, 6, 9, 14, 22, 23, 24, 25, 31).

Ever since the Gates study over twenty-five years ago (9), we have known that the test-study mehod of teaching spelling, when properly used, is superior to the study-test. Gates suggested that study-test might be used in grade two. Subsequent studies done recently clearly show that, using the test-study method with an immediate correction of the test, the test-study method is superior to the study-test method even in grade two (14, 25).

In order to determine the extent of incidental learning relative to spelling words, the first step must be to find out which words are already known. This is done by testing. Children need have no fear of tests if they understand that tests serve an important instructional function in addition to the function of measurement (22).

Anyone concerned with individualized instruction in spelling desires immediate knowledge of which words which students need to study. From the standpoint of interest and efficient study, each child should concern himself only with those words he does not know how to spell. By testing before study, attention is focused immediately upon the job at hand, misspelled words.

In spite of all the evidence showing the superiority of testing before study, current instructional materials and methods typically use the study-test method. This lag between what is *known* and what is *done* in spelling instruction is discouraging.

2. Because of incidental learning, a special time need not be set aside for the study of spelling (6, 16, 17, 21, 23).

This issue is related to the previous one, but extends the utilization of incidental learning to the erroneous conclusion that little or no systematic study is necessary for developing spelling ability. In classes where "spelling is taught all day," rather than in a systematic fashion, spelling results are rarely anything but inferior (6, 21, 23).

Lack of systematic instruction and systematic use of inferior methods undoubtedly constitute the major causes of low spelling achievement. When children can be shown which words they need to study and the results of efficient study, there is little need for concern over meaningful hard work. It is time to put a premium on a job well done.

3. Words can be learned more readily if they are presented in context (5, 6, 13, 21, 23, 24, 32).

The important relationship of reading context to meaning is well known to most teachers and parents. Likewise, many (but not all) good teachers are good spellers. The over-simplification and misapplication of these two factors has resulted in widespread presentation of spelling words in contextual form. We have known for thirty-five years that the contextual presentation of spelling words is inferior to the list presentation (24), yet many teachers and authors of spelling materials persist in using the inferior method.

There is no argument about the value of context to identifying word meanings in reading. There is considerable argument about the value of context to correct spelling. The issue of teaching the meaning of every word before learning to spell it will be discussed as the fourth issue.

It is more than a little surprising that so few persons have noticed the spuriousness of the context method of presentation. True, context clues are quite necessary to efficient reading. *But*, the context of spelling is in writing. The spelling needs of each individual differ according to what he is trying to write. To have each pupil *read* a concocted paragraph containing some spelling words not only negates the principles of individual instruction, but directs attention away from the real business of spelling and writing (6, 21, 23).

The combined effects of the study-test method and contextual presentation of words have been shown to be consistently inferior to the test-study and list presentation of words. Why then must we continue to use such methods?

4. In order to learn to spell, the meaning of each word must be taught (6, 16, 23).

This is another example of the attempts to make use of the correlations between reading and spelling and the erroneous extension of context clues in reading to the area of spelling. When a child reads a word, he does so to the extent the symbol has meaning for him. When a child is expressing himself in writing, he is trying to communicate his meaning through written symbols.

In teaching spelling, we are trying to enable the child to write the symbols correctly. His context is the writing of ideas. For the person attempting to read the child's writing, the context is whatever has been written. Of course, handwriting needs can hardly be separated from spelling needs.

Most courses of study in spelling consist of the two to three thousand high-frequency words in terms of child and adult use. Almost every child has had these words in his speaking and listening vocabularies for a number of years before he learns to read. Meaning is rarely a problem with these high-frequency words. Why then, when learning to spell, should each child have to listen to the development of meanings he already knows? To do so is a wasteful procedure.

When children do not know the meaning of a word, the word usually is not in the central core of high frequency words. Obviously, individual pupils many times go far beyond this central core, even as early as grade three. This is where meanings and the use of such references as the dictionary should be taught.

5. Each child should have his own list of words to study rather than any general course of study (2, 4, 6, 15, 16, 20, 21, 23, 27, 29, 30).

This kind of statement generally grows out of the concern for individualized instruction. It is too bad that so little attention is paid to the fact that the words of greatest frequency of use for both children and adults are pretty much the same (2). Although it is quite true that writing vocabularies are individualized, the two to three thousand words of highest frequency are pretty much the same for everyone.

It is at the point where pupils need to depart from the central core of words that individual vocabularies needed for writing begin to show wide differences in scope. Indeed, it is the qualitative differences in vocabulary that set the fine writer apart from the mediocre ones (21, 23). As more and more opportunities for composition are provided, wider differences in vocabulary needs becomes apparent. It is in the opportunities and needs for writing that the benefits of integrated approaches have great promise.

However, for the central core of two to three thousand words (sometimes called the "security segment"), it is a waste of time to set up "individual" spelling lists for children. The same words appear time and time again. When children need words beyond the central core, this is where the individual list becomes valid (23).

Related to this problem is the logical but incorrect notion that so many new words of high frequency are coming into the language that any list is out of date the day it is printed. Evidence concerning "new" words is discussed more at length in a later article (See: What's New in Words These Days?).

6. Just spell the word the way it sounds (6, 11, 16, 18, 19, 21, 23, 26, 28).

Thiss staytmeant iz enuff too mayk won shreak (sic). Despite some very interesting evidence on similar phonetic elements in spelling words (11, 26), the perfidious nature of the English language makes most attempts to teach spelling by phonetic generalizations questionable (6, 16, 23). Nevertheless, many well meaning parents and teachers advise children to spell words the way they sound. The difficulty is that so many words, particularly polysyllabic words, just are not spelled the way they sound.

One of the most common types of misspellings is the phonetic misspelling. Thus we get *shur* for *sure; lettrs* for *letters; trie* for *try; fue* for *few; coll* for *call; uv* for *of; pensl* for *pencil; therd* for *third; forth* for *fourth; theese* for *these; past* for *passed* (and vice versa) ; *red* for *read; arithmatic* for *arithmetic;* and *mayks* for *makes.* One can see from this that a child making these mistakes could well be following the direction to spell the words the way they "sound."

It is unfortunate for would-be spellers that for all the sounds we need to

spell, our English alphabet has but twenty-six letters. In addition to this limitation, there are three relatively useless letters included in the twenty-six: *c* (spells
k or *s* sounds), *q* (spells *k* sound), and *x* (spells *eks*, *k*, and *z* sounds).

Like many worthwhile things, there does not seem to be any shortcut to
learning to spell. Although some phonetic generalizations hold true consistently,
e.g., initial consonant sounds like *b*, time is better spent in learning to spell
needed words rather than learning generalizations. This is true for most spelling
rules (16).

7. Spelling tests may be considered of minor importance in modern spelling methods (1, 3, 5, 7, 12, 16, 21, 23, 27).

Education is still trying to recover from overconcern about the effect of
tests upon the whole child. Certainly the atmosphere of fear that sometimes
accompanies testing is not desirable, but the solution is to remove the undesirable atmosphere rather than forego all testing. In fact, one reason for the
current attitudes toward tests is the failure to understand the instructional functions of tests in addition to the function of measurement.

Like many things, tests are not inherently bad, but they can be misused
with unfortunate results (21, 22, 23). When used as part of the test-study
method with the corrected test technique, spelling tests have been found to be
the most effective single method of learning to spell (14, 21, 23, 25).

Pretesting a group of children using a sample of the words to be studied
during the year shows which children need considerable systematic study of
spelling and which might well be excused from study. Testing at the beginning
of each unit of work is the only way the individual child knows for sure which
words he needs to study.

With such obvious desirable uses of spelling tests, one wonders why some
consider them subversive, undemocratic, and bases for undesirable competition.
Each of us is "tested" every day in some way. How else do we and others evaluate our effectiveness in order to improve the quality of our contributions to society? It is this testing or "proof of the pudding" that shows the way to better
things.

References

1. Ayer, Fred C. "An Evaluation of High-School Spelling." *Sch Rev* 59:233-36;
   1951. No. 4. (April)
2. Davis, Bennie Joe. "A Study of the Vocabulary Overlap Between Words Written
   by Children and Words Written by Adults." Master's thesis. The University of
   Texas, January, 1954. 142 p.
3. Doyle, Andrew M. "A Study of Spelling Achievement." *Cath Educ R* 48:171-4;
   1950.

4. Fitzgerald, James A. *A Basic Life Spelling Vocabulary*. Milwaukee: Bruce Pub. Company, 1951. 161 p.

5. Fitzgerald, James A. "Research in Spelling and Handwriting." *J of Educ Res* 22:89-95; 1952.

6. Fitzgerald, James A. *The Teaching of Spelling*. Milwaukee: Bruce Publishing Company, 1951. 233 p.

7. Fox, William H., and Eaton, Merrill T. *Analysis of the Spelling Proficiency of 82,833 Pupils in Grades 2 to 8 in 3,547 Teaching Units of the City Schools in Indiana*. Indiana University, Bulletin of the School of Education, Vol. 22, No. 2. 1946. p. 1-45.

8. Furness, Edna L. "Pink Pills for a Pale Spelling Situation." *Am Sch Bd J* 133: 17-18; July, 1956.

9. Gates, Arthur I. "An Experimental Comparison of the Study-Test and Test-Study Methods in Spelling." *J Ed Psychol* 22:1-19; 1931. No. 1. (June)

10. Greene, Harry A. *The New Iowa Spelling Scale*. State University of Iowa, 1954. 178 p.

11. Hanna, Paul R., and Moore, James T. Jr. "Spelling—From Spoken Word to Written Symbol." *El Sch J* 53:329-37; 1953. No. 6. (Feb.)

12. Harris, Oliver E. "An Investigation of Spelling Achievement of Secondary-School Pupils." *Educ Adm and Supv* 34:208-19; 1948.

13. Hawley, W. E., and Gallup, Jackson. "The 'List' versus the 'Sentence' Method of Teaching Spelling." *J Ed Res* 5:306-10; 1922.

14. Hibler, Gladys H. "The Test-Study Versus the Study-Test Method of Teaching Spelling in Grade Two: Study I." Master's thesis. The University of Texas, January, 1957. 48 p.

15. Horn, Ernest. *A Basic Writing Vocabulary*. University of Iowa. Monographs in Education, First Series, No. 4. 1926. 225 p.

16. Horn, Ernest. "Research in Spelling." *El Eng R* 21:6-13; 1944. No. 1. (Jan.)

17. Horn, Ernest. "The Incidental Teaching of Spelling." *El Eng R* 14:3-5, 21; 1937. No. 1. (Jan.)

18. Horn, Ernest. "Phonetics and Spelling." *El Sch J* 57:424-32; 1957. No. 8. (May)

19. Horn, Ernest. "Phonetics and Spelling." *J Ed* 136:233-35, 246; 1954.

20. Horn, Ernest. "The Validity and Reliability of Adult Vocabulary Lists." *El Eng R* 16:129-34, 138; 1939. No. 4. (April)

21. Horn, Thomas D. "That Straw Man: The Spelling List." *Elem Sch Eng*, XXIX, No. 5; 265-267; 1952.

22. Horn, Thomas D. "The Effect of the Corrected Test on Learning to Spell." *El Sch J* 47:277-85; 1947. No. 5. (Jan.)

23. Horn, Thomas D., and Otto, Henry J. *Spelling Instruction: A Curriculum-Wide Approach*. University of Texas, *Bur of Lab Sch Pub* No. 2, Austin, 1954. 160 p.

24. McKee, Paul G. *Teaching and Testing Spelling by Column and Context Forms*. Doctor's thesis. State University of Iowa, 1924. 166 p.

25. Montgomery, Margaret A. "The Test-Study Method Versus the Study-Test Method of Teaching Spelling in Grade Two: Study II." Master's thesis. The University of Texas, January, 1957.

26. Moore, James T. Jr. *Phonetic Elements Appearing in a Three-Thousand Word Spelling Vocabulary*. Doctor's thesis. Stanford University, 1951.

27. National Conference on Research in English. (J. Conrad Seegers, Chrm.) "Vocabulary Problems in the Elementary School." *Seventh Annual Research Bulletin*. Scott, 1939. 60 p.

28. Petty, Walter T. *An Analysis of Certain Phonetic Elements in a Selected List of Persistently Difficult Spelling Words.* Doctor's thesis. State University of Iowa, 1955. 656 p.

29. Rinsland, Henry D. *A Basic Vocabulary of Elementary Children.* Macmillan, 1945. 636 p.

30. Thorndike, Edward L. *The Teacher's Word Book.* Teachers Col., 1921. 134 p.

31. Tyson, Ivernia M. *Factors Contributing to the Effectiveness of the Corrected Test in Spelling.* Doctor's thesis. State University of Iowa, 1953. 261 p.

32. Winch, W. H. "Additional Researches on Learning to Spell." *J Ed Psychol* 7:93-110; 1916.

41 Evaluation of Five Methods of Teaching Spelling— Second and Third Grades

Hale C. Reid

In this essay, Reid states schools compromise between direct spelling instruction and a more functional incidental approach. But he raises questions about the relative value of five different methods of the teaching of basal spelling word lists and generalized spelling skills.

What were the results and conclusions of the Reid study? What implications might it have for spelling instruction? The reader may wish to compare the Reid findings with those of Schoephoerster, cited in Selected References for Part Six. Other articles about how particular approaches influence spelling achievement are by Byers, Hall, Petty, Radaker, and Russell.

There is controversy among educators over placing emphasis on direct, systematic spelling instruction versus what might be called a more functional, incidental approach. Many school systems employ a compromise between the two extremes, but wide individual differences exist among teachers in applying locally recommended spelling methods.

The investigation reported herein arose from informal experimentation in the Cedar Rapids, Iowa, schools. It used a variety of methods to raise questions about the relative merits of different approaches to the teaching of the basal word list and generalized spelling skills. Five specific spelling methods involving various combinations of direct and incidental teaching were investigated, with twenty minutes spent daily on the directed teaching of spelling.

Method 1, Test-Study-Test

This followed recommendations in the basal spelling text, *Spelling We Use*.[1] The majority of the teaching time was confined to dictation-type testing,

From *The Instructor* 75:6-77; 82-83; March 1966. Reprinted by permission from *The Instructor* © F. A. Owen Publishing Company and Hale C. Reid, formerly Director of Elementary Education, Cedar Rapids City Schools, Cedar Rapids, Iowa.

oral proofreading, and reporting of test scores. Teachers as a rule did not make application of generalized spelling skills.

Method 2, Word Perception with Test

This program utilized the same basal word list and applied the principles of *word perception* skills taught in reading in order to teach the child to learn additional words through (1) the substitution of one-, two-, and three-letter beginnings; (2) the substitution of medial vowel elements; (3) the addition of word endings with and without change in the root form; and (4) the utilization of syllabic parts. A spelling guidebook[2] for Grades 2 and 3 was prepared, consisting of a series of lessons based on the weekly lessons presented in *Spelling We Use*. Every variation of a basic word presented in the lesson is contained in the guidebook. Consequently, a basal weekly list of fifteen words may be extended to a weekly list of some thirty to fifty words when the lesson is completed.

Method 3, Word Perception Without Test

This is the same as Method 2 except that the weekly test was eliminated.

Method 4, Proofreading and Correcting

This extended the basic composition program to fifty minutes each day. The child's own, independently written compositions formed the basis from which spelling lessons were taught without using a basal list of spelling words. The method employed the application of phonetic skills, dictionary skills, and self-checking in relation to all the language arts which are taught at this grade level. Each day the children wrote an original composition independent of teacher help. Some children wrote on the chalkboard, others wrote at their desks. After completion of the individual composition, each child proofread his story, checking it for errors by using punctuation, capitalization, and usage charts, and the dictionary for a check on his spelling. Pairs of children checked compositions together for errors in spelling, punctuation, capitalization, and other language usage skills and made corrections whenever necessary. The classmate proofreader printed his initials at the end of the composition which was then ready for the class to discuss. During the language arts period the author read his work, receiving positive comments and constructive criticisms from his classmates.

Method 5, The Workbook

A spelling workbook[3] was used to teach the same basal word list as Methods 1, 2, and 3, and employed a weekly review test. The workbook lessons were developed so that the pupils could take over routine, thus freeing the teacher for individual pupil instruction. All lessons were planned in terms of the Test-Study-Test method.

Procedures

For the investigation, five classrooms per method per grade were used, for a total of fifty classrooms. Classrooms were selected from the 149 available, and assigned to a method on the basis of teacher preference, judgments of teacher quality, and estimated achievement level. Teacher preference was obtained through a questionnaire with first and second choices indicated. An index, to determine teacher quality, was based upon ratings which were made independently by three members of the administrative staff. The average level of achievement of the *Iowa Tests of Basic Skills* was estimated for each class group on the basis of results for previous classes, similarly constituted, in the same building. By using three factors—teacher preference, teacher quality, and estimated pupil achievement level—initial differences were controlled as much as possible.

During the experiment, teachers continued to conduct the 30-minute daily common correcting and proofreading language program (standard procedure in the school system) augmented by a 20-minute period in which the assigned experimental spelling method was taught. In order to clarify the experimental method for each participating teacher and to assure strict adherence to the assigned method, in-service meetings were held in conjunction with a carefully planned series of observations carried out by a trained observer.

Three separate criterion tests were devised for Grades 2 and 3 classes. The first two were used both as pre- and posttests. The third was employed as a posttest only. The first test was composed of *words specifically taught* under the Test-Study-Test and Workbook methods, and was a sample of 60 words for Grade 2 and 60 words for Grade 3 selected from the textbook and workbook. These words had correctness-of-response percentages of less than 50 on the *New Iowa Spelling Scale*. The 60 words for Grade 2 were arranged into three subtests of approximately equal difficulty for ease of administration and for purposes of obtaining estimates of test reliability. The test for Grade 3 was divided into two subtests of equal difficulty in a similar fashion.

In an attempt to measure the effectiveness of methods in developing generalized spelling skills, another test was devised from a selection of high social utility words *not* specifically taught under any of the methods from the *New*

Iowa Spelling Scale, with correctness-of-response percentages of less than 35. A set of 60 words arranged into three equally difficult subtests of 20 words each formed the Grade 2 test and a different set of 60 words arranged into two subtests comprised the Grade 3 test.

A third criterion test, designated as a "Sensitivity to Error" test, was devised for each grade which required proofreading ability in recognizing spelling errors in context.

The relative overall effectiveness of methods was determined by making comparisons between class means on the final test, adjusted by methods of analysis of covariance in terms of initial test performance, IQ, and Teacher Quality Index. In order to determine whether methods were equally suitable for pupils at different levels of ability, further comparisons of scores were made for pupils at different IQ levels.

Results and Conclusions

The results of all six major comparisons (2 grades × 3 criterion tests) were highly significant statistically, and the methods were not equally effective. Results are shown below.

	GRADE 2 Method					GRADE 3 Method				
	1	2	3	4	5	1	2	3	4	5
Test of Words Specifically Taught										
Method 1 (T-S-T)		+		+			−	−		
Method 2 (WPWT)	−		−			+				
Method 3 (WPWOT)		+		+	+	+				
Method 4 (C P)			−							
Method 5 (WB)	−		−							
Test of Words Not Specifically Taught										
Method 1 (T-S-T)		+		+				+	+	
Method 2 (WPWT)	−		−	+				+	+	
Method 3 (WPWOT)		+		+		−	−			
Method 4 (C P)	−	−	−		−	−	−			−
Method 5 (WB)				+					+	
Sensitivity to Error Test										
Method 1 (T-S-T)			−		−		−		−	
Method 2 (WPWT)			−		−	+			−	
Method 3 (WPWOT)	+	+							−	
Method 4 (C P)						+	+	+		+
Method 5 (WB)	+	+							−	

A plus sign indicates a significant difference (five per cent level) favoring the method at the left over the method indicated at the top of the column. Twenty-seven of the 60 comparisons were statistically significant. Six favor the Test-Study-Test method, five the Word Perception with Test method, eight the Word Perception without Test method, four the Proofreading and Correcting method, and four the Workbook method.

The results are somewhat inconsistent from grade to grade. Some of these differences are difficult to understand or explain. Also, results for the different criterion measures do not always agree with what might reasonably have been expected. For example, it might have been expected that the Test-Study-Test and Workbook methods would have been somewhat superior to the others on the test of words specifically taught, but there is little or no evidence to support this hypothesis. On the other hand, the superiority of the Proofreading and Correcting method over others in Grade 3 on the Sensitivity to Error test might have been predicted.

In general, the Test-Study-Test and Word Perception methods were somewhat superior to the Proofreading and Correcting method and the Workbook method. On the two list-dictation tests, all eight of the significant differences favored the former three methods over the latter two. However, when the Sensitivity to Error test was the criterion, only three differences favored the former; five favored the latter.

The fact that methods as different as Test-Study-Test and Word Perception proved to be so nearly equally effective under conditions of supervised, enlightened teaching in nearly optimum situations, suggests that effectiveness of spelling instruction is not so much a matter of method but rather of how adequately the method is implemented. The fact that none of the methods was *consistently* superior to the others suggests that teachers be encouraged to develop a method which they feel they can employ most adequately. From the comments of the participants about the difficulties of avoiding "contamination" of one method with others, it is quite likely that in most instances this would involve a combination of methods. The results of this study suggest the conditions under which elements of the methods investigated might be employed.

Footnotes

1 Horn, Ernest, Ashbaugh, Ernest J. and Thomas D. Horn. *Spelling We Use, Grade 2.* New York: J. P. Lippincott, 1959. 63 pp.; Horn, Ernest, Ashbaugh, Ernest J. and Thomas D. Horn. *Spelling We Use, Grade 3.* New York: J. P. Lippincott, 1959. 80 pp.

2 Crane, Helen C. *Spelling Guidebook, Grade 2.* Cedar Rapids Public Schools. 1962. 49 pp.; Crane, Helen Co. *Spelling Guidebook, Grade 3.* Cedar Rapids Public Schools. 1962. 49 pp.

3 Horn, Ernest, Ashbaugh, Ernest J. and Thomas D. Horn. *Spelling We Use, Grade 2.* New York: J. P. Lippincott, 1959; Horn, Ernest, Ashbaugh, Ernest J. and Thomas D. Horn. *Spelling We Use, Grade 3.* New York: J. P. Lippincott, 1959.

42　Searching Linguistics for Cues in the Teaching of Spelling

Richard E. Hodges and E. Hugh Rudorf

The linguistic axiom that printed letters (graphemes) in words represent sounds (phonemes) in spoken words has intrigued educators who have seen it as a clue to improving spelling instruction. This article reports the research phases on phoneme-grapheme correspondences completed in 1964 by a group study conducted at Stanford University under the direction of Dr. Paul R. Hanna and supported by the Cooperative Research Branch of the U.S. Office of Education.

What insights into the American-English orthography were found? How do various factors—such as position of a phoneme in a syllable, the syllabic stress, and 'internal constraints'—affect the spelling of a word? What other morphological and syntactical elements also need to be considered? Can elementary school children be expected to spell linguistically regular words with the same consistency suggested by computer findings? Has the linguistic approach been adopted by commercial spelling textbooks? Do you know of any research studies which have explored children's spelling achievement under such a program? Related articles cited in Selected References for Part Six are those by Hanna and Hanna on the psychological aspects of spelling and those by Hodges and Stevens on spelling reform.

The relationship of linguistics to spelling instruction

Linguistic approaches to spelling instruction can be traced back well over a quarter of a century (1); however, the general introduction of linguistic principles into the school spelling curriculum has not been widespread in the English-speaking world. Typically, the teaching of spelling has been predicated on the assumption that there is little relationship between the way words are said and how they are spelled so that each spelling word requires a separate act

From *Elementary English* 42:527-533; May 1965. Reprinted with permission of the National Council of Teachers of English and Richard E. Hodges, Assistant Professor, University of Chicago, Chicago, Illinois, and E. Hugh Rudorf, Associate Professor, University of Nebraska, Lincoln. Footnotes have been renumbered.

of learning. Consequently, lists of spelling words for class study have been selected largely on the basis of the utility of these words in children's and adults' writings (3, 11).

Statistical analysis of phoneme-grapheme correspondences, on the other hand, suggests a considerably different rationale for spelling instruction. An early research into the consistency with which the 3,000 most frequently used words in children's writing are spelled was initiated by Paul R. Hanna of Stanford University in 1950. This research revealed that the phonemes (sounds) of the 3,000 words are regularly represented by certain graphemes (letters) approximately 80 per cent of the time (12). More recently, with the advent of computer technology, other investigators have attempted to analyze the orthography by linguistic techiques for their own particular purposes; and these studies, too, have indicated that large numbers of words have relatively consistent phoneme-grapheme (sound-to-letter) relationships (4, 8).

What are some of the linguistic assumptions which underlie these kinds of investigations, and what do these investigations imply for the teaching and learning of American-English spelling?

First of all, the American-English orthography is an *alphabetically* constructed system for the writing of spoken words. Many languages use this type of orthography in which each of the phonemes (sounds) of the spoken code has from one to several graphemes (letter symbols) which represent it when spoken words are encoded (translated) into written forms. Ideally, an alphabetic orthography would have one, and only one, grapheme to represent each phoneme. Thus, if a spoken language used forty different phonemes, the written code would also have exactly forty different graphemes. Some languages (*e.g.*, Hawaiian, Finnish, and Italian) come close to achieving this ideal. The American-English language, however, does not attain this criterion (10).[1] Through the processes of borrowing words (including their spellings) from other languages, through changes in the way sounds are pronounced without changing the way they are spelled, and through historical accidents of printers' preferences or dictionary-makers' errors, the orthography has acquired many more letter repesentations for phonemes than are necessary.

The problem of learning to spell in most spelling classes centers on the assumption that there are very few useful rules to determine which graphemes do in fact represent the sounds of spoken words. Thus, a child learning to spell cannot with certainty predict how a particular sound will be spelled when it occurs in a specific word; hence, he needs to be helped to learn the spellings of words largely by principles other than the basic principles of sound-to-letter correspondences (6).[2]

These assumptions have been widely held, largely because there was no massive evidence to support the contention that most American-English phonemes are spelled with reasonable consistency. The Hanna-Moore study of

3,000 words seemed too narrow a sample of the American-English lexicon (the total stock of words existing in the language) (7). Examining more closely additional thousands of words, it was suggested, would verify that the orthography was inconsistent to the point that the Hanna-Moore findings would be deemed unreliable. Other investigators offered findings which were disparate with the conclusions of Hanna and Moore. Bost, for example, applied Moore's phoneme data to 1,148 representative words from Books 3 and 6 of the Horn-Ashbaugh series and found lower percentages of consistency, *e.g.*, 45.7 per cent for vowels and 35.7 per cent for all phonemes (2).

A study of phonological relationships between sound and letter

To clarify this and related issues, an intensive study was launched in 1962 at Stanford University of the relationships between phonemes and graphemes in over 17,000 different words (13). Under the direction of Hanna, and with the collaboration of the authors, this research sought not only to examine the degree of consistency of phoneme-grapheme relationships in these 17,000 words, but to analyze the structure of the American-English orthography in general. Using modern computer technology, it became possible to examine the structure of the orthography to a degree never before attempted nor possible by the hand-analysis methods of previous studies of the orthography.

What kinds of insights into the American-English orthography were found? Most important, perhaps, it was demonstrated in Phase I (9)[3] that the orthography is actually a far more consistent reflection of spoken language than had been assumed, particularly when the several components of the phonology (sound system) underlying the orthography are examined. It is true that most phonemes have more than one way of being represented in writing. And it is equally true that, taking into account the way phonemes are spelled in large numbers of *different* words, it is difficult to sort out measures of consistency. But phonemes occupy *positions* in syllables and in monosyllabic words, and when phoneme-grapheme correspondences are tabulated in terms of their occurrences in these positions, a remarkable amount of consistency is found. Furthermore, when the amount of stress given to syllables in these 17,000 words is considered, even more consistency between phonemes and their graphemic representations is evident.

This statistical examination of the orthography, Phase I, does not necessarily presume that the results obtained are in themselves adequate to justify a firm claim for a linguistic approach to spelling instruction. In the first place, the fact that a phoneme is represented by a given grapheme over 80 per cent of the time in some position in stressed and unstressed syllables does not tell how useful this information may be in the spelling of *words*. Secondly, increasingly restricting the tabulations of phoneme-grapheme correspondences to particular positions in stressed and unstressed syllables means that the obtained results are generalizable to fewer numbers of words.

Beyond these restrictions, the statistical examination made in the course of the study ascertained that the great majority of phonemes in spoken American-English are indeed consistently represented in writing when the main phonological factors underlying the orthography are taken into consideration: 1) position in syllables, 2) syllabic stress, and 3) internal constraints. In addition, this thorough analysis of the relationship between phonemes and graphemes indicates that other kinds of linguistic factors are determinants of the ways in which some words are spelled. And further, the evidence obtained from the Phase I investigation made it possible to design a second computer program which takes the findings of this first study and uses them to *predict* the spellings of some 17,000 different words.

Predicting the spelling of American-English words

This second computer program, Phase II (14),[4] it should be emphasized, relies upon phonological factors alone for its spelling "rules." Three factors which determine the choice of a graphemic option are: 1) the simple phoneme-grapheme relationships, 2) the effect of position of a phoneme in a syllable, and 3) the effect of syllabic stress upon choice of graphemic option. A fourth phonological factor is utilized, a factor designated "internal constraints" or "environmental factors." For example, while the spelling of the phoneme /f/[5] can be predicted only some 74 per cent of the time on the basis of the first three factors, it is seen from the data in the Hodges study that when this phoneme follows the phoneme /s/, it is *always* spelled <ph> rather than <f> (e.g., *sphere, sphinx*). Thus, the immediate environment of the phoneme limits the choice of graphemic options which may represent it.

An algorithm (a set of rules or symbols defining a process) was therefore developed which utilizes the data from the Hodges study and adds observable factors of internal constraints. For each phoneme a set of rules was constructed which indicated which spelling of that phoneme should be used under various conditions of position, stress, and environment.

The algorithm was then utilized to process the 17,000 words from their phonemicization to their graphemic representation. This processing was expected to show: 1) how many and which words in the corpus could be spelled accurately by the use of oral-aural cues alone; and 2) how many of the words could not be so spelled. Further, the program was constructed to list these words according to the number of spelling errors made and to identify the particular phonemes producing the misspellings.

What are some of the results obtained from this computer run? Of the total number of words, 8,346 (49 per cent) were spelled correctly. An additional 6,332 (37.2 per cent) of the words were spelled with only one error, 1,941 (11.4 per cent) with two errors, and 390 (2.3 per cent) with three or more errors.

Morphological and syntactical elements of spelling

The power of the algorithm, and the phonological approach to spelling, is strengthened when the error list is examined. A glance at these words and types of errors involved indicates that many of these errors may not constitute a serious spelling problem. Many of them could be obviated with the mastery of simple morphological rules (morphology is the study of word formation—the combination of phonemes into meaningful units; roots, affixes, and inflection). For example, the factor of compounding in the formation of words obscures certain rules with regard to position. One rule which this study confirms states that when the long /a/ sound occurs in final position in a word, it is in almost all cases spelled <ay>. But in spelling the word *playground* on phonological cues alone, we obtained the spelling *plaground*. *Play*, however, was spelled correctly, as was *ground*. Because it can be assumed that a child who can spell both of·these words can also spell the compound word *playground*, this type of error in the phonological spelling may be discounted. However, field tests of such assumptions which involve children have not yet been reported. Other morphological factors such as affixation and assimilation can also be taught as additional spelling cues which, when combined with a sense of the phonological base of the orthography, should help the child to spell correctly many hundreds, if not thousands, of the words contained in the printout of error lists.

One further morphological factor which may be utilized in producing correct spelling can also be identified from preliminary scanning of the error lists. Misspellings of certain phonemes can be seen which form a pattern, and these patterns can often be related to the origin of the root word. Families of words from French, Spanish, Italian, or Greek and Latin can be identified.

The teaching of etymology has been generally omitted in the elementary school spelling program. The research here reported lends weight to the suggestion that it might well be a fruitful area of investigation. The evidence indicates that the bulk of the words in a typical elementary school program can be spelled on a phonological basis and a smaller, but still significant, number of words can be spelled correctly by combining phonological and morphological factors such as compounding and affixation. It seems a reasonable hypothesis that an analysis of the relatively few words remaining to be learned by reliance upon other cues might indicate that knowledge of a few important roots from various foreign languages could be a significant factor to enable the child to spell additional numbers of words. For example, a child who learns the spellings and meanings of *phono, photo,* and *graph* can spell additional numbers of words in which these root forms are included.

Finally, of course, as was expected, there does remain a residue of words that must simply be mastered by eye and hand learning methods. These words fall into two broad categories: 1) certain words, a limited number, whose graphemic correspondence to the phonemes is so irregular that they cannot be attacked by phonological or morphological means—words such as *one, acre, iron,* and some of the nautical terms like *forecastle;* and 2) the homonyms or homophones such as *bear* and *bare.* Quite obviously, there is nothing in either phonology or morphology which can help one to distinguish between the spellings of two different words with the same pronunciation. Here we must proceed to a third primary source of information, the syntactic or semantic level of language.

A model of American-English orthography

Thus, out of this Stanford research project there begins to appear a basis for analyzing the structure of the orthography of the American-English language. We see how such a structure emerges on empirical grounds; it is also quite defensible upon a logical basis. Linguists have long emphasized the fact that what we refer to as a *language* is a system of *oral* symbols. Writing, the orthography, is a surrogate for the oral language; it is, in effect, a symbol for a symbol. Therefore, the structure of the oral language should be reflected in the orthography.

Linguists typically analyze the structure of language on three levels: phonology, morphology, and syntax. Thus, an orthography will reflect phonological, morphological, and syntactical components. The influence of each of these components will depend upon the nature of the written form of the language; that is, whether it is logographic (word) writing, syllabic (syllable) writing, or alphabetic (sound-to-letter) writing. A word-writing system (such as the Chinese) would depend primarily upon morphological and syntactical factors, while an alphabetic writing system would, by definition, be determined primarily at the phonological level. Thus, we can give a definitional model for the spelling of American-English: *The orthography of American-English is determined by a set of rules for unit phoneme-grapheme relationships based, with decreasing productivity, upon three levels of analysis—phonological, morphological, and syntactical.* The phonological level can be further divided into the components of position, stress, and environmental factors; the morphological level can be subdivided into components of compounding, affixation, and word families. This model may be summarized in tabular form as follows:

Phoneme-grapheme relationships determined by:
1. Phonological factors
   1.1 Position
   1.2 Stress
   1.3 Environmental factors
2. Morphological factors
   2.1 Compounding
   2.2 Affixation
   2.3 Word families
3. Syntax

That the assumptions upon which this model is based are sound has been demonstrated by the Stanford spelling research project (13). Individual phoneme-grapheme relationships, though not in terms of whole *words*, can be predicted with an accuracy of 89.6 per cent by use of the phonological cues contained in the algorithm. Equally interesting is the statistical evidence that eight phonemes (/â/ as in *care*, /ē/ as in *here*, /o͞o/ as in *food*, /o͝o/ as in *foot*, /û/ as in *urn*, /ə/ as in *circus*, syllabic /'n/ as in *button* and /z/ as in *zebra*) can be identified which cause a large majority of the spelling problems. When these are considered separately, the percentage of predictability of the remainder rises to over 91 per cent. The implication of this for development of a spelling curriculum is obvious.

It must be emphasized that neither the definitional model nor the algorithm is intended to be solely prescriptive of a spelling curriculum. What has been demonstrated at this stage of the research is that the orthography reflects the structure of the oral language upon which it is based. It suggests that regularities exist in the relationship between phonological elements in the oral language and their graphemic representations in the orthography, and that a pedagogical method based upon oral-aural cues to spelling may well prove to be more efficient and powerful than present methods which rely primarily upon visual and hand learning approaches. The next stage of research is to compare the effect of a linguistic approach on learning to spell with other methods.

Summary and Implications

We have seen that by relying upon phonological cues alone we can spell over 8,300 words correctly from the research list of 17,000 words. Consider this in relation to the typical spelling program for the elementary school which contains in a series of textbooks from grade two through grade eight some 3,000 words which are in the main taught as separate learning acts.

Greene and Petty in the 1963 edition of their *Developing Language Skills in the Elementary School* state that ". . . the ability to spell one word is distinct from the ability to spell other words . . ." (5). From these Stanford research studies, one evidently can hypothesize that even a limited knowledge of the phonological relationships between the sounds and the letters of the orthography can provide the power to spell literally thousands of words and that other abilities relating to morphology and syntax may give the pupils the ability to spell the vast majority of the words in their oral vocabularies.

Much work yet needs to be done. The algorithm must be examined to determine how words should be selected to help the pupil to arrive inductively at the generalizations that would help him to translate oral cues into writing.

The error lists need to be examined to determine what morphological and morphophonemic factors can be utilized in a spelling curriculum to add to the pupil's ability to combine meaningful units into words for his writing needs.

Finally, the words which the pupil needs that depart markedly from the basic alphabetic nature of the orthography need to be identified and introduced into the curriculum at appropriate points with a heavy reliance upon visual and haptical learning techniques.

These new insights into the nature of the American-English orthography are currently being matched by increasing insights into the nature of the language learning process. Developers of spelling programs will need to take into account the best available generalizations regarding both the content of the curriculum and appropriate instructional processes; that is, the selection of words which best exemplify the alphabetic principles underlying the orthography and methods of teaching-learning which most effectively help children to apply their learnings to their writings.

In addition, material changes in the conventional means of evaluating children's spelling abilities will undoubtedly need to be made, because both what is learned and how this learning is accomplished may be quite different in a linguistically oriented spelling program.

Footnotes

[1] For a further discussion of past and current efforts to revise the orthography so that there is a more consistent "fit" between the phonemes of speech and the graphemes of writing, see: Richard E. Hodges, "A Short History of Spelling Reform in the United States," *Phi Delta Kappan*, 7 (April, 1964), 330-332.

[2] See Jean S. and Paul R. Hanna, "Spelling as a School Subject: A Brief History," *The National Elementary Principal*, 38 (May, 1959), 8-23, for an elaboration of various ways in which weekly spelling lists have been developed in order to stress similarities among words other than phoneme-grapheme correspondences.

[3] This dissertation, referred to in this article as Phase I, is the first of a series of studies to be completed as part of a continuing research project in spelling initiated at Stanford University; it is available from USOE as part of the Project 1991 report.

[4] This dissertation, referred to in this article as Phase II, is the second of a series of

studies to be completed as part of a continuing research project in spelling initiated at Stanford University; it is available from USOE as part of the Project 1991 report.

⁵ / / indicates a phoneme (sound) ; < > indicates a grapheme (letter).

References

1. Bloomfield, Leonard, *Language*. New York: Henry Holt and Co., 1933. 564 pp.
2. Bost, Theda, "An Application of Moore's Phoneme Data to the Spelling of 1,148 Words," unpublished study. Austin: The University of Texas, 1952 (unpaged).
3. Fitzgerald, James A., *A Basic Life Spelling Vocabulary*. Milwaukee: The Bruce Publishing Company, 1951. 161 pp.
4. Garvin, Paul L. and Edith C. Trager, "The Conversion of Phonetic into Orthographic English: A Machine Translation Approach to the Problem," *Phonetica*, 2 (1964), 1-18.
5. Greene, Harry A. and Walter T. Petty, *Developing Language Skills in the Elementary School*. Second edition. Boston: Allyn and Bacon, Inc., 1963. 572 pp.
6. Hanna, Jean S. and Paul R. Hanna, "Spelling as a School Subject: A Brief History," *The National Elementary Principal*, 38 (May, 1959), 8-23.
7. Hanna, Paul R. and James T. Moore, Jr., "Spelling—From Spoken Word to Written Symbol," *Elementary School Journal*, 53 (February, 1953), 329-37.
8. Higginbottom, Eleanor, "A Study of the Representations of English Vowel Phonemes in the Orthography," *Language and Speech*, 5 (1962), 67-117.
9. Hodges, Richard E., "An Analysis of the Phonological Structure of American-English Orthography," unpublished doctoral dissertation. Stanford, California: Stanford University, 1964. 625 pp.
10. ———, "A Short History of Spelling Reform in the United States," *Phi Delta Kappan*, 7 (April, 1964), 330-32.
11. Horn, Ernest, *A Basic Writing Vocabulary*. Iowa City: University of Iowa Monographs in Education, First Series, No. 4, 1926.
12. Moore, James T., Jr., "Phonetic Elements Appearing in a Three Thousand Word Spelling Vocabulary," unpublished doctoral dissertation. Stanford, California: Stanford University, 1951. 69 pp., plus appendices.
13. *Phoneme-Grapheme Relationships Basic to Cues for Improvement of Spelling*. USOE Cooperative Research Project No. 1991. Stanford, California: Stanford University (available from the United States Office of Education).
14. Rudorf, E. Hugh, "The Development of an Algorithm for American-English Spelling," unpublished doctoral dissertation. Stanford, California: Stanford University, 1964. 974 pp.

43 Phonetics and Spelling

Ernest Horn

In this essay, Horn arrives at the conclusion that "little justification is found for the claim that pupils can arrive deductively at the spelling of most words. . . . There seems no escape from the direct teaching of the large number of common words which do not conform in their spelling to any phonetic or orthographic rule."

How does Horn arrive at his conclusion? To what extent does Horn's contention agree and/or disagree with those by Hodges and Rudorf in the previous article? What implications for research and instruction do Horn's findings suggest? For an analysis of this article and the preceding one, see Hodges, cited in Selected References for Part Six. For another view of the generalization controversy on spelling instruction, see Yee's article. Other research studies which shed some light on the matter are those by Aaron, Petty, Radaker, and Russell.

English spelling is tough. Efforts to alleviate its difficulty have been the serious concern of many scholars for more than four hundred years. Any help, even though small, should therefore be welcomed by everyone. It is essential, however, that any proposed plan be soundly grounded in all essential related evidence if it is to be more than a passing fad.

Some of the claims recently made for the contribution of phonics to spelling, and the related proposal to spell by "word analysis, sounding, and logical reasoning by analogy," do not, unfortunately, appear to be so grounded. There is considerable evidence to suggest that well-planned instruction in sound-to-letter and letter-to-sound associations in appropriate relation to other learning procedures may be of benefit both in spelling and in reading. This is all the more reason for making sure that any plan for such instruction should be critically formulated on the basis of adequate evidence on all the important factors related to such instruction.

From *Elementary School Journal* 57:424-432; May 1957. Reprinted from "Phonetics and Spelling" by Ernest Horn by permission of The University of Chicago Press © 1957 by The University of Chicago Press and Ernest Horn, Emeritus Professor of Education, The University of Iowa, Iowa City.

There are at least six types of evidence which should be considered in appraising the potential contributions of phonic instruction to spelling: (1) evidence on the uniformity or the lack of uniformity in pronunciations; (2) evidence on the ways in which the various sounds are spelled; (3) data from investigations of children's attempts to spell the sounds in common words; (4) evidence on the influence of word patterns and of the ways in which sounds are spelled in different word relationships; (5) evidence on the operation of the laws of association and of negative and positive transfer; (6) findings from the research on teaching generalizations, such as spelling rules. This article is chiefly concerned, however, with the first three types of evidence.

The Influence of Pronunciation on Spelling

In an article the claim is made that the pupil who has been taught to relate sounds and written symbols can "arrive deductively at the spelling of most words that he can pronounce" (1:337). This seems to imply that there is only one acceptable way to pronounce a word. The fact is that a very considerable portion of words have more than one accepted pronunciation and many have three or more. An inspection of several thousand words sampled systematically from Kenyon and Knott's *A Pronouncing Dictionary of American English* (4) indicates that at least a third of the words in that dictionary have more than one accepted pronunciation. Moreover the authors state in the Preface, "Almost certainly we have omitted many 'good' pronunciations" (4:v). If the spelling of a word is phonetically regular in one pronunciation, it is not likely to be in another.

Regional differences in both formal and informal speech are readily recognized. The three chief speech regions in the United States are Eastern, Southern, and General American ("General American" refers to the rest of the country outside the East and South). Variations in pronunciations among these regions are recorded in *A Pronouncing Dictionary of American English*. Further differences are found in the speech of northern England, southern England, and Scotland. Yet, with few exceptions, words are spelled the same in all these regions in the United States and Great Britain.

There have been marked changes in the pronunciation of English words, especially in vowel sounds, but only to a small extent has the spelling been changed to conform to the changes in pronunciation. There are some words, although a small percentage of the total, that have had their pronunciations changed to conform to their spelling.

An important distinction in considering the relation of phonetics and spelling is that between platform speech or public reading and the speech that has been called "the familiar, cultivated colloquial." Phoneticians warn against the mistaken idea that "colloquial" is synonymous with "bad." On the contrary, this style, which has been termed "the speech of well-bred ease," is considered by Kenyon and others to be the most important of all styles (3:12-17, 4:xv-xvi). It is certainly the most important in its effect on spelling since it is the language that the pupil commonly hears and speaks.

The Consistency with Which Sounds Are Spelled

Many modern spelling books recommend that, in learning to spell a word, the pupil should pronounce it carefully and should notice closely how each syllable or part is spelled. But observing how each sound in a word is spelled *as a method of learning a word* is a different thing from attempting to spell it by sounding, by analogy, or by spelling each sound in the way in which it is most commonly spelled, all of which involve the application of some sort of generalization.

The usefulness of teaching any generalization in spelling, whether phonetic or orthographic, is limited by the number of words covered by the generalization and the number of words which are exceptions to it. It is important, therefore, to have adequate information on these two points. In order to secure such information for the present study, it was necessary to select, first, the list of words to be analyzed and, second, the dictionary or dictionaries which were to be the source of authority on pronunciations. For the first, the ten thousand words in the writer's *A Basic Writing Vocabulary* (2) were chosen because the analysis of this number of words, while laborious, was practicable and because these words, with their repetitions, make up more than 99 per cent of the running words written by adults. Samplings made from Rinsland's *A Basic Vocabulary of Elementary School Children* (6) indicate that the results here reported would not vary greatly from those that would be obtained from an analysis of that vocabulary. They would probably not be very different from the results that would be obtained from an analysis of an equally extensive list of the words most frequently found in reading.

A succession of dictionaries were used as sources of pronunciation, according to their availability and suitability to the problem at hand. The pronunciations of the words containing the sounds given in Table 1 are from the *Thorndike Century Junior Dictionary* and the *Thorndike-Barnhart Junior Dictionary*, the latter being substituted upon its publication. In Table 2 the *Thorndike-Barnhart Dictionary* was used for the sound of *oi* as in *boil*, *ou* as in *out*, and long *u* as in *use*, but the other sounds were tabulated on the basis of the pronunciation given in *A Pronouncing Dictionary of American English*. In Table 3 the Thorndike dictionaries were used for all the consonant sounds except *ch*, *ng*, *sh*, and *y*. Kenyon and Knott's *A Pronouncing Dictionary of American*

English was the authority for the pronunciation of *ch*, *ng*, and *y*. The sound *sh* was originally tabulated from *Webster's Elementary School Dictionary*, but the recorded pronunciations were later checked against Kenyon and Knott. The data on the spelling of some of the sounds as here reported may vary from what would be found if one dictionary were used alone, but certainly not to an extent

Table 1

The Most Common Spellings of Certain Vowel Sounds

Thorndike-Barnhart Symbol	Webster Symbol	Number of Occurrences of the Sound	Number of Different Spellings	Most Common Spellings	Examples	Number of Occurrences	Per Cent of Occurrences
ā	ā	1,237	14	a-e	date	636	51.40
				a	angel	249	20.13
				ai	aid	192	15.52
				ay	day	89	7.19
ē	ē	859	14	ea	each	263	30.62
				ee	feel	221	25.72
				e	evil	176	20.49
				e-e	these	56	6.52
				ea-e	breathe	34	3.96
e	ĕ	1,917	7	e	end	1,763	91.97
				ea	head	86	4.49
ō	ō	691	15	o	go	333	48.19
				o-e	note	179	25.90
				ow	own	95	13.75
				oa	load	54	7.81
ô	ô	497	11	o	office	281	56.54
				a	all	83	16.70
				au	author	60	12.07
				aw	saw	30	6.04
u̇	o͝o	108	4	oo	book	61	56.48
				u	put	36	33.33
				ou	could	7	6.48
				o	woman	4	3.70
ü	o͞o	371	16	u	cruel	93	25.07
				oo	noon	87	23.45
				u-e	rule	61	16.44
				o-e	lose	30	8.09
				ue	blue	27	7.28
				o	to	19	5.12
				ou	group	15	4.04
u	ŭ	721	6	u	ugly	548	76.01
				o	company	126	17.48
				ou	country	30	4.16

that would greatly change the practical significance of the evidence. The frequency of certain sounds would vary considerably if all accepted pronunciations were used.

In tabulating the various spellings of any sound, each occurrence of the sound was counted. Since some words contain the same sound two or more times, the number of words containing the sound is less—but, in most cases, not much less—than the number of occurrences.

Making such counts is not a purely objective, routine task. Many decisions must be made as matters of judgment, especially in the case of words containing silent letters. Some of these letters were earlier pronounced, as the *k* in *knife*, the *g* in *gnaw*, and the *gh* in *light;* others are capricious accidents in the history of spelling. In some instances, as when final silent *e* makes the preceding vowel long or *g* and *c* soft, the problem is relatively simple. In words in which the silent *e* is needed to show a long vowel and also a soft *g* or *c*, the silent *e* was counted as helping to spell both the vowel and the consonant sounds. In the word *range*, for instance, if silent *e* were omitted, the word would be *rang*. In many words, however, silent letters have no function, but, since all letters in a word must be written, each silent letter was assigned to some sound. In certain types of words the assignment of these letters was somewhat arbitrary. It could hardly be otherwise, since in many words the silent letters are not only phonetically superfluous but even, as in the case of silent *e* in the word *definite*, actually misleading. The policy in all cases was to consider the problems pupils face in spelling the sounds.

Findings of the Study

Tables 1, 2, and 3 contain sounds for which (1) the commonest spelling makes up less than 90 per cent of the total spellings of the sound or (2) even when the commonest spelling makes up more than 90 per cent of the total, other spellings are found in a large number of words.

Two vowel sounds of special spelling difficulty are not included in Table 1: the obscure vowel sound (*schwa*), as in the second syllable of *separate*, and the short *i* sound, as in *hit*. These are the two vowel sounds most frequently heard in the English language. They are troublesome to tabulate because they are so frequently alternate pronunciations in unaccented syllables of the same letter or letter combinations. The pronunciations in *A Pronouncing Dictionary of American English* were used in investigating the spelling of these sounds.

The short *i* sound (ɪ) is spelled at least fifteen ways in common words and only in a little more than half the time with the letter *i* alone. Examples are (in one accepted pronunciation): *i* (*bit*), *e, y* (*pretty*), *ie* (*mischief*), *ui* (*build*),

Table 2

The Most Common Spellings of the Stressed and Unstressed Syllabic r's (ɜ, ə), the Diphthongs oi, ou, and Long u, and the Syllabic Consonants l and n*

Sound	Symbol in International Phonetic Alphabet	Number of Occurrences of the Sound	Number of Different Spellings	Most Common Spellings	Examples	Number of Occurrences	Per Cent of Occurrences
Stressed syllabic r...	ɜ	430	12	er	her	160	37.21
				ur	church	93	21.63
				ir	first	63	14.65
				or	world	34	7.91
				ear	heard	26	6.05
				our	courage	24	5.58
Unstressed syllabic r	ə	1,044	11	er	better	720	68.97
				or	favor	165	15.80
				ure	picture	72	6.90
				ar	dollar	62	5.94
oi	ɔɪ	107	2	oi	oil	63	58.88
				oy	boy	44	41.12
ou	aʊ	225	2	ou	out	165	73.33
				ow	cow	60	26.67
u	ju	376	11	u	union	167	44.41
				u-e	use	130	34.57
				ue	value	29	7.71
				ew	few	17	4.52
Syllabic l..	l̩	478	10	le	able	247	51.67
				al	animal	163	34.10
				el	cancel	34	7.11
				il	civil	16	3.35
Syllabic n..	n̩	171	8	en	written	79	46.20
				on	lesson	33	19.30
				an	important	18	10.53
				in	cousin	17	9.94
				contractions	didn't	12	7.02
				ain	certain	10	5.85

* This table does not contain the sound of long *i* as in *ice*, although it is diphthongal. It is spelled in at least a dozen ways.

ey (*money*), *a* (*character*), *ay* (*Monday*), *u* (*busy*), *ee* (*been*), *ai* (*portrait*), *ei* (*foreign*), *ia* (*marriage*), *o* (*women*) and *ea* (*forehead*). There are other spellings in less common words.

The short *i* is also pronounced in many words in which the vowel sounds,

Table 3

The Most Common Spellings of Thirteen Consonant Sounds

Sound	Number of Occurrences of the Sound	Number of Different Spellings	Most Common Spellings	Examples	Number of Occurrences	Per Cent of Occurrences
ch	357	5	ch	church	212	59.38
			t(u)	picture	91	25.49
			tch	watch	42	11.76
			ti	question	11	3.08
f	1,117	7	f	feel	936	83.80
			ff	sheriff	91	8.15
			ph	photograph	57	5.10
j	484	10	ge	strange	161	33.26
			g	general	138	28.51
			j	job	118	24.38
			dge	bridge	26	5.37
k	2,613	11	c	call	1,681	64.33
			k	keep	290	11.10
			x	expect, luxury	164	6.28
			ck	black	159	6.08
			qu	quite, bouquet	113	4.33
l	2,590	5	l	last	2,205	85.14
			ll	allow	294	11.35
			le	automobile	84	3.24
m	1,712	7	m	man	1,500	87.62
			me	come	112	6.54
			mm	comment	66	3.86
n	4,007	8	n	no	3,724	92.94
			ne	done	170	4.24
ng	998	3	ng	thing	880	88.18
			n	bank, anger	116	11.62
s	3,846	9	s	sick	2,568	66.77
			ce	office	323	8.40
			c	city	315	8.19
			ss	class	299	7.77
			se	else	149	3.87
			x(ks)	box	140	3.64
sh	829	17	ti	attention	423	51.03
			sh	she	242	29.19
			ci	ancient	47	5.67
			ssi	admission	36	4.34
t	4,277	6	t	teacher	3,522	82.35
			te	definite	424	9.91
			ed	furnished	179	4.19
			tt	attend	145	3.39

Table 3—The Most Common Spellings of Thirteen Consonant Sounds—Continued

Sound	Number of Occurrences of the Sound	Number of Different Spellings	Most Common Spellings	Examples	Number of Occurrences	Per Cent of Occurrences
y*	530	13	u	union	190	35.85
			u-e	use	155	29.25
			y	yes	55	10.38
			i	onion	44	8.30
			ue	value	42	7.92
			ew	few	17	3.21
z	1,792	8	s	present	1,473	82.20
			se	applause	183	10.21
			ze	gauze	64	3.57

* The *y* sound is the first element in the diphthongal sound long *u*. In many words where the long *u* sound follows a consonant—for example, *d (duty)* and *t (tune)*—the sound of *y* occurs in only one of two or more pronunciations.

from their word patterns (vowel, consonant, and silent *e;* or two adjacent vowels), might be expected to be long. Examples are *furnace, mountain, favorite, minute* (time), and *coffee.*

The *schwa* sound is found in at least one accepted pronunciation in more than half of the multisyllabic words in the ten thousand commonest words. It is a very frequent sound in the speech of people in the East and South who do not pronounce their *r*'s unless the *r* is followed immediately by a vowel sound. It is spelled with almost any vowel or vowel digraph, hence in many different ways. The multiplicity of possible choices makes it difficult to spell.

Unaccented syllables are a special problem. They are difficult to spell for two reasons: (1) they are less distinctly pronounced, the vowel sounds, especially, being weakened, and (2) in a great many words, as pointed out above, the obscure vowel sound, *schwa* (ə), or the short *i* is substituted for the vowel sounds which might be inferred from the printed letters.

Three other difficulties should be noted: silent letters, double letters, and the fact that syllabication in the pronunciations does not always conform to the conventional syllabication in the dictionary entries. If one includes letters not pronounced in digraphs, as in *please* or *boat,* and double letters where only one is pronounced, all but four letters of the alphabet (*j, q, v,* and *x*) are silent in some words. A systematic sampling of the words in the *Thorndike-Barnhart Junior Dictionary* indicates that probably at least half of the words in that dictionary contain silent letters. It is not likely that a pupil, by applying phonic "principles" or by "logical reasoning by analogy," can decide to insert a letter which neither spells nor helps to spell any sound.

More than a sixth of the ten thousand words most frequently written contain double letters. There is, of course, a rule for doubling or not doubling when adding suffixes, but the problem of double letters is not limited to adding suffixes. Double letters are far more frequent in the body of words.

The evidence here reported was compared with that furnished in an unpublished dissertation by Moore and summarized in an article by Hanna and Moore (1). The results agree rather closely as to the most frequent spelling of the sounds but differ considerably in some instances as to the percentage which each spelling of a sound makes up of the total and as to the number of different spellings. These differences may be due in part to differences in the nature and extensiveness of the list analyzed by the writer (ten thousand words as compared to three thousand) and especially to the fact that this longer list contained a greater number of multisyllabic words and hence more unaccented syllables. It is to be expected that more double letters and more *schwa* and short *i* sounds would be found in multisyllabic words.

There are marked differences, however, in the significance attached to the evidence by the writer and by Hanna and Moore. They state, "The letter or combination of letters most frequently used to represent a phoneme is called the regular spelling" (1:333). This use of "regular" is at variance with the common meanings of the term, which imply a greater uniformity and fewer exceptions than are exhibited by the commonest spellings of the sounds reported above or the spellings of the same sounds in Moore's investigation. It is easy, in discussing the evidence, to slip over from this specialized definition of "regular" to the misleading use of the term to mean regular in the sense of dictionary definitions. The authors also state "that for almost every sound . . . there is what might be called a 'highly regular' spelling" (1:330). The spelling of the thirty sounds cited above can scarcely be called "regular" and certainly not "highly regular." Neither the evidence here presented nor that given by Moore appears to warrant the statement that variants from the commonest spellings of these sounds are rare (1:337).

The data cited in Tables 1, 2, and 3 and in the paragraphs on the sounds of ə and ɪ show that these thirty sounds are spelled in many ways and that the commonest spelling accounts for too low a percentage of the total spellings to be called "regular" in the usual meaning of the term. Nine words out of ten contain one or more of these sounds. There are fifteen sounds in the tables that are spelled with the commonest spelling less than 60 per cent of the time. The frequency with which the sounds occur and the number of exceptions should be taken into account. The sound of long *a* (ā), for example, was found 1,237 times, with 601 exceptions to the commonest spelling; the sound of *k* was found 2,613 times, with 932 exceptions; and the sound of *s* in *sick*, 3,846 times, with 1,278 exceptions. One is hardly justified in calling spellings "regular" or in teaching the commonest spellings as principles or generalizations when the exceptions are numbered not merely by the score but by hundreds.

Implications for Research and Instruction

With so many different spellings of these sounds from which to choose, it would be strange indeed if pupils did not spell unlearned words in a variety of ways. They do. In an early experiment by the writer, 195 pupils in Grades I and II, all of whom had been taught phonics as one approach to reading, spelled *circus* in 148 ways. *Tease* was spelled in 44 ways. The "best" spellings were *tes, teas, tease, tees,* and *teez*. Subsequent investigations have shown a wide variety of misspellings even for more mature pupils who had had much greater experience in both writing and reading. Masters (5), for example, in an analysis of the attempts of 200 students in each of Grades VIII, XII, and XVI to spell 268 difficult words selected from 5,000 words of high frequency, found *miscellaneous* to be spelled in 153 ways—113 ways in Grade VIII, 40 in grade XII, and 22 by college students. An inspection of the attempts to spell these 268 words shows that the majority of the most common misspellings are analogically reasonable in the sense that the individual sounds were spelled in ways that represent the correct spelling of the sounds in other words. Examples are *adequate—adequit, amiable—aimiable, deny—denigh, scandal—scandle*. Additional examples, all reported as common misspellings by elementary school children, are: *aid—ade, asleep—asleap, before—befour, boat—bote, busy—bizzy, crumb—crum, force—forse, honor—honer, mystery—mistory, tongue—tung*. Pupils need no encouragement to misspell by utilizing analogic spellings.

Attempts to account for a pupil's choice of a spelling of an unlearned word at a given time are largely conjectures. Why did one pupil, in attempting to spell *awful*, write *offul*, while others wrote *aufull, offel,* or *offle?* There must have been some influence or influences that, if known, would explain why these particular spellings of the sounds were written. Presumably any of the laws of association may operate in a given attempt to spell, and sometimes in combination. Both common sense and the evidence from research suggest that, when a number of reasonable choices are available, responses are uncertain.

The preceding discussions underestimate, rather than exaggerate, the complications which confront children in attempting to spell. How much more complicated the factors are can readily be seen by reading standard works on phonetics and philology, and treatments of transfer and the laws of association in the psychological literature. It is not the purpose of this article, however, to disparage the use of phonetics in teaching either reading or spelling. Its purpose is rather to call attention to types of evidence which should be considered in designing any plan for emphasizing sound-to-letter relationships, either for experimental purposes or for classroom use.

It seems important that children should learn the *ways*, not *the* way, in which each sound is spelled. This should at least eliminate many misspellings in which the sounds are spelled in ways in which they are never correctly spelled. Children should learn how to spell the principal prefixes and suffixes and should know how to add these to base words. They should also learn such orthographic aids as apply to large numbers of words with few exceptions.

The recognition of the importance of giving careful attention to the ways in which sounds are spelled is not new. For more than thirty years, authors of many series of spelling textbooks have recommended that, in learning a word, the word be carefully pronounced and that the pupil should note how each part or syllable is spelled. These procedures in themselves should promote an understanding of how sounds are spelled, but they are not the same as teaching principles or generalizations. As pointed out above, the criteria for deciding whether a phonetic generalization is possibly worth teaching are that it should apply to a large number of words and that it should have few exceptions, certainly not hundreds of exceptions.

What results should be expected from emphasizing as generalizations or principles the commonest spelling of sounds that have a large number of exceptions? Would pupils tend to spell these sounds in all words by the commonest spellings? If they should, as research has shown, they would misspell more words than they now do. Would it usefully sensitize children to deviant spellings? Would it give them a misplaced confidence in utilizing these commonest spellings, which would lead to disillusionment and therefore to a decrease in interest in spelling? These possibilities have not been adequately explored.

There are some characteristics of English spelling, however, that exhibit considerable consistency. Most of these pertain to word patterns, syllables, meanings, word positions, the adding of suffixes, and the influence of sounds or letters adjacent to the sound to be spelled. Most consonant sounds, whether single sounds, as the *b* in *bed,* or initial blends, as the *bl* in *black,* are regularly spelled at the beginning of words. The most important exceptions are the sounds of *f* as in *fun* or *physics, k* as in *cup* and *keep, s* as in *city* and *sad,* and *j* as in *jump* and *gem.*

Some consonant sounds, however, that are spelled regularly at the beginning of words are spelled in many other ways in other word positions. For example, the sound of *sh* is regularly spelled with *sh* at the beginning and end of words, but in other word positions it is spelled more often in other ways than with *sh.* The sound of *k* at the beginning of a word or a syllable is, with few exceptions, spelled with *c* before *a, o, u, r,* and *l,* but with *k* before *e, i,* and *y.* It is spelled in many other ways at the end of words and syllables. The letters *l* and *f* are, with very few exceptions, doubled at the end of monosyllables when preceded by a single short vowel. Other consistencies could be cited for the spelling of sounds in certain word relationships.

Some help, moreover, may be obtained from the knowledge of word patterns, at least in preventing obvious blunders. For example, it is not too much to expect that children should know not to spell *mad* m-a-d-e or *made* m-a-d, but note how the sound of *ade* is spelled in *aid, weighed, suède, stayed,* and *obeyed.* Actually, writing final silent *e* to indicate a long vowel sound is only one of four very common ways of showing vowel length, and long vowel sounds are more often spelled in other ways than this. Examples of other ways are: open syllables, *fatal;* double letters, *deep;* and digraphs, *boat.* There are many words, however, in which these four devices do not spell long vowel sounds. Examples are *definite, machine, been,* and *head.*

When the evidence, on both the consistency and the irregularities of English spelling, is critically and realistically assessed, little justification is found for the claim that pupils can arrive deductively at the spelling of most words they can pronounce. There seems no escape from the direct teaching of the large number of common words which do not conform in their spelling to any phonetic or orthographic rule. One must be exceedingly credulous to believe that authorities with the most complete knowledge of the English language (philologists, phoneticians, and lexicographers) have been in error in pointing out the serious lack of conformity between spoken words and their printed symbols, have been unaware of such orthographic and phonetic regularities as exist in the language, or would have so strongly urged that English spelling be simplified if its difficulties could be removed or largely alleviated by the teaching of phonetic and other orthographic aids.

References

1. Hanna, Paul R., and Moore, James T., Jr. "Spelling—From Spoken Word to Written Symbol," *Elementary School Journal,* LIII (February, 1953), 329-37.
2. Horn, Ernest. *A Basic Writing Vocabulary.* University of Iowa Monographs in Education, First Series, No. 4. Iowa City: State University of Iowa, 1926.
3. Kenyon, John S. *American Pronunciation.* Ann Arbor, Michigan: George Wahr Publishing Co., 1950.
4. Kenyon, John S., and Knott, Thomas A. *A Pronouncing Dictionary of American English.* Springfield, Massachusetts: G. & C. Merriam Co., 1949.
5. Masters, Harry V. "A Study of Spelling Errors: A Critical Analysis of Spelling Errors Occurring in Words Commonly Used in Writing and Frequently Misspelled." Unpublished Doctor's dissertation, State University of Iowa, 1927.
6. Rinsland, Henry D. *A Basic Vocabulary of Elementary School Children.* New York: Macmillan Co., 1945.

44 The Relative Efficiency of the Various Approaches to Writing with the Left Hand

E. A. Enstrom

This report by Enstrom deals with the relative efficiency of various approaches to writing with the left hand.

What criteria were used as a basis for evaluating the various techniques? What were the findings of the researcher? Which adjustments appeared to hold the greatest promise for success?

A previous report, taken from an unpublished dissertation by the writer,[1] covered the extent of the use of the left hand in handwriting. It was found that 11 per cent of pupils in grades one through six preferred the left hand. Among boys, 12.5 per cent used the left hand, and among girls, 9.7 per cent. This second report will deal with the relative efficiency of the various approaches to writing with the left hand.

The Literature

In a study of 108 references dating from 1847 to the present, the writer found no mention of left-handedness until the year 1915. These references included (1) handwriting instruction books for pupils and adults, (2) teachers' manuals in handwriting, (3) books devoted exclusively to handwriting, and (4) courses of study dealing with handwriting.

From the first mentioning of the problem in 1915,[2] there has been a gradual increase in reference to left-handedness. The literature, to the present, revealed six different approaches to the problem. The suggested slope of letters varied from the more easily read forward slant, to vertical, and to questionable

From *The Journal of Educational Research* 55:573-577; August 1962. Reprinted with permission of Dembar Educational Research Services, Inc., and E. A. Enstrom, Director of Research, Peterson Handwriting, Greensburg, Pennsylvania.

backhand. Yet, with all of the disagreement and dearth of understanding, there were no research attempts to find better answers to the problem confronting the teacher of this segment of the school population. West[3] even recommended such a study as early as 1927, but the suggestion went unheeded.

Techniques Actually Used by Left-Handed Writers

The writer began his search for methods actually used by children in classrooms with the aid of a camera and sketch pad. Careful notes were taken of likenesses and differences among the techniques employed by these writers. Grades five through eight were selected for this phase of the study. It was felt that in these more advanced grades, habits would be well set, resulting in techniques of writing that were established sufficiently to permit comparative evaluation.

The two-year study of this phase of the problem revealed that more classifiable methods and variations were in use than were listed in the literature. Instead of six approaches, the writer found 15 different techniques that could be classified and that were used frequently enough to be tested for relative efficiency.

The classroom observer will discover that there are two general groups attempting to write with the left hand: those who keep the writing hand below the writing line (Group I in the writer's study) and those who approach from the left side of the paper and more or less "hook" the wrist while writing (Group II). A careful look will reveal many differences among pupils found in each group.

In Group I, there were six different classifiable variations taking into account, (1) the relationship between the lower edge of the paper and the front edge of the desk, (2) the angle formed between the arm axis and the paper ruling, and (3) the direction of the movement which determined leverage (or lack thereof) and slope (slant, or lack thereof) in the written product. For details of Group I techniques, with variations, see the plate entitled "Group I."

Group II, consisting of the loosely termed "hookers," included nine classifiable techniques. Variations were found (1) in the placing of the paper in relation to the front edge of the desk (which also affects body posture), and (2) the extent to which the wrist is turned on edge and "flexed" during the writing process. Some writers keep the wrist on edge sufficiently to facilitate a hinge action at the joint as the basic movement supporting the writing. Others keep the wrist flat (probably the result of teacher instruction directed to right-handed writers) that permitted only poor wrist movement. Still others may be classified as being approximately half-way between these two extremes. Descriptions of each of these adjustments are found on the plate entitled "Group II."[4]

A comparison of the frequency of the use of techniques showed that certain adjustments held preference by pupils in both Groups I and II. In Group I,

Group I

Writing-hand-below-the-writing-line adjustments. All these adjustments are relatively smear-free.

I –C

Paper is not turned enough to be the reverse of right-handed placement. Angle between the arm axis and paper ruling is less than 90°. Writing slope varies but is downward (usually very irregular).

I –D₁

Reverse of right-handed position. Arm axis is 90° with paper ruling. Downward strokes are directed toward elbow, "into the sleeve." Writing slope approaches vertical and is usually somewhat irregular.

I –D₂

Reverse of right-handed position. Arm axis is 90° with paper ruling. Slant strokes are directed downward and outward (leftward). Slant is generally forward and uniform.

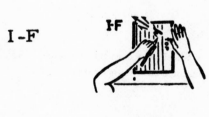

I –E

Paper is turned more to the right (clockwise) than the reverse of right-handed placement. Arm axis angle with paper ruling is greater than 90°. Slant motion is a sideward (leftward) push of the writing arm. Slant is uniformly forward.

I –F

Extreme turning of the paper. Paper ruling is 90° (plus or minus 5°) with the front edge of the desk. Slant motion is a sideward (leftward and upward) push of the writing arm. Slant is generally forward and uniform.

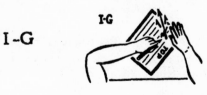

I –G

Very extreme turning of the paper. Paper ruling is greater than the 90° (above). Angle between top of paper and the front edge of the desk is usually between 50° and 30°. Slant is a sideward (upward) push of the writing arm. Slant is generally forward and uniform.

Group II

Writing-hand-above-the-writing-line adjustments. Inherent smearing possibility exists with all these writing techniques.

Adjustments numbered II-A. Paper is turned leftward as for right-handed placement. These are the three basic hooked wrist techniques.

I I -Aa

Wrist is turned on edge enough to permit maximum flexing.

I I -Ab

Wrist is somewhat flattened. Less flexing—more finger movement.

I I -Ac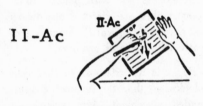

Wrist is flat. Practically no flexing —all finger or whole arm movement, or mixture of two.

Adjustments numbered II-B. Same as II-A except that the paper ruling is generally parallel with the lower edge of the desk (plus or minus 5°).

I I -Ba

Wrist is turned on edge enough to permit maximum flexing.

I I -Bb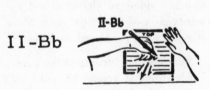

Wrist is somewhat flattened. Less flexing—more finger movement.

I I -Bc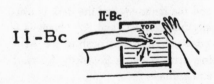

Wrist is flat. Practically no flexing —all finger or whole arm movement, or mixture of two.

Adjustments numbered II-D. Same as II-A but paper is turned rightward (clockwise) as for "correct" left-handed placement, yet wrist is still hooked.

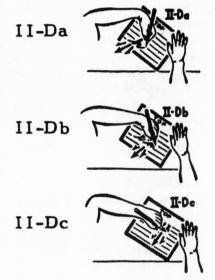

II-Da Wrist is turned on edge enough to permit maximum flexing.

II-Db Wrist is somewhat flattened. Less flexing—more finger movement.

II-Dc Wrist is flat. Practically no flexing —all finger or whole arm movement, or mixture of two.

the most frequently used technique, it was later found, held high advantage in both speed and quality. In Group II, a less desirable technique was used more frequently. With advancing grades, however, it was found that this less desirable method tended to convert into the most desirable approach for this often condemned group.

Evaluation of the Adjustments

The criteria used as a basis for the evaluation of the various techniques employed were (1) the quality of the handwriting product, (2) the rate of writing, (3) ability to produce neat, smear-free papers, and (4) healthful body posture considerations. In addition to the study of the quality of papers produced and the time required in writing them, notes regarding smearing tendency and possible health hazards were made during the initial study and classification of all left-handed writers.

Every precaution was taken in the evaluation phase of the work to make sure that each pupil was actually using his classified technique. Testing for speed was done by using the best combined recommendations for such testing. Whole classes were tested and left-handed writers were not aware that the testing concerned them. Quality scores were obtained through the use of the Ayres Scale[5] with trained experts rating the scrambled papers five separate times.

The average of the five ratings was used as the final quality score with special precautions taken for any rare discrepancies. None of the persons scaling the papers had information as to which of the fifteen techniques was used by the writer of any given page. Two different samples were used in the quality testing: (1) The rate test where the pupils were instructed to write "as well as you can, as fast as you can," and (2) an additional sample where the pupils were merely asked to write as well as they could. Favorable comparison here showed that the original instructions had been followed.

Scope of the Study

At first it was thought that the study would be sufficient in scope if 400 left-handed writers were classified and evaluated for efficiency. However, upon breaking down the four grades into a possible fifteen different adjustments in each, it was thought advisable to extend the study by at least 200 more cases. After this had been done, it was then further decided that, to remove all possible doubt regarding findings, 500 additional cases would be studied, tested, compared, and included. After the elimination of any cases that would possibly interfere with valid findings (pupils using two different techniques, handicapped pupils unable to follow testing instructions, etc.), 1,103 usable left-handed writers were included in the final evaluation. This proved more than ample in securing the desired information.

It should also be mentioned that the findings were obtained from schools where handwriting is generally well taught through a program of in-service help consisting of workshops, class visitations and demonstrations by resource personnel available at scheduled intervals during the school term.[6] The chief objective of the study was to find the efficiency potential of each adjustment in use.

Findings: Relative Efficiency of Various Techniques

In Group I, the I-E adjustment (not taught in the area prior to the testing, but discovered by pupils in the group) also rated highest in quality and in rate of all six Group I techniques. In each grade, pupils using this approach ranked much higher than the quality norms set for the grade. The same was true for speed scores in all grades except eighth, where the rate finding was the same as the norm. (The exceedingly high quality here apparently slowed the speed to some extent.)

The I-D$_2$ adjustment (taught in the area) was next in frequency of use, was above grade standard in quality, but below rate standards in grades five and seven, almost at the rate standard in grade six, and above in grade eight. The general picture here, while good, was not as favorable as in I-E.

The I-F technique (not taught, but discovered by pupils) fluctuated more in findings than the two previous adjustments. It was above quality standards in grades five, six and seven; below in eight. It was below rate standards in grades five and six; above in seven and eight.

The frequently recommended (in the literature) I-D$_1$ technique (pulling the arm "into the sleeve") was at quality standard in grade five, but well below standard in grades six, seven, and eight. In rate, grade five was slightly below standard, grade six further below, but grades seven and eight were above. This speed, however, resulted in the previously mentioned very low quality scores for these two grades. In spite of its frequent recommendation, there is nothing to suggest that this adjustment should be taught to left-handed pupils as a means of solving their writing problems.

The other two adjustments in Group I (I-C and I-G) were so poor (or fluctuated so much) as to warrant no consideration at all.

In Group II, only one approach can be recommended, and then with some reservations. This more desirable "hooked" technique was used by 20 per cent of pupils in this classification. This approach is II-Aa, and showed very high quality with above standard rate in all grades except grade five. However, there are two inherent drawbacks to this solution: (1) The side of the hand does not move readily across the page, particularly if the hand tends to perspire. (2) Since the hand, vigorously flexing, moves through the work written, there is always danger of smearing—again, more so if the hand perspires. All other Group II approaches were either low in speed and quality, fluctuated greatly, or presented possible health hazards (stooped shoulders, twisted backs, etc.), so cannot be considered desirable.

Conclusions: Adjustments Holding the Greatest Promise for Success

In Group I, half of the six adjustments can be considered generally good in four efficiency considerations: (1) quality, (2) rate, (3) freedom from smearing, and (4) posture. Of the remaining, one adjustment (I-G) is erratic because of too few cases; another, the frequently recommended I-D$_1$ approach, is very low in quality, and still another, the I-C, is very low in both quality and rate.

The best Group I adjustments, in order of desirability, are:

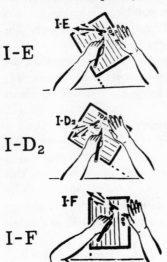

I-E

I-D₂

I-F

These three success-producing techniques make up approximately 69 per cent of Group I writers.

In Group II, only one adjustment out of nine can be considered good, and then with reservations. It is:

II-Aa

While this adjustment, used by only 20 per cent of the group, ranks high in both quality and rate, inherent weaknesses exist and, under less than favorable conditions, can be very handicapping. These weaknesses, as mentioned, are the difficulty of sliding the side of the hand forward in carrying the writing across the page, and smearing tendencies under conditions that cause hand perspiration.

The remaining 80 per cent of Group II writers use modifications in the adjustment that cannot be recommended, either from (1) the efficiency standpoint in quality, rate, or even greater tendency to smear, or (2) from physical health considerations. They seem to have little to recommend them.

It can be concluded that Group I techniques are best, all things considered, and should be taught at beginning stages in writing. Adjustment II-Aa is the most desirable of the "hooked" group and all advanced grade hookers who are unable, or do not desire, to make major changes should be helped to modify their approach to conform most nearly with this more desirable technique..

Footnotes

[1] Enstrom, E. A., *The Extent of the Use of the Left Hand in Handwriting and the Determination of the Relative Efficiency of the Various Hand-Wrist-Arm-Paper Adjustments*, unpublished Ph.D. dissertation: University of Pittsburgh, 1957. Dr. Herbert T. Olander was advisor.

[2] Zaner, C. P., *Zaner Method Writing, Arm Movement, Teacher's Manual No. 4, 5*, Columbus, O.: Zaner and Bloser Co., 1915, 14.

[3] West, Paul V., *Changing Practice in Handwriting Instruction*, Bloomington, Ill.: Public School Publishing Co., 1927, 55-56, 133.

[4] In addition, a more detailed description of each adjustment is found in the original dissertation for those wish to delve into the problem even further. See 1., above: 24-26, 45-60.

[5] Ayres, Leonard P., *Measuring Scale for Handwriting, Gettysburg Edition*, Princeton, N.J.: Cooperative Test Division of Educational Testing Service.

[6] The Peterson System of Directed Handwriting, Greensburg, Pa.

45   Simplified Handwriting
for Today

Gertrude Hildreth

A respected authority on language arts instruction turns iconoclast and challenges the traditional view that cursive writing has advantages over manuscript style and argues that the need to change from manuscript to cursive (or add cursive) may not exist.

Why is a change in style of handwriting required in the primary school years? After reading this article, to what extent do you believe the transition is necessary? Might some advantages accrue from one simplified style as opposed to the present day dual style? The articles by Anderson and Groff corroborate Hildreth's argument while those by Lewis and Templin deal with handwriting instruction in general. E. Horn, cited in Selected References for Part Six, analyzes areas of needed research in handwriting.

In spite of typewriters and telephones, handwriting continues to serve for convenient communication and record making. The older generation learned to write a flowing cursive hand by dint of persistent practice at school. From the early 1920's when manuscript style writing was introduced (a style similar to typing), school beginners learned these simple letter forms which could be used for expressive writing almost from the first lesson. Originally, the new style was presumed to be the pupil's permanent hand, with no suggestion that at midpoint in learning a changeover to cursive style writing would be required. However, as the new style passed the experimental stage and became widely adopted by public school systems, a transition to cursive style writing was required in the later primary period, sometimes as early as the end of second grade.

In the meanwhile, another change in writing usage was taking place. The business world with increasing frequency requested people to "print" important information in filling out application blanks and other documents.

From *Journal of Educational Research* 56:330-333; February 1963. Reprinted with permission of Dembar Educational Research Services, Inc., and Gertrude Hildreth, Visiting Professor, American University, Beirut, Lebanon (Brooklyn College, Brooklyn, New York).

Cursive Style   Manuscript Writing

BLOCK PRINTING

Was the frequency of this request due to the greater volume of forms to be processed, or was it because we were becoming more careless in handwriting? Whatever the cause, this matter brings up the question of handwriting skills suited to our practical writing needs today, and the methods of school instruction required to produce the best results.

How do people respond when requested to "print" while filling out business papers? To the older generation, "printing" can mean only slow, painstaking block lettering, but younger people are inclined to interpret "print" as manuscript style writing learned in the primary grades, often referred to there as "printing." Some people simply turn to a handy typewriter when requested to print.

During recent years, clerks employed in stores in the larger cities have been taught block printing and are required to use it in making out all sales slips and other memoranda, a slow process for many, judging from the effort neat block printing requires.

In order to check up more fully on this situation, a study was made of the handwriting of college students who were requested to print while filling out registration cards for the fall term, 1961, at Brooklyn College, New York. This required the printing of full name, address, and other information. Records were obtained for two classes of junior year undergraduate students in education courses and two classes of graduate students in education courses, who, for the most part, had several years of teaching experience and training in elementary school work. Of the total of 103 students in these four classes, ten were men.

The table indicates the handwriting response made by these students when

Class	Block Printing	Manuscript Style	Manuscript and Block Lettering	Cursive Style	Typing	Totals
Junior Year I	16	14	1	1		32
Junior Year II	16	12	1		1	30
Graduate I	5	20	4	1		30
Graduate II	3	26		2		31

they were requested to print. The cursive style writers must have forgotten the request to print. The junior year students were in the age range 18-19, the graduate students in their 20's and 30's, for the most part. The men uniformly block-printed except for one who typed. An inspection of the registration blanks proved that some of the letters in block printing were scarcely legible and the students had to be asked to give their names.

These results indicate that the undergraduates did block printing or wrote in manuscript style in about 50-50 proportions, while the graduate students showed more inclination to do manuscript style writing. The difference is due to the fact that graduate students in elementary education have brushed up on manuscript style or learned it in their methods courses in the senior year, and those who teach in the primary grades use it daily in classroom instruction, whereas the undergraduates have not had elementary methods courses and have had no experience in teaching handwriting. The men in these classes were high school teachers lacking elementary methods and teaching experience in the elementary grades.

When the students were queried about handwriting instruction in the grades, most of these young people indicated that they had first learned manuscript style (printing) and had changed over before the end of the primary period.

A bulletin, *Teaching Handwriting*, states that the changeover from manuscript style to cursive writing is standard practice throughout New York City except in special cases.[1] For a few children, the physically immature, the left-handed, the slow learners, those with motor handicaps, the partially seeing children, the authorities recommend continuing with manuscript writing. Most children make the change in the third grade. Some children, this publication states, may not be ready until the fourth grade or later. The bulletin goes on to say that when the children have acquired facility in both styles, they use cursive for most writing activities and manuscript for those situations in which it is most appropriate. Block printing or lettering is widely taught in high school shop and drafting courses. In some cases, children have been changed back and forth more than once in moving from one city to another and even in elementary schools within the same school system.

Although the New York City bulletin properly uses the term "manuscript writing" in referring to primary instruction, teachers, parents, and the children themselves refer to this unjoined letter style as "printing," not only in New York City but throughout the country. The children are said to be learning "to print"; the term "handwriting" is not used. We are told, "Now they're only printing. Next year the children will be taught to write." This misleading terminology is unfortunate, since it gives the impression that manuscript style is not actual handwriting, and that it must inevitably be discarded.

Most people who elect to "block print" in responding to the request "please print" write in an unaccustomed, unpracticed hand since block printing is not taught in the elementary school and only a few learn it in high school. Consequently, the writer must necessarily slow down and print laboriously.

Reasons for the Change-Over

Why is a change-over in style of handwriting universally required in the primary grades today? The reasons given are that manuscript style is slower than cursive style at maturity and that most parents object to the continuance of babyish printing, in part because it is said to be slower and also because it does not look "educated" enough for the middle and upper students. Another reason is that teachers in the intermediate and upper grades have had no instruction in teaching manuscript writing at an advanced level.

Research studies dating back 30 and 40 years, comparing the results of manuscript writing and cursive style, have demonstrated that manuscript style is not necessarily slower than cursive style with equal amounts of practice through the elementary grades.[2] There is no reason why manuscript should be slower if children beyond the primary grades practice for fluency and rhythm. The writer found that upper graders who had always used manuscript style and did extensive expressive writing actually wrote faster than their classmates who had always used cursive style.

The belief that manuscript style must be slower is due to the fact that children who learn and use manuscript have generally been "contaminated" at some time or other with cursive style instruction, and they have not been drilled as thoroughly to develop fluency as those who are taught the traditional cursive style.

The parents' request for the change-over is insistent only in the brief span of grades four to six or slightly over. They willingly accept manuscript writing for their children in the primary grades because of the demonstrated advantages for young children in the beginning stages of learning to read and write. They freely consent to a "change-back" to manuscript writing or to instruction in block lettering or typing in the junior high school to insure neater, more legibly written papers. Typical parents regard cursive style writing as a symbol of traditional academic schooling, the acquisition of a skill that demonstrates the child's increasing scholastic maturity. Manuscript style writing is regarded as an infantile stage which must be abandoned for a more grown-up accomplishment.

Another argument for the change-over is that teachers in the intermediate and upper grades have not been trained to build mature writing habits from the children's manuscript learned in the primary grades; hence, they are unable to assist the children in developing rhythm and fluency. Furthermore, there are few good teaching materials for manuscript style in the upper grades and no training courses that give instruction in teaching advanced writing in simplified styles.

In the days when the upper grade teacher's chief task in handwriting instruction was to help a child improve cursive handwriting habits that were fairly well established by the intermediate grades, the problem was to assist individual children who presented some special difficulty for one reason or another; but today, upper grade teachers must not only assist individual children with handwriting problems, but also teach a new style to the entire class.

Objections to the Change-Over

A change-over from manuscript style writing learned in the primary grades to cursive style beyond that point is both wasteful and unnecessary. Since the psychology of learning proves that first-learned skills tend to persist and to interfere with later-learned related skills, pupils must be thoroughly retaught and drilled in the new forms to prevent reversion to earlier forms and to offset interference of the earlier manuscript writing practice. The partially learned, hastily written cursive writing may break down or never really be perfected in the upper grades. The data cited above suggest how readily young people in teacher training courses can change back to manuscript style when occasion requires.

A massive reteaching effort is required to "retool" primary grade handwriting just at the time that children have gained considerable control over simple letter forms and are beginning to enjoy expressing their ideas in writing. After nearly three years or more of practice in simple, clear-cut letter forms they are required to learn a new style with different letter strokes and joined letters. There is no such thing as a natural transition from manuscript style writing to cursive, because the letter strokes in the two styles are distinctly different for at least half of the letters. Here are some illustrations:

Teachers say that the children are changed over when they are "ready to make the change." However, no school-age child is ever as ready to change abruptly to a new motor habit as he is to continue in the accustomed motor patterns. A change-over at this point entails psychological interference. Although most children are successfully retrained within a short time, the children show by their behavior and comments that they resist the change, whether consciously or not.

Although at the point of the change-over the pupils have already had several years' experience in learning to write, now they must be treated more like beginners learning a new skill. This entails different problems for the upper primary and intermediate grade teacher than teaching the six-year-old beginner to write cursive style. Practice from the point of the change-over must be as thorough as in the early grades. Time that is needed in the middle and upper grades for improvement in expressive writing and written work in the content studies must be given to drill to perfect the new writing habits.

The Need of Simplified All-Purpose Handwriting Styles

The confused situation in present-day handwriting practices raises the question whether it is possible to devise a clean-cut style of handwriting that is highly legible, can be written fluently without fatigue; handwriting that need not be changed over in an intermediary stage, but can be developed to a point of high proficiency through systematic instruction by the end of the elementary school period. The answer is decidedly "yes," judging from observations of adults who learned manuscript style in the first place, practiced to perfect it, and have never changed over.

Simplified writing styles can be just as fluent and rhythmical as cursive writing with systematic practice continued until mature habits are established. Upper grade teachers who have taught handwriting as maturation of primary grade manuscript writing have found satisfaction in the ease with which children are taught and the excellent results achieved.

It is not necessary to maintain skill in two different styles, one for fluent writing, the other for the occasion when "printing" is better. With a slightly modified manuscript hand, it is entirely possible to write with good speed and still produce clean, neatly written script. There is no question that simplified styles have advantages, too, for adult illiterates and non-English speaking people learning to read and write English.

The school child's chief use of handwriting is for school papers and reports; the adult most commonly uses handwriting for his informal letters and memoranda. A clear-cut manuscript style is well suited for all these writing purposes.

Instead of making a complete change-over from manuscript to cursive letter forms, just a few slight adjustments are needed for maturation of the manuscript style writing learned in the primary grades. Mr. George Thompson, a British handwriting authority, has devised a slight-slant, slightly joined style which he refers to as "Italic script." This style is developed from the children's primary grade manuscript style writing without any basic changes in letter forms or strokes. Mr. Thompson has prepared a copy book with directions for developing fluent, rhythmical writing in this simplified style, writing that is fluent as well as legible and beautiful.[3] The pupil slants his paper when writing on a flat surface and may or may not slant the writing, depending on his personal inclinations.

Even though the quality of writing continues to be good, systematic and continuous practice is needed throughout the elementary grades to step up the rate of writing and to automatize rhythmical writing habits.

Simplified writing styles done with modern tools are by no means lacking in individuality. Each child's writing, as he matures, increasingly mirrors his own personal adjustments and preferences with no essential difference in basic letter styles. At maturity, individual variability in the established writing hand is always apparent.

During the past thirty years or so, a period of rapid change in elementary education, experimental work in handwriting has been at a virtual standstill. Now with new-style handwriting tools and the frequent demand for clear-cut writing, a vigorous program of research is needed to appraise existing practices and to try out new methods. This experimentation should be carried out on a broad basis in all types of schools, and it should be accompanied by an educational program for parents to acquaint them with new practices in teaching handwriting.

Footnotes

[1] *Teaching Handwriting*, Curriculum Bulletin No. 3, 1960-61 (New York: Bureau of Curriculum Research, Division of Elementary Schools, Board of Education, 1961).

[2] Gertrude Hildreth. "Manuscript Writing After Sixty Years," *Elementary English*, XXXVII (January 1960), pp. 3-13.

[3] George Thompson. *Better Writing*, Puffin Picture Book, No. 96 (Middlesex, England: Penguin Books, Ltd., 1954).

Part Seven

Curriculum Topics and Resources

This part considers the issues of special aspects of the instructional program, involving both children and materials. In considering variations from the norm, instructional materials are necessarily adjunct features or ways of dealing with human variability. Thus this section treats such topics as methods of teaching English to the deprived and bilingual child as well as the teaching of foreign language to English-speaking children; programmed material, mass media, particularly educational television; other educational media as instructional tools; the typewriter as an educational aid; and the paperback and children's periodicals.

It is evident more study needs to be made of speech characteristics of deprived children (though there are some data as reported in other parts of this anthology) and ways of developing an awareness of children that many of these practices constitute a social liability. One proposal is that standard English be regarded as a second language and that a language-laboratory approach be used for teaching standard English more effectively to these children. With about 25 per cent of the school population in the United States bilingual, it is obvious that attention should be focused upon special problems and what teachers can do to alleviate problems of these children. Many questions are raised about the ever-increasing number of programs involving foreign language instruction in the elementary school, making the topic worthy of study. All agree that second language teaching should be done well or not at all, but what is meant by "done well"?

Everyone stands in favor of ways of individualizing instruction. What programmed materials are available to provide another promising avenue toward individualization of instruction? Reflecting the increased concern for programmed instruction, two volumes, *Program '62* and *The Use of Programmed*

Instruction in U. S. Schools, survey in detail available programs and their uses in schools. Both are available from the Superintendent of Documents, Washington, D. C. 20025. To keep educators abreast of current developments, there is a bi-monthly bulletin, *Programed Instruction,* which may be ordered from the Center for Programed Instruction, Inc., 365 West End Avenue, New York, N. Y. 10024.

Many teachers subscribe to and make use of communication media (television, paperbacks, newspapers, and magazines) prepared especially for the young. Nearly one thousand titles of paperback books suitable for elementary school children are annotated in *Paperback Book Guide for Elementary Schools,* New York: R. R. Bowker Company, 1180 Avenue of the Americas, 1966. As to television teaching, two programs in the Cincinnati Public Schools deserve mention. An excellent study guide is available for classroom teachers.

Certainly, many of the possibilities exist for approaches as suggested in the preceding two paragraphs, even though they may not exist at this time in many localities.

Unfortunately, lack of published articles appears in the use of audio-visual resources with language arts instruction (*i.e.,* filmstrips, charts, records, films, tape recorders, overhead projectors, listening devices, etc.). Likewise articles dealing with specific suggestions for adjusting language instruction for the extreme achievers, advanced and the slow-learning, are scarce. (For the enrichment program, see Burns, Paul C., "Research for the Library-Minded Mentally Advanced Language Arts Pupils," *Elementary English,* 39 (May 1962), 427-428 and "Elementary School Language Arts Library—A Selected Bibliography," *Elementary English,* 41 (December 1964), 879-884.) The topic of diagnosis and remediation of language problems seemed too broad for this anthology. For those interested, the following articles are suggested:

Fitzgerald, James A., "A Crucial Core Vocabulary in Elementary School Language and Spelling," *American School Board Journal,* 103 (July 1941), 22-24.

Fitzgerald, James A., "Spelling . . . Diagnosis and Remediation," *National Elementary Principal,* 38 (May 1959), 27-30.

Furness, Edna Lue, "Diagnosis and Remediation of Handwriting," *Elementary English,* 32 (April 1955), 224-228.

———, "A Remedial and Developmental Program in Listening," *Elementary English,* 32 (December 1955), 525-531.

———, "A Remedial and Developmental Speech Program," *Elementary English,* 32 (May 1955), 289-295.

———, "Pupils, Pedagogues, and Punctuation," *Elementary English,* 37 (March 1960), 184-189.

———, "Pupils, Teachers, and 'Sentence Sense,'" *Education,* 86 (September 1965), 12-17.

———, "Pupils, Teachers, and Telltale Verbs," *Education,* 87 (October 1966), 111-116.

Johnson, Leslie W., "One Hundred Words Most Often Misspelled by Children in the Elementary Grades," *Journal of Educational Research*, 44 (October 1950), 154-155.

Manual for Interpreting Iowa Language Abilities Test, Yonkers-on-Hudson: World Book Company, 1948 (See for "spelling"; sentence sense"; "language usage"; "capitalization"; and "punctuation").

Zaner-Bloser staff, *Handwriting Faults and How to Correct Them*, Columbus, Ohio: The Zaner-Bloser Company, n.d.

The reader needs to be alert for the possibility of articles on such topics as educational media, differentiation of instruction, and remediation of language difficulties which may be published subsequent to the date of this anthology.

The reason for the omission of articles dealing with ungraded classrooms, team teaching, middle schools, and the like is not that they are unimportant, but most of these are administrative arrangements and appear to have had little influence on language arts instruction. Teachers and materials seem to be the best hope to achieve some semblance of individualization. Also the editors of this anthology decided against inclusion of articles or essays dealing with administrative arrangements unless *specifically* related to language arts instruction. In brief, this book did not intend to suggest the efficacy of one kind of classroom or school organization over another, but rather to emphasize the classroom activities.

The issues raised by the articles in Part Seven are worthy of serious consideration. For few, if any, of the possibilities explored by the articles in this part are there reasonably clear proposals or partial answers at present. The task of strengthening this vital aspect of the language arts program cannot, then, be taken lightly, and to execute it well will call for the expenditure of a great deal of thought and effort.

46 Some Approaches to Teaching Standard English as a Second Language

Charlotte K. Brooks

Linguists have long been aware of varied speaking styles and the inherent cor-rectness of each one in certain situations. Brooks, out of a background of per-sonal experiences, writes convincingly of children "who have language or dialect problems . . . and are told by their teachers that their language is not 'correct.' "

Why does the writer differentiate between the 'culturally different' and the 'culturally deprived'? Defend or attack the two assumptions posed by the writer. Can children be expected to switch back and forth from 'natural' to 'standard' English depending upon the situation? What are your tentative answers to the 'unanswered questions'? Is Brooks consistent with the theses presented by Roberts and Kurath in Part Two of this anthology? Readers may also want to refer to articles by Allen, Clubb, Golden, Granite, Green, and Newton cited in Selected References for Part Seven.

Linguists say that all languages and dialects are really of equal merit, and that good language is simply language which gets the desired effect with the least trouble for the user.

I am concerned at this moment, deeply concerned, about two kinds of children who have language or dialect problems and who are told by their teachers that their language is not "correct."

Two Kinds of Children

Like many others, I have taught and now watch with a troubled mind two other kinds of pupils: the culturally different and the culturally deprived. I am

From *Non-Standard Speech and the Teaching of English* (ed. by William A. Stewart), Center for Applied Linguistics, 1964, pp. 24-32. Reprinted with permission of Center for Applied Linguistics and Charlotte K. Brooks, Supervising Director of English, Washington, D. C. Public Schools.

concerned because I think that in spite of a growing awareness of the long neglected problems of these childrens, educators have not yet learned the best ways of dealing with them. And unless teachers of the language arts salvage the youngsters and do so very early in their school lives, these potentially useful citizens will be lost forever to all education and will become the problems, the drop-outs, the hangers-on, the failures. In our rapidly changing, automation-geared land, we can no longer afford such losses.

I said "two kinds of children" quite purposefully, because I want to differentiate sharply between two groups: the culturally different and the culturally deprived. Many people, even those who have made careful studies of the needs of children who perform below par, tend to lump the two groups together. In Washington, D.C., where partly through tracking we have attempted to help children who are retarded in school, basic classes sometimes have not only these children but also the mentally subnormal and the emotionally maladjusted. A careful reading of newspapers and magazines and attendance at professional meetings has elicited for me the not too surprising information that all over this land totally unlike kinds of culturally different and culturally deprived children are thus grouped. Too often there is little consideration given to the great differences among them or to the best approaches to teaching them.

Limitations of space and time will prevent my fully exploring the variations among these children and all of the approaches that can be used in teaching them. I shall concern myself with the users of nonstandard English among the culturally different and the culturally deprived, and with some approaches to teaching them standard English as though it were a second language.

It must be mentioned, however, that among the culturally different should be listed the perfectly intelligent, even superior, non-English speaking children; some immigrants from country or rural community to big cities; pupils with physical or emotional problems; pupils from other English speaking countries; in short, all who differ from the average child of middle or upper level American city or suburb. No teacher must make the error of considering these different children necessarily deprived. They have rich cultural heritages and can offer much to their fellow pupils and teachers if sensible approaches are used.

The culturally deprived child

What, then, is the culturally deprived child? There is some overlapping because the culturally deprived child may also be culturally different. He is the child who has been isolated from those rich experiences that should be his—isolated by poverty, by meagerness of intellectual resources in his home and surroundings; by the incapacity, illiteracy, or indifference of his parents, guardians, or community. He may have come to school without ever having had his mother sing him the traditional lullabies, with no knowledge of nursery rhymes, fairy stories, or the folklore of his country. He may have taken few trips—perhaps his only one the cramped, uncomfortable trip from the lonely shack on the tenant farm to the teeming, filthy slum dwelling—and probably he knows nothing of poetry, music, painting, or even indoor plumbing. He may live in the slums; he may reside in the suburbs. He may fool the observer with his quiet and cleanliness; he may create disgust with his dirty appearance and crude manners. He may disturb because of his loud, vulgar ways or frustrate because of his sullen silence. He may infuriate with his intransigent, delinquent activities. He may be the child of a minority group; a product of inferior schools staffed by inadequate, poorly prepared, or—to him, at least—culturally different (or indifferent) teachers. Here, I am concerned about the child of potentially average or above average ability from a home poor in every way, culturally and financially: an almost inarticulate user of non-standard English.

Since being relatively happy and successful in the middle and upper reaches of the English speaking world requires the ability to use standard English, and since the old ways of attempting to teach this use have not been notably successful, other ways must be tried. In order to prepare for experimentation in this area, I have visited schools in which English is being taught as a foreign language, have watched speech and language arts teachers at work on elementary and secondary levels, and have talked with and observed the work of teachers of the culturally different and the culturally deprived. At least one teacher of English in Washington is now designing a research project in which she will teach standard English as a second language. Others are interested.

The First Assumption

This is my first assumption: that standard English can be taught successfully as though it were a second language to children who speak nonstandard English as a result of cultural differences and/or cultural deprivation.

Why do I assume that this can be done? Many teachers of the language arts, themselves the products of the so-called middle classes, teach as though linguistic science did not exist; as though standard English speech and usage were historically and geographically fixed and immutable, with certain well-known laws that always have been and always must be obeyed. Textbooks—those best of all authorities—have blandly stated these laws and teachers have inexorably taught them. Nice little girls and good little boys have easily learned and practiced these correct forms because, invariably, this is the kind of usage that they have always heard and seen. The basal readers—those boring little books—have pictured their milk-cum-vitamin way of life. Later, these children have identified with the characters of stories in school and in the stories their parents and teachers have encouraged them to borrow from the libraries. Their parents and teachers have talked in identical socially acceptable ways; lived in the same kinds of worlds. With few problems in the language arts, these children have moved from elementary to the secondary school, and then usually to college and to professional careers.

The others? On entering school they have learned very quickly how unlike the socially accepted pattern they are. Dress, manners, speech, all have been inferior and must be changed. The stories—even the pictures in the books—have not usually been about their lives; the language spoken by the teachers and prescribed by the grammar books has not been theirs. The teacher, often without scientific language training, has set himself up as a language expert and has attempted to remodel the child in his own image. One linguist maintains that this kind of teacher is a quack and should be just as liable to prosecution as the medical fraud. The nonstandard speaker, meeting this snobbery in school, is puzzled and thrown off the track.

Teachers have said, for example: "Her speech reflects her personality traits," or "Careless, sloppy speech reveals a careless, sloppy person." And the nonstandard pupils have often believed this, and have shrunk or have resisted learning.

Let us consider now examples of the kinds of pupils whom I am discussing.

The culturally different child

Carlos is culturally different. His parents, born in New York City, are the children of parents born in Puerto Rico. Because one grandparent lives in the home, Spanish is often spoken there, although the parents are able to speak English. They have little money, but Carlos and his family love music and dancing, and often attend free concerts or go to art galleries. The grandfather has shared his store of tales and poetry with the boy, and sometimes takes him on long rides into the country, or to beaches and parks. Carlos has even visited Puerto Rico, where another grandparent lives. But the boy does not say much in school because he is shy and is not sure that he has always the correct English word. His teachers in primary school, harrassed with overcrowded classes, few materials, and little training in dealing with the culturally different, "lumped" him with other Puerto Rican children in a slow class.

Fortunately, the program described in the October 18, 1963 *Christian Science Monitor* came to the rescue before it was too late. A trained volunteer now works with Carlos, often in this way. The boy picks up an interesting picture.

"I *hab* a tree, with *leebs*," says Carlos.

"Yes, you *have* a tree, with *leaves*," replies the teacher. "Say *have-leaves*."

"Have-leaves," repeats Carlos, learning the "v" sound in English.

Because this boy already knows some English, he needs mainly to have someone take an interest in him to draw out what he knows, to involve him in the life around him, to help him share with others orally and in writing his valuable contributions, and to correct some speech difficulties.

Mary: culturally deprived

Mary, on the other hand, is a culturally deprived child. A small brown girl whose mother moved north with her family of nonworking husband and six children, Mary seldom opens her mouth in her first-grade classroom deep in the slums of a big city. Mary's mother is too tired at the end of a long working day to do much more than the minimum amount of housework. She says little except to reprimand; the father, seldom present, says nothing, unless he is cursing in a drunken fury. The rooms are small, noisy, and unclean. Loud parties are given constantly, cars and trucks clash by; sirens, dogs, radios, and television assault the ear, and Mary long ago learned to "turn herself off." *Conditioned inattention* they call it when Mary cannot "turn herself on" in school. Apathetic, vacant, she seems stupid. She is not—yet.

A special language arts program . . . may save Mary. In Washington, and in other cities with such programs, trained teachers work with pupils like this girl. Such children can become interested in fascinating objects like many bells with different sounds, and can learn to listen, to talk, and to write about them. They are given new experiences—something else to talk and write about. Unlike Carlos, Mary must be taken, after a careful pre-planning, to fire stations, museums, concerts, art galleries, the zoo, the country. Like Carlos, though, she can be taught standard English as a second language.

Mary may say, "Dis here a leaf."

The teacher can reply, "This is a leaf, Mary. Put your tongue between your teeth and say 'th.'" (The teacher will surely *not* say "You have a lazy tongue." That kind of value judgment would defeat her purpose, and would simply deflate, in the time-honored way, the already nearly defeated child.)

Mary, enjoying this special attention and not told she is wrong at every word, will try. And she will learn to say *this, teeth, that,* and other standard English sounds and words. I know, for I have seen this done.

The Second Assumption

My second assumption is based upon the first. If standard English is taught as a second language, it is not necessary to reject the first, the nonstandard English.

With Carlos this is fairly easy. Most people realize that non or minimal English speaking persons must retain the first language for use in the home and sometimes in the community. They even accept with equanimity those errors in English usage that come obviously from primary use of the other language: *leebs* for *leaves*; "I no want to go," and such interesting dialects as Pennsylvania Dutch and Cajun. How many teachers, though, are able to accept the nonstandard *dis* and *hisn* of the nonstandard Marys? For Mary *will* use "corrupt and incorrect" English. She will be affected by her community and her peers more than she will be affected by her teachers. She will say:

You done it.
That's hisn, but I ain't sure.
It's me.
I didn't see nobody.

This language will get the desired effect in Mary's community with the least difficulty for its user, while

You did it.
That is his, but I am not sure.
It is.
I didn't see anybody.

from Mary would cause an embarrassing sensation in the home and among her friends, although Miss Fidditch would approve, undoubtedly.

Perhaps Mary can use both kinds of language, each at its appropriate time, if her teacher will show her the way. Must the teacher reject the nonstandard English as wrong, and with it Mary's family, her friends, and her values? Many teachers feel that they must change the language of children like these. They have tried. How successful have they been?

Some Unanswered Questions

Here I shall pose other questions for your consideration, questions which I shall not answer, except indirectly, but questions which I hope you will study and attempt to answer for yourselves.

What right has a person to impose his cultural pattern upon another? How does the teacher know that his *is* the right way? What does the teacher know about the history of his language? Does he know the truth about *shall* and *will*, the double negative (perfectly right, by the way, in Spanish), the possessive; *ain't I?* Who made the rules, and who changes them? Who decides upon standard American English? Does it differ regionally in America: is it different from standard British English?

After a year spent teaching English in Birmingham, England, I revised many of my own attitudes about pronunciation (Birming*ham*, Alabama; Birmingh'm, England), spelling, usage, punctuation, and meaning. I learned to spell *labor*, l-a-b-o-u-r, to say *contró-versy* and *a* to *zed*, to put a comma after the salutation of a business letter and to use *Esq.* and *Yours faithfully;* to say "The team are ready," and to know that napkins are *diapers* after my husband brought some home for use at my first grand English high tea! I met men and women from Wales, many of whom speak their own Celtic tongue among their countrymen. At my school there were six who spoke English well—though almost always with a musical lilt—but kept Welsh as a "first language." They had no trouble shifting from one to the other at will, or from formal to informal —and sometimes nonstandard-British English. Most of us move from formal to informal American English quite as readily. Will not pupils, if their own "first language" is not rejected, learn and shift into standard English when such a shift is required by circumstances?

Another question. If, as linguists say, "Languages change; they do not become corrupted or decay," must not the teacher of the language arts stop being dogmatic about what is right?

Before briefly summarizing some of the suggested approaches in a final statement, may I reiterate my reason for feeling that these rather tentatively suggested and not yet completely tried suggestions are needed?

Constant drill has not, we know, taught correct usage to those who habitually use nonstandard English. Red pencils have seldom changed the ways of resistant pupils. Why, then, should teachers not exploit the tremendous psychological lift implicit in the idea of acceptance by saying to Carlos and to Mary,

> I accept you and your language. Use it when you need it for communication with your family and friends. But, if you really want to be a free and successful participant in other areas of this American life, why not learn the language spoken there: standard English?

The teacher must, of course, fit this little speech to the age and mental ability of the pupil, but perhaps he can with one stroke destroy the barrier to communication built by the usual, unknowingly insensitive, rejection. Perhaps with the same stroke he can build a foundation for the kind of teaching he must do. The initial acceptance can lead to some of the approaches I shall mention.

(Incidentally, if language laboratories are used in this program as they are for the foreign languages, we in the language arts should be in an excellent position to request some of the NDEA funds now going into other languages. Too, if linguistic science is truly a science—and I believe it is—we have a second reason for requesting participation in the NDEA grants.)

What, then, may we do?

We should not reject the first language of any child, but must accept the linguists' request that we leave his language alone, and teach him a second language as though it were a foreign tongue.

We should point out as early as possible in the child's school career that there are certain advantages in learning and using standard English. Specific examples should be pointed out.

Culturally deprived children might be started earlier in school—perhaps in a pre-kindergarten or nursery school—so that they can be given some of the rich experiences that are not now being provided by the home or the community.

The same media used for teaching foreign languages should be used for teaching standard English as a second language: interesting objects and pictures, tape recorders, records, television programs, language laboratories, films, and new textbooks based upon the findings of linguistic science.

Teachers and pupils must learn the history of the language, and must understand what standard English really is.

Books, especially basal readers and grammar books, must be revised to include more material directed toward the culturally different and the culturally deprived.

I hear Miss Fidditch cry, "We must teach them never to use a preposition to end a sentence with." Or is it a wail that soon she will not be needed? She mustn't worry; there will be plenty for her to do. Pupils will still have to be taught to read well and critically, to speak clearly, to write accurately, and to avoid those mechanical errors in the use of English which interfere with communication. But these errors are found everywhere, not just among the different and the deprived.

Edwin Sauer says in *English in the Secondary School,*

> . . . the really serious language faults of our time are more likely to be heard in high places than in low. The gardener who says to his employer, 'I ain't hardly got no room for them tulip bulbs,' will be understood. . . . But what can a reader do with a statement like this from a top industrial executive: 'Gentlemen: In re your communication as to the expediency of our continued controls of merchandisable materials, may we state that, pursuant to many requests . . .'?

If Miss Fidditch can help eliminate jargon, gobbledegook, tautology, euphemisms, and clichés in addition to what has already been suggested, she will have a more than full-time job.

Culturally different and cuturally deprived pupils, like Carlos and Mary, may well be happier and more successful sayin' what comes natur'lly where this is perfectly acceptable, but learning to use standard English in the appropriate situations. And, if the natural talk is not rejected completely, and the standard English taught from the beginning witih the very best approaches used in teaching a foreign language, Miss Fidditch and teachers of the language arts may be happier and more successful, too.

At least it is worth trying.

47   Methods for the Bilingual Child

Doris C. Ching

Bilingual children have some peculiar problems of their own and present some unique instructional difficulties. In this essay, Ching summarizes experimental studies concerned with methods of teaching the bilingual child and draws some implications from these findings for the classroom teacher.

What specific techniques are suggested for the bilingual child in the primary years? Should special classes in the study of English be provided for some pupils? What would be the curriculum for such classes? What are some details about special methodology for these children which you feel is needed if classroom teachers are to successfully cope with bilingual children? What difficulties are presented by the fact that many bilingual children can also be legitimately classified as disadvantaged? Why do you suppose there are no articles listed in Selected References which also deal with this topic?

The problems of the bilingual child continue to be of interest and concern to educators. Bilingualism is still prevalent in our large metropolitan areas, in the rural areas of the Middle West, in the five southwestern states, and in Hawaii.

When the term *bilingualism* is used, there is frequently a vagueness of meaning attached to it. Some people think of a bilingual as an equilingual, a person who can perform proficiently in all aspects of both languages. However, when the term *bilingualism* is used in its broadest sense, it is considered without qualification as to the degree of difference between the two languages or systems known; it is immaterial whether the two systems are "languages," "dialects of the same language," or "varieties of the same dialect" (11).

Thus, a bilingual's achievement may be limited to one aspect of a language, dialect, or variety of a dialect, such as understanding, speaking, reading, writing; or he may have varying degrees of ability in all these aspects. Actually, bilingualism and monolingualism can be thought of as opposite extremes of a

From *Elementary English* 42:22-27; January 1965. Reprinted with permission of the National Council of Teachers of English and Doris C. Ching, Associate Professor, California State College, Los Angeles, California.

continuum, with a continuum for each aspect of language, dialect, or variety of a dialect (8).

Teachers who work with bilingual children are often confronted with pupils who have handicaps in relation to the language background necessary for successful reading. Investigation has revealed that bilingual children enrolled in the first four grades of the elementary school have difficulties with meanings of words in readers. Before the child with a language handicap can begin to read successfully, he must command a meaningful English vocabulary based on the interests of his age group and including the concepts needed in beginning reading. The task confronting the teacher of a child such as this is much greater than that of a teacher of English-speaking children. The bilingual child with a language handicap needs to receive special attention and instruction (10).

Various methods of teaching the bilinguals in different parts of the United States have been used, and there have been numerous articles with many suggestions for helping the bilingual child overcome his language deficiencies. Unfortunately there has been a paucity of carefully designed experimental studies concerned with this aspect of the problem of bilingualism; that is, trying to find the best methods that teachers can use to help bilingual children. The studies bearing on this topic which could be located and which have implications for the classroom teacher of bilingual children are summarized below.

Pioneer Experimental Studies

Fuller (3) conducted a four-year study in which successive groups of children in the kindergarten of the Grant School in San Jose, California, were given special language training. Units of work, games, visual aids, and dramatizations were utilized for vocabulary building. The understanding and speaking of the English language was emphasized in all activities. The effectiveness of the special language training given to pupils in the kindergarten was measured by comparing twenty-nine pupils with no speech training and thirty pupils with a year of speech training in the kindergarten as to amount of failure and reading ability during the early elementary school years. The results showed that pupils with special language training in kindergarten made fewer failures in the first grade than those without special training and made better scores on reading tests (names of tests used were not given) when they were tested after three years of schooling. However, because the children were not equated on intelligence, it is difficult to interpret the findings of this study. Fuller concluded that "the problem of providing adequate educational opportunities for those children who are handicapped in language by reason of foreign parentage is of such importance as to warrant further intensive study and experimentation under conditions where more factors can be controlled with larger groups of pupils than was possible in this study. Such research should yield rich returns in the solution of the problem of providing those school experiences which are necessary to meet the needs of pupils with language handicaps."

Unfortunately, though many educators have recognized this need for special methods, there has not been much carefully controlled experimentation in this area.

The San Jose Experimental School study (7), however, seems to have been a carefully planned experimental study. It was carried on over a period of eight years in New Mexico. The subjects of the experiment were 2,312 pupils in the first through the eighth grades. All the children came from Spanish-speaking homes. The battery of tests administered to San Jose and also to two control schools (with 1,331 and 1,320 pupils respectively) included individual and group intelligence tests and various achievement tests. The children in the control schools were Spanish-speaking and of the same general background as the San Jose youngsters, the number of pupils per teacher was about the same, and the length of the school term was approximately the same, so the author declared that the type of educational program was the large differential factor.

In the school program adopted at San Jose, special emphasis was given to reading and oral English. Extensive room libraries were provided, the work in social sciences was considered as one part of the reading program, and a minimum vocabulary list was taught the first-grade child before the regular work was undertaken.

A comparison of the relative achievements of the three schools in the achievement tests administered; that is, the Gates Reading Test and the New Stanford Achievement Test, showed that when the schools were compared grade by grade according to the averages of the medians for five years, San Jose was in the lead on the Gates by differences which were large enough to prove that they were real and not chance differences. On the Stanford, San Jose was again superior although the differences were not statistically reliable until the fifth grade. However, this report is difficult to interpret because data concerning intelligence were not presented. Furthermore, there was no measure of the extent of bilingualism present in the children studied.

In another study, Herr (4), like Fuller, was interested in the effect of pre-first-grade training on the bilingual child's achievement when he entered elementary school. This study was somewhat of an improvement on Fuller's because the investigator attempted to equate the children on vocabulary ability, home environment, chronological age, and intelligence. The first two factors were equated by "subjective analysis," and the Pintner-Cunningham Primary Intelligence Test was used to equate the children on intelligence. Two groups of five-year-olds were selected from nine towns in New Mexico. The control group did not attend school and was subjected to no special training, while the experimental group attended school and received special training directed toward the development of their vocabulary, auditory perception, and visual perception.

Another form of the Pintner-Cunningham Intelligence Test was given to both the control and experimental groups when they entered the first grade, and the results showed that the IQ's of the children in the experimental group had increased by 29.91 points (from 66.01 to 95.92), while those of the control group had increased by only 9.56 points (from 68.9 to 78.46). However, since the intelligence tests were verbal and the children had only a limited English vocabulary, the results serve merely as a basis for comparison and diagnosis and not as a true measure of intelligence.

Both groups were introduced to reading in the first grade through the use of experience charts and the preprimer was used when the pupil showed a definite desire to read. At the end of the school year the Metropolitan Achievement Test was given to both groups, and the results showed that all the children in the control group attained a grade placement of 1.5 or below in reading achievement, while in the experimental group 20% achieved a grade placement of 2.1 or over, 67% had 1.9 or over, and not one received a grade placement below 1.5. The investigator concluded that Spanish-American children with pre-first-grade training have a decided advantage over the children who do not have the experience of pre-first-grade training, and that such training is an important factor in success in learning to read and could eliminate a large percentage of failures in the lower grades.

It is unfortunate that Herr did not also give the children a non-verbal intelligence test and that she did not use some of the various measures available for measuring extent of bilingualism instead of just doing it by "subjective analysis." However, the investigator must be commended for her efforts toward a carefully controlled experimental study.

Recent Experimental Studies

The experimental phase of J. Cayce Morrison's *The Puerto Rican Study* (5) is one of the more recent research studies concerning methods of teaching bilingual children. The study was conducted in the first, fourth, and seventh grades of seven schools. In each experimental class one half hour was given to teaching English to Puerto Rican pupils selected as language learners. Language learners were those Puerto Rican children who were not able to communicate effectively in English in the school situation. During the half hour period the teacher emphasized one of three variants of methods. These were: vocabulary, structure or language pattern, and experience. Each teacher used three types of materials: (1) resource units with suggestions for helping the child who needed help in learning English; (2) variant brochures which were manuals of procedure that described the variant to be emphasized and suggested devices, illustrative English-language-learning situations, procedures, and practices; and (3) variant supplements which provided the specific words, the structural patterns or the experiential situations to be developed from day to day.

The testing program was carried on at the beginning and near the close of the school year to obtain measures of pupils' learning in understanding spoken English and in speaking, reading, and writing English. The Gates Reading Test was used to measure English reading ability and all other tests used were constructed by those involved in the study. Data were reported separately for the fourth and seventh grades, but none were given for the first grade. The total numbers of language learners assigned to the experimental classes were 146 in the fourth grade and 462 in the seventh grade. Comparisons were made of the differential gains between variant groups and of the gains from pre-testing to post-testing. The results of the study led the author to conclude that "the three variants had differential strengths, and that all variants were weak in promoting development of English reading skills. The strength of an experiential emphasis seems to be in the area of improving the pupil's ability to understand spoken English. The strength of the vocabulary emphasis is in improving the pupil's ability both to speak and to write English. The strength of a structural emphasis is in improving the pupil's ability to write English. For any one goal, a particular variant may be more effective. For an integrated attack on all four areas of English—understanding, reading, writing, and speaking—a combination of the three emphases together with a more direct attack on reading would seem to be most desirable."

Unfortunately no control group was used in this study and the mental ability of the pupils in the variant groups was not measured. The Puerto Rican pupils may have made gains in the four areas of English without the special instruction and emphasis on teaching English, and the intelligence variable may have had an influence on the results of the study. These factors must, therefore, be considered when interpreting the results of this study.

In another recent study by Ching (2), a remedial English program was carried on with third-grade bilingual children over a period of six months. The subjects of this investigation were 246 children, 123 each in the experimental and control groups. The experimental and control groups were comparable to each other in regard to chronological age, intelligence, reading and English language ability, and various factors of their personal and environmental backgrounds. The testing instruments used to secure data during the pre-testing and post-testing were the California Short-Form Test of Mental Maturity, the California Reading Test, and two original tests devised by the investigator, the Written English Test and the Oral English Test.

The experimental language program was carried on in the experimental classrooms twenty minutes daily for a six-month period. Approximately two weeks were spent on each of the ten lessons in this program. The lessons were primarily oral in nature. Each lesson was devoted to the correction of a specific type of error in usage and consisted of six main parts: oral drill with sentences; dramatizations; stories; and games which gave the children practice in the correct use of the words being emphasized; and regular checks and regular reviews of what had been taught.

Comparisons of the final scores of the experimental and the control groups in reading and in written and oral English tests showed that the experimental group was significantly superior to the control group in reading and English language ability. Over the six-month period the experimental group made gains in reading and written English which were significantly greater than those of the control group and only the experimental group made a significant gain in oral English.

Other Methods Used with Bilinguals

The preceding are all that can be presented in the way of research reviews in methods for bilingual children. However, the professional literature reveals other methods of teaching bilingual children that have been tried in different parts of the United States. These methods are summarized in an article by Burbeck (1).

Patterson and Johnson (6) of Santa Barbara, California, worked with a Mexican group using both the informal methods of experience-activity charts and the textbook method of teaching reading. Their conclusions were that these children learned more words from their own charts than from the textbooks and ready-made materials.

Stone (9) made a survey of a school system in California consisting of thirteen schools where there was a considerable number of Mexicans and Italians. Stone felt that the reasons for failure among these children were that the course of study was inflexible, that the material used was too difficult, and that too much time was being devoted to formal vocabulary drills. His experiences with bilingual children led him to conclude that the experience-activity method of teaching reading gave the children a poor start in reading.

Here we have conflicting findings and ideas as to the best methods to use with bilinguals. The reasons for this apparent disagreement may be the manner in which the experience-activity method was used and the different purposes for which it was used. In Patterson and Johnson's study the children may have learned more words from the charts because they had developed the charts themselves from the background of their own experiences and, therefore, the words in the reading material were meaningful and real to them. However, the experience-activity method has its shortcomings as well as its advantages. Although it may be valuable in building interest in reading, in laying the foundation for certain reading mechanics, and in developing comprehension, it cannot be used to teach all children to read because experiences are varied and, therefore, vocabulary to express such experiences must be varied. Consequently, vocabulary is introduced at such a rapid rate that only the exceptional child can keep pace. The teacher can control the vocabulary to some extent, but the control necessary for adequate repetition demands skill and time that the average teacher cannot afford. In addition, expression is stilted by too much control. Stone probably concluded that the method was not a good one for bilinguals because of these reasons. Actually the use of experience charts is a sound method, providing it is not the only method used for developing reading skills with bilingual children.

In the La Jolla School in southern California a method called "incidental" was tried for seven years with "very satisfactory progress." The children were Mexican and Japanese and entered school with scarcely any knowledge of the English language. The curriculum in this school consisted of the study of nature and industrial activities, the enjoyment of songs and stories (through retelling, dramatization, and other activities), and handiwork. Formal subjects, such as arithmetic and grammar, were not taught. Very little writing was done in the primary grades. In this way the teaching of English was incidental, for the main objective was the "improvement of pupils' activities in normal life." It was reported that when this group was tested on formal subjects, the norms compared favorably with average American schools.

One can easily see how the incidental method can be used to advantage in the elementary grades, especially at the primary levels, because it can help to enrich the child's background of experiences and give him many opportunities for oral speaking; but if the method were used for an indefinite period of time, the child would be penalized in other aspects of his school work. There is no reference as to where Burbeck learned about the above situation, and a search of the literature in this area has not uncovered it. It would be of interest to know which test was given to the group in which the norms of the group compared favorably with average American schools, the grade level of the group that was tested, the length of time during which the children were taught by the incidental method, and whether or not the children attended classes in regular schools after they had gained a sufficient knowledge of English.

In Seattle, Washington, Japanese-American bilinguals were segregated and placed in special groups. In their school program, emphasis was placed on pitch and intonation of speech, drill on exercises for the speech organs to obtain correct articulation of English, and drills on the sounds of the letters. Each child progressed at his own rate, and at the end of one and a half to two years, he was able to enter the grade in his own district in which he belonged. At the time the report was written, none of the children had had to return to the special classes for additional work.

There was no description as to the extent of bilingualism present in the children; but the above method, it seems, would be insufficient for children with little knowledge of English. Such children would also need many opportunities for oral speaking and various experiences to broaden their concepts.

Thus, we see that several different methods have been tried with bilinguals in the United States. There is a need now for carefully controlled experimental studies using each of the different methods or combinations of methods to appraise the effectiveness of each with bilingual children. In these studies there should be valid pre-test and post-test measurements of ability and achievement, followed by rigorous and searching statistical analyses of the data. There should also be adequate measurements and descriptions of bilingualism present in the children studied and specific definitions and descriptions of the methods of teaching used to improve the bilingual children's language and reading, as well as the progress, if any, shown by the bilinguals as a result of such methods being used.

References

1. Burbeck, Edith, "Problems Presented to Teachers of Bilingual Pupils," *California Journal of Elementary Education*, 8 (August, 1939), 49-54.
2. Ching, Doris C., "Effects of a Six Month Remedial English Program on Oral, Writing, and Reading Skills of Third-Grade Hawaiian Bilingual Children," *Journal of Experimental Education*, 32 (Winter, 1963), 133-145.
3. Fuller, Lorraine, "The Effect of Kindergarten Speech Training on Primary Grade Progress and Achievement of Children with Foreign Language Handicaps," *California Journal of Elementary Education*, 4 (February, 1936), 165-173.
4. Herr, Selma E., "The Effect of Pre-First Grade Training upon Reading Readiness and Reading Achievement among Spanish-American Children," *Journal of Educational Psychology*, 37 (February, 1946), 87-102.
5. Morrison, J. Cayce, *The Puerto Rican Study, 1953-1957*. New York: Board of Education, 1958.
6. Patterson, Inez and Hazel M. Johnson, "Methods for Mexicans," *Sierra Educational News*, 33 (September, 1937), 12.
7. San Jose Experimental School, *We Learn English: A Preliminary Report of the Achievement of Spanish-Speaking Pupils in New Mexico*. Albuquerque: University of New Mexico, 1936.
8. Singer, Harry, "Bilingualism and Elementary Education," *Modern Language Journal*, 40 (December, 1956), 445-446.
9. Stone, Clarence R., "How to Adapt Reading Instruction to the Varying Needs of Children," *California Journal of Elementary Education*, 5 (February, 1936), 91-99.
10. Timothy, Sister M., "The Reading Problem of a Bilingual Child," *Elementary English*, 41 (March, 1964), 235-237.
11. Weinrich, Uriel, *Languages in Contact: Findings and Problems*. New York: Publication of the Linguistic Circle of New York, 1953, 1-2.

48 Is the Teaching of Foreign Languages in the Elementary School Worthwhile?

Donna Hussain

Hussain introduces a controversial issue: should foreign languages be taught in the elementary school? "What knowledge is of most worth?" is an old— and ever-recurring—question for elementary school teachers. Time and cost are other priority considerations. The reader may not agree with Hussain's conclusion, but he will find it a thought-provoking article.

Defend or attack Hussain's position as to analysis of each of the five objectives. Should the second language be provided for all children or only some children? Which children? At what age? By what instructional medium? Two articles cited in Selected References for Part Seven which also deal with aspects of foreign language instruction in the elementary school are by Moskowitz and Riestra.

A recent trend in American education has been the introduction of foreign languages in the elementary schools. Propaganda promoting a language program at the elementary level besets today's educators. Professional journals are filled with articles outlining teaching techniques. Teacher-training institutions include methods courses in foreign languages in their curricula. Inservice training programs are common among school districts. Even television has moved into the language field and prepared introductory lessons for elementary pupils with supplemental lesson guides for the teacher. The popularity of the language program with parents has lessened public attack on the quality of American education at the time when our schools have been unfavorably compared with other educational systems.

It is noteworthy that effective implementation of the language program is

From *Elementary English* 40:821-824; December 1963. Reprinted with permission of the National Council of Teachers of English and Donna Hussain, Las Cruces, New Mexico.

the subject commonly discussed rather than consideration of the inherent merits of the program. The value of elementary language instruction seems to be taken for granted. But have the objectives of the program been subjected to a thorough critical evaluation? Have we analyzed the ability of public schools to meet these objectives? Let us stop to consider whether the teaching of foreign languages at the elementary level is truly worthwhile.

Among the objectives most commonly propounded in support of the elementary language program are the following.

1. Children, unabashed mimics, with ease acquire a foreign tongue. Their still flexible palate enables them to mouth words which later become more difficult to pronounce. At the same time they enjoy experimenting with sounds and are not embarrassed, bored, or readily discouraged at the repetitious attempts necessary for perfecting an accent. Training of the ear and palate is one of the prime objectives of language instruction at the elementary level.

2. Social awareness is augmented by a language program. With the learning of a language comes understanding of a different way of life. Elementary schools make a point of integrating music, art, map studies, literature, *etc.*, with the formal language training so that the child is introduced to a culture as well as to a verbal tongue. In addition, children may be able to discern forces that have molded their own communities through language study. For example, in California the study of Spanish leads to an awareness of Spanish influences in community life.

3. An early introduction to foreign languages gives a child a background for intensive study at the high school level. Most American children have little experience with a foreign tongue in childhood and the plunge as a high school freshman into the grammatical complexities of another language is overwhelming. An understanding of the concept of language itself plus hearing and using a language is necessary before a grammatical approach to that language is meaningful. High schools rarely have time to provide the student with this background.

4. It is asserted that children with language training in elementary school will proceed at a faster rate in high school language courses than those without such an experience. High schools will, of course, review previous learnings but through effective grouping the child with background training should be able to cover more material than the ordinary pupil.

5. A final role of the elementary school in teaching language is one of stimulating interest. Language at this level is taught through activities children enjoy, such as songs, games, stories, *etc.* A very favorable attitude toward foreign language study is established at this level which should have beneficial effects on the high school program.

How well can the elementary school achieve these objectives? Let us consider each of these objectives in order.

Objective: To provide the child with the opportunity of learning and re-producing foreign sounds accurately.

Ideally the elementary school should employ bilingual teachers if the child is to have a truly meaningful language experience. A teacher's proficiency in the language is essential if a verbal approach to language is to be stressed. The bilingual teacher is also able to use foreign words at various times during the school day so that basic expressions soon become an integral part of the child's vocabulary. Learning is then not confined to a regularly scheduled language period.

Of course, many school districts cannot hire linguists to staff their faculties, for they lack both funds and a field of qualified applicants from which to choose. It is therefore common practice for districts to employ a special language teacher to visit classrooms once, or possibly twice a week. However, in teaching children a language, repetition and constant usage is essential. A special teacher simply lacks sufficient time for adequate instruction and must rely heavily on the classroom teacher for follow-up. The teacher, with a smattering knowledge of the language and undoubtedly an American accent, factors which have made her an unqualified language teacher in the first place, thus becomes the primary teaching agent. This is the basic weakness of hiring specialists.

The use of educational television for language instruction with follow-up lessons by the classroom teacher is also a common practice. Teachers who have used this system point out the difficulty of hearing new sounds through this media. There is no way to check whether the class has understood correctly and is reproducing the words accurately. Lessons can't be adapted to the speed or special needs of a class. The unqualified teacher is again responsible for the follow-up with all the limitations mentioned above.

In summary, elementary districts cannot meet the objective of training the child in hearing and reproducing sounds without being staffed by bilingual teachers. The unqualified teacher cannot be expected to succeed in a verbal approach to a foreign language.

Objective: To increase social awareness through language study.

Without doubt the study of a foreign language does increase social awareness. However, the social studies program can teach these social concepts effectively in far fewer class hours. For example, at the sixth grade most states introduce the western hemisphere. This is not strictly an academic approach for songs, dances, a limited Spanish vocabulary, and social customs are also learned. The desired social values are taught while eliminating time-consuming repetition and drill necessary in foreign language study.

Objective: To provide a background language experience so that a grammatical language approach in high school is meaningful.

That most high school freshmen are ill-prepared for the study of foreign languages is a well recognized fact. Certainly the language program at the elementary level under the direction of qualified teachers can be extremely effective in providing pupil preparedness. However, in the absence of bilingual elementary teachers, two alternative programs are recommended for providing pupils with language background.

First, it should be recognized that most freshmen undertake a grammatical study of another tongue without any understanding of the grammatical base of English. Oblique and nominative cases, transitive and intransitive verbs, differentiating between imperfect and past tenses: all sound as foreign to the pupil as the foreign words themselves. It is therefore recommended that an elementary and junior high program be established which would provide the student with grammatical concepts. This would contribute substantially to success in the study of another language as well as increasing competence in our mother tongue.

A second recommended program for establishing language background is the introduction of a comparative language course at the junior high level. A study of word forms and sentence constructions for expressing similar ideas in two or three different languages would be useful in establishing the important concept that English can't be translated word for word. Pupils could become familiar with the character, form, and sound of several languages. With this base, the decision of which language to study in high school would be far more rational, and necessary background for successful language study would be provided.

Rather than utilize class time for poor language instruction at the elementary level, time desperately needed for an effective program in the three R's, let us prepare the student for foreign language study by a junior high course in comparative languages and intensified English grammatical instruction.

Objective: To provide basic language learnings which will enable children to acquire a greater degree of language competency than is now possible through the regular high school program.

A speaking knowledge of a language can be retained only through usage. Even fluency in one's mother tongue can be lost through disuse. Since foreign languages are taught by the verbal approach in elementary schools, the program must be a continuous one if the instructional time spent is to be worthwhile. All too frequently, however, the elementary program is discontinued by junior highs due to heavy course loads and difficulties in scheduling. In the two years before language instruction is reintroduced, forgetting and unlearning take place to a high degree. Language background will, of course, be of value to the pupil, for relearning is far less painful than attacking new material. However, unless the junior high schools establish a language program, the amount of time spent at the elementary level can hardly be justified.

Consistency of language instruction is also hindered by the mobile American society. Frequent class turnover makes continuity of instruction impossible. Each year the teacher must adjust the program so that newcomers can participate. This means learning beginning material and basic expressions all over again. Children with no previous language experiences or those who have been taught another language prevent the class from making substantial progress with new material. Until a statewide or nationwide program is initiated, this problem will plague the elementary school.

It should also be recognized that most high schools give a choice of several languages to incoming freshmen. The child who selects a tongue different from the language studied at the elementary level derives limited values from his previous instruction. The applicable merits of his language experience, *i.e.*, developing a concept of language and social awareness, can be acquired in other areas as outlined earlier in this discussion.

Objective: To stimulate interest in foreign languages.

Certainly interest is stimulated in foreign languages through an elementary language program. Learning activities are "fun" at this level and a favorable attitude toward future language study is established. However, we certainly cannot justify the time spent in language instruction on this basis alone.

Conclusion

Elementary teachers agree that the school day is too short to cover all subjects adequately. Time limitations force teachers to slight basic areas. The introduction of a foreign language means a further trimming of the program, except in those few exceptions where the school day is extended for the purpose of special language instruction. Can we justify the time spent in elementary schools for language instruction?

If foreign languages were taught through the medium of bilingual teachers, if the program were state or nationwide, and if language instruction were continuous through the elementary and junior high schools, this writer would endorse the program wholeheartedly. The learning involved could compensate even for a reduced program in other subject areas.

However, the language program as operational in most districts today fails to satisfy most of its objectives. The weaknesses of the program far outweigh its merits. Without utilizing limited class time for foreign language study, many of the same basic objectives can be satisfied through other programs.

Is the teaching of foreign languages in the elementary school worthwhile? Under the present system, No!

49   A Programmed Course in Spelling

Alice K. Edgerton and Ruth W. Twombly

Programming of instruction is not a new approach or method of teaching, but it is still a controversial topic. This essay reports on programmed materials developed and used for spelling instruction in an attempt to provide an avenue toward individualized instruction.

Could the children learn to spell successfully using the program? Did the program help the children spell accurately 'where it counts'? What were the reactions of the children and teachers to the programmed instruction? If you were attempting a similar study, what changes would you make in the experimental design? What aspects of language arts instruction other than spelling lend themselves to a programmed approach? Are you aware of commercially available programmed materials suitable for elementary school language arts instruction? See the articles by Blake and Johnson cited in Selected References for Part Six for other ways to individualize spelling instruction.

Is a programmed course in spelling more effective than a course taught in the traditional way? The public schools of Weston, Massachusetts, decided to find out. In 1960–61, the elementary schools in this community began a programmed course in spelling for third-grade pupils (1).

The program had several purposes: to allow each child to work on his own level and at his own rate; to give each pupil a greater feeling of independence by allowing him to teach himself and to note his own progress; to increase the probability of success in learning so that most pupils would enjoy spelling; and to allow the teacher to devote the time saved to more complex subjects.

What type of machine was used?

The machine used in the program was designed by an elementary-school principal and constructed by a high-school teacher of industrial arts, both of

From *Elementary School Journal* 62:380-386; April 1962. Reprinted from "A Programmed Course in Spelling" by Alice K. Edgerton and Ruth W. Twombly by permission of The University of Chicago Press(© 1962 by The University of Chicago Press), Alice K. Edgerton, Reading Consultant, Waltham, Massachusetts, and Ruth W. Twombly, Public Schools, Weston, Massachusetts.

Weston. The machine consisted of a simple box with a slot at the top through which the pupil fed a piece of paper 8½ × 11 inches.

Each page had five frames of questions (and answers). As soon as the pupil completed an answer, he turned the knob of the machine to bring the correct answer into view. Thus his learning was reinforced immediately. The pupil proceeded from one frame to the next until the five frames on the page were completed. He could not turn the knob backward to change his answers.

The authors agree with B. F. Skinner when he wrote:

> The machine itself, of course, does not teach.. It simply brings the student into contact with the person who composed the material it presents. It is a labor-saving device because it can bring one programmer into contact with an indefinite number of students. This may suggest mass production, but the effect upon each student is surprisingly like that of a private tutor. The comparison holds in several respects: (a) There is a constant interchange between program and student. Unlike lectures, textbooks, and the usual audio-visual aids, the machine induces sustained activity. The student is always alert and busy. (b) Like a good tutor the machine insists that a given point be thoroughly understood, either frame by frame or set by set, before the student moves on. Lectures, textbooks, and their mechanized equivalents, on the other hand, proceed without making sure that the student understands and easily leave him behind. (c) Like a good tutor the machine presents just that material for which the student is ready. It asks him to take only that step which he is at the moment best equipped and most likely to take. (d) Like a skillful tutor the machine helps the student to come up with the right answer. It does this in part through the orderly construction of the program and in part with techniques of hinting, prompting, suggesting and so on, derived from an analysis of verbal behavior. (e) Lastly, of course, the machine, like the private tutor, reinforces the student for every correct response, using this immediate feedback not only to shape his behavior most efficiently but to maintain it in strength in a manner which the layman would describe as 'holding the student's interest' (2: 143).

How were the spelling words chosen and grouped?

The spelling words for this program were chosen on the basis of frequency of use in writing in third grade. They were compiled from lists prepared by Henry D. Rinsland, E. W. Dolch, and James A. Fitzgerald (3, 4, 5).

If a word followed a phonetic or a structural principle, it was included in a group of words of the same nature. For instance, the units included such categories as "short vowel words," "words ending in twin consonants," and "words with the *ai*, *ay*, or *oa* vowel teams." This kind of grouping, it was felt, might help the child not only to spell new words, but to read them as well. To point out exceptions to the rules, non-phonetic words in common use were included in the program.

How were the frames constructed?

The frames were constructed with several principles in mind. Words used in the directions were kept at a second-grade reading level. More difficult words —such as *directions, underline,* and *syllable*—were placed on a special page, which the child examined before turning to the machine. If a child had trouble with the vocabulary he was free to get help from another child.

To make sure the pupil read the directions for each exercise, the wording was varied. At one time the pupil might be asked to circle the vowels. At another time he might be asked to underline them.

The prompts, or cues, given for each word were also varied. The pupil might be asked to write words that rhyme with the cue word. For the cue word *cake,* he might write the rhyming words *bake* and *make.* The pupil might be asked to begin or to finish a word, and draw pictures to illustrate. A frame of this kind might show: __eep or chur__. In response, the child might insert letters to spell *sheep* and *church.* The pupil might be asked to fill in a word omitted from the context: The giraffe has a long n___. Or the pupil might be asked to find little words in words: *arm* in *warm,* or *all* in *small.*

Words were presented from two to seven times in the unit. How many times a word was presented depended on how difficult it was.

Simple drawings were used in various ways. A frame might show a picture of a nest, and the pupil might be asked to choose from a list of words those that had the vowel sound of the word that was illustrated.

Drawings were also used to explain words in a sentence. One frame presented the sentences: "Jack sailed his boat along the coast." "In winter it's fun to coast downhill." To bring out the two meanings of the word *coast,* each sentence was accompanied by a drawing. The drawing for the first sentence showed a boat sailing along the coast. The drawing for the second sentence showed a boy coasting down a hill.

When a word was programmed for the last time, the pupil was asked to write the word for the picture, with no cues other than the picture to help him.

In short, the units were as varied as possible, to prevent carelessness and to maintain interest.

What procedures were used?

An average unit of work was made up of fifteen to twenty words, programmed in sequential steps. One unit might be made up of fifty to sixty frames. The pupil's first step was to complete from fifteen to twenty-five frames of the unit. His second step was to take a word test in which he was asked to identify pictures of the words he had studied or to supply the word missing from the context. For example, he looked at a picture of a train and wrote *train,* or he read "The color of snow is _____" and wrote *white.*

Pupils who missed more than one word on this test returned to the teaching machine and finished the remaining thirty-five frames in the unit. The frames had enough practice material to insure reasonable success on the posttest. Few pupils failed a second time.

The third and final step consisted of writing sentences heard through earphones attached to a tape recorder.

Each taped lesson began with hints for good writing. Here is one set of reminders: "By now you are in the habit of writing in a good position, of holding your pencil correctly, of tilting your paper, and of resting your arm on the desk. Have you noticed how these good habits help to improve your writing?"

Pauses between phrases were long enough to allow most pupils to finish. Because each pupil had previously had many opportunities to spell each word on the programmed pages, he usually remembered the correct spelling of the words on these tests.

How did the experimental and the control classes compare?

Classes in the Weston elementary schools are grouped heterogeneously. An IBM machine is used to form the groups on the basis of scores on the California Test of Mental Maturity. Pupil scores on the Kuhlmann-Anderson Intelligence Tests were also available. As Table 1 shows, no significant differences appeared between the control group and the experimental group on the basis of intelligence quotient.

Table 1

Mean Intelligence Quotients and Mean Grade Equivalent Scores in Spelling for Pilot, Experimental, and Control Groups

Group	Number of Pupils	Mean Intelligence Quotient	Mean Grade Equivalent Score September	Mean Grade Equivalent Score June	Difference in Years and Months
Pilot..............	24	111	3.5	4.8	1.3
Experimental	60	112	3.8	5.2	1.4
Control	66	110	3.7	4.6	.9

In September, at the beginning of the school year, three groups of eight children each were used as pilot groups to test the spelling units as they were developed. For these groups, the teachers chose children whose achievement in spelling was average and children who had reading and spelling problems. It was felt that if the units were revised so that such children could understand the directions, work with the pictures, and use the tape recorder, success in the classroom would be more probable. These pupils were of great value as critics.

In planning for revisions, the programmer took her cue from Skinner, who wrote: "A trial run of the first version of a program quickly reveals frames which need to be altered or sequences which need to be lengthened. One or two revisions in the light of a few dozen responses work a great improvement" (2: 151).

In December, after the pilot groups had tried several complete units, the program was extended to a classroom of thirty pupils. The pilot groups continued to criticize new units as they were developed for classroom use. In January a second classroom began to use the machines, and by April the children in three of the six third-grade classrooms in Weston were participating.

There was no programmed spelling in the three remaining third-grade classrooms in Weston. The children in these classrooms (half of the third-grade enrollment in the town) composed the control group. They were taught spelling by the usual textbook method.

Was the evaluation continuous?

The responses of the children in the pilot group were scrutinized daily. If clarification proved necessary, items were reworded or pictures redrawn. For example, some children saw the picture for *leg* and wrote *knee*, for *stone* and wrote *rock*, for *pup* and wrote *dog*. However, these difficulties did not occur in sentence dictation when the word was heard in context over the tape recorder.

Most word tests consisted of two parts. Part 1 included words that had been introduced in the programmed pages. Part 2 included a small number of new words that illustrated a phonetic or structural rule that had been presented. For example, in one unit the pupil was asked to spell the word *rope*. The children had been taught that many one-syllable words that have a long vowel sound end with silent *e*. If the child applied the rule, he could spell the word, even though it was not on the spelling list for third grade.

How well children followed directions could also be determined, for the children wrote all tests and sentence dictation in individual notebooks. The children corrected these tests themselves. The review tests, however, were corrected by the teacher. This periodic inspection allowed the teacher to evaluate each child's progress and encouraged careful work.

The children were not under pressure for time. Even when they were taking sentence dictation on the tape recorder, enough time was provided for everyone. Each sentence was presented four times: it was read as a sentence, repeated in short phrases, repeated as a sentence; and finally the seven or eight sentences in the exercise were read in sequence to allow the child to proofread.

How were spelling gains measured?

Spelling gains were measured by the Buckingham Extension of the Ayres Spelling Scale. The Ayres thirty-word test from the L Scale was given in September to all third-grade children. The M Scale was given in June. The results were converted to grade equivalent scores.

What results were obtained?

An analysis of grade equivalent scores between September and June shows a mean gain of thirteen months for the pilot group, fourteen months for the experimental group, and nine months for the control group. The results are shown in Table 1. These gains show an average improvement of four months for the pilot group and five months for the experimental (machine-taught) groups. That is, for each month during which the children in the experimental group used the machines, they gained a month over and above normal expectations. That these gains are significant is indicated by a critical ratio of 2.27 and a probability of .02.

Gains were restricted by the fact that the final test was too easy for the children in the experimental group, many of whom scored one hundred. Moreover, many pupils started the machine program late. Before the final test only about a third of the experimental pupils had completed the programmed course. A full year of programmed spelling for third-graders might result in a two-year gain in spelling achievement.

Did the programmed course give the pupils a greater feeling of independence, success, and enjoyment? The response of the pupils was unreservedly enthusiastic. They were greatly disturbed whenever anything prevented their having a spelling lesson.

One teacher said, "Spelling, ordinarily a tedious subject, became a delight." Another teacher remarked, "Children found spelling was fun and truly enjoyed it."

The children were quick to master the handling of materials, machines, word tests, and recording of scores.

Carefully selected third-graders proved capable of operating the tape recorder. The children considered this assignment a great honor and enforced strict regulations of their own. They often set up the equipment before school and stored it at the end of the lesson.

But there were difficulties. Children were tempted to spend too much time telling other members of the group what they could or could not do. At times too many bosses emerged. It was not always easy for the teacher to conduct a reading class with one group of pupils while another group was occupied with spelling. But when the pupils were taking sentence dictation by tape, all was still enough to hear the proverbial pin drop.

Was much time saved by this method? Yes, the teachers were unanimous on this point. The time the pupils saved was devoted to enrichment reading. The time the teachers saved was used for class preparation for reading and other subjects. These two important by-products of the programmed course, while not reflected in spelling improvement as such, are gains worthy of consideration.

What problems did the teachers encounter?

In a questionnaire at the end of the school year, they reported that the tape recorder had the greatest trouble potential. The children had to become fairly adept with the recorder because they were required to select from the tape the sentence tests appropriate to the unit they were studying. This was not easy when several groups were at various points in the program. The problem was less troublesome after tape chairmen were appointed.

While eight pupils used the machines by themselves at a separate table, the teacher taught reading to a second group, and the remaining children did seatwork. Three twenty-minute periods were required before the entire class completed spelling study. The problem of scheduling was not an easy one.

Perhaps the biggest shortcoming was the costly consumption of paper. The type of machine used in the program required pupils to write directly on the programmed sheets.

Was the experiment continued?

The 1960–61 programmed spelling experiment was considered successful by pupils, teachers, and administrators. Funds were therefore budgeted for an item analysis of all frames and for revision of the programmed material. The analysis and the revision were carried out in the summer of 1961. Seven third-grade classrooms using sixty-four machines became involved in the new program.

Because of the high consumption of paper, the machine was redesigned. The new machine makes it possible for each pupil to write his responses on a roll of adding-machine tape. With this machine, programmed material can be re-used.

The Weston teachers involved in programmed instruction are inclined to agree with Skinner when he wrote:

In assigning certain mechanizable functions to machines, the teacher emerges in his proper role as an indispensable human being. He may teach more students than heretofore—this is probably inevitable if the world-wide demand for education is to be satisfied—but he will do so in fewer hours and with fewer burdensome chores (2: 156).

As a result of the third-grade experiment, a programmed spelling course was begun in fourth-grade classrooms in Weston.

References

1. The program was financed through a grant from the Ford Foundation Fund for the Advancement of Education.
2. B. F. Skinner. "Teaching Machines," *Teaching Machines and Programmed Learning: A Source Book*, pp. 137-58. Edited by A. A. Lumsdaine and Robert Glaser. Washington: Department of Audio-Visual Instruction, National Education Association, 1960.
3. Henry D. Rinsland. *A Basic Vocabulary of Elementary School Children.* New York: Macmillan Company, 1945.
4. E. W. Dolch. *Better Spelling.* Champaign, Illinois: Garrard Press, 1942.
5. James A. Fitzgerald. *The Teaching of Spelling.* Milwaukee: Bruce Publishing Company, 1951.

50   Teaching of English in the Mass Media

Samuel L. Becker

Even though the title of this essay uses the term 'mass media,' it focuses upon the teaching of English via educational television, both commercial and closed-circuit. Also, while considerable emphasis in this article is directed at secondary and college levels, it provides a view of the present and future possibilities of such approaches at the elementary school level.

What contributions may be made by the television medium to attainment of goals in various facets of the language arts program? How do you interpret the fact that many comparative studies have been able to show no difference in achievement between TV and non-TV students? Is this a factor for or against TV? Choose one topic and outline goals, content, and methods for an experiment utilizing one of the mass media. (See the article in Part One, "The Classroom Teacher as a Researcher.") Additional information about TV as a medium for language arts instruction is contained in the article by Miner cited in Selected References for Part Seven.

With the increasing use of mass media, particularly television, for instruction in English, it is essential that the research on such use be reviewed and evaluated as a guide for teachers and researchers in the area. Because the bulk of the recent research has been concerned with television, the focus will be upon research in this medium.

Until the advent of television, instructors in colleges and universities were distinguished in this field primarily by their reluctance to use any of the mass media in their classes. The rapidly rising enrollments which accompanied the maturation of television, coupled with the lure of research money from the Fund for the Advancement of Education and the U. S. Department of Health, Education, and Welfare, has caused this situation to change. For example, since

From *Elementary English* 38:250-258; April 1961. Reprinted with permission of the National Council of Teachers of English and Samuel L. Becker, Professor of Speech, The University of Iowa, Iowa City.

1954 the television medium has been utilized for formal campus instruction in English composition at San Francisco State College (26), Purdue University (23), New York University (14), and the State University of Iowa (2). English literature has been taught via television at New York University (20), Los Angeles City and Valley Colleges (12), and the State University of Iowa (3). Courses in speech have been taught wholly or in part by television at Pennsylvania State University (16), the State University of Iowa (3), the University of Illinois (8), the University of California at Los Angeles (4), Wayne State University (11), Los Angeles City and Valley Colleges (12), and the University of South Dakota (24). Innumerable colleges and universities have telecast such courses to the general public.

Television programs specifically produced for English or speech instruction in the public schools have been tried in Evanston (Illinois) (6), Schenectady (New York) (1), St. Louis (13), Dade County (Florida) (10), Washington County (Maryland) (9), Lincoln (Nebraska) (15:62-65), Detroit (15), San Diego (25), New York (21), Philadelphia (22), Norfolk (Virginia) (17), Southwestern Indiana (27), and Oklahoma City (18). These, of course, are only a sample.

There are many ways in which we could categorize the research which has been done on the above in-school uses of television. Because the most fruitful research in the long run tends to be that which focuses upon important educational goals, we will examine recent research according to what it tells us of the ability of the television medium to contribute to the attainment of some of the major goals of English instruction.

Reading

In the area of reading, the research evidence indicates no consistent differences between television-aided instruction and conventional instruction for either secondary school or college students. Scores on a literature test for students taking a television-correspondence course in twelfth grade English in Nebraska did not differ significantly from scores of students taking the course in conventional fashion. However, significant differences were found favoring non-television students on a Mechanics of English test and an English Comprehension test (15). In Washington County, Maryland, where reading was taught to elementary students in the first through the third grades wih the aid of television, the children *reported* that television helped them to learn better (9:17-18). At Evanston, Illinois, where television-supplemented instruction in English-speech was given to tenth grade students, the researchers reported that test scores of the experimental students on ability to read and interpret a short story were "about like the scores of a group of students with comparable I.Q.

scores in regular English classes" (6:20). The State University of Iowa found no significant differences in the reading rate and comprehension of freshmen taught Communication Skills in part by television recordings and those taught in more conventional ways (2:14). Oklahoma City reported no significant differences between television and control students in American Literature classes on comprehension and appreciation or interpretation of literary materials (19:10). When Modern Literature was taught in part by television to college students at Iowa, no significant differences in learning were found when the television students were compared with either small discussion sections or with combination lecture-discussion sections of the course. The criterion measure was an essay examination on the knowledge and understanding of literature (3:20-21). New York University found no significant difference in the literary comprehension of students taught English partly via television and those taught in conventionally small groups (14:18). In an early study in which The Literature of England was taught in part by television at New York University, the tentative conclusion from a comparison of course grades was that "the A and B students profited about equally from the two kinds of learning situations; that the average and poorer students . . . may have learned better (from the televised instruction)" (20:26). Los Angeles and Valley Colleges found no significant difference between students who received Introduction to Literature instruction by television and those who received it in other ways (12:12-13).

No television studies were found which compared groups on the basis of skill in outlining, literary appreciation, or acquisition of criteria for evaluating literature or public address.

Listening

Instructional television research which seemed to consider listening as a course goal was even more sparse. At Evanston, it was found that the scores of television students on the STEP Tests of Ability to Listen were not significantly different than for other English students with comparable I.Q. scores (6:20). It was also reported that television did not "prevent the growth of a wide range of interests in the activities of the course" at Evanston. These activities included literature, theatre, and the media. This interest was checked by means of questionnaires and attendance at plays (6:21). At Detroit, it was found that students who had received instruction in American Literature by means of television scored significantly higher on a listening test than did those who received their literature instruction in a more conventional manner (15:49). With freshman Communication Skills students, Iowa found no significant differences between television-kinescope students and control students on gain in listening ability (2:14). In Dade County, Florida, senior high school students indicated that note-taking was more difficult at first and they had to listen more intently in television courses than in other courses (10:45-46).

None of the reported television studies indicate a concern with student gain in comprehension or appreciation of dramatic forms, or in acquisition of criteria for evaluating what is heard.

Speaking

Five studies were found which were concerned with systematically testing the effects of teaching speech-making by television. At Evanston, television students made "generally adequate progress in the . . . ability to speak effectively" and "liking" for and "self-confidence in doing so." However, the television students were more often rated lower "in aspects of speaking related to content and thinking" (6:20-21). At Pennsylvania State University it was found that "that was little difference" between the grades earned by students receiving part of their basic speech course instruction by television and those receiving all of it in conventional ways (16:4). At Los Angeles and Valley Colleges, where experimental students in Public Speaking and Voice and Diction received one-third of their classroom instruction by television, no significant differences were found in the speech tests of these and students receiving all of their instruction in regular classes (12:12-13). At Iowa, no significant differences were found in speech ratings between students receiving the principles of communication from television recordings and those receiving comparable material from their regular classroom instructors or from readings (2:14). A somewhat unique use of television for speech instruction was tried at the University of California at Los Angeles. In an effort to improve physical delivery, each student was permitted to view himself on a television monitor while delivering three speeches. The researchers reported that "the TV monitor as employed did not lead to greater than normal progress in skills of physical delivery" (4:128).

No studies involving the use of television for speech instruction have reported an evaluation of student achievement in recognizing the social and psychological factors involved in communicating with people of different backgrounds, or in knowledge or practice of discussion with its accompanying interpersonal problems. However, in regard to the latter, the researchers at Hagerstown have reported some pertinent findings from non-speech courses taught by television to sixth and eighth graders.

A preliminary investigation of group structure was made using sociometric techniques in sixth and eighth grade classes in television and non-television schools. The study revealed that group structure seems to change with television resulting in fewer "isolates.". . . (The) type, frequency, and direction of participation seems to change in the television classroom. The traditional pattern of teacher-student participation in which the classroom teacher asks questions or gives directions and the pupils respond is altered. The teacher on the television screen seems to upset this pattern. The students respond to him and then project or transfer their discussion to other students in the classroom and a natural give-and-take situation is encouraged. Some students who took little part in classroom activities prior to the introduction of television were now taking an active part in the discussions that followed the telecasts (9:18).

Writing

More research appears to have been done on the teaching of writing by means of television than the teaching of any of the other skills of communication. Experiments have been reported on three college and two high school courses in which at least one of the goals was the teaching of English composition. Results of an experiment with a composition course at Purdue University indicated that conventionally taught students tended to achieve slighly better ratings on their test themes than students who received two-thirds of their instruction by television. The results, however, were not consistent nor was a consistent pattern found between level of student ability (as assessed by the freshman orientation English test) and achievement in theme writing (23:12-17). At New York University, where the experimental students received three-fifths of their English composition instruction via television, inconsistent results were again obtained. When student achievement in theme writing was tested for each of three levels of initial theme writing ability, it appeared that television instruction may have been somewhat more effective for the low ability students while conventional instruction may have been more effective for the high ability students (14:16-17). This is in contradiction to some educational research which seems to indicate that, if method of instruction makes a difference, it is usually for the low ability students (and not for those of high ability). In the Iowa experiment, in which somewhat less than one-fourth of the instruction in Communication Skills was by means of television recordings, no consistent differences were found between the television and non-television students in achievement in theme writing. Neither was a significant interaction found which would indicate that students of differing academic ability were affected differently by the various means of instruction (2:14-15). In the English-speech course taught partially by television at Evanston, students made "at least as high marks" on written composition tests as non-television students in the preceding year, "and at least as high and perhaps higher marks than might have been expected on the basis of I.Q. scores" (6:19-20). Television students appeared to do somewhat more poorly than other tenth grade English students on the Mechanics of Expression test in Oklahoma City (19:11). No significant difference on the language arts examination was found between television and non-television students in Philadelphia (22:21). Only one published report was found by this writer of a controlled experiment on the teaching of English by television in which no supplementary instruction was carried on in the school. Ninth grade English composition was telecast to two St. Louis public schools for thirty minutes a day, five days a week for one semester. There were 122 students viewing the broadcasts as a group in one school, 146 in the other. "One experienced teacher was in each room to receive assignments and meet any unforeseen occurrences—but not to teach in the usual sense of the word. She was assisted by a college graduate who was not a professional teacher." In addition, classes of 70 and 98 second-grade students viewed lessons in spelling for twenty minutes a day, five days a week, over a period of two semesters. Again an experienced teacher was in charge of each of the two rooms but did not teach. In English composition, "there was a suggestion that they (the television students) made slightly better gains." In second grade spelling, the television and the conventionally taught students "did equally well in a test of second grade words, but when they were tested on words considered above the usual second grade level, the conventionally taught students did better than those in the experiment" (26:34-35).

None of the televison research on writing instruction appears to have included a consideration of such criteria as the ability to evaluate one's own work, motivation to write, or what might be called "writing fright" (the counterpart of speech fright and probably at least as important a hindrance to effective communication).

Limitations of Existing Research

Let us summarize the weaknesses in the existing research on utilizing television in English instruction.

In no case was there sufficient control to enable effects to be attributed to a single cause and thus to be repeatable at will. There consistently have been more differences between the experimental groups and control groups in these studies than simply the presence or absence of television. There appears to be only one published report of a controlled experiment in which the televised instruction was not supplemented by more conventional classroom instruction, and the classroom supplementation of the electronic presentations has been different from the activity going on in the control classrooms at comparable times. Admittedly, optimum instruction by television involves a complex of factors but, in the experimental stage when we are trying to learn as much as possible about these phenomena, the wisdom of confounding these factors is questionable. Confounding the effects of the medium with the effects of supplementary activity makes it virtually impossible to determine what the effect of television per se has been. Also, because of this, where contradictory research results have been obtained, there is little chance to find the probable reasons for the differences.

Related to the failure to isolate variables has been the failure to repeat studies with comparable goals, students, and procedures. We are dealing with laws of probability in the social sciences and it is only through duplication of experiments that we are able to increase the precision of these laws. The fact that there has been *one* instance in which college freshmen were able to recall the principles of communication better or learned to write themes better when they received the principles of such communication from listening to a class-room teacher or when they received them from viewing a television presentation does not permit us to generalize with confidence about the relative merits of these media for communicating, even to college freshmen. One of the axioms which we learn early in experimentation is that anything can happen *once*. Until studies are repeated, we have little chance of developing laws for this type of classroom learning.

We have no evidence yet of the effect of television instruction over a long period of time, after a student has been receiving part of his instruction in this way over a four or five year period or longer and any novelty effect has been dissipated. Presumably, some evidence on this point will be forthcoming soon from Pennsylvania State University where a large number of courses have been taught by television since 1954 (7) and from the five year study in Washington County, Maryland (9). There is some evidence scattered through the literature that students must learn to learn from television, that teachers must learn to teach by television, and that student attitudes toward televised instruction be-come more favorable with experience in receiving instruction in this way. All of these would seem to indicate that learning may increase proportionately with time. Whether these differences would be great enough to overcome loss of the novelty effect or whether these differences truly will be found to exist when they are isolated and examined systematically is not known at this time.

In the studies which have employed criterion measures other than simple retention tests, the kinds of measuring instruments used tend to be unreliable. This makes it extremely difficult to obtain statistically significant differences between groups, even when there may truly be such differences. For example, methodological studies have consistently shown low reliability for theme and speech ratings except in those cases where an impractical number of raters was used or where the raters were given lengthy training in rating the specific phenomenon. This may well account for some of the many "no significant differ-ences" found in instructional television studies. To improve our research in this area we must obtain more precise measurement, which means better measur-ing instruments and procedures.

Another important weakness of the research which has been concerned with using television for teaching English is that some of the major goals of such instruction apparently have been ignored in the evaluations. The requirements for meaningful research in instructional television are the same as the requirements for almost any sound educational research. One must begin with course goals, plan experimental conditions which one believes will best meet these goals, and then test whether these specific goals were obtained. Too often, a decision has been made simply to use television or, having television, to use it in some particular way. We plan our procedures and content for the course and then start to worry about how to test the effect of the procedures or the retention of the content. It seems a wasteful procedure to worry about whether students can be taught some sort of behavior better via television than via some other medium until we have some knowledge, or at least some testable hypotheses, about the way such behaviors are learned.

None of the above is meant to be a condemnation of recent research in instructional television. These investigations have contributed to our knowledge of learning and can contribute much more. The weaknesses of this research have been the weaknesses of the bulk of educational research. Television is an excellent means for observing what goes on in the classroom. It may prove to be the only means by which some of the more basic issues may be studied.

Suggestions for Future Research

So where do we go from here? What kinds of research most need doing? What kinds will be most helpful to us in understanding the ways in which television can be useful in English instruction? What kinds can help us learn to teach better? Classroom research conducted by the regular teacher is highly important at this point, because a great deal of the needed research in teaching English by television can probably be *best* done by the classroom teacher. Important contributions can be made in this area without large research teams or vast experience in research. One should have, however, a familiarity with the research which has been done, both on the teaching of English and on utilization of the media for instruction. One should also be able to describe accurately the conditions under which the experiment was done so that other teachers or researchers can duplicate the instruction or experiment and expect to come up with the same results. Most important, and generally most difficult, one should be able to approach the research with objectivity, a willingness to search for all of the facts and to accept them when they are found.

One of the kinds of research which can often best be done by teachers in the field is the duplication of experiments done in only one or two school systems. Until some of the teaching methods which have been tried in one or two places are experimented with in many places, by many different teachers, with various kinds of students, and various kinds of school situations, we will have little idea of the applicability of the present findings.

Classroom teachers can also make important contributions to our knowledge of motivating students in English. If there is virtue in any usage of the television medium for instructional purposes, its use for motivational purposes would appear to be foremost. The professional researcher is well aware that learning and memory are dependent in part upon motivation. The question of the *specific kinds* of experience which will encourage students to write or speak better, or to read better books, can probably best come from the classroom teacher who has been faced with the problem of motivating various kinds of students and who has, in most cases, tried many types of procedures for this purpose and observed the results. Television provides an opportunity to try additional procedures or, possibly, to make some of the procedures tried in the classroom more effective.

Another kind of media research which often can grow out of the experiences of the classroom teacher is that which focuses upon the attitudes, skills, or knowledge which children have trouble getting from books or the usual classroom work. A knowledge of these problem areas, coupled with a knowledge of media research, should make it possible to come up with hypotheses about ways in which television or the other media can help to solve the problem. Once such hypotheses are developed and put in operational terms, the most important and difficult part of the research is done.

Though there has been a great deal of research comparing "conventional" (whatever that means) to "televised" instruction, little attention has been given to the problem of the best way to use television, or any of the other media, once the decision is made that there is something to be gained by media use. In spite of the impression one might get from reading the research literature, television is not a *method* of instruction, it is a *medium* capable of transmitting and being used with many different methods. An infinite number of studies need to be done to compare various methods of using television. Not only must various content and techniques of programming be studied, but various methods of integrating the televised material with other work in the classroom must be compared.

Whichever of these problems you decide to attack, start with some specific educational goals. Do not think in terms of the content of a course or courses. Decide what it is that the student should be able to do and know at the end of the year which he does not now. Try to make these goals as specific as possible. For example, do not say that the student should be able to appreciate literature. This cliché of the profession has little meaning to the teacher who wants to know what to teach or how to teach it and little meaning to the researcher who wants to find out whether it has been learned. Goals must be defined in terms of ob-

servable behavior. For example, you might decide that "appreciation of literature" means in part that, given a choice, a student will read T. S. Eliot instead
of Bret Harte, or perhaps vice versa. Or you might mean that a student will vol-
untarily start reading more books, without their being assigned in school. Or
you might mean that a student can indicate some of the basic insights of the
authors whose works he reads. These are not necessarily good definitions of
"appreciation of literature," but they are descriptions of behavior which can
be observed objectively. Objectivity means, in this case, stating goals and
measures as descriptions of behavior that can be counted or observed by any
observer.

Once this is done, think of all of the experiences which may help students
to reach the goals. Consider at this point not only what you have done in the
past, or what has been done by others, but every possible experience which
might be carried out in an ideal situation. It would appear that our educational
systems will be undergoing dramatic changes in the next few decades. What
seems completely impossible at this point may be quite practical within a very
short time. In other words, this is the stage at which the most imaginative thinking needs to be done. There are many standard methods for teaching each aspect
of English. On the other hand, it is almost certain that these standard methods
do not exhaust the field, that there are methods as yet unthought of or, at least,
untried.

Along with the experiences which may help students to reach the outlined
goals, you must consider, obviously, the course content.

Once the goals, content, and methods are defined, you have the information needed to plan your experiment intelligently. For example, you will be able
to see which methods cannot be carried out with conventional classroom instruction and which might be done with one or more of the media. You will be able
to see which types of content are difficult to learn under present classroom conditions and how some of the media could be helpful. You will be able to see which
goals are not now being adequately met and which may be if approached differently. I have explained elsewhere (5:23-29) a technique for making this analysis. The technique is essentially the formation of a three dimensional diagram
with goals along one dimension, content along another, and methods along the
third. Such a structure helps not only to solve the problems above but is an aid
in devising measuring instruments for it permits the researcher to "see" what
content and method combinations are to achieve each goal.

Worry little or not at all about "controls" or statistics. The suggested purpose is to explore combinations of methods utilizing the vast wealth of mass
media with which we are surrounded. This may mean bringing the media into
the classroom, or it may mean supplementing your teaching with outside assignments. It means, at any rate, that we keep ourselves aware, week to week and day

by day, of the fare available, and furthermore, that we allow our imagination to be free to devise ways of teaching well.

References

1. Ambrosino, Michael J., Dunstand, William H., and Haake, Bernard F., "The Schenectady Experiment." Schenectady, New York: The Schenectady Public Schools, Undated. Mimeographed.
2. Becker, Samuel L., Dallinger, Carl A., Crosby, Harry H., and Gold, David, *Communication Skills: An Experiment in Instructional Method.* Iowa City: The State University of Iowa, August, 1958.
3. ———, Dunlap, Rhodes, and Gerber, John C., "A Comparison of Three Methods of Teaching Modern Literature." Iowa City: The State University of Iowa, June, 1957. Mimeographed.
4. ———, "Teaching Speech by Television? Some Historical Notes," *Central States Speech Journal,* XI (1960), 126-130.
5. ———, "We Need a Stronger Research Base," *Opportunities for Learning: Guidelines for Television,* ed. Alexander Frazier and Harold E. Wigren, NEA, Washington, D.C., 1960, 23-29.
6. Carpenter, William, Fair, Jean, Heald, James, and Mitchell, Wanda, "The Use of Closed Circuit Television at Evanston Township High School." Evanston, Ill.: Evanston Township High School, Undated. Mimeographed.
7. Carpenter, C. R., and Greenhill, L. P., *An Investigation of Closed Circuit Television for Teaching University Courses, Report Number 2.* University Park: The Pennsylvania State University, Spring, 1958.
8. Cobin, Martin T. and Clevenger, Theodore, Jr., "An Experiment in Open Circuit Television Instruction in the Basic Course in Oral Interpretation," *Speech Monographs,* XXVI (1959), 149-154.
9. *Closed Circuit Television Teaching in Washington County 1958-1959.* Hagerstown, Maryland: The Board of Education, March, 1959.
10. "The Dade County (Greater Miami) Educational Television Project." Miami, Florida: Dade County Board of Education, Undated. Mimeographed.
11. Ellery, John B., "A Pilot Study of the Nature of Aesthetic Experiences Associated with Television and Its Place in Education." Detroit: Wayne State University, January 15, 1959. Mimeographed.
12. "An Evaluation of Closed-Circuit Instructional Television in Los Angeles City College and Los Angeles Valley College, Final Report." Los Angeles City School Districts, Division of Extension and Higher Education, 1959. Multilithed.
13. Herminghaus, Earl G., "An Investigation of Television Teaching." St. Louis: The St. Louis Educational Television Commission and the St. Louis Public Schools, September, 1956. Mimeographed.
14. Klapper, Hope Lunin, *Closed Circuit Television as a Medium of Instruction at New York University, 1956-1957.* New York: New York University, October, 1956.
15. "The National Program in the Use of Television in the Public Schools." New York: The Fund for the Advancement of Education, January, 1959. Multilithed.

16. Nelson, Harold, "The Use of Closed-Circuit Television in Teaching the Basic Speech Course," *The Speech Teacher*, VII (1958).
17. "The Norfolk City Experiment in Instructional Television, The Evaluation Report for the 1958-1959 School Year." Norfolk: Norfolk City School Board, 1959. Mimeographed.
18. "Oklahoma City's Secondary School Report on Television Teaching for 1958-59." Oklahoma City: Board of Education, Undated. Mimeographed.
19. "Oklahoma City Analysis of Achievement Test Results, 1958-1959." Oklahoma City: Board of Education, Undated. Mimeographed.
20. Pollock, Thomas Clark, *Closed Circuit Television as a Medium of Instruction, 1955-1956*. New York: New York University, October, 1956.
21. *Progress Report on Educational Television, New York State Educational Department Experiment:* "Instructional Television." Albany, New York: State Education Department, August 30, 1957.
22. "Second Report of the National Experiment of Television Teaching in Large Classes . . . 1958-1959." Philadelphia: Philadelphia Public Schools, Undated. Mimeographed.
23. Seibert, W. F., "An Evaluation of Televised Instruction in College English Composition." Lafayette: Purdue University, July, 1958. Mimeographed.
24. Skaine, James C., "A Study Evaluating the Conventional and Televised Lecture Methods as Employed in the Speech I Course at the State University of South Dakota." Vermillion: University of South Dakota, 1958. Mimeographed.
25. Stanley, DeG., "Educational Television Programs and Evaluations, 1954-1955." San Diego, California: San Diego City Schools, June 30, 1955. Mimeographed.
26. *Teaching by Television*. New York: The Ford Foundation and the Fund for the Advancement of Education, 1959.
27. "Testing Results." Evansville: Southwestern Indiana Educational TV Council, 1959. Mimeographed.

51   Educational Media

Robin Aurelius

Much technology is now available for teachers of language arts and this article suggests some media and some of their possibilities.

Which of the media mentioned have you used in the language classroom with children? For what purpose and with what result? What uses of various media can you suggest in addition to the ones mentioned? For example, one of the more significant contributions of video-tape recording is the possibility of analyzing (self-evaluating) one's own performance—seeing yourself as others see you. Other articles germane to this topic in Selected References for Part Seven have been written by King, Miner, Murray and Karel. Also see the article by Duker in Selected References for Part Three.

A notion prevails that teachers despise and ignore educational training systems, and that they deplore the necessity of operating and maintaining the newer electronic equipment and machinery available to the teaching art.

It may be more accurate to observe that teachers are not aware of the technology now being used successfully to improve and expand the teaching of reading, speech and writing skills. It is the purpose of this article to report some of the possibilities which could actually ease teacher load and vastly expand media for the teaching of language.

Motion picture

The 16-millimeter film has long been a leader in dramatic and dynamic mass communications. Gone are the days of heavy-handed and didactic handling of the media; now emerge new dimensions with color and quality sound reproduction. Commercial producers are supplying more lively material. Educational film critics (and television critics who have promoted the burgeoning

From *California Teachers Association Journal* 63:35 ff; March 1967. Reprinted with permission of California Teachers Association and Robin Aurelius, Media Consultant, San Francisco, California.

National Educational Television network) have helped to create a more selective and discriminating market.

The recent improvement of quality of 8-millimeter film and equipment has encouraged many teachers and students to produce their own educational films and documentary reports, including single concept film loops for self-study aids. Students in one high school made their own feature film of a dramatic production at a cost of only $50.

Video-tape recorder

A broader use of film is the video-tape recorder, which has the advantage of immediate playback. Within the past year units have been developed which are priced well within school budget limitations. It is possible to tape superior telecasts from commercial or educational stations and retain them permanently in a library. Fledgling actors may be video-taped for immediate critical analysis. Children with speech defects may be taped for future research or consultation.

Tape is particularly effective for collecting visual effects that are stretched out in time, such as the progress of a drama or poetry-reading student. The new equipment has simplified controls and self-correcting devices which should reduce the distaste of a nontechnical teacher.

Students of foreign languages can observe the peculiar facial expressions and gestures of native speakers, aiding them to communicate naturally in that language.

Audio tape recorder

Stereo has now added a second channel which, used with music, can be used to control a slide projector—or it can provide a master channel for comparison with a student channel. Used in connection with a switching console and combinations of headphones and microphones, they create an electronic classroom or language laboratory. It is an excellent tool for the correction of voice quality and accent.

A recent addition to the recorder called a "responsor" allows the student to hear his own voice and the master tape without having to wind back the tape. The "responsor" is an electronic logic device that holds back recorded information until the precise and immediate moment that the student needs it for effective learning reinforcement.

The ordinary stereo recorder is also being used in drama classes in the same fashion as the "music minus one" records. Just as the young musician plays his solo instrument along with a professional group, so the student actor may speak his lines in the company of recorded professionals. His part has been shifted to the second channel, where he may listen to it at will.

Rich sources of recorded materials, both on film and record, are now available from commercial or university sources which have recorded the representative sounds of the century, such as the voices of Presidents and poets. Many FM radio stations which use these educational recordings often make materials available to schools for copying—or they ask a reasonable fee when copyright applies.

Film strips

35-millimeter projections have long been popular in schools. With the advent of control track tape, voice and picture can be synchronized.

Reading drills on filmstrip are effectively used with a sync-track on the recorder, so that the flashed word comes ahead of the sound, and the sound gradually dies away. The erase factor makes it possible to change the tape or correct it periodically. It is possible for students to tell the story of the picture without using the voice track.

Radio

Often described as the stepchild of educational media, radio suffers from overuse of advertising gimmickry. In its early days live symphonies and operas were brought into classrooms via the airwaves. But now quality tape recorders and discs are more reliable.

After the trashy post-war period (and the cries of pain which accompanied it), many communities supported stations which featured mature programming; the "quality audience" is here to stay. Serious intellectual discussions are becoming more commonplace. Listener participation via phone, still often on the infantile level, offers opportunities for experimentation.

FM radio is generally doing a great deal to lift the level of the home environment and to provide the motivation to study, read, and discuss ideas. Many stations print programs far in advance of airing and they are useful in scheduling programs of educational value.

Telephone

Business men were the first to see the value of long distance telephone and conference calling, but not until lately have educators found appropriate adaptations. It is possible to employ a famous poet or philosopher and have his words heard simultaneously in many lecture halls. Students have held conference calls instead of seminars, actually much less expensive than travel. Bed-ridden students can call at appropriate times to be hooked in to their classroom, even participating in the class discussions. Music can be transmitted by special "hi-fi" telephone lines that are free of hums, clicks, and interruptions.

Computers

At first used only for processing records, computing flexible class schedules, and other clerical tasks, new uses for computers in education are now being explored. Several important computer "languages" offer this possibility.

Given the potentially large memory units of present generation computers, a teacher can build up the contents of an extended period of learning with the occasional aid of an experienced programmer. A series of questions can be asked and a wide variety of verbal answers can be evaluated by the computer. Following previously recorded instructions, the computer can then extend, delete, or review portions of the knowledge, depending on the student's needs.

All transactions may be typed on a continuous roll of paper which the student may save for review, or it can be recorded on magnetic tape for the teacher's review. To spread the cost per student, computer time may be shared by whole classrooms of students at individual consoles. Consoles are simple teletype machines hooked up to ordinary telephone lines. The computer may be effectively adapted to other teaching devices, including video tape recorders, color slides, motion pictures, and visual displays.

Microprinting

Basically the technics of microprinting are related to microfilm, now standard equipment in libraries the world over. Microfiche is an adaptation, using film cards (usually 3×5 or 4×6 inches in size) on which 50 pages or more of a book may be recorded. A mammoth library can thus be stored in small space, subject to instant recall. Research can be accomplished quickly and in an orderly way. Scanning on a small screen may be simplified by shifting the image for examination of details.

That educational technology is opening new doors to teachers of language is clearly evident. For the imaginative teacher of literature, speech, and reading the possibilities for use of the new media are almost limitless. Perhaps those limits will be reached only when the human brain refuses to learn.

52 The Electric Portable Typewriter as an Instructional Tool in Fourth Grade Language Arts

Jack Yuen, Lawrence Carrillo, Corwin Bjonerud, and Dewey Chambers

This article reports findings of a research study about the typewriter as an instructional tool.

What general findings are reported? How might future studies help with yet unanswered questions? The article by Capehart and McNish cited in Selected References for Part Seven summarizes findings from previous research studies about the typewriter—how much it improves learning; when it should be introduced; what materials and methods are most effective; and who should teach it.

Introduction and Background

Careful research dating back many years has established the fact that typing can be taught effectively to elementary school students (4, 8, 9, 11, 12). Other studies have attempted to relate the skill of typing to progress in the language arts. The effect of typing on spelling in the schools has been studied often (2, 8, 17), and most of these studies and others (1, 16) relate typing to reading skill and vocabulary as well. The latest investigations in this area have attempted to relate elementary typewriting instruction to learning in still other language arts, such as creative writing (13, 15). Articles have appeared which emphasize the typewriter as a method of teaching reading to children (3, 10).

All of these attempts reflect a concern among educators to improve the curriculum by the addition of a skill which does not detract from other areas of study, but rather makes higher efficiency possible in learning. Several recent articles by Erickson (5), Hart (7), and Rowe (13) have indicated their feeling

From *Elementary English* 39:101-108; February 1962. Reprinted with permission of the National Council of Teachers of English and Professors Yuen, Carrillo, and Bjonerud, San Francisco State College and Chambers, University of Pacific, Stockton, California.

that typing *belongs* in the elementary school. They would seem to concur in the belief (backed by their own research) that typing ability contributes to language learnings of all kinds.

One of the questions asked often in the research is that of the proper age at which to begin instruction in typing (6, 12, 14). The consensus seems to be that the optimum age at which to introduce typing is eight to nine years. It is possible to teach an interested child much earlier, but without curiosity and determination in all the individuals in the class, it is probably not an efficient procedure. Continual *use* of the typewriter after the introductory course is also recommended.

With the advent of the electric portable, some of the problems with muscular coordination are eliminated, and efficient instruction at an early age is possible (13). The ease of handling such a machine would suggest the possibility of even better results in correlated learnings in the language arts area.

Purposes of the Study

In the elementary school, the curriculum in the language arts includes four major facets: listening, speaking, reading, and writing. Each of these facets is closely related to the others, and instruction which facilitates improvement in one is likely to benefit the others. It would seem that instruction in typing might benefit several specific areas in language, such as spelling, sentence structure, punctuation, reading, and possibly others. One of the purposes of this study is to ascertain the effect of the skill of touch typewriting as a vehicle for learning the language arts in elementary school.

Secondly, this research attempts to determine the relative value of the electric portable typewriter in the acquisition of typing skill by elementary school pupils. And, third, materials which are appealing to younger students, but which teach typing efficiently, need to be developed *in use*.

The Situation

The experiment was set in the Frederic Burk Elementary School in San Francisco, California. This is the demonstration school for San Francisco State College, but is a community school having a pupil population selected only by living area. In general, the school population may be characterized as urban upper middle class, having above average ability, but having rather more than average tensions.

All of the teachers in this school are exceptional teachers, selected as "demonstration teachers" after experience elsewhere. The class size is small (average pupil-teacher ratio of 22-1), the school library and school plant in general are well above average, so that pupils have some advantages not otherwise found in most California schools.

The fourth grade selected for the initial year of the study was divided into three classrooms. A separate room was used for typing instruction (called the Typewriting Laboratory), since the wires were laid on the floor in order to avoid extra expense.

Four extra typewriters were placed in the regular classroom for the experimental group, two of them in front and two in the back of the room, where there were regular electrical outlets. Those near the front were next to the "library corner" and the language arts display area. These typewiters were for use at any time, but especially during "free activity." Children used them for spelling drill, to copy from books, to write personal letters, and for any other writing purpose they desired, so long as this did not interfere with regular classroom activity. The manufacturer of the electric portable, Smith-Corona Marchant, Inc., provided the typewriters.

Procedures

The original plan of the study was to: (1) have three groups to be kept separate for the three years of the study; (2) provide typing instruction for one group at fourth grade placement (Group A), for a second group at fifth grade placement (Group B), and maintain the third group (Group C) as a control group throughout; (3) test at the beginning of the experiment with the regular achievement tests and at the end of each year of the three years; and (4) attempt to maintain as consistent a program as possible for the groups, except for the inclusion of the typing, which would be a part of the regular time allotment for language arts.

This plan has been carried out for one year, but it will not be possible to continue it in the original form. With changes in school population, the classes have become too small, and during next year the total group will be in two fifth grades instead of three. Consequently, the study is being written up at this stage, with a plan to continue for one more year rather than two, providing typing instruction for the children who have not been included in the experimental group (typing) during this first year.

In general, the plan for the experimental group was as follows:

(1) The regular classroom teacher (who could type to some degree, but had no training in the teaching of typing) would give, during the regular class time, special instruction on the typewriters for his class. The group met in 30 minute sessions three times per week for this purpose. As soon as the mechanics were mastered, no more special time would be devoted to instruction in typing, but the typewriter would be used as a tool in regular classroom work.

(2) Teaching materials were developed, based upon primary grade reading and spelling vocabulary, so that unfamiliar words would not be encountered in beginning stages.

(3) As soon as the mechanics of typing were mastered, the emphasis on materials would be toward creative writing, composing, and the use of the typewriter in spelling and vocabulary work. Exercises provided for use with the machine would, even in beginning stages, emphasize the individual use of the skill rather than the skill itself.

(4) Students could be sent to the Typing Laboratory individually or in groups to work only if they had sufficient ability to work in this way. That is, it was necessary for the mechanics to be mastered first, and then for them to be responsible citizens in using the machines to do the job.

(5) As a pre- and post-test, the language skills section of Form 1 of the *Iowa Test of Basic Skills* would be administered in October and in June, and the significance of difference of scores between the experimental and control groups calculated.

(6) The *SRA Achievement Tests* would also be administered in October, and these results compared with a second form of the same test given in the following February.

Results

The results are presented here in three categories—Mechanics, Language Arts, and Impression, since the major purposes of this study were to test results in the two areas of skill development, and the impressions of the teacher would seem to add a further dimension.

Mechanics

In general, no difficulties were encountered with the mechanical aspects. Learning to type with the electric portable seemed to be, if anything, easier for these fourth graders than for adults. After only six hours of instruction on the typewriter, the mechanics had been completed, and after ten hours of instruction, adequate mastery had been achieved. This included all letters of the alphabet (presented in known words), spacing between words, capitalization, and the use of the question mark, the comma, and the period. By this time, the children could type faster than they could write in longhand.

Interest was very high, and although two of the children suffered broken arms in the first few months of the experiment, they returned to school with their arms in casts, and found no real difficulty in continuing with their typing.

After a total of thirty-two hours of using the typewriter (only the first ten hours of this could be considered as actual typing instruction, since the rest was

Table I

**Results of One-Minute Timed Writing on the Electric Portable
with Fourth Graders After Thirty-Two Hours of Instruction**

Name	Words #1	Words #2	Phrases
Elaine	13/1	16/3	15/0
Wendy	19/1	26/1	28/2
Linda	14/0	14/3	16/1
Tom	11/1	15/1	18/1
Steve	22/1	22/2	23/1
George	21/4	23/7	29/3
Kurt	22/2	28/1	32/2
John	20/2	22/1	24/2
Cindy	26/1	32/1	35/1
Bobby	15/1	17/4	20/1
Debbie	22/0	26/2	26/0
Mark	14/3	18/1	16/2
Judy	12/2	14/2	18/0
Jimmy	12/3	16/5	20/3
Sally	25/0	26/3	20/1
Terry	20/4	20/8	27/4

(Note: The first figure represents the number of words or phrases in the timed writing, the second figure the number of errors. Two other members of the class were absent.)

using the typewriter with regular school work), a one-minute speed test was taken. Table I shows the results. Speed varied widely, some of the pupils typing twice as fast as they could write by hand, and others at about the same speed.

Language arts

All three classes were tested in February with the *SRA Achievement Tests* in Spelling, Capitalization-Punctuation, and Grammar Usage. The results are shown in Table II. Due to the fact that the original test results with the experi-

Table II

**SRA Achievement Test Results After Four Months
of Typewriting Instruction
(Grade Placement Means)**

Sub-Test	Experimental Group		Control Group		Control Group	
	October	February	Oct.	Feb.	Oct.	Feb.
Spelling	4.8	5.9	5.7	6.1	5.7	6.4
Capitalization-Punctuation	3.8	6.2	5.4	6.4	5.5	6.7
Grammar Usage	3.5	6.1	5.8	6.4	5.8	6.8
	Mean Gain = 2.05 years		Mean Gain = .53 years		Mean Gain = .97 years	

mental class were so much lower than the others, and that the classes seemed to be very much the same in spite of these test scores, these apparent gains were assumed to be invalid. However, these results did tend to confirm the opinion held by the experimenters that the experimental group was most certainly not of any higher quality than the control groups, and if anything, somewhat less better equipped at the beginning of the experiment.

After a full school year, the *Iowa Test of Basic Skills* was re-administered, and the results subjected to statistical analysis. Results are shown in Tables III and IV. In Table III the means are shown for the experimental and control

Table III

Means in Grade Equivalents for Experimental and Control Groups Iowa Test of Basic Skills

Group	Spell.	Capit.	Punct.	Lang. Us.	Total	Average Total Gain	Number of Students
			October, 1960				
Exp.	5.38	4.79	5.74	5.66	5.37		17
Cont. #1	5.06	5.20	5.56	6.20	5.59		14
Cont. #2	5.07	4.71	5.34	6.45	5.26		18
			June, 1961				
Exp.	6.51	6.98	7.92	6.78	6.99	1.62	17
Cont. #1	5.74	5.92	6.33	6.75	6.14	.55	14
Cont. #2	6.01	6.16	6.70	5.76	6.33	1.07	18

Table IV

Experimental Group and Two Control Groups' F-Scores Through Analysis of Variance on the Raw Scores on the Subtests of the Iowa Tests of Basic Skills

Subtest	June, 1961 Value of F	October, 1960 Value of F
Punctuation	3.878*	.158
Spelling	.690	.499
Language Usage	.848	.978
Capitalization	.833	.723

* Difference significant at greater than .05 level of confidence

sections; in Table IV the mean raw scores from the subtests of the experimental group were compared to the mean scores of the two control classes through analysis of variance.

Impressions

Following are the impressions of the teacher, a person who has had a number of years teaching experience at the intermediate grade level, and should be qualified to make judgments of this type.

1. The experience helped build listening skills. In order to keep up with the group, they needed to listen very carefully. In addition, because of the interest in the approach, the ability to pay attention to the task of writing for a long period of time grew considerably.

2. The 'eye sweep' improved. The children developed much greater skill than expected in keeping their eye on the line of print. They paid much more attention to the configuration of the individual words, also.

3. The typewriting program provided an excellent 'shot in the arm' for all of the language skills. The children showed real 'intrinsic' motivation for grammar. They wanted to know how to do it properly —the typing gave a real reason for knowing how.

4. They *wanted* to express themselves with the typewriter—it was no effort to get them to write. As a result, it was excellent motivation for the polishing of creative writing efforts. Writing on the typewriter seemed more like 'real' writing, and the bulletin board displays showed this, both in volume and quality. If we had some way to measure growth in creative writing, this would be one of the best results.

Other impressions by the school administration and the college faculty acting as consultants were:

1. There was much more attention to neatness of papers than is usual at this grade level.

2. The children, because of their interest in the project and the typewriters, needed much less direction than expected.

3. The new methods of presenting the keyboard and the new materials developed seemed to be quite effective at this age level. The "try-outs" of classroom methods and materials should prove valuable for others attempting elementary school typing.

4. Considerable evidence of teacher interest in wanting to include the use of the typewriter into the school curriculum.

5. Ready acceptance by parents of the typing program. It is interesting to note that parents displayed an almost "for granted" attitude toward the introduction of the typewriters in the elementary school.

Conclusions

Although this is a tentative report, presented in the middle of an experiment, it would seem that there are some conclusions possible, which would perhaps be subject to revision as the experiment proceeds, but which definitely show in the results to the present time.

1. There is no difficulty in teaching children in the fourth grade to type on the electric portable typewriter. They would seem to learn the skill with less instruction than if they were adults.

2. Teaching children typewriting at this early age gives them a mechanical skill which is helpful in expression. It is a skill which they will be able to use throughout their school career, and possibly throughout their lifetime.

3. If children can type in the fourth grade, new creative possibilities are added to the language arts program. In addition, some skills which are rather difficult to motivate (such as the skill of proper punctuation) become important to the children, and therefore easier to teach.

4. Habits of neatness and proper expression come more naturally to children through the use of the typewriter than through handwriting.

5. Following these same children through the next two years of elementary school should show other results which are not now obvious. . . .

6. In general, the language arts skills seem to be learned to a somewhat higher degree with the typewriter than without the typewriter. All teachers in this study were exceptional teachers, and the previous teachers of these children had also been outstanding. Under these circumstances, any results approaching significance are especially important.

References

1. Baty, Wayne M. "Incidental Learning of Vocabulary in Beginning Typewriting Classes." Doctoral Dissertation, University of Southern California, 1958. 162 pp.
2. Beavers, Blanche Elizabeth. "Typewriting as an Aid to Learning in the Elementary Grades." Master's Thesis, University of Oklahoma, 1940. 61 pp.
3. Chamberlain, John. "Reading at Age Three." *The Wall Street Journal*, May 12, 1961.
4. Colahan, Wayne John. "Touch Typewriting in Two Elementary Schools." Master's Thesis, University of Chicago, 1935. 41 pp.
5. Erickson, Lawrence W. "The Typewriter—A Tool of Learning in the Elementary Grades." *The Balance Sheet*, October, 1960. Vol. 42, pp. 52-59.
6. Haefner, Ralph. *The Typewriter in the Primary and Intermediate Grades*. New York: The Macmillan Co., 1932. 329 pp.
7. Hart, Leo B. "Typing Belongs in the Elementary Curriculum." *Business Education World*, January, 1960. Vol. 40, No. 5, pp. 9-11.
8. Heffernan, E. P. "Relationship Between the Ability of Elementary School Pupils to Use the Typewriter and Sex, Chronological Age, Mental Age, Spelling Ability, Reading Ability." Master's Thesis, University of Pittsburgh, 1932. 90 pp.
9. Hutchings, Mabel Maxine. "A Study of Typewriting as Offered in Elementary Schools." Master's Thesis, Northwestern University, 1948. 105 pp.

10. "O.K.'s Children." *Time*, November 7, 1960, p. 103.
11. Olson, M. Adeline. "Grade Pupils Become Proficient Typists." *The Balance Sheet*, October, 1955, pp. 56-57, 65.
12. Ricketts, Mary Carmichael. "Typewriting for the Lower Grades." *The Balance Sheet*, March, 1950, pp. 292-94.
13. Rowe, John L. "An Experiment in Teaching Portable Electric Typewriting to Third and Fourth Grade Students." *The College of Education Record*, University of North Dakota, pp. 21-32, Vol. 44, No. 2.
14. Smith, Harold H. "How Young is 'too young to type?'" *Business Education World*, April, 1957, pp. 34, 43. Vol. 37.
15. *The Manual Portable Typewriter as an Instructional Tool in the Elementary School Classroom.* Port Chester, New York, Royal McBee Corporation. 24 pp.
16. Unzicker, Cecelia. "An Experimental Study of the Effect of the Use of the Typewriter on Beginning Reading." *Teachers College, Columbia University, Contributions to Education # 610*, 1934. 95 pp.
17. Wood, B. D. and F. N. Freeman. *An Experimental Study of the Educational Influences of the Typewriter in the Elementary School Classroom.* New York: The Macmillan Co., 1932. 214 pp.

53   Big Boom in Paperbacks

Margaret Bierbaum

This article focuses on a new educational dimension in the language arts program, the 'paperback.' Bierbaum lists the values of paperbacks and then gives specific titles of available paperbacks.

Why must teachers be careful in selection of paperbacks? How can paperbacks be utilized most successfully in elementary school classrooms? Of what value are paperback book clubs? Why do some people object to such clubs? Must teacher guidance be exercised when pupils purchase books from these clubs? The reader's attention is called to other articles dealing with this topic which are cited in Selected References for Part Seven.

Many of the large book companies are rendering a valuable service to an entire generation of young Americans with comparatively inexpensive paperbacks. Although the first paperbacks, as we know them, were produced by Pocket Books in the early 1930s, the paperback boom did not gather momentum until about 1959. That year, 6,500 titles were listed. In 1963 there were 22,800 items; at this writing there are over 35,000 available titles. Also, the quality of the paperback for educational use has improved.

Thus far, the majority of paperbacks published for schools have been for the junior high, high school, and college. However, in a poll of 25 major publishing houses, more than half the companies expressed considerable interest in paperbacks for elementary schools and are planning their publication. A dozen or more companies have already put out paperback editions of many works for use in the elementary grades.

Today the teacher finds the same categories of pupils that her predecessor did a generation ago: (1) A small percentage of children apparently born with the need and love of books. A child of this group starts to read on his own, often before he enters school. (2) The great majority who learn to read in

From *Grade Teacher* 83:85; 88; 89; 90; November 1965. Reprinted from Grade Teacher Magazine by permission of the publishers (Copyright November 1965 by Teachers Publishing Corporation) and Margaret Bierbaum, Reading Specialist, Burr Farms Schools, Westport, Connecticut.

school. Most students are in this category. And (3) those few who are reluctant readers; they are slow to grasp the meaning of the printed page and, unless something happens, they will never be enthusiastic readers.

Miracles happen

But none of these children is immune to the possibility of a miracle. It happens on the day one of them picks up a book, one particular book, which serves as a key to unlock some hidden corridor of the mind, to fill some deep, unsuspected need. Thanks to the availability of paperbacks, there is a greater possibility of this miracle occurring.

Compact school libraries

Here is where the paperbacks do their job so well. The school library (if, indeed, there is one) is often in use during most of the school day as a classroom and is not always accessible to the student. There should be a classroom library and since few school boards are affluent enough to provide each teacher with 300 or 400 hardcover books, the answer is paperbacks. The student usually has a few minutes before school, after school, and during the day when his assignments are finished. Here he can browse and make a selection. The books take up little room, they are easily displayed and, most important, they are *read*. Many teachers have no idea how many disciplinary problems can be solved by the acquisition of a room library.

Paperbacks should be considered expendable. A great deal of the school budget is used for such items. No one questions the purchase of crayons, paper, pencils, etc., although these things are consumed with use. In fact, the very *lack* of permanence in paperbacks makes for a constant re-evaluation of the curriculum.

Individualized reading

The reason for the paperback "explosion" can probably be traced to individualized reading. A new approach to reading has been developed by most teachers throughout the country. It is a program of enrichment reading, but with a great deal more structure and direction than was given to it in the past. Individual reading gets away from the "lock step" of a basal approach, although many teachers combine the two with excellent results. (See "An Individualized Program of Enrichment Reading" in *Grade Teacher*, November, 1963.)

To foster this program, the largest number of books in the room library should be fiction and should include paperback editions of novels that have delighted youngsters for years: *Captains Courageous, Heidi, The Arabian Nights,*

Rebecca of Sunnybrook Farm, The Wizard of Oz, Lassie Come Home, Alice in Wonderland, the Mark Twain classics, *Charlotte's Web, Black Beauty, Swiss Family Robinson,* to name a few. Then there are the modern favorites in paperback, like *The Young Viking, Eddie's Pay Dirt, Encyclopedia Brown, Henry and the Paper Route, First to Ride,* and *Silver for General Washington.* Dell Publishing Company has produced some excellent paperbacks in their Laurel Leaf Library. Besides *Robinson Crusoe* and *Treasure Island,* etc., they have some extremely good new titles such as *Chucklebait,* an anthology of humorous short stories (fifth and sixth grades) and *Turning Point, Tales of Daring and Decision.*

The Macmillan Publishing Company is offering excellent selections for upper-grade readers in their new Acorn series. It's gratifying to see the ever popular *Caddie Woodlawn* in paperback. Other worthwhile titles in the series are included in the list of recommended selections that accompanies this article.

Screwball, published in 1963 by Grosset and Dunlap, one of the most popular and heartwarming stories to come out in a decade, is now in paperback. *Karen* (Dell), the story of a child afflicted with cerebral palsy who overcame her handicap to a remarkable degree, is an inspiring book for good sixth grade readers.

As our taste in literature changes, we can discard books that have outlived their usefulness. Recently I visited a school where a set of hardbound copies of *Man Without a Country* had been issued to students. This dreary story of a mythical naval officer, banished to 55 years of seagoing imprisonment, was originally a piece of popular fiction written by a retired clergyman 100 years ago. It somehow became embalmed in school reading programs for generations. Why then, is this undistinguished tale still being studied in spite of the fact that the United States, five wars later, has produced truly great fiction that presents the moral of the story much better? Simply because the copies are hardbound, standard school property, and teachers feel duty-bound to issue them. The same investment today would buy *five* to *10* paperbacks, better written.

Some companies have recently produced paperbacks in areas other than fiction, for use as textbooks, entitled *Call Them Heroes.* Developed by the New York City Board of Education, each book has stories of men and women of that city who are dedicated to helping humanity while overcoming personal obstacles of poverty, prejudice and language. The books are written for the sixth grade level.

There is a particularly good literature series in paperback entitled *Prose and Poetry for Young Readers and Writers* (L. W. Singer). The series (for the fourth grade) has selections from *Alice in Wonderland,* along with some enchanting poems, a short introduction to fantasy and poetry, and the complete *Pinocchio.* The fifth and sixth grade series are equally good.

Educators agree that the social studies curriculum is in a constant state of change. Since few agree on what concepts should be taught at the fourth, fifth and sixth grade levels, and in view of the constantly changing world situation, consideration should be given to the use of paperbacks in teaching this subject. One social studies unit developed by Follett Publishing Company is *Exploring New England,* and deals with the geography, climate and natural resources of this area. At $1.95 a copy, it is worth examining. In addition, units of study are available on Canada, Latin America, Western Europe, the Soviet Union, Asia, North Africa, etc., from Prentice-Hall at $1.28 per unit.

An excellent supplementary social studies text is the paperbound edition of *Sailors, Whalers and Steamers* (Lane). The text is crisp, the pictures striking and at $1.50 it is a good investment.

Many upper elementary science teachers have on hand the *How and Why Paperback Series* (Wonder Books) which cover practically all units taught at this level: astronomy, weather, magnets and magnetism, etc. Several copies of each would enable students to borrow them for assignments and special projects. Science paperbacks are also published by the Webster Publishing Company and the Golden Press.

Inspiration from pictures

An outstanding paperback for teaching creative writing to sixth graders is *Stop, Look and Write* by Leavitt and Sohn (Bantam). This book contains over 100 pictures, each carefully chosen for teaching aspects of writing. The student studies the picture and then composes a piece of creative writing about it.

For the teacher in search of creative projects, there is an excellent paperback series entitled *Young Artists* (Merrill), for grades one through eight.

Should the school library stock paperbacks? In the past, most school librarians held fast to the theory that they were duty-bound to order only hardcover books. Dorothy A. McGinniss, executive secretary of the American Association of School Librarians, has pointed out that school libraries should have paperbacks for the same reason classrooms should have them. They are appealing, more portable and less formidable to read. The narrow width of the page cuts down the perception span so that the child's reading is much faster.

No librarian can stock the required number of certain books. *The Story of Helen Keller* is a good example. He can, however, buy a few hardcover copies plus a half-dozen paperback copies and can then begin to meet the demand. And a rack for paperbacks takes up little of the library's precious space. Librarians who plan to order paperbacks for their libraries should obtain a copy of Bowker's *Paperbound Books in Print* as a reference.

With a book-centered learning environment in the classrooms and library, and with the help and encouragement of understanding teachers, most of our students will have every opportunity to become enthusiastic lifetime readers.

Paperbacks for Fourth, Fifth, and Sixth Grades

Fiction

The Mysterious Schoolmaster	Anckarsvard	Harcourt, Brace & World
The Witch Family	Estes	"
The Comeback Guy	Frick	"
Here's a Penny	Haywood	
No Children, No Pets	Holland	Scholastic Book Services
Trolley Car Family	Clymer	"
Double Trouble for Rupert	Parkinson	"
Blue Ribbons for Meg	De Leeuw	"
A Room for Cathy	Woolley	"
Snow Treasure	McSwigan	"
Emily San	Reynolds	"
The Enormous Egg	Butterworth	
Cheaper by the Dozen	Gilbreth	Bantam
The Pearl	Steinbeck	"
Road Rocket	Felsen	
Jabberwocky	Carroll	Dell
The Selfish Giant	Wilde	"
Karen	Killilea	"
With Love from Karen	Killilea	"
Around the World in 80 Days	Verne	"
Chucklebait	Scoggin, ed.	
Wizard of Oz	Baum	Scholastic
Davey Logan, Interne	Felsen	Berkley
Great Sport Stories	Masin	"
Bambi	Salten	Tempo
Winning Pitcher	Porter	"
Screwball	Armer	"
Understood Betsy	Canfield	
Caddie Woodlawn	Brink	Macmillan
The Captain's Daughter	Coatsworth	"
Brown Wolf & Other Jack London Stories	London	"
The Raft	Trumbull	Pyramid
Wild Bill Hickok	O'Connor	Ace
Born Free	Adamson	Macfadden
Forever Free	Adamson	"
The Family Nobody Wanted	Doss	Monarch

Classics

Kidnapped	Stevenson	Dell
Black Beauty	Sewell	"
Treasure Island	Stevenson	"
Swiss Family Robinson	Wyss	"
Call It Courage	Sperry	Scholastic

Heidi	Spyri	Scholastic
Anne of Green Gables	Montgomery	Grosset
Rebecca of Sunnybrook Farm	Wiggin	"
Captains Courageous	Kipling	Bantam
Huckleberry Finn	Twain	"
A Christmas Carol	Dickens	Washington Sq. Press

Animal

Star of Wild Horse Caynon	Bulla	Scholastic
Yellow Eyes (lion)	Montgomery	"
Black Storm	Hinkle	"
Born to Race	Perrin	"
Champion Dog, Prince Tom	Fritz	"
Outlaw Red	Kjelgaard	"
Shamrock Queen	Henry	"
Incredible Journey	Burnford	Bantam
The Red Pony	Steinbeck	"
Mutts, Mongrels and Mischief	Coates, ed.	Pyramid
National Velvet	Bagnold	Tempo
Lassie Come Home	Knight	"
Big Book of Horse Stories	Cooper, ed.	Berkley

Mystery

Black Spaniel Mystery	Cavanna	Scholastic
Deadline at Spook Cabin	Miller	"
Ghostly Trio	Smith	"
Mystery at Shadow Pond	Jane	"
Great Ghost Stories	Stern	Washington Sq. Press
Boys' Book of Great Detective Stories	Haycroft, ed.	Berkley
Great Tales of Horror	Sohn, ed.	Bantam
The Mystery of the Aztec Idol	Carr	Macmillan
Mystery Island	Blyton	"

Biography

Abe Lincoln Gets His Chance	Cavanah	Scholastic
Lonely Crusader (F. Nightingale)	Woodham-Smith	Bantam
The Miracle Worker (Helen Keller)	Gibson	"
A Day in the Life of President Kennedy	Bishop	"
They Fought for the Sky (Pilots—WWI)	Reynolds	"
Upon from Slavery	Washington	Dell
Marco Polo	Komroff	Washington Sq. Press
Story of Helen Keller	Hickok	Tempo
JFK—Boyhood to White House	Lee	Fawcett
We Seven	Astronauts	Pocket Books
Thomas Alva Edison	Clark	Berkley

Historical—Fact

Kon Tiki	Heyerdahl	Pocket Books
Lost Cities and Vanished Civilizations	Silverberg	Bantam
A Night to Remember	Lord	"
Alone	Byrd	Ace
Windjammer Story	Villiers	Scholastic

Historical—Fiction

The Cabin Faced West	Fritz	Scholastic
Silver for General Washington	Meadowcroft	"
Young Viking	Coggins	"
First to Ride	Crowell	"
Becky Landers, Frontier Warrior	Skinner	Macmillan

Science—Fact

100 Great Scientists	Greene	Washington Sq. Press
Alligators & Crocodiles	Zim	Scholastic
Dinosaurs	Bloch	"
First Men in the World	White	"
Hurricanes & Twisters	Irving	"
Never Cry Wolf	Mowat	Dell
Our Friend the Atom	Haber	"
150 Science Experiments Step by Step	Viorst	Bantam

Science—Fiction

Danny Dunn and the Anti-Gravity Paint	Williams	Scholastic
Miss Pickerell and the Geiger Counter	MacGregor	"
Miss Pickerell Goes Underseas	MacGregor	"
The Time Machine	Wells	Berkley
Twenty Thousand Leagues Under the Sea	Verne	Bantam
Voyage to the Bottom of the Sea	Sturgeon	Pyramid
Journey to the Center of the Earth	Verne	Ace

Publishers of Paperbacks

Ace Books, Inc., 1120 Avenue of the Americas, New York, N.Y. 10036
Bantam Books, Inc., 271 Madison Ave., New York, N.Y. 10016
Berkley Publishing Corp., 15 E. 26th St., New York, N.Y. 10010
R. R. Bowker Co., 1180 Avenue of the Americas, New York, N.Y. 10036
Dell Publishing Co., Inc., 750 Third Ave., New York, N.Y. 10017
Fawcett World Library, Fawcett Pl., Greenwich, Conn. 06830

Follett Publishing Co., 1010 W. Washington Blvd., Chicago, Ill. 60607
Golden Press, Inc., 850 Third Ave., New York, N.Y. 10022
Grosset and Dunlap, Inc., 51 Madison Ave., New York, N.Y. 10022
Harcourt, Brace & World, Inc., 757 Third Ave., New York, N.Y. 10017
Lane Magazine & Book Co., Menlo Park, Calif. 94025
J. P. Lippincott, Washingon Sq., Philadelphia, Pa. 19105
Macmillan Co., 60 Fifth Ave., New York, N.Y. 10022
Charles E. Merrill Books, Inc., 1300 Alum Creek Dr., Columbus, Ohio 43216
Monarch Books, Inc., 529 Fifth Ave., New York, N.Y. 10017
Pocket Books, Inc., 630 Fifth Ave., New York, N.Y. 10020
Prentice-Hall, Inc., Englewood Cliffs, N.J. 07632
Pyramid Books (Macfadden), 444 Madison Ave., New York, N.Y. 10016
School Book Services, 425 Park Ave., S., New York, N.Y. 10016
School Paperback Institute (Pub. School Paperback Journal), 124 E. 40th St., New
    York, N.Y. 10016
Silver Burdett Co., Park Ave. & Columbia Rd., Morristown, N.J. 07960
L. W. Singer Co., 249 W. Eric Blvd., Syracuse, N.Y. 13202
Tempo Books (Grosset-Dunlap), 1107 Broadway, New York, N.Y. 10010
Washington Square Press, Inc., 630 Fifth Ave., New York, N.Y. 10020
Webster Publishing, 1154 Reco Ave., St. Louis, Mo. 63126
Wonder Books, 51 Madison Ave., New York, N.Y. 10010

54   Children's Magazines and Periodicals: A selective bibliography

Earl E. Edmondson

This article by Edmondson provides an annotated selected listing of magazines and periodicals for boys and girls. In the use of such materials, there is a need for pupil guidance in skills of periodical reading such as developing the idea that an item is not necessarily correct because it is in print; skimming and scanning; reading with an awareness of the writer's point of view; studying different parts of the periodical; and evaluating and comparing magazines and periodicals.

What types of periodicals interest boys and girls in the primary school years? Intermediate school years? What is the role of periodicals in the language arts program? Of what value can be magazines published in English speaking nations other than USA? Foreign language periodicals? For a comprehensive listing of periodicals for children and youth, see Horn's article cited in Selected References for Part Seven. And for suggestions on how to help pupils read and understand newspapers, see the articles by Burns and Van Ness.

Magazines and periodicals, for the past one hundred years, have materially contributed to the education and enlightenment of boys and girls of the United States. Currently, children's magazines and periodicals are published in vast numbers. When classified according to type, the magazines present a wide range of content: religious, general, school, foreign language, and foreign periodicals in English. The following magazines are some of the many that boys and girls may profit from reading:

General

American Girl, The; $3.00; ages 10-16; Publisher—Girl Scouts of America, 830 Third Avenue, New York 22. Sports, grooming, dress, international friendship, dating, today's girl interests, Girl Scouts, nature, fiction, non-fiction.

From *Claremont Reading Conference, Thirtieth Yearbook,* 1966, pp. 215-220. Reprinted with permission of Malcolm P. Douglass, editor, and Earl E. Edmondson, Principal, Norwalk-La Mirada Unified School District, California.

American Junior Red Cross News; $1.00; ages 6-12; Publisher—American National Red Cross, 18th and D Street, N.W., Washington, D.C. Animals, holiday, other nations, nature, science, international assistance and friendship, helping our fellow man, fiction, non-fiction.

Boys' Life; $3.00; ages 8-19; Publisher—Boy Scouts of America, New Brunswick, New Jersey. Scout information, adventure, comic book section, large dramatic illustrations, lively stories, much advertising, craft ideas, fiction, non-fiction.

Calling All Girls; $3.50; ages 7-12; Publisher—Parents' Institute, 52 Vanderbilt Avenue, New York 17, New York. Fiction, non-fiction—meets interests of today's girl.

Child Life Magazine; $4.00; ages 3-12; Publishers—Child Life, Inc., 36 Federal Street, Boston 10, Mass. Stories, sketches, photographs, puzzle pictures, wide interest material, fiction, non-fiction.

Children's Activities; $4.00; ages 5-12; Publisher—Child Training Association Inc., 1111 South Wabash Avenue, Chicago 5, Illinois. Articles, stories, paper and pencil activities, poems, play, fiction, non-fiction.

Children's Digest; $3.50; ages 5-12; Publisher—Parents' Magazine Press, Inc., 52 Vanderbilt Avenue, New York 17, New York. Things-to-do, stories, book reviews, riddles, puzzles, extracts of books, reprints.

Children's Playmate Magazine; $3.50; ages 6-9; Publisher—Children's Playmate Magazine, Inc., 3025 E. 75th Street, Cleveland 4, Ohio. Stories, art and craft activities, non-fiction, fiction.

Geographic School Bulletins; $2.00; ages 9-15; Publisher—School Service Division, National Geographic Society, 1146 16th Street, N.W., Washington 6, D.C. Geographic articles about the countries and peoples of the world, photographs in color, excellent material.

Highlights for Children; $6.00; ages 3-12; Publisher—Highlights for Children, 968 Main Street, Honesdale, Penn. Fiction, non-fiction, things-to-do, editorials, guide for parents and teachers, stories, pictures, puzzles, music, science, poems, book reviews.

Humpty Dumpty's Magazine; $3.50; ages 3-7; Publisher—Parents' Institute, 52 Vanderbilt Avenue, New York 17, New York. Fiction, riddles, puzzles, poems, tell-me, stuffed with material.

Jack and Jill; $3.50; ages 5-10; Publisher—Curtis Publishing Co., Independence Square, Philadelphia 5, Penn. Fiction, non-fiction, plays, stories, letters from readers, serial story, folk tales, paper dolls.

Model Airplane News; $4.00; ages 7-up; Publisher—Air Age, Inc., 551 Fifth Avenue, New York 17, New York. Non-fiction, hobbies, airplane news plans.

Nature and Science; $1.65 (minimum order: 10); Publisher—The American Museum of Natural History, Central Park West at 79th Street, New York, N.Y. 10024. Science and nature experiments, puzzles, articles, explanations.

Children's magazines published in English speaking nations other than the United States of America

Young people enjoy reading English language magazines published abroad. The following magazines present varied format and content and are designed for differing age levels. Through these magazines boys and girls can learn much about their English speaking friends.

Australia

School Magazine; monthly; Publisher: New South Wales Department of Education, Sydney, New South Wales, Australia; fourpence per copy; ages, elementary grades; stories and articles. This magazine is supplementary to the literature instruction program in the schools.

England

Elizabethian; monthly; Publisher: Periodical Publications, Ltd., 2 Breams Bldg., London, E.C. 4, England; one year, $4.00; ages 10-18; fiction, non-fiction, travel, clubs, books, fashions; probably England's finest teen-age magazine.

England

Meccano Magazine; monthly; Publisher: Meccano Magazine, Bins Road, Liverpool 13, England; write for subscription rate; ages 12-18; hobbies, stamps, jokes, clubs, articles, models.

India

Sunshine; monthly; Publisher: Children's Sunshine Concerns, 6 Parvati Villas Road, Poona L. Poone, India; one year, $2.00; ages 10-15; geography, science, fiction, cartoons, puzzles, games, stamps, letters; "the magazine for boys and girls" of Asia with a world view, printed in English and used by boys and girls throughout Asia as an aid to learning a second language.

Israel

Israel Horizon; monthly; Publisher: The Youth and Hechalutz Department of Zionest Organization, P.O. Box 92, Jerusalem; 12 issues, $3.00; ages 15-19; stamps, art, archeology, education, people, special topics, for the mature reader.

New Zealand

The Students' Digest; also *Junior Student;* Publisher: L. J. Cronin, Colonial Mutual Building, Customhouse Quay, Wellington, New Zealand; rates upon request; current events, science, history, puzzles, people, stamps, geography, government. These magazines are designed primarily to supplement school classroom use.

Foreign language periodicals for children published in United States of America, Canada, England

The following magazines are recommended because, although published in English speaking countries, they are specifically designed for the English speaking children who are learning a second language.

German

Glukanf; monthly; Publisher: The House of Grant Ltd., 29 Mobile Dr., Toronto 16, Canada; one year, $1.50; ages 12-16; general subject matter for beginning reader.

French

Ca Va; nine times yearly; Publisher: The House of Grant Ltd., 29 Mobile Dr., Toronto 16, Canada; one year, $1.25; ages, for beginning readers of French; pictures, cartoons, crossword puzzles, stories, vocabulary activities.

French

Francois; bi-monthly; Publisher: Jeunesse Etudiante Catholique, Inc., 430 Sherbrooke East, Montreal 24, Quebec, Canada; one year, $1.50; ages, boys 10-15; general stories and articles.

Italian

Giornalino, Il; monthly; Publisher: Pierina B. Castiglione, 30 W. 12th Street, New York 11, New York; one year, $1.00; ages 12-18; photographs, articles, poetry, vocabulary exercises, recipes.

Spanish

American Junior Red Cross News (Spanish Edition); monthly; Publisher: American National Red Cross, 18th and D Streets, N.W., Washington, D.C.; one year, $1.00; ages 9-16; fiction, non-fiction, poems, photographs, excellent illustrations.

Children and youth learning a second language can facilitate the growth of foreign language skills by utilizing the materials provided by magazines published in other nations in the languages of those countries. The following magazines constitute a selected list and is, by no means, complete. Your local librarian can provide "The Dobler International List of Periodicals for Boys and Girls," which is most comprehensive.

Argentina (Spanish)

Billiken; weekly; Publisher: Editorial Atlandia, Azopardo 579, Buenos Aires, Argentina; one year, $4.00; ages 8-14; fiction, non-fiction, games, puzzles, hobbies.

Dutch

Kris Kras; bi-weekly; Publisher: Stichting, Kinderbelegan, Stadionweg 21, Amsterdam 7, Holland; one year, 15 f; ages 7-13; fiction, non-fiction, crafts, plays, hobbies.

French

Tintin, Le Journal des Jeunes; weekly; order from European Publishers Representatives, Inc., 132 West 43rd Street, New York 36, New York; one year, $14.25; ages 10-15; well illustrated, cartoons, articles, games, science, clubs, hobbies.

French

TOP Realities Jeannesse; weekly; Publisher: Realities, 133 Champs-Elysees, Paris, France; one year, $12.00; ages 13-19; profusely illustrated, broad variety, cross-section of French living.

German

Rasselbande; weekly; order from German News Co., 200 E. 86th Street, New York 28, New York; one year, $9.25; illustrated weekly for boys and girls between 10-17 years, very comprehensive in content.

Italian

Topolino; weekly; order from Italian Publications, Inc., 132 West 43rd Street, New York 36, New York; one year, $12.00; ages 10-14; cartoons, articles, games, stories, biography, science.

Polish

Na Prezelaj; monthly; order from European Publications Representative, Inc., 132 West 43rd Street, New York 36, New York; one year, $5.00; ages 10-15; a generalized children's magazine.

Swiss

Schweizer Kamerad; Publisher: Pro Juventute, Seefeldstrasse 8, Zurich 8, Switzerland; 5.80 Swiss francs; ages 9-14; articles, drawings, photos.

Turkish

Dogan Kardes, Mecmussi; monthly; Publisher: Dogan Kardes Yayinlari, Divanyolu, Instanbul, Turkey; ages 8-12; stories, cartoons, articles, poems.

Resources

Several standard references will serve to inform readers about available magazines. *The Dobler World Directory of Youth Periodicals,* 1966, Lavinia G. Dobler, New York, New York: Schultz Publishing Company, 80 Fourth Avenue, New York, New York, 10003, is currently the latest publication. The latest references are:

Ayer and Sons Directory of Newspapers and Periodicals, N.W., 1965, 97th year. Philadelphia; West Washington Square, 19106.

Dobler International List of Periodicals for Boys and Girls, 1960. New York: Murill Fuller, Post Office Box 193, Grand Central Station 17.

Evaluating Library Resources for Elementary School Libraries, 1962. Mary Virginia Gaver and Marian Scott. New Brunswick, New Jersey: SSH Press.

Guide to Children's Magazines, Newspapers and Reference Books, 1962. Association for Childhood Education International, 3615 Wisconsin Avenue, N.W., Washington, D.C.

Magazines for School Libraries: Bibliography, 1965. Chicago: American Association of School Librarians, 50 East Huron Street, 60611.

Magazines for School Libraries, 1950. Laura K. Martin. New York: The H. W. Wilson Company, 1950 University Avenue, 10452.

Magazines in the Classroom, 1960. Washington, D.C.: National Education Association, 1201 Sixteenth Street, N.W.

101 Plus Magazines for Schools, Grades 1-12, 4th Edition, 1964. Ruth Ethel Cundiff (comp.). Nashville, Tennessee: Tennessee Book Company.

Reader's Guide to Periodical Literature, 1965. New York: The H. W. Wilson Company, 950 University Avenue, 10452.

Subject Index to Children's Magazines, 1965. Meribah Hazen (ed.). Madison, Wisconsin: 301 Palomino Lane, 53705.

Ulrich's Periodicals Directory, 10th ed., 1963. Eileen Graves (ed.). New York: R. R. Bowker Company, 1180 Avenue of the Americas, 10036.

Part Eight

Evaluation of Language Learnings

This part is devoted to evaluation of language learnings. It represents a plea that teachers take suggestions about evaluation to heart. Too often, elementary school teachers use only general standardized achievement tests and teacher-made tests as the testing and evaluation program.

If this be true, the issue of this part would be enhanced by a study of the uses and misuses, values and limitations of standardized language arts tests. Perhaps what is really needed are suggestions on comparing achievement with child language-development data (inter-child evaluation) and suggestions on measuring improvement (intra-child evaluation).

In the total evaluation program, far too many teachers begin the teaching act without diagnosing the present status of pupils, indicating a need for diagnostic inventory procedures. Evaluation should always be based upon previously accepted goals and involves the determining of the extent to which these goals have been achieved. Planning, acting, and evaluating are continuous steps in the teaching-learning process.

Specifically, the articles included in this anthology consider the problems of general assessment of (a) pupil growth in language (Manning); (b) oral language and listening activities (Kopp); (c) children's composition (Strickland); (d) literature programs (Irwin); and (e) children's responses to literature (Young).

55   Assessing Pupil Growth in Language

John C. Manning

In this article, Manning examines three aspects of the problem of assessing language growth in pupils and offers some practical suggestions.

What suggestions are offered for assessing listening, speaking, spelling, and language mechanics? What are the uses and limitations of standardized language arts tests you may have used? Of what value are diagnostic and evaluative data for a class or a pupil? Of what value in assessing pupils' language growth are studies such as Smith's and Loban's in Part Two of this anthology and DeLawter and Eash's in Part Three? Articles by Diederich, Feldt, Fitzgerald, Odom, and Olson cited in Selected References for Part Eight are pertinent to this topic.

The search for methods of appraising the English language development of pupils has a rich history of continuing experimentation and a somewhat limited heritage of accomplishment. Most successful have been those efforts to measure the quantitative aspects of English language achievement. Studies of the size of the four functional vocabularies, efforts to control the vocabulary content in basal reading systems, and contemporary studies of the effects of redundancy on comprehension skills development merit universal acceptance in our sometimes all too tolerant behavioral science.

Less successful and subject to arbitrary definitions and subjective evaluations have been those efforts to assess the qualitative aspects of English language growth. Factors affecting creativity, development of the higher mental processes, imaginative and elaborative thinking abilities are terms which frequently appear in the professional literature but are seldom defined to the satisfaction of the educational fraternity.

From *Reading and the Related Arts*, A Report of the Twenty-first Annual Conference and Course on Reading, University of Pittsburgh, 1965, pp. 103-110. Reprinted with permission of Donald L. Cleland (ed.), and John C. Manning, Associate Professor, University of Minnesota, Minneapolis.

It is generally accepted that many factors of heredity and environment significantly affect the development of a hearing, a speaking, a reading, and a writing vocabulary. Component analysis of those background factors has not shown clear cause-effect relationship on any variable examined with relation to a language outcome.

Cultural deprivation does affect language growth; to what extent is open to conjecture.

Physiological factors do affect achievements in speaking and reading; evidence of the relationship between hyperopia (farsightedness) and reading disability can be established. Legions of excellent readers with this same eye impairment, however, cast doubt on this seemingly logical causal relationship.

Neurological impairments of various types may be diagnosed in pupils who fail in our schools and in those students whose language achievements are superior.

The possibilities for investigation of these various sub-strata factors are limitless and will, no doubt, as we move to a more scientifically oriented profession, provide a fertile field for interdisciplinary studies of English language learning.

The effectiveness of standardized testing instruments has done much to advance the possibilities for controlled experimental research in English language development. Many areas of language growth, however, such as reference and research ability, improvement of oral reporting, ability to organize materials, improved quality of written expression, enrichment of concepts and development of pupil interest in language defy the best intentioned efforts of both psychologist and educator.

These opening remarks have been intended to emphasize the complexity of the task which confronts the classroom teacher and to reinforce the thesis that what knowledge exists in our discipline is often contradictory, often not appropriate to practical application and often without a theoretical base, inductively constituted, which cornerstones every profession except our own.

This paper will lightly examine three aspects of the problem of assessing language growth in pupils:

1. Background factors affecting English language development.
2. Normal English language development.
3. Uses and limitations of standardized testing instruments and more pointedly examine selected informal classroom procedures which may be used to improve the teaching of the English language arts.

Background Factors Affecting Language Development

The main argument for intensifying research in this area is that hopefully we will be able to provide a status profile for each pupil on entrance to school that will have immediate practical value for compensatory and intensive instruction in areas of anticipated language deficiency.

Four major tasks must be accomplished if this situation is to eventuate:

1. Specialization of research efforts to determine cause-effect relationships in each sub-strata area through interdisciplinary approaches.
2. The development of needed, and the refinement of existing, measurement instruments.
3. The full utilization of computer systems for analysis of Status Profiles.
4. The use of these same electronic systems for programming educational materials in appropriate intensity to accommodate individual differences among pupils.

Normal Language Development

It would be presumptious to suppose that valid analysis could be made of the many variables affecting normal language development within the limits of this paper. The complexity of the interrelationships among physiological capacity, environmental conditioning, and intellectual components including psychological-emotional aspects precludes the possibility of a satisfactory treatment here.

I do, however, wish to make brief comment on two significant problems of contemporary importance.

Ample research evidence exists concerning the size of the various functional vocabularies utilized by pupils at various chronological and mental age levels. We speak of normal language development as a sequence of accomplishments in acquiring a hearing vocabulary, a speaking vocabulary, a reading vocabulary and a writing vocabulary appropriate to the satisfaction of our social needs. The extent to which individual pupils utilize these vocabularies varies widely, especially with regard to mental age factors.

It is difficult to find curriculum programs reflecting these language differences. Seemingly, we have not appreciated the fact that elaborative thinking abilities, critical thinking skills and creative thinking attainments can be improved through listening tasks and reflected in the improved speaking accomplishments of pupils. All too many intermediate and secondary school language arts programs revolve around grammar workbooks, written composition assignments and reading comprehension tasks poorly adjusted to the vocabulary abilities of students and ill suited to the full utilization of the communicative media of our time.

The so-called "dropout" problem is aggravated by our reluctance or seeming inability to desire more efficient educational programs in the listening-speaking areas. With automation so emphatically upon us, it is ill advised to concentrate on industrial art or craft programs for terminal pupils in our secondary schools.

A second matter concerns our national commitment, philosophically and economically, to the educational improvement of the culturally deprived. Obviously, language development is of major importance in this endeavor.

A distinction should be made between those vocabularies which are learned somewhat naturally—the hearing and the speaking vocabularies, and those which are learned more formally—the reading and the writing. One difficulty in improving the educational level of the culturally deprived child is that a natural sequential development must be artificially accelerated to overcome language deficiencies and thus insure academic success in the lower primary grades.

The various "Projects Headstart" which I have observed in Texas and in California, and the various local projects courageously started without federal aid, do not, in most instances, regard some basic linguistic principles in language development and thus do not make maximum use of the additional school time which such projects financially afford. Entirely too much effort is expended on experiential activities related to concept development and entirely too little on formal instructional procedures to develop pupil proficiency with English phonology and syntax.

The vocabulary of our English language is not its most difficult component and such concept deficiencies are easily overcome. Those skills learned through oral-aural methods, specifically phonology and syntax, should constitute our major effort in formal language and reading readiness activities designed to overcome language deficiencies caused by socio-economic disadvantage.

Uses and Limitations of Standardized Tests

As a procedure for assessing the language development of individual pupils, the use of standardized tests has obvious advantages in measuring certain reading and writing abilities and glaring limitations in the listening-speaking areas. It would be unfair to criticize standardized testing in the main since a general fault is the use and interpretation of such measures rather than their content or professional intent.

Again, quite realistically, improved methods of correction and diagnostic appraisal must be fashioned before maximum use of such devices will be made. All too often such standardized tests are used solely as achievement measures, and the burden of correction and estimate of grade placement is assigned to the classroom teacher. The dubious motive purports that such correction procedures will result in a more sensitive understanding of the pupils enrolled in any given class. That such understandings *can* and *do* occur is not at question here;

that such understanding must come by such debilitating clerical procedures is professionally reprehensible.

Again, I would hope that economical individual school computer systems, impersonal enough to be objective and discriminating enough to hold valuable the unique development of each child, will soon be an integral part of the school facility.

Informal Classroom Procedures for Assessing Language Growth

A distinction is generally made between hearing capacity and listening ability. The former is more frequently defined in physiological terms while the latter refers more specifically to a communication skill. The following remarks relate to this latter classification.

Among the many reasons for assessing the listening abilities of pupils, two are of major significance:

1. A test of listening comprehension will provide suitable evidence of the capacity to read.
2. A test of listening comprehension is useful in determining the functional level for pupil participation in both skills and content subject areas.

In lieu of more formalized procedures, a listening comprehension test is a simple diagnostic measure which may be used to determine the reading capacity of individual pupils with reading disabilities.

Paragraphs, generally narrative or factual in style, may be selected from basal readers of various grade levels. These paragraphs should vary in length from a grade one selection of perhaps twenty-five words to an eighth grade selection of approximately 125 words. Comprehension questions may then be devised appropriate to each paragraph. Four or five questions would be sufficient for the grade one selection to perhaps seven or eight for the grade eight paragraph.

Contrasting the pupil's ability to answer questions following teacher reading of the paragraphs with the pupil's ability to read paragraphs of a similar type but different content will roughly approximate the degree of retardation in reading.

Such information regarding pupil deficiencies should be encouraging for it provides evidence that with properly adjusted educational materials, intensive teaching efforts and teacher dedication to the possibilities of increased achievement, improvement is possible. Further, when such information is professionally presented to parents, it can provide cautioned encouragement and do much to relieve parental anxiety concerning the mental abilities of the academically failing child.

The measurement of listening as a functional ability in various skill and content subject areas may be effected with slightly more elaborate procedures.

The graded paragraph format may again be used, but the content and style of both paragraphs and comprehension questions would change to suit the purposes of the measurement. Graded paragraphs to measure problem solving abilities could be employed, those measuring critical thinking abilities could be used, *while graded paragraphs in the various content areas could be used* as a measure of listening ability for the purposes of following directions, drawing inferences and conclusions, and for ability to determine main idea and logical sequence.

The instructional implications should be obvious; pupils with reading disabilities could benefit from listening skills instruction and classroom activities adjusted to comprehension level.

The matter of attention and persistence in learning is intimately associated with listening abilities. More than likely, pupil inattention in grade one is a major cause of learning disability and also the major symptom of inappropriate instructional procedures. All too often the use of pictures, simple visual directions and routine completion exercises aggravate the inattention problem.

Primary grade teachers could improve the listening abilities of pupils by decreasing the number of demonstrative pronouns used in giving oral directions and by increasing the number of subordinate units and qualifiers used in the assignment of classroom lessons.

At the intermediate and upper grade levels, major improvement in listening ability can be effected through the use of listening study guides which clearly specify the purposes for listening. Oral reporting activities, discussion procedures, and teacher presentation in content areas should be preceded by instructions for improving the efficiency of listening and accompanied by opportunities for pupil-written responses during the conduct of such oral activities.

Assessing Levels of Speaking Ability

The reluctance of many pupils to meaningfully participate in speaking activities in our classrooms no doubt stems from two major causes:

1. A self judgment that what is known by the pupil is not significant enough or pertinent enough to be shared.
2. An attitude of self consciousness or fear having root somewhere in that forest of experiences which affects all human behavior for good or ill.

Both problems are difficult to overcome instructionally and more than likely, each of us suffer in some degree from both.

The classroom teacher may gain some insight into the interests and speaking abilities of individual pupils (and the two are more than casually related) through the use of pictures of various types. Some pupils will readily respond to pictures narratively charged; other pictures more abstractly constituted and stimulus questions such as "What do you think will happen next?" "Why do you think the little girl is so happy?" might yield less enthusiastic results.

Some pupils operate well if the speaking activities are on a rather explicit level; others more imaginative, though not necessarily more intelligent, function well with more implicit motivations.

Following are examples of pictures and appropriate stimulus questions in order of increasing abstraction:

Picture	Initial Stimulus Question
1. Children playing	Tell me what the children are doing.
2. Dock or terminal scene	Tell me what is happening here.
3. Family on a picnic	What do you think mother is saying? Father? etc.
4. Boy and his father getting into an auto	What do you think is going to happpen?
5. Child gazing out a window	What do you suppose this little girl is thinking?

In a sense, procedures of this kind, rather grossly, measure various thinking abilities as well as speech proficiency. It is difficult, however, to devise clean measures which evaluate one and not, by inference, the other.

Two major instructional adjustments may be made for pupils with limited speaking vocabularies:

1. Adjustment of the speaking task to the demonstrated level of pupil facility.
2. Adjustment of group size to encourage increased pupil participation in oral activities.

Assessing Pupil Growth in Oral Reading

The question of the amount of oral reading proportionate to the amount of silent reading in developmental programs continues to plague the profession and has in past decades provided speaker, orator, and scholar with opportunities to extol the virtues of one and the vices of the other and vice versa.

Aside from certain aesthetic values, the purpose of oral reading is the diagnosis of word recognition errors of individual pupils. As such, certain procedures may be followed to instructional advantage.

When word recognition errors are made during oral reading, two entries should be made by the teacher, the actual error of the pupil and the correct lexical item from the text being read. Errors recorded should be reviewed periodically to determine the "pattern of error" for more effective word recognition instruction in subsequent reading lessons.

Assessment of the individual pupil's "pattern of error" is the important element for effective reteaching and word skills instruction. It is necessary, therefore, that errors be recorded over an extended period of time and that each individual pupil's errors be recorded separately. A tabbed stenographer's notebook is excellent for this purpose.

A symbol system should be devised for accurate recording of the following common error types: mispronunciations, words pronounced for pupils, insertions of words, additions to words, and omissions.

The recording activities should be clearly explained to pupils and the objectives of such recording of error should be demonstrated by sensitive and effective reteaching. I do not support the point of view that such recording methods stir latent feelings of insecurity and failure. Such feelings unfortunately arise when pupils do not understand teacher behavior, do not understand the reasons for their failure, and see no improvement in their subsequent reading attempts.

Similarly, the level of the text being used should come into serious question if too many errors need to be recorded. More than one pupil error in every twenty running words should alert the teacher to a reappraisal of the level of the text being used. If no errors are made by pupils, a similar reappraisal would be in order.

It is my contention that parents should be directly and early informed of the specific causes of reading failure. It is of questionable value to chronicle the symptoms of disability such as poor attitude, poor study habits, lack of motivation, daydreaming and the like. The use of such terms, more often than not, gives parents wide latitudes for conjecture and supposition and ultimately may emotionally stretch the deficiency beyond the point of educational remediation.

Most reading disabilities are not complicated beyond the understanding of classroom teachers. Conscientious recording of pupil errors, periodic review of such deficiencies and intensive remedial instruction at the point of word recognition weakness can, and in most cases will, provide failing pupils with a first full measure of success.

The problem we, as educational practitioners, have not confronted is the development of remedial materials in sufficient quantity, largely pupil directed and corrected, which when intensively used will assist the classroom teacher in overcoming reading deficiencies.

Developmental programs of reading instruction as presently constituted are clearly not enough. Instructional materials development, branched to include language-experience instruction, intensive phonics instruction, linguistic instruction and intensive kinesthetic-tactile instruction must be appreciated by the publishers of basal reading materials if we are to be successful in eliminating reading failure from our schools.

Assessing Pupil Growth in Written Language

My final remarks will relate to measurement in spelling and correction for mechanics of language factors.

We are moving as a profession, I think, to a clearer understanding of the contribution which other academic disciplines can provide with regard to subject matter content. The contribution of linguistics to spelling instruction is a case in point.

I am reasonably certain that the number of spelling words introduced per week, the manner of presentation, the type of word presented, and the speller exercises have not changed appreciably in the last three decades. The merit of this contention should be questioned since perhaps at some future time an opportunity to amplify the position will be afforded your speaker.

A major cause of spelling failure is an excess in the number of words presented for individual pupil mastery. It is even more fundamental than that perhaps; it is in the presentation of a spelling list at all.

If a child is failing to learn to read, I see little merit in introducing a spelling list. More appropriate, perhaps, would be the use of the reading vocabulary words as spelling words and instructionally provide visual memory training with those words during the spelling period.

Teachers may justify a modification in the number of spelling words presented to pupils failing in reading using the following simplified classification system:

Words may be classified as:

Content words:	nouns, verbs, adjectives, and adverbs
Function words:	articles, prepositions, conjunctions, word auxiliaries, connectives

Words may be sub-classified as:

Colorful:	words that evoke mental images (grandfather, canoe, dog, etc.)
Abstract:	words which do not evoke mental images (whenever, because, however)
Phonetically regular:	words in which a one-to-one correspondence exists between the phonemes and the graphemes (mud, sod, tub)
Phonetically irregular:	words in which an irregular phoneme-grapheme correspondence can be found (most of the words in our language)

A content, colorful, phonetically regular word, therefore, would, in most instances, be more readily mastered in spelling than a function, abstract, phonetically irregular word. Though the point is highly generalized, the classroom implications for instruction should be clear.

A modification in the manner of presenting words in spelling tests might also prove valuable in assessing spelling power.

Spelling words may be presented orally by definition as one phase of a test and then by actual word in another phase. A two columned sheet may be used. Spaces for words not known by definition should be left blank in the first column and then attempted in the second column when the teacher provides the word stimulus.

Rationale for this method rests on the assumption that when we want to write, we have some ideas to communicate, and like Pirandellos "Six Characters" we go searching for the words which best express our thoughts.

And finally, correction procedures for written language.

All too often there is little articulation in the written language program in our schools. The method following is supported by the theory that pupils develop writing skills at various rates of progress and that intensive remedial instruction is necessary to overcome mechanics of language deficiencies. The method is further contingent for success on the preparation of educational materials of sufficient quantity in the specific sub-skills areas of capitalization, punctuation usage and spelling.

A first problem is to determine the level of corrections; that is, the type of correction mark and the position of that mark relative to the specific error. Obviously, the classroom teacher must begin at a level appropriate to the number of errors made by individual pupils; the greater the total number of errors in proportion to total running word count, the lower the level of correction which should be employed.

Level I   Correction at the point of error with the correction item.

    J   to
    (john sat down too eat.)

Level II   Correction at the point of error by symbol.

    X   X
    (john sat down too eat.)

Level III Correction at the line of error.

    (2X john sat down too eat.)

Level IV   Correcting by indication of the total and type of error.

    (2p, 2c, 2u, meaning 2 punctuation, 2 capitalization and 2 usages errors)

Level V   Indication by numeral of the total number of mechanics errors without indication as to type.

Level VI   Pupil self-proofreading.

The teacher correction procedures at whatever level conducted should be followed by intensive practice specific to the sub-skills weakness. For this purpose, quantities of practice materials of increasing difficulty should be catalogued by skill, and be readily available for pupil practice and self-correction.

The road to excellence in instructional practice is arduous and professionally demanding.

No developmental language programs thus far outlined will serve all learning needs for all pupils.

No standardized or informal tests thus far designed will assess all language deficiencies.

No teacher education programs thus far operative or envisioned will adequately prepare practitioners for all instructional possibilities.

And certainly no profession has ever undertaken a task so monumental as the development of universal literacy with so optimistic an attitude of eventual and certain success.

56　The Evaluation of Oral Language Activity: Teaching and learning

O. W. Kopp

In this essay, Kopp treats an extremely difficult problem—assessment of oral language skills, listening and speaking. Language expression is difficult to evaluate since it is both a process and a product. Because of more tangible aspects of writing, written composition may be more easily evaluated by classroom teachers. But the difficulty inherent in oral language measurement should not encourage teachers to make only a cursory appraisal. The explicit purpose of this article is to provide practical procedures for a teacher in diagnosing and measuring abilities in oral expression.

What standardized evaluative instruments are available for appraisal of the skills and products of listening and speaking? What are several informal means for evaluating listening and speaking? If feasible, develop a scale and use it in rating a pupil's speaking ability. Kelly reports an informative study on the validity of standardized listening tests in an article cited in Selected References for Part Eight.

"When I go to school, I'm going to learn to read and write." This comment reflects the aspirations of most four-year-olds about to enter the magic land of school. Their concern is centered upon the two language arts known to them. After all, they already know how to speak and listen.

Also, unfortunately, too many teachers fail to recognize the need to teach speaking and listening. The term "language arts" refers to a quarternary discipline, but too often in actual practice the language arts are reduced to a binary discipline.

It is understandable and logical that much concerted effort is directed toward the teaching of reading and writing. At the same time, it is incompre-

From *Elementary English* 44:114-123; February 1967. Reprinted with permission of the National Council of Teachers of English and O. W. Kopp, Chairman of Elementary Education, Teachers College, University of Nebraska, Lincoln.

hensible and illogical to assume that no further improvement is needed in the skills of speaking and listening.

Just how important is oral communication? Man in all his wisdom has discovered only two ways to settle differences—by using words or by using weapons. Democratic, peaceful resolution of problems involves discussion; listening is necessarily half of this dualism. Our world is one in which oral communication is a vitally necessary tool for understanding and learning; it frequently dominates as the primary mode of communication.

In the hope that more teachers may wish to do a better job in the teaching of speaking and listening, pertinent research has been reviewed with the aim of giving direction to the teaching of oral communication. Attention must also be given to the knowledge available from research which will assist teachers in diagnosing and measuring abilities in the oral language skills and give direction to their improvement.

Listening

Very little disagreement about the feasibility of teaching listening exists. Duker's extensive bibliography on listening is prefaced by a statement that listening can be improved by proper teaching.[1] Shane and Mulry, after examining many references on listening, also conclude that listening can be taught and evaluated.[2] Hatfield comments that advances in teaching English include the realization that ". . . listening is an art as complex as reading and is improvable through instruction and guided practice."[3] The National Council of Teachers of English has stated that listening should be taught because it is the most used of the language arts, it is often poorly done, and evidence suggests that listening habits may be improved through training.[4]

Berry urges teachers to chart their inquiry regarding listening into four major areas.[5] She suggests:

1. A frank analysis of your own listening experience.
2. A thoughtful study of the listening situation in your classroom.
3. A development in children of concern for their own listening competence.
4. A development of the problem in relation to communication, with listening playing its essential role—not as a value in itself but as a means to the more important meeting of minds.

Other writers agree with Berry that the first step in teaching listening is for the teacher to examine his own listening habits. Nichols has devised a self-rating scale to be used in making an analysis of one's poor listening habits.[6]

Brown has stated, "The most basic and most important element for auding competence is possessing and imparting a reliable concept of what it is that the student is being asked to improve."[7] A student must first recognize his deficiencies and then set up a plan for doing something about them.

Experiences should be provided to encourage children's use of the scientific method of inquiry into listening as well as into other subject areas. The following questions are examples of the kinds of topics which could be used as springboards for pupil discussions and pupil investigations:

1. How does listening differ from hearing?
2. What are some good listening habits?
3. What are some poor listening habits?
4. How do good listeners help a speaker?
5. How does a speaker's personality affect a listener?
6. Why does the same word often mean different things to different people?
7. How can a listener guard against accepting falsehoods for the truth?
8. How do the experiences you have had in your lives affect your listening?
9. How can wide reading improve listening habits?
10. How can you learn to tell which ideas are most important and which ones are least important?

Evaluation, of necessity, must be based upon a standard. For listening this standard is the "good listener"—one who has a wide range of interests, respect for other people and their viewpoints, and the ability to delay his own reactions. The poor listener often precludes further listening by reacting instantaneously, vigorously, and without critical thought.

Stromer suggests the following as examples of poor listening habits: tuning out one's mind; thinking we already know what is going to be said; looking for mannerisms of the speaker instead of listening; doing other things while supposedly listening; and hearing words instead of ideas.[8]

To evaluate accurately a child's listening performances, the teacher needs to recognize the importance of several factors.

1. He must take into consideration factors accounting for individual differences:
   a. Intelligence and aptitude.
   b. Reading comprehension ability and vocabulary development.
   c. Cultural background.
   d. Interests.
   e. Personality traits.
2. He must consider factors relating to attention as preparation for auditory perception:
   a. Physiological sensitivity and fatigue.
   b. Psychological sensitivity and concentration.
   c. Readiness to respond.

     d. Interference of distracting elements.

     e. Training of the sense organs.

3. He must consider other personal factors determining what one perceives:

     a. Individual needs.

     b. Perceiving what one wishes to perceive.

     c. Personal bias and prejudices.

An analysis of listening problems should include diagnosis of possible hearing difficulties and a consideration of total adjustment, including personality, an element which has been found to be closely related to listening ability.[9] An analysis of listening problems should also include an assessment of the vocabulary development of the child. The teacher needs an awareness of the vocabulary development of the child and an awareness of the quality and quantity of the child's listening and speaking both in and out of school.[10, 11]

In the evaluation of listening, both formal and informal tests may be used. One is not a substitute for the other. Standardized tests or teacher-made tests can be used to evaluate such skills as listening for directions, listening for word meaning, listening to draw conclusions, listening for immediate recall of details, listening to identify the main point, and listening to identify sequence.

Standardized tests have the advantage of providing for comparison with a norm; interpretation by percentile ranks and scores; known reliability, validity, and difficulty; predetermined relationships to other test instruments; and ease of administration and scoring.[12] Brown believes that appropriate test instruments must be developed for all levels if we are to reach a needed understanding of listening.[13]

Standardized listening tests for the lower elementary grades have been almost nonexistent. The *Sequential Tests for Educational Progress* (STEP) include a listening test, but this test is not appropriate below grade four. However, Wright devised and standardized a listening test for grades two through four, which has been used by others and found reliable for grades two and three but is considered too easy for most children in grade four.[14]

Informal evaluative techniques can be designed to fit specific classroom situations. Brown reported the use of informal evaluation in three of the most common listening situations—casual listening, purposeful listening, and notetaking while listening. Students were able to assess their listening efficiency as the result of tests given in each situation. Purposeful listening resulted in better comprehension than casual listening. Notetaking seemed to lower comprehension at the time, but retesting showed that notetaking delayed forgetting.[15]

Even in the early primary grades children can formulate standards for listening and judge whether or not their performances meet their own standards. Self-evaluation checklists such as the following can help children become aware of the many factors involved in listening.

Checking Up on My Listening

	Yes	No
1. Did I remember to get ready for listening?		
a. Was I seated comfortably where I could see and hear?		
b. Were my eyes focused on the speaker?		
2. Was my mind ready to concentrate on what the speaker had to say?		
a. Was I able to push other thoughts out of my mind for the time being?		
b. Was I ready to think about the topic and call to mind the things I already knew about it?		
c. Was I ready to learn more about the topic?		
3. Was I ready for "take-off"?		
a. Did I discover in the first few minutes where the speaker was taking me?		
b. Did I discover his central idea so that I could follow it through the speech?		
4. Was I able to pick out the ideas which supported the main idea?		
a. Did I take advantage of the speaker's clues (such as first, next, *etc.*) to help organize the ideas in my mind?		
b. Did I use my extra "think" time to summarize and take notes— either mentally or on paper?		
5. After the speaker finished and the facts were all in, did I evaluate what had been said?		
a. Did this new knowledge seem to fit with the knowledge I already had?		
b. Did I weigh each idea to see if I agreed with the speaker?		

If you marked questions *NO*, decide why you could not honestly answer them *YES*.

Wilt emphasized the importance of pupil participation when she stated: "Children learn best those things they live and do; they learn from each other. They cannot learn how to speak by listening entirely to the teacher speak, nor can they learn to listen to their peers when they seldom have the opportunity to listen to their peers."[16]

Listening to recordings of various regional speech patterns can focus the pupil's attention on similarities and differences. Listening to tape recordings of their own voices can lead students to the realization that each individual has his own personal idiolect. Simple diagrams which show rising and falling pitch help children become aware of the intonation patterns of our language.

Each year of school should find each child progressing toward increasingly sophisticated levels of speaking and listening maturity. Each child should become more and more aware of the characteristics of good listening and his own strengths and weaknesses relative to these standards. He should realize that good listeners must have an interest in people, hear people out, respect the other person's rights to express an opinion, have an interest in the points of view of others, and be interested in broadening his own viewpoints.

Upper elementary children are capable of evaluating their own listening powers by using the following criteria:

Do I
Hold the thread of a discussion in mind?
Listen to content even though it does not affect me directly?
Watch for transitional phrases?
Try to discount bias in a speaker?
Disagree with a speaker courteously?
Reserve judgment in listening to different viewpoints in discussion?
Indicate by my remarks that I have turned over in my mind the
ideas of others?[17]

Kegler has suggested that pupils keep logs of their listening activities. Analysis of these logs will prove helpful in the evaluation of listening experiences.[18]

Charting the flow of discussion may help students to recognize the importance of "equalizing" their roles as speakers and listeners. Such an activity helps develop an understanding of the communication process, emphasizes the principles of effective communication, and provides practice in the use of communication skills. Through interaction, students are given a chance to sharpen their skills as well as to exchange ideas and viewpoints.

Frazier pointed out that listening can also be taught and evaluated by means of pupil conversations and group discussions in which the teacher and pupils analyze the role of the listener and how it is being fulfilled.[19] Pupils can also determine how the group leader's role differs from that of the participants.

The alert elementary school teacher will find countless ready-made opportunities to evaluate listening as children plan units of work, give reports, give directions and make announcements, tell or read stories, and speak in verse choirs.

The evaluation of listening should also include an analysis of the school environment by such questions as the following:

1. Is the classroom climate favorable for good listening?
2. Does each child feel secure and feel that his contribution is important?
3. Is there a real purpose for listening?
4. Is the seating arrangement adequate?
5. Is frequent pupil participation encouraged?
6. Is the length of presentation appropriate for the attention span of the pupils?
7. Are children encouraged to set standards for self-evaluation?
8. Do children have the opportunity to use what they hear?

Dale has stressed the importance of making the classroom a place in which listening or not listening matters to the student. He states that to teach listening effectively it is necessary for teachers to:

1. Regard communication as sharing;
2. Earn the right to speak by listening;
3. Create mood or disposition for others to speak;
4. Move from the simple to the complex;
5. Teach evaluation of the logic of a speech; and
6. Teach critical listening.[20]

The statement, "That to which the child is asked to listen in school should be worthy of time and thought," also emphasizes this view.[21] The school's task is to teach the child to listen objectively, appreciatively, and critically. Specific lessons for the primary purpose of teaching listening are stilted and artificial, according to Wilt. She recommends using many regular classroom activities for teaching listening skills.[22]

As a means of developing more effective listening by pupils, Dawson and Zollinger suggest that the teacher take advantage of opportunities for listening; that the classroom atmosphere be relaxed, comfortable, quiet, and thus conducive to listening; that pupils be prepared for what they are about to hear; that they be led to expect meaning whenever they listen; that opportunities be arranged for the reproduction of the materials listened to; that the children set up standards for effective listening; and that they be guided in the evaluation of what they hear.[23]

Gardner believes that "in order to listen alertly and intelligently one needs to cultivate patience, discipline, and a deeply rooted interest in others."[24] These same qualities are necessary if one hopes to teach others to listen. Even though the best way to teach listening may not yet have been established by research, everything possible should be done to improve students' listening skills.

Teaching the skills of listening involves awareness of the importance of listening; knowledge of the abilities, skills, understandings, attitudes, and appreciations acquired through the spoken word; assessment of the present listening abilities and habits of pupils; and provision for direct, systematic instruction in listening.[25]

Speaking

A recognition of the importance of oral communication and a realization that speaking is a part of this dualism foster a desire to improve speaking through teaching. The child enters school able to speak; but there are obvious deficiencies in his speaking skills. The need to teach speech or speaking has been accepted for many years; however, emphasis upon it and recognition of its importance have varied from time to time. Also, the swing of the educational pendulum has focused attention on different phases of speech teaching—correction of physiological deficiencies, improving mechanics of speaking, encouraging public speaking, *etc.*

Wagner, in a survey of speech programs, notes the increasingly broad interpretation of speech and lists the criteria which he finds are being used to evaluate the adequacy of speech programs:

1. Provision for all pupils
2. Provision for the handicapped
3. Interpretation of speech as social behavior
4. Realism in scope and sequence
5. Development of ethical standards for speech.[26]

Because the same kinds of speaking—conversation, discussion, reporting, *etc.*—are used at all age levels, difficulties are inherent in defining the scope and sequence of a speech program. Beauchamp feels that the main areas for emphasis should be mechanics, individual performance, and performance as part of a group.[27]

Teachers need a well planned guide to use in comparing the levels of progress of the individual pupils within their classrooms. Dawson and Zollinger recommend that these standards be formulated by a committee of teachers and give an example of a sequential listing of goals worked out by teachers of the Portland, Oregon, public schools.[28]

The level of development of speaking skills varies from individual to individual. However, Strickland states:

The standards which evolve from experience and advance progressively from level to level follow this general sequence.
1. Emphasis on freeing the individual and encouraging him to participate
2. Emphasis on increasing recognition of responsibility to others and the development of group consciousness
3. Emphasis on interplay of ideas and meeting of minds
4. Emphasis on responsibility for the value and the truth of one's remarks
5. Emphasis on the improvement of personal techniques such as voice and mannerisms
6. Emphasis on training for leadership in the carrying on of group processes.[29]

Evaluation of speech is a special problem, for "the transitory and usually unrecorded nature of oral communication makes systematic evaluation of it difficult."[30] A dearth of standardized tests of oral communication skills and abilities exists; therefore, it has been suggested that "in listening and speaking little dependence can be placed on standardized tests" and that "teacher-pupil-made tests, simple rating scales, tape recordings, children's own records, and observations of teachers can provide for emphasis on the improvement by each individual child in the course of each school year."[31]

The importance of the use of simple rating devices—comparison of voice recordings over time or comparison of voice recordings to a scale such as Netzer's—is discussed in *The English Language Arts*, but little has been done as a follow-up to these suggestions.[32] The view generally held is that regardless of the evaluative technique used, "Methods of appraisal should be devised by teachers actually working with children, and in some of the procedures the pupil should participate in rating himself or others."[33]

Teacher-child relationship, motivation, and classroom atmosphere are important factors to be considered.[34, 35] Bolz suggests the following questions as a guide for teacher self-evaluation:

Do I recognize the need for children to practice oral expression?
Do I consistently provide opportunities for children to communicate orally?
Am I willing to work with children where I find them—willing to work patiently and understandingly with a shy child?
How can I improve my own skills in oral expression? Do I set a good example in my speech—enunciating clearly, speaking comfortably and easily, organizing my thoughts logically?
Do I listen to children? Do I give them my complete attention? Do I respond fully to their questions and comments?[36]

Hopkins believes that ". . . attainment of 'self-confidence' has been overplayed as an object of the speech course. . . . Of greater importance is his (the pupil's) knowledge of language, his skill in its use, his ability to contribute something of worth, his sense of values as expressed in the oral communication situation."[37]

Criteria for evaluation of pupil progress might be similar to Pronovost's listing of attitudes and abilities to develop in a speaking situation:

1. A desire to contribute worthwhile ideas effectively.
2. The ability to use words which express ideas clearly and accurately.
3. The ability to select and organize ideas effectively.
4. The ability to use voice and articulation so that speech will be heard and understood easily.
5. The ability to use appropriate posture, bodily actions, and visual aids.
6. The ability to adapt speech behavior and speech organization to group situations such as conversations and discussions.
7. The ability to communicate thought and mood in oral reading, choral speaking, and dramatic activities.[38]

One committee suggests that progress is being made toward the goals of speech teaching when the child shows a ". . . growing awareness of the responsibilities of both the listener and the speaker; an appreciation of the effects of oral language on oneself and others; a growing sensitivity to the influence of different purposes for communication on oral language activity; alertness to various clues and cues that are an integral part of oral communication; and growing effectiveness in discussions as shown by an increasing awareness of the importance of courtesy and relevance as well as the responsibility of knowing when to speak and when to listen."[39]

Tidyman and Butterfield have warned that one cannot stress all skills and abilities at one time, but should stress the specific language goal most needed by the individual or the group.[40] When making an evaluation, it is important to remember that specific comments about strong or weak points contribute more to growth than weak generalities.[41]

The mechanics of evaluation frequently present a problem to the teacher. The suggestion has been made that designated symbols be used as a "shorthand" notation for evaluation of individual pupils during a speaking situation; for example:

l   contributions notably relevant, pertinent
+   contributions notably for effectiveness of vocabulary, analogy imagery (as well as relevance)
g   good generalizations (induction)
e   concrete examples of illustrations of concept being discussed; application of a principle (deduction)
o   irrelevant attention-getting, foolish, ineffective oral language.[42]

Keeping a record of evaluations made of each pupil on an individual card provides opportunity for individual diagnosis and for showing evidence of progress over a period of time.

A comparison of the teacher's evaluation of speaking performance to the pupil's evaluation can lead to a better understanding of strengths and weaknesses. Checklists such as the following might be used.

Student's Speech Checklist

I. How do I sound?
   a. Is my voice pleasant to hear?
   b. Can others understand the words I say?
   c. Is my voice neither too loud nor too soft?
II. Is my speech interesting to others?
   a. Do I use a variety of expressions and words?
   b. Do I explain things so others understand my ideas?
   c. Do I use language correct for each speaking situation?
   d. Do I remember to take my turn to speak—talking neither too much nor too little?

I can improve my voice and speech by _____

Teacher's Speech Checklist

I. Student's voice.
   a. Is the voice pleasant?
      If not, how would you describe it? _____
   b. Are articulation and enunciation satisfactory?
      If not, what needs to be improved? _____
   c. Is volume appropriate for each occasion?

If not, is it too loud or too soft? _____

II. Student's speech.

    a. Does speech show a variety of expressions and vocabulary?
       If not, what needs improving? _____

    b. Does speech give evidence of care-thinking?
       If not, what seems to be the reason? _____

    c. Is usage acceptable?
       If not, what faults are most common? _____

    d. Is there evidence that personality problems hamper speech quality?
       If yes, what seems to be the problem? _____

Examples of the use of dual evaluation checklists for individual speaking situations can be found in *Children and Oral Language*.[43]

Self-evaluation based on pupil-set standards has often been recommended.[44, 45, 46] Such pupil-set standards might be similar to the following:

Do others listen when you tell a personal experience?
Can people follow the directions you give?
Can you take part in discussion without becoming angry or making others angry?
Are you tolerant and respectful of others' viewpoints?
Can you ask for information so that it is willingly given?
Are you accurate and thorough in reporting what you hear or read, so that you give true understanding to others?
Do you like to listen when others talk?[47]

Not only can children set up overall standards for improving speaking skills, but they can be led to formulate standards for each type of speaking occasion—conversation, discussion, reporting, *etc.* Examples of such pupil-set standards can be found in Dawson and Zollinger[48] and Strickland.[49]

Evaluation of the progress of pupils should be done with basic goals kept in mind. "As in other areas of the curriculum, a wide range of individual differences is apparent. The purpose is not to eliminate these differences—not to make every child an orator—but to help each pupil to say those things which are important to him."[50]

"When I went to elementary school I learned to read, write, *speak*, and *listen*." It is to be hoped that this will be the comment of the adolescent of the future. With concerted teaching effort, including effort based upon adequate evaluation, it certainly should be.

Footnotes

[1] Sam Duker, *Listening Bibliography*. New York and London: The Scarecrow Press, Inc., 1964.

[2] Harold G. Shane and June Grant Mulry, *Improving Language Arts Instruction*

Through Research. Washington, D.C.: Association for Supervision and Curriculum Development, 1963, pp. 102-110.

3 Wilbur Hatfield, "Advances in the Teaching of English," *NEA Journal,* 45 (February, 1956) 90-92.

4 National Council of Teachers of English, *Language Arts for Today's Children.* New York: Appleton-Century-Crofts, Inc., 1954, pp. 71-105.

5 Althea Berry, "Experiences in Listening," *Elementary English,* 28 (March, 1951) 130-32.

6 Ralph G. Nichols, "How Well Do You Listen?" *Education,* 75 (January, 1955) 302.

7 Don P. Brown, "And Having Ears They Hear Not," *NEA Journal,* 39 (November, 1950) 587.

8 Walter F. Stromer, "Learn How to Listen," *This Week Magazine,* 16 (February 21, 1960) 13-15.

9 Walter F. Stromer, "Listening and Personality," *Education,* 75 (January, 1955) 322-26.

10 Don P. Brown, "Teaching Aural English," *English Journal,* 39 (March, 1950) 128-36.

11 Margaret B. Parke, "Children's Ways of Talking and Listening," *Childhood Education,* 29 (January, 1953) 223-30.

12 Don P. Brown, "Evaluating Student Performance in Listening," *Education,* 75 (January, 1955) 316-21.

13 *Ibid.*

14 Evan Leonard Wright, "The Construction of a Test of Listening Comprehension for the Second, Third and Fourth Grades," unpublished doctoral dissertation, Washington University, 1957. *Dissertation Abstracts,* 17 (October, 1957) 2226-27.

15 Brown, *loc. cit.*

16 Miriam E. Wilt, "Let's Teach Listening," *Creative Ways of Teaching the Language Arts.* Champaign, Illinois: National Council of Teachers of English, 1957.

17 Wilt, *op. cit.,* p. 88.

18 Stanley Benjamin Kegler, "Techniques in Teaching Listening for Main Ideas," *English Journal,* 45 (January, 1956) 30-32.

19 Alexander Frazier, "The Teaching of Listening: A Memo to Teachers," *Elementary English,* 35 (February, 1958) 111-12.

20 Edgar Dale, *Audio-Visual Methods in Education.* New York: Dryden Press, 1954.

21 Miriam E. Wilt, "Listening Skills Can Be Improved," *Instructor,* 72 (January, 1963) 6.

22 Miriam E. Wilt, "The Teaching of Listening and Why," *Educational Screen,* 31 (April, 1952) 144-46.

23 Mildred A. Dawson and Marian Zollinger, *Guiding Language Learning.* Yonkers, New York: World Book Company, 1957, pp. 160-92.

24 John W. Gardner, "The Art of Listening," *Saturday Review,* 39 (June 2, 1956) 46.

25 Harold A. Anderson, "Teaching the Art of Listening," *School Review,* 57 (February, 1949) 63-65.

26 Guy Wagner, "What Schools Are Doing—Improving the Speech Program," *Education,* 8 (February, 1963) 380-82.

27 George A. Beauchamp, *The Curriculum of the Elementary School.* Boston: Allyn and Bacon, Inc., 1964, pp. 95-99.

28 Dawson and Zollinger, *op. cit.,* pp. 138-59, 249-307.

29 Ruth G. Strickland, *The Language Arts in the Elementary School,* Second Edition. Boston: D. C. Heath and Co., 1957, p. 185.

30 National Council of Teachers of English, *The English Language Arts.* New York: Appleton-Century-Crofts, Inc., 1952, p. 431.

31 Helen K. Mackintosh (Editorial Chairman), *Children and Oral Language.* Washington, D.C.: Association for Childhood Education International, Association for Supervision and Curriculum Development (NEA); Newark, Delaware: International Reading Association; Champaign, Illinois: National Council of Teachers of English, 1964.

[32] National Council of Teachers of English, *op. cit.*, pp. 431-33.

[33] Mackintosh, *op. cit.*, p. 29.

[34] National Council of Teachers of English, *op. cit.*, p. 433.

[35] Carrie Rasmussen, *Speech Methods in the Elementary School*, Revised. New York: The Ronald Press Company, 1962.

[36] George C. Bolz, "Promoting Oral Expression," *National Elementary Principal*, 42 (April, 1963) 41-43.

[37] Thomas A. Hopkins, "The Spoken Word," *Education*, 84 (November, 1963), 166-69.

[38] Wilbert Pronovost, *The Teaching of Speaking and Listening in the Elementary School*. New York: Longmans, Green and Co., 1959, pp. 3-4.

[39] Mackintosh, *op. cit.*, p. 12.

[40] Willard F. Tidyman and Marguerite Butterfield, *Teaching the Language Arts*. New York: McGraw-Hill Book Company, Inc., 1959, pp. 38-63, 235-53.

[41] Mackintosh, *op. cit.*, p. 31.

[42] *Ibid.*

[43] *Ibid.*, pp. 29-30.

[44] Robert M. Bloom, "A Program for Oral English," *Elementary English*, 41 (February, 1964) 158-64.

[45] Mildred A. Dawson, *Teaching Language in the Grades*. Yonkers, New York: World Book Company, 1951, pp. 177-78.

[46] Dawson and Zollinger, *loc. cit.*

[47] Dawson, *op. cit.*, p. 154, citing Idelle Boyce and Ethel Mabie Falk, "Judging by Results," *Childhood Education*, 14 (January, 1938) 200.

[48] Dawson and Zollinger, *loc. cit.*

[49] Strickland, *loc. cit.*

[50] Bolz, *op. cit.*, p. 43.

Bibliography

Anderson, Harold A., "Teaching the Art of Listening," *School Review*, 57 (February, 1949) 63-65.

Beauchamp, George A., *The Curriculum of the Elementary School*. Boston: Allyn and Bacon, Inc., 1964, pp. 95-99.

Berry, Althea, "Experiences in Listening," *Elementary English*, 28 (March, 1951) 130-32.

Bloom, Robert M., "A Program for Oral English," *Elementary English*, 41 (February, 1964) 158-64.

Bolz, George C., "Promoting Oral Expression," *National Elementary Principal*, 42 (April, 1963) 41-43.

Brown, Don P., "And Having Ears They Hear Not," *NEA Journal*, 39 (November, 1950) 587.

———, "Evaluating Student Performance in Listening," *Education*, 75 (January, 1955) 316-21.

———, "Teaching Aural English," *English Journal*, 39 (March, 1950) 128-36.

Dale, Edgar, *Audio-Visual Methods in Education*. New York: Dryden Press, 1954.

Dawson, Mildred A., *Teaching Language in the Grades*. Yonkers, New York: World Book Company, 1951, pp. 105-35, 151-87.

———, and Marian Zollinger, *Guiding Language Learning*. Yonkers, New York: World Book Company, 1957, pp. 138-92, 249-307.

Duker, Sam, *Listening Bibliography*. New York and London: The Scarecrow Press, Inc., 1964.

Frazier, Alexander, "The Teaching of Listening: A Memo to Teachers," *Elementary English*, 35 (February, 1958) 111-12.

Gardner, John W., "The Art of Listening," *Saturday Review*, 39 (June 2, 1956) 46.

Greene, Harry A. and Walter T. Petty, *Developing Language Skills in the Elementary Schools*. Boston: Allyn and Bacon, 1963, pp. 481-561.

Hatfield, Wilbur, "Advances in the Teaching of English," *NEA Journal*, 45 (February, 1956) 90-92.

Hopkins, Thomas A., "The Spoken Word," *Education*, 84 (November, 1963) 166-69.

Kegler, Stanley Benjamin, "Techniques in Teaching Listening for Main Ideas," *English Journal*, 45 (January, 1956) 30-32.

Mackintosh, Helen K. (Editorial Chairman), *Children and Oral Language*. Washington, D.C.: Association for Childhood Education International, Association for Supervision and Curriculum Development (NEA); Newark, Delaware: International Reading Association; Champaign, Illinois: National Council of Teachers of English, 1964.

National Council of Teachers of English, *The English Language Arts*. New York: Appleton-Century-Crofts, Inc., 1952.

———, *Language Arts for Today's Children*. New York: Appleton-Century-Crofts, Inc., 1954, pp. 71-143.

Nichols, Ralph G., "How Well Do You Listen?" *Education*, 75 (January, 1955) 302.

Parke, Margaret B., "Children's Ways of Talking and Listening," *Childhood Education*, 29 (January, 1953) 223-30.

Pronovost, Wilbert, *The Teaching of Speaking and Listening in the Elementary School*. New York: Longmans, Green and Co., 1959.

Rasmussen, Carrie, *Speech Methods in the Elementary School*, Revised. New York: The Ronald Press Company, 1962.

Shane, Harold G., *Research Helps in Teaching the Language Arts*. Washington, D.C.: Association for Supervision and Curriculum Development, 1955, pp. 68-72.

Shane, Harold G. and June Grant Mulry, *Improving Language Arts Instruction Through Research*. Washington, D.C.: Association for Supervision and Curriculum Development, 1963.

Strickland, Ruth G., *The Language Arts in the Elementary School*, Second Edition. Boston: D. C. Heath and Company, 1957, pp. 116-97.

Stromer, Walter F., "Learn How to Listen," *This Week Magazine*, 16 (February 21, 1960) 13-15.

———, "Listening and Personality," *Education*, 75 (January, 1955) 322-36.

Tidyman, Willard F. and Marguerite Butterfield, *Teaching the Language Arts*. New York: McGraw-Hill Book Company, Inc., 1959, pp. 38-63, 235-53.

Wagner, Guy, "What Schools Are Doing—Improving the Speech Program," *Education*, 83 (February, 1963) 380-82.

Wilt, Miriam E., "Let's Teach Listening," *Creative Ways of Teaching the Language Arts*. Champaign, Illinois: National Council of Teachers of English, 1957.

———, "Listening Skills Can Be Improved," *Instructor*, 72 (January, 1963) 6.

———, "The Teaching of Listening and Why," *Educational Screen*, 31 (April, 1952) 144-46.

Wright, Evan Leonard, "The Construction of a Test of Listening Comprehension for the Second, Third and Fourth Grades," unpublished doctoral dissertation, Washington University, 1957. *Dissertation Abstracts*, 17 (October, 1957) 2226-27.

57 Evaluating Children's Composition

Ruth G. Strickland

Strickland examines the assessment of children's written expression. She discusses types of evaluation; methods of evaluating composition at different levels of the school program; and evaluating individual and class growth in composition.

What evaluative ideas are found in common as presented by Strickland and Kopp? What standardized evaluative instruments are available for appraisal of the skills and product of written expression? If feasible, develop a scale and use it in rating a pupil's written composition.

The headmaster of a school on the fringe of London has a delightful method of helping children to evaluate their own growth in written expression. As is true of most schools in England, each child in this school has in his desk several notebooks in which he writes for different purposes. One notebook may be his diary, another for work in the social studies, another for "sums," and the like. Each child has one notebook that is his "rough" book. In it he may try out any ideas or write anything he wishes, even to lampooning the teacher, because this book is private—no one looks into it without being invited to by its owner. As each child in the school finishes a book he has written other than his "rough" book, he takes it to the office of the headmaster. Together they look it over to see how much the child has improved from the first page to the last. After they have discussed it the child leaves his finished book in the office and goes back to his classroom with a new book and the determination to make this one even better. The headmaster keeps and binds together all of the books a child has finished from age six to the age of eleven-plus, when he goes on to secondary school. Some time during the first term in secondary school the children are invited back to their primary school in groups of six or eight to look over their accumu-

From *Elementary English* 37:321-330; May 1960. Reprinted with permission of the National Council of Teachers of English and Ruth G. Strickland, Research Professor of Education, Indiana University, Bloomington.

lation of notebooks with the headmaster, then to take them proudly home as a record of their growth through six years.

A great deal has been written regarding standards for the evaluation of children's writing. Teachers often feel defeated and frustrated as they see children content to do work that is less than their best in spite of the teacher's efforts. It would appear that the key to good work may lie not in the standards the school sets for the children's writing, but in the standards each child is helped to set for himself, because those are the standards he takes with him out into life after he leaves the realm of the teacher's authority. Showing respect for children's compositions by keeping them in some sort of permanent form which makes possible both self-evaluation by the child and evaluation by the teacher over a period of time long enough to show growth is one method of helping children to take pride in their growth and motivating them to stretch upward to new heights.

The Art of Writing

The art of writing as of speaking consists in having something to say and knowing how to say it. It is taken for granted that what one has to say should be worth the effort of speech or the far greater effort of writing. Content and style must be thought of together since in any good composition content should determine form. Few people would agree with the statement quoted from a 1941 report to the Glasgow Education Authority which declared that, ". . . it is not the duty of the examiner in English to assess the worth of the subject-matter of composition. His concern is not with the thing said but with the saying of it" (27, p. 119). Teachers who wish to help children become writers turn their attention first to what the child wishes to say and his purpose in saying it, and, last to an appraisal of the form in which the ideas are set forth. "Good English," says Vicars Bell, is "that which is forceful, direct and intimate writing of a style peculiar to the writer." Correct English is "that which is composed, spelt, and punctuated according to the best usage" (2, p. 77). Good English is the child's first need. It is impossible to correct or improve a pupil's expression until he offers enough of it to work with. When it is flowing as freely as he is capable of at the time, he is ready for help with form and correctness.

Writing is one of the language arts, and it is highly dependent for its growth on the growth in the other language arts. The quality of writing is closely related to the quality of speech. While an occasional secondary school student or adult writes better than he talks, it is a rare child who writes, at least in the early grades, any better than he talks. Few write as well as they talk. If a child rarely uses a complete or grammatically standard sentence and still more rarely twists his tongue or his mind around a compound or complex sentence, his written sentences will be as weak as those he speaks. The sentence structure and grammar a child brings to school are those of his home and neighborhood. He has learned them thoroughly by the time he enters school at the age of five or six. Many years of intensive effort will be required to change them.

Writing is a form of expression; therefore, the writer must have something to express. The subject matter and the ideas for writing are obtained through observing, listening, reading and other types of experience. The quality of what is expressed in writing depends upon the quality of thinking that undergirds it. If the ideas a child expresses orally are meager, immature, and lacking in clarity, his writing will exhibit all of these problems in even greater measure.

Essential Types of Evaluation

Evaluation of composition in the schools requires looking at composition in a variety of ways and from a number of angles. No one type of evaluation will serve the needs of any teacher or any class or school. At least six types of evaluation will serve the needs of any continuous application and some for periodic application. 1. There is the evaluation of a piece of writing. Teachers and pupils do this in one way or another practically every day. 2. There is the evaluation of the growth of an individual child from day to day, within the school year, and from year to year throughout his school life. 3. Teachers are concerned with the growth of the class as a whole and with comparisons among classes. 4. Administrators and supervisors as well as teachers are concerned with the quality of composition within an entire school. 5. Both the school and the teacher evaluate methods of teaching writing. 6. There is periodic evaluation of the total curriculum in writing within grade levels, within the school as a whole, and within the school system. Parents, employers who hire the school's product, and the general public are concerned with the quality of writing the school produces, but their concerns will be dealt with only indirectly in this article.

Evaluating a piece of writing or many of them is an almost daily occurence at all levels of schooling beyond first grade. How it is done depends on the level of maturity of the writer, the purpose for which the writing is done, and the needs of the writer at the time. Evaluating the growth of a child is a longitudinal process and is the task of all teachers who deal with the teaching of English. Evaluation of the writing of a class is a continuous process though some measures may be applied only intermittently. Studies of the quality of composition in an entire school or school system, evaluation of methods of teaching, and of the total curriculum in writing may be periodic studies carried on by the entire staff at stated times or as need arises.

Methods of evaluating composition differ at the different levels of the school's program. The emphasis placed on content and on form depends on the stage the pupil has reached. In the earliest grades children may furnish the content, but the teacher assumes full responsibility for the form in which it is set out. By the end of the secondary school pupils are expected to assume responsibility for both content and form. A good program of evaluation is accomplished through adjusting criteria and methods of evaluating to the level and needs of the individual, class, or school being studied.

The Beginning Stage of Composition

Young children's first compositions are dictated for the teacher to write. Frequently this dictation is guided by the teacher's comments and questions and thus represents both child and teacher. The teacher is responsible for the form which the material takes on the paper, its spelling, punctuation, and arrangement. The child furnishes the ideas and expresses them in his own way with a minimum of guidance. At this stage, the teacher's evaluation of the child's composition deals with the quality of the child's ideas and the evidence these offer of the richness or meagerness of his background of experience as well as with his powers of expression. The purpose of evaluation is clearly that of determining where the child stands with regard both to content for composition and skill in expression so that the teacher knows where to start her guidance and how to proceed with it. Her comments regarding what the child dictates are designed to draw him out, to help clarify his thinking, and to aid him in expressing his meaning.

Anecdotal records help the teacher of beginners to study each child's language ability and his needs. These records tend to show the child's attitude toward himself, the freedom and ease with which he speaks, and the quality and maturity of his language and of his thinking. They make clear the child's needs so that the teacher can devise means of meeting them.

The child's own evaluation of his composition lies in the satisfaction he finds in watching the teacher transfer his words to the paper and the use to which his contribution is put. Since expression is not forced and the child himself determines its content, the values for him are found in satisfying expression and in the concepts of form that emerge as he sees his words take shape under the teacher's hand. The message of the composition is the most important item for consideration in the mind of the child and should be kept so.

These same values obtain as the child begins to write his composition for himself. Spelling, capitalization, punctuation, and arrangement on the paper are guided by the teacher as she helps the child to say in writing what he wants to say. All types of writing tend to be managed in this way as long as children need such help though emphasis on independence and the use of self-help resources—word lists, picture dictionaries, models, and guide sheets for headings and the like—are encouraged as the child is ready for them. The teacher's evaluation of the child's progress is a continuous one. The personality traits that the child shows, the amount of help he needs, his growth in interest, in initiative, in sustained attention to the writing task, in independence, as well as in technical skills of handwriting and spelling are all a part of the evaluation. The teacher's observation of the child's behavior, her anecdotal records, and the writing the child produces form the materials for evaluation. Though the teacher evaluates the child's writing for content and for form, what is happening to the child is more important than what he produces.

The lack of controlled research concerned with evaluation of the compositions of young children points to the fact that personality development and development of ability to write are completely interwoven. Grading papers and assigning marks or ratings to them is completely inappropriate at this stage. Also inappropriate is the assigning of writing which the child is to do independently and turn in for the teacher's comments. All writing of any consequence should be done when the teacher is free to guide and to help while the child writes. This early stage in learning to write is a critical one. If a child is asked to write only when he has something to write, has a purpose for writing, and can write with all the help he needs, he is on the way to becoming a writer. Every teacher of older children and every adult knows that there are people in any group who dislike and actually dread attempting any writing task. It appears true that for many, if not most of them, aversion to writing was developed at least in part by unwise requirements during this critical early period. Children who, during this period, find satisfaction and fulfillment in writing go on to achieve at higher levels. Those who find writing a laborious, discouraging and distasteful experience carry throughout their lives the attitudes built during this period unless at some later time a wise and understanding teacher takes active steps to build in these individuals a sense of personal worth and confidence in the worth of their ideas.

Every piece of writing produced by a child in the primary grade is a reflection of the oral work that goes on in that grade. A former inspector in Her Majesty's service in England has declared, ". . . the atmosphere and general attitude that give rise (to good writing) are almost always those of constant conversation and oral alertness. It may be safely said that if a teacher is having difficulty with the written English of his school, and finds the children wooden, unresponsive, and unwilling to put their thoughts on paper, the first thing he should look at is the oral side; it is probable that the fault is there" (6, p. 65). Evaluation of the child's level of operation in oral work must accompany evaluation of his ability to write and probably should actually precede it. The two cannot be separated because one is clearly the outgrowth of the other.

A recent study throws light on children's use of sentences in their speech and therefore indicates what they are potentially capable of in their writing.

Templin (21), in a study which brings up to date the earlier studies of Davis (7) and McCarthy (14), found that children today use longer responses and fewer one-word responses than did children of three to eight years of age twenty to thirty years ago. This difference becomes significantly greater when the older subjects are compared. Children of upper socio-economic status groups consistently used longer remarks than did children from lower socio-economic status groups. When the sentence usage of the eight-year-old sample was taken as a measure of terminal status over the five-year span studied, there was a decrease in the proportion of incomplete sentences, little change in the use of sentences without a phrase, and an increase in the use of all types of sentences that involve increasing complexity of sentence structure such as coordination or subordination (21, p. 103, 104). It is interesting to note that Templin found no essential differences in the use of various types of sentences by boys and girls. Of particular significance is the fact that the structure of adult grammar has already imposed the pattern of word selection upon children by the age of three.

An early study by Betzner shows the range of content and form found in original compositions dictated by children (3). It would be interesting to know how different such dictated composition might be today if children used the entire range of the possibilities they are capable of conceiving. Television, travel in parents' cars, books available in every supermarket, and the breadth of other experiences available to children today may have pushed their potential limits considerably higher.

Types of Written Composition

Several types of writing emerge as the curriculum in writing expands through the grades. These can be roughly distinguished as personal and creative, utilitarian, and critical and intellectual. Utilitarian writing is found at all age levels as an integral part of school work. Personal and creative writing are encouraged from the beginning and form an important part of the curriculum in writing from the primary grades upward. Critical writing is found infrequently in the early grades but appears occasionally even there as children indicate in writing their reaction to characters and episodes in stories they have read or heard.

Many teachers maintain that the bulk of work designed to develop skill in dealing with form and correctness should be done on the practical, utilitarian writing. The elementary school child should be encouraged to do as much free, creative writing as he is willing to do. Unless this is to be kept for permanent use or enjoyment it is not corrected and put into final form but merely shared with the group through reading aloud by the author or the teacher. Creative writing may take the form of imaginative stories, poems, plays, or, with the older children, essays though it may be of the personal sort represented by personal letters, anecdotes, descriptions, and narratives based on personal experience. Utilitarian writing, on the other hand, is a service-type of writing growing out of classroom needs and activities. It may take the form of business letters, announcements, reports, direction and how-to-do-it papers, and the like. Critical writing consists of expression of thought and opinion by means of short editorials, book reports, critiques of literature, and research papers. Usually these are treated as teaching-learning experiences which call for reworking and refinement of original drafts.

Writing in the Middle Grades

Children in the middle grades do a number of kinds of writing and for a widening number of purposes. The emphasis on imaginative, creative writing continues with thought given to what makes it interesting and how to achieve it. Class discussion of quality may include attention to an opening sentence or paragraph which catches attention and interest, a plot that is built up in an interesting manner, and a conclusion that is clear and satisfying. Through discussion and comparison of their own stories with those in books they become increasingly good judges of quality. Revision may follow evaluation or the child may lay aside this attempt and try to incorporate points of improvement into his next effort. Writing, sharing, evaluation by the class and self-evaluation are closely interwoven. The teacher enters into the class discussion to raise children's sights regarding techniques, help them appreciate the growth of the child who finds writing difficult, and to spur the competent or gifted child on to higher levels of aspiration.

Personal writing that is to be shared with the group or used to serve a purpose—an anecdote, a report of experience, or possibly a personal letter may be evaluated and revised if the occasion warrants it. This may be done by the teacher with the individual child or it may serve as material for class discussion depending on the teacher's judgment of the worth of such discussion to the child or the group.

Utilitarian writing that is to serve a class or individual purpose is usually carried through several stages of refinement. After the material for the report, announcement, or business letter has been assembled, the pupil writes a rough draft, reads it for clarity, completeness and satisfactory presentation of content, reads it again for form to catch and remedy any problems of spelling, punctuation, and the like. He may then take it to the group or the teacher for reading and criticism before turning out a final, carefully executed draft.

In the middle grades, as in the primary grades, evaluation is a part of the writing process. It is an integral part of the entire teaching-learning scheme.

Assigning writing tasks, grading them and marking the errors, and handing the papers back to the pupils is profitless activity because it omits the best opportunities for teaching while interest is at high level. The end result of such procedure is usually little actual teaching and still less learning. At intervals, a set of papers may be studied by the teacher to determine the progress of the class as a whole, to assess her own teaching methods, and to compare the work of the class with that of other classes or with available norms.

Watts recommends the assignment of three-sentence compositions as a method of developing disciplined writing. He would require children from time to time to write all that is of interest or importance to them about a topic in no more and no fewer than three sentences. This compels children to exercise their judgment and skill for a perfectly definite purpose. They learn through this exprience to get quickly off the mark, to distribute ideas among the sentences, and to give thought to sentence construction and emphasis. The sentences children write differ according to age and maturity. Class discussion and evaluation of the product provide children with goals to work toward in their writing yet allow for individual differences in style as well as maturity. Watts has devised a three-sentence written composition scale for judging the maturity of such compositions (22, pp. 141-142).

Development of sentence structure and "degree of grammaticalness" (a useful phrase coined by the structural linguists) enter into any appraisal of the growth of writing competence in the middle grades. The most informative research on the development of the sentence in the writing of children is doubtless that of LaBrant (12) who analyzed the writing of over a thousand pupils from eight years upward, with a view to classifying the various types of dependent clause used at different ages. She found: (1) that dependent clauses increased in frequency as writers became more mature and that at the same time writing increased in complexity and clarity of thought; (2) that the relation between sentence-complexity and chronological age was closer than between sentence-complexity and mental age, suggesting that experience plays an important part in the mastery of language; and (3) that the dependent clauses least used were noun clauses and adverbial clauses of condition, concession, place, purpose, result, and comparison. These constituted at each mental level less than 6 per cent of all clauses used.

One wonders whether this record would be different if elementary schools placed less emphasis on formal grammar and more on an approach suggested by the studies of the structural linguists and their analysis of English. As children progress in maturity they can be led to realize that sentences can be made to express thoughts with increasing clarity and interest by the addition of movables of a variety of sorts. The simple subject-predicate sequence, "Tom came," can be enriched by the addition of movables which tell where, when, why, how and for what purpose, as in the following examples: "Tom came home yesterday to visit his parents." "Yesterday, because it was their anniversary, Tom came home to visit his parents and surprise them with the gift of a new car." Changing the verb in the predicate slot adds new possibilities, as in: "Because yesterday was their anniversary, Tom flew home to surprise his parents and delight them with his unexpected visit." Children learn how to weave ideas together into well-constructed longer sentences through opportunity to play with movables and arrange them in different positions in relation to the two essential slots, subject and predicate. They detect the fact that a change in position may alter emphasis or create a new shade of meaning. Intonation and meaning determine punctuation within the written sentence (9, 17, 22).

While it is true that length of sentence and number of dependent clauses are indicative of growth beyond the simple sentence, mere increase in the number of dependent clauses must not be overweighted as evidence of progress in the use of language. It may be found that a single sentence pattern is used over and over again as it is in the folk story, "This is the house that Jack built." Use of a variety of types of subordination represents a higher level of skill than much use of only a few forms. As children's writing skill advances they tend to use simple sentences containing prepositional phrases and infinitive expressions in place of clauses (22). Examples such as the following begin to appear: "To his surprise, the boy returned quickly," in place of "He was surprised that the boy returned quickly"; or "Being very tired, he sat down to rest," in place of "He sat down to rest because he was very tired." Compression and use of fewer words may be evidence of greater sophistication and command of language than the use of a larger number of words.

Children of middle and upper grades learn to plan their composition with increasing skill, to utilize many resources for the gaining of content and ideas and to use effectively the dictionary, handbooks of form and style, and other self-help resources. Careful proofreading follows the writing of a first draft and making a final copy climaxes the effort of making the necessary revisions in expression of ideas, statement of fact, sequence, phraseology, and spelling. The making of the final copy provides the writer with the experience of putting every part of his work into shape that will be a credit to him. It reinforces what he learns from the corrections he has made. While these final steps may seem to some children laborious and distasteful, if the purpose for which the writing is done is one that the child can identify with, he tends to view his final product with real satisfaction. Self-evaluation with recognition of personal needs and awareness of personal growth can be encouraged through utilizing children's writing in a variety of satisfying ways and in the kind of longitudinal overview provided for by the English headmaster mentioned at the beginning of the article.

Composition in the Secondary School

In 1917 the Hosic report on English in the secondary school criticized the program in composition as too ambitious, formal and literary, too little concerned with speech and too much concerned with grammatical and rhetorical analysis (11). It recommended a broad range of composition activities with attention to both utilitarian and imaginative writing. It called for more emphasis on practical activities and less on the purely literary, more time devoted to actual writing and less to theory. It foreshadowed present day emphasis on oral expression and on the teaching of functional grammar.

Many writers from that time to the present have reiterated the points made in this early report. There have been far more studies of composition on the secondary level than on the elementary. These are admirably summarized in the section on English in *Encyclopedia of Educational Research* (18). The trends which developed from early studies were brought into focus in *An Experience in English* (10), published in 1935. This publication marked what was probably the first attempt to describe growth sequences from kindergarten through twelfth grade. That a unified program throughout this span has not been achieved is evidenced by the fact that the Conference on Basic Issues in the Teaching of English held in 1959 listed as one of its major recommendations the development of such a unified program on a nation-wide scale.

Emphasis on grammar still holds a large place in the composition program of the secondary school though there is little agreement as to its value and the weight it should carry in the total program. The research on grammar is well summarized and thoughtfully evaluated by DeBoer in this series. An attitude that appears to be growing in England as well as in the United States is set forth by Smith. "The plain fact is that no one ever wrote a whit the better for having an outdated English Grammar open by his side, and it should be realized that the grammarians' efforts to reconcile ever-changing usage with their set formulae must inevitably leave them well in the rear of current practice. . . . The belief that one can write and speak well only out of a background of grammatical knowledge is a strongly held superstition" (19, pp. 130-131).

A question asked by the members of the Conference on Basic Issues in the Teaching of English participated in by members of the American Studies Association, College English Association, Modern Language Association, and National Council of Teachers of English is, "Could national standards for student writing at various levels be established, and what would be their value?" The Conference recognizes that evaluation of student writing is difficult. "Some teachers," they admit, "mark only mechanical and grammatical errors, leaving students with the impression that learning to write is a negative matter—the avoidance of such errors. Others go too far in the other direction and grade very subjectively, leaving the student with the impression that the art of writing well is merely the knack of appealing to the tastes and whims of his particular teacher." Reconciling these differences and helping teachers understand what writing is and how it can be developed may prove more valuable than any sort of norm. The research that is available indicates what every teacher knows— that the range of ability in any class is very wide. It would appear on the surface that national norms are unworkable though research might prove that some type of scale, flexibly applied, would be useful.

Evaluating a Piece of Writing

Any manuscript written by a student should be written for a definite audience and should reach its audience. Some papers are written for the class, some for the teacher. In any case there should be some reaction to what has been written. If the paper has been written for the class the author may read it himself, or the teacher may read the whole or selected parts of it to the class. Often, the author prefers to have the teacher read it and lead the discussion regarding it. If, in the reading, the teacher corrects unacceptable usage this is in itself a way of teaching that is highly acceptable to the author. The author's name should not be divulged unless he is willing to have it known. The evaluation may be more fruitful without it.

Good discussion, LaBrant says, takes time for thought (13). Students should be encouraged to take a moment for thinking before commenting on a composition that is read to them. At all times, the first comments should deal with the message of the paper and the purpose it is designed to serve. Evaluation should not result in rating the paper *good* or *bad*. It should deal with the thought that is conveyed, and young people should be led to realize that a *good* paper is one that does something important to the reader or hearer. All discussion should encourage the author to continue writing and to write increasingly well.

Marking papers that have been handed in calls for the same care and the same attention to the psychological reaction of the writer that is true of class discussion. Red-penciling errors and putting down a grade is profitless expenditure of the time and energy of the teacher. A less well-trained person than he could do that. The student who receives a paper with many errors marked and a poor grade rarely studies his problems and corrects the errors. In consequence, the same errors appear on the next paper and the next.

The comments on a student's paper should cause him to dig a little deeper, think through his topic and his purpose more carefully, and put his thoughts down more clearly and accurately. Attention must include form as well as content. If the writer is clear about his purpose and knows what he has to say, he usually writes in complete sentences, but if the thinking lacks clarity the writing will present the same problem.

Evaluating the Growth of an Individual

Case studies of children's progress in reading are found in many books but similar studies of children's writing are rare. Probably the most extensive and inclusive studies available in the literature are those of the Bronxville children studied by Burrows and others (5). These studies present detailed sketches of each child as a person with all his strengths and problems and the traits that are uniquely his. The samples of the child's writing are fitted into their setting and portray the growth taking place in the child himself as well as in the writing.

Some principals have selected samples of children's writing added each year to the children's folders in the official cumulative file. The series of compositions from a school in Baltimore which appears in the chapter on Writing in the book *Language Arts for Today's Children* (15) is such a collection. Through it one can see growth in power to compose sentences, to spell, to write and to express ideas clearly and vividly. The emergence of individual style is interesting to trace.

Many teachers arrange a folder for each child in which samples of his work are accumulated. Children find as much interest in the accumulation as the teacher and frequently come to her, a paper in each hand, to say, "Look, this is the way I wrote a way back last fall. Don't you think I'm doing better now?" Children find great satisfaction and real motivation in evidence that they are growing in power. The teacher's evaluation of each child's progress is always with reference to himself—the distance from the point at which he started to the point which he has achieved. Children are not judged by the application of an arbitrary standard nor expected to attain an established norm. Each child's work is judged with relation to his own potential. Slow children develop pride in what they can accomplish, and gifted children are encouraged to expand their powers as rapidly as their capacity permits.

Surveying Composition in a School

An evaluation of composition in a class or school is a composite of appraisal of each individual's ability to communicate his thoughts and feelings in various written forms appropriate to his purpose, to the specific occasion, and to the reader whom he intends to reach. Since the language act grows out of the experience of the individual, the situation in which the act is performed, and the skill of the individual in the situation, exact measurement is extremely difficult. Language power and thought power, Smith states (19), go hand in hand. One cannot be assessed without attention to the other. Language is a social instrument which cannot be isolated and measured in the same sense that spelling or arithmetic skill can be measured. For these reasons, evaluation in language has remained an inconclusive field of educational research.

Whether the evaluation being attempted is evaluation of the work of a class or of a school or school system some of the variables must be identified as a starting point for the building of criteria. Smith (20) used the following in her study of the English program in the elementary schools of New York: the wealth and originality of ideas and the facility of expression in handling the mechanics of language. The three variables that are almost certain to appear in any list of criteria are content, logical sequence, and mechanics of expression.

The administrative and supervisory staffs of a school or school system study the status of composition at intervals or as need arises. A setting may be arranged within which all children will write, possibly in response to a film, a dramatization, or some school-wide occurrence. Witty and Martin report a study of compositions children wrote in response to a film (24). An administrator may ask for a set of papers from a class or sets from all the classes in a school or school system. Papers may be evaluated by a committee and analyzed for content, mechanics, and style. Seattle has a program of evaluation which is geared to their course of study (16). Portland, Oregon, carries on a program of city-wide evaluation (25). Composition scales are difficult to devise because of the social content of writing. The survey committees which evaluate the compositions tend to devise their own rating scheme to fit the situation and the type of composition which was required.

One standardized test may be of limited service in a school survey of composition skills. The *Language Arts* tests of the SRA Achievement Series for grades 4-6 and 6-9 constitute a basic literacy measure in the form of a proofreading test of capitalization, punctuation, and usage.

No single measure can be accepted as accurately portraying the level of development of any writer. Several kinds and units of writing from each individual should be examined before passing judgment on writing skills.

The purpose of evaluation is to find weaknesses to be strengthened and strengths to be expanded, refined, and deepened. Any program of evaluation comes back finally to the individual. Since growth in writing is closely tied up with all other aspects of individual growth, the individual must be strengthened in order to strengthen his writing. Expanding the individual's contacts, deepening his insights, helping him to think more clearly and feel more deeply— all these will improve the content of his writing. Individual help with problems of form in which he is weak will improve his handling of mechanics.

Children can learn to take pride in their own good writing, and to recognize quality in the writing of others. It is thus that standards for composition become the writer's own and take on lasting value.

References

1. Applegate, Mauree, *Helping Children Write*. New York: International Textbook Company, 1948.
2. Bell, Vicars, *On Learning the English Tongue*. London: Faber and Faber, 1953.
3. Betzner, Jean, *Content and Form of Original Composition Dictated by Children from Five to Eight Years of Age*. Contributions to Education No. 442. New York: Teachers College, Columbia University, 1930. (53 p.)
4. Burrows, Alvina T., *Teaching Composition: What Research Says to the Teacher*, No. 18. Department of Classroom Teachers, American Educational Research Association of the National Education Association. Washington, D.C.: The Association, 1959.
5. Burrows, Alvina T. and others. *They All Want to Write*. Revised Edition. New York: Prentice-Hall, Inc., 1952.
6. Cutforth, J. A., *English in the Primary School*. Oxford, England: Basil Blackwell, 1954.
7. Davis, Edith A., "Mean Sentence Length Compared with Long and Short Sentences as a Reliable Measure of Language Development," *Child Development*. 8:69-79 (1937).
8. DeBoer, John J., "Grammar in Language Teaching," *Elementary English*. 36 (October, 1959), 413-421.
9. Francis, W. Nelson, *The Structure of American English*. New York: The Ronald Press Company, 1958.
10. Hatfield, W. Wilbur (Ed.), *An Experience Curriculum in English*. New York: D. Appleton-Century Co., 1935.
11. Hosic, James F. (Comp.), *Reorganization of English in Secondary Schools*. Washington: Government Printing Office, 1917.
12. LaBrant, Lou, *A Study of Certain Language Developments in Children*. Genetic Psychology Monographs, No. 5, November, 1933. Clark University, Worcester, Mass.
13. LaBrant, Lou, *We Teach English*. New York: Harcourt, Brace and Company, 1951.
14. McCarthy, Dorothea, *The Language Development of the Preschool Child*. University of Minnesota Institute of Child Welfare Monograph, No. 4, University of Minnesota Press, Minneapolis, 1930.
15. National Council of Teachers of English, Commission on the Curriculum, *Language Arts for Today's Children*. NCTE Curriculum Series, Vol. II. New York: Appleton-Century-Crofts, Inc., 1952.
16. Olson, Helen F., "Evaluating Growth in Language Ability," *Journal of Educational Research*. 39 (1945), 241-253.
17. Roberts, Paul, *Patterns of English*. New York: Harcourt, Brace and Company, 1956.
18. Searles, John R. and Robert G. Carlson, "English," *Encyclopedia of Educational*

Research, pp. 464-470. Third Edition. Edited by Chester W. Harris. New York: The Macmillan Company, 1960.

19. Smith, A. E., *English in the Modern School.* London: Methuen and Company, Ltd., 1954.
20. Smith, Dora V., *Evaluating Instruction in English in the Elementary Schools of New York.* Chicago: Scott, Forsman and Company, 1941.
21. Templin, Mildred C., *Certain Language Skills in Children: Their Development and Interrelationships.* Child Welfare Monograph Series, No. 26, University of Minnesota Press, Minneapolis, 1957.
22. Watts, A. F., *The Language and Mental Development of Children.* London: George G. Harrap and Company, Ltd., 1944. Boston: D. C. Heath and Company, 1947.
23. Whitehall, Harold, *Structural Essentials of English.* New York: Harcourt, Brace and Company, 1956.
24. Witty, Paul and William Martin, "An Analysis of Children's Compositions Written in Response to a Film," *Elementary English.* 34:158-63; March, 1957.
25. Zollinger, Marion, "Developing Competence in Writing," *The English Journal.* 41 (1952), 411-415.

58 Evaluating Elementary
Literature Programs

Martha E. Irwin

Irwin addresses herself to the question of "what is a good overall program for children's literature in the elementary school." Her research report describes tentative criteria—involving (a) provisions for literature in the curriculum and (b) classroom activities.

Could this checklist serve as a model for a similar one used to evaluate other aspects of the language arts curriculum? Which components seem most susceptible to valid evaluation using this type of instrument? If feasible, use the Irwin checklist to evaluate the literature program in your school.

> The best means of the evaluation of the success of a school program
> is not a score on a standardized test but rather the amount and quality
> of the materials children read (5).

Russell's statement implies that the ultimate aims of a reading program cannot be objectively tested. Lennon supports the conclusion in his review of the measurable aspects of reading instruction (4). This fact does not, however, release us from the responsibility of determining the effectiveness of our attempts to help children become true readers.

In conducting our evaluation, we can learn much by observing the habits and reactions of children in their leisure as well as during the opportunities which are provided for them to read and discuss books. But suppose our informal assessment reveals that the quantity and the quality of the students' reading is not what we would desire. Of course, many interrelated factors could underlie the results or the lack of results, but let us confine our attention to the factors within the school program. To do so, we must ask what is a good overall program for children's literature in the elementary school.

From *Elementary English* 40:846-849; 888; December 1963. Reprinted with permission of the National Council of Teachers of English and Martha E. Irwin, Associate Professor of Education, Eastern Michigan University, Ypsilanti. References have been renumbered.

Determining Tentative Criteria

Part of a recent study by the author was devoted to developing a set of tentative criteria that might be used in evaluating a local program (3).

Several steps were involved in the establishment of the criteria. The professional writings on literature in the elementary school and the standards for school libraries were reviewed. Language arts and library authorities were asked to name schools in which they judged there were good literature programs. The principal of each school named was asked to respond to a questionnaire regarding the details of the program in his or her building. Each provision in the fifty-eight schools for which the principals responded (the "criterion schools") was classified as to desirability according to the percentage of schools in which it was found.

From the basic criteria established by the fifty-eight criterion schools and from the recommendations of language arts and library authorities, the following check list has been devised. Part One of the check list can be used to aid in the evaluation of a literature program on a building or system-wide level. Part Two can be used in the same way as well as in individual classrooms. The weighted values are suggested according to the degree of desirability, with the "highly desirable" provisions given three points, the "desirable" provisions two points, and the "helpful" provisions one point. For some of the items a rater should use a value smaller than the value listed instead of considering the evaluation on a completely fulfilled or no-score basis.

Tentative Check List for Evaluating
Elementary School Literature Programs

Part One. Provisions for literature in the curriculum	Maximum value
A. Facilities and materials (18)	
1. A central school library	3
2. Seating space in library for 45-55 students	3
3. A book collection of 6,000 to 10,000 books (enrollment 250-500 students)	3
4. Annual book expenditure of $4 to $6 per student	3
5. Ample supply of audio-visual materials, including films, filmstrips, and records	3
6. Trained librarian in building	3
B. Use of facilities and materials (30)	
1. Extensive use of central library	3
2. Regular library periods for classes	3
3. Teachers accompany classes to library	3

    4. Responsibility for teaching library skills shared by teachers and librarians   3
    5. Several activities included in regular library periods:
        a. Guided book-selection   3
        b. Browsing and free reading   3
        c. Storytelling   3
        d. Assigned research and reports   3
        e. Teaching of library skills   3
    6. Extensive use of classroom collections   3

C. Administrative provisions (9)

    1. Curriculum guide for literature or for language arts, including literature   2
    2. Curriculum guide for reading, including literature   1
    3. Specific or suggested time allotment   2
    4. "Self-contained" classes for literature   2
    5. Individualized approach to literature   2

D. In-service activities (27)

    1. Supervisor or consultant in language arts and/or reading   2
    2. Much teacher participation in ordering books   3
    3. Some use of pamphlets and brochures to teachers   3
    4. Some use of book exhibits and fairs for teachers   3
    5. Some use of speakers   3
    6. Some use of teacher discussion groups about literature and its uses   3
    7. Some demonstration teaching of literature   2
    8. Local studies of children's interests   1
    9. Magazines available for reference:
        a. *Elementary English*   3
        b. *School Library Journal*   1
        c. *The Horn Book*   1
        d. *Library Journal*   1
        e. *The Reading Teacher*   1

E. Provisions to acquaint parents with program (11)

    1. Lists of suitable books   3
    2. Book exhibits or fairs   3
    3. Speakers or discussions   3
    4. Pamphlets on literature and recreational reading   2

F. Evaluating and reporting pupil development (6)

    1. Elimination of grades in literature as a separate subject   3
    2. Informing parents of growth in literature (other than by grades)   2
    3. Cumulative record of books read by individual children   1

Part Two. Classroom activities

A. Grades one and two (55)

    1. Daily reading to class by teacher   3
    2. Much use of quiet periods for reading   3

	Maximum value
3. Much use of art activities	3
4. Much use of bulletin boards and exhibits	3
5. Much use of dramatizations	3
6. Occasional use of creative writing	3
7. Occasional informal book discussions	3
8. Occasional oral book reports	3
9. Occasional use of audio-visual aids	3
10. Occasional use of literature in science and social studies	3
11. Limited use of choral reading	3
12. Limited use of puppetry	2
13. Limited use of tours of public library	2
14. Limited use of written book reports	2
15. Little or no analysis of literature	2
16. Limited use of book or literary clubs	1
17. Yearly inventories of children's interests	1
18. A variety of informal evaluation techniques:	
a. Records of books read by children	3
b. Class discussions (evaluations of)	3
c. Teacher observations of habits and attitudes	3
d. Pupil-teacher conferences	3

B. Grades three through six (58)

1. Daily reading to class in grades 3-4	2
2. Occasional reading to class in grades 5-6	2
3. Extensive use of quiet periods for reading	3
4. Much use of art activities	3
5. Much use of bulletin boards and exhibits	3
6. Much use of written book reports	3
7. Much use of creative writing	3
8. Much use of informal book discussions	3
9. Much use of oral book reports	3
10. Occasional use of dramatizations	3
11. Occasional use of audio-visual aids	3
12. Occasional use of literature in science and social studies	3
13. Limited use of choral reading	3
14. Limited use of book or literary clubs	2
15. Limited use of puppetry	2
16. Limited use of tours of public library	2
17. Some analysis of literature	2
18. Yearly inventories of children's interests	1
19. A variety of informal evaluation techniques:	
a. Records of books read by children	3
b. Class discussions (evaluations of)	3
c. Teacher observations of habits and attitudes	3
d. Pupil-teacher conferences	3

Library Facilities

The American Library Association standards (1) are evident in sections A and B of Part One of the check list. The criterion schools were found to be above the national average in library facilities but they are not up to the recommended standards. For example 81 per cent have central school libraries with an average collection of 4,768 books and an average annual per pupil expenditure of $2.20. Over half of the 81 per cent have a full-time librarian and over three-fourths have either a full-time or a part-time librarian. The results of this survey point to the importance of library facilities to a literature program but they also reveal that schools can develop programs which gain recognition even with substandard facilities and, in some cases, with no school libraries at all. (However, the criterion schools without libraries in the buildings rely heavily upon public facilities and classroom collections.)

Classroom Organization

The investigation of the administrative provisions in the criterion schools led to some interesting observations which are not included within section C of Part One of the check list.

A large percentage (82.8) of the criterion schools report that they have a required basal reader or readers. The most common means of incorporating literature into the elementary curriculum is a form of individualized reading within the self-contained classroom, found in over two-thirds (67.2 per cent) of the criterion schools. The phrase "a form of individualized reading" is used to show that various interpretations of the term "individualized reading" exist. The data in this study suggest that an individualized approach is used to stimulate interest in literature and to guide children in selecting and appreciating materials suited to their abilities and interests, while the development of reading skills is carried on primarily in the basal reader program. In other words, the criterion schools have not found it necessary to choose between a basal reader program and individualized reading, but have found a combination approach satisfactory.

Classroom Activities

The principals of the criterion schools were asked to indicate which activities are used in their schools as well as to estimate the extent of their usage. Because of the element of judgment involved in the principals' responses and in the author's classifications, the amounts of use of the classroom activities listed in Part Two of the check list are defined in general terms. "Occasional" use of audio-visual aids, for example, is not necessarily equal to "occasional" oral book reports. However, the listing does indicate that a range of activities is desirable and that within the range some activities should be used much more often than others.

One would also want to remember that the check list represents a survey of general practices only and that within each category named there are many adaptations. Before searching for a new way to introduce children and literature, one might first determine if the general classes of activities suggested by the criterion schools have been incorporated into the program being evaluated. One might want to determine further if the activities are routine or if they are enlivened through variations such as those suggested in many excellent references (2).

Summary and Conclusions

An attempt has been made to determine the elements of a good program in children's literature as reported by principals of schools judged to have strong programs. The check list which has resulted, although subject to the limitations of the survey questionnaire technique, may provide guidelines for a teacher or school desiring to evaluate a local program.

However, the evaluation should not overlook a most significant factor. This factor is undoubtedly present in the criterion schools and, like the ultimate aims of a reading program, is not amenable to objective testing. Behind each good program must be an enthusiastic classroom teacher with a wide knowledge of children's literature as a distinct category of children's books utilizing techniques which inspire rather than prescribe.

References

1. American Association of School Librarians, *Standards for School Library Programs*. Chicago: American Library Association, 1960.
2. Applegate, Mauree, *Easy in English*. Evanston, Illinois: Row, Peterson and Company, 1960.
3. Irwin, Martha Ellen, *Children's Literature Programs in Elementary Schools*. Unpublished doctoral dissertation, Western Reserve University, 1963.
4. Lennon, Roger T., "What Can Be Measured?" *The Reading Teacher*, 15 (March, 1962) 326-337.
5. Russell, David H., *Children Learn to Read*. Boston: Ginn and Company, 1961.

59   Evaluation of Children's Responses to Literature

Doris Young

In this article, Young attempts to measure children's responses to literature. These responses (and findings from research and further questions) are categorized: (1) emotional, imaginative responses; (2) responses of understanding and insight; (3) responses to literature as a discipline; and (4) responses to literature in the child's creative work.

The quality of a pupil's reaction to literature and what it does for him can best be evaluated by the teacher who is sensitive to the child's thinking and feeling. What 'action research' would you like to undertake to discover whether children are growing toward the accepted goals?

In one of the "Peanuts" cartoon strips, Schulz presented one kind of response to literature as Lucy summarized Snow White. Lucy stalks along as she says: "This Snow White has been having trouble sleeping, see? Well, she goes to this witch who gives her an apple to eat which put her to sleep. Just as she's beginning to sleep real well . . . you know, for the first time in weeks . . . this stupid prince comes along and kisses her and wakes her up." Linus then remarks, "I admire the wonderful way you have of getting the real meaning out of the story."[1] Expressing the "real meaning" is but one response to literature. Response to literature is also evident as it satisfies a child's need. For example, in *Home from Far*, Little describes this response: "Usually when Jenny was sent to her room, she felt it was cheating to read. You forgot all about whatever you had done wrong two minutes after you opened a book. But now she jumped off the bed and went to the bookcase. She wanted a sad book. She was not ashamed of crying over people in a story. She chose *The Birds' Christmas Carol* and curled up in the chair next to the window. Soon she was in another world, where

From *Library Quarterly* 37:100-109; January 1967. Reprinted from "Evaluation of Children's Responses to Literature" by Doris Young by permission of The University of Chicago Press (© 1967 by The University of Chicago Press) and Doris Young, University of Hawaii, Honolulu.

Mother, the two Michaels, and the nightmare of fear she had felt when she had been trapped by the fire could not follow her."[2]

Evaluation begins with recognition that the child's "real meaning" and other responses are internal evaluations. He decides to give attention by evaluating his environment; he evaluates as he selects elements to remember, allows feelings to flow, or permits the alchemy of imagination to work its wonders. However, the concern of this paper is external evaluation. A brief definition of evaluation as a process will be followed by examples of four categories of responses. There is no attempt here to summarize research; the intent is to indicate kinds of investigations that have been made. The analysis will lead to questions that need to be answered.

Evaluation as a Process

The first step in the process of evaluation is identification of the kinds of responses that might be observed. Concurrently, it is necessary to make some judgments about the kinds of changes it would be desirable to make as the child spends time in the elementary school. The child does "spend" his time, and educators have no right to insist that he waste this precious coin of life. Thus, the objectives we select are of prime importance. Determining objectives is a part of evaluation. Instead of a synonym for measurement, it is considered to be "a continuous process of inquiry, based upon criteria co-operatively developed in the school-community, which lead to warranted conclusions with respect to how successfully the school is studying, interpreting, and guiding socially desirable changes in human behavior."[3] Thus, the design of instruments to gather evidence and the collection and interpretation of evidence about behavior are but parts of a total process. Some educators would urge us not to attempt the measure of responses to literature. They are afraid that the intangible elements, like love, will disappear with analysis. Others fear written tests of cognitive development may overbalance the objective of enjoyment of literature. There is concern that procedures designed for research might become the major teaching strategy. These fears are unjustified if the concept of evaluation of a total situation is kept in mind. Krathwohl and others[4] point out the dangerous "erosion" of educational objectives that are not evaluated. Failure to identify objectives in terms of behavior in both the cognitive and affective domain will only result in further "time-stealing" school activities.

Evidence of Children's Responses to Literature

Every teacher or librarian is aware of the varied responses of children to literature. Children react differently to the very act of reading or listening. An

individual reads for different purposes at different times. Closely related to
these interests and attitudes is the category of emotional experience of literature. Meanings and understandings form another category of responses related to a particular selection. A fourth type of response is in the cognitive
domain—knowledge of literature as a field. The child's creative products reflect further responses to the experience of literature. All of these responses are
components of that elusive term, appreciation.

Interests, attitudes, preference

The children respond

The following expressions reveal some of children's interests and attitudes:
"How many books do you have to read to go to the summer party?"
"Aw, that's a baby book."
"But horse stories are for girls!"
"Nope. I just read science books."
"The author of my book is Elizabeth Speare. The title is *The Bronze Bow*.
It's a Newbery book on the list. It has 254 pages. The main character is Daniel.
The setting is Galilee. I liked it because it had lots of fights. That's my report."
  " 'I chatter, chatter as I flow,
    To join the brimming river,
   For men may come and men may go,
    But I go on forever.'
"That's my 100 lines!" (The fourth grader had completed his memoriza-
tion assignment in the middle of the poem, and sat down with a "clump.")

Investigators report

Concerned with the development of citizens who are readers, the school
must ask "what does the child do?" as well as "what can he do?" Many studies
of reading interests and preferences have been made. For example, Norvell's
study of 24,000 children revealed that children do not like what adults think
they should or do enjoy.[5] One problem with this study was that there was no
investigation of the literature available to the children. Kindergarten children
studied by Cappa responded by asking to hear the story again, by looking at
the book, or through creative interests.[6] Interests of boys in grades four through
six were obtained through interviews by Stanchfield.[7] We do have evidence regarding content interests according to age and sex. Interests in poetry have been
investigated by Mackintosh in 1932,[8] Kyte in 1947,[9] and recently by Pittman.[10]   In these studies, children selected favorite poems among those read
by the teacher. Wells found that adolescents' preferences for humorous literature
were influenced by cultural level.[11] In schools having a higher cultural level,
satire and whimsy received greater appreciation. Absurdity ranked first, slap-

stick second, satire third, and whimsy fourth. Gaver developed measures for studying effectiveness of centralized library service.[12] Sixth graders maintained complete reading records for nearly four months. Concerned with quality as well as quantity, I developed an instrument to determine levels of maturity in reading.

Further questions

There have been few, if any, longitudinal studies of reading interests and attitudes. What will be the effect of the libraries made possible by federal funds? What are the opportunities for responding to literature? How do differences in these opportunities affect attitudes and interests? What would be the effect of more co-operative planning of the school librarian and public librarian? What teaching strategies will create a more open response toward varied types of literature? What poems will children select, read to the class, and memorize when given an opportunity to read from many sources?

These are questions to be investigated about groups. Each teacher and each librarian must be concerned with study of the unique patterns of interest of each reader. What records can be maintained easily? What information about reading and listening experiences should become part of the cumulative record? How shall this information guide their work with boys and girls?

Emotional, imaginative response

The children respond

The internal response as the child interacts with visual and auditory symbols may be reflected in overt behavior, or it may be recalled through introspection. Yet, introspection cannot be considered a true account of the process. These responses illustrate behaviors that reflect emotional response:

"Oh!"—on a rising note of surprise as second graders see the picture of Tico's golden wings. Surprise, joy, beauty are surmised.

"Read it again!" after hearing, "Once there was an elephant/who tried to use the telephant/..."

"I cried when Biddy died—she was so wonderful. . . . And I really liked Peter," says a child after reading *Mountain Born* by Yates. However, it was the unspoken word, the look of mutual understanding that passed between teacher and pupil that reflected the deeper satisfaction.

"I want to read you this poem—not the class, just you," announced the child who wanted to share McCord's "This Is My Rock."

"It was awful—just terrible when they were beating the Greyhound," reported a nine year old who reflected some of his horror. Yet he liked the book and commented he felt he had really read a "grown up" book now.

————. This space can only indicate the sudden intake of breath when a nine year old turned a page of *In a Spring Garden* to experience the glowing color of Keats's background for the poem by Issa, "Just simply alive,/Both of us, I/And the poppy/...."

"Listen now, I want to tell you about this book, *Island of the Blue Dolphins*. How many have read it? I've read it three times. It's well, sort of a girl's book, but not really. Well, do you *know* about it, what it *really means?*" The fourth grader continued to discuss the plot, characterization, and theme of a book that had deep significance to him.

Evidence of research

Varied methods have been used to identify and measure emotional response to literature. Hruza used a galvanometer and a pneumograph to note changes as college students listened to fifteen poems.[13] However, introspection indicated some subjects who showed large galvanic reactions were unaware of emotional reaction. This study also showed there was a greater reaction when the subject matter was related to personal experience. Broom also used a galvanometer to determine emotional reactions to specific words.[14] Other investigators attempted to identify responses through recall of feelings experienced as a selection was heard or read. Valentine asked graduate students to recall the degrees of pleasure, imagery, and details experienced while hearing poetry.[15] He found that imagery or a deliberate attempt to create a visual image may interfere with pleasure. Letton also used the retrospective-verbalization technique in a study of ninth graders' oral reports of their thoughts during reading of poetry.[16] After telling what he thought as he read, the student was asked to look at "thought units" from the poems and tell what he thought about and felt when reading that part of the poem. In 1935, Pooley urged that measures of appreciation be devised and noted that "any measuring instrument which rests exclusively upon the student's ability to identify and explain the sources of appreciation without first measuring his inarticulate sensitivity to them is not a valid test."[17] Indeed it is this "inarticulate sensitivity" that has been neglected. Perhaps the work of Hess in measuring dilation and constriction of the pupil of the eye will give a method for study of inner responses.[18]

The effect of the child's stage of development has been explored by Peller.[19] She suggested the importance of literature that supports daydreams for both boys and girls in the latency stage and believed that sex differences are of great importance. Loban's study of social sensitivity among adolescents revealed that the reader tended to identify with the character most like himself.[20]

An example of a study of overt responses of two to four year olds as they listened to stories was made by Smith.[21] Such items as laughter, smiling, nodding approval, and annoyance behavior were checked.

There are descriptive accounts but scant research in the field of bibliotherapy.

Collier and Gaier have published reports of investigations of college students' childhood preferences for literature.[22] Cultural and sex roles are apparently influential factors, and literature may affect acceptance of role. Very little is known about the relationship of literature and psychological development. Peller suggested that a child may have a crucial experience through a daydream in a story at a time when he is under stress.[23]

Needed research

Perhaps our first concern should be that teachers become more aware of emotional responses to literature and provide opportunities for the child to express his feelings in an atmosphere of "psychological safety." We need to know more about the nature of the experience of literature. What occurs in the process of "identification" with a character? What factors lead to empathy, imagination, identification? What is the relation of self concept to imaginative response?

Responses of understanding and insight

Literal comprehension is not essential for response to sensory images, rhythm, or rhyme; perhaps some readers feel they "stand in the shoes" of a character without fully comprehending the situation. However, literal comprehension is the foundation for understanding implied meanings and for perception of relationships. As children gain insight into man's relationships with nature, with other men, and with the supernatural they gain self-knowledge. There is a very close relationship of the cognitive and affective responses as values are internalized and as understanding of the human condition is applied to life experience.

Children's responses

The following excerpts are from tape recordings of group and individual discussions of books. Frequently, we can see the child fumbling for words to cage fledgling thoughts: "I just didn't know what it would be like to be deaf. David was lost, and he couldn't even tell anybody." The ten year old had gained insight into problems of a deaf person through reading *David in Silence* by Robinson. "I think Swimmy had to change, you know, he had to swim slower to be the eye. And I think he worried about, well, some little fish might not stay in that place . . . and, uh, it wouldn't be easy." A second grader was perceiving some problems of leadership as he reflected upon *Swimmy* by Lionni. A sixth grader was thinking through the implications of *Harriet the Spy* by Fitzhugh. "No, Harriet wasn't exactly like anybody I know. Who would need a nurse at her age? And in most schools I think you'd have to do your homework instead of writing. But I know about, well, like telling the truth, even if it makes people mad, and . . . some kids are like that, well—before you learn, and it's well, hard to decide." In another discussion, of Holm's *North to Freedom*, the same reader said: "David shouldn't have told the younger children about things being so awful—like you can't trust people . . . and, well, that things are bad. They'll find out, but, like—if I told Laurie about awful things, she'd never go to play, maybe—or she'd be afraid."

Findings from research

To assess children's understandings of literal and implied meanings we can utilize reading-comprehension tests and vocabulary tests, but there is a need for instruments to measure literary meanings. Garrison and Thomas asked sixth graders to write what they thought a poem was about after hearing it read.[24] They found a significant relationship between vocabulary ability and discovery of theme, reader participation, and sensory imagery. Weekes presented forty-one poems in original and simplified versions to 412 sixth graders.[25] Figurative language presented more difficulty than "involved sentence structure." She found that actual experience could be a favorable or unfavorable factor in understanding the poem. Foreman held the view that basic appreciation is "a concept of the reality and humanness of the characters in a story; the awareness of story purpose and trend; the pictures which are stimulated by the author's description and completed through the child's experience."[26] The interview method was used to determine meanings seventh graders obtained from excerpts from three prose selections. He developed scales to classify responses to such questions as, "If you were going to paint a picture, what would you put in? Were there any people you would like to know or be with?" In Skelton's study of intermediate-grade children's interpretations of poems, 49 per cent of the responses were denotative interpretations and 35 per cent were meanings "read into" the poem.[27] Most of the children did not go beyond reporting of the details of the four poems read to them.

Tests were developed by Logasa and McCoy to determine high school students' ability to discover themes in poetry. A test of literary comprehension and appreciation is available for high school students.[28] The studies of critical reading underway at The Ohio State University[29] will provide some instruments that should prove useful.

Further questions

Most of the investigations have used poetry or excerpts from longer works. We need to study meanings children derive from total works. What selections are appropriate for a measure of literary understandings? When a child returns to a selection in a year or two years, what additional insights will be evident? What is the effect of wide reading upon discovery or understanding of themes? Do particular teaching strategies result in higher levels of insight?

Responses to literature as a discipline

The child's reaction to a specific selection is influenced by his knowledge of literature, authors and illustrators, genre, the craft of writing, and criteria for evaluation. Each discipline does have its mode of inquiry, but in literature there is no one "method of literary study."

Responses of children

The following examples of children's responses indicate the beginning of awareness that each selection is a part of a larger body of literature: "This is a fantasy," announced a third-grade reviewer of *The Borrowers Aloft* by Norton. He was implying certain expectations and criteria in recognizing the literary genre. When a large poster copy of the poem, "Brooms," was displayed with the poet's name, second graders expressed interest, "Oh, Dorothy Aldis! We know her poems." Familiarity with the poet established a "set" for the new poem. Upon hearing *Baba Yaga,* by Small, a seven year old said, "It's like Hansel and Gretel—you know, the children in the oven, and the pot in this story." To the question, "What are you reading today?" Lissa replied, "A Nancy Drew—oh, I know it really isn't good writing—but it's fun, and everybody else reads Nancy Drew." Lissa was aware of criteria as we discussed Nancy Drew plots and characterization, but she also wanted to be accepted by her peers. "I know why the South Wind has to be the baker—because a south wind is warm—and he says 'bites' because the north wind bites your fingers." A second grader volunteered this response to Lindsay's "The Moon's the North Wind's Cooky." "This book isn't as good as *The Loner,*" remarked the ten year old who had just read Wier's new book, *Easy Does It.* His reasons for the statement were supported by evidence. A critic of *The Spider Plant* by Speevack commented, "It just wouldn't be that way. I don't think everybody would come to the play—and they just wouldn't suddenly start being nice." These kinds of responses include what has been called critical reading. The reader separates fact from fiction, draws inferences, recognizes the author's point of view. He evaluates structure of plot, validity of theme, authenticity of setting, depth and realism of characterization, use of figurative language. His awareness of the form and arrangement of symbols in creating the total effect is a part of this kind of response to literature.

Evidence from research

In the thirties there was a surge of interest in testing "appreciation" of literature. To many of the investigators, appreciation was considered recognition of merit. Carroll's high school subjects were asked to rate prose selection,[30] and Speer's sixth graders ranked poetry according to merit.[31] Howells and Johnson devised a test in which high school pupils selected a line of poetry that most nearly fitted the poem.[32] A test designed by Eppel also asked pupils to select the best line of poetry when one was omitted.[33] In Burton's short-story test three possible endings were presented for student selection.[34] The Logasa-McCoy tests attempted to assess ability to identify rhythm and trite and fresh expressions, for example. Very little attention has been given the problem of assessing the elementary school child's knowledge of or awareness of types of literature, sound effects of language, metaphor, plot structure, or characterization.

Huus presented a summary of research related to development of taste in literature in the elementary school.[35] However, many articles cited were descriptive accounts; the majority of the studies were old; there were very few investigations of children in primary grades.

Problems for investigation

At the present time we do not know what knowledge of literature children possess at the end of elementary school, or at different age levels. What criteria do children use in evaluating the prose and poetry they encounter? What *can* they learn about modes of inquiry? This question should be followed by the question, What *should* they learn about the process of literary criticism in the elementary school? How can a local school system establish guidelines in terms of "standard literary works" children should know, yet provide the flexibility needed for special group and individual needs? An example of a kind of question facing the curriculum-makers is that of biblical literature; if children are to be familiar with the body of literature, with literary allusions, should Bible stories be included in the program? What materials could be used?

How children express awareness of literary style is another kind of question. Before an analysis of teaching materials and methods can be made, it will be necessary to develop instruments to assess such responses. At the present time a committee of the National Council of Teachers of English is developing one instrument. Challenged to develop a paper-pencil instrument for grades four to six, the committee has faced the problems of identifying and limiting kinds of responses that could be assessed in this way. We need to know, for example, how responses differ when the selection is read silently by the child and when he hears it read aloud by the teacher. What selections are appropriate for such an instrument? What cues or activities will elicit children's understanding of a selection and their sensitivity to the ways in which the total effect was created by the writer?

Responses to literature in the child's creative work

A fourth category of response to literature is the response evidenced in the child's own creative work. The experience of literature becomes part of the child's resources for communicating *his* responses to his environment.

Examples of children's responses

"Creative work" as viewed in this context does not have to be a tangible product. There is creativity in discussion, for example, when children make comparisons, evaluate, and juxtapose ideas in new relationships. Recordings could be analyzed to identify this type of creativity, but the following examples reflect ways literature may become a catalyst for tangible creative endeavors: "I made a hat like Jennie's," said a first grader as she displayed a creation of her own after hearing Keats's story, *Jennie's Hat.* "Once upon a time in a faraway land . . ." begins a child's story patterned after the folk tales he had heard. "Now you're Robin Hood, and I'm Little John," the director of backyard dramatic play was overheard to say. "Beyond the fence is Sherwood Forest." "This is a haiku poem I wrote. Can you help me make it sound better in the last line?" requests a sixth grader. In a letter to Taro Yashima, "I think you know just how it is to be a lonely little girl."

Needed research

To respond to literature with deeper awareness, children need to experience the problems and pleasures of attempting to communicate their experiences. In this paper, we can neither explore nor summarize the research related to creativity. It should be noted that the University of Nebraska curriculum project has been concerned, in part, with the effect of literature upon composition. Further studies of children's writing, painting, and dramatizations are needed to identify responses related to experience with literature.

Teachers and Librarians as Evaluators

Teachers and librarians have always evaluated children's responses to literature in informal ways. Perhaps they have been satisfied to enjoy the comradely glow when a child finds pleasure in a book they enjoyed. They are happy when they observe good readers seeking and discovering the "realms of gold" in literature. Seldom have there been attempts to discover why some children reach out, why others who can read just as well do not really enter the world of books.

Teachers and librarians do not need to wait for the psychologists and educators to present research. In recent years the concept of "action research" has been neglected, but this approach is needed now more than ever before. Librarians and classroom teachers can work together to evaluate the various components of appreciation. They can develop and maintain cumulative records of children's reading interests. They can maintain anecdotal records of the child's use of literary models or allusions to literature in his own writing. Analysis could be made of oral and written book reviews at different times during the year. Records can be made of overt responses as a child reads. Anecdotes could include introspective comments as "I know how it feels," "I have done this." Time can be planned for conferences and small-group discussions so there is opportunity to listen to the child's interpretation of a book. As instruments become available to aid them in gathering evidence about pupil behavior, teachers can use such instruments with wisdom, just as they use intelligence tests, achievement tests, and sociograms to aid in understanding the whole child. The process of evaluation of children's responses to literature must gain priority among the present professional tasks if the school is to plan the kind of literature program needed to prepare the adults of the twenty-first century.

Footnotes

1 Charles Schulz, "Peanuts," United Features Syndicate, Inc.

2 Jean Little, *Home from Far*, illus. Jerry Lozare (Boston: Little, Brown & Co., 1965), p. 81.

3 Harold G. Shane and E. T. McSwain, *Evaluation and the Elementary Curriculum* (rev. ed.; New York: Henry Holt & Co., 1958), p. 60.

4 David R. Krathwohl, Benjamin S. Bloom, and Bertram B. Masia, *Taxonomy of Educational Objectives. The Classification of Educational Goals. Handbook II: Affective Domain* (New York: David McKay Co., 1964), p. 16.

5 George W. Norvell, *What Boys and Girls Like To Read* (Morristown, N.J.: Silver Burdett Co., 1958).

6 Dan Cappa, "Kindergarten Children's Responses to Storybooks Read by Teachers," *Journal of Educational Research*, 52 (October, 1958), 75.

7 Jo M. Stanchfield, "Boys' Reading Interests as Revealed through Personal Conferences," *Reading Teacher*, 16 (September, 1962), 41-44.

8 Helen K. Mackintosh, "A Critical Study of Children's Choices in Poetry," *University of Iowa Studies in Education*, Vol. 7, No. 4 (1932).

9 George C. Kyte, "Children's Reactions to Fifty Selected Poems," *Elementary School Journal*, 47 (February, 1947), 331-39.

10 Grace Pittman, "Young Children Enjoy Poetry," *Elementary English*, 43 (January, 1966), 56-59.

11 Ruth E. Wells, "A Study of Taste in Humorous Literature among Pupils of Junior and Senior High Schools," *Journal of Educational Research*, 28 (October, 1934), 81-91.

12 Mary Virginia Gaver, *Effectiveness of Centralized Library Service in Elementary Schools (Phase I)* (Report of the research study conducted at Rutgers University under contract no. 489, SAE-8132 with the U.S. Office of Education [New Brunswick, N.J.: Rutgers University, Graduate School of Library Service, 1960]).

13 Thelma E. Hruza, "An Investigation of Some Factors in the Appreciation of Poetry" (unpublished Ph.D. dissertation, George Peabody College for Teachers, 1940).

14 M. E. Broom, "A Study of Literature Appreciation," *Journal of Applied Psychology*, 18 (1954), 357-63.

15 C. W. Valentine, "The Function of Images in the Appreciation of Poetry," *British Journal of Psychology*, 14 (October, 1923), 164-91.

16 Mildred C. Letton, "Individual Differences in Interpretive Responses in Reading

Poetry at the Ninth Grade Level" (unpublished Ph.D. dissertation, University of Chicago, 1958).

[17] Robert C. Pooley, "Measuring the Appreciation of Literature," *English Journal*, 24 (October, 1935), 631.

[18] Eckhard H. Hess, "Attitude and Pupil Size," *Scientific American*, 212 (April, 1965), 46-65.

[19] Lili E. Peller, "Daydreams and Children's Favorite Books," in J. F. Rosenblith and Wesley Allinsmith (eds.), *The Causes of Behavior: Readings in Child Development and Educational Psychology* (Boston: Allyn & Bacon, 1962), pp. 405-11.

[20] Walter Loban, "A Study of Social Sensitivity (Sympathy) among Adolescents," *Journal of Educational Psychology*, 44 (February, 1953), 102-12.

[21] Lois Z. Smith, "Experimental Investigation of Young Children's Interest and Expressive Behavior Responses to Single Statement, Verbal Repetition, and Ideational Repetition of Content in Animal Stories," *Child Development*, 1 (March, 1930), 247-54.

[22] Mary J. Collier and Eugene I. Gaier, "Adult Reactions to Preferred Childhood Stories," *Child Development*, 29 (March, 1958), 97-103.

[23] Peller, "Reading and Daydreams in Latency, Boy-Girl Differences," *Journal of the American Psychoanalytic Association*, 6 (January, 1958), 57-70.

[24] K. C. Garrison and M. Thomas, "A Study of Some Literature Appreciation Abilities as They Relate to Certain Vocabulary Abilities," *Journal of Educational Research*, 22 (December, 1930), 396-99.

[25] Blanche E. Weekes, "The Influence of Meaning on Children's Choices of ˙ ₜry," *Contributions to Education*, No. 354 (New York: Teachers College, Columbia U versity, 1929).

[26] Earl R. Foreman, "An Instrument To Evaluate the Literary Appreciation of Adolescence" (unpublished Ph.D. dissertation, University of Illinois, 1951), p. 4.

[27] Glenn Skelton, "A Study of Responses to Selected Poems in the Fourth, Fifth, and Sixth Grades" (unpublished Ph.D. dissertation, University of California, Berkeley, 1963).

[28] Mary Willis and H. A. Domincovich, *Cooperative Literary and Appreciation Test* (Princeton, N.J.: Educational Testing Service, 1943).

[29] Charlotte Huck, Martha King, Beatrice Ellinger, and Willavene Wolfe, "The Critical Reading Ability of Elementary School Children" (U.S. Office of Education Project OE 2612 [Columbus, Ohio: The Ohio State University]).

[30] Herbert A. Carroll, "A Method of Measuring Prose Appreciation," *English Journal*, 22 (March, 1933), 184-89.

[31] Robert K. Speer, "Measurement of Appreciation in Poetry, Prose and Art and Studies in Appreciation," *Contributions to Education*, No. 362 (New York: Teachers College, Columbia University, 1929).

[32] Thomas H. Howells and A. A. Johnson, "A Study of Metre-Sense in Poetry," *Journal of Applied Psychology*, 15 (1931), 539-44.

[33] E. M. Eppel, "A New Test of Poetry Discrimination," *British Journal of Educational Psychology*, 20 (June, 1950), 111-16.

[34] Dwight L. Burton, "The Relationship of Literary Appreciation to Certain Measurable Factors," *Journal of Educational Psychology*, 43 (November, 1952), 436-39.

[35] Helen Huus, "Development of Taste in Literature in the Elementary Grades," *Development of Taste in Literature* (Champaign, Ill.: National Council of Teachers of English, 1962).

Part Nine

Selected References

During the search for possible selections to be included in this book, it soon became evident to the editors that a large number of valuable and significant articles would have to be omitted. Hence this selected reference listing.

We do not pretend that the items are a comprehensive listing of all the possible ones. Just as a book of readings is designed to supplement—rather than substitute for—existing textbooks, so is the following bibliography intended to supplement those bibliographic items cited in existing textbooks, although there may be considerable overlap. While emphasis has been placed on recency of publication, other criteria have been used as well. We hope that the reader will find them as informative as we have.

Part One: Introduction

Artley, A. Sterl, "Research Concerning Interrelationships Among the Language Arts," *Elementary English*, 27 (December 1950), 524-537.
Burns, Paul C., "Language Arts Research That Should Make a Difference," *Elementary English*, 31 (March 1964), 279-284.
Carlsen, G. Robert, "Conflicting Assumptions in the Teaching of English," *English Journal*, 49 (September 1960), 377-386.
Clymer, Theodore, "Research Design in the Language Arts," *Elementary English*, 39 (April 1962), 349-352.
Figurel, J. Allen, Gertrude Crampton, and Richard Elder, "Emerging Instructional Procedures in English," *Education*, 85 (January 1965), 259-265.
Haven, Julia Mason, "The Role of Government in Improving Language Arts Instruction," *Instructor*, 75 (March 1966), 64-65.

Jones, Daisy M., "Curriculum Development in Elementary Language Arts: Current Trends and Issues," *Elementary English*, 41 (February 1964), 138-148.

Nelson, Lois A., "Modes of Teaching Leadership During Language Instruction," *Elementary School Journal*, 66 (November 1965), 92-96.

Sabol, James W., "An Experiment with Inductive Language Study," *Patterns and Models for Teaching English*, Champaign: National Council of Teachers of English, 1964, 1-4.

Schiller, Andrew, "The Coming Revolution in Teaching English," *Harper's Magazine*, 229 (October 1964), 82 ff.

Squire, James R., "New Directions in Language Learning," *Elementary English*, 39 (October 1962), 535-544.

——, "Preparing the Elementary Teacher to Teach Language," *National Elementary Principal*, 40 (September 1965), 22-25.

Strickland, Ruth G., "Some Issues in the Teaching of English," *Phi Delta Kappan*, 41 (May 1960), 332-335.

——, "Innovations in the Language Arts," *National Elementary Principal*, 43 (September 1963), 53-60.

"The Instructor Reports the First National Survey on the Status of Language Arts," *Instructor*, 75 (March 1966), 31-33.

Wachner, Clarence W., "Detroit Great City School Improvement Program," *Elementary English*, 41 (November 1961), 734-742.

Part Two: Language Learning and Linguistics

Bacher, June, "Needed for Language Growth: A Nourishing Diet of Experiences," *Elementary English*, 42 (February 1965), 185-188.

Burrows, Alvina T., "Children's Language: Insights for the Language Arts," *National Elementary Principal*, 40 (September 1965), 16-21.

Carroll, John B., "Words, Meanings and Concepts," *Harvard Educational Review*, 34 (April 1964), 178-202.

Cazden, Courtney, "Subcultural Differences in Child Language: An Interdisciplinary Review," *Merrill Palmer Quarterly*, 12 (July 1966), 185-219.

Chafe, Wallace L., "The Nature of Language," *National Elementary Principal*, 40 (September 1965), 11-15.

Chomsky, Noam, "The Current Scene in Linguistics: Present Directions," *College English*, 27 (May 1966), 587-595.

Church, Joseph, "Language in Childhood," *Childhood Education*, 39 (September 1962), 19-22.

DeBoer, John, "Some Sociological Factors in Language Development," *Child Development and the Language Arts*, National Conference on Research in English, National Council of Teachers of English, 1963, 6-16.

Deutsch, Martin, "The Role of Social Class in Language Development and Cognition," *American Journal of Orthopsychiatry*, 35 (January 1965), 78-88.

Deutsch, Martin, and Estelle Cherry-Peisach, "A Study of Language Patterns," *Instructor*, 75 (March 1966), 95 ff.

Hamp, Eric P., "The Science of Linguistics and Language Teaching," *Teachers College Record*, 62 (April 1961), 550-561.

Hunt, Kellogg, "Recent Measures in Syntactic Development," *Elementary English*, 43 (November 1966), 732-739.

Kenyon, John S., "Cultural Levels and Functional Varieties of English," *College English*, 10 (October 1948), 31-36.

Laird, Charlton, "Structural Linguistics: Notes for a Devil's Advocate," *College English*, 24 (November 1962), 93-97.

Lefcourt, Ann, "Linguistics and Elementary School Textbooks," *Elementary English*, 40 (October 1963), 598-601.

McCarthy, Dorothea, "Language Disorder and Parent-Child Relationships," *Journal of Speech and Hearing Disorders*, 19 (December 1954), 514-523.

McDavid, Raven I., "The Cultural Matrix of American English," *Elementary English*, 42 (January 1965), 13-21.

———, "American Social Dialects," *College English*, 26 (January 1965), 254-260.

May, Frank B., "The Effects of Environment on Oral Language Development: I and II," *Elementary English*, 43 (October, November 1966), 587-595; 533-546.

Menyuk, Paula, "Syntactic Rules Used by Children from Preschool Through First Grade," *Child Development*, 35 (June 1964), 533-546.

Metz, F. Elizabeth, "Poverty, Language Deprivation, and Language Ability," *Elementary English*, 43 (February 1966), 129-133.

Ponder, Eddie G., "Understanding the Language of the Culturally Disadvantaged Child," *Elementary English*, 42 (November 1965), 769-774; 794.

Rosenbaum, Peter S., "On the Role of Linguistics in the Teaching of English," *Harvard Educational Review*, 35 (Summer 1965), 332-348.

Strickland, Ruth G., "How Children Learn Their Language," *Childhood Education*, 39 (March 1963), 316-319.

———, "Implications of Research in Linguistics for Elementary Teaching," *Elementary English*, 40 (February 1963), 168-171.

Tibbetts, A. M., "Rebuttal," *College English*, 22 (April 1960), 516-517.

Tilley, Winthrop, "Linguistics: Stern-Faced Science or Deadpan Frivolity?" *Elementary English*, 44 (February 1967), 158-159.

Wetmore, Thomas H., "The English Language," *Elementary English*, 37 (February 1960), 113-115; 117.

Wilson, Theda M., "Helping the Disadvantaged Build Language," *National Elementary Principal*, 40 (November 1965), 43-46.

Part Three: Listening and Speaking

Anderson, Harold M., and Robert J. Baldauf, "A Study of a Measure of Listening," *Journal of Educational Research*, 57 (December 1963), 197-200.

Bany, Mary, "A Discussion Technique for Settling Conflicts," *Elementary English*, 35 (April 1958), 233-236.

Bloom, Robert M., "Program for Oral English," *Elementary English*, 41 (February 1964), 158-164.

Brown, Charles T., "Three Studies of the Listening of Children," *Speech Monographs*, 32 (June 1965), 129-138.

Brown, Kenneth L., "Speech and Listening in Language Arts and Textbooks: Parts I and II," *Elementary English*, 44 (April, May 1967), 336-341; 461-465.

Canfield, G. Robert, "How Useful Are Lessons on Listening?" *Elementary School Journal*, 62 (December 1961), 147-151.

Cox, Philena and Rosalind Hughes, "Effective Choral Speaking and Reading," Ginn and Company Contributions to Reading, No. 9, 1957.

Crocker, Laurel M., "Using the Flannel Board with Stories," *Elementary English*, 38 (October 1961), 404-405.

Curry, Herbert L., "Howz Yer Speechin'?" *Elementary School Journal*, 60 (October 1959), 270-273.

DeCarlo, Mary, "Techniques of Teaching Oral Communication" in *Reading and the Related Arts*, A Report of the Twenty-first Annual Conference and Course on Reading, University of Pittsburgh, 1965, pp. 47-57.

Duker, Sam, "Basics in Critical Listening," *English Journal*, 51 (November 1962), 565-567.

———, "An Annotated Guide to Audiovisual Aids Available for the Teaching of Listening," *Audiovisual Instruction*, 10 (April 1965), 320-322.

Emerick, Lonnie, "Speech Improvement in the Kindergarten," *Education*, 84 (May 1964), 565-568.

Fry, Charles L., "Training Children to Communicate to Listeners," *Child Development*, 37 (September 1966), 675-685.

Gallegos, B. Barton, "Toward Better Speech," *Elementary School Journal*, 62 (April 1962), 348-353.

Graubard, Paul S., "Pantomime: Another Language," *Elementary English*, 37 (May 1960), 302-306.

Hoffman, Miriam, "Our Listening Center Livens Language Arts," *Elementary School Journal*, 63 (April 1963), 381-385.

Hollingsworth, Paul M., "The Classroom Teacher as a Speech Teacher", *Education*, 85 (January 1965), 270-273.

Horrworth, Gloria L., "Listening: A Facet of Oral Language," *Elementary English*, 43 (December 1966), 856-864.

Kane, Peter E., "Role Playing for Educational Use," *Speech Teacher*, 13 (November 1964), 320-323.

Knox, Al, "The Classroom Teacher and the Stuttering Child," *Phi Delta Kappan*, 44 (December 1962), 136-137.

Leutenegger, Ralph R., "What We Have Learned About Stuttering in the Past Twenty-five Years," *Speech Teacher*, 9 (January 1960), 23-30.

Lewis, George I., and Ann Kemmerling Burkhart, "Creative Dramatics: A Selective Bibliography," *Elementary English*, 39 (February 1962), 91-100.

Lewis, Maurice S., "Teaching Children to Listen," *Education*, 80 (April 1960), 455-459.

Loban, Walter, "Oral Language Proficiency Affects Reading and Writing," *Instructor*, 75 (March 1966), 97 ff.

Lundsteen, Sara, "Critical Listening—Permanency and Transfer of Gains Made During an Experiment in Fifth and Sixth Grades," *California Journal of Educational Research*, 16 (November 1965), 210-216.

Manolakes, George, "Oral Language and Learning," *Elementary English*, 40 (November 1963), 731-734.

Munkres, Alberta, "Oral Communication," *Education*, 82 (October 1961), 72-76.

Ogilvie, Mardel, "Oral Communication in Elementary School Living," *Speech Teacher*, 6 (January 1957), 43-47.

Petrie, C. R., "What We Don't Know About Listening," *Journal of Communication*, 14 (December 1964), 248-251.

Petty, Walter and Roberta Starkey, "Oral Language and Personal and Social Development," *Elementary English*, 43 (April 1966), 386-394.

Petty, Walter T., "Listening: Directions for Research," *Elementary English*, 39 (October 1962), 572-577.

"Research Critiques," *Elementary English*, 44 (April 1967), 405-410.

Sawyer, Richard P., "Better Speech for Better Reading," *Elementary School Journal*, 65 (April 1965), 359-365.

Siks, Geraldine B., "Creative Dramatics for Children," Ginn and Company Contributions to Reading, No. 26, 1961.

Sister M. Millicent, "Creative Dramatics in the Classroom," *Elementary English*, 40 (April 1963), 382-385; 389.

Part Four: Literature and Creative Writing

Allen, Robert L., "Written English is a 'Second Language,' " *English Journal*, 55 (September 1966), 739-746.

Bateman, Donald R., "More Mature Writing Through a Better Understanding of Language Structure," *English Journal*, 50 (October 1961), 457-460.

Beghe, Theodore L., "And Gladly Teach: Make Room for Literature," *National Elementary Principal*, 40 (November 1965), 30-35.

Boesen, Sister Mary Theodore, "Developing Maturity in Writing," *Instructor*, 75 (March 1966), 103 ff.

Burrows, Alvina T., "Encouraging Talented Children to Write," *Education*, 88 (September–October 1967), 31-34.

Carlson, Ruth Kearney, "An Originality Story Scale," *Elementary School Journal*, 65 (April 1965), 366-374.

——, "Sparkling and Spinning Words," *Elementary English*, 41 (January 1964), 15-21.

Duff, Annis, "The Literary Heritage of Childhood, *Wilson Library Bulletin*, 33 (April 1959), 563-570.

Evertts, Eldonna L., "Composition Through Literature," *The Instructor*, 75 (March 1966), 105-108.

Hildreth, Gertrude, "Early Writing as an Aid to Reading," *Elementary English*, 40 (January 1963), 15-20.

Hill, Mary Evelyn, "Creative Writing: First Steps," *Elementary School Journal*, 60 (May 1960), 433-436.

Howell, Miriam M.,"Differentiating Variables in Compositions of Seven-Year-Olds," *Elementary School Journal*, 57 (December 1956), 145-149.

Huck, Charlotte S., "What Is Children's Literature?" *Elementary English*, 41 (May 1964), 467-470.

——, "Discovering Poetry with Children," Chicago: Scott-Foresman and Company, 1964.

——, "Planning the Literature Program for the Elementary School," *Elementary English*, 39 (April 1962), 307-313.

——, "Literature's Role in Language Development," *Childhood Education*, 42 (November 1965), 147-150.

Jacobs, Leland B., "More Than Words," *Childhood Education*, 37 (December 1960), 160-162.

Jenkins, William A., "Illustrators and Illustrations," *Elementary English*, 41 (May 1964), 492-499.

Korey, Ruth Anne, "Children's Literature for Integrated Classes," *Elementary English*, 43 (January 1966), 39-42.

LaBrant, Lou, "Writing—Most Difficult of the Language Arts," *NEA Journal*, 47 (March 1958), 189-190.

Lieberman, Phyllis and Sidney Simon, "Values and Student Writing," *Educational Leadership*, 22 (March 1965), 414-421.

McClelland, David C., "Values in Popular Literature for Children," *Childhood Education*, 40 (November 1963), 135-138.

Martin, Marvin, "All Writing Should Be Creative," *Elementary School Journal*, 63 (December 1962), 132-135.

Martin, William, "Some Stories Should Be Memorized," *Elementary English*, 34 (March 1957), 167-170.

May, Frank B., and B. Robert Tabachnick, "Three Stimuli for Creative Writing," *Elementary School Journal*, 67 (November 1966), 307-313.

Miller, Helen Rand, "Children as Poets," *Childhood Education*, 39 (March 1963), 333-335.

Miller, Marnie, "What Creative Writing Can Tell a Teacher About Children," *Elementary English*, 44 (March 1967), 273-274.

Neville, Emily, "Social Values in Children's Literature," *Library Quarterly*, 37 (January 1967), 46-52.

Parke, Margaret B., "Composition in the Primary Grades," *Elementary English*, 36 (February 1959), 107-121.

Personke, Carl, "A Gauntlet Retrieved," *Elementary English*, 45 (April 1968), 464-467.

Ross, Ramon, "Cultivating Taste in Children's Literature," *Education*, 86 (September 1965), 22-26.

Sawyer, Ruth, "How to Tell a Story," Chicago, Illinois: F. E. Compton Company, Division of Encyclopaedia Britannica, Inc.

Sister Mary Nora and Ruth French, "What Are Some Resources for the Teacher of Children's Literature?" *Elementary English*, 41 (May 1964), 516-525.

Smith, Dora V., "The Children's Literary Heritage," *Elementary English*, 41 (November 1964), 715-727.

Snedaker, Mabel, "Enjoying Poetry with Children," Ginn and Company's Contributions to Reading, No. 121, 1961.

Squire, James R., "The Teaching of Writing and Composition in Today's School," *Elementary English*, 41 (January 1964), 3-14.

Taylor, Winnifred F., and Kenneth C. Hoedt, "The Effect of Praise Upon the Quality and Quantity of Creative Writing," *Journal of Educational Research*, 60 (October 1966), 80-83.

Thornley, Gwendella, "Reading Poetry to Children," *Elementary English*, 39 (November 1962), 691-698.

———, "Storytelling is Fairy Gold," *Elementary English*, 45 (January 1968), 67-79; 88.

Tiedt, Sidney W., "Self-Involvement in Writing," *Elementary English*, 44 (May 1967), 475-479.

———, and Iris M. Tiedt, "Imaginative Books Inspire Imaginative Writing," *Elementary School Journal*, 66 (October 1965), 18-21.

Withers, S., "Creativity in English—A Dissent," *Phi Delta Kappan*, 42 (April 1961), 311-314.

Wittick, Mildred Letton, "Correctness and Freshness—Can Children's Writing Have Both?" *Elementary School Journal*, 60 (March 1960), 295-300.

———, "Improving Written Composition," *National Elementary Principal*, 40 (November 1965), 14-18.

Witty, Paul and William Martin, "An Analysis of Children's Composition Written in Response to a Film," *Elementary English*, 34 (March 1957), 158-163.

Wyatt, Nita, "Research in Creative Writing," *Educational Leadership*, 19 (February 1962), 307-310.

Part Five: Words and Their Use

Binney, James, "Linguistics and Grammar in the Classroom Today," *College English*, 23 (March 1962), 492-494.

Bostain, James C., "Dream World of English Grammar," *NEA Journal*, 55 (September 1966), 20-22.

Cameron, Jack R., "Tradition, Textbooks, and Non-English Grammar," *Elementary English*, 33 (April 1956), 216-219.

Ching, Doris C., "Toward Better English Usage," *Elementary School Journal*, 65 (November 1964), 81-86.

Conlin, David A., "Form and Function: A Quandry," *English Journal*, 49 (October 1960), 457-463.

Corbin, Richard, "Grammar and Usage: Progress but Not Millennium," *English Journal*, 49 (November 1960), 548-555.

DeBoer, John, "Grammar in Language Teaching," *Elementary English*, 36 (October 1959), 413-421.

Dykema, Karl W., "Where Our Grammar Came From," *College English*, 22 (April 1961), 455-465.

Evans, Bergen, "Grammar for Today," *Atlantic Monthly*, 205 (March 1960), 79-82.

Everhart, Rodney W., "Why Not Teach Children Semantics?" *Elementary English*, 34 (December 1957), 548-551.

Francis, W. Nelson, "Revolution in Grammar," *Quarterly Journal of Speech*, 40 (October 1954), 299-312.

Geist, Robert J., "Structural Grammar and the Sixth Grade," *American Speech*, 31 (1956), 5-12.

Gleason, H. A., Jr., "What Grammar?" *Harvard Educational Review*, 34 (Spring 1964), 267-281.

Groff, Patrick J., "Is Knowledge of Parts of Speech Necessary?" *English Journal*, 50 (September 1961), 413-415.

Hatfield, W. Wilbur, "Helping Students See Their Language Working," *English Journal*, 56 (January 1967), 67-73.

Hayes, Curtis W., "Syntax: Some Present-Day Concepts," *English Journal*, 56 (January 1967), 89-96.

Heffron, Pearl M., "Our American Slang," *Elementary English*, 39 (May 1962), 429-434.

Jacobs, Roderick A., "A Short Introduction to Transformational Grammar," *Education*, 86 (November 1965), 138-141.

Johnson, Falk S., "Grammars: A Working Classification," *Elementary English*, 44 (April 1967), 349-352.

Joos, Martin, "Standards in the Community Language," *National Elementary Principal*, 40 (September 1965), 26-33.

Lamberts, J. J., "Basic Concepts for Teaching from Structural Linguistics," *English Journal*, 49 (March 1960), 172-176.

Lees, Robert B., "The Promise of Transformational Grammar," *English Journal*, 52 (May 1963), 327-352.

Lewis, Norman, "How Correct Must Correct English Be?" *Harper's Magazine*, 198 (March 1949), 68-74.

Lorge, Irving and Jeanne Chall, "Estimating the Size of Vocabularies of Children and Adults: An Analysis of Methodological Issues," *Journal of Experimental Education*, 32 (Winter 1963), 147-157.

McDavid, Raven I., "Dialectology and the Classroom Teacher," *College English*, 24 (November 1962), 115-116.

Malmstrom, Jean, "Linguistic Atlas Findings Versus Textbook Pronouncements on Current American Usage," *English Journal*, 48 (April 1959), 191-198.

May, Frank B., "Composition and 'The New Grammar,'" *Elementary English*, 44 (November 1967), 762-764; 767.

Mooney, P., "Generative Grammar in Grade 4," *Catholic School Journal*, 66 (March 1966), 61-63.

Moyer, Haverly O., "Can Ear-Training Improve English Usage?" *Elementary English*, 33 (April 1956), 216-219.

Norman, Arthur, "This Most Cruel Usage," *College English*, 26 (January 1965), 276-282.

Pooley, Robert C., "Grammar in the Grades?" *NEA Journal*, 47 (September 1958), 422.

Postman, Neil, "Creative Inquiry and the Teaching of Grammar," *Elementary English*, 37 (February 1960), 90-92.

Robinson, Helen M., "Vocabulary: Speaking, Listening, Reading, and Writing," in *Reading and the Language Arts*, Supplementary Educational Monographs, No. 93, Chicago: University of Chicago Press, 1963, pp. 167-176.

Schuster, Edgar H., "How Good Is the New Grammar?" *English Journal*, 50 (September 1961), 392-397.

Strickland, Ruth, "Teaching of Grammar," *National Elementary Principal*, 40 (November 1965), 58-62.

Tibbetts, A. M., "Real Issues in the Great Language Controversy," *English Journal*, 55 (January 1966), 28-38.

Wolfe, Don M., "Grammar and Linguistics: A Contrast in Realities," *English Journal*, 53 (February 1964), 73-78.

Womack, Thurston, "Teachers' Attitude Toward Current Usage," *English Journal*, 48 (April 1959), 186-190.

Part Six: Spelling and Handwriting

Aaron, I. E., "The Relationship of Selected Measures to Spelling Achievement at the Fourth and Eighth Grade Levels," *Journal of Educational Research*, 53 (December 1959), 138-143.

Ames, Wilburn S., "A Comparison of Spelling Textbooks," *Elementary English*, 42 (February 1965), 146 ff.

Andersen, Dan W., "Handwriting Research: The Concern for Handwriting Style," *Elementary English*, 42 (February 1965), 115-119.

Blake, Howard E., "Studying Spelling Independently," *Elementary English*, 37 (January 1960), 29-32.

Bonney, Margaret K., "Sound and Sense in Spelling," *Elementary English*, 42 (March 1965), 243-246.

Bremer, Neville H., "Ways to Improve Spelling in Elementary Grades," *Elementary English*, 38 (May 1961), 301-307.

Byers, Loretta, "The Relation of Manuscript and Cursive Handwriting to Accuracy in Spelling," *Journal of Educational Research*, 57 (October 1963), 87-89.

Enstrom E. A., and Doris C. Enstrom, "Teaching for Greater Legibility," *Elementary English*, 41 (November 1964), 859-862.

Fitzgerald, James A., "What Words Should Children Study in Spelling?" *Education*, 79 (December 1958), 224-227.

Frasch, Dorothy K., "How Well Do Sixth-Graders Proofread for Spelling Errors?" *Elementary School Journal*, 65 (April 1965), 381-385.

Freeman, Frank N., "On Italic Handwriting," *Elementary School Journal*, 60 (February 1960), 258-264.

Groff, Patrick J., "Preference for Handwriting Style by Big Business," *Elementary English*, 41 (November 1964), 863-864.

Hall, Norman, "The Letter Mark-Out Corrected Test," *Journal of Educational Research*, 58 (December 1964), 148-157.

Hanna, Paul R., and Jean S. Hanna, "Applications of Linguistic and Psychological Cues to the Spelling Course of Study," *Elementary English*, 42 (November 1965), 753-759.

———, and J. T. Moore, "Spelling—From Spoken Word to Written Symbol," *Elementary School Journal*, 53 (February 1953), 329-337.

———, and others, "Needed Research in Spelling," *Elementary English*, 43 (January 1966), 60-66.

Hildreth, Gertrude, "Manuscript Writing After Sixty Years," *Elementary English*, 37 (January 1960), 4-13.

Hodges, Richard E., "A Short History of Spelling Reform in the United States," *Phi Delta Kappan*, 45 (April 1964), 330-332.

———, "Case for Teaching Sound-to-Letter Correspondences in Spelling," *Elementary School Journal*, 66 (March 1966), 327-336.

———, "The Psychological Bases of Spelling," *Elementary English*, 42 (October 1965), 629-635.

Horn, Ernest, "Questions for Research on Handwriting," *Elementary School Journal*, 62 (March 1962), 304-312.

Johnson, Dorothy, "S-P-E-L-L-I-N-G Self-Taught from Magnetic Tape," *Elementary School Journal*, 63 (November 1962), 79-82.

Lamana, Peter A., "A Summary of Research on Spelling As Related to Other Areas of the Language Arts," *Journal of the Reading Specialist*, 6 (October 1966), 32-39.

Lewis, Edward R., and Hilda P. Lewis, "Which Manuscript Letters Are Hard for First Graders?" *Elementary English*, 41 (December 1964), 855-859.

Noble, J. Kendrick, "Handwriting Programs in Today's Schools," *Elementary English*, 40 (May 1963), 243-246.

Personke, Carl and Lester Knight, "Proofreading and Spelling: A Report and a Program," *Elementary English*, 44 (November 1967), 768-774.

Petty, Walter T., "Handwriting and Spelling: Their Current Status in the Language Arts Curriculum," *Elementary English*, 41 (December 1964), 839-845.

Radaker, Leon D., "The Effect of Visual Imagery upon Spelling Performance," *Journal of Educational Research*, 56 (March 1963), 370-372.

Russell, David H., "Auditory Abilities and Achievement in Spelling in the Primary Grades," *Journal of Educational Psychology*, 49 (December 1958), 315-319.

————, "A Second Study of the Characteristics of Good and Poor Spellers," *Journal of Educational Psychology*, 46 (March 1955), 129-141.

Schoephoerster, Hugh, "Research into Variations of the Test-Study Plan of Teaching Spelling," *Elementary English*, 39 (May 1962), 460-462.

Templin, Elaine, "Handwriting—the Neglected 'R,' " *Elementary English*, 37 (October 1960), 386-389.

Yee, Albert, "The Generalization Controversy on Spelling Instruction," *Elementary English*, 43 (February 1966), 154-161.

Part Seven: Curriculum Topics and Resources

Allen, Virginia F., "Teaching Standard English as a Second Dialect," *Teachers College Record*, 68 (February 1967), 355-370.

Anderson, Marion, "Using the Dictionary in the Elementary Classroom," *Elementary English*, 41 (April 1964), 334-339.

Burns, Paul C., "Language Arts Methods and Materials for the Disadvantaged Youth," *Bulletin of Education*, 20 (Spring 1966; Lawrence, Kansas: University of Kansas, School of Education), pp. 113-122.

————, "How to Read and Judge a Newspaper," *Grade Teacher*, 82 (March 1965), 107-108; 121.

Capehart, Bertis and Margaret McNish, "The Typewriter as an Instructional Tool," *National Elementary Principal*, 38 (February 1959), 23-26.

Clubb, Merrel D., "Standard English as a Foreign Language," *Elementary English*, 38 (November 1961), 497-501.

Durham, Virginia, "English Enrichment: Challenging the Talented Before Junior High," *Clearing House*, 34 (February 1960), 333-336.

Fillmer, Henry T., "Programmed Instruction in Elementary English," *Elementary English*, 40 (December 1963), 833-837.

Golden, Ruth, "Ways to Improve Oral Communication of Culturally Different Youth," *Improving English Skills of Culturally Different Youth*, Washington, D. C.: U. S. Government Printing Office, 1964, pp. 100-109.

Granite, Harvey R., "Language Beacons for the Disadvantaged," *Elementary School Journal*, 66 (May 1966), 420-425.

Green, William D., "Language and the Culturally Different," *English Journal*, 54 (November 1965), 724-733.

Horn, Thomas D., Audrey Fisher and James L. Lanman, "Periodicals for Children and Youth," *Elementary English*, 43 (April 1966), 341-358.

King, Paul E., "Multisensory Teaching Tools and the Very Young Language Learner," *Audiovisual Instruction*, 11 (October 1966), 639-641.

LaBrant, Lou, "Lifetime Reading and the Paperback Book," pp. 13-22 in *Paperbacks in the Schools*, edited by Alexander Butman, Donald Reis, and David Sohn, New York: Bantam Books, 1963.

Lake, Marjorie F., "A Fifth Grade Publishes the School Newspaper," *Elementary English*, 40 (January 1963), 31-34.

McGinniss, Dorothy A., "Paperbacks in the School Library," pp. 122-130 in *Paperbacks in the Schools*, edited by Alexander Butman, Donald Reis, and David Sohn, New York: Bantam Books, 1963.

Merryman, Donald, "Resources for Teaching Language," *National Elementary Principal*, 40 (November 1965), 73-78.

Miner, Adah L., "Elementary Speech Taught from the Skies," *Speech Teacher*, 11 (January 1962), 21-25.

Moore, Walter J., "The Contribution of Lexicography to the Teacher of Language Arts," *Elementary English*, 41 (April 1964), 388-394.

Moskowitz, Gertrude, "Janus Rears His Head in FLES," *Elementary School Journal*, 63 (March 1963), 329-335.

Murray, Walter I., and Newman Rose Karel, "Utilizing Television in Teaching Children's Literature," *Education*, 82 (January 1962), 309-311.

Newton, Eunice Shaed, "Planning for the Language Development of Disadvantaged Children and Youth," *Journal of Negro Education*, 33 (Summer 1964), 264-274.

Norvell, George W., "The Challenge of Periodicals in Education," *Elementary English*, 43 (April 1966), 402-408.

Nunally, Nancy, "Magazines and Newspapers for Children," *Childhood Education*, 42 (April 1966), 517-521.

Pooley, Robert C., "The School Dictionary: Source Book for the Study of English," *Elementary English*, 41 (April 1964), 380-383.

Porter, W. E., "Mass Communication and Education," *National Elementary Principal*, 37 (February 1958), 12-16.

Riestra, Miguel and Charles E. Johnson, "Changes in Attitudes of Elementary School Pupils Toward Foreign-Speaking Peoples Resulting from the Study of a Foreign Language," *Journal of Experimental Education*, 33 (Fall 1964), 65-72.

Torrance, E. Paul, "Ten Ways of Helping Young Children Gifted in Creative Writing and Speech," *Gifted Child Quarterly*, 6 (Winter 1962), 121-127.

Van Ness, Marjorie, "Getting to Know a Newspaper," *Grade Teacher*, 84 (March 1967), 104 ff.

Wilt, Miriam E., "Organizing for Language Learning," *National Elementary Principal*, 45 (November 1965), 6-13.

Wolfson, Bernice J., "The Promise of Multiage Grouping for Individualizing Instruction," *Elementary School Journal*, 67 (April 1967), 352-362.

Worth, Walter H., and J. Harlan Shores, "Does Nonpromotion Improve Achievement in the Language Arts?" *Elementary English*, 37 (January 1960), 49-52.

Part Eight: Evaluation of Language Learnings

Diederich, Paul B., "How to Measure Growth in Writing Ability," *English Journal*, 55 (April 1966), 435-449.

Feldt, Leonard S., "The Reliability of Measures of Handwriting Quality," *Journal of Educational Psychology*, 53 (December 1962), 288-292.

Fitzgerald, James A., "Evaluating Spelling Ability, Progress, and Achievement," *Education*, 77 (March 1957), 404-408.

Kelly, Charles M., "An Investigation of the Construct Validity of Two Commercially Published Listening Tests," *Speech Monographs*, 32 (June 1965), 139-143.

McKey, Eleanor F., "Do Standardized Tests Do What They Claim to Do?" *English Journal*, 50 (December 1961), 607-611.

Malstrom, Jean, "A Progress Report on Textbook Analysis," *English Journal*, 51 (January 1962), 39-43.

Odom, R. R., "Capitalization and Punctuation: A Diagnostic Test," *California Journal of Educational Research*, 15 (March 1964), 68-75.

Olson, Helen F., "Evaluating Growth in Language Ability," *Journal of Educational Research*, 39 (December 1945), 241-253.

Index of Names

Index of Topics